DATE DUE

DEMCO 38-296

2000
The Supreme Court Review

2000
The

"Judges as persons, or courts as institutions, are entitled to
no greater immunity from criticism than other persons
or institutions . . . [J]udges must be kept mindful of their limitations and
of their ultimate public responsibility by a vigorous
stream of criticism expressed with candor however blunt."
—*Felix Frankfurter*

". . . while it is proper that people should find fault when
their judges fail, it is only reasonable that they should recognize the
difficulties. . . . Let them be severely brought to book,
when they go wrong, but by those who will take the trouble
to understand them."
—*Learned Hand*

THE LAW SCHOOL

THE UNIVERSITY OF CHICAGO

Supreme Court Review

EDITED BY

DENNIS J. HUTCHINSON
DAVID A. STRAUSS
AND GEOFFREY R. STONE

THE UNIVERSITY OF CHICAGO PRESS

CHICAGO AND LONDON

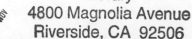

INTERNATIONAL STANDARD BOOK NUMBER: 0-226-36249-3

LIBRARY OF CONGRESS CATALOG CARD NUMBER: 60-14353

THE UNIVERSITY OF CHICAGO PRESS, CHICAGO 60637

THE UNIVERSITY OF CHICAGO PRESS, LTD., LONDON

© 2001 BY THE UNIVERSITY OF CHICAGO, ALL RIGHTS RESERVED, PUBLISHED 2001

PRINTED IN THE UNITED STATES OF AMERICA

The paper used in this publication meets the minimum requirements of American
National Standard for Information Sciences–Permanence of Paper for Printed
Library Materials, ANSI Z39.48-1984. ⊗

CONTENTS

RICHARD A. POSNER

FLORIDA 2000: A LEGAL AND STATISTICAL ANALYSIS OF THE ELECTION DEADLOCK AND THE ENSUING LITIGATION

The Supreme Court's dramatic decision in *Bush v Gore*,[1] which ended the 2000 presidential election deadlock by stopping the hand recount ordered by Florida's highest court, leaves many political and legal questions open, but four are salient:

> 1. Was Gore the "real winner," in some meaningful sense, of the Florida popular vote for President?
> 2. Whether he was or not, was the Court's decision unjust, partisan, or imprudent?
> 3. In evaluating a Supreme Court decision in a momentous, high-visibility case such as this, what weight if any should be given to pragmatic considerations? Stated otherwise, in such a case, where does law end and politics begin?
> 4. What should be done to minimize the likelihood of deadlock in future presidential elections?

The last question is not academic or premature. It will not do to say that because the last deadlocked presidential election took

Richard A. Posner is Judge, U.S. Court of Appeals for the Seventh Circuit, and Senior Lecturer, University of Chicago Law School.

AUTHOR'S NOTE: I thank Bryan Dayton for his very helpful research assistance, and Christopher DeMuth, John Donohue, Frank Easterbrook, Eldon Eisenach, Elizabeth Garrett, Pamela Karlan, Larry Kramer, Lawrence Lessig, Michael McConnell, Edward Morrison, Eric Posner, Eric Rasmusen, Stephen Stigler, and Cass Sunstein for their very helpful comments on earlier versions of this article. For a more detailed discussion of the subject of this article, see my book *Breaking the Deadlock: The 2000 Election, the Constitution, and the Courts* (2001).

[1] 121 S Ct 525 (2000) (per curiam).

place 124 years ago (the Hayes-Tilden election of 1876), we have plenty of time to think of ways of preventing a repetition. In the thirty-four presidential elections since 1868 (the date of the first post–Civil War presidential election), there have been two deadlocks. That is a nontrivial 6 percent of the presidential elections in this period. Realism counsels assigning a similar probability of deadlock to the presidential election four years from now—or maybe even a higher probability, since, with the growing professionalization of political campaigning, close elections may well be more frequent in the future than they have been in the recent past. The better both parties are at gauging voter sentiment, appealing to voters, and assembling winning coalitions, the likelier they are to fight to a near tie.

The first and fourth questions (who really won and how can future deadlocks be averted) are related, and I discuss them together in Part I. Part II discusses the litigation. The first and second questions (who really won and should the U.S. Supreme Court have intervened) are also related. If the hand recount ordered by the Florida supreme court in its second opinion was improper, as the Court ruled, then it is clear that Bush received more *legal* votes than Gore, and that is all that matters so far as the legality of Bush's selection as President is concerned. I argue in Part II that although the Supreme Court's second opinion (the one that terminated the recount) leaves much to be desired—unsurprisingly, in view of the time pressure under which the Court acted and the internal political pressure to find a ground that would command more than a bare majority—its decision is not the outrage that the Court's liberal critics have charged. This conclusion depends partly on legal doctrine but partly too on the statistics of the vote and the mechanics of counting and recounting, the subject of Part I, and on the answer to the question, which is one of jurisprudence and constitutional theory, how far the Supreme Court should consider the practical consequences of alternative decisions.

I. The Deadlock

A. Statistical Analysis

After the machine recount of the Florida votes, after a few completed hand recounts (mainly in Volusia County), and after the addition to the tally of the late-arriving overseas ballots, Bush was ahead by only 930 votes out of almost 6 million votes that had been cast and counted in Florida for a presidential candidate.[2] The secretary of state of Florida, Katherine Harris, wanted to stop there and certify Bush the winner by 930 votes. As a result of judicial action described in Part II, however, additional hand recounts were conducted that shrank Bush's lead although they did not eliminate it completely. The hand recounts were stopped by the Supreme Court's decision of December 12 (by which time Bush's unofficial lead had fallen below 200 votes) before they could be completed. Whether there should have been any hand recounts, and if so how they should have been conducted, and with what likely result if they were conducted properly, are the focus of this section of the paper.

Bush's original margin of 930 votes out of 6 million made the Florida presidential election a statistical tie. This is an important concept, and let me explain it briefly, after which I shall consider whether Gore would have been likely to prevail in a fair hand recount.

Since the counting of millions of ballots by any method is liable to error, a razor-thin margin of victory establishes merely a probability, and not necessarily a very high one, that the victor actually received more votes than the vanquished. That is why recounts are fairly common in U.S. elections. Despite widespread criticisms, the machine count in Florida, at least as corrected by the machine recount, was fairly accurate. In Broward County, where the hand recount was conducted in a way calculated to maximize—indeed, I'll argue, to exaggerate—the estimate of the number of errors made in the machine count, fewer than 2,000 out of more than half a million votes were deemed not to have been recorded for either Gore or Bush as a result of machine error. Whether the rejection of these votes by the machine really could be called "error" is doubtful, but I postpone that question. The point for now is that 2,000 miscounted ballots is less than one-half of 1 percent

    [2] My voting statistics are drawn from the briefs and judicial opinions in the litigation challenging the election results, from the report of the machine count in a table published in the *New York Times* (national ed; Nov 27, 2000), p A15, and from Gwyneth K. Shaw, Jim Leusner, and Sean Holton, *Uncounted Ballots May Add Up to 180,000: Election Officials Said Confusion, Mistakes and Protests All Contributed to Votes Being Thrown Out*, Orlando Sentinel (Nov 15, 2000), p A1.

of the votes cast. Projected to the state as a whole, that error rate implies that about 30,000 votes statewide were erroneously not recorded. If those votes were representative of the entire Florida vote assumed to be a tie, then counting them accurately would be very unlikely to change (and of course should not change) the result; there would be only a 5 percent probability that the statewide vote for Bush or Gore would change by more than 174 votes.[3] But if the 30,000 are not a random sample of the entire vote and an infallible counter would have counted 60 percent of these votes for Gore, he would have won the election in Florida by about 5,000 votes, while if the infallible counter would have counted only 51 percent of the uncounted votes for him, Gore would have lost, given Bush's 930-vote machine-count lead, by more than 300 votes. These possibilities prevent our knowing on the basis of the machine vote who really won.

Whether the margin of error would have been narrowed by recounting the votes by hand depends in part on the accuracy of hand counting compared to machine counting. Neither method is categorically superior to the other. Machines can be poorly designed, defectively manufactured, and inadequately maintained, and as a result make many errors. Human counters can be fatigued, biased, or simply unable to infer the voter's intent, with any approach to certainty, from a ballot that the machine refused to count; so they can make many errors too—some deliberate, which is beyond a machine's capacity. One would have to know a lot about the specific machines and the specific hand counters to decide which method was more accurate. Republicans were entitled to be concerned about hand recounts by canvasing boards dominated by Democrats, and Democrats about hand recounts by Republican-dominated boards.

The closeness of the statewide results made it unlikely that hand counting, even if more accurate than machine counting, would break the statistical tie unless it produced a very large margin for one of the candidates. Suppose that hand counting is twice as accurate as machine counting, so that the margin of likely error would shrink to .25 percent in a hand recount (this is still assuming that

---

[3] Imagine flipping a fair coin 30,000 times. There would be a 95 percent probability that the number of heads and tails would be 15,000 plus or minus 174, since any greater deviation would be more than two standard deviations from the mean of 15,000.

the Broward County hand recount yielded an accurate estimate of
the number of votes miscounted by the machine). In other words,
about half the 30,000 votes statewide that I'm assuming were miscounted by the machine would have been recovered as votes for
one of the presidential candidates. Gore would have had to receive
from an honest recount more than 53 percent of these 15,000 recovered votes to overcome Bush's 930-vote lead. At 53 percent to
Bush's 47 percent, Gore would have picked up a net of 900 votes.

He would have been unlikely to prevail by such a margin in a
complete, accurate statewide recount. The fact that Gore did not
request a recount in any counties besides Broward, Palm Beach,
Miami-Dade, and Volusia is evidence that he didn't think a recount in any of those other counties would have yielded net gains.
It is true that he offered to agree to a statewide recount if Bush
would agree to abide by the results, but he must have known that
Bush would refuse, since the agreement would have entailed the
surrender by Bush of options that he possessed to thwart a recount
that went against him, notably the Florida legislature's appointing
its own slate of electors, pledged to Bush.

In not seeking a statewide recount initially, Gore may have been
concerned with the delay that a statewide recount would cause.
But this would not have been a reason for asking for a recount in
just four counties rather than in five or six or eight or some other
number larger than four though well short of sixty-seven, the total
number of counties in Florida. Since the recounts in the counties in which Gore did not request recounts would not have produced perfect ties, it is a fair inference that he thought that recounts in those counties would have produced a net gain for Bush,
though maybe a smaller one than the gains that the recount in
the Democratic-selected counties produced for Gore. "Maybe"
becomes "probably" if we assume that Bush would have requested
a statewide recount had he expected it to favor him; but the assumption may be erroneous. He may not have made such a request
because it would have tended to validate the hand-recount method,
and he could not be certain how such a recount conducted statewide would turn out, whereas he was certain that he had won the
machine-tabulated vote. From his perspective, he had won the toss
and now his opponent wanted to toss again, using a different but
not a more balanced coin. Still, the possibility that Gore would
have received 53 percent of the miscounted votes statewide cannot

yet be excluded. But this is on the assumption that the Broward hand recount was meaningful.

Gore would probably have overcome Bush's lead if the recounts had been confined to the four counties picked by him and if in addition they had been administered in accordance with the criteria used by the Broward County canvasing board. Gore's net gain of 582 votes in the Broward County recount represented .15 percent of his total votes there. That is, for every 10,000 votes Gore had received in the machine count in Broward County, the hand recount had netted him fifteen more votes over Bush. If the votes he received in the machine count in Palm Beach and Miami-Dade counties are multiplied by the same percentage and added to his net gain in Broward, his aggregate net gain from hand recounting is 1,480 and overcomes Bush's 930-vote lead.[4]

But the 1,480 figure is unreliable as a guide to who "really" won the election:

1. Democrats dominated the canvasing boards of all four counties. Close calls were therefore likely to favor Gore. Close calls were inevitable if the criteria used by Broward County were used in the other counties as well.[5]

2. The canvasing boards' political complexion made it likely that they would use criteria (namely, the Broward criteria) that maximized the number of votes recovered from the ballots that the machine tabulation had not counted. For as long as the recovered ballots divided in roughly the same proportions as the machine-counted ballots, the more ballots that had been rejected in the machine tabulation that were recovered in the hand recount the greater would be Gore's net gain. Suppose that in some precinct Gore had 7,000 votes in the machine tabulation and Bush 3,000, and 300 had been rejected in the machine tabulation, so

---

[4] Volusia County completed its hand recount before the November 14 statutory deadline for the completion of recounts (see Part II), and therefore the 98-vote net gain that it produced for Gore was included in calculating Bush's 930-vote margin. As we'll see, the Volusia recount probably produced an excessive net gain for Gore.

[5] This point helps to place in perspective *Delahunt v Johnston*, 671 NE2d 1241 (Mass 1996), where the Supreme Judicial Court of Massachusetts upheld a hand recount of punchcard ballots against objections that the recount counted dimples as votes. The recount was conducted by a judge, and judges in Massachusetts are not elected. The Supreme Judicial Court's opinion is brief, moreover, and does not explore the full range of potential objections to counting dimples even when the counter's competence and freedom from bias are conceded.

that Gore led Bush in the machine-tabulated vote by 4,000 votes. If now the 300 were counted as votes, and they split in the same proportion as the votes that had been included in the tabulation, Gore would get 210 more votes and Bush ninety more, increasing Gore's lead by 120 votes. Gore of course led in all four counties.

3. Palm Beach refused to use the Broward criteria, and Miami-Dade seemed reluctant to do so. (I don't know what criteria Volusia County used.) Had Miami-Dade used Palm Beach rather than Broward criteria, Gore would have received fewer than 1,480 votes, though probably enough to overtake Bush's lead, as we will see.

4. Many of the disputed ballots could not be objectively read as votes, although the Republicans were on weak ground in arguing that *no* hand count of *any* rejected ballot could be read so. A hanging or swinging chad, that is, a chad that though punched remains dangling from the ballot by one corner (a hanging chad) or two corners (a swinging chad), is pretty good evidence of an intent to vote for the candidate whose chad was punched—provided, of course, that the voter did not also punch the chad of another candidate for the same office. But inferring a voter's intentions from a merely dimpled chad, or a chad only one of whose corners has been separated from the ballot (a "tri-chad"), is chancy. Broward County counted all dimpled chads and tri-chads in the undervotes (ballots that the machines had recorded as containing no vote for a presidential candidate). Yet a faint dimple might be created by the handling of the ballot or by its being repeatedly passed through the vote-counting machines. Or the voter may have started to vote for the candidate but then changed his mind, perhaps realizing he had made a mistake. There were many undecided voters in the 2000 presidential election, some of whom may have gone into the voting booth still undecided and, in the end, "decided" they couldn't make up their minds which presidential candidate to vote for. And no doubt some voters, probably many more than the undecideds, misunderstood or simply neglected to comply with the ballot instructions, even though the instructions were clear (including the instructions for voting the punchcard ballot) and if followed would assure that the vote would be counted. In the counties that used punchcard machines, not only was the voter instructed to punch a clean hole through the ballot (no dimples); he was also told to turn the ballot over after

removing it from the voting machine and to make sure there were no bits of paper stuck to it, that is, no dangling chads. But to follow instructions you have to be able to read them, and not all voters are literate.

The punchcard method of voting also requires a minimum of manual dexterity, and some voters lack even that. But emphasis properly falls on "minimum." The punchcard voting machine consists of an empty tray on which the ballot (which has roughly the consistency of an airline boarding pass) is placed. Since the chad is perforated and there is empty space beneath the ballot, it takes no strength to punch a clean hole through the chad, provided the machine is not defective.

The undervotes were only a tiny fraction of the total number of votes cast. We are talking about the tail of a distribution of voting competence. The average performance in the tail may be quite different from that in the center of the distribution. It would not be surprising if a large fraction of the votes cast by the people in the tail had been cast by undecided, confused, clumsy, illiterate, or inexperienced (first-time) voters. The inference of voter error or indecision in casting punchcard ballots is especially compelling in the case of ballots in which the voter punched through the chads of all the other candidates except the presidential candidates, indicating that the punchcard voting machine itself was not defective. This was the ground on which the Palm Beach County canvasing board decided eventually to exclude such ballots from the recount totals while including those that had several, though apparently the number could be as small as three, dimpled chads.[6] This was also why it would have been wrong for the Miami-Dade County canvasing board, had it decided to count dimples, to recount only the 10,750 undervotes. Some of the ballots that had been counted for the presidential candidate whose chad had been punched through may have contained a hanging chad in another presidential candidate's chad. A hand recount would discover that the voter had voted for two presidential candidates (had cast, in other words, an "overvote"), voiding the ballot. We know there were lots of overvotes (ballots automatically—though, as we'll see, not infalli-

---

[6] Trial Transcript, 2000 WL 1802941, at *104 (Dec 2, 2000) (testimony of Judge Charles Burton, chairman of the Palm Beach canvasing board), in *Gore v Harris*, 2000 WL 1790621 (Fla Cir Ct Dec 4, 2000), affirmed in part and reversed in part, 772 So2d 1243 (Fla 2000) (per curiam).

bly—rejected in the machine tabulation); and a ballot in which the voter punched both presidential chads yet left one dangling is as persuasive evidence that the voter tried to vote for both candidates as a dangling chad in an undervote is evidence that the voter tried to vote for that candidate. It would not take a large percentage of overvotes by dangling chads, out of the more than 600,000 cast in Miami-Dade County, to offset defective ballots among the 10,750 undervoted ballots.

According to exit polls, at least 1 percent of the voters in Miami-Dade County voted for other offices but not the presidency.[7] If we assume that 6,000 (1 percent of the total vote in Miami-Dade) of the 10,750 undervoted ballots are those in which the voter made a deliberate choice not to vote for President, then fewer than 5,000 remain to be allocated between Bush and Gore. But that is too many also. It must include many ballots that were irrevocably spoiled: the voter wanted to vote for President but failed to do so because of an error that no recount could dispel.[8]

In sum, a hand recount, unless very conservative criteria of vote recovery are used, is bound to introduce new errors.

5. And correct old ones? Surprisingly, this is far from certain. We must ask, What exactly is a voting "error" recoverable by a hand recount? An error, and even more clearly an error curable by a hand recount, is not a natural kind, like a blade of grass. It is a legal category. The category might be limited to an error in the machine tabulation: the ballot contains a cleanly, completely punched-through vote for Gore and for no other presidential candidate, yet the counting machine somehow failed to record it as a vote for Gore. There is no evidence that such errors were common or favored Bush over Gore. They make the best fit with the ordinary meaning of an error in tabulating the vote, however— and correcting them is an objective process. You just look for a cleanly, completely punched-through vote for one and only one presidential candidate.

---

[7] One estimate is 1.5 to 2 percent. *Election 2000: The Florida Vote*, CNN Live Event/Special, Nov 28, 2000, 10 p.m. EST, Transcript 00112809V54 (remark by Tom Fielder of the *Miami Herald*).

[8] The 1 percent estimate that I am using may be too high, however; inaccuracy in exit polling was apparently one reason for the erroneous projection on the evening of November 7 that Gore had won Florida. Howard Kurtz, *Errors Plagued Election Night Polling Service*, Washington Post (Dec 22, 2000), p A1.

At the other extreme, a recoverable error might be, in addition, any improperly marked ballot that a human counter *thinks* (or says he thinks) contains an indication of whom the voter intended to vote for. That was Broward County's concept, and it is dangerously subjective.

In between is the concept of recoverable errors as including, besides ballots in the first category, improperly marked ballots that contain objective indicia of the voter's intention to vote for a particular presidential candidate. This was the concept that the Palm Beach County canvasing board eventually settled on when it decided to count as votes all dislodged chads plus dimpled chads in ballots that had at least three dimples. The idea was that three dimples composed a pattern suggestive of a deliberate effort to vote for the dimpled candidates. Maybe; but a more conservative method would have been to count dimples only in ballots in which no chads had been punched through, a pattern more clearly consistent with the voter's having tried to punch through and been thwarted, perhaps by a chad buildup or some other defect in the voting machine.

The method or rather methods used by the Palm Beach County canvasing board produced either 176 or 215 extra votes for Gore; the Florida supreme court declined to decide which number was correct. Assume the higher one was. It was .08 percent of the votes that the machine had counted for Gore in Palm Beach County. Had the Broward and Miami-Dade canvasing boards used the Palm Beach method and produced the same percentage of additional votes for Gore, he would not have overtaken Bush's lead. His total gain in all three counties would have been only 788 votes (215 in Palm Beach as mentioned, 263 in Miami-Dade, and 310 in Broward).[9] With politically neutral counters, if there are such animals, this number would be even smaller, though probably not much smaller, as the Palm Beach counters appear to have been conscientious. The 168 additional votes that Gore netted in Miami-Dade from the first 20 percent or so of the recounted precincts before the recount was interrupted are a meaningless figure, because these precincts are far more heavily Democratic than the county as a whole. Had Miami-Dade completed a hand recount

---

[9] In addition, he would have had a net gain of only 78, not 98, votes in Volusia County, reducing his overall net gain from 788 to 768.

using Palm Beach rules, Gore could have overtaken Bush only if Broward's 582-vote gain for Bush from counting dimples were allowed to stand. Gore's total gain would then have been 1,060 (263 in Miami-Dade, 582 in Broward, and 215 in Palm Beach).

Already journalists and political activists are recounting the disputed ballots. But these recounts are unlikely to reveal who "really" won, because of the subjectivity of hand-counting punch-card ballots, the biases of counters, and, underlying both points, the fact that what shall count in a hand recount as a vote is a contestable issue, both of law and of judgment.

Of the disputed votes awarded to either Gore or Bush that yielded Gore's net gain of at most 215 votes in Palm Beach County, 61 percent went to Gore and 39 percent to Bush, compared to a 62/38 percent split of the total machine-counted Palm Beach vote. This undermines the earlier suggestion that Gore might have received 53 percent of the votes recovered in a state-wide hand recount. More likely he would have received no more than 50 percent, his total in the machine count, and then of course he would not have overcome Bush's lead. This point also underscores the meaninglessness of the 168-vote gain for Gore from the partial recount in heavily Democratic precincts in Miami-Dade County. He received 70 percent of the additional votes recorded by the recount, though his margin in the county as a whole was only 53 percent; a complete recount might well have reduced the 70 percent to 53 percent.

An alternative method of estimating how many recovered votes each candidate might have received in a completed hand recount in the four counties would be to compare Gore's vote gain in Palm Beach County with the number of disputed ballots in that county, 14,500. His maximum net gain of 215 votes from those ballots was 1.5 percent of the number of votes he received in the machine count. Had he received the same percentage vote gain from the 10,750 undervotes in Miami-Dade County, he would have had a net gain of only 161 in that county, compared to 263 by my earlier method. And even the 161-vote estimate is inflated. Gore received a lower percentage of the total Gore-Bush vote in Miami-Dade County—53 percent, compared with 62 percent in Palm Beach County. If a 24 percent margin (62–38) would have yielded Gore 161 extra votes over Bush, a 6 percent margin (53–47) would have yielded him only forty.

TABLE 1

REGRESSION OF SPOILED BALLOTS

Independent Variable	Coefficient	t-Statistic
Ballot	−.008	−1.350
Where counted	**.040**	6.495
Income	.000	.258
Hispanic	.008	.290
Black	.039	1.262
Literacy	**−.230**	−3.077
Over 64	**−.149**	−3.534
Under 25	−.159	−1.513
Constant	.221	4.314

$R^2 = .78$
Adj. $R^2 = .74$
$F = 23.35$
Prob. $> F = .000$
$N = 63$

It might make sense to average the machine-count and hand-recount results on the theory that if their errors are independent, averaging the two results will cause many of the errors to cancel out. But averaging Bush's 930-vote machine lead with a smaller but still positive lead for Bush obviously would not swing the election to Gore.

Some further light is cast on these issues by regression analysis. In Table 1, the dependent variable is the percentage of spoiled ballots in each county,[10] and the independent variables are factors that might be expected to influence that percentage. The variables

---

[10] I use "spoiled" loosely to include undervotes as well as overvotes, though some undervotes are deliberate. The source of the demographic data used in Tables 1 through 4 is U.S. Census Bureau, *Population, Demographic, and Housing Information from the 1990 Census*, http://quickfacts.census.gov/qfd/states/12000.html. The source of the literacy data is Florida Literacy Coalition, *The Florida Literacy Data and Statistics Handbook* 7 (Florida Dept. of Education, n.d.) (1992 data) (the literacy measure I use is one minus "the percentage of adults functioning at the lowest level of literacy," id.). The sources of the ballot and counting data are Shaw, Leusner, and Holton (cited in note 2), and Brooks Jackson, *Fact Check: Examining Florida's "Undervote"* (Nov 30, 2000), http://www.cnn.com/2000/ALLPOLITICS/stories/11/30/jackson.undervote/index.html and http://www.cnn.com/ELECTION/2000/resources/ballot1.html. The variance across counties in the percentage of spoiled ballots is very great, ranging from less than two-tenths of 1 percent to more than 12 percent, with a mean of 3.9 percent and a standard deviation of 3.1 percent.

for "ballot" and "where counted" are dummy variables[11] that take, respectively, a value of 1 if the ballot was a punchcard ballot and 0 if it was not, and 1 if the votes are counted at the county's election office and 0 if they are counted at the precinct level and the totals are forwarded to the county office. When the vote is counted in the precinct, the counting machine may be programmed to reject the ballot if it contains an undervote or an overvote and to let the voter revote. So it is not surprising that when the counting takes place at the county rather than the precinct level there is a statistically significantly higher spoilage rate. What is surprising is that when other explanatory variables are taken into account, the use of the punchcard ballot does not result in a higher spoilage rate—and the percentage of elderly residents of a county actually reduces that rate. Income, race, and Hispanic ethnicity are not significant factors, but literacy is highly significant—the lower the literacy rate in a county, the higher the percentage of spoiled ballots.[12] The lack of significance of the design of the ballot, and the significant effect of literacy, are evidence that the undervotes and overvotes are the result mainly of voter error rather than of defects in the voting machines.[13] The instructions were clear—if you could read.

The results change, however, when undervotes and overvotes are regressed separately on the independent variables. This is done in Table 2. These regressions are not strictly comparable to the regression in Table 1 because of missing data; data for only fifty-two counties are available, compared to data for sixty-three counties in Table 1. However, the means and standard deviations in the two data sets are almost identical, which suggests that the two sets are quite comparable. Table 2 indicates that where the ballots are counted (whether at the precinct level or at the county level) is crucial for overvotes but not for undervotes. It is easier to spot an overvote as an error and thus invite the voter to vote again than to spot an undervote as an error, since an undervote may be

---

[11] That is, dichotomous variables, variables that can take a value of only 0 or 1.

[12] Some of these variables, however, are highly correlated; for example, the correlation between black and literacy is −.55, and between black and income −.32.

[13] The regression equation as a whole has a high explanatory significance, as shown by the high R^2, Adjusted R^2, and F value. The number of observations is fewer than the number of counties because of missing data for four of the counties. Coefficients whose sign is statistically significant at the conventional 5 percent significance level are in boldface.

TABLE 2

SEPARATE REGRESSIONS OF OVERVOTES AND UNDERVOTES

INDEPENDENT VARIABLE	(1) OVERVOTES		(2) UNDERVOTES	
	Coefficient	t-Statistic	Coefficient	t-Statistic
Ballot	−.014	−1.971	.012	5.245
Where counted	.032	4.751	.000	.216
Income	−.000	−.090	−.000	−1.458
Hispanic	.031	.849	−.013	−1.057
Black	.085	1.720	.000	.017
Literacy	−.173	−1.673	−.001	−.021
Over 64	−.075	−1.257	−.024	−1.209
Under 25	−.146	−.887	−.047	−.843
Constant	.157	2.130	.027	1.068

$R^2 = .66$ $R^2 = .48$
Adj. $R^2 = .59$ Adj. $R^2 = .38$
$F = 10.31$ $F = 4.94$
Prob. $> F = .000$ Prob. $> F = .000$
$N = 52$ $N = 52$

deliberate (the voter didn't want to vote for President), whereas an overvote must be accidental. Hence the significant negative sign of the "where counted" coefficient in equation (1) but not in equation (2). And notice that the punchcard ballot actually reduces the percentage of overvotes after correction for the other variables. But equation (2) supports the critics' claim that the punchcard ballot increases the incidence of undervotes. None of the other variables besides type of ballot is significant in either of the regressions in Table 2 at the conventional 5 percent level, but two of them, black and literacy, are significant at the 10 percent level in equation (2); the larger the black population and the lower the literacy level, the higher the incidence of undervotes even after other factors are taken into account.

Taken together, the two equations provide only weak support for the Democrats' claim that the punchcard machines used in the Florida election were defective. If voters have difficulty punching through, this would tend to increase the number of undervotes yet reduce the number of overvotes, so that the net percentage of spoiled ballots might not be greater—the implication of Table 1,

TABLE 3

NATURAL-LOG REGRESSIONS OF OVERVOTES AND UNDERVOTES

INDEPENDENT VARIABLE	(1) OVERVOTES		(2) UNDERVOTES	
	Coefficient	t-Statistic	Coefficient	t-Statistic
Ballot	.327	.714	**1.290**	4.064
Where counted	**1.699**	3.771	**.639**	2.046
Income	−1.584	−.946	−1.902	−1.641
Hispanic	−.061	−.274	−.161	−1.050
Black	−.123	−.277	.408	1.324
Literacy	**−9.547**	−2.146	−.820	−.266
Over 64	−.294	−.320	−.253	−.399
Under 25	.835	.523	−.157	−.142
Constant	8.940	.510	12.993	1.070
	R^2 =.53		R^2 =.54	
	Adj. R^2 = .44		Adj. R^2 = .46	
	F = 6.07		F = 6.39	
	Prob. > F = .000		Prob. > F = .000	
	N = 52		N = 52	

where the ballot variable had no statistically significant effect on the percentage of spoiled ballots.

The variables (other than the dummies) can be transformed into natural logarithms to reduce the weight of extreme observations, which may be unrepresentative. When this is done (see Table 3), the equation in Table 1 is unchanged, but the equations in Table 2 are changed somewhat. In the overvote equation, the ballot variable becomes insignificant, but the literacy variable becomes significant (and negative) at the conventional 5 percent significance level, just as in Table 1. In the undervote equation in Table 3, the only significant change is that the where-counted variable becomes statistically significant at the 5 percent level and, as expected, positive: undervotes are more likely when votes are counted at the county level, as there is then no possibility that the error will be caught before the voter leaves the voting place and that the voter will have an opportunity to revote.[14]

---

[14] Consistent with my earlier suggestion that it is easier to spot an overvote than an undervote, the coefficient of the "where counted" variable is almost three times as large in the overvote log regression as in the undervote log regression.

The log transformations thus strengthen the inferences from the original regressions. However, in the overvote equation in Table 3 is some support for the view that Gore probably did win the popular vote in Florida if legal votes can (as a matter of law) be recovered from spoiled ballots. If it is assumed that less literate voters are both more likely to overvote and more likely to vote Democratic, and that the overvote would tend to take the form of punching Gore's chad and then writing in Gore's name in the place for write-in candidates, a recount of overvotes could be expected to produce a net gain for Gore. The Gore team believed that this type of overvoting had occurred in Duval County and cost Gore a significant number of votes.[15] Yet it was Bush rather than Gore who complained that to recount undervotes and not overvotes was an unsound procedure, and Gore defended the Florida supreme court's decision (see Part II) to recount only undervotes. Moreover, some of the gains that Gore obtained in the four counties that he sought recounts in may have been from recovered overvotes.

The suggestion that a hand recount of overvotes would have helped Gore is supported by a final statistical transformation—weighting the observations by the population of each county. The smaller a county's population, the more likely random factors are to influence the number of spoiled ballots—and the population of Florida counties varies from less than 6,000 to almost 2 million. Table 4 redoes Table 2, substituting weighted for unweighted regressions.[16] Notice that, although the undervote equation is virtually identical to the undervote equation in Table 2, the only variable in the overvote equation that is statistically significant at the conventional 5 percent level is race. (Whether counted at the county rather than the precinct level is, however, significant at

---

[15] Richard T. Cooper, *A Different Florida Vote—In Hindsight*, Los Angeles Times (Dec 24, 2000), p A1; see also Andres Viglucci, Geoff Doughterty, and William Yardley, *Florida Black Voters Shortchanged*, Pittsburgh Post-Gazette (Dec 31, 2000), p A12. According to Cooper, Gore's team did not discover the overvote problem in Duval County in time to request a recount there. Cooper's finding that a not insignificant number of overvotes contained a write-in and a mechanical vote for the same presidential candidate is supported in Mickey Kaus, *Almost Everything We Thought about the Florida Recount Is Wrong!* Slate (Dec 28, 2000), http://slate.msn.com/code/kausfiles/kausfiles.asp?Show=12/28/2000&idMessage=6758.

[16] An alternative would be to weight by number of votes cast per county, but that turns out to yield materially identical results.

TABLE 4

NATURAL-LOG REGRESSIONS OF OVERVOTES AND UNDERVOTES

INDEPENDENT VARIABLE	(1) OVERVOTES		(2) UNDERVOTES	
	Coefficient	t-Statistic	Coefficient	t-Statistic
Ballot	.003	.370	**.011**	5.828
Where counted	.013	1.719	.001	.567
Income	.000	.419	.000	.778
Hispanic	−.029	−1.597	.002	.331
Black	**.209**	3.426	.011	.730
Literacy	−.095	−.947	−.026	−.977
Over 64	−.012	−.169	−.008	−.434
Under 25	−.160	−1.013	−.014	−.337
Constant	.064	.757	.019	.847
	$R^2 = .53$		$R^2 = .73$	
	Adj. $R^2 = .44$		Adj. $R^2 = .68$	
	$F = 6.02$		$F = 14.25$	
	Prob. $> F = .000$		Prob. $> F = .000$	
	$N = 52$		$N = 52$	

the 10 percent level.) Black voters are more likely to cast overvotes, and since we know that black voters heavily favored Gore, recovered overvotes would probably favor Gore. It is curious, therefore, that the Democratic recount efforts were focused entirely on undervotes, leaving Republicans to argue that overvotes should be recounted as well. For completeness, I note that when Table 1 (the regression of spoiled ballots, that is, of undervotes plus overvotes) is redone on a weighted basis, the ballot variable remains insignificant and the where-counted variable significant, but the literacy variable recedes to significance at the 10 percent level and the race variable becomes highly significant, both in the predicted direction. Table 4 implies, however, that the racial effect is limited to overvotes.

B. THE BUTTERFLY BALLOT AND A TAXONOMY OF VOTING-RELATED ERRORS

Some voters in Palm Beach County who cast ballots that the machine counted were misled by the "butterfly" punchcard ballot used in that county and mistakenly voted for Buchanan when they meant to vote for Gore.[17] The ballot was the brainchild of the Democratic supervisor of elections for the county. The reasons for its butterfly design (i.e., candidates listed on both sides of the ballot rather than all on one side) were both to enable the candidates' names to be printed in large type, in consideration of the number of elderly voters in the county, and to place before the voter all the candidates for each office on one page, without need to turn the page, so that the voter would not vote before realizing that there were other choices; presumably overvotes would be less common. Another ballot design, while less confusing, would have disenfranchised an unknown number of voters who had poor eyesight, or cast their vote before realizing that there were additional candidates for the same office on the next page of the ballot, or cast two votes for candidates for the same office because they didn't realize that candidates for the same office were on different pages. Even if, as is widely and for all I know correctly believed, the butterfly design was on balance a mistake, it was an irremediable one for purposes of the 2000 election—not only because there was no reliable method of determining within any reasonable deadline for selecting Florida's electors the actual intent of these voters, but also because altering an election outcome on the basis of the confusing design of the ballot would open a Pandora's box of election challenges.

The problem with the butterfly ballot underscores the sheer variety of voting-related errors, and it will be useful to pause here and summarize the different types:

1. *Error in tabulation.* An impeccably completed ballot may fail to be counted as a vote because of a defect in the design, construction, or operation of the tabulating machinery or process (the tabulation might be done by hand). There were few if any errors in the machine tabulation of the Florida presidential votes, at least after the machine recount. Hand tabulation, as we know, is prone to error.

2. *Unspoiled ballot, voter error.* This was the butterfly problem. The ballot was completed and tabulated correctly, but did not reflect the voter's actual intention. Such errors, it is agreed, could not be corrected in time to affect the outcome of the 2000 election.

---

[17] The reports by the media that these were mainly elderly Jewish voters is undermined by my regression results, which suggest that age does not lead to mistakes in voting.

3. *Spoiled ballot, pure voter error.* The voter misread or misapplied the instructions, and as a result cast a ballot that the tabulating machinery would not record as a vote. This was the focus of the hand recounts.

4. *Spoiled ballot, defective voting machine.* The voter could not cast a ballot that the tabulating machinery would record as a vote because the voting machine (not the tabulating machine) was defective—for example, cluttered with chads from previous ballots, making it difficult or impossible for later voters to punch their ballots all the way through.

C. REFORM

If my analysis thus far is correct, leading to the conclusion that the vote in Florida for President is best described as a statistical tie, the lesson for the future is a simple one: increase the accuracy of voting machines and recount procedures and (for the sake of the confused, inept, or inexperienced voter, if it is considered important as a matter of democratic theory or social peace to facilitate their voting) the clarity (legibility, intelligibility, ease of use, etc.) of the ballot in order to reduce the probability of statistical ties. The more accurate the voting machinery, the less likely such a tie is; if the machinery were perfectly accurate, a statistical tie would occur only if the leading candidates received the identical number of votes, which is extraordinarily unlikely. The less accurate the count, the more likely that a difference of a few hundred votes will be interpreted as a tie because the margin of error is also hundreds of votes. To minimize confusion and arbitrary disparities, moreover, the voting technology should be uniform throughout each state rather than varying from county to county.

One might hope that the states would take this lesson to heart without prodding or coercion by the federal government. But that may be too optimistic. Incumbents may oppose any reform—having won with the existing voting technology, they may be afraid to take a plunge into the unknown by changing it; they may even be convinced that it favors them.[18] This conjecture is supported by the fact that the inadequacies of election administration have

---

[18] See, e.g., John Mintz and Dan Keating, *A Racial Gap in Voided Votes: Precinct Analysis Finds Stark Inequity in Polling Problems*, Washington Post (Dec 27, 2000), p A1.

been well known for a very long time,[19] yet little has been done to ameliorate them.

If the states will not improve the accuracy of their vote counting, their alternative is to insist that voters comply strictly with the ballot instructions. The instructions issued with the Florida punchcard ballots were clear, and if they had been followed carefully there would have been few dangling or dimpled chads. There was, it is true, evidence presented at the trial of the contest proceeding (see Part II) that some of the punchcard voting machines may have been defective; the example I gave earlier was a buildup of chads in the receptacle under the ballot that might have made it difficult to punch through. But undervotes resulting from such defects are properly regarded either as voter errors or as joint machine-voter errors, since the voter who has read the directions will know that if he has failed, for whatever reason, to punch through, the machine is defective and he should speak to a precinct worker. A pure machine error is one that the voter could not spot, for example, a failure of the machine to record the votes on an impeccably punched-through ballot. Those errors appear to be vanishingly small, even in the case of punchcard ballots. That is why the literacy and "where counted" variables are so significant in the regressions.

One of the much-discussed reforms, a national ballot for presidential elections, would probably be a mistake. Because all national elections coincide with elections for state and local officials, the voter would have to be given two ballots. This would confuse many voters, slow up the voting and the counting process, and create additional errors in counting. An even greater objection is to prematurely nationalizing the presidential-ballot issue, the kind of mistake many people think the Supreme Court made in deciding *Roe v Wade*[20] in favor of a federal right of abortion rather than leaving the regulation of abortion to the states. Just as *Roe* propelled abortion to the top of the national agenda by identifying it as an issue to be decided at the national level, so a national ballot

---

[19] "Almost everyone agrees that states generally must do a better job" in election administration. Jeanne Richman and Robert Otis, *State Control of Election Administration*, in Richard J. Carlson, ed, *Issues of Electoral Reform* 117, 118 (1974).

[20] 410 US 113 (1973).

would become a focus of political dispute over the conduct and result of elections. The parties would fight over every feature of the ballot and the counting mechanism, and the loser would blame the ballot and its designers for his loss. The electoral process would become a cockpit of partisan wrangling, and public faith in the reliability of the process would be eroded. An advantage of our federal system is that many contentious issues can be diffused across a multitude of different state systems rather than becoming a magnet for high-visibility nationwide political strife.

Nor is the Florida deadlock an argument for abolishing the Electoral College. On the contrary, if Presidents were elected by popular vote, a nationwide recount might have been unavoidable in 2000 because Gore's margin was so small. He received 51 million votes and Bush 50.5 million,[21] a difference of one-half of one percent, which if a popular-vote plurality were the method used for electing the President would have incited calls for a national recount on the same grounds that Gore argued for a Florida recount. There is little doubt that if Bush's people nosed around heavily Democratic precincts throughout the nation they would come up with colorable arguments about voter and tabulation error that might have determined the election. A national recount would be a nightmare. Nevertheless, the nationwide popular vote in this election, unlike the Florida vote, was not a statistical tie. If we assume that nationwide the machine error rate is no higher than the maximum estimate of the error rate of the widely criticized Florida punch ballot, which I said was .5 percent, then the total undercount was only 500,000 votes. Even if Bush had managed to snag 100 percent of these votes in a recount, he would not have overcome Gore's 540,000-vote lead.

I do not deny that the Electoral College has anachronistic features. Its creation reflected concerns about the administrability of a nationwide popular election that have no current validity, and also reflected expectations that have proved unfounded that the contingent election procedure ordained by the Constitution— election of the President by the House of Representatives (the most democratic component of the governmental structure created

---

[21] David Stout, *The 43rd President: The Final Tally: Gore's Lead in the Popular Vote Now Exceeds 500,000*, New York Times (national ed; Dec 30, 2000), p A11.

at Philadelphia in 1787) if no candidate received a majority of electoral votes—would be used frequently.[22] But to anticipate Part II,
finding new functions for old provisions is a familiar technique of
government. The Electoral College reduces the uncertainties that
would afflict a system in which the President was determined by
the nationwide popular vote. These uncertainties could also be
reduced by the adoption of a national ballot, but that solution
has its own drawbacks, as I have explained. The much-criticized
weighting of the votes in the Electoral College, which is identical
to that in Congress (each state has as many electoral votes as it
has representatives plus senators), is faithful to the original compromise that enabled the Constitution to be ratified and assures
that candidates will have cross-regional appeal. A feasible reform,
however, might be to amend the Constitution to require states to
appoint electors by popular election and to require the electors to
vote in accordance with the result of that election.

A more questionable reform would be to require that each state's
electoral vote be divided among the presidential candidates in proportion to their share of the popular vote. This would reduce the
likelihood that the popular-vote winner would, as in 2000, lose
in the Electoral College. But it would increase the likelihood of
deadlocks. It is easier to determine who is the winner of the popular vote in a state than to determine his actual share of the vote,
a determination that might be required for the allocation of the
state's electoral votes between him and his opponent.

II. The Litigation

I called the tie in the Florida popular vote for President a
"statistical" tie, not a tie *simpliciter*. The difference is important.
If it were a real tie, something would have to be done to break it.
It was not a real tie; Bush won when the U.S. Supreme Court in
Bush v Gore rebuffed the legal challenge that Gore had mounted
in the Florida courts. Gore had tried to show that the election in

---

[22] See Neal R. Peirce and Lawrence D. Longley, *The People's President: The Electoral College
in American History and the Direct Vote Alternative* (rev ed 1981); Shlomo Slonim, *The Electoral College at Philadelphia: The Evolution of an Ad Hoc Congress for the Selection of a President*,
73 J Am Hist 35 (1986). But since each state's delegation would have one vote, the contingent procedure isn't actually very democratic, as was discovered in 1824, when Andrew
Jackson lost in the House, although he had the most popular and electoral votes.

Florida hadn't really been a tie, that he had won it. This is very doubtful, as we have just seen.

Bush v Gore has been ferociously attacked,[23] yet less because of what it said (that the recount procedure decreed by the Florida supreme court on December 8 was unconstitutional, a view to which seven of the nine Justices subscribed) than for what it did (forbidding a further recount and thus confirming Bush's lead in the certified vote total) and for who did it, namely, the five most conservative Justices, assumed by liberal critics to have partisan motivations. I want to postpone the issue of motivation and consider the soundness of the Court's decision to reverse the Florida supreme court, and of the remedy the Court decreed.

There is such a thing as judgment in advance of doctrine. Experienced judges may have a strong intuition about how a case should be decided yet have difficulty matching the intuition to existing doctrine. Such tensions play a creative role in legal growth and change. *Bush v Gore* may someday be seen as such a case.

A. THE RUN-UP TO BUSH V GORE

The litigation that culminated in the Supreme Court's decision was complex though compressed, involving numerous provisions of state and federal law and eight major judicial decisions.[24] We must work through its stages carefully, beginning with Florida's election statute.[25] The counties are required to submit their vote totals to Florida's secretary of state within seven days of the election, which meant, in 2000, by November 14,[26] except that as a consequence of federal law, overseas ballots are to be counted if received up to the tenth day after the election, and added to the

---

[23] See, e.g., Jeffrey Rosen, *Disgrace: The Supreme Court Commits Suicide*, New Republic (Dec 25, 2000), p 18.

[24] I count as major the decision by Florida circuit judge Lewis on November 17, 2000, upholding the Florida secretary of state's refusal to extend the deadline for hand recounting beyond November 14; the state supreme court's reversal of that decision on November 21; the U.S. Supreme Court's vacation of the decision of the state supreme court on December 4; circuit judge Sauls's dismissal of the contest proceeding the same day; the reversal of that dismissal by the Florida supreme court on December 8; the U.S. Supreme Court's stay of that decision the next day; the Florida supreme court's decision on December 11 purporting to clarify the November 21 decision; and the U.S. Supreme Court's reversal of the Florida supreme court's December 8 decision on December 12.

[25] Fla Stat, tit IX, esp. chs 101, 102.

[26] Fla Stat § 102.111(1).

seventh-day totals.[27] Up to that seventh day, a candidate may "protest" the result of the election in a county as "being erroneous" and "may . . . request . . . a manual recount," and the county canvasing board "may authorize" it.[28] This hand recount is of just a sample of precincts; but if it "indicates an error in the vote tabulation which could affect the outcome of the election,"[29] the board must take further corrective action, which can include a hand recount of all the ballots cast in the county.[30] Should this recount not be completed by the seventh day, the results of the recount "may be ignored" by the secretary of state.[31] Once she has received the county totals and certified the winner of the election, the loser can "contest" the outcome by filing a lawsuit. If he can show in the contest suit that enough "legal votes" were rejected in the count on which the secretary of state relied to "change or place in doubt the result of the election," the court can "provide any relief appropriate under such circumstances."[32] No vote is to be declared invalid if, though the ballot is "damaged or defective," there is "a clear indication of the intent of the voter as determined by the canvassing board."[33]

None of the recounts sought by Gore, except the one in Volusia County,[34] was complete by November 14, and the secretary of state said she would refuse to consider them. Her view was that unless there was evidence of fraud or statutory violations, or some disaster (a hurricane, for example) that had interrupted the recount, the seven-day statutory deadline for the submission of the county's votes should be firm.[35] She implicitly interpreted the statutory term "error in the vote tabulation" to mean a failure of the tabula-

---

[27] See *Palm Beach County Canvassing Board v Harris*, 772 So2d 1273, 1288 and n 19 (Fla 2000) (per curiam).

[28] Fla Stat §§ 102.112(1), 102.166(1), (4)(a), (4)(c).

[29] Fla Stat § 102.166(5).

[30] Fla Stat § 102.166(5)(c).

[31] Fla Stat § 102.112(1). The preceding section (§ 102.111(1)) says "shall be ignored," creating the only real inconsistency in the statute. I have no quarrel with the Florida supreme court's preferring "may," which was also the position taken by the secretary of state.

[32] Fla Stat §§ 102.168(3)(c), (e)(8).

[33] Fla Stat §101.5614(5).

[34] See note 4 above.

[35] Her statement is quoted in *Palm Beach County Canvassing Board v Harris*, 772 So2d 1220, 1226 n 5 (Fla 2000), vacated and remanded under the name *Bush v Palm Beach County Canvassing Board*, 121 S Ct 471 (2000) (per curiam).

ting machine to count properly marked ballots, rather than miscounts due to voters' failing to follow instructions or to complain to a precinct worker if the voter couldn't comply with the instructions because the voting machine was defective. The many dimpled and dangling chads were the result of voters' either failing to follow the instructions or, if the voting machine itself was defective, failing to seek the assistance of one of the precinct election workers. Under the Florida election statute, only errors in the tabulation of the vote warrant the canvasing board's ordering a hand recount of the county's votes. If voter error, not being an error in tabulation, is not a valid ground for recounting rejected (or all) ballots, there was no possible justification for extending the statutory deadline for the submission of a county's votes in order to permit an effort to recover votes from ballots rejected because of voter error. The only reason the county canvasing boards needed extra time was to complete the laborious hand recounts that are necessary to ascertain the clear intent of the voter in a ballot the voter spoiled.

On November 21, the Florida supreme court reversed the secretary of state and extended the November 14 deadline for protest recounts to November 26.[36] This decision was unwise; it was the catalyst of the legal and political mess that roiled the nation for the ensuing three weeks. It was also unsound, a patent misreading of the election statute. By postponing the certification to November 26, the court postponed the commencement of the contest proceeding until then.[37] This compressed the time for completing such a proceeding to a degree that made completion by any realistic deadline infeasible. By moving the boundary between the protest and contest phases the court had squeezed the contest phase virtually to death. The unwisdom of such a squeeze argues for the secretary of state's statutory interpretation, which was in any event a straightforward reading of "error in the vote *tabulation*." That doesn't sound like an error by the voter, as distinct from an error by the mechanical or human tabulator. The tabulating machinery used in the punchcard counties is designed not to tabulate dimpled or otherwise unpunched-through ballots; how therefore could its failure to count such ballots be thought an error in tabulation?

---

[36] *Palm Beach County Canvassing Board v Harris*, note 27 above.

[37] See Fla Stat § 102.168(2).

Since that "failure" is built into the design of the tabulating machinery, to call it an error or defect in the tabulation of the vote would make hand recounts mandatory in all close elections, something the statute cannot reasonably be read to contemplate. Since many elections, especially at the lower levels of government, are very close, it would hardly pay to invest in voting machines if all close elections had to be recounted by hand—a state would be well advised in that event to use hand counting exclusively.

The absence of a postmark on some absentee ballots of military personnel, however, a defect that the secretary of state did not think invalidated those ballots, was akin to a tabulating error. The voter does not affix the postmark. The overseas voters had followed instructions to the letter and had thus done all they could reasonably have done to cast a legal vote; the screw-up was in the transmission process.[38]

It is important to keep in mind that the punchcard voting machine does not *tabulate* votes. The machine is just the platform for the ballot, designed to enable the voter to signify his vote by punching holes. After voting he removes the ballot from the machine, and the votes on it are then recorded by another machine, the machine that counts the ballots. As I have emphasized, an error in the vote tabulation is an error by the tabulating machinery, or by hand counters if the tabulating machine breaks down and the votes are counted by hand instead. Distinguishing between errors in voting and in tabulation is important because the voter is complicit in the former error whereas the latter error is invisible to the voter. If the punchcard machine doesn't work and as a result the voter does not emerge with a fully punched-through ballot, he should know, if he's read the directions, that he has a spoiled ballot and he should request a fresh ballot and a properly operating voting machine. It is easy to understand why a state might not want its canvasing boards to be forced to undergo the bother of hand recounts, let alone the agony of hand recounts protracted beyond the seven-day statutory limit for the submission of a county's votes, merely because voters fail to follow instructions.

---

[38] The Democrats, after being accused of being anti-military, decided not to make an issue of the absence of postmarks on military ballots. Some other irregularities in the processing of overseas ballots were challenged, but the Florida courts rebuffed the challenge. See *Jacobs v Seminole County Canvassing Board*, 773 So2d 519 (Fla 2000) (per curiam).

The statute does not specify the circumstances if any in which the secretary of state is required or even permitted to include in her certification of the election results the results of a recount not completed by the statutory deadline. But the statute authorizes her to interpret the statute,[39] implying that her interpretation if reasonable is conclusive. Katherine Harris's interpretation, which excluded voter error as a ground for extending the deadline, was reasonable and should therefore have been conclusive on the Florida supreme court. Indeed, it was the natural and sensible interpretation of "error in the vote tabulation," which, to repeat, is the only basis in the statute for a complete hand recount of a county's votes.

The statute also provides that the secretary of state may ignore recount results received after the seventh day following the election. This implies that she has discretion to ignore results not barred by the statute (e.g., a hand recount conducted because of an error in the vote tabulation that might have affected the outcome of the election) as well as being compelled to ignore those that are barred.[40] So even if she erred in her statutory interpretation, erred therefore in thinking her hands tied by the statute and therefore failed to exercise her discretion to ignore or not to ignore late recount results designed to correct voter error, the court should have directed her to exercise her discretion; that is the normal remedy for a failure to exercise discretion.[41] The fact that Harris is a Republican and that her rulings favored Bush's candidacy did not disentitle those rulings to the usual deference; Florida had for good or ill made the secretary of state an elected official.

---

[39] Fla Stat § 97.012(1).

[40] As Judge Lewis explained in upholding Katherine Harris's refusal to include late recount results, "Florida law grants to the Secretary [of State], as the Chief Elections Officer, broad discretionary authority to accept or reject late filed returns. The purpose and intent of my Order was to insure that she in fact properly exercised her discretion, rather than automatically reject returns that came in after the statutory deadline. On the limited evidence presented, it appears that the Secretary has exercised her reasoned judgment to determine what relevant factors and criteria should be considered, applied them to the facts and circumstances pertinent to the individual counties involved, and made her decision." *McDermott v Harris*, 2000 WL 1714590 (Fla Cir Ct Nov 17, 2000), reversed under the name *Palm Beach County Canvassing Board v Harris* (note 27 above).

[41] See, e.g., *Chathas v Local 134 IBEW*, 233 F3d 508, 514 (7th Cir 2000); *Channel v Citicorp National Services, Inc.*, 89 F3d 379, 387 (7th Cir 1996); *Campanella v Commerce Exchange Bank*, 137 F3d 885, 892 (6th Cir 1998). As the court said in *Channel*, "Because he held that § 1367(a) did not authorize the exercise of supplemental jurisdiction, [the district judge] did not exercise the discretion § 1367(c) confers. It belongs to him rather than to us, so we remand for its exercise." 89 F3d at 387.

The justices of the Florida supreme court thought themselves at liberty to strong-arm the election statute because they considered it internally inconsistent, inasmuch as it allows a recount to be sought right up to the seventh day after the election even though a recount requested on the last day could not be completed by the end of that day, the deadline for certification. There is no inconsistency. If the recount is not requested promptly after the election and so cannot be completed by the seventh day, the losing candidate has mainly himself to blame for not having acted faster; and the only consequence is to force him back on his remedy of filing a contest proceeding.

The appearance of inconsistency is a result of the court's mistaken interpretation of "error in the vote tabulation." If, as the secretary of state believed, this just refers to a breakdown of the tabulating process, meaning that perfectly unspoiled ballots just have not been counted, the hand recount should not take much time at all. It will be obvious at a glance which candidate received the vote on those ballots. Judgment, disagreement, and resulting delay come into play only when, because the ballot was spoiled, the voter's intention is an enigma.

On December 8, the Florida supreme court would, as we shall see, rule in effect that the certification has no presumptive validity, and if this is right (it is not, as we'll also see), the disappointed candidate loses little by being hurried through the protest phase and into the contest phase of the challenge to the election. To allow the deadline for certification to be postponed hands him a Pyrrhic victory by truncating the contest period. But the more important point, to repeat, since the December 8 ruling was erroneous, is that the only thing that would make the seven-day period for the submission of a county's votes unreasonably short, other than extraordinary circumstances fortunately not present such as fraud or some natural disaster, would be a desire to recover spoiled ballots as votes, a process that is time consuming because of its subjectivity. The secretary of state was entitled in the exercise of her discretion in the interpretation and application of the statute to conclude that wanting to recover votes from ballots spoiled by the voter was not a proper reason for an extension of the statutory deadline—especially in a presidential election, where delay in certifying the results of the election could cause chaos, as we shall see.

Against this it can be argued that since the statute regulates all elections in Florida, and only the presidential election is time sensitive (because of the nature of the office and because of the tight federal statutory and constitutional deadlines for casting and counting electoral votes), to interpret the statute to make it "work" for presidential elections is to let the tail wag the dog. And it is true that the statute fixes no deadline for the completion of contest proceedings. But it fixes a tight deadline for the certification of the winner after any protests. The legislature recognized the desirability of resolving all election disputes as soon as possible so that the "winner" does not exist in a kind of limbo during much of his term of office. Moreover, it is precisely in adapting the statute to the exigencies of a presidential election that the secretary of state might have been expected to be given a freer rein in statutory interpretation and application. Her decision not to delay the certification of the winner of the presidential election deserved considerable deference, it received none.

The Florida supreme court acknowledged, indeed emphasized, that both in interpreting the statute differently from the secretary of state and in casting aside her discretionary authority, it was appealing to a higher law than the statute. It derided "sacred, unyielding adherence to statutory scripture"[42] and "hyper-technical reliance upon statutory provisions"[43] and said that "the abiding principle governing all election law in Florida" was to be found in the statement in Florida's constitution that "all political power is inherent in the people."[44] The court was using the Florida constitution, or perhaps some principle of natural law, to trim the statute. "[T]he will of the people is the paramount consideration. . . . This fundamental principle, *and* our traditional rules of statutory construction, guide our decision today."[45]

But Article II of the U.S. Constitution provides that each state shall pick presidential electors "in such Manner as the Legislature thereof shall direct."[46] Not as the *state* shall direct, but as the state *legislature* shall direct. On December 4, the U.S. Supreme Court

---

[42] 772 So2d at 1227–28, quoting *Boardman v Esteva*, 323 So2d 259, 263 (Fla 1975).

[43] 772 So2d at 1227.

[44] Id at 1230, quoting Fla Const, Art I, § 1.

[45] Id at 1228 (emphasis added, footnote omitted).

[46] US Const, Art II, § 1, cl 2.

vacated and remanded the Florida supreme court's decision of November 21 in a unanimous opinion strongly intimating that a state court cannot, by appeal to the state's constitution, limit the power granted the state's legislature by Article II.[47] This does not mean that a state court has no legitimate role to play in the selection of electors, even if there is no express delegation to it by the legislature. The court could decide, for example, whether the election law had actually been adopted by the state legislature. Nor does it mean that what the Florida supreme court did was not "interpretation," a word of almost infinite plasticity. It means only that Article II may circumscribe (not extinguish) the authority of a state court to construe state legislation governing the appointment of the state's presidential electors. Normally, it is true, the U.S. Supreme Court defers to a state supreme court's interpretation of the state's statutes. But if Article II grants authority to state legislatures, maybe it authorizes the Court to protect the prerogative thus granted. When the Constitution designates a particular organ of state government as the presidential election rulemaker, it becomes a question of federal law whether the state judiciary has allowed the designated organ to decide the manner in which the state shall select its presidential electors. By assigning to state legislatures the task of determining the manner by which federal electors would be determined, Article II may reasonably be interpreted as federalizing disputes over whether the authority thus granted to state legislatures has been usurped by another branch of state government.

The provisions of the Florida constitution, like all the amendments to date of the U.S. Constitution, are approved by the legislature before being submitted for ratification, in Florida by the electorate. But that doesn't make the Florida constitution an election statute. We don't say that because Congress approves a constitutional amendment before the amendment is ratified, the amendment is a congressional enactment. Nor does a legislature, by approving a constitutional provision that will be interpreted by the courts, authorize those courts to revise the provision. The courts can invalidate it, or interpret it reasonably, but they are not to rewrite it, that is, interpret it unreasonably.

In claiming authority to limit the freedom of a state court in

---

[47] *Palm Beach County Canvassing Board v Harris*, 121 S Ct 471, 474 (2000) (per curiam).

interpreting the state's statute governing the manner of appointing presidential electors, the Court quoted from its 1892 decision in *McPherson v Blacker* a brief and enigmatic dictum that the words "in such Manner as the Legislature thereof shall direct" "operat[e] as a limitation upon the State in respect of any attempt to circumscribe the [state's] legislative power."[48] This dictum is weak authority for the December 4 decision, but we'll see that the decision can be defended by reference to a role that can reasonably be assigned to the "Manner Directed" Clause.

The Court sent the case back to the Florida supreme court for clarification of the basis of that court's interpretation of the election statute, and also for clarification of that court's view on whether the state legislature had wanted to comply with the "safe harbor" provision of Title III of the U.S. Code. If so, this presumably would limit the court's power to change preexisting Florida election law, because it is a precondition of the safe harbor that "final determination of any controversy or contest concerning the appointment of all or any of the electors of such State . . . shall have been made . . . pursuant to such [state] law *existing on said day*," that is, the day of the election, November 7.[49] Changing the existing law would not be a "violation" of the section; it would merely forfeit the safe harbor. But if the legislature *wanted* the safe harbor, the court's action in changing the law would compound the violation of state law, in further violation of federal law if Article II, section 1, clause 2 indeed limits a state judiciary's freedom to interpret the statute that prescribes the manner of appointing the state's presidential electors.

The Florida supreme court dithered. By the time it responded to the U.S. Supreme Court's request for clarification a week later (December 11),[50] the appeal from its second decision (issued on December 8, four days after the remand from the U.S. Supreme Court) had already been argued in the U.S. Supreme Court. The timing of the clarification was thus curious—it was as if Florida's

---

[48] 146 US 1, 25 (1892). The Court in *McPherson* had also quoted with approval a Senate report of 1874 which stated that the power conferred on state legislatures by the "Manner Directed" Clause "cannot be taken away from them or modified by their state constitutions." Id at 35.

[49] 3 USC § 5 (emphasis added).

[50] *Palm Beach County Canvassing Board v Harris*, 772 So2d 1273 (Fla 2000) (per curiam).

supreme court justices had waited to see whether the U.S. Supreme Court Justices would tip their hand in questioning the lawyers at the oral argument of the appeal from the December 8 decision.

The purported clarifying opinion, which recast the original opinion, that of November 21, as an exercise in conventional statutory interpretation and added that therefore the court had not changed the election statute and so had not jeopardized the safe harbor or violated Article II, was suspect for additional reasons besides the timing:

1. The court abandoned reliance on the Florida constitution without comment and specifically without explaining why its original opinion had placed such heavy weight on the constitution if the outcome had been dictated, as the December 11 opinion claims, by conventional principles of statutory interpretation.

2. It failed to explain why it had relied in its December 8 decision on the vacated decision of November 21.

3. It stated that the "plain meaning" of the statutory term "error in the vote tabulation" encompasses an error resulting from a voter's mistake that made his ballot unreadable by the machine.[51] I am not a "plain meaning" buff myself, but if that was to be the governing principle of statutory interpretation it supported, as we have seen, the secretary of state's interpretation rather than the court's.

4. By committing itself in its December 8 decision to another adventurous expansion of the election statute, it prejudged, as a practical matter, the propriety of its earlier adventurous expansion of the statute. Without looking foolish, it could not have said on December 11, the very day on which the appeal from its December 8 decision was being argued in the U.S. Supreme Court, "Oops, we goofed! The logic of the U.S. Supreme Court's opinion of December 4 requires us to vacate our decision of December 8." In any event, the attempt at clarification came too late to allow the lawyers to brief and argue its bearing on the about-to-be-decided appeal to the U.S. Supreme Court.

In defense of the delay, it might be argued that since the case had moved from the protest to the contest phase, it was no longer

---

[51] Id at 1283.

important whether the Florida court had erred in extending the statutory deadline for the completion of recounts during the pro-test phase from November 14 to November 26. But it was impor-tant. The extension had caused a reduction in Bush's lead as certi-fied by the secretary of state, the lead that the contest aimed to reduce further, from 930 votes to 537 votes by the inclusion of the results of the Broward recount, which was completed between the fourteenth and the twenty-sixth. The difference might have proved decisive in the recount that the Florida supreme court ordered on December 8 had that recount gone through to completion.

In speaking of the Florida supreme court's decisions of Decem-ber 8 and 11, I have gotten ahead of myself, and so let me retrace my steps a bit. After the secretary of state had on November 26, the date of the expiration of the extended deadline for certification following protest, certified Bush as the winner of the presidential election in Florida, albeit with the diminished lead of 537 votes, Gore had brought suit against the canvasing boards of Palm Beach and Miami-Dade counties, contesting the election results in those two counties. After a trial on December 2 and 3, state circuit judge Sauls had dismissed Gore's suit.[52] Judge Sauls ruled that Gore had failed to show that the canvasing boards had abused their discre-tion, the Palm Beach board in its methods of recounting or the Miami-Dade board in deciding not to complete the recount that it had begun. Gore's hopes seemed dashed. For even if Sauls was reversed, it seemed impossible that the contest proceeding could be completed by December 12, the accepted deadline (as we'll see), just one week away. But Gore appealed, and on December 8 the Florida supreme court reversed.[53] This was a surprise—not only because it was so late in the day, but also because the Democrats' efforts to establish pervasive defects in the voting machines had fallen short at the trial, because the Democrats were attacking de-cisions by canvasing boards dominated by Democrats and a ruling by a Democratic judge, and because it had become clear at the

---

[52] *Gore v Harris*, 2000 WL 1790621 (Fla Cir Ct Dec 4, 2000). Gore also challenged the certified vote totals in Nassau County, but the rejection of this challenge was affirmed by the Florida supreme court. *Gore v Harris*, 772 So2d 1243, 1260 (Fla 2000) (per curiam).

[53] *Gore v Harris*, 772 So2d 1243 (Fla 2000) (per curiam).

trial that hand recounts of spoiled ballots are largely standardless and probably inherently subjective.[54]

Judge Sauls had interpreted the state election statute as making contest proceedings judicial proceedings to review administrative action. The purpose of the contest trial was thus to determine whether the canvasing boards, the agencies charged with tabulating election results, had abused their discretion in failing to conduct a hand recount in a certain way (i.e., the Broward way, sought by Gore), or at all (the Miami-Dade County canvasing board had begun a hand recount, then changed its mind and stopped). Unless, perhaps, overvotes were recounted (see Part I), which Gore was not seeking, there was no reason to believe that the result of the election in either county would change in favor of Gore if reasonable recounting protocols were followed, of which the most favorable to Gore that could be considered reasonable was Palm Beach's three-dimples procedure. And so Judge Sauls was on solid ground in concluding that there had been no abuse of discretion by the election officials and therefore that there was no occasion to order a further recount. By reversing him and holding that the decisions of canvasing boards on whether to conduct hand recounts are entitled to no deference, the Florida supreme court ruled in effect that any doubts that might warrant a canvasing board in conducting a recount at the protest stage *compelled* the court at the contest stage to order (in fact to conduct itself or under its supervision) a hand recount. This ruling made the protest a meaningless preliminary to the contest and expanded, without any basis in the statute, the power of the courts relative to that of the officials—the members of the canvasing boards and the secretary of state—to whom the legislature had assigned the conduct and supervision of elections, including election recounts (and, incidentally, the power of the supreme court relative to that of the trial court). And while the statute limits the canvasing boards to correcting errors in the vote tabulation, the opinion authorizes judges in contest cases to conduct recounts intended to rectify voter errors as well. The court, even though it lacks staff and experience for counting and interpreting ballots (especially thousands or tens of thousands of mil-

---

[54] See, e.g., Trial Transcript (note 6 above), at *90–104 (testimony of Judge Charles Burton).

lions of ballots), becomes the primary vote tabulator, rather than the election officials. This is all upside down.[55]

As well as enlarging the grounds for a contest, the court set the threshold for awarding relief in a contest at an implausibly low level. No human or machine fault in the conduct of the election, and no external circumstances (such as a natural disaster) that might interfere with the conduct of the election or with the tabulation, had to be shown. It was enough that the election had been close and that a hand recount using unspecified criteria might recover enough undervotes to change the outcome.[56] Successful contests, in the sense of contests eventuating in judicial orders for selective or comprehensive hand recounts, would become the norm in close elections.

On November 21, the Florida supreme court had extinguished the secretary of state's discretion. On December 8, it extinguished the canvasing boards' discretion. The court said in effect: if the election is close and we think there were a lot of voter errors, we have carte blanche to order any mode of recount that strikes us as likely to recover a substantial number of the rejected votes.

Turning to remedy, the court ordered that the 215 votes that Gore had gained in the Palm Beach recount (or 176—the court left it to the trial court to decide which number was correct), plus the 168 that he had gained from the partial recount in Miami-Dade County, be added to Gore's net certified total. The court thus was changing that total after the deadline (November 26) that it itself had set for determining the certified vote totals after the completion of the protest recounts. The results of Broward County's recount, which had been completed within the extended deadline of November 26, had already yielded Gore a net gain of 582 votes. Other late recounts had netted Bush a few votes, but since his certified lead had already shrunk, mainly because of the Broward recount, to 537 votes,[57] the addition of the partial Palm Beach

---

[55] As forcefully argued by the chief justice in his dissenting opinion. *Gore v Harris* (note 53 above), at 1263–65. See also Brief of the Florida House of Representatives and Florida Senate as *Amici Curiae*, Dec 10, 2000, pp 3–16, in *Bush v Gore*, No 00–949, 121 S Ct 525 (2000) (per curiam).

[56] *Gore v Harris* (note 53 above), at 1255.

[57] This became, in the end, after the contest proceeding was dismissed by the Florida supreme court in the wake of the U.S. Supreme Court's decision of December 12, Bush's official popular-vote margin.

and Miami-Dade results reduced his lead to 154 votes if the higher figure for Palm Beach (215 rather than 176) was used. The court ordered a hand recount of all the remaining undervotes not only in Miami-Dade but throughout the state, estimated at 60,000.[58] No overvotes were to be recounted, however.

The trial before Judge Sauls had made clear, if it was not already, that the hand recounts conducted in the wake of the 2000 election in Florida had been neither uniform nor reliable. What had been recounted were mostly ballots that voters had failed to complete correctly, rather than correctly completed ballots that the machine had missed. There were Broward rules for determining the likely intent of the voter who had cast a spoiled ballot, which favored Gore unduly, as I explained in Part I, and there was a medley of different Palm Beach rules. (It was unclear what rules the Miami-Dade canvasing board had used.) Palm Beach's three-dimples rule had emerged after the recount had begun; earlier iterations had been a "sunshine rule"—light must be visible through the chad hole—and a "no dimples" rule, the rule followed by the Palm Beach canvasing board in previous election recounts.[59] Yet while acknowledging that "practical difficulties may well end up controlling the outcome of the election"[60]—that is, might terminate the contest proceeding before its completion—the Florida supreme court gave Gore the votes he had gained in Miami-Dade County before the recount was interrupted, even though the precincts counted were unrepresentative. The stunning implication (probably unintended) was that if the recount could not be concluded because of shortness of time, and Gore were ahead in the recount when time ran out, he would be declared the winner of the election even if the disputed ballots in precincts likely to favor Bush had not yet been recounted. For the court had given Gore the votes he had received in Miami-Dade's partial recount even though the full recount might *never* be completed ("practical difficulties may well end up controlling the outcome of the election").

---

[58] The reason this figure, to which should be added an estimated 110,000 overvotes statewide, exceeds the 30,000 figure that I estimated in Part I to be the maximum number of machine errors statewide is that 30,000 is an estimate of the number of errors that a hand recount would correct, that is, an estimate of the number of votes recoverable from the spoiled ballots. Many spoiled ballots remain inscrutable even after the most imaginative inspection.

[59] Trial Transcript (note 6 above), at *91–104.

[60] *Gore v Harris* (note 53 above), at 1261 n 21.

Without pretending that the hand recounts to date had used uniform or consistent criteria, the court nevertheless failed to prescribe uniform criteria for the statewide recount that it was ordering. It thus was ordering a recount that, as we saw in Part I, would carry no assurance of even minimal accuracy. Critics of the U.S. Supreme Court's intervention in the election deadlock blame this on the Court, which they argue impaled the Florida court on the horns of a dilemma. If that court left the statutory standard ("clear indication of the intent of the voter") undefined, it was inviting the equal-protection challenge that in fact became the ground on which it was reversed; but if it defined the standard, it would be violating Article II as interpreted in the U.S. Supreme Court's first opinion.

The argument is unsound. There is a difference between changing the meaning of a statute and filling in empty spaces in the statute. The Florida election law fixed a deadline that the state's supreme court changed. The law did not specify what type of spoiled ballot might contain a "clear indication of the intent of the voter." That was a gap in the statute that a court applying normal principles of statutory interpretation might fill. The Florida court could, moreover, have justified the laying down of precise criteria for recounting by reference to the Equal Protection Clause of the Fourteenth Amendment, the ground later embraced by seven Justices of the U.S. Supreme Court. To conform Florida election law to the requirements of federal constitutional law would not raise questions under Article II. Although *McPherson v Blacker* had described the power of the state legislatures over the appointment of electors as plenary, a later decision made clear that federal constitutional amendments limit that power.[61] This creates, it is true, a theoretical possibility that by invoking the constitutional jurisprudence of the U.S. Supreme Court concerning voting rights, the Florida supreme court (if nimble) could have reasoned that to save the constitutionality of the state election law it would have to interpret it to require the hand recounting of dimpled and other machine-rejected ballots. But given the vagaries of hand counting spoiled ballots, such reasoning would be untenable. There are limits, too, to the degree to which a court can

---

[61] *Williams v Rhodes*, 393 US 23 (1968); see Michael J. Glennon, *When No Majority Rules: The Electoral College and Presidential Succession* 27–30 (1992).

revise a statute to save its constitutionality; the power to invalidate an unconstitutional statute is not the power to rewrite it.

An alternative explanation for why the Florida supreme court declined to specify a uniform standard to guide the hand recount that it was ordering was that the Broward standard was indefensible, yet if the court rejected it but at the same time included the results of the Broward recount in Gore's vote, as it was obviously minded to do, the court would be accepting the results of a standard that it had just rejected. Better to say nothing about the standard than to grasp that nettle—or so it may have seemed to the Florida court independently of the U.S. Supreme Court's decision of December 4.

Ordering only undervotes recounted was another highly questionable feature of the Florida supreme court's December 8 decision. Gore's gains in the Broward, Palm Beach, Miami-Dade, and Volusia recounts that had already been conducted, gains the Florida supreme court had as it were credited to Gore's account, may well have included recovered—perhaps mistakenly recovered—overvotes. An overvote (voting for more than one candidate for the same office) is less likely to be recovered by a hand recount than an undervote is—if the voter has voted for two candidates for the same office, there is no objective method of determining which one he intended to vote for—but no stronger statement is possible. If the chad for one candidate is cleanly punched through, and the chad for his rival is slightly dislodged because the voter started to vote for the rival and then realized that he was making a mistake, the machine might read the second dislodgement as a vote and void the ballot. Or, as we know, if the voter both punched a candidate's chad and wrote the candidate's name in the space provided for write-in votes, the machine would automatically reject the ballot even though the voter's intent in such a case is clear; recall that Gore's team believed that this type of mistake, which a hand recount would cure, had cost him significant votes in at least one county. With an estimated 110,000 overvotes statewide and the election so close, even a tiny overvote recovery rate could prove decisive.

And so the refusal to order the overvotes recounted could not be justified, except possibly because of the shortness of time; and subject to the same qualification, all votes in the four counties in which Gore had picked up additional votes from the hand recount should have been recounted, not just those the machine count had failed to award to one of the presidential candidates. For some of those votes may have been true, unrecoverable overvotes, where, as I explained in Part I, the voter had punched through the chads for two presidential candidates but one of the chads had been left hanging, and as a result the machine, which can't be relied on to count hanging chads as votes, had failed to invalidate the ballot but a hand recounter would have invalidated it. For that matter, except for lack of time, all 6 million votes cast in the Florida election should have been recounted, since the result of recounts in strongly Democratic counties could not be generalized to the entire state.

Yet even the bobtailed recount ordered by the court could not have been completed in time. The court treated the deadline for recounting the votes and certifying the results as December 12, since under federal law a certification made after that could be challenged in Congress when the electoral votes were counted in January.[62] There was no way in which 60,000 votes could be recounted by the twelfth yet allow time for the contestants' lawyers to challenge, and a judge to review (and his rulings to be appealed and the appeal briefed and argued and decided), the decisions made by the counters on particular ballots, especially when the counters would be using different criteria for what constituted a "legal vote." One is tempted to speculate that the court was either planning abbreviated judicial review of the recount or expecting the recount to fizzle and wanting to avoid the blame for that happening.

When time is of the essence, some curtailment of normal procedural rights is excusable. But the lack of time had been caused by the court itself, when in violation of the statute it had extended the deadline for the protest recounts to November 26 and as a result had caused the commencement of the contest proceeding to be postponed from November 15 to November 27.

If one puts the December 8 opinion side by side with the Florida election law and asks whether the former can be said to derive by a *reasonable* process of interpretation from the latter without the assistance of the "people power" provision of the Florida constitu-

---

[62] 3 USC § 5. This is subject to the qualification explained in the text accompanying note 49 above.

tion, the answer would appear to be "no," as the chief justice of that court, concluding that the majority had indeed violated Article II, remarked in dissent.[63] The "Manner" of appointing Florida's electors prescribed in the majority opinion (and in the court's earlier opinion of November 21) was not the manner that had been directed by the Florida legislature when it enacted the election law. The legislature could have said in that law that electors are to be picked by the state's supreme court after it knows and maybe doesn't like the result of the election, using a standard of the voter's unclear intent and the principles of natural law even when there is no reason to suppose that an infallible hand recount would reverse the result of the election. But the legislature didn't say anything like that. The only explicit delegation of authority in the statute is to state and local election officials. There is an implicit delegation to the courts to interpret the election law when it is unclear, but what the Florida supreme court did with the statute was so freewheeling as to raise a serious question of conformity with Article II of the U.S. Constitution, which places the authority to determine the manner of appointment of a state's presidential electors in the state's legislature.

Granted, the Florida statute is vague when it comes to relief. The court in a contest proceeding that finds that enough "legal votes" were rejected to "change or place in doubt the result of the election" can "provide any relief appropriate under such circumstances."[64] "Appropriate" is not defined; it has been left to the courts to work out on a case-by-case basis. But even a term as vague as "appropriate" does not give a court carte blanche. If no reasonable person could consider the relief ordered by the Florida supreme court on December 8 appropriate, then, once again, the court had violated the statute rather than merely interpreted it.

B. BUSH V GORE: THE CONSTITUTIONAL GROUNDS

When the case returned to the U.S. Supreme Court, a majority of seven decided that the recount decreed by the Florida court was indeed unconstitutional. But the ground was that such a recount would deny Florida voters equal protection of the laws, because

---

[63] Id at 1258 (dissenting opinion).

[64] See note 32 above and accompanying text.

the lack of precise standards to guide the recounters would inevitably result in different voters' votes being weighted differently. I do not find this ground compelling. The conduct of elections has been confided to local government—to counties and, indeed, to a considerable extent, to precincts. Different counties in the same state often use different equipment, methods, ballots, and instructions, generating different sources and rate of error; and ballots are often counted differently in different precincts, and, perhaps more important, as we saw in Part I, differently when they are counted at the county level rather than at the precinct level. Such differences had not previously been thought to deny equal protection of the laws and if they are now to do so this portends an ambitious program of federal judicial intervention in the electoral process, a program the Supreme Court seems, given the haste with which it acted, to have undertaken without much forethought about the program's scope and administrability. The last thing we need is more election litigation.

The concept of entitlement that underlies the equal protection ground can also be questioned. If my dimple was not counted in the original election and yours was, what exactly is my complaint? Neither dimple should have been counted, and a lawbreaker is on weak ground in complaining that he has been punished but some other lawbreaker has gotten off scot-free. Selective prosecution, unless based on invidious grounds, is not a denial of equal protection. The differences here were not deliberate or invidious; they were the accidents of long-established, if careless and ramshackle, local voting practices.

Or if I was a good boy and punched my chad clean through, and you only dimpled your chad, what is my complaint if your dimple is counted as a vote, when if the county had used a better voting technology (better from the standpoint of minimizing rejections), or even had counted votes at the precinct level rather than at the county level, you would have had no difficulty casting a clearly legal vote? To the extent that the inclusion of the Broward recount totals in Gore's vote could be thought a partisan act akin to vote fraud, the equal protection argument was stronger. But if all the recounts were conducted by neutrals, the lack of standards to guide the counters, while anarchic, would not be invidious. On this theory, the only or principal thing wrong, from the standpoint of equal protection, with the Florida supreme court's opinion of

December 8 was the inclusion of the Broward County recount results.

A better Fourteenth Amendment argument is that an irrational method of determining the outcome of an election is a denial of due process of law.[65] The Florida supreme court's refusal to establish a precise standard to guide the recounters, at the same time that it accepted both the Broward and the Palm Beach recount results even though they had been based on inconsistent methodologies, can fairly be described as irrational, even perhaps as the near equivalent of ballot-box stuffing. Maybe future cases will read *Bush v Gore* as standing for little more than this. Yet even this would not be an inconsequential doctrinal step—the creation of a federal duty to use uniform *precise* criteria in a recount. The Florida statutory criterion, "clear indication of the intent of the voter," which the state's supreme court refused to elaborate, is uniform as stated; the problem is that it is too vague to assure uniformity of application.

Having found that the Florida supreme court had acted unconstitutionally, the Court had next to decide on the remedy. Five Justices held that because the Florida supreme court had repeatedly suggested that the state legislature would have wanted to take advantage of the safe harbor for certifications completed no later than December 12, that was the deadline, and so no further recount was permissible under Florida law.[66] The Florida supreme court had indeed indicated that it regarded the twelfth as the deadline for the recount.[67] Alternatively, the Supreme Court might have said that no further recount was feasible given the Florida legislature's undoubted desire that Florida have a slate of electors in the Electoral College, a desire that could not as a practical matter have been realized by December 18, the date prescribed by federal law for the electors to vote.[68] Whether electoral votes cast later count is unclear. It would be up to Congress, the electoral-vote counter, to decide in the first instance, and it might decide

---

[65] As held in *Roe v Alabama*, 43 F3d 574, 580–81 (11th Cir 1995), and *Griffin v Burns*, 570 F2d 1065 (1st Cir 1978).

[66] In accordance with this ruling, the Florida supreme court dismissed Gore's suit. *Gore v Harris*, 773 So2d 524 (Fla 2000) (per curiam).

[67] See, e.g., *Gore v Harris* (note 53 above), at 1261–62 and nn 21–22; *Palm Beach County Canvassing Board v Harris*, 772 So2d 1273, 1281–82, 1288–91 (Fla 2000) (per curiam).

[68] 3 USC § 7.

to count votes cast by a rival slate appointed by the Florida legislature.[69] Or it might decide to count no electoral votes from Florida, thus raising the unresolved question whether "a majority of the whole number of Electors appointed" in the Twelfth Amendment is a majority of the electoral votes counted, or an absolute majority of electoral votes. (Florida would have appointed electors—in fact two sets of them!) If the former, Gore would be the President-elect if Florida's electoral votes were not counted, and in the latter case the House of Representatives would pick the President-elect (and so Bush would win).

In opposition to the suggestion that electoral votes cast after December 18 may not count, it can be pointed out that if a state's electoral votes are not received in Washington by the fourth Wednesday in December (December 27 in 2000), inquiry is to be made of the state,[70] and this might seem to imply that votes can be cast after the eighteenth. But the section of Title III that provides for this inquiry is captioned "Failure of certificates of electors to *reach* President of the Senate or Archivist of the United States" (emphasis added). This sounds like a concern with a failure in delivery, not a failure to vote. The electors cast their votes in their home states and mail the results to Washington, rather than going to Washington to vote; and this provision of Title III dates back to 1887, when transcontinental mail service was not fully dependable.

Moreover, if read to permit electoral votes to be cast after December 18, Title III may violate Article II, section 1, clause 3 of the Constitution, which provides that the day on which the electors vote "shall be the same throughout the United States." December 18 was Electoral College election day in 2000.[71] And nor-

---

[69] Title III, in a section that dates back to 1845 (Act of 1845, 5 Stat 721), provides that if the state fails to make a choice for electors on the day prescribed by law (November 7), the legislature can appoint them later. 3 USC § 2. If continued uncertainty about the result of the November 7 election were deemed a failure to have chosen electors on that day, then presumably the Florida legislature could select its own slate, which, given the composition of the legislature, would have been a slate pledged to Bush.

[70] 3 USC § 12.

[71] It is true that 3 USC § 1 requires that each state appoint its electors on the first Tuesday after the first Monday in November of the fourth year following a presidential election—in other words, on "election day" in the popular sense (November 7, 2000, for example)—and that authority for this provision derives from Article II, section 1, clause 3. See *Foster v Love*, 522 US 67, 69–70 (1997). But to infer that the only temporal uniformity required is in the appointment of the electors would be error. The clause reads in its entirety, "The Congress may determine the Time of chusing the Electors, and the Day on which they shall give their Votes; which Day shall be the same throughout the United

mally, of course, a voter who does not vote on election day loses his right to vote in the election. That is what clause 3 seems to say. It is true that in 1960 Hawaii, as the result of a recount, appointed its electors after the statutory deadline, yet its votes were counted. But as its votes had no effect on the outcome of the election, there was no reason to make an issue of the state's tardiness.

So December 18 may have been the deadline after all, unless changed by Congress. A responsible recount could not have been concluded by December 18. We must imagine the U.S. Supreme Court on December 12 ordering the Florida supreme court to conduct the recount in a manner soberly designed, in conformity with Florida's election law, to identify ballots containing a clear indication of the voter's intent. The court would have required several days to establish criteria. Would they be Broward rules? Palm Beach rules? Which Palm Beach rules? The court would have had to ask for briefs on the question, the parties having been notably unhelpful up to then with respect to the recount criteria— the Democrats because they did not want to invite close judicial inspection of the Broward rules, without which Gore would be unlikely to overtake Bush, and the Republicans because they were adamant against any form of hand recount.

Had criteria been adopted by December 15 and the recount restarted that day and completed the next, only two days before the eighteenth would have remained for the courts to evaluate what would undoubtedly have been hundreds of challenges to the decisions of particular counters. That would have been too little time. The U.S. Supreme Court, an abler group of judges than the Florida supreme court and with better staff support, was under such time pressure that the opinions that the Court issued concerning the Florida deadlock do not satisfy even those commentators who agree with the decisions themselves. But even if the recount had been completed and new totals certified by the eighteenth without concern for the niceties of judicial review and due process of law, the infirmity of the process would have assured a rancorous struggle in Congress when a Gore slate (assuming the recount resulted in a court order that the secretary of state certify Gore's slate) was

---

States." Section 1 of Title III derives from the "Time of chusing the Electors" provision. The same-day requirement applies to the casting of the electoral votes by the electors, not to the appointment of the electors.

challenged. Florida's legislature would by then have appointed a Bush slate. Congress was required by federal law to meet to count the electoral votes on January 6.[72] Its choice of whose slate to accept if there were competing slates (or what to do if it rejected both slates) might have led to further proceedings in the Supreme Court. Had the wrangle in Congress dragged on for two weeks, the speaker of the House or (if he refused to resign from the House) the president pro tem of the Senate (with the same qualification), ninety-eight-year-old Strom Thurmond, would have become acting President on January 20, serving until the winner of the 2000 presidential election was somehow determined.[73]

The outcome of the Hayes-Tilden election, which took place on November 8, 1876, was not determined until March 2, 1877, four months later and only two days before the inauguration.[74] Title III was passed ten years later in an effort to head off a future such dispute, but it is unclear whether it could have headed off the dispute arising from the 2000 election deadlock. For if the Senate and the House of Representatives fail to agree on which electoral votes to count (a likely eventuality, since the House of Representatives in the Congress that met on January 6 was controlled by the Republicans and the Senate in effect by the Democrats because Vice President Gore presided over the Senate until January 20 and thus would cast tie-breaking votes), Title III provides only that "the votes of the electors whose appointment shall have been certified by the executive of the State, under the seal thereof, shall be counted."[75] Supposing that Florida's governor certified the Bush slate but the Florida supreme court declared his certification a nullity and ordered him to certify the Gore slate, and he refused, which slate would be the legitimate one? To complicate matters still further, the constitutionality of Title III, portions of which seem, as we have noted with reference to the dead-

---

[72] 3 USC § 15.

[73] See 3 USC §§ 19(a),(b). Next in line, if Hastert and Thurmond both refused the crown, would be the Secretary of State, followed by the Secretary of the Treasury. Id, § 19(d). But the Secretary of State, Madeleine Albright, being foreign-born, would not have been eligible; and so Lawrence Summers would have become the acting President if, the election still unresolved on January 20, Thurmond passed.

[74] See Paul Leland Haworth, *The Hayes-Tilden Disputed Presidential Election of 1876* 280–81 (1966).

[75] 3 USC § 15.

line for submission of electoral votes, to be in tension with Article II and the Twelfth Amendment, has never been authoritatively determined.

Consideration of the practicalities of continued recounting is notable by its absence from the opinions of the dissenting Justices in *Bush v Gore*. They were content to leave the matter to be resolved by Congress in January—or later, for that matter. I cannot see the case for precipitating a political and constitutional crisis merely in order to fuss with a statistical tie that, given the inherent subjectivity involved in hand counting spoiled ballots, can never be untied. Had the responsibility for determining who would be President fallen to Congress in January, there would have been a competition in indignation between the parties' supporters, with each side accusing the other of having stolen the election. Whatever Congress did would have been regarded as the product of raw politics, with no tincture of justice. The new President would have been deprived of a transition period in which to organize his administration and would have taken office against a background of unprecedented bitterness. His "victory" would have been an empty one; he could not have governed effectively. The scenario that produces this dismal result is conjectural. But that there was a real and disturbing *potential* for disorder and temporary paralysis (I don't want to exaggerate) seems undeniable. That is why the Supreme Court's decision was greeted with relief by most of the nation.

In fairness to the dissenters, they could point to Title III as Congress's carefully crafted response to the possibility of presidential election deadlocks. And Title III vests Congress, not the federal courts, with the authority to resolve specific such deadlocks. A President selected by Congress, because of an electoral deadlock, would have more democratic legitimacy than one selected by the Supreme Court. Remember that Title III provides that if the House and the Senate can't agree on which slate of electors to accept (if there is more than one), the slate certified by the governor prevails. To head off a collision between court and governor, the Florida legislature had only to withdraw judicial jurisdiction over its appointment of electors.

But the legislature might not think of this way of sealing a Bush slate. And even if it did, with the governor of Florida the brother of presidential candidate Bush and with Gore having by hypothesis prevailed in the popular vote in Florida as well as nationwide, the election of Bush to the presidency by such a means would poison his tenure in the office. There are also the unresolved doubts about the constitutionality of Title III, specifically whether Congress can authorize electoral votes to be counted that were cast after Electoral College electoral day, December 18, which Article II decrees "shall be the same throughout the United States."

The dissenters may have had a simpler and sunnier expectation, that remanding the case to the Florida supreme court for the continuation of the recount *if that court wished* would have the same effect as terminating the recount because the Florida court would quickly realize that there wasn't enough time to establish a precise uniform standard for the recount in order to comply with the Supreme Court's ruling on equal protection, conduct the recount, and still preserve a reasonable opportunity for judicial review. But there would have been three dangers in relying on the Florida court to take the hint. First, it might not do so, having already turned down the opportunity to end the agony when it reviewed Judge Sauls's decision. It might endeavor to rush the process through to completion, somehow, by December 18, or even let it continue past that date. It might even, by analogy to what it had done with the partial recount results in Miami-Dade County, certify a winner on the basis of an incomplete statewide recount of the undervotes.

Second, the Florida court might have terminated the contest proceeding after the recount but before the completion of judicial review. If the unreviewed recount had shown Gore ahead, this would have done substantial and unjustified political harm to Bush. For he would have had no opportunity to challenge the result of the recount, however meritorious the basis of his challenge might be; the case would have become moot. One suspects that by December 12, even before the Supreme Court's decision, most of Gore's supporters had lost hope that he would be President and their objective had become to cast enough doubt on the legitimacy of Bush's election to undermine him and the Republicans generally.

Third, the U.S. Supreme Court would have lost the credit it earned from the general public for having brought the election deadlock to a sharp and welcome end. It might instead have been accused of playing cat and mouse with the Florida supreme court—remanding, a second time, for a process that it knew to be futile.

C. BUSH V GORE: THE REMEDY

So the Supreme Court took the pragmatic route, cut the Gordian knot, and let Bush get on with the transition and with governing. But there can be such a thing as an excess of pragmatism; and the remedy decreed by the five-Justice majority has a "gotcha!" flavor, as if the U.S. Supreme Court had outsmarted the Florida supreme court by nailing that court with its perhaps unconsidered suggestion that December 12 was the deadline under Florida law for designation of the state's electors. And by terminating the recount, the Supreme Court was providing no relief to voters whose votes had not been counted but would have been under constitutionally adequate uniform criteria, though such voters were as much victims of the denial of equal protection that the Court had just found as voters whose valid votes were diluted by the improper recovery of spoiled ballots cast by other voters.

With more time, however, the Supreme Court could have tied the remedy to Article II in a way that would have provided a more convincing rationale for its decision than the route taken. There was an air of non sequitur to ruling that the Florida supreme court had violated the Constitution by failing to prescribe uniform criteria for a recount, yet terminating the recount rather than permitting it to go forward under proper criteria. But if Article II barred the recount because the state supreme court had had no statutory basis for ordering a recount, whatever the criteria to be used in the recount, proper relief required barring the recount, period.

Remedial considerations to one side, there is more to be said in favor of the Article II ground for reversing the Florida court than was said by the concurring Justices, who embraced that ground, or by Bush's lawyers. Not enough to make it conclusive but enough to make it respectable as well as to confirm its superior fit with the relief ordered, and these are relevant considerations in light of the vilification of the Court's decision by its liberal critics.[76]

---

[76] See, e.g., Rosen (note 23 above), and the editorial in the same issue of the *New Republic*, entitled "Unsafe Harbor," in which we read of "the Republican larcenists, in and out of robes, who arranged to suppress the truth about the vote in Florida and thereby to make off with the election of 2000. . . . [M]orally and historically speaking, we have witnessed

Think back to the word "Legislature" in section 1, clause 2 of Article II. One of the most hotly debated issues at the constitutional convention in 1787 was how to select the President. Popular vote, appointment by Congress, appointment by state legislatures, appointment by state governors—all these possibilities were discussed before the idea of selection by electors came into the picture, and then there was debate over how the electors were to be selected. A number of the delegates favored appointment of the electors by popular election, but in the end the convention left the matter to the states by the "Manner Directed" Clause.[77] I have not discovered why the clause says "Legislature" rather than "State." One possibility is that the draftsmen wanted to negate any inference that the states were required to use popular election to select electors; it would be up to each state legislature to decide.[78] But probably the word "Legislature" in the "Manner Directed" Clause has no more intended force than the same word in Article I, section 4,[79] where it seems to have been used simply because the legislature is the branch of government that makes laws. Yet one thing courts do all the time is find contemporary functions for old legal categories, pouring new legal wine into old bottles. A lesson of the 2000 election deadlock is that the word "Legislature" may be the key to heading off future such fiascoes by unequivocally denoting the site within state government of the power to appoint electors. The train wreck that the Supreme Court's decision may have averted would have been the result of uncertainty about which branch of Florida's government had the last word in fixing the rules for the appointment of the electors.

---

an outrage." New Republic (Dec 25, 2000), p 9. When one recalls the public comments made by professors of constitutional law during the postelection litigation, it becomes apparent that the academic practice of constitutional law is as political as the judicial practice. Liberal professors who spend their time trying to find a satisfactory rationale for decisions that they like, such as *Roe v Wade*, made no effort to salvage *Bush v Gore*, while conservative professors found themselves unaccustomedly supportive of a decision that whatever its merits, which obviously I think not inconsiderable, cannot avoid the label "activist," since it expands federal judicial power without clear warrant in constitutional text or precedent. But the politicization of constitutional-law scholarship is a story for another day.

[77] The pertinent debates are summarized in Tadahisa Kuroda, *The Origins of the Twelfth Amendment: The Electoral College in the Early Republic, 1787–1804*, ch 1 (1994).

[78] For a hint of this interpretation, see David A. McKnight, *The Electoral System of the United States: A Critical and Historical Exposition of Its Fundamental Principles* 42 (1878).

[79] "The Times, Places and Manner of holding Elections for Senators and Representatives, shall be prescribed in each State by the Legislature thereof."

Concretely, was it the legislature or the courts? More precisely, was it the legislature subject to the normal judicial power to fill statutory gaps and resolve statutory ambiguities, or the courts in the exercise of a plenary power of "interpretation"?

Had the Supreme Court not intervened, the interbranch dispute might not have been resolved until January, when Congress would, had Gore won the recount and the Florida supreme court ordered the governor of Florida to cast Florida's electoral votes for Gore, have been faced with two slates—unless the governor defied the court; and that was possible too. If I am right that this would have been a miserable denouement, one unprovided for in the Constitution,[80] unreliably addressed by Title III, yet imperative to avert, there is much to be said for an interpretation of "Legislature" in Article II that by curtailing gubernatorial and state judicial involvement in the selection of electors except to the extent that the legislature clearly delegates a role in that selection to the governor or the courts, minimizes the risk of an interbranch dispute over selection of electors that might spill over into January. Had this been the Court's ground, the remedy of stopping a recount not authorized by Florida's election law would have followed naturally.

The suggested interpretation of the "Manner Directed" Clause is not compelled by case law, legislative history, or constitutional language. But neither is it blocked by any of these conventional interpretive guides. And it is consistent with the concern expressed at the convention and in the ratifying debates with preventing the choice of the President by cabals, agents of foreign powers, other intriguers, or corrupt devices. That concern informs the provisions of Article II that require the electors to vote in their home states rather than congregating to vote and that require all the electoral votes to be cast on the same day.[81] Interpreting the "Manner Directed" Clause to forbid a state's governor or courts to change the electoral rules laid down by the legislature likewise operates to re-

---

[80] Article II, section 1, as amended by the Twelfth Amendment, makes provision for the situation in which no candidate receives a majority vote of the electors, but it makes no provision for resolving disputes over the appointment of electors. Title III provides for resolution by Congress (if the safe-harbor provision is inapplicable), 3 USC § 15, but of course is not part of the Constitution.

[81] US Const, Art II, § 1, cls 2, 4. See Max Farrand, ed, *The Records of the Federal Convention of 1787*, vol 2, p 500 (rev ed 1937); Kuroda (note 77 above), at 11, 21; Peirce and Longley (note 22 above), at 22, 27, 29; Slonim (note 22 above), at 52–53.

duce malign influences on the selection of electors. Of course, there will be debate over whether the state supreme court has engaged in statutory interpretation so free as to amount to "changing" the rules, but the principle is more important than the application. If the Florida legislature wants to lengthen the interpretive reach of the state's supreme court, it can do so (it can for that matter, if it wants, authorize the court to appoint the state's electors); but it must make clear that it is doing this.

I am aware of the irony of interpreting the Constitution broadly to force state courts to interpret their election laws narrowly. But critics of the Court's decision should ask themselves the following question: Had the Florida supreme court said that because the state's election law did not in the court's view provide a satisfactory resolution to the deadlock, the judges would appoint the state's electors, would these critics acknowledge that the court would be violating Article II? If so, the only question is whether what the Florida supreme court did do is sufficiently close to my hypothetical example to have justified the U.S. Supreme Court in reversing. It is possible both to view the Florida court as having abused its discretion in "interpreting" the state's election law and to view Article II as making such an abuse a matter of federal concern. We needn't lose sleep over the possibility that since the same state statute governs challenges to presidential and all other elections, the Florida court could apply different interpretive principles to protests and contests of presidential elections than to protests and contests of other elections, including other federal elections. That would be nothing new. A state court faced with a vague state statute regulating the use of public property may interpret the statute broadly when the use does not involve conduct potentially protected by the First Amendment, but narrowly (if by doing so the court can save the statute's constitutionality) when the use does involve such conduct.

Granted, even if the Florida supreme court, whether under compulsion of Article II or otherwise, had upheld the secretary of state and, later, when the contest proceeding was conducted, had managed to find a ground for reversing Judge Sauls that was consistent with the Florida election statute, the Republican-dominated state legislature might still, had Gore prevailed in the recount, have appointed a slate of electors pledged to Bush, and in that event there might well have been a January crisis. But this prospect was unlikely for a reason that provides additional support for the Article II ground of reversal. What would have given the Florida legislature a colorable, or at least politically defensible, basis for appointing a Bush slate, had the U.S. Supreme Court not terminated the recount, was the fact that a court composed entirely of Democrats (the Florida supreme court) had changed the election rules after the election. By doing so the court had challenged the legislature, and a response could be anticipated. The "Manner Directed" Clause can head off presidential election crises by preventing one branch of state government, disappointed perhaps by the result of the presidential election, from changing the outcome by changing the election rules after the result is known, provoking an interbranch struggle that is a recipe for chaos. This interpretation is buttressed by the provision of Title III that requires the governor of the state to transmit the list of the state's electors to Washington.[82] If the governor is not bound by the rules laid down by the state legislature, there is again the specter of competing slates of electors and no certain method of choosing between them.

If the Florida court did not change the rules in violation of Article II, moreover, the appointment of a slate of electors by the state legislature might be unlawful. Title III authorizes such appointment if the state "has held an election for the purpose of choosing electors" but the election has "failed to make a choice."[83] That is an apt description of the situation in which the outcome of the election is mired in controversy when the safe-harbor deadline for choosing a state's electors arrives. Title III provides the mechanism (appointment of the state's electors by the state legislature) by which the controversy can be bypassed and the new President selected by the Electoral College without the intervention of Congress. If, however, the state's electors have been determined in the manner directed by the legislature (namely, in the case of Florida, by popular election, not election by the legislature), then a subsequent attempt by the legislature to appoint the electors could be thought inconsistent with Article II and therefore enjoined, and again an interbranch conflict would be averted—though this assumes the constitutionality of Title III.

Nothing is more infuriating than changing the election rules

---

[82] 3 USC § 6.

[83] 3 USC § 2.

after the election results under the existing rules are known. Those are banana-republic tactics. If we set to one side the appointment of electors by a legislature dissatisfied with the outcome of the popular election, a clearly improper step if the election was conducted under the preexisting rules, we see that the "Manner Directed" Clause of Article II can be used to curb such abuses by limiting the making of the rules for the appointment of the state's presidential electors to the organ of government that operates prospectively, which is the legislature. Courts operate retrospectively. The Florida courts were asked not to set new standards for future elections but to determine the outcome of the 2000 election. The state's highest court assumed the power, arguably in violation of the "Manner Directed" Clause, to change the rules for that election that had been laid down by the legislature. Once the outcome of a close election is known, the choice of a method of recounting likely to change the outcome is all too easy. Legalities aside, if there was one critical misstep, one avoidable precipitant of the (fortunately later averted) postelection crisis, it was the Florida supreme court's decision of November 21, which by displacing the secretary of state's discretionary authority invaded the legislative prerogative of establishing the rules for selecting presidential electors.

D. CRITICISMS OF THE SUPREME COURT'S INTERVENTION

Three criticisms of the U.S. Supreme Court's decisions remain to be considered. The first is that the Court, to avoid entanglement in a partisan struggle and thus preserve its image of being above the political fray, should have taken advantage of its right to decline to take a case without giving any reason and thus not have intervened at all. But if I am right that the Florida supreme court may well have been violating the Constitution, and if, as seems likely, without the Court's intervention the deadlock would have mushroomed into a genuine crisis, the Court's refusal to intervene might have prompted the question, What exactly is the Supreme Court good for if it refuses to examine a likely constitutional error that if uncorrected will engender a national crisis? We might call this the reverse political-questions doctrine. Political considerations in a broad, nonpartisan sense will sometimes counsel the Court to abstain, but sometimes to intervene. It is not an ordinary court, however much it may pretend to be one in an effort to insulate itself from political criticism.

Judges worry about expending their political capital, which is to say narrowing the margin of protection from other branches of government that they obtain by being thought by the public to personify the judicial virtues and thus, of distinct relevance in an election case, to be "above" politics. Judges seem not to worry *that* much about spending down their capital, judging from the frequency with which they accuse each other of being "result-oriented," tendentious, and downright lawless. Still, it is a concern, particularly at the highest level of the judiciary. But before criticizing a judge for an expenditure of his political capital, or more crudely for deliberately courting a loss of prestige, we should ask what he bought with his expenditure. (We should also ask whether it isn't a natural tendency of judges to exaggerate the value of their prestige to society.) *Bush v Gore* may have done less harm to the nation by reducing the Supreme Court's prestige than it did good for the nation by averting a significant probability of a presidential selection process that would have undermined the presidency and embittered American politics more than the decision itself did or is likely to do. Judges unwilling to sacrifice some of their prestige for the greater good of the nation might be thought selfish. The trade-offs become particularly favorable to intervention if one believes that, had the Court abstained in December, it might well have been dragged back into the presidential selection process in January, facing multiple appeals from rulings in the Title III proceedings that might have followed a completed recount. If it had ducked *then*, it might have invited comparison to Nero fiddling while Rome burned.

The second criticism is of the Supreme Court's action in staying the recount on December 9. A stay is proper only if the party seeking it would suffer irreparable harm were it denied. Critics say the only harm to Bush was the embarrassment he would have suffered had the recount continued and showed Gore overcoming his lead, a merely "political" harm against which courts do not grant a remedy, and that in any event the irreparable harm to Gore from the interruption of the recount was greater. The first point is unsound and the second misleading. In a political contest, the harm from allowing an unconstitutional recount to continue is bound to be political; what other harm could there be? Why can't a court be realistic about the stakes in a political contest? Concern with the political impact of Bush's having a certified vote lead was presumably what led Gore's forces to press to delay the certification, though by doing so they compressed the time for the contest proceeding. Had they not objected to the secretary of state's insistence on adhering to the statutory deadline of November 14, they could have filed the contest proceeding on the fifteenth rather than, by virtue of the Florida supreme court's having extended the deadline to November 26, on the twenty-seventh, with time quickly running out.

And while Gore indeed suffered more harm from the grant of the stay than Bush would have from a denial, the decision whether to grant or deny a stay does not depend only on the balance of harms. It depends also on the likely outcome of the appeal.[84] If it was certain that the Florida supreme court would be reversed, the harm to Gore from stopping the recount was irrelevant. By December 9, the Supreme Court Justices had become deeply immersed in the case, and it was unlikely that another round of briefs and oral argument by lawyers on the point of exhaustion would change the Justices' views.

The harm to Bush from the denial of a stay would have been particularly difficult to justify if, as I am speculating, the dissenters may have thought that the effect of remanding the case to the Florida supreme court would be the termination of the contest proceeding short of decision. For that would open up the possibility of a recount favoring Gore yet impossible for Bush to challenge, however compelling his grounds, because the contest proceeding had been dismissed after the recount was complete.

It was not only political harm to Bush that the stay averted, but

---

[84] For example, *Hilton v Braunskill*, 481 US 770, 776 (1987); *McClendon v City of Albuquerque*, 79 F3d 1014, 1020 (10th Cir 1996); *Michigan Coalition of Radioactive Material Users, Inc. v Griepentrog*, 945 F2d 150, 153 (6th Cir 1991), reversed on other grounds, 954 F2d 1174 (1992) (en banc); *Cuomo v NRC*, 772 F2d 972, 974 (DC Cir 1985). Cases dealing with the standard for the grant or denial of a preliminary injunction (closely analogous to a stay pending appeal) make clear that a "sliding scale" is to be used under which the greater the movant's showing of likelihood of success on the merits, the less he need show that the balance of harms favors his position. *Gentala v City of Tucson*, 213 F3d 1055, 1061 (9th Cir 2000); *Sofinet v INS*, 188 F3d 703, 707 (7th Cir 1999); *Serono Laboratories, Inc. v Shalala*, 158 F3d 1313, 1317 (DC Cir 1998); *Ross-Simons of Warwick, Inc. v Baccarat, Inc.*, 102 F3d 12, 19 (1st Cir 1996); *Roland Machinery Co. v Dresser Industries*, 749 F2d 380, 387 (7th Cir 1984). The *Griepentrog* and *Cuomo* decisions explicitly apply the sliding-scale approach to stays.

political harm to the Supreme Court. Suppose the recount had gone ahead and shown Gore the winner of the popular vote in Florida, and *then* the Court had stepped in (perhaps to break a deadlock in Congress over rival slates of electors) and ruled in favor of Bush. There would then be no ambiguity about the Court's being responsible for the selection of the forty-third President, whereas now there is, since no one can be sure what the recount would have shown; the media recounts now under way cannot credibly declare an official winner. So maybe the Court minimized the damage to its political capital. Maybe the Justices are better politicians than their critics.

The third criticism is that in embracing the equal protection ground for reversing the Florida court, the Supreme Court's five-Justice majority was going against the grain, and this shows that the decision was partisan. The five Justices are "conservative," and "conservative" judges don't "like" the Equal Protection Clause. This is a crude characterization, but let me accept it for the sake of argument. These Justices might have preferred to base their decision on Article II; three of them, in a concurrence, embraced it as an alternative ground. But there were obvious tactical advantages to adopting a ground that would attract two of the liberal Justices, creating a solid bipartisan majority for the bedrock proposition that the Florida supreme court had acted unconstitutionally and could not continue with the recount along the lines it had laid down.[85] The Court's two most liberal Justices, who dissented from the ruling that equal protection had been denied, were put in the uncomfortable position of rejecting an equal protection claim— and, as liberals, they are supposed to "like" the Equal Protection Clause. The two other liberal Justices, who dissented from the remedy while agreeing that the Florida supreme court had acted unconstitutionally, were put in the uncomfortable position of being unwilling to avert a potential political and constitutional crisis by allowing the deadlock to continue past December 12 and probably past December 18 as well, or even January 6. In a case so politically fraught, a bit of *Realpolitik* affecting only the ground of decision and not the decision itself should be tolerable to anyone

---

[85] This leaves unexplained, however, why Justices O'Connor and Kennedy did not join the concurrence.

who takes a pragmatic approach to adjudication. *Fiat justicia ruat caelum* is not a workable motto for the U.S. Supreme Court.

I do not think the four Justices who dissented in whole or in part did the Court a service by accusing the five-Justice majority of having impaired public confidence in the impartiality of the judiciary. Such an accusation, however heartfelt, is what is called fouling one's own nest. It has also the element of a self-fulfilling prophecy: by telling the world that the decision would undermine public confidence in the courts, the dissenters made it more likely that the decision would indeed undermine public confidence in the courts. It was a gratuitous blow to the Court's prestige, justifiable if at all by the prospect that it makes credible the threat of future such blows, a threat that might in the long run curb any "activist" impulses of the majority, though this seems unlikely.

The dissenters were, consciously or not, reminding the public that the Justices had a conflict of interest of sorts in ruling on a case that would decide who would become President (more precisely that *might* decide this, since Bush might well have become President anyway, by virtue of Republican control of the Florida legislature and the U.S. House of Representatives, even if Gore had won the recount). Judges are not indifferent to who their colleagues are, and specifically to whether their colleagues agree with them on the big issues; and as there may be vacancies on the Supreme Court in the next four years, the current Justices are unlikely to be indifferent to who the next President is. But this is as true of the four liberal Justices as it is of the five conservative ones. For the four to insinuate that the five had impure motives is to live in a glass house and throw stones. But the conflict of interest was there, and it will forever cast a shadow over a decision that in other circumstances might have garnered considerable professional support. If I am right that the Court was in a no-win situation, that damage to the judiciary was inevitable once Gore decided to bring the courts into the process of presidential selection rather than accepting the machine recount or the decisions of the county canvasing boards, judges' ire should be directed not at each other but at him.

Only the very naive believe any more that ideology plays only a small role in constitutional adjudication at the Supreme Court level. But there is a difference between political ideology and partisan politics,[86] and it has been many years since the Justices have been accused of voting on party lines. That is precisely the accusation being leveled in liberal circles against the Justices in *Bush v Gore* (the parallel charge is leveled in conservative circles against the Florida supreme court), and it is based in part on the fact that the Justices seem to have been voting against their ideological proclivities. (For which ordinarily they would be complimented!) But this is true only in part. Close beneath the surface of the legal issues in the postelection litigation are intertwined issues of personal responsibility, demotic power, governmental paternalism, and judicial discretion that divide Left and Right. Almost certainly the vast majority of the ballots that the machines refused to count were rejected because of voter error. The voter had not followed the directions, although they were quite simple and clear at least for anyone who could read. Illiterates are permitted to vote, but some conservatives may think it rather an excess of democracy for illiterates to hold the electoral balance of power. And on the other side of the ideological divide, liberals might want to point out that Bush won on a technicality, Gore having received a popular-vote majority nationwide and being the undoubted second choice of most of Nader's supporters, who gave Nader 97,000 votes in Florida.[87] Small-d as well as capital-D democrats will add that the Congress, which would have ended up selecting the President if the Supreme Court had kept its hands off, is a more democratic institution than the Court. The Florida supreme court's invocation of the "people power" provision of the Florida constitution should resonate with Democrats.

A conservative might say that the Democrats were urging that the Florida voters whose ballots had been rejected be relieved from their errors through the beneficent intervention of government officials who would try to guess what the voters would have done had they followed directions. Government would ascertain and effectuate the popular will. When Gore's attempt was thwarted by a Republican elected official (the Florida secretary of state), Gore's supporters turned to the state courts, appealing to free-wheeling

---

[86] See generally Richard A. Posner, *The Federal Courts: Challenge and Reform*, ch 10 (1996).

[87] Buchanan and the Libertarian Party candidate, Browne, together received only 38,000 votes; presumably Bush would have been the second choice of most of these voters. The other presidential candidates received only a smattering of votes.

interpretive principles that enable aggressive judges to override even rather clearly expressed legislative designs. The use of the "people power" clause of the state constitution to revise the state election law was a conservative's nightmare of constitutional free interpretation. All power to the people is not a conservative slogan, and Rousseau, he of the "popular will," is a conservatives' bête noire. Hostility to democratic excess and to judicial activism may not sort well, but that is as much a problem for liberals, who tend to couple enthusiasm for democracy and even populism with a passionate commitment to broad democracy-limiting interpretations of constitutional rights, as for conservatives. My point is only that there were plenty of reasons, whether good or bad, besides the party identity of the litigants for conservative Supreme Court Justices to want to reverse the Florida supreme court and liberal Justices to affirm it. And there was sufficient play in the legal joints to enable either side to write a professionally respectable opinion justifying its preferred outcome, though limitations of time may have prevented either side from actually doing so.

III. Conclusion

But what if the critics are right, and the Supreme Court did not have adequate grounds for halting the recount ordered by the Florida supreme court? It is natural to think that, if so, an injustice was done. But this is far from clear. To begin with, even with Bush's lead carved down to as few as 154 votes by the Florida supreme court's decision of December 8, it is unclear whether Gore would have prevailed in the recount ordered by that court. It is true that all he needed was to pick up a few more than that number of votes from the 9,000 not yet recounted in Miami-Dade County, assuming the other 50,000 or so undervotes statewide that had not yet been recounted would have split evenly. We do not know what rule the Miami-Dade canvasing board would have used had it resumed recounting. But recall from Part I that if it had used Palm Beach rules on all 10,750 disputed ballots in Miami-Dade County, it probably would have given Gore only 263 additional votes—fewer than 100 more than the 168 vote gain that the Florida supreme court had already given Gore in its December 8 opinion. Had Gore gained only 100 more votes, Bush would still have won, albeit by as few as fifty votes.

Still, Gore might have prevailed in the recount—but only by virtue of the Florida supreme court's having butchered the election statute. Whether that court misinterpreted the state's election law, and whether the U.S. Supreme Court should have intervened, are separate questions; and the answer to the first question is simpler than the answer to the second. The Florida supreme court did misinterpret the state law. (It is no more presumptuous to accuse a state court of misinterpreting its state's law than to accuse a federal court of misinterpreting federal law.) In fact, the court's decisions of November 21 and December 8 made a hash of that law. Maybe the U.S. Supreme Court should have kept its nose out of the dispute, either as a matter of prudence or because a federal basis for intervention was wanting. But the fact that a decision may be immunized from further review doesn't make it correct. Abstention by the federal courts would not have erased the fact that the Florida supreme court had erred grievously in interpreting the Florida election law. It should not have extended the deadline for hand recounting that had been fixed by the secretary of state, or interpreted "error in the vote tabulation" to include a voter's error in voting, or reversed Judge Sauls's dismissal of the contest proceeding, or denied the discretionary authority of the state and local election officials, or authorized relief in a contest proceeding on the basis merely that the election was close and there were a number of undervotes, or credited Gore with the Broward and the partial Miami-Dade recount results, or ordered a statewide recount of undervotes but not overvotes, or tolerated inconsistent and subjective criteria in hand recounting. In all these respects it was violating Florida law. Had Gore been declared the winner on the basis of the recount ordered by the Florida court on December 8, he would have owed his victory to legal error, whether or not legal error that the U.S. Supreme Court should have corrected. The result of the Court's intervention was, therefore, at the least, rough justice; it may have been legal justice as well.

MICHAEL C. DORF
AND BARRY FRIEDMAN

SHARED CONSTITUTIONAL
INTERPRETATION

In *United States v Dickerson*,[1] the Supreme Court reaffirmed *Miranda v Arizona*,[2] stating that it was "a constitutional decision," and thus not subject to congressional overruling.[3] A contrary judgment would have had enormous symbolic significance, as *Miranda* is one of the best-known legacies of the Warren Court. In penning the opinion for a seven-two majority in *Dickerson*, Chief Justice Rehnquist reassured the legal community and the nation at large that this pillar of the Warren Court's criminal procedure revolution would remain standing.[4]

Michael C. Dorf is Professor of Law, Columbia University School of Law. Barry Friedman is Professor of Law, New York University School of Law.

AUTHORS' NOTE: We gratefully acknowledge the very useful comments and suggestions of Sherry Colb, Samuel Issacharoff, Yale Kamisar, Larry Kramer, Debra Livingston, Henry Monaghan, Gerald Neuman, Robert Post, George Thomas, and Richard Uviller. Research assistance was ably provided by Scott Chesin, Jason Cooper, and Jeremy Saks. Special thanks go to Lisa Mihajlovic and Geoffrey Stone.

[1] 120 S Ct 2326 (2000).

[2] 384 US 436 (1966).

[3] *United States v Dickerson*, 120 S Ct 2326, 2329 (2000).

[4] This is not to say that current criminal procedure doctrine is in any way a straightforward extension of the rest of the Warren Court's views. Although cases like *Miranda* and *Mapp v Ohio*, 367 US 643 (1961), have not been overruled, the Burger and Rehnquist Courts have undermined Warren Court legal doctrines through, inter alia, a variety of rules that reduce or eliminate the penalty that law enforcement must pay for violating suspects' or defendants' rights. See Carol Steiker, *Counter-Revolution in Constitutional Criminal Procedure? Two Audiences, Two Answers*, 94 Mich L Rev 2466, 2469 (1996) ("The edifice constructed by the Warren Court governing investigative techniques . . . remains surprisingly intact. Rather than redrawing in any drastic fashion the line between constitutional and unconstitutional police conduct, the Supreme Court has revolutionized the consequences of deeming conduct unconstitutional.")

Most of the legal community saw *Dickerson* as an important case about criminal procedure, but the decision's far greater significance may lie in its implications for the shared institutional process of determining constitutional meaning. Even as it prescribed the now-familiar warnings that must precede custodial interrogation, the *Miranda* Court abjured any intention to subject law enforcement to a "constitutional straightjacket,"[5] and thus invited "Congress and the States to . . . search for . . . other procedures which are at least as effective [as the Court-prescribed warnings] in apprising accused persons of their right of silence and in assuring a continuous opportunity to exercise it."[6] On its face the *Dickerson* opinion appears a strong statement of judicial supremacy in constitutional interpretation, but the *Dickerson* Court nonetheless reiterated *Miranda*'s "invitation" to other constitutional actors to fashion equally effective safeguards for Fifth Amendment rights.[7]

Dickerson thus invites examination of the following question: What role might nonjudicial institutions and officials play in determining the meaning of the Constitution? Suppose that Congress or the states were to accept the invitation to devise alternatives to the warnings prescribed by the Court. Is the Supreme Court prepared to entertain such alternatives, and thus permit others to share in the task of interpreting the Constitution? And how should the *Miranda* Court's invitation to Congress and the states be understood in the light of recent decisions narrowing federal power in favor of state sovereignty?

Dickerson and the somewhat bewildering array of recent federalism decisions provide an appropriate opportunity to explore the relative roles of the Court, Congress, and the states in matters of constitutional interpretation. Although the Court of late has displayed a self-aggrandizing tendency, we believe there nonetheless is, within existing doctrine, substantial room for institutional dialogue about the meaning of the Constitution.[8] We explore that constitutional space and how it might be employed as a model

---

[5] *Miranda v Arizona*, 384 US 436, 467 (1966).

[6] Id.

[7] *Dickerson*, 120 S Ct at 2334.

[8] See Barry Friedman, *Dialogue and Judicial Review*, 91 Mich L Rev 577 (1993) (envisioning creation of constitutional meaning as a dialogic process).

of shared constitutional interpretation. We emphasize two themes throughout: first, there is, and ought to be, considerable opportunity for shared constitutional interpretation; and second, this cooperative process can work only if all constitutional actors are sufficiently humble about their own conclusions and respectful of the pronouncements of the others.

We begin, necessarily, with the question of precisely what *Miranda* and *Dickerson* held. We say "necessarily" because it is apparent from *Dickerson* and other recent Supreme Court decisions that the Court will not tolerate tampering by other actors with what the Court views as constitutional bedrock. As the *Dickerson* Court said, ". . . Congress may not legislatively supersede our decisions interpreting and applying the Constitution."[9] The important question after *Dickerson*—and in any case in which other constitutional actors seek to share with the Court the job of defining the scope of the Constitution—is where the freedom of action lies.[10]

Our concern here is not whether *Miranda* was correct as an original matter.[11] For all the ambiguity *Dickerson* leaves, it makes clear that *Miranda* is here to stay. With that starting point, we ask how *Miranda* and *Dickerson* are best understood. In our view, these cases stand for the proposition that suspects have a constitutional right to some procedures that are adequate to inform them of the right to remain silent in the face of custodial interrogation, and a consti-

---

[9] 120 S Ct at 2332 (citing *City of Boerne v Flores*, 521 US 507 (1997)).

[10] Of late, there has been a veritable flood of commentary disparaging judicial supremacy and urging that greater attention be paid to the role of nonjudicial actors in constitutional interpretation. For a representative sampling, see Akhil Reed Amar and Alan Hirsch, *For the People: What the Constitution Really Says About Your Rights* (1998); Louis Fisher and Neal Devins, *Political Dynamics of Constitutional Law* (2d ed. 1996); Richard Parker, *"Here, the People Rule": A Constitutional Populist Manifesto* (1994); Mark Tushnet, *Taking the Constitution Away from the Courts* (1999). Although we have some sympathy for the notion of shared constitutional interpretation, see Michael C. Dorf, *Supreme Court 1997 Term, Foreword: The Limits of Socratic Deliberation*, 112 Harv L Rev 4, 60–73 (1998) (advocating "provisional adjudication" that expressly authorizes experimentation); Friedman, 91 Mich L Rev at 580 (cited in note 8) ("the everyday process of constitutional interpretation integrates all three branches of government"), we think some of this work sweeps too far in denying the Court's supremacy with regard to constitutional interpretation.

[11] See Albert W. Alschuler, *A Peculiar Privilege in Historical Perspective: The Right to Remain Silent*, 94 Mich L Rev 2625 (1996) (arguing against a right to silence on normative and historical grounds); Akhil Reed Amar and Renee B. Lettow, *Fifth Amendment First Principles: The Self-Incrimination Clause*, 93 Mich L Rev 857 (1995) (same); R. Kent Greenawalt, *Silence as a Moral and Constitutional Right*, 23 Wm & Mary L Rev 15 (1981) (arguing for a right to silence only in the face of interrogation on slight suspicion).

tutional right to procedures that provide a continuous opportunity to exercise the right to remain silent.[12] The four particular warnings set forth in *Miranda* are not constitutionally required "in the sense that nothing else will suffice to satisfy constitutional requirements."[13] Equally effective procedures could be substituted for the warnings. However, *Dickerson* and *Miranda* hold that the Fifth Amendment requires some safeguard that is at least as effective. The federal statute at issue in *Dickerson*, 18 USC § 3501, did not satisfy that requirement because it essentially restored the status quo prior to *Miranda*. That is the basic, and basically sound, rationale of *Dickerson*.

This understanding of *Dickerson* as *constitutional* interpretation makes it possible to sidestep most of the academic debate about whether the Court has the authority to promulgate "prophylactic rules" or "constitutional common law"[14]—doctrines that are not required by the Constitution but crafted by the Court to protect underlying or core constitutional requirements.[15] It is possible to

---

[12] Implicit in the right to be informed of a right to silence, of course, is a right to silence itself. That right appeared to receive explicit protection a year before *Miranda* in *Griffin v California*, 380 US 609 (1965) (prohibiting an inference of guilt from a suspect's silence in the face of police questioning). Some post-*Miranda* cases appear to be inconsistent with a Fifth Amendment right to silence. See *Baxter v Palmigiano*, 425 US 308, 316–20 (1976) (in prison disciplinary proceeding, permitting adverse inference from silence); *Fletcher v Weir*, 455 US 603 (1982) (in criminal trial, permitting admission of post-arrest silence for impeachment purposes). These cases can probably be reconciled with *Miranda*, however. *Baxter* reflects the Court's general unwillingness to apply the Fifth Amendment to civil proceedings, while *Fletcher*'s problems, whatever they may be, are of a piece with *Harris v New York*, 401 US 222 (1970), discussed below. See Part I.C.

[13] *Dickerson*, 120 S Ct at 2335.

[14] Compare Henry P. Monaghan, *The Supreme Court 1974 Term—Foreword: Constitutional Common Law*, 89 Harv L Rev 1 (1975) (explaining how the Court might legitimately be seen to have the power to make law beyond what the Constitution requires); Martha A. Field, *Sources of Law: The Scope of Federal Common Law*, 99 Harv L Rev 883 (1986) (less tentatively, same); Daniel J. Meltzer, *Deterring Constitutional Violations by Law Enforcement Officials: Plaintiffs and Defendants as Private Attorneys General*, 88 Colum L Rev 247, 287–95 (1988) (same, also less tentatively); David A. Strauss, *The Ubiquity of Prophylactic Rules*, 55 U Chi L Rev 190 (1988) (same, taking prophylaxis as paradigm rather than exception) with Joseph D. Grano, *Prophylactic Rules in Criminal Procedure: A Question of Article III Legitimacy*, 80 Nw U L Rev 100 (1985) (challenging the legitimacy of most common law and prophylaxis).

[15] A typical example is David Huitema, *Miranda: Legitimate Response to Contingent Requirements of the Fifth Amendment*, 18 Yale L & Policy Rev 261 (2000). In Huitema's view, the Fifth Amendment touchstone is voluntariness, but the *Miranda* rule is nonetheless a justified prophylactic measure because courts cannot accurately distinguish voluntary from involuntary confessions. See id at 269–70. See also Lawrence Crocker, *Can the Exclusionary Rule Be Saved?* 84 J Crim L & Criminol 310, 312 (1993); John Kaplan, *The Limits of the Exclusionary Rule*, 26 Stan L Rev 1027, 1029–30, 1055 (1974).

see why the academy and the Court both tried to understand *Miranda* in these subconstitutional terms, but the case can be explained equally effectively without raising the legitimacy concerns that prophylaxis and constitutional common law trigger: *Miranda* can be justified purely in terms of the Court's incontestable power to interpret the Constitution. Adequate safeguards for the right to remain silent during custodial interrogation are *constitutionally* required.

Hence, two principles frame the balance of this article as well as the process of shared constitutional interpretation. On the one hand, *Miranda* is a constitutional decision, and the Court has made clear repeatedly that neither Congress nor state officials can defy or repeal a judicial decision construing the Constitution.[16] On the other hand, *Miranda* and *Dickerson* both explicitly invited Congress and the states to take action in response to those decisions. What is it we can learn about the process of cooperative interpretation from this invitation?

After tracing the tortured doctrinal path from *Miranda* to *Dickerson*, Part I poses this question by offering a hypothetical congressional response to the "invitation." Suppose Congress were to pass a statute governing all custodial interrogation by federal agents. The statute, which we dub the "Anti-Coercion and Effective Custodial Interrogation Act" ("ACECIA"), provides that: before custodial interrogation by federal authorities commences, the suspect must be informed of his right to remain silent; prior to the institution of adversarial proceedings, a suspect has no right to have an attorney present during federal custodial interrogation; all federal custodial interrogation must be videotaped; and no statement that results from federal custodial interrogation is admissible in a federal criminal trial unless the interrogation was videotaped and the statement was voluntary.

Although ACECIA departs substantially from the scheme set forth in *Miranda*, it is plausibly an alternative procedure that both informs the suspect of his right to remain silent and, through the videotaping requirement, ensures a continuous opportunity to exercise it. Part I uses this example to explore the questions of who

---

[16] See *Boerne*, 521 US at 516–29 (1997) (equating the Constitution's meaning with the Court's doctrine); *Cooper v Aaron*, 358 US 1, 18 (1958) ("[T]he federal judiciary is supreme in the exposition of the law of the Constitution.").

decides whether an alternative procedure is as effective as the default set by *Miranda* and according to what criteria. We conclude that there may be more than one way to safeguard constitutional rights, that if Congress wishes to be heard in this dialogue it must act sensibly in drafting alternatives, and that the Court ought then to consider such alternatives respectfully. The debate over the meaning of *Miranda* and the constitutionality of Section 3501 has not reflected mutual respect, but we can envision a dialogue about protecting Fifth Amendment rights that does.

Part II turns from the relative powers of Court and Congress to those of Congress and the states. Here we imagine that Congress goes further, affirmatively requiring the states to employ its favored safeguard, videotaping. Would such a "National Anti-Coercion Act" ("NACA") be valid against the claim of a state that wished to adhere to the original *Miranda* warnings? Part II asks where Congress derives the authority to impose such an obligation on the states. The answer, we conclude, is Section 5 of the Fourteenth Amendment. After the recent decisions narrowly construing Section 5,[17] adding constitutional safeguards at the Court's express invitation would seem one of the few valid uses of that congressional power. We next use a variant of ACECIA and NACA (with yet another acronym) to clarify the sense in which Section 5 acts as a one-way ratchet.

Assuming that Congress has the affirmative power to impose a videotaping requirement on the states, we ask the further question whether doing so would violate the anticommandeering principle of *New York v United States*[18] and *Printz v United States.*[19] Perhaps, pursuant to *Reno v Condon*,[20] the videotaping requirement could be understood as preemptive regulation rather than as an affirmative command. But even if not, we conclude on Supremacy Clause grounds that if the obligation were phrased simply as a rule of substantive law applicable in state court, it would not violate the anticommandeering principle.

---

[17] See *United States v Morrison*, 120 S Ct 1740, 1755–59 (2000); *Kimel v Florida Bd. of Regents*, 120 S Ct 631, 644–50 (2000); *Florida Prepaid Postsecondary Educ. Expense Bd. v College Savings Bank*, 527 US 627, 636–47 (1999); *Boerne*, 521 US at 516–36 (1997).

[18] 505 US 144 (1992).

[19] 521 US 898 (1997).

[20] 120 S Ct 666 (2000).

Despite the power of Congress to impose rules of this nature on the states, Congress should hesitate to do so, for the same sort of reasons that the Court should take seriously congressional attempts to define "equally effective" constitutional safeguards. The whole point of the no-straightjacket language from *Miranda* is to encourage experimentation by a variety of jurisdictions. By imposing a uniform national rule, NACA would defeat the purpose of recognizing a zone of experimentation. Just as the Supreme Court ought to be respectful of procedures besides the ones it has devised for guaranteeing rights, Congress should hesitate to exercise its Section 5 power where doing so stifles state and local innovation.

Finally, suppose that a state were to pass its own ACECIA applicable to state actors. If the federal ACECIA is valid, as we suggest in Part I, is this valid as well? Part III concludes that because the key to upholding any set of procedures for safeguarding the right to remain silent is the conclusion that those safeguards are adequate, and not who envisioned or enforced those safeguards, then just as Congress may devise safeguards equal or superior to those devised by the Court, so can the states. But here too we return to the point about respect and humility. Rather than taking up *Miranda*'s "invitation," most state officials did nothing, or attacked *Miranda* as outside the Court's power. The Supreme Court of late has created a very different environment for federalism as a laboratory for experimentation. Whether that experiment will succeed depends not so much upon the Court, but upon whether the states eschew the use of their autonomy to curtail individual rights (as has too often been the case in the past) and become serious partners in the process of governance and constitutional interpretation.

Ultimately this article is about shared constitutional experimentation, and the institutional humility and respect necessary to foster it. Because constitutional meaning is so wrapped up in broader questions of governance, constitutional interpretation should be a shared endeavor among (at the least) all the branches of the national, state, and local governments. Each branch brings to the process both a constitutional role and a set of institutional advantages (and vantages). For the process to work, however, each actor must display humility and treat the pronouncements of other actors respectfully, granting them the weight they deserve. The response to the *Miranda* invitation demonstrates this process at its

worst; the response to the *Dickerson* invitation that we envision
here suggests a better alternative.

I. The Constitution, the Supreme Court, and Everyone Else

In 1966, in *Miranda v Arizona*, the Supreme Court held
that a criminal defendant's confession cannot be admitted in evidence unless interrogating officers follow certain procedures, including providing the suspect with the now-familiar *Miranda*
warnings. In the years following, the *Miranda* decision was criticized continually,[21] and its survival often appeared in doubt. *United
States v Dickerson* reaffirmed *Miranda*, putting to rest, at least for
the foreseeable future, the fate of this constitutional landmark.

Yet matters are not as simple as they seem, for *Dickerson* leaves
us no more certain than did *Miranda* about precisely what the
Constitution requires regarding a suspect's rights during police interrogation. Moreover, *Dickerson* does nothing to eliminate the
confusion created by *Miranda*'s invitation to other political actors
to develop an alternative to the *Miranda* regime.

At issue in *Dickerson* was the constitutionality of Section 3501,
a congressional statute enacted to replace *Miranda*. Section 3501
essentially imposed the "voluntariness" test as the sole standard
for evaluating the constitutionality of confessions, while making
the failure to provide warnings one factor in the determination
whether, in any given case, a confession was unlawfully compelled.[22] *Dickerson* invalidated Section 3501, but at the same time

---

[21] See note 31.

[22] 18 USC § 3501 provides:

Admissibility of confessions

(a) In any criminal prosecution brought by the United States or by the District
of Columbia, a confession, as defined in subsection (e) hereof, shall be admissible
in evidence if it is voluntarily given. Before such confession is received in evidence,
the trial judge shall, out of the presence of the jury, determine any issue as to
voluntariness. If the trial judge determines that the confession was voluntarily
made it shall be admitted in evidence and the trial judge shall permit the jury to
hear relevant evidence on the issue of voluntariness and shall instruct the jury
to give such weight to the confession as the jury feels it deserves under all the
circumstances.

(b) The trial judge in determining the issue of voluntariness shall take into
consideration all the circumstances surrounding the giving of the confession, including (1) the time elapsing between arrest and arraignment of the defendant
making the confession, if it was made after arrest and before arraignment, (2)
whether such defendant knew the nature of the offense with which he was charged

restated *Miranda*'s invitation to other political actors to provide a meaningful alternative to the *Miranda* regime.[23]

After *Dickerson*, confusion lingers over what it means to say that *Miranda* formulated a "constitutional rule," and what freedom that statement leaves other constitutional officials in responding to the decision. The Court in *Dickerson* repeatedly invoked the idea of a constitutional rule in explaining why Congress could not overturn *Miranda*'s requirements. But if *Miranda* is a constitutional rule, and if Congress cannot overturn constitutional rules, then what does the *Miranda/Dickerson* "invitation" invite Congress and the states to do?

Ambiguity about the foundation of *Miranda* provided the basis upon which Justice Scalia's biting dissent took the *Dickerson* Court to task. The Supreme Court only has the power to decide cases based on the Constitution, Justice Scalia explained.[24] But *Miranda*'s many progeny (and the many Justices who wrote those decisions)

---

or of which he was suspected at the time of making the confession, (3) whether or not such defendant was advised or knew that he was not required to make any statement and that any such statement could be used against him, (4) whether or not such defendant had been advised prior to questioning of his right to the assistance of counsel; and (5) whether or not such defendant was without the assistance of counsel when questioned and when giving such confession. The presence or absence of any of the above mentioned factors to be taken into consideration by the judge need not be conclusive on the issue of voluntariness of the confession.

(c) In any criminal prosecution by the United States or by the District of Columbia, a confession made or given by a person who is a defendant therein, while such person was under arrest or other detention in the custody of any law enforcement officer or law enforcement agency, shall not be inadmissible solely because of delay in bringing such person before a magistrate [magistrate judge] or other officer empowered to commit persons charged with offenses against the laws of the United States or of the District of Columbia if such confession is found by the trial judge to have been made voluntarily and if the weight to be given the confession is left to the jury and if such confession was made or given by such person within six hours immediately following his arrest or other detention: Provided, That the time limitation contained in this subsection shall not apply in any case in which the delay in bringing such person before such magistrate or other officer beyond such six hour period is found by the trial judge to be reasonable considering the means of transportation and the distance to be traveled to the nearest available such magistrate or other officer.

(d) Nothing contained in this section shall bar the admission in evidence of any confession made or given voluntarily by any person to any other person without interrogation by anyone, or at any time at which the person who made or gave such confession was not under arrest or other detention.

(e) As used in this section, the term "confession" means any confession of guilt of any criminal offense or any selfincriminating statement made or given orally or in writing.

[23] See *Dickerson*, 120 S Ct at 2334.

[24] See id at 2338 (Scalia dissenting).

expressly denied the constitutional status of *Miranda*. If *Miranda* is constitutionally grounded, Justice Scalia insisted, then the many intervening decisions cannot be justified. If *Miranda* is not constitutionally compelled, then the Court should have upheld Section 3501 because it clearly complied with the core Fifth Amendment command that confessions not be "compelled." As Justice Scalia saw it, one or the other must be true.[25]

As we explain, we believe *Miranda can* be understood as a constitutional decision. Thus Justice Scalia is wrong in seeing the situation in binary terms. Justice Scalia would put the Court to a stark choice: overrule its intervening decisions or uphold Section 3501. But as we will make clear, Section 3501's unconstitutionality does not necessarily doom the Court's entire *Miranda* jurisprudence.

Where Justice Scalia is on firm ground, however, is in criticizing the Court's frequent resort to *ipse dixit*. *Miranda* and its progeny reveal two sides of the modern Court. On the one hand, *Dickerson* is a relatively small step in the Court's recent insistence on judicial hegemony with regard to constitutional interpretation.[26] On the other hand, *Miranda*'s progeny reveal a result-oriented Court that has too little care for the coherence of its own jurisprudence. Unfortunately, *Dickerson* continues this trend.

Dickerson was a devil of the Court's own doing. *Miranda* was not an altogether popular decision, but it was a constitutional one, and cultural respect for the Constitution and the Court led to general adherence to the rule. The Justices themselves undermined the rule, in part by their eagerness to slice pieces off whenever possible, but worse by saying peculiar things like, "these procedural safeguards were not themselves rights protected by the Constitution"[27] and "the rule . . . is our rule, not a constitutional command."[28] As we explain below, *Miranda* is best understood as guaranteeing adequate procedural safeguards rather than any particular set of safeguards, but that is a far more modest principle than the one the Court espoused in some post-*Miranda* cases: that nothing

---

[25] See id at 2342.

[26] See *Boerne*, 521 US at 516–29 (1997); *Seminole Tribe of Florida v Florida*, 517 US 44 (1996). See generally Laura S. Fitzgerald, *Beyond Marbury: Jurisdictional Self-Dealing in Seminole Tribe*, 52 Vand L Rev 407, 408–09 (1999) (noting the Court's preference for its own power and disdain for Congress).

[27] *Michigan v Tucker*, 417 US 433, 444 (1974).

[28] *Arizona v Roberson*, 486 US 675, 688 (1988) (Kennedy dissenting).

Miranda required flowed from the Constitution itself. The Court took the tack it did because prevailing in individual cases assumed greater importance to some, sometimes a majority, of the Justices than maintaining its institutional role. And in doing so the Court diminished respect for its own decisions.[29]

A. THE PUZZLE OF MIRANDA

As many have observed, *Miranda* reads more like a legislative edict than a judicial decision.[30] It begins by announcing a statute-like holding, then supports and fleshes it out in a committee report–like opinion. The decision was vilified instantly,[31] and yet the *Miranda* warnings today are household words, appearing frequently in the popular media. The Court in *Dickerson* is right that *Miranda* is embedded in our culture.

But what is *Miranda*, and what did it hold? These questions hardly were posed by Section 3501's frontal attack on the rule. Prior to *Miranda* the constitutional test for a confession was whether it was voluntary under the totality of the circumstances. In enacting Section 3501, Congress seized on *Miranda*'s statement that the decision was not a "constitutional straightjacket" and that it would govern only in the absence of alternatives. However, Con-

---

[29] One particularly troubling manifestation of this disrespect is the practice of police officers questioning suspects "outside *Miranda*." In this practice, police officers intentionally ignore *Miranda*, knowing that any statement obtained can be used for impeachment purposes pursuant to *Harris v New York*, 401 US 222, 225 (1971), or for other purposes consistent with the *Miranda* exceptions the Court has fashioned. See Transcript of Deputy District Attorney Devallis Rutledge, in *Videotape: Questioning "Outside Miranda"* (Greg Gulen Productions 1990), excerpted in Charles D. Weisselberg, *Saving Miranda*, 84 Cornell L Rev 109 at 189–92 (1998). There is simply no way to interpret *Miranda* as a decision permitting such questioning. To do so makes a mockery of the constitutional right at stake, but the Court's own treatment of *Miranda* has encouraged this sort of behavior. In addition to its general denigrations of *Miranda*, in *Oregon v Hass*, 420 US 714 (1975), the Court thought that questioning outside *Miranda* was a mere "speculative possibility." Id at 723. Even if that were true in 1975, it no longer is. See Richard A. Leo and Welsh S. White, *Adapting to Miranda: Modern Interrogators' Strategies for Dealing with the Obstacles Posed by Miranda*, 84 Minn L Rev 397, 460 (1999) (noting that "[a]t least two state courts have held that even statements obtained after an interrogator's deliberate misrepresentation as to the admissibility of the suspect's statement may be introduced for the purpose of impeachment," although one state court has ruled such statements inadmissible as a due process violation).

[30] Louis Michael Seidman, *Brown and Miranda*, 80 Cal L Rev 672, 678 (1992).

[31] For an instructive description, see Otis H. Stephens, Jr., *The Supreme Court and Confessions of Guilt* 165 (1973). See generally Fred P. Graham, *The Self-Inflicted Wound* 245 (1970).

gress simply returned to the original constitutional rule, and added the *Miranda* warnings as factors in determining voluntariness.[32]

Thus, *Dickerson* was an easy case, because no matter what *Miranda* held, Section 3501 seemed to flout it. *Miranda* emphasized the compulsion inherent in custodial interrogation, and clearly stated that any alternative had to be "equally effective" in ameliorating this compulsion and safeguarding a suspect's rights. Section 3501 provided no alternative, equally effective or otherwise. It was a slap at the Court,[33] and if any Court was likely to slap back, it was this one. For the Court that in recent years has given us *Seminole Tribe of Florida v Florida*,[34] *Plaut v Spendthrift Farm, Inc.*,[35] *City of Boerne v Flores*,[36] and other decisions favoring its own power at the expense of Congress, Section 3501 was a gnat that ran into the windshield of whatever it was that *Miranda* held.

Yet *Miranda*'s holding is elusive, and time has made it only more so. Some of the numerous post-*Miranda* decisions arguably have expanded upon *Miranda*'s safeguards, such as the rule in *Edwards v Arizona*[37] that once a suspect requests counsel, the police may not initiate any further questioning, even with regard to another offense.[38] But many more decisions have cut back on what might have seemed the constitutional core of *Miranda*. *Michigan v Tucker*[39] and *Oregon v Elstad*[40] held that the "fruits" of *Miranda* violations did not have to be excluded from evidence,[41] *Harris v New York*[42] held that statements taken in violation of *Miranda*

---

[32] See Yale Kamisar, *Can (Did) Congress "Overrule" Miranda?* 85 Cornell L Rev 883, passim (2000).

[33] See id at 895.

[34] 517 US 44 (1996) (holding that the Indian Commerce Clause does not grant Congress power to abrogate state's sovereign immunity).

[35] 514 US 211 (1995) (broadly construing the principle that Congress cannot retroactively change the law applicable to a litigated case).

[36] 521 US 507 (1997) (holding that Congress's power under Section 5 of the Fourteenth Amendment is strictly remedial and preventative).

[37] 451 US 477 (1981).

[38] See id at 484–85.

[39] 417 US 433 (1974).

[40] 470 US 298 (1985).

[41] See id at 308; *Tucker*, 417 US at 450.

[42] 401 US 222 (1971).

could be used for impeachment purposes,[43] *New York v Quarles*[44] held that voluntary responses to interrogation without warnings were admissible if the interrogation was necessary to protect the public safety,[45] and so on.

What further complicated the meaning of *Miranda* was the Court's own constant rhetorical undermining of the decision. The Court consistently denied the constitutional basis of *Miranda*. *Miranda* came to be understood, in the Court's own words, as a "prophylactic."[46] The Constitution prohibited compelling statements from an accused, and admission of compelled statements would violate the core constitutional requirement, but in order to safeguard that right, the Court had adopted these broader rules. A violation of the particular rules themselves barred use of a statement so obtained, but only to the extent required by the Court's decisions. And for the most part, that area of limitation shrank over time.

B. THE "PROPHYLAXIS" APPROACH

The Court's post-*Miranda* decisions, and parallel developments with regard to the Fourth Amendment exclusionary rule, understandably led to exploration of the idea of a prophylactic rule.[47]

---

[43] See id at 226.

[44] 467 US 649 (1984).

[45] See id at 655.

[46] See *Duckworth v Eagan*, 492 US 195, 203 (1989); *Connecticut v Barrett*, 479 US 523, 528 (1987); *Oregon v Elstad*, 470 US 298, 305 (1985); *New York v Quarles*, 467 US 649, 654 (1984).

[47] Most of the academic literature accepts the legitimacy of prophylaxis, with the debate focusing on how to justify it. See, e.g., Strauss, 550 Chi L Rev at 195 (cited in note 14) (equating prophylaxis with ordinary constitutional interpretation); Brian K. Landsberg, *Safeguarding Constitutional Rights: The Uses and Limits of Prophylactic Rules*, 66 Tenn L Rev 925, 949–63 (1999) (offering different justifications for different forms of prophylaxis); Monaghan, 89 Harv L Rev at 21 (cited in note 14) (viewing prophylaxis as a form of federal common law); Kamisar, 85 Cornell L Rev at 943 (cited in note 32) (accepting, *arguendo*, Monaghan's view, but distinguishing those aspects of *Miranda* that are constitutionally required); Huitema, 18 Yale L & Policy Rev at 265 (cited in note 15) (justifying prophylaxis addressed to risks of constitutional violations and activities that chill the exercise of constitutional rights). But see Grano, 80 Nw U L Rev 100 (cited in note 14) (rejecting the legitimacy of most prophylaxis); Joseph D. Grano, *Miranda's Constitutional Difficulties: A Reply to Professor Schulhofer*, 55 U Chi L Rev 174 (1988) (same).

Some commentators also distinguish between prophylactic rules and per se rules. See Wayne R. LaFave, Jerold H. Israel, and Nancy King, *Criminal Procedure* §§ 2.9(d), 2.9(e) (2d ed 1999); Archibald Cox, *The Role of Congress in Constitutional Determination*, 40 U Cin L Rev 199, 250–52 (1971).

For more than thirty years, the Court imposed *Miranda* on the states, but denied that it was a constitutional command. Similarly with regard to the Fourth Amendment, the Court frequently has denied that the exclusionary rule was compelled by the Constitution, giving it power to taper the remedy as it wished.[48] Yet, the remedies could not coherently be explained as an exercise of the Court's supervisory power over the federal courts because they applied to the states, despite their assertedly nonconstitutional nature. The Court's own explanation for this apparent anomaly was the notion of prophylactic rules. *Miranda* and the Fourth Amendment exclusionary principle were not constitutional commands, but prophylactic safeguards.

The first and perhaps still best attempt to understand the jurisprudence of prophylaxis was Henry Monaghan's *Harvard Law Review* foreword, "Constitutional Common Law."[49] Monaghan's central point was that much of what appears to be the Supreme Court's constitutional jurisprudence "is best understood as something of a quite different order—a substructure of substantive, procedural, and remedial rules drawing their inspiration and authority from, but not required by, various constitutional provisions."[50] In Monaghan's view, *Miranda* could be justified on utilitarian grounds as just this sort of constitutional common law. But key to Monaghan's entire understanding was that because these rules were not themselves constitutionally required, they were "subject to amendment, modification, or even reversal by Congress."[51] In that light, Monaghan would have granted Congress wide (but not unlimited) authority over the contours of *Miranda*.

The subsequent scholarly literature of prophylaxis typically makes one of two common "moves." One, typified by David

---

[48] See *United States v Calandra*, 414 US 338, 348 (1974) (holding the exclusionary rule inapplicable to grand jury proceedings because it is "a judicially created remedy designed to safeguard Fourth Amendment rights generally through its deterrent effect, rather than a personal constitutional right of the party aggrieved."); *Stone v Powell*, 428 US 465 (1976) (for the same reason holding that habeas corpus relief is unavailable where state prisoner alleges that evidence was admitted in violation of the Fourth Amendment exclusionary rule); *United States v Leon*, 468 US 897 (1984) (for the same reason permitting admission of evidence obtained in good faith reliance on a defective warrant).

[49] See Monaghan, 89 Harv L Rev 1 (cited in note 14).

[50] Id at 2.

[51] Id at 3.

Strauss's "The Ubiquity of Prophylactic Rules,"[52] argues that the structure of the *Miranda* rule is not so different from many other areas of constitutional law because constitutional decisions frequently go beyond the core constitutional command.[53] The point of Strauss's move essentially is to normalize *Miranda*. He thus equates it, for example, with the Court's strict treatment of content regulation under the First Amendment, which Strauss understands as regulating beyond the bounds of what the amendment literally requires to avoid government violation of free speech guarantees.[54]

A competing move subjects the idea of a prophylactic rule to harsh analysis, carving out a small realm where such prophylaxis might be acceptable, but for the most part deeming it illegitimate. Typical is Joseph Grano's "Prophylactic Rules in Criminal Procedure: A Question of Article III Legitimacy."[55] Grano contends that some rules that have been understood as prophylactic could be reconceptualized as constitutionally required, either as a matter of procedural due process[56] or some specific constitutional command.[57] This reconceptualization may solve the legitimacy problem in general, but Grano concludes that "any attempt to provide a constitutional foundation for [*Miranda* itself] would be strained and ultimately unconvincing."[58]

Although scholarship since the Monaghan article has helped to clarify the propriety of certain judicial decisions, we think that the analytic value of the concept of prophylaxis is limited because ultimately it asks the wrong question.[59] Perhaps we may be accused of sidestepping an important discussion, but in our view the critical question is not how to justify judicial rulings that go beyond what

---

[52] See Strauss, 55 U Chi L Rev 190 (cited in note 14).

[53] See generally id.

[54] See id at 197.

[55] See Grano, 80 Nw U L Rev 100 (cited in note 14).

[56] See id at 157–62.

[57] See id at 162–63.

[58] Id at 163.

[59] Compare Dorf, 112 Harv L Rev at 72 (cited in note 10) ("reflecting on the large role of doctrinal prophylaxis [in the Strauss approach] may lead us, by a seeming paradox, to discard the dichotomy of core versus prophylactic norms.").

the text and history of the Constitution strictly require. In a post-Realist world, there is no shortage of justifications for courts making law. In our view, analysis focuses most usefully on what steps nonjudicial actors may take in response to judicial decisions, however they are justified. This, incidentally, was the focus of Monaghan's original work. His Foreword was not so much an attempt to justify constitutional common law as an effort to explore its mutability. We believe this is the right approach.[60]

C. A MORE TRADITIONAL SOLUTION: MIRANDA AND ITS PROGENY AS CONSTITUTIONAL LAW

Miranda can be explained without resort to prophylaxis,[61] as an exercise of the Court's traditional authority to interpret the Constitution in the course of deciding cases. There are two ways of understanding *Miranda* as ordinary constitutional interpretation.

One understanding is that the entire procedure mandated by *Miranda* is part of the right embodied in the Fifth Amendment. Such an interpretation is unassailable from a legitimacy standpoint, except perhaps among originalists. We do not mean to say that this necessarily is a correct interpretation of the Constitution. We mean only that the Court regularly determines what the Constitution means, and it is not helpful to challenge *Miranda*'s legitimacy by pointing out that the "traditional" rule under the Fifth Amend-

---

[60] We would apply the same approach to an often equally bewildering problem, that of constitutional remedies. Indeed, sometimes it is difficult even to tell whether what is being discussed is a prophylactic rule or a constitutional remedy. Is exclusion of a confession based on a *Miranda* violation an application of the prophylactic rule, a remedy for an earlier violation of the *Miranda* right, or both? All that is clear is that commentators perceive similar problems of authority and scope. For a sampling of work on the relationship between rights and remedies, see William C. Heffernan, *Foreword: The Fourth Amendment Exclusionary Rule as Constitutional Remedy*, 88 Geo L J 799 (2000); Richard H. Fallon, Jr. and Daniel J. Meltzer, *New Law, Non-Retroactivity, and Constitutional Remedies*, 104 Harv L Rev 1733 (1991); Barry Friedman, *When Rights Encounter Reality: Enforcing Federal Remedies*, 65 S Cal L Rev 735 (1992); Daryl J. Levinson, *Rights Essentialism and Remedial Equilibration*, 99 Colum L Rev 857 (1999). For a more comprehensive catalogue, see Friedman, supra, at 736 n.4.

[61] We do not address whether other categories of cases now understood in prophylactic terms could be reconceptualized. See, e.g., *Colter v Kentucky*, 407 US 104, 116 (1972) (treating as prophylactic the Court's decision in *North Carolina v Pearce*, 395 US 711 (1969), which established a presumption of vindictiveness in cases in which a trial judge imposed a harsher sentence upon resentencing after a reversal than in the first instance).

ment was voluntariness.[62] Although the traditional rule under the Sixth Amendment implied no obligation on the state to provide counsel,[63] *Betts v Brady*[64] imposed such an obligation under special circumstances,[65] and that rule was in turn superseded by *Gideon v Wainwright*.[66] Constitutional rules evolve.[67] We do not observe many people claiming that *Gideon* was illegitimate, which perhaps suggests some connection between perceived correctness and perceived legitimacy.

There is some support for this understanding of *Miranda* both in the decision itself and in subsequent cases. *Miranda* establishes two fundamental propositions: first (as had seemed clear since *Bram v United States*[68]), the Fifth Amendment applies in the sta-

---

[62] Thus, Justice White, who dissented in *Miranda*, nonetheless forcefully defended its legitimacy in a speech before the chief justices of the state courts. See Justice Byron R. White, *Recent Developments in Criminal Law*, Address Before the Nineteenth Annual Meeting of the Conference of Chief Justices (Aug. 3, 1967), in Council of State Governments, *Proceedings of the Nineteenth Annual Meeting of the Conference of Chief Justices* (1967), quoted in Kamisar, 85 Cornell L Rev at 908–09 (cited in note 32).

[63] The first case in which the Court hinted at any obligation on the state to provide appointed counsel was *Powell v Alabama*, 287 US 45 (1932), and even there the defendants' ignorance, the capital charge, and the potential availability of retained counsel all suggest an extremely limited right.

[64] 316 US 455 (1942).

[65] Id at 473 ("while want of counsel in a particular case may result in a conviction lacking in . . . fundamental fairness, we cannot say that the [Fourteenth] Amendment embodies an inexorable command that no trial for any offense, or in any court, can be fairly conducted and justice accorded a defendant who is not represented by counsel.").

[66] 372 US 335 (1963). See also *Argersinger v Hamlin*, 407 US 25 (1972) (finding a right to counsel in misdemeanor and petty cases for which the defendant is imprisoned); *Scott v Illinois*, 440 US 367 (1979) (finding no right to counsel where state statute authorizes punishment of imprisonment but imprisonment is not imposed); David A. Strauss, *Common Law, Common Ground, and Jefferson's Principle* (manuscript on file with authors), at 30 (noting mere coincidence between the language of the Sixth Amendment and the rule of *Gideon v Wainwright*, 372 US 335 (1963)).

[67] A variety of theories exist that seek to legitimize the evolution of constitutional rules, but no matter what the relative merits of these theories, the fact of evolution is impossible to deny. For a sampling of the relevant theories, see Bruce Ackerman, 1 *We the People: Foundations* (1991) (constitutional moments); Michael C. Dorf, *Integrating Normative and Descriptive Constitutional Theory: The Case of Original Meaning*, 85 Geo L J 1765 (1997) (pragmatic eclecticism); Barry Friedman and Scott B. Smith, *The Sedimentary Constitution*, 147 U Pa L Rev 1 (1998) (development through experience over time); Larry Kramer, *Fidelity to History—and Through It*, 65 Fordham L Rev 1627 (1997) (same); Lawrence Lessig, *Understanding Changed Readings: Fidelity and Theory*, 47 Stan L Rev 395 (1995) (translation); David A. Strauss, *Common Law Constitutional Interpretation*, 63 U Chi L Rev 877, 884 (1996) (common law development).

[68] 168 US 532 (1897).

tionhouse; and second, custodial interrogation is inherently coercive. In light of these conclusions, *Miranda* held that something needs to be done to ensure that police custodial interrogation does not violate the Fifth Amendment, and that something was recognition of the panoply of "rights" identified in *Miranda*. Subsequent to *Miranda*, the Court has spoken of the Fifth Amendment "right" to counsel[69] and, more generally, has equated the full panoply of *Miranda* rights with the Fifth Amendment itself.[70]

There are two problems with this interpretation. First, if the many elements of *Miranda* are all part of the Fifth Amendment right, then it is difficult to understand the meaning of *Miranda*'s invitation to develop "fully effective" alternative safeguards.[71] Second, as Justice Scalia observed, this understanding of *Miranda* collides with subsequent decisions, such as *Michigan v Tucker*,[72] which are difficult to reconcile with the idea that *Miranda* is a constitutional rule.

But there is an alternative understanding of *Miranda* that makes sense of the "invitation." Under this understanding, *Miranda* decided only what *Dickerson* identified as *Miranda*'s core holding: that the Fifth Amendment requires "apprising accused persons of their right of silence and . . . assuring a continuous opportunity to exercise it."[73] Thus, what the Fifth Amendment requires is not every aspect of the *Miranda* procedure, but only that an accused learn of the right not to speak with the police, and that the interrogation take place in a manner that permits the suspect to exercise that right at any time.

This also is a plausible understanding of the Fifth Amendment. Whether one can be said to possess a right of which he is ignorant is a difficult question, and just because the Court has answered

---

[69] See, e.g., *Edwards v Arizona*, 451 US 477, 481 ("*Miranda* thus declared that an accused has a Fifth and Fourteenth Amendment right to have counsel present during custodial interrogation.").

[70] See *Dickerson*, 120 S Ct at 2334 n 5 (citing *Withrow v Williams*, 507 US 680, 691 (1993); *Illinois v Perkins*, 496 US 292, 296 (1990); *Butler v McKellar*, 494 US 407, 411 (1990); *Michigan v Jackson*, 475 US 625, 629 (1986); *Moran v Burbine*, 475 US 412, 427 (1986); *Edwards*, 451 US at 481–82).

[71] *Miranda*, 384 US at 478–79.

[72] 417 US 433 (1974). See also *Oregon v Elstad*, 470 US 298, 308 (1985) (treating *Tucker* as holding that fruit of poisonous tree doctrine does not apply to *Miranda* violations).

[73] *Dickerson*, 120 S Ct at 2334 (quoting *Miranda*).

that question affirmatively in some areas (for example, consent to
search under the Fourth Amendment)[74] does not mean it cannot
be answered in the negative with regard to the Fifth Amendment
right. Knowing and intelligent waiver is the standard for trial
rights,[75] and the Court and commentators regularly draw the connection between what goes on during police questioning and the
subsequent trial.

Nor is there anything especially odd about the right applying
at the stationhouse. Indeed, by its terms the right should apply to
any governmental conduct, no matter where it occurs. A confession that is a product of torture, for example, would plainly violate
the Fifth Amendment (as well as Due Process) even if it took place
in a home. Finally, it requires little to insist that the right remain
effective throughout interrogation; whether or not custodial police
interrogation carries with it quite the coercive effect the *Miranda*
Court suggested, custodial interrogation undoubtedly places some
substantial pressure on suspects to confess.

We favor this interpretation of *Miranda*, even though it too runs
afoul of several post-*Miranda* decisions. This problem is not as
large as Justice Scalia takes it to be, however, for solving it requires only that the Court retract some of its ill-considered dicta
and rethink the rationales of several decisions. Whether the post-
Miranda decisions are viable depends upon whether any given outcome can be explained by the interpretation we have offered of
Miranda. This in turn requires of the Supreme Court only that it
work on a case-by-case basis to justify its holdings in constitutional
terms.[76]

Under this approach, some post-*Miranda* decisions clearly are
defensible.[77] On the other hand, some post-*Miranda* decisions

---

[74] See *Schneckloth v Bustamonte*, 412 US 218 (1973).

[75] See *Johnson v Zerbst*, 304 US 458, 464 (1938); see also *Schneckloth*, 412 US at 235
(distinguishing between waiver of trial rights and other situations in which a person may
fail to invoke "a constitutional protection").

[76] Donald Dripps engages in a similar endeavor, arguing that all of the cases relying on
a "prophylactic" interpretation of *Miranda* can be squared with the decision itself. See
Donald Dripps, *Miranda Caselaw Really Inconsistent? A Proposed Fifth Amendment Synthesis*,
17 Const Comm 19 (2000). While we are not persuaded that Dripps succeeds in squaring
all of the cases with *Miranda*, his endeavor is the correct one.

[77] *New York v Quarles*, for example, held that a *Miranda* violation is excused if the public
safety demands that a subject be questioned immediately without warnings. See 467 US
649 (1984). See id at 656–57. Few rights are absolute, and all *Quarles* does is to acknowledge
that some balancing is appropriate.

are more dubious,[78] and some will present difficult cases.[79] The Court will have to overrule, reconceptualize, or at least further justify some of its rights-expanding decisions as well as its rights-contracting ones.[80]

---

[78] *Michigan v Tucker* is a good example. If *Miranda* is a constitutional rule, and if in fact it violates the Constitution to fail to warn a suspect of the right to remain silent, then it is difficult to see how we can avoid excluding the fruits of unwarned statements. To be sure, if one thought that unlawfully coercive interrogation completed a *Miranda* violation in the way that an illegal search completes a Fourth Amendment violation, one might also think that neither suppression of the confession nor its fruits is constitutionally required. A damages remedy might suffice. However, in assuming that *Miranda*'s core is a constitutional rule, we have been assuming that the core includes the right to suppression of a confession obtained in violation of *Miranda*. If that is so, there appears to be no good reason to distinguish the confession from its fruits.

One might question why it necessarily follows that the fruits of constitutional violations must be excluded, but the proper focus of attention is on the relationship between the violation and the fruit, not on some wholesale rule. The confession obtained from a tortured suspect is "just" the fruit of the violation. So is the witness discovered through that same torture, and the buried murder weapon (whether located from the suspect's testimony or from that of the witness the suspect identified). The Supreme Court's doctrine accounts for these distinctions by, inter alia, permitting the introduction of evidence if the causal chain between government misconduct and the evidence has been attenuated, see *Wong Sun v United States*, 371 US 471 (1963), or if the fruit is evidence likely to have been discovered anyway, see *Nix v Williams*, 467 US 431 (1984). We do not mean to endorse any particular decision regarding the fruit of the poisonous tree doctrine; our point is that those doctrines should be applied consistently when a constitutional violation is at stake.

[79] A good example is *Harris v New York*, which held that statements inadmissible in a case-in-chief because of a *Miranda* violation can nonetheless be admitted for impeachment purposes. See 401 US 222, 226 (1970). Whether a balancing of the interest in preventing perjury against the Fifth Amendment right justifies the rule most likely will have to be decided on a case-by-case basis if it applies at all. See id at 225–26 (discussing competing value of excluding perjury). *Oregon v Elstad* presents another thorny problem. See 470 US 298 (1985). *Elstad* held that if a suspect made a statement in violation of *Miranda*, a subsequent statement made shortly thereafter is admissible if *Miranda* warnings are administered before the second statement and the first statement is not involuntary. See id at 314. But that decision becomes difficult to justify in light of *Brown v Illinois*'s holding that the *Miranda* warnings are not talismanic. See *Brown v Illinois*, 422 US 590, 603 ("Miranda warnings, alone and per se, cannot always make the act sufficiently a product of free will to break, for Fourth Amendment purposes, the causal connection between the illegality and the confession."). Given that the Fifth Amendment is in part about a concern for voluntariness, it is difficult to understand why administering the warnings would be talismanic for Fifth Amendment purposes, but not so for the Fourth Amendment. *Elstad* perhaps could be explained, but Justice O'Connor's opinion for the Court relies on the nonconstitutional understanding of *Miranda*, and that will not wash. See *Elstad*, 470 US at 306 (stating that the *Miranda* exclusionary rule "sweeps more broadly than the Fifth Amendment itself").

[80] One candidate for further explanation under the narrowed interpretation of *Miranda* is *Edwards v Arizona*, holding that once the Fifth Amendment "right" to counsel is invoked, the suspect cannot even be questioned following a second set of warnings by different officers as to a different offense. See 451 US 477, 484–45 (1981). Because the Fifth Amendment, like the Sixth Amendment, tends to be treated as offense-specific, some more reasoning is necessary to maintain the *Edwards* holding. Perhaps the Court could provide such an explanation, but it has not done so.

D. MIRANDA AFTER DICKERSON: SHARED CONSTITUTIONAL
    INTERPRETATION

This discussion still leaves unanswered how we should understand all the rules in *Miranda* that seem to go beyond this understanding of the decision. Was the Court entitled to speak about
the "right" to counsel and insist that counsel be provided to indi-
gents? Isn't this the very sort of prophylaxis that we already have
said is unnecessary to make sense of the case?

The answer to this question turns out to be related to what *Miranda*'s invitation meant, that is, what Congress and the states can
do after *Dickerson*. What if Congress decided after *Dickerson*, or
after *Miranda* for that matter, that it wanted to take the Court up
on its invitation to try something different? As we have seen, if
every aspect of *Miranda* is constitutionally required, the invitation
seems empty. But even though *Dickerson* describes some aspects of
Miranda as constitutionally required, it does not go this far.
Rather, it treats the invitation as having meaning.

Suppose that in the aftermath of *Dickerson* Congress passed
the "Anti-Coercion and Effective Custodial Interrogation Act"
("ACECIA"). The statute mandates that any suspect taken into
custody by federal officers must be told of the right to remain
silent before any interrogation commences, that any such interrogation must be videotaped from beginning to end, and that counsel
may *not* attend the interrogation (except, of course, after the onset
of adversarial criminal proceedings).[81]

ACECIA is but one of several possible responses Congress
might offer to *Miranda/Dickerson*. Others are easily imagined, such
as requiring that all interrogation take place before a magistrate,
or dispensing with police-administered warnings altogether but
forbidding any custodial interrogation without the presence of the
suspect's attorney. The point is that Congress could devise several
ways of dealing with interrogations that do not accord the full panoply of *Miranda* guarantees, but address the twin concerns of informing a suspect of the right to remain silent and ensuring compliance with this right throughout the interrogation.[82]

In order to determine what the Court might say about such a

---

[81] See *Massiah v United States*, 377 US 201 (1964); *Brewer v Williams*, 430 US 387 (1977).

[82] See Kamisar, 85 Cornell L Rev at 912 (cited in note 32).

congressional response, we need only return to *Miranda* itself. The Court's opinion is revealing in a way that has received little attention. For the opinion does not simply extend an "invitation," but also characterizes its approach not as a "rule," but as a "guideline."[83] The Court explains that it granted certiorari "to explore some facets of the problems . . . of applying the privilege against self-incrimination to in-custody interrogation, and *to give concrete constitutional guidelines for law enforcement agencies and courts to follow.*"[84] The Court sets out its "holding" at the outset, and that holding is only that the prosecution may not use statements made in custodial interrogation "unless it demonstrates the use of procedural safeguards effective to secure" the privilege.[85] And "[a]s for the procedural safeguards to be employed, *unless other fully effective means are devised to inform the accused persons of their right of silence and to assure a continuous opportunity to exercise it*" the specific *Miranda* guidelines are required.[86] The Court then devotes an entire paragraph to encouraging governmental bodies to devise their own ways of safeguarding the right.[87] At least twice more, the Court repeats the holding and re-extends the invitation.[88]

In other words, the best way to understand *Miranda* is not as mandating specific procedures, but as laying down a right and creating a safe harbor for those charged with respecting it. According to *Miranda*, the Constitution requires the government to inform suspects of their right to remain silent and to safeguard that right throughout the interrogation. Other actors are then encouraged to develop alternative ways to achieve these goals.

From this discussion it ought to be apparent that the problem is not so much with *Miranda*, but with the way subsequent decisions have characterized *Miranda*, both under-enforcing and over-enforcing the guidelines. Indeed, *Miranda*'s "invitation" serves only to make explicit what is always implicit—that it is always open to political actors to offer a competing vision of the requirements of the Constitution. After the Supreme Court held unconstitu-

---

[83] 384 US at 442.

[84] Id at 441–42 (emphasis added).

[85] Id at 444.

[86] Id at 444–45 (emphasis added).

[87] See id at 467.

[88] See id at 478–79, 490.

tional Texas's prosecution of a flag burner,[89] Congress was entitled to, in effect, urge the Court to reconsider that judgment, by enacting a federal law that attempted to prohibit burning the American flag,[90] just as the Court, in turn, was entitled to reject Congress's plea.[91] There is, admittedly, a sensitive and difficult constitutional line between appropriate testing of constitutional bounds and defiance. That is the problem that was presented in *Cooper v Aaron*[92] and some of the more extreme responses to *Roe v Wade*.[93] But generally a legislature passing laws subject to the ordinary process of judicial review will be on the permissible side of the line.

Of course, in the end the say is the Court's. The Court stated as much in *Miranda*, pointing out that "the issues presented are of constitutional dimensions and must be determined by the courts."[94] But this, standing alone, is nothing but the rule of *Marbury*, in its most modest form. In a case involving admission of a confession, a court must determine whether admission is consistent with constitutional commands.

In light of these familiar understandings, it becomes clearer what the Court should do with ACECIA. The Court should weigh ACECIA against the rule that *Dickerson* defines as the heart of *Miranda*. The Court should ask whether the ACECIA procedures are as effective as the *Miranda* warnings at informing suspects of their right to silence and ensuring a continuous opportunity to exercise that right. The procedures of ACECIA seem to measure up.[95] In-

---

[89] See *Texas v Johnson*, 491 US 397 (1989).

[90] See Flag Protection Act of 1989, 103 Stat 777, codified at 18 USCA § 700 (Supp 1990).

[91] See *United States v Eichman*, 496 US 310 (1990).

[92] 358 US 1 (1958).

[93] 410 US 113 (1973).

[94] 384 US at 490.

[95] While the videotaping of confessions will in the vast run of cases be enough to assure that both the *Miranda* and voluntariness components of the Fifth Amendment are met, there may be cases that require further elaboration of the statute or the constitutional rule. Perhaps the Court will find that a defendant subjected to hours and hours of interrogation could not have exercised free will. Perhaps the Court will conclude from a particular videotape that the process of interrogation so strained the suspect that he or she was not sufficiently of right mind to confess. Perhaps gaps in the videotape or the chronology from the time of arrest to the time of an incriminating statement will suggest that the police engaged in illegal practices when the machine was not recording. See *Stephan v State*, 711 P2d 1156, 1164 (Alaska 1985) (excluding the defendant's statement where "a police officer, in his own discretion, chose to turn the recorder on twenty minutes into the interview rather than at the beginning"); Wayne T. Westling and Vicki Waye, *Videotaping Police Interrogations: Les-*

forming the suspect of the right to silence is a key component of *Miranda/Dickerson*, and videotaping provides adequate protection of the right to continuous exercise of the privilege.[96]

Note, however, that the ultimate answer will emerge in the context of specific cases addressing whether particular suspects were adequately informed of their right to silence and whether they were the beneficiaries of procedural safeguards adequate to ensure a continuous opportunity to exercise it.[97] This is as it should be, and perhaps where *Miranda* went wrong. The appropriate complaint about *Miranda* is not that it departed from the traditional involuntariness test, for as we have seen, rights evolve. But the *Miranda* Court could have worked itself through to its essential holding on a case-by-case basis. Whether or not this was a necessity—and recognizing, ironically, that the bright-line nature of the *Miranda* decision might have done law enforcement a favor—the Court would have been subjected to less criticism had it worked incrementally.[98]

The most difficult part of ACECIA is the denial of counsel. This too might survive constitutional scrutiny after *Dickerson*, for most

---

sons from Australia, 25 Am J Crim L 493, 533–34 (1998) (describing the Australian experience).

[96] See Paul G. Cassell, *Miranda's Social Costs: An Empirical Reassessment*, 90 Nw U L Rev 387, 487 (1996) ("Videotaping interrogations would certainly be as effective as *Miranda* in preventing police coercion and probably more so."). Of course, nothing in *Miranda* prevents federal or state officials from videotaping confessions in addition to providing counsel and all of the standard warnings. See Stephen J. Schulhofer, *Miranda's Practical Effect: Substantial Benefits and Vanishingly Small Social Costs*, 90 Nw U L Rev 501, 556 (1996). By enacting ACECIA Congress would be making a judgment that videotaping should substitute for, rather than supplement, a right to counsel and the accompanying warnings. Compare Philip E. Johnson, *A Statutory Replacement for the Miranda Doctrine*, 24 Am Crim L Rev 303, 306, 313 (1987) (proposing audiotaping or videotaping as a recommended measure, possibly to be made mandatory after a period of study).

[97] See generally Harold J. Krent, *How to Move Beyond the Exclusionary Rule: Structuring Judicial Response to Legislative Reform Efforts*, 26 Pepperdine L Rev 855, 871–74 (1999) (discussing Supreme Court evaluation of a similar question—alternative remedies to exclusion under the Fourth Amendment—in the context of specific cases). Although the ultimate determination regarding any set of procedures would thus await concrete cases, declaratory relief should be liberally available to ensure that government officials do not engage in widespread illegal activity and to assure those same officials that a proposed set of alternative safeguards will not be ruled categorically inadequate. See Michael C. Dorf and Charles F. Sabel, *A Constitution of Democratic Experimentalism*, 98 Colum L Rev 267, 462–64 (1998) (urging a variant on the latter to avoid stifling experimentation by governments fearful of judicial overturning of convictions).

[98] Compare Ruth Bader Ginsburg, *Speaking in a Judicial Voice*, 67 NYU L Rev 1185, 1198–1205 (1992) (making the same point with respect to *Roe*).

of the Court's decisions treat the right to counsel as existing only in the service of the Fifth Amendment's commands, not as a core part of that Amendment, and the videotaping requirement should achieve the central goal of providing counsel in this setting.[99]

What is more interesting to us than any particular answer the Court might provide is how much room proper constitutional process should leave for other actors. *Miranda*'s "invitation" was quite specific, but the Congress that enacted Section 3501 did not take it seriously. Congress simply denied the Court's interpretation of the Constitution. Thus, the Court's invalidation of the statute in *Dickerson* is not surprising. But a serious legislative effort along the lines of ACECIA would deserve serious consideration by the Court.

II. Congress, the States, and Constitutional Power

The controversy in *Dickerson* raised a question of separation of powers—a contest between Congress and the Court. In this part we consider the implications of *Dickerson* in the contest between the states and the federal government. We conclude that the power granted to Congress by *Dickerson* gives it substantial control over the states, but consistent with our themes of shared interpretation, experimentation, humility, and respect, we believe Congress should be reluctant to exercise its power in a manner that limits state choices. Inherent in that conclusion, of course, is our belief (discussed in Part III) that just as Congress has power after *Dickerson* to pass legislation altering *Miranda*'s guidelines, so too do the states.

A. CONGRESSIONAL POWER TO SUPPLEMENT MIRANDA

Consider now a variant of ACECIA, the "National Anti-Coercion Act" ("NACA"). It states, "Absent a demonstration that videotaping was not possible in a particular case, no statement that

---

[99] Obviously the statutory rule would fail if the confession were taken after the Sixth Amendment right to counsel attached. And admittedly there is ambiguity in the case law—from *Escobedo v State of Illinois* if not before—as to whether there is an independent right to counsel in the custodial interrogation setting. See 378 US 478 (1964). Some of the continuing ambiguity arises from the fact "that *Miranda* did not build on the approach taken in *Escobedo* as much as it *displaced* it." Kamisar, 85 Cornell L Rev at 885 n 3 (cited in note 32) (emphasis in original).

is the product of custodial interrogation shall be admissible as evidence against the maker of that statement in any state or federal court unless the entire period of custodial interrogation, beginning with a warning that the suspect has the right to remain silent, was videotaped."[100] Unlike ACECIA, which substitutes alternative procedures for three of the four *Miranda* warnings, NACA supplements the warnings. In addition, and more importantly for present purposes, whereas ACECIA applies only to the federal government, NACA applies to the states as well. Under NACA, states would be permitted to give the full *Miranda* warnings *in addition to* videotaping custodial interrogation, but could not refuse to use videotaping. Is this constitutional?

1. *The commerce power.* From 1937 through 1995, the Supreme Court took an expansive view of Congress's power to regulate interstate commerce.[101] Of particular note, the commerce power was used regularly to justify civil rights legislation.[102] Most observers assumed that to sustain federal regulatory power over some activity it was necessary only to explain how that activity was connected to interstate commerce, and, of course, in a modern economy every activity is, in some measure, so connected. Accordingly, it came to be assumed that Congress could enact virtually any law under its commerce power.[103]

Thus, until recently, one might have tried to justify NACA under the Commerce Clause. The argument might have gone something like this: By requiring the videotaping of custodial inter-

---

[100] Those readers who are skeptical that Congress would ever pass a statute that seems to extend a new right to suspects may wish to imagine further that NACA responds to some widely publicized police scandal or is packaged with other measures that crack down on crime.

[101] In *NLRB v Jones & Laughlin Steel Corp.*, 301 US 1 (1937), the Court upheld the National Labor Relations Act of 1935. As the four dissenters noted, in affirming Congress's power to regulate manufacturing, the Court departed from a stricter view of the Commerce Clause that had prevailed earlier in the century. See *NLRB v Friedman-Harry Marks Clothing Co.*, 301 US 58, 78 (1937) (McReynolds dissenting from decisions in several cases) (objecting to federal regulation of "purely local industry beyond anything heretofore deemed permissible."). The Court did not again strike down a law as beyond the scope of the Commerce Clause until its decision in *United States v Lopez*, 514 US 549 (1995).

[102] See, e.g., *Katzenbach v McClung*, 379 US 294 (1964); *Heart of Atlanta Motel, Inc. v United States*, 379 US 241 (1964).

[103] See, e.g., Laurence H. Tribe, *American Constitutional Law* 313 (2d ed 1988) ("The doctrinal rules courts currently employ to determine whether federal legislation is affirmatively authorized under the commerce clause do not themselves effectively limit the power of Congress.").

rogation, NACA increases the demand for videotape, for video recording devices, and for employees who operate video recording devices. The tape and the recording devices are articles of commerce that move in an interstate market, and some people will cross state lines to find work operating the video recording devices. Accordingly, the argument concludes, NACA regulates interstate commerce.

United States v Lopez[104] and *United States v Morrison*[105] make clear that this sort of argument no longer works. Whatever the outer boundaries of the Commerce Clause after these decisions, NACA is outside them.

Arguably, *Lopez* itself, which struck down the Gun Free School Zones Act, held merely that Commerce Clause legislation must in fact regulate something that has a "substantial effect" on interstate commerce,[106] and indicated that without such a requirement Congress's powers may seem to be without limit. However, *Morrison*, which invalidated the civil remedy provision of the Violence Against Women Act (VAWA), restates the constitutional test formalistically. *Morrison* requires that if Congress regulates some activity because of its substantial effects on interstate commerce, the regulated activity must be "some sort of economic endeavor."[107]

The fact that NACA would have an effect on interstate commerce is thus irrelevant. The same was true of the Gun Free School Zones Act and VAWA. Like firearm possession and gender-motivated violence—the activities Congress sought to regulate in *Lopez* and *Morrison*, respectively—neither custodial interrogation nor the introduction of evidence at a criminal trial is likely to strike

---

[104] 514 US 549 (1995).

[105] 120 S Ct 1740 (2000).

[106] There are two other branches of the commerce power: the regulation of the "channels" and "instrumentalities" of interstate commerce, neither of which was applicable in *Lopez*, see id at 559, and neither of which is applicable here.

[107] *United States v Morrison*, 120 S Ct 1740, 1750 (2000) (citing *Lopez*, 514 US at 559–60). *Lopez* may have made sense as an attempt to define the permissible boundaries of congressional regulation under its enumerated powers, but *Morrison*—at least as it was written—signals a regrettable return to pre-1937 formalism. Moreover, *Morrison* seems in some ways an attempt by the Chief Justice to resuscitate his opinion in 1976 in *National League of Cities v Usery*, 426 US 833 (1976). That would be unfortunate, given that the constitutional structure does seem to imply an attempt to define enumerated powers, whereas *National League of Cities'* notion of a traditional state function, see id at 849–52, finds no place in the Constitution. See Thomas R. McCoy and Barry Friedman, *Conditional Spending: Federalism's Trojan Horse*, 1988 Supreme Court Review 85, 114 (1988).

the Court as "economic activity" or as having a "substantial effect" on interstate commerce. Accordingly, NACA presents a fairly easy case under current doctrine. It is not authorized by the Commerce Clause.

2. *The "Morgan" power.* Section 5 of the Fourteenth Amendment is a plausible source of congressional power to enact NACA. It authorizes Congress "to enforce, by appropriate legislation," the substantive provisions of the Fourteenth Amendment. One of those substantive provisions is the Due Process Clause, which, through the incorporation doctrine, is the basis for applying the Fifth Amendment to the states.

Katzenbach v Morgan[108] was probably the high-water mark of the Section 5 power. In that case, the Court upheld a provision of the federal Voting Rights Act forbidding states to condition the vote of any person educated in a Puerto Rican Spanish-instruction school on English literacy, notwithstanding the fact that the Court had earlier upheld a state-imposed English literacy test.[109] The Court reasoned that Section 5 grants Congress the power to "enforce" the Fourteenth Amendment independent of any adjudicated violation of its terms,[110] and Congress could reasonably have determined that proscribing English literacy tests was necessary to combat state-sponsored discrimination in voting. The Court was emphatic, however, that "§ 5 grants Congress no power to restrict, abrogate, or dilute the[ ] guarantees" of the Fourteenth Amendment,[111] even as it authorizes Congress to go beyond what the courts require. Section 5 was thus a "ratchet."[112] Congress could add to but not subtract from the protection the Court itself afforded constitutional rights.

But what kind of ratchet is Section 5? Does it authorize Congress to define the content of the substantive provisions of the

---

[108] 384 US 641 (1966).

[109] See id at 649 (distinguishing *Lassiter v Northampton Election Bd.*, 360 US 45 (1959)).

[110] See *Morgan*, 384 US at 648–49.

[111] Id at 651.

[112] See William Cohen, *Congressional Power to Interpret Due Process and Equal Protection*, 27 Stan L Rev 603, 613 (1975); Douglas Laycock, *RFRA, Congress, and the Ratchet*, 56 Mont L Rev 145, 152–69 (1995); Matt Pawa, *Comment: When the Supreme Court Restricts Constitutional Rights, Can Congress Save Us? An Examination of Section 5 of the Fourteenth Amendment*, 141 U Pa L Rev 1029, 1062–69 (1993); Lawrence G. Sager, *Fair Measure: The Legal Status of Underenforced Constitutional Norms*, 91 Harv L Rev 1212, 1230 (1978).

Fourteenth Amendment independent of the Court's own jurisprudence, and then enact legislation designed to "enforce" the Congressional interpretation? The Court approved that approach with respect to Congress's power to enforce the Thirteenth Amendment in *Jones v Alfred H. Mayer Co.*,[113] and parts of *Morgan* appeared to acknowledge a parallel enforcement power under the Fourteenth Amendment.[114] Individual Justices strongly criticized this view of the Fourteenth Amendment, however, in two post-*Morgan* cases.[115]

The Rehnquist Court's interest in defending state sovereignty against what it considers congressional overreaching spelled doom for the substantive ratchet theory. After all, a substantive ratchet is inconsistent with the spirit, if not the letter, of the Court's insistence in *Lopez* that there are limits to Congress's affirmative powers. Virtually any law, indeed, any human action, can, on some rational understanding, be seen to deprive someone of life, liberty, property, or equality; thus, a congressional power to enforce Congress's own definition of the substantive provisions of the Fourteenth Amendment could well become the sort of plenary congressional power that the *Lopez* Court was at pains to reject under the Commerce Clause.

Unsurprisingly, just two years after *Lopez*, the Court formally renounced the substantive ratchet theory.[116] *City of Boerne v Flores*[117] held that Section 5 did not authorize the enactment of the Religious Freedom Restoration Act[118] (RFRA), which required that laws of general applicability be subject to strict judicial scrutiny in those instances in which they imposed a substantial burden on religion. Because the Court had previously ruled that such generally applicable laws do not trigger heightened scrutiny,[119] the Court

---

[113] 392 US 409 (1968).

[114] See *Katzenbach v Morgan*, 384 US 641, 653–56 (1966).

[115] See *EEOC v Wyoming*, 460 US 226, 262 (1983) (Burger dissenting) ("Allowing Congress to protect constitutional rights statutorily that it has independently defined fundamentally alters our scheme of government."); *Oregon v Mitchell*, 400 US 112, 205 (1970) (Harlan concurring in part and dissenting in part); id at 296 (Stewart concurring in part and dissenting in part).

[116] See *Boerne*, 521 US at 519–29.

[117] 521 US 507 (1997).

[118] Pub L No 103-141, 107 Stat 1488 (1993), codified at 42 USC § 2000bb (1994).

[119] See *Employment Div. v Smith*, 494 US 872 (1990).

deemed RFRA an impermissible effort to exercise a substantive ratchet power.

Boerne nonetheless recognized that Section 5 grants Congress a remedial ratchet power, that is, a power to enact remedial or preventative measures for what the Court itself would consider to be violations of the Fourteenth Amendment, even if the Court would not itself require the specific remedial or preventative measures.[120] That recognition was necessary to reconcile *Boerne* with *Morgan* and other cases, and more importantly, to avoid rendering Section 5 nugatory.

The Court's simultaneous disavowal of a substantive ratchet and recognition of a remedial ratchet in *Boerne* gave rise to an obvious difficulty: how to distinguish the two. In *Morgan*, for example, the Court characterized the challenged provision as either a remedy for official discrimination or an extension of substantive protection against voting discrimination beyond what the Court had required. The mechanism the Court used in *Boerne* for discerning permissible remedial measures from impermissible efforts to ratchet up substantive constitutional protection was a means/ends test. There must be a "congruence and proportionality" between what the Court would recognize as a constitutional violation and the means Congress chooses to remedy or prevent that violation;[121] otherwise, the Court will assume that Congress is merely dressing a substantive ratchet in remedial garb.

Is NACA congruent and proportional to violations of the Fifth Amendment? That depends on how close a fit between means and ends is demanded. Even after *Lopez* and *Morrison*, the general standard for determining whether an Act falls within one of Congress's enumerated powers is the quite deferential necessary-and-proper test of *McCulloch v Maryland*:[122] "Let the end be legitimate, let it be within the scope of the constitution, and all means which are appropriate, which are plainly adapted to that end, which are not prohibited, but consist with the letter and spirit of the constitution,

---

[120] See *Boerne*, 521 US at 518 ("Legislation which deters or remedies constitutional violations can fall within the sweep of Congress' enforcement power even if in the process it prohibits conduct which is not itself unconstitutional and intrudes into 'legislative spheres of autonomy previously reserved to the States.'" (quoting *Fitzpatrick v Bitzer*, 427 US 445, 455 (1976)).

[121] *Boerne*, 521 US at 519.

[122] 17 US (4 Wheat) 316, 421 (1819).

are constitutional."[123] The Court has applied the necessary-and-proper test quite deferentially when Congress has invoked its powers to enforce the Thirteenth and Fifteenth Amendments,[124] and one might therefore expect similar deference in the Fourteenth Amendment context.

However, in four recent cases the Court has held that federal laws were not justified under the Section 5 power.[125] This pattern suggests that congruence and proportionality is a demanding standard.[126] Nevertheless, NACA satisfies the standard the Court has applied in the recent Section 5 decisions.

---

[123] Id at 421.

[124] See *Jones v Alfred H. Mayer Co.*, 392 US 409, 443–44 (1968) (Thirteenth Amendment); *South Carolina v Katzenbach*, 383 US 301, 326 (1966) (Fifteenth Amendment); *City of Rome v United States*, 446 US 156, 175 (1980) (Fifteenth Amendment).

[125] See *Morrison*, 120 S Ct 1740 (2000); *Kimel v Florida Bd. of Regents*, 120 S Ct 631 (2000); *Florida Prepaid Postsecondary Educ. Expense Bd. v College Savings Bank*, 527 US 627 (1999); *Boerne*, 521 US 507.

[126] Contrasting *Boerne* with a Fifteenth Amendment case, *City of Rome v United States*, 446 US 156 (1980), suggests that congruence and proportionality is a stricter test than necessary and proper. In *Rome*, as in *Boerne*, Congress sought to substitute what could be described as a disparate impact test for a judicially mandated purposeful discrimination test. Applying the necessary-and-proper test, the Court deferred to Congress's chosen means in *Rome*; applying the congruence and proportionality test, the Court invalidated Congress's handiwork in *Boerne*. See Laurence H. Tribe, 1 *American Constitutional Law* 933–36 (3d ed 1999).

Is the Court justified in applying a stricter standard of review to legislation under Section 5 of the Fourteenth Amendment than under the other Civil War Amendments (not to mention Congress's powers under Article I, Section 8)? One might reconcile the cases by noting that, unlike the Fourteenth Amendment Section 5 power, the power to enforce the Fifteenth Amendment does not pose a risk of becoming a plenary power. The Fifteenth Amendment is limited to a much narrower subject matter—race discrimination in voting—than the Fourteenth Amendment. Hence, it could be argued, the Court can afford to grant Congress greater deference under the Fifteenth Amendment than under the Fourteenth.

Although this line of argument may work for the Fifteenth Amendment, it does not work for the Thirteenth Amendment. Under *Jones*, "Congress is free, within the broad limits of reason, to recognize whatever rights it wishes, define the infringement of those rights as a form of domination or subordination and thus an aspect of slavery, and proscribe such infringement as a violation of the Thirteenth Amendment." Tribe, 1 *American Constitutional Law* at 927 (cited above). And because the Thirteenth Amendment contains no state action requirement, this means that "Congress would possess nearly plenary authority under the Thirteenth amendment to protect all but the most trivial individual rights from both governmental and private invasion." Id. Accordingly, the difference in wording and subject matter among the Thirteenth, Fourteenth, and Fifteenth Amendments does not justify the narrower approach that the Court has lately taken toward the Fourteenth.

Nonetheless, we do not mean to suggest that the Civil War Amendment cases are strictly irreconcilable with one another. For example, one could think that *Boerne* and *Rome* are both rightly decided. Given our nation's long history of racial discrimination in voting, in 1965 (the date of passage of the Voting Rights Act), it was entirely plausible for Congress to conclude that many or most changes in voting rules that have a disparate racial impact are in fact motivated by official racial animus, even if specific proof of such animus is unavailable in particular cases. By contrast, in 1993 (the date of passage of the Religious

In *Florida Prepaid Postsecondary Education Expense Board v College Savings Bank*,[127] the most restrictive of the Section 5 decisions, the Court held that Section 5 did not authorize Congress to subject nonconsenting states to suit in federal court for violating patent rights. Although the Court accepted that patent rights are "property" within the meaning of the Fourteenth Amendment Due Process Clause,[128] the Court nonetheless found a lack of congruence and proportionality. Selectively citing procedural due process cases, the Court asserted that a patent violation by the state violates due process only if the state fails to provide an adequate remedy.[129] Because Congress had compiled what the Court considered insufficient evidence that states were failing to provide remedies for their own patent violations, the Court found a lack of congruence and proportionality.[130]

Standing alone, *Florida Prepaid* is deeply troubling: it appears to abandon any notion that the Court and Congress are partners in enforcing the Constitution. Why was Congress's Section 5 "preventative" power insufficient to justify the statute? The Court's answer is that the remedy was not, in its view, necessary to protect constitutional rights.[131] But necessity cannot be the touchstone under Section 5, for by hypothesis Congress may enact measures that

---

Freedom Restoration Act), Congress had no reason to believe that any but a tiny handful of the generally applicable laws that, from time to time, impose substantial burdens on the free exercise of religion were adopted out of religious animus. The *Boerne* Court itself appeared to endorse this distinction between race and religion. See, e.g., *Boerne*, 521 US at 531 ("In contrast to the record which confronted Congress and the judiciary in the voting rights cases, RFRA's legislative record lacks examples of modern instances of generally applicable laws passed because of religious bigotry. The history of persecution in this country detailed in the hearings mentions no episodes occurring in the past 40 years."). Thus, the different outcomes in *Rome* and *Boerne* could be taken to mean that the Court applied a consistent standard of review, which the Voting Rights Act satisfied and the Religious Freedom Restoration Act did not. The outcomes alone do not logically entail that the Court applied different standards.

[127] 527 US 627 (1999).

[128] See id at 642.

[129] See id at 642–43 (citing *Zinermon v Burch*, 494 US 113, 125 (1990); *Parratt v Taylor*, 451 US 527, 539–31 (1981); *Hudson v Palmer*, 468 US 517, 532–53 (1984); id at 539 (O'Connor concurring). As the dissent observed, these cases only establish that negligent deprivations of property do not violate the Due Process Clause if there is an adequate state postdeprivation remedy; a willful deprivation is a completed Due Process violation at the moment it occurs. See *Florida Prepaid*, 527 US at 653 (Stevens dissenting) (citing *Daniels v Williams*, 474 US 327, 332–34 (1986)).

[130] See id at 643–44.

[131] See Tribe, 1 *American Constitutional Law* at 958 (cited in note 126).

go beyond what the Court itself deems necessary. In *Florida Prepaid* the Court appears to have forgotten the purpose of the congruence and proportionality test: to distinguish between legitimate and sham remedial or preventative measures. There was no serious argument in *Florida Prepaid* that Congress had, as in RFRA, attempted to redefine the substance of constitutional rights. Accordingly, the Court should have deferred to Congress. Instead, it apparently mandated "something between intermediate and strict scrutiny"[132] of Congressional enactments pursuant to the Section 5 power.

Florida Prepaid is an aberration. The Court's other recent Section 5 cases are not quite so constricting. In particular, last Term's decision in *Kimel v Florida Board of Regents*[133] used the congruence and proportionality test for its original purpose: to smoke out a Congressional effort to exercise a substantive ratchet power.[134] It is striking that, despite the division within the Court over questions of federalism, none of the Justices have questioned the congruence and proportionality test in principle.[135] We believe this

---

[132] Id at 959.

[133] 120 S Ct 631 (2000).

[134] In *Kimel* the Court held that the Age Discrimination in Employment Act (ADEA) could not be justified under the Section 5 power. Age discrimination, in the Court's view, is unconstitutional only if irrational, and Congress had identified no pattern of age discrimination, much less a pattern of irrational age discrimination. See id at 649. In this respect, the ADEA was plausibly understood as an illicit attempt by Congress to treat age as a suspect classification in the face of judicial decisions holding that it is not. See *Gregory v Ashcroft*, 501 US 452, 473 (1991); *Vance v Bradley*, 440 US 93, 102–03 (1979); *Massachusetts Board of Retirement v Murgia*, 427 US 307, 317 (1976) (per curiam). To be sure, age discrimination, like most forms of discrimination, is subject to mere rational basis scrutiny out of deference to Congress and state legislatures. By reserving heightened scrutiny for the most invidious forms of discrimination, the Court leaves room for the operation of the democratic process. Arguably, a parallel principle of respect for a coordinate branch of government should mean that Congress is also entitled to deference when it determines that age discrimination is sufficiently invidious to warrant a legislative solution. But this argument leads ultimately to the very substantive ratchet theory that *Boerne* rejected, and thus it is not surprising that the *Kimel* Court (implicitly) rejected the argument.

[135] By contrast with *Florida Prepaid*, in neither *Kimel* nor *Boerne* was there any dissent from the application of the congruence and proportionality test itself. In *Boerne*, the dissenters objected to the Court's interpretation of the Free Exercise Clause, rather than its insistence that Congress had gone beyond that interpretation. *Boerne*, 521 US at 544–45 (O'Connor dissenting); id at 565 (Souter dissenting); id at 566 (Breyer dissenting). In both *Florida Prepaid* and *Kimel*, Justices Stevens, Souter, Ginsburg, and Breyer objected to the doctrine, first announced in *Seminole Tribe*, that permits Congress to abrogate state sovereign immunity when acting pursuant to the Section 5 power but not when acting pursuant to its Article I powers. But only in *Florida Prepaid* did these same four Justices object further to the way in which the majority applied the congruence and proportionality test. In *Morrison v United States*, the Court held that Section 5 did not authorize the provision of the

agreement[136] stems from the fact that *Boerne*'s original judgment—
that RFRA was an effort to expand substantive protection for free
exercise rights rather than to remedy or prevent religious discrimination—was basically sound.

What implications do the recent cases have for Congress's
power to supplement *Miranda*? If, as *Florida Prepaid* suggests, the
Section 5 power may be exercised only if an act of Congress is,
in the Court's view, necessary to remedy or prevent a recognized
constitutional violation, NACA's requirement that all custodial interrogation be videotaped would be plainly unconstitutional, for
Miranda and *Dickerson* make clear that the *Miranda* warnings are
sufficient to satisfy the Constitution.

Moreover, both *Florida Prepaid* and *Morrison* criticize Congress
for enacting statutes that apply nationwide when the underlying
problem might have been restricted to particular states or re-
gions.[137] To the extent that these criticisms state a constitutional
requirement, NACA would need to be limited to those places for
which there was evidence before Congress of a pattern of coerced
confessions—and even that might not be sufficient for a targeted
NACA, given the presumptive adequacy of the *Miranda* warnings.

Nonetheless, we think that NACA, even if applicable nationwide, would be valid under Section 5. As indicated above, *Florida
Prepaid* is aberrational in the standard it applies. The Court's rulings in each of its other recent decisions rejecting Congress's efforts to use the Section 5 power are plausibly understood to rest

---

Violence Against Women Act that created a federal civil remedy for victims of gender-
motivated violence. 120 S Ct 1740 (2000). The Court relied mainly on nineteenth-century
precedents invalidating Acts of Congress that sought to regulate private conduct pursuant
to Section 5. See id at 1756 (discussing *United States v Harris*, 106 US 629 (1883) and the
Civil Rights Cases, 109 US 3 (1883)). The Court then rejected the claim that Congress
had provided a right of action against private actors as the means by which persons who
would otherwise face official discrimination in state courts could circumvent that constitutional wrong. See id at 1758–59. Two of the dissenters did not reach the Section 5 question,
as they would have sustained the law under the Commerce Clause. Justice Breyer, writing
for himself and Justice Stevens, expressed doubt about the soundness of the Court's Section
5 analysis, see id at 1778–80 (Breyer dissenting), although not about the congruence and
proportionality test itself. See id at 1779 (distinguishing *Boerne*).

[136] Accord Robert C. Post and Reva B. Siegel, *The Uncertain Future of Federal Antidiscrimination Law: Morrison, Kimel, and the Dismantling of Congressional Section 5 Powers* 2 (draft
on file with authors) ("This silence is remarkable.").

[137] *Morrison*, 120 S Ct at 1759 (contrasting VAWA with statutes "directed only to the
State where the evil found by Congress existed"); *Florida Prepaid*, 120 S Ct at 646–47
("Congress did nothing to . . . confine the reach of the Act by . . . providing for suits only
against States with questionable remedies or a high incidence of infringement.").

on the view that Congress was attempting to exercise a substantive ratchet power it lacks: in *Boerne*, Congress expanded free exercise protection; in *Kimel*, it attempted to recognize a new suspect class; and in *Morrison*, it lifted the state action requirement. Thus, with the exception of *Florida Prepaid*, congruence and proportionality has been a test of congressional motivation—asking whether Congress was really enacting permissible remedial and preventative measures or illegitimately attempting to change the substantive meaning of the Constitution.

There can be little doubt that NACA is designed as a remedial and preventative provision. To be sure, one could characterize NACA as creating a substantive right to videotaping, but that characterization would not make sense in context. Presumably, Congress would enact NACA in order to implement the Fifth Amendment rights of suspects subject to custodial interrogation, not to establish videotaping as a right in itself.[138] Thus, if the congruence and proportionality test is applied properly, NACA should satisfy it.[139] For far from an effort to circumvent Court-set limits, NACA responds to the Court's direct invitation to Congress in *Miranda* to devise alternative safeguards.

To be clear, we are not saying that the *Miranda* invitation by itself authorizes NACA. It is possible to read that invitation as applying to Congress and the states, respectively, each in its own sphere. On this reading, the Court invited each state to devise its own alternative procedures, while Congress would devise alternative procedures only for federal agents. However, as even Justice

---

[138] Contrast RFRA, in which Congress thought that substantial burdens on religion imposed by generally applicable laws were (unconstitutional) harms in themselves.

[139] Furthermore, *Florida Prepaid* may be less of an obstacle than it at first appears. Notwithstanding the Court's acknowledgment that patents are property for purposes of the Due Process Clause, in *Florida Prepaid* as in the other recent Section 5 cases, one senses that the Court viewed Congress as attempting to evade limits the Court had set. A law granting remedies for patent infringement is, in some intuitive sense, most clearly an exercise of Congress's Article I powers, see US Const, Art I, § 8, cl 8, bearing at best a tangential relationship to the Civil War Amendments. Having decided (quite erroneously in our view) that Congress may abrogate state sovereign immunity when acting pursuant to its power to enforce the Civil War Amendments but not its Article I powers, see *Seminole Tribe*, the *Florida Prepaid* Court was understandably reluctant to permit Congress to treat what looked like an Article I matter as falling within the Section 5 power. On this view, the Court was right (within its own erroneous assumptions) to see the Patent Remedy Act as incongruent with and disproportionate to a Fourteenth Amendment violation, even if the Court—in a now all too familiar move—chose to explain why in a way that aggrandized its own power at the expense of Congress.

Scalia recognized in his *Dickerson* dissent, through Section 5, the Constitution grants Congress a "limited power to supplement its guarantees . . . ."[140] In our view, NACA would satisfy the congruence and proportionality requirement.[141]

B. COULD CONGRESS CONSTITUTIONALLY PROHIBIT DEFENSE ATTORNEYS FROM ATTENDING CUSTODIAL INTERROGATIONS OF THEIR CLIENTS?

Suppose Congress determined that videotaping custodial interrogation would solve only half of the problem, and that if states continued to provide a right to counsel at such interrogations some otherwise admissible confessions would be lost. We already have suggested that Congress could bar attorneys in federal cases, but could it bar them in state cases as well?

Let us imagine that Congress enacts the "National Anti-Coercion and Effective Custodial Interrogation Act." "NACECIA" requires that all custodial interrogation be preceded by the warning that a suspect has the right to remain silent and requires that all custodial interrogation be videotaped. But NACECIA forbids state agents from delivering the other *Miranda* warnings and from allowing attorneys to be present during pre-indictment custodial interrogation.

Like NACA, NACECIA can only be sustained as an exercise of the Section 5 power,[142] but viewed from that perspective, NACECIA is highly problematic. The effect of NACECIA would be to bar three of the four *Miranda* warnings and to bar attorneys

---

[140] Dickerson, 120 S Ct at 2345.

[141] What other statutes would be authorized under the Court's view of Section 5 remains an open question. For example, in *Zurcher v Stanford Daily*, 436 US 547 (1978), the Court held that neither the First Amendment nor the Fourth Amendment requires any heightened showing of need by law enforcement in order to obtain a warrant to search a newspaper's premises for evidence of third-party wrongdoing. Congress responded by enacting the Privacy Protection Act of 1980, 42 USC § 2000aa, which affords the institutional media and their employees with protection against searches and seizures beyond what the Constitution (as interpreted in *Zurcher*) requires. As a regulation of law enforcement officials rather than the media, the Act may fall outside the scope of the Commerce Clause, and as an apparent attempt to expand the Court's definition of the substantive right protected by the Fourth Amendment, the Act may likewise exceed the Section 5 power.

[142] NACECIA would not pass muster under the Commerce Clause for the same basic reason that NACA would not: the regulated activity is not economic activity. Both *Lopez* and *Morrison* clearly reject the claim that a law designed to cut crime is, ipso facto, a regulation of interstate commerce.

from attending custodial interrogation. But if NACECIA reduces the level of protection to which suspects are entitled, in what sense is NACECIA an effort to "enforce" the Fourteenth Amendment? This looks very much like an attempt to "restrict, abrogate, or dilute" rights, a power that the Court in *Katzenbach v Morgan* insisted is not encompassed within Section 5.

Or does it? Section 5 authorizes enforcement measures. If, taken as a whole, NACECIA works as well as or better than the standard *Miranda* warnings, perhaps NACECIA can legitimately be said to enforce the Fifth Amendment (through the Fourteenth). On this view, the fact that NACECIA limits the supererogatory measures states might otherwise employ does not distinguish it from other federal laws that preempt contrary state practices. Comprehensive federal statutes routinely block state efforts to "over-enforce" the very policies that appear to underlie the federal statutes themselves.[143]

What about the Court's concern in *Morgan* about restriction, abrogation, or dilution? Section 5 gives Congress no power to *violate* the Fourteenth Amendment. For example, Congress could not, in the guise of enforcing the Equal Protection Clause, mandate racial segregation in public schools. That Congress lacks this power follows both from the fact that Congress lacks a substantive power to define the Fourteenth Amendment (per *Boerne*) and, more fundamentally, from the basic tenets of *Marbury v Madison*.

But to deny that Congress may authorize rights violations is not to say that the Section 5 power prevents Congress from eliminating remedies the Court has itself required. In our view, no such separate limit to Congress's remedial Section 5 power exists. If some set of procedures is constitutionally required, then of course Congress cannot dispense with them. But as *Miranda* shows, the Court can declare some set of procedures (P_1) to be a constitutionally adequate response to some set of risks—a safe harbor— even though it would be prepared to uphold some other set of procedures (P_2). A proponent of NACECIA might thus contend that Congress should be permitted to conclude that P_2, understood

---

[143] See, e.g., *Crosby v National Foreign Trade Council*, 120 S Ct 2288 (2000) (economic sanctions for human rights abuses by foreign government); *United States v Locke*, 120 S Ct 1135 (2000) (oil tanker regulations); *City of Burbank v Lockheed Air Terminal, Inc.*, 411 US 624 (1973) (aircraft noise).

as a comprehensive remedial scheme, is preferable to P$_1$. Other than the *ipse dixit* in *Morgan*—which may be best understood as barring only Congress's power to violate the Constitution—there is nothing in existing case law to rule out this understanding of the enforcement power. If it were accepted, NACECIA would fall within the Section 5 power so long as the NACECIA procedures themselves are as effective as the *Miranda* safeguards.

C. THE ANTICOMMANDEERING PRINCIPLE

Before concluding that Congress can constitutionally enact NACA (not to mention NACECIA)[144] we must consider the doctrine that prohibits Congress from "commandeering" state legislative and executive officials.[145] In another branch of its burgeoning federalism jurisprudence, the Court held in *New York v United States*[146] and *Printz v United States*[147] that Congress may not commandeer the agencies of state government to regulate on behalf of the federal government. By requiring state officials to videotape custodial interrogation, NACA appears to "direct the functioning of the state executive" in violation of *Printz*.[148] If Congress cannot direct state law enforcement officials to perform background checks on prospective handgun purchasers, as *Printz* holds, how can Congress direct state law enforcement officials to videotape custodial interrogations?

The proper approach appears to come from contrasting *Printz* with last Term's unanimous decision in *Reno v Condon*.[149] In *Condon*, the Court upheld the Driver's Privacy Protection Act,[150] notwithstanding the fact that compliance with the Act would "require time and effort on the part of state employees,"[151] because the Act "'regulated state activities,' rather than 'seeking to control or in-

---

[144] For simplicity, this section only considers NACA.

[145] See *New York v United States*, 505 US 144 (1992) (holding that Congress may not direct the states to enact legislation); *Printz v United States*, 521 US 898 (1997) (holding that Congress may not compel state executive officers to carry out federal law).

[146] 505 US 144 (1992).

[147] 521 US 898 (1997).

[148] Id at 932.

[149] 120 S Ct 666 (2000).

[150] 18 USC §§ 2721–25.

[151] *Reno v Condon*, 120 S Ct 666, 672 (2000).

fluence the manner in which states regulate private parties.'"[152]
The term "commandeering" implies that rather than doing its own
work, the federal government is attempting to compel the states
to do the federal work. As regulatory objects, by contrast, the states
are subject to, rather than the agents of, a federal regulatory
scheme.

In practice, however, the line between regulation of the states
and impermissible commandeering may be difficult to draw. Both
the background check requirement in *Printz* and the prohibition
on the release of driver information in *Condon* take the form of
commands to state actors, and both laws have a substantial regulatory impact on private parties: In *Printz* the effect is to delay or
deny permission for a seller and purchaser of a handgun to complete their transaction; in *Condon* the effect is to prevent commercial advertisers and others from obtaining drivers' private information.

One might understand the *Printz/Condon* distinction in terms of
acts and omissions. The Brady Act forced state officials to take
actions regarding third parties where they might have preferred to
do nothing; the Driver's Privacy Protection Act prohibited the
state from acting with respect to third parties where they would
have preferred to act (by selling driver information to commercial
purchasers). But given all the complex ways in which the modern
state interacts with its citizens, there may nonetheless be doubts
whether the act/omission distinction can do the work that *Printz*
and *Condon* seem to require.[153]

Even if the *Printz/Condon* distinction is defensible, NACA presents a borderline case. On the one hand, videotaping suspects cannot reasonably be characterized as "regulation" of those suspects.
NACA tells state actors what they must do; it does not tell state
actors what they must tell private parties to do or not to do. Thus,
in terms of *Condon*, NACA appears unobjectionable. On the other
hand, if the *Printz/Condon* distinction is an act/omission distinction, NACA seems to fall on the wrong side of the line. It com-

---

[152] Id (quoting *South Carolina v Baker*, 485 US 505, 514–15 (1988)).

[153] Indeed, the *Condon* Court itself recognized that the imposition of affirmative obligations on the states is "an inevitable consequence of regulating a state activity." 120 S Ct
at 672 (quoting *South Carolina v Baker*, 485 US 505, 514 (1988) (internal quotation marks
omitted)). See also Matthew D. Adler and Seth F. Kreimer, *The New Etiquette of Federalism:
New York, Printz, and Yeskey*, 1988 Supreme Court Review 71, 95–102 (1998).

mands state officials to take an affirmative measure—videotaping custodial interrogation. We need not resolve this ambiguity, however, because Congress could impose the equivalent of NACA regardless of whether it falls on the *Printz* or the *Condon* side of the line.

NACA would be constitutional if Congress phrased it as a substantive rule of law governing confessions.[154] The rule would read something like this: "No statement made during custodial interrogation shall be admissible against the maker of the statement in a criminal trial in any state or federal court unless the custodial interrogation was videotaped." This rule would not run afoul of the anticommandeering principle because so long as a federal law is within federal competence—as we concluded NACA would be under the Section 5 power—there is no constitutional obstacle to putting it in the form of a rule that state courts must abide.[155]

Long before *Miranda*, it was settled that state courts could not utilize evidence obtained in violation of federal law. Thus, the predecessor rule to *Miranda*, which barred the admission into evidence of involuntary confessions, was routinely invoked to invalidate convictions that rested upon such confessions.[156] Applying broader substantive understandings, *Miranda* itself and the Fourth Amendment exclusionary rule have the same structure. Further, the principle is not limited to criminal proceedings. Under *New York Times v Sullivan*,[157] a public official can prevail in a defamation action only by proving the defendant's reckless disregard for the truth.[158] If state law permits recovery on a showing of mere falsehood, *Sullivan* displaces the state standard.

---

[154] Current doctrine also suggests that Congress could impose NACA as a conditional exercise of the spending power, see *New York*, 505 US at 167 (distinguishing commandeering from conditional spending), although it remains to be seen whether this power will survive the *New York/Printz* line of cases. Compare *Printz*, 521 US at 918 ("We of course do not address [statutes that arguably utilize conditional spending]; it will be time enough to do so if and when their validity is challenged in a proper case.").

[155] We do not contend that there is some general federal power to fashion rules of evidence or procedure for state courts. Our claim is far more limited: If a rule of law falls within the scope of one of Congress's enumerated powers, requiring state courts to comply with it is not independently objectionable on federalism grounds.

[156] See, e.g., *Brown v Mississippi*, 297 US 278 (1936); *Chambers v Florida*, 309 US 227 (1940); *Ward v Texas*, 316 US 547 (1942).

[157] 376 US 254 (1964).

[158] See id at 279–80 (imposing "a federal rule that prohibits a public official from recovering damages for a defamatory falsehood relating to his official conduct unless he proves that the statement was made with 'actual malice'—that is, with knowledge that it was false or with reckless disregard of whether it was false or not.").

Nor is the supremacy of federal law in state court limited to constitutional as opposed to statutory law. Quite apart from the rule of *Testa v Katt*, requiring state courts to be open on a nondiscriminatory basis to federal causes of action,[159] the availability of federal law—whatever its source—as a shield against contrary state action is the very core of federal supremacy.

Thus, in the furtherance of its enumerated powers, Congress has not hesitated to enact substantive rules that are applicable in state court. For example, the Soldiers' and Sailors' Relief Act of 1940[160] requires state (as well as federal) courts[161] to suspend various judicial proceedings by or against active duty members of the U.S. military. Congress's unquestioned power to provide for the national defense permits such a rule.

Similarly, Title III of the Omnibus Crime Control and Safe Streets Act of 1968[162] mandates the remedy of exclusion from state (as well as federal) court proceedings for violations of the substantive terms of the Act,[163] which prohibit some conduct that the Fourth Amendment would allow. Most prominently, Title III applies to private actors.[164] Although some courts have declined to apply the exclusionary remedy to private violations of the Act,[165] that approach is not universal.[166] In any event, no court has ever suggested that an exclusionary remedy for private violations would be beyond Congress's power. Assuming the substantive provisions of Title III are authorized under the Commerce Clause or the Section 5 power, a statutory exclusionary rule is unobjectionable.

---

[159] 330 US 386 (1947). According to the *Printz* Court, *Testa* is consistent with the anti-commandeering rule because state courts differ from state executives and state legislatures in two crucial respects. First, the literal language of the Supremacy Clause binds state judges to federal law. See *Printz*, 521 US at 928–29. Second, the Madisonian compromise, under which Congress was free to create no lower federal courts, meant that the Framers contemplated assigning some federal tasks to state court judges. See id at 907. We have doubts whether these points sufficiently distinguish *Testa* from *New York* and *Printz*, but as we explain in the text, that is irrelevant to the present discussion, as the validity of a federal rule of inadmissibility applicable in state court does not rest on the *Testa* power.

[160] 5 USC § App 501 et seq.

[161] See 5 USC § App 511(4).

[162] Pub L No 90-351, 82 Stat 212, codified at 18 USC §§ 2510–22 (1994 & Supp IV 1998).

[163] See 18 USC § 2515.

[164] See 18 USC § 2511.

[165] See, e.g., *United States v Liddy*, 354 F Supp 217 (DDC 1973).

[166] See, e.g., *United States v Grice*, 37 F Supp 2d 428 (D S Car 1998) (applying exclusionary remedy in accordance with the Act's plain language).

The same is true for NACA. So long as it is authorized by an affirmative power of Congress, there is no obstacle to Congress phrasing it as a rule of inadmissibility for the state courts.[167]

D. CONGRESSIONAL HUMILITY AND STATE EXPERIMENTATION

To suggest that Congress *could* impose NACA (or NACECIA) on the states is not to suggest that it *should* do so. Congress should refrain from imposing such requirements on the states. Congress should respect the value of experimentation and hesitate to conclude that any one solution is correct.

With regard to NACECIA, the issue is whether states ought to be free to offer greater protection to individuals than the Constitution requires. There is a long tradition of such freedom, and recent years have seen an increase in the willingness of state courts to extend state constitutions beyond the bounds of the federal Constitution.[168] For example, the Supreme Court of Alaska has held "that an unexcused failure to electronically record a custodial interrogation conducted in a place of detention violates a suspect's right

---

[167] NACECIA is a different story, however. There is no plausible way to phrase the attorney ban as an exclusionary rule.

[168] See, e.g., Helen Hershkoff, *Positive Rights and State Constitutions: The Limits of Federal Rationality Review*, 112 Harv L Rev 1131 (1999) (positive rights under state constitutions); Robert A. Schapiro, *Identity and Interpretation in State Constitutional Law*, 84 Va L Rev 389 (1998) (examining justifications for independent state constitutional law); James A. Gardner, *The Failed Discourse of State Constitutionalism*, 90 Mich L Rev 761 (1992) (acknowledging the trend but criticizing its legitimacy). The trend was sparked in part by a plea from Justice Brennan, see William J. Brennan, Jr., *State Constitutions and the Protection of Individual Rights*, 90 Harv L Rev 489 (1977), who later applauded state courts' willingness to protect civil liberties to a greater extent than the U.S. Supreme Court. See William J. Brennan, Jr., *The Bill of Rights and the States: The Revival of State Constitutions as Guardians of Individual Rights*, 61 NYU L Rev 535, 550–52 (1986). See also Judith S. Kaye, *Dual Constitutionalism in Practice and Principle*, in 3 *Benjamin N. Cardozo Memorial Lectures* 1401, 1415 (1995). The movement has not been all in one direction, however. For example, the Florida Constitution protects against unreasonable searches and seizures as well as excessive punishments, but both provisions now contain express limitations that prevent the Florida courts from interpreting them more liberally than the U.S. Supreme Court interprets their federal counterparts. See Fla Const Art I, §§ 12, 17. See also Cal Const Art I, § 24 ("This Constitution shall not be construed by the courts to afford greater rights to criminal defendants than those afforded by the Constitution of the United States, nor shall it be construed to afford greater rights to minors in juvenile proceedings on criminal causes than those afforded by the Constitution of the United States."). As a matter of judicial practice, other states follow nearly the same course, see Gardner, 90 Mich L Rev at 788–90 (cited above) (discussing Massachusetts, Virginia, and Louisiana cases). For a defense of this "lockstep" approach, see Earl M. Maltz, *Lockstep Analysis and the Concept of Federalism*, 496 Annals Am Acad Pol & Soc Sci 98, 99 (1988).

to due process, under the Alaska Constitution."[169] The Supreme Court of Minnesota reached the same conclusion in the exercise of its supervisory power.[170] States should be free to extend their protections for civil liberties beyond those mandated by the federal Constitution.

III. THE STATES' INTERPRETIVE ROLE

In Part I we concluded that ACECIA would be constitutional, or at least that some Act of Congress that substitutes one or more procedures for one or more of the *Miranda* warnings must be constitutional. Suppose that a state were to adopt its own version of ACECIA. Would it be valid as well?

A state version of ACECIA plainly would be constitutional. After all, in *Miranda* itself, the Court invited "Congress *and the States*" to develop alternative safeguards. More important than this *ipse dixit*, however, are the premises behind that invitation. In the Court's view, the Constitution requires an adequate safeguard to ensure the right to silence and the right to a continuous opportunity to exercise that right. If ACECIA or some other set of procedures satisfies the constitutional standard, it should make no difference whether those procedures are put in place by Congress or the states.[171]

Perhaps, however, ACECIA's validity rests on a principle of deference to Congress in particular. The Court might conclude that the *Miranda* warnings are more effective than the safeguards set forth in ACECIA, but nonetheless uphold ACECIA out of respect for Congress's superior ability to find facts. On this view, the Court might uphold a federal ACECIA but not a state or local ACECIA.[172]

---

[169] *Stephan v State*, 711 P2d 1156, 1157 (Alaska 1985). This doctrine is not, strictly speaking, a response to the *Miranda* Court's invitation to develop alternative safeguards, because Alaska does not treat videotaping as a substitute for the right to counsel. It treats videotaping as a wholly additional requirement under Alaska law. See id at 1160.

[170] See *State v Scales*, 518 NW 2d 587, 592 (1994).

[171] This same logic suggests that localities—including the major metropolitan police forces most involved in custodial interrogation—also ought to be free to devise their own alternative safeguards.

[172] If the Court first upheld the federal ACECIA, a question would arise as to whether states, in enacting their own ACECIAs, would be permitted to ride piggy-back on that judgment. Compare *Richmond v J. A. Croson*, 488 US 469, 504–06 (1989) (finding Richmond's invocation of Congressional findings with respect to the national market inadequate

We find this distinction unpersuasive. If *Miranda* and *Dickerson* hold that the Constitution guarantees procedures that are no less effective than the *Miranda* warnings, the Court should not approve procedures that, in *its* best constitutional judgment, fail to satisfy that standard. As recent Commerce Clause cases correctly establish, congressional findings can inform the Court's constitutional judgment; they cannot substitute for it.[173] And if Congress can adduce evidence that a federal ACECIA is constitutionally adequate, there is no reason why a state legislature or even a particular police department cannot adduce similar evidence in support of a state or local ACECIA.

More fundamentally, *Miranda*'s invitation was a call for experimentation, and in our system of government, the states and their subdivisions are the quintessential "experimental laboratories."[174] Fifty states and thousands of smaller jurisdictions can attempt a wide variety of approaches without committing the nation as a whole to a single, potentially inadvisable path.[175] That states and localities provide an appropriate *situs* for experimentation seems especially true with respect to custodial interrogation, because the vast majority of law enforcement officials are state rather than federal actors.

Prior to the Warren Court's nearly full incorporation of the criminal procedure provisions of the Bill of Rights against the states, the Constitution was often interpreted to apply a stricter standard to the federal government than to the states.[176] In part

---

to support a local affirmative action program) with id at 546–48 (Marshall dissenting) (arguing that Richmond should have been permitted to rely on Congressional findings).

[173] See *Morrison*, 120 S Ct at 1752 ("[T]he existence of congressional findings is not sufficient, by itself, to sustain the constitutionality of Commerce Clause legislation."); *Lopez*, 514 US at 557 n 2 (quoting *Hodel v Virginia Surface Mining & Reclamation Assn., Inc.*, 452 US 264, at 311 (1981) (Rehnquist concurring in judgment)) ("Simply because Congress may conclude that a particular activity substantially affects interstate commerce does not necessarily make it so.").

[174] See *New State Ice Co. v Liebmann*, 285 US 262, 311 (1932) (Brandeis dissenting) ("It is one of the happy incidents of the federal system that a single courageous state may, if its citizens choose, serve as a laboratory; and try novel social and economic experiments without risk to the rest of the country."). See also Barry Friedman, *Valuing Federalism*, 82 Minn L Rev 317, 397–401 (1997); Larry Kramer, *Understanding Federalism*, 47 Vand L Rev 1485, 1499 (1994) (arguing that capital and taxpayers act as incentives for local governments to experiment); Michael W. McConnell, *Federalism: Evaluating the Founders' Design*, 54 U Chi L Rev 1484, 1498–1500 (1987) (book review) (exploring economic arguments underlying state innovation).

[175] See David L. Shapiro, *Federalism: A Dialogue* 85–88 (1995).

[176] See, e.g., *Wolf v Colorado*, 338 US 25 (1949); *Palko v Connecticut*, 302 US 319 (1937).

this difference was justified on textual grounds: the open-ended Due Process Clause was deemed consistent with a wider variety of procedures than the more detailed guarantees of the Fourth, Fifth, and Sixth Amendments. But the divergence was also based on principles of federalism. Although jot-for-jot incorporation means that states no longer have greater freedom than the federal government to experiment at the core of constitutional guarantees, the principles of federalism that animated the pre–Warren Court approach to criminal procedure retain their vitality. It would stand those principles on their head to say that Congress has a greater power to experiment than the states.[177]

Having conceded the power of states and their subdivisions to enact their own versions of ACECIA, we conclude by recasting observations we have made earlier in other contexts. The Court's revival of federalism in recent years has met skepticism in some quarters. The basis for this skepticism is concern about the states' often appalling use of their constitutional powers to limit individual liberties. Unfortunately, the reaction of state officials to Warren Court initiatives, of which *Miranda* was no exception, easily leads one to wonder if federalism's invitation was simply to license such behavior.

States (and their subdivisions) can and should attempt to operate within the space of shared constitutional interpretation to innovate in ways that meet the twin goals of protecting constitutional liberty and fostering effective governance. These are not always easy goals

----

[177] The conclusion that a state ACECIA would be no less valid than a federal ACECIA may also vindicate our decision to sidestep the debate over the legitimacy of constitutional common law that envelopes so much academic discussion of *Miranda*; for that conclusion illustrates that the term "constitutional common law" is a misnomer when applied to describe the Court's requirement of the *Miranda* warnings. The term "common law" captures the idea of judge-made law that is subject to legislative revision. However, at least since *Erie R. Co. v Tompkins*, 304 US 64 (1938), it has been understood that common law is the law of a particular jurisdiction. If constitutional common law were really common law in this sense, it would clearly be federal common law—in which case it would be revisable by Congress alone, for state legislatures have no power to create federal law. Yet, as we have seen, the *Miranda* warnings should be revisable by the states no less than by Congress. See Dorf and Sabel, 98 Colum L Rev at 454–55 (cited in note 97).

The term constitutional common law is misleading in a second way as well. True common law can be altered at will by the legislature. If, for example, a state high court recognizes a novel cause of action, the state legislature can wholly abolish that cause of action. But of course this is exactly what Congress attempted to do through 18 USC § 3501. The field of maneuver for Congress and the states authorized by *Miranda* and *Dickerson* is tightly circumscribed by the requirement that federal, state, and local law enforcement officials must observe some set of procedures as effective as the *Miranda* warnings.

to reconcile, and it is undeniable that state officials have in the past sometimes exercised excessive zeal in their efforts to eliminate crime. But there are limits under our constitutional system to how we accomplish these ends, and states therefore ought to respect fundamental constitutional concerns as well. That is the basis of sound partnering.

IV. Conclusion

Miranda establishes a *constitutional* right to procedures that are adequate to inform a suspect of his right to remain silent in the face of custodial interrogation and a *constitutional* right to procedures that provide a continuous opportunity to exercise the right to remain silent throughout custodial interrogation. Congress or the states can constitutionally enact substitute procedures for three of the four *Miranda* warnings, and arguably a videotaping requirement that dispenses with the right to counsel and the accompanying warnings qualifies as a satisfactory set of substitute procedures.

Notwithstanding the last decade of decisions narrowing the powers of Congress in favor of the states, Congress could mandate the videotaping of all custodial interrogation through a rule of inadmissibility applicable in state and federal courts. A federal statute barring attorneys from custodial interrogation by state officers might, if combined with the videotaping requirement, fall within the scope of Congress's power to enforce the Fourteenth Amendment, but even if it did, it might nonetheless be invalid as a violation of the anticommandeering rule.

Beyond these considerations of constitutionality lie deeper questions of policy. We do not purport to know whether videotaping or some other procedure would be an improvement over the *Miranda* warnings. Our primary aim has been to set forth the considerations relevant to allocating authority to decide what constitutes an adequate procedural safeguard.

How should Congress use the authority allocated it? In our view, even if Congress has the power to bar attorneys from interrogation by state officers, it should not exercise that power. There is a long tradition of states providing more protection for civil liberties than the federal Constitution requires.[178] Congress should not lightly override that tradition.

A simple videotaping requirement presents a closer question. Like any uniform national approach, it would stifle experimentation. For that reason, we think that in the first instance Congress should impose such a requirement only on federal agents. If substantial experience under such a regime proves successful, it might then appropriately be extended to the states.

This last point has implications for the Court as well. Suppose experience shows that videotaping leads to fewer confessions that cause concern and more admissible ones. We put aside the difficult question of exactly how one measures these effects; let us assume that videotaping satisfies whatever standard of proof the Court might demand.[179] If videotaping is shown to be more effective than the *Miranda* warnings and no more burdensome to the legitimate needs of law enforcement, why should the *Miranda* warnings continue to constitute a safe harbor? In these circumstances, it would be appropriate for the Court to raise the bar and require videotaping or its equivalent as a constitutional minimum. In this way, the Court could show respect for the capacity of political actors to improve upon the Court's own judgment about what satisfies the constitutional standards it has announced.

---

[178] See note 171. The Framers' willingness to rely on state courts to protect individual rights was reflected in the Madisonian compromise. See note 162; *Atlantic Coast Line R.R. Co. v Brotherhood of Locomotive Engineers*, 398 US 281, 285 (1970) ("Many of the Framers of the Constitution felt that separate federal courts were unnecessary and that the state courts could be entrusted to protect both state and federal rights.").

[179] We are also putting aside the question of how a jurisdiction would be able to accumulate sufficient experience to demonstrate the adequacy of a videotaping regime, given that any procedures other than the standard *Miranda* warnings could be subject to an immediate challenge. For a proposed solution to this problem, see Dorf and Sabel, 98 Colum L Rev at 462–65 (cited in note 97).

SAMUEL ESTREICHER AND

MARGARET H. LEMOS

THE SECTION 5 MYSTIQUE,
MORRISON, AND THE FUTURE OF
FEDERAL ANTIDISCRIMINATION LAW

In *United States v Morrison*,[1] the Supreme Court held that Congress lacks the power under both the Commerce Clause and Section 5 of the Fourteenth Amendment to enact a provision of the Violence Against Women Act creating a civil remedy for the victims of gender-motivated violence.[2] *Morrison* is but one of a recent string of cases in which the Court has attempted to delineate judicially enforceable limits on Congress's authority to legislate in furtherance of the substantive guarantees of the Fourteenth Amendment.[3]

Samuel Estreicher is Professor of Law, New York University. Margaret Lemos is a J.D. candidate, New York University School of Law, 2001; Law Clerk to Hon. Kermit Lipez, U.S. Court of Appeals for the First Circuit, 2001–2002.

AUTHORS' NOTE: Thanks are due to Norman Dorsen, Chris Eisgruber, Marci Hamilton, Larry Kramer, and Larry Sager for their comments on an earlier draft of this Article. While we are sure that we have not been able to respond fully to their criticisms, we owe them greatly for their thoughtful suggestions.

[1] 120 S Ct 1740 (2000).

[2] Pub L No 103-322, Tit IV, § 40302, 108 Stat 1941-1042 (1994) (codified at 42 USC § 13981 (Supp IV 1998)).

[3] See *Kimel v Fla. Bd. of Regents*, 120 S Ct 631 (2000) (holding that Congress lacked power under Section 5 to abrogate state sovereign immunity for suits under the Age Discrimination in Employment Act, 29 USC §§ 621–34 (1994 & Supp IV 1998)); *Fla. Prepaid Postsecondary Educ. Expense Bd. v College Savings Bank*, 527 US 621 (2000) (same, for suits under Patent Remedy Act, 35 USC §§ 271(h), 296(a) (1994)), *City of Boerne v Flores*, 521 US 507 (1997) (striking down Religious Freedom Restoration Act, Pub L No 103-141, 107 Stat 1488 (codified at 42 USC § 2000bb (1994)) as beyond the scope of Congress's Section 5 power).
Several commentators have argued that the federal balance is best protected by the politi-

These cases appear at first glance to depart from the spirit, if not the letter, of relevant precedent; indeed, last Term marks the first time since Reconstruction that the Court has held that antidiscrimination laws fall outside of the reach of Congress's Section 5 authority.

The Court's recent Section 5 jurisprudence has met with both confusion and consternation in the legal academy. In particular, several commentators have faulted the Court for what they see as its unduly crabbed understanding of Congress's ability—and authority—to act as a partner to the courts in giving meaning to constitutional guarantees.[4] While we agree with much of what has been written on the subject, we believe that a closer look at the cases leading up to *Morrison* reveals that they are, in the main, justifiable. *Morrison* is troubling precisely because it cannot be squared with the reasoning of these earlier cases. In order to understand what is wrong about *Morrison* and right about the cases that preceded it, a clear understanding of Congress's Section 5 power is called for. Much rides on the Court's willingness to reexamine some of the aspects of its decision in *Morrison*, lest ill-founded concerns regarding the balance of power both between Congress and the courts and between the federal government and the states result in a narrowing of the scope of federal antidiscrimination law, and in the capacity of the national government to address problems of inequality.[5]

---

cal processes, and that the judiciary need not (and should not) play a role in policing its bounds. See, e.g., Jesse Choper, *Judicial Review and National Political Process* (1980); Larry D. Kramer, *Putting the Politics Back into the Political Safeguards of Federalism*, 100 Colum L Rev 215 (2000); Larry Kramer, *Understanding Federalism*, 47 Vand L Rev 1485 (1994); Herbert Wechsler, *The Political Safeguards of Federalism: The Role of the States in the Composition and Selection of the National Government*, 54 Colum L Rev 543 (1954). The current Court, however, seems intent on finding some judicially enforceable limits on Congress's power. Accordingly, as good limits are better than bad ones, we proceed on the assumption that such limits do indeed exist, and attempt to explain where they should lie.

[4] See, e.g., David Cole, *The Value of Seeing Things Differently: Boerne v. Flores and Congressional Enforcement of the Bill of Rights*, 1997 Supreme Court Review 31, 59–71; Douglas Laycock, *Conceptual Gulfs in City of Boerne v. Flores*, 39 Wm & Mary L Rev 743, 763–67 (1998); Michael McConnell, *Institutions and Interpretation: A Critique of City of Boerne v. Flores*, 111 Harv L Rev 153, 169–74, 184–89 (1997); Robert C. Post and Reva B. Siegel, *Equal Protection by Law: Federal Antidiscrimination Legislation after Morrison and Kimel*, 110 Yale L J 441, 509–22 (forthcoming 2000).

[5] The Section 5 question has taken on added importance in recent years due to the Court's apparent willingness to impose nontrivial limits on Congress's authority to regulate commerce, confining the permissible reach of commerce-based enactments to regulation of "economic," as opposed to social, conduct. See *Morrison*, 120 S Ct at 1750–52; *United States v Lopez*, 514 US 549, 567 (1995). Since the Justices' famous 1937 "switch in time

The debate over Congress's enforcement power under Section 5 has been clouded by two fundamental misconceptions of the nature of that power. The first source of confusion stems from the Fourteenth Amendment's peculiar structure, which invests Congress and the courts with complementary authority to see that its substantive provisions are enforced against the states. It is widely understood that the power of the courts to "enforce" the provisions of the Constitution necessarily embraces the power to interpret those provisions. Accordingly, the judicial act of enforcement is inextricably linked to the power of the courts to "say what the law is."[6] Section 5 thus seems to pose a constitutional conundrum. On the one hand, Congress's power to enforce the Fourteenth Amendment could be understood to mirror that of the courts. Congress, on this view, enjoys broad authority independently and authoritatively to interpret the meaning of the constitutional provisions it "enforces." Such definitional authority, however, seems to violate well-settled principles of separation of powers, and indeed to call into question the supremacy of the Constitution, for if Congress can alter constitutional meaning through ordinary legislation, then "[s]hifting legislative majorities could change the Constitution and effectively circumvent the difficult and detailed amendment process contained in Article V."[7]

Separation of powers concerns, therefore, might lead us to give

---

that saved nine," which heralded a willingness to give expansive readings to congressional authority, especially under the Commerce Clause, it commonly had been thought that the reach of federal authority was essentially a "political" question. Congress could be expected, under this view, to intrude on state interests no more than necessary to address national problems, because the very structure of the national government provided ample safeguards for the states. As long as the Court was prepared to view congressional authority in these terms, the precise reach of Congress's Section 5 power was not a matter of great practical urgency. Thus, the civil rights laws enacted in the 1960s—which one would have thought were the natural province of Section 5 power—were sustained by the Court as instances of Congress's power to regulate interstate commerce. See *Katzenbach v McClung*, 379 US 294 (1964); *Heart of Atlanta Motel v United States*, 379 US 241 (1964). Even though these laws were principally about equality rather than commerce, interstate commerce was found implicated, for example, in every workplace having fifteen or more employees. See Civil Rights Act of 1964, Tit VII, 42 USC § 2000e(b) (1994). Section 5 authority was, of course, in the background in these cases, but both Congress and the Court found it unnecessary to reach that issue given the capacious reading the Justices were prepared to accord to Congress's authority to regulate interstate commerce. The Court's recent cases limiting Congress's power under the Commerce Clause suggest that antidiscrimination legislation can no longer rest comfortably on the commerce power, bringing to the fore the reach of its authority under Section 5.

[6] *Marbury v Madison*, 5 US (1 Cranch) 137, 177 (1803).

[7] *City of Boerne v Flores*, 521 US 507, 529 (1997).

a much more limited scope to Congress's Section 5 enforcement power. On this view, the courts' interpretations of the Fourteenth Amendment would mark both the floor and the ceiling of constitutional protections; Congress may neither restrict those protections nor enhance them. Its authority to enforce the provisions of the Fourteenth Amendment would include only the power to codify the courts' constitutional holdings. Congress's contribution to the scheme of constitutional protection would lie in its ability to fashion complex or wide-reaching remedies for those constitutional violations identified by the courts in particular cases.

This narrow understanding of Congress's Section 5 power still seems unsatisfactory, however, because it denies Congress any independent role in determining "whether and what legislation is needed to secure the guarantees of the Fourteenth Amendment."[8] For this reason, the Court consistently has stated that Congress's Section 5 power is not restricted to legislating against those state actions a court would find unconstitutional if asked.[9]

Here we find ourselves at an apparent impasse: Either Congress can interpret the Constitution in the same way courts do, or Congress never can engage in any independent interpretation. The former solution gives Congress too much interpretive authority; the latter too little. But this is a false conflict if we understand that whatever "interpretation" inheres in Section 5 legislation is in no sense a species of constitutional adjudication, and in no sense derogates from judicial supremacy over the meaning of the Constitution. There is a difference between what, for example, the Equal Protection Clause requires of its own force and thus is a matter of self-enforcement by the courts, and what sort of legislation might be "appropriate" to ensure full practical enjoyment of the constitutional values that inhere in the Equal Protection Clause,

---

[8] *Katzenbach v Morgan*, 384 US 641, 651 (1966).

[9] See, e.g., *United States v Morrison*, 120 S Ct 1740, 1755 (2000) (stating that Congress's Section 5 power includes authority to "'prohibit conduct which is not itself unconstitutional'" (quoting *Boerne*, 521 US at 518)); *Kimel v Fla. Bd. of Regents*, 120 S Ct 631, 644 (2000) (noting that Congress's power to enforce Fourteenth Amendment includes authority to remedy and prevent constitutional violations by prohibiting conduct that "is not itself forbidden by the Amendment's text"); *Morgan*, 384 US at 648 ("A construction of § 5 that would require a judicial determination that the enforcement of the state law precluded by Congress would violate the Amendment, as a condition of sustaining the congressional enactment, would depreciate both congressional resourcefulness and congressional responsibility for implementing the Amendment.").

as interpreted by the courts. Once we recognize that statutorily enhancing a constitutional guarantee is not the same thing as changing it, the institutional conflict suggested by the Fourteenth Amendment's grant of concurrent authority to enforce its substantive provisions dissolves from view. It is possible, therefore, to respect separation of powers while according Congress an important role in giving practical meaning to constitutional guarantees.

Section 5 is perplexing, not only because of separation of powers concerns, but also because the potential sweep of congressional authority threatens to upset the federal balance. As a general matter, Section 5 should raise no more federalism concerns than any other of Congress's enumerated powers. Any legislation—whether based on Section 5 or Article I—will result in an expansion of the federal power and a corresponding restriction of that of the states.[10] In one sense, however, Section 5 *is* different. In *Fitzpatrick v Bitzer*,[11] the Court held that Congress may abrogate the states' Eleventh Amendment immunity from suit when it exercises its Section 5 enforcement power. Then, in *Seminole Tribe v Florida*,[12] the Court made clear that Section 5 is the *only* basis for such authority: Congress cannot subject nonconsenting states to suit under the Commerce Clause, for example.[13]

The rationale of *Fitzpatrick* was reasonably straightforward. Given that the Fourteenth Amendment constitutes an explicit expansion of the powers of the federal government and a consequent diminution of state sovereignty,[14] Congress's power to legislate pursuant to Section 5 could not readily be limited by

---

[10] It has been suggested that because the due process guarantee of the Fourteenth Amendment protects all "life, liberty [and] property," US Const, Amend IV, § 1, Congress's Section 5 power, if not properly limited, could overtake the states entirely, rendering them mere instrumentalities of congressional will. But Congress's Section 5 power is not unlimited, for, as we demonstrate below, Congress can act only in areas of heightened constitutional concern, as identified by the Court either in advance of or subsequent to legislation. See Parts I.B, III.B.

[11] 427 US 445 (1976).

[12] 517 US 44 (1996).

[13] Id at 63–73 (holding that Congress lacks power under Article I to subject nonconsenting states to suit in federal court). See also *Alden v Maine*, 527 US 706 (1999) (extending *Seminole Tribe*'s sovereign immunity bar to suits brought against states in their own courts).

[14] See *Fitzpatrick*, 427 US at 456 ("When Congress acts pursuant to Section 5, not only is it exercising legislative authority that is plenary within the terms of the constitutional grant, it is exercising that authority under one section of a constitutional amendment whose other sections by their own terms embody limitations on state authority.").

the principles of sovereign immunity embodied in the Eleventh Amendment.[15] The Court's recent Section 5 cases demonstrate, however, that what the Court giveth, the Court taketh away. Because the Court has vested Congress with more power to restrict state sovereignty—by abrogating sovereign immunity—under Section 5 than under Article I, it now seems prepared to subject Section 5–based legislation to more searching scrutiny in order to protect against congressional overreaching.

The Eleventh Amendment question does raise the practical stakes, and the Court is right to insist that particular legislation represent an appropriate exercise of Section 5 power. But concern over the states' immunity from suit should not drive the Section 5 inquiry. Congress's role in enforcing Fourteenth Amendment guarantees, when appropriately exercised, works "no invasion of state sovereignty"[16] because that sovereignty is limited by the amendment. The central task, therefore, should be to work out appropriate ground rules for Section 5 authority that give full effect to the design of the Framers, rather than hobble the capacity of the national legislature in order to shield the states from suit.

In this article, we argue that Congress's power to legislate pursuant to Section 5 should be analyzed, like legislation enacted under Article I, under the deferential necessary and proper standard. In accordance with that standard, Congress should be accorded substantial deference both in its identification of valid ends of national legislation and in its choice of the means by which to achieve its goals. Section 5, properly understood, raises no more separation of powers concerns than any other grant of power to Congress. Any limits on Congress's Section 5 power, therefore, should stem, not from an artificial distinction between legislation that is "substantive" in effect and that which enforces (but does not purport to change) the constitutional guarantees in question, but from a theory of the appropriate objects of Section 5 legislation.

We argue that Congress acts within its Section 5 power when it seeks to ensure full enjoyment of constitutional rights the Court

---

[15] See id at 454–56. See also *Alden*, 119 S Ct at 2267 ("[I]n adopting the Fourteenth Amendment, the people required the states to surrender a portion of the sovereignty that had been preserved for them by the original Constitution, so Congress may authorize private suits against nonconsenting states pursuant to its § 5 enforcement power.").

[16] *Ex Parte Virginia*, 100 US 339, 346 (1879).

has identified (or is prepared to identify). Thus, Congress is not limited to codifying the Court's constitutional decisions, but can legislate within the areas of constitutional concern the Court has marked out. That is, the Court's interpretations of Section 1 of the Fourteenth Amendment provide the starting point for Section 5–based legislation; Congress can create statutory rights beyond what the Constitution requires of its own force when it finds such extra-constitutional protections to be necessary in order to effectuate the more general constitutional values recognized by the Court.

In Part I.A, we discuss the Court's early explications of the Section 5 power in *Katzenbach v Morgan*[17] and the cases that followed it. *Morgan*, we explain, has spawned a great deal of confusion in that it can be taken to imply that Congress has power under Section 5 to alter the meaning of the constitutional provisions it enforces. The question raised in *Morgan* regarding whether Section 5 accords Congress a definitional role with respect to constitutional meaning was answered definitively in the negative in the Supreme Court's recent decision in *City of Boerne v Flores*.[18] In Part I.B, we discuss the *Boerne* decision, and argue that, while the *Boerne* Court was correct to identify a separation of powers problem with the Religious Freedom Restoration Act,[19] the problem was more limited than the Court suggested. We then turn to the congruence and proportionality test introduced in *Boerne*, and explain how the test was used (until *Morrison*) to identify and assess the ends of Section 5–based legislation, rather than question the means Congress employs in the service of objectives properly within the scope of its Section 5 authority.

In Part II, we address the Court's decision in *Morrison*, which, we argue, was marred by two crucial errors. First, the Court misunderstood the state action limitation in Section 1 of the Fourteenth Amendment; second, the Court misapplied the congruence and proportionality test, transforming it from a tool to divine whether Congress's objectives were constitutionally proper into a limitation on the means Congress permissibly may adopt to achieve otherwise valid legislative ends. Finally, in Part III, we apply our proposed framework to the Americans with Disabilities

---

[17] 384 US 641 (1966).

[18] 521 US 507 (1997).

[19] Pub L No 103-141, 107 Stat 1488 (1993) (codified at 42 USC § 2000bb (1994)).

Act[20] so as to illustrate the role of Section 5 as a basis for federal antidiscrimination legislation to enforce values the Court has identified under Section 1.

I. The Mystique of Section 5

The Fourteenth Amendment is something of a constitutional anomaly. Like the provisions of the Bill of Rights, the first section of the Fourteenth Amendment prohibits certain governmental incursions on individual rights; these prohibitions are self-executing and enforceable by the courts. However, the Fourteenth Amendment does more than guarantee citizens a set of negative rights against the government. Rather, the Fourteenth Amendment—like the Thirteenth and Fifteenth—contains an affirmative grant of power to Congress to enforce its prohibitions.[21] It envisions an important role for the federal government in giving full effect to the rights it guarantees. Given our tendency to think of the Court as the primary protector of individual rights, it is easy to forget that the main purpose of the Reconstruction Amendments was to enlarge the power of Congress.[22] Although the drafters of the amendments were careful to ensure that the judiciary would have the power to compel adherence to the self-enforcing provisions of these amendments,[23] they believed that federal legislation pursuant to the amendments' enforcement provisions was necessary in order to make them "fully effective."[24]

Section 5's grant of power to Congress to "enforce, by appropriate legislation," the Fourteenth Amendment raises deep and puzzling questions regarding the proper role of Congress in interpreting and effectuating constitutional guarantees. Although Congress has broad enforcement power under Article I—power that, unconstrained, could reach countless facets of daily life—the potential sweep of congressional authority under the Fourteenth

---

[20] 42 USC § 12101 et seq (1994 & Supp IV 1998).

[21] US Const, Amend XIV, § 5 ("The Congress shall have the power to enforce, by appropriate legislation, the provisions of this article.").

[22] *Ex Parte Virginia*, 100 US at 345 ("It is the power of Congress which has been enlarged."). See also text accompanying notes 28–29.

[23] See notes 187–95 and accompanying text.

[24] *Ex Parte Virginia*, 100 US at 345.

Amendment is nothing short of breathtaking.[25] Section 5 thus requires us to think seriously about how meaningfully to confine congressional power under Section 5 while remaining faithful to the structure of the amendment, which unquestionably means to enlist the power of the federal government in ensuring that its guarantees of liberty and equality enjoy full practical effect.

A. KATZENBACH V MORGAN'S TWO RATIONALES

What, then, does it mean for Congress to "enforce" the provisions of the Fourteenth Amendment? The Court first addressed this question in *Ex Parte Virginia*,[26] in which it upheld a statute prohibiting state officials from excluding citizens from jury service on account of their race.[27] Emphasizing that the Reconstruction Amendments "were intended to be, what they really are, limitations of the power of the states and enlargements of the power of Congress,"[28] the Court explained that Section 5 vests Congress with expansive authority to give effect to the guarantees of the Fourteenth Amendment:

> Whatever legislation is appropriate, that is, adapted to carry out the objects the amendments have in view, whatever tends to enforce submission to the prohibitions they contain, and to secure to all persons the enjoyment of perfect equality of civil rights and the equal protection of the laws against State denial or invasion, if not prohibited, is brought within the domain of congressional power.[29]

As this language suggests, Congress would seem to enjoy the same broad power under Section 5 as under the Necessary and

---

[25] See, e.g., Cole at 54–55 (cited in note 4) (noting that, because most provisions of Bill of Rights have been incorporated into Fourteenth Amendment's guarantee of due process, Congress's Section 5 authority conceivably could support legislation imposing additional warrant requirements to enforce Fourth Amendment, requiring provision of legal counsel in all interrogatories pursuant to Fifth Amendment, or prohibiting the regulation of obscenity under First Amendment).

[26] 100 US 339 (1879).

[27] Act of March 1, 1875, ch 114, § 4, 18 Stat 336 (codified as amended at 18 USC § 243 (1994)).

[28] *Ex Parte Virginia*, 100 US at 345.

[29] Id at 345–46.

Proper Clause of Article I.[30] Under the standard set forth by Chief Justice Marshall in *McCulloch v Maryland*,[31] Congress traditionally is accorded substantial discretion in choosing the means by which to pursue permissible legislative goals: "Let the end be legitimate, let it be within the scope of the constitution, and all means which are appropriate, which are plainly adapted to that end, which are not prohibited, but consistent with the letter and spirit of the constitution, are constitutional."[32]

The lesson of *McCulloch* is not limited, however, to deference to congressional choice of means. Marshall's famous admonition that "it is a constitution we are expounding"[33] did not, as is commonly assumed, speak to the authority of the judiciary to read meaning into the Constitution's vague pronouncements. Rather, in the context of *McCulloch* (which, after all, upheld the constitutionality of legislation creating the Bank of the United States), those words counseled judicial deference to Congress's rational identification of legitimate legislative ends. The Constitution is painted in broad strokes, Marshall reminds us, and within the rough outline the document itself provides, Congress should be accorded wide discretion in identifying the need for federal legislation and the appropriate means to effectuate constitutional guarantees.

The Court affirmed this reading in *Katzenbach v Morgan*.[34] Explicitly linking congressional authority under Section 5 to the unquestionably plenary grants of Article I, including the Necessary and Proper Clause, the Court made clear that Congress's Section 5 authority is not limited to prohibiting acts identified by the Court as unconstitutional.[35] In other words, the question whether a legislative "end" is "legitimate" under *McCulloch* does not turn

---

[30] See *Katzenbach v Morgan*, 384 US 641, 650 (1966) ("By including § 5 the draftsmen sought to grant to Congress, by a specific provision applicable to the Fourteenth Amendment, the same broad powers expressed in the Necessary and Proper Clause, Art. 1, § 8, cl. 18."). See also Part II.B (explaining that the history of Fourteenth Amendment supports this reading).

[31] 17 US (4 Wheat) 316 (1819).

[32] Id at 421.

[33] Id at 407.

[34] 384 US 641 (1966).

[35] See id at 648 (rejecting argument that legislation cannot be sustained as "appropriate" under Section 5 unless it prohibits governmental action that the Fourteenth Amendment, as interpreted by Court, forbids of its own force).

on whether the Court has interpreted the Fourteenth Amendment to require the same result by its own force.

If Congress were limited under Section 5 merely to prohibiting constitutional violations under Section 1 of the Fourteenth Amendment, the Court would have been compelled to invalidate the provision of the Voting Rights Act of 1965 at issue in *Morgan*. Section 4(e) of the Voting Rights Act[36] prevented the states from enforcing a literacy requirement for voting in the case of persons educated in American-flag schools in which the predominant classroom language was other than English; its primary effect was to bar New York from applying an English literacy requirement to New York City residents from Puerto Rico. However, the Court previously had held in *Lassiter v Northampton Election Board*[37] that state literacy qualifications for voting do not, on their face, violate the Fourteenth and Fifteenth Amendments. Accordingly, the Attorney General of New York argued that Congress could not prohibit under the fifth section of the Fourteenth Amendment state action the Court was unwilling to proscribe under the first.[38] The Court rejected this narrow view of Section 5 authority: "Correctly viewed, section 5 is a positive grant of legislative power authorizing Congress to exercise its discretion in determining whether and what legislation is needed to secure the guarantees of the Fourteenth Amendment."[39] The proper inquiry, therefore, was whether the Court could "perceive a basis" for the congressional determination that an occasion justifying national legislation was present.[40]

In his opinion for the Court, Justice Brennan offered two distinct rationales for holding section 4(e) to be "appropriate legislation" to "enforce" the Fourteenth Amendment, notwithstanding the facial validity of state literacy barriers. Under the first rationale, which might be termed "remedial" or "preventative," Congress is empowered by Section 5 to enact preventative measures reaching conduct that does not expressly violate the Fourteenth

---

[36] Voting Rights Act of 1965, § 4(e), Pub L No 89-110, 79 Stat 439 (codified as amended at 42 USC § 1973b(e) (1994)).

[37] 360 US 45 (1959).

[38] See *Morgan*, 384 US at 648.

[39] Id at 651.

[40] Id at 653. Compare *Katzenbach v McClung*, 379 US 294, 303–04 (1964) ("[W]here we find [that Congress had a] rational basis for finding the chosen regulatory scheme necessary to the protection of commerce, our investigation is at an end.").

Amendment in order to ensure practical enjoyment of the amendment's guarantees as well as to remove obstacles to the states' performance of their obligations under the amendment. Justice Brennan reasoned that Section 4(e) "may be viewed as a measure to secure for the Puerto Rican community residing in New York nondiscriminatory treatment by government—both in the imposition of voting qualifications and the provision or administration of governmental services."[41] Thus, despite the absence in the record of any actual discrimination by New York in the provision of such services, the *Morgan* Court held that Congress appropriately could act in a prophylactic fashion to ensure that Puerto Ricans have the political power that will enable them "better to obtain 'perfect equality of civil rights and the equal protection of the laws.' "[42]

Justice Brennan's remedial justification was supported by the Court's ruling earlier that term in *South Carolina v Katzenbach*[43] upholding, as "appropriate legislation" under the Enforcement Clause of the Fifteenth Amendment,[44] provisions of the Voting Right Act[45] that authorized the suspension of literacy tests and other practices in particular states even though discriminatory application of such requirements had not been demonstrated for all of the covered jurisdictions.[46] The *South Carolina* Court, while noting that Congress could not reach "evils not comprehended by the Fifteenth Amendment,"[47] rejected a narrow and "artificial" reading of the Fifteenth Amendment that would limit Congress's power to generally forbidding violations of the amendment and perhaps crafting additional sanctions for such violations.[48] Instead, it emphasized, as it would again in *Morgan*,[49] that the framers of the Reconstruction Amendments intended that "Congress was to

---

[41] *Morgan*, 384 US at 652.

[42] Id at 653 (quoting *Ex Parte Virginia*, 100 US 339, 346 (1879)).

[43] 383 US 301 (1966).

[44] US Const, Amend XV ("The Congress shall have the power to enforce this article by appropriate legislation.").

[45] 42 USC §§ 1973i, 1973j(a)–(c) (1994).

[46] See *South Carolina*, 383 US at 329–30.

[47] Id at 326.

[48] Id at 327.

[49] *Katzenbach v Morgan*, 384 US 641, 648 & n 7 (1966).

be chiefly responsible for implementing the rights created" by those amendments.[50]

The second, and more controversial, rationale offered by the *Morgan* Court was that Section 5 confers independent authority on Congress to find that a state practice violates the Fourteenth Amendment even if the Court is unwilling to make the same determination.[51] This second rationale suggests that Congress has power under Section 5 to determine the substantive scope of the Fourteenth Amendment, and accordingly typically is referred to as Morgan's "substantive" theory.

It is unclear, however, that the *Morgan* Court meant what its words have been taken to imply. Some commentators point to Justice Brennan's statement that "it is enough that we perceive a basis upon which Congress might predicate a judgment that the application of New York's English literacy requirement . . . constituted an invidious discrimination in violation of the Equal Protection Clause"[52] as evidence that the Court accorded Congress some substantive or definitional[53] authority with respect to the meaning of the Fourteenth Amendment.[54] But since *Morgan* involved what was essentially an alienage classification restricting the exercise of voting, a judicially denominated "fundamental right,"[55] Justice Brennan's second rationale could be read narrowly to acknowledge only that Congress's power under Section 5 allows it to subject a state's justification for such a classification to its own demanding scrutiny.[56] Under this reading, Congress's superior fact-finding re-

---

[50] *South Carolina*, 383 US at 326. As the Court later explained in *City of Rome v United States*, 446 US 156, 173 (1980), the holding in *South Carolina* made clear "that Congress may, under the authority of § 2 of the Fifteenth Amendment, prohibit state action that, though in itself not violative of § 1, perpetuates the effects of past discrimination."

[51] See *Morgan*, 384 US at 656.

[52] Id.

[53] For our view that the terms "substantive" and "definitional" mean different things and should not be confused, see Part I.B.1.

[54] See, e.g., Daniel O. Conkle, *The Religious Freedom Restoration Act: The Constitutional Significance of an Unconstitutional Statute*, 56 Mont L Rev 39, 47–48 (1995); Eugene Gressman and Angela C. Carmella, *The RFRA Revision of the Free Exercise Clause*, 57 Ohio St L J 65, 70 n 17 (1996).

[55] See *Harper v Va. Bd. of Elections*, 383 US 663, 667 (1966) (citing *Reynolds v Sims*, 377 US 533, 561–62 (1961); *Yick Wo v Hopkins*, 118 US 356, 370 (1886)).

[56] See *City of Boerne v Flores*, 521 US 507, 528 (1997) (suggesting that *Morgan*'s second rationale turned on whether Court could "perceive[] a factual basis on which Congress

sources would enable it to override a state justification that the Court, necessarily engaging in a more limited inquiry because of institutional constraints, might sustain.

Nor does a definitional role for Congress necessarily follow from Justice Brennan's famous "ratchet" limitation on Section 5–based legislation. In his *Morgan* dissent, Justice Harlan accused the majority of clothing Congress with "the power to define the substantive scope of the [Fourteenth] Amendment," and thus "to exercise its Section 5 'discretion' by enacting statutes so as in effect to dilute the equal protection and due process decisions of this Court."[57] Rather than deny that the majority opinion recognized any definitional authority in Congress, Justice Brennan responded only to Justice Harlan's suggestion that Congress could, pursuant to its Section 5 powers, restrict constitutional protections established by the Court:[58] "We emphasize that Congress' power under § 5 is limited to adopting measures to enforce the guarantees of the Amendment; § 5 grants Congress no power to restrict, abrogate, or dilute these guarantees."[59]

Some have understood this language to support a broad definitional role for Congress under the auspices of Section 5.[60] Yet, again, it is not clear that this is the best reading of *Morgan*. It does not follow from the fact that Congress cannot dilute constitutional protections that it is free to enlarge them. Moreover, the fact that Congress has discretion to reach conduct that the Fourteenth Amendment does not prohibit of its own force does not mean that Congress has any authority to define the meaning of the Fourteenth Amendment. Rather, it simply means that, within the constitutional framework set forth by the Court, Congress is entitled to substantial deference; it may enact appropriate legislation re-

---

could have concluded that New York's literacy requirement 'constituted an invidious discrimination in violation of the Equal Protection Clause'" (quoting *Morgan*, 384 US at 656)).

[57] *Morgan*, 384 US at 668 (Harlan dissenting).

[58] See id at 651 n 10 ("[Section] 5 does not grant Congress power to exercise discretion in the other direction and to enact 'statutes so as in effect to dilute equal protection and due process decisions of this Court.'").

[59] Id.

[60] See, e.g., Thomas W. Beimers, *Searching for the Structural Vision of City of Boerne v. Flores: Vertical and Horizontal Tensions in the New Constitutional Architecture*, 26 Hastings Const L Q 789, 797 (1999); Stephen L. Carter, *The Morgan "Power" and the Forced Reconsideration of Constitutional Decisions*, 53 U Chi L Rev 819, 830 (1986); Brief for Petitioner at 38, *City of Boerne v Flores*, 521 US 507 (1997) (No 95-2074).

sponsive to due process and equal protection concerns that the
Court itself has identified.[61] Indeed, nothing in *Morgan* grants to
Congress anything more than another fairly generous basis of legislative authority, analogous in breadth to the Commerce Clause
and other powers enumerated in Article I. What *Morgan*, and
South Carolina before it, accomplished was to bring Section 5–
based legislation within the *McCulloch* tradition of deferential review of congressional authority to legislate as against the reserved
powers of the states.

Four years after *Morgan*, the Court had occasion to reevaluate
the scope of congressional power under Section 5. In *Oregon v
Mitchell*,[62] the Court reviewed the 1970 amendments to the Voting
Rights Act, which lowered to eighteen years the age barrier for
voting in state and federal elections.[63] The case provided an ideal
test for Congress's supposed definitional authority. Because the
Court already had recognized voting as a fundamental constitutional right,[64] a definitional theory would argue that Congress
could interpret the Constitution to prohibit an arbitrary judgment
that maturity in voting does not occur until twenty-one years of
age. In *Mitchell*, however, a sharply divided Court ruled against
the assertion of Section 5 authority for state elections. Four Justices squarely rejected the notion that Congress has any authority
to define the substantive requirements of the Constitution, while
Justice Black cast the deciding vote on non–Fourteenth Amendment grounds.[65] Only Justice Brennan, writing also for Justices

---

[61] Once we understand that Congress has no power under Section 5 (or any other provision of the Constitution, for that matter) to define the meaning of the Constitution, Justice
Brennan's ratchet footnote makes sense: Legislation that purported to restrict constitutional
rights would, in fact, authorize constitutional violations and so would be invalid on that
ground. An example of such legislation is the proposed Human Life Bill, S 158, 97th Cong,
1st Sess, 127 Cong Rec S8429 (daily ed July 24, 1981), introduced in Congress in 1981 as
a response to the Court's ruling in *Roe v Wade*, 410 US 113 (1973). The bill would have
prohibited federal courts from invalidating or restraining the operation of state laws prohibiting abortions—laws the Court had held violate the Constitution. The problem with the
Human Life Bill was not that it would have redefined the meaning of the Constitution
(for there is no reason to think a statute could do so), but that it explicitly authorized
unconstitutional state action and shielded such action from judicial review. See Samuel
Estreicher, *Congressional Power and Constitutional Rights: Reflections on Proposed "Human Life"
Legislation*, 68 Va L Rev 333 (1982).

[62] 400 US 112 (1970).

[63] Voting Rights Act Amendments of 1970, Pub L No 91-285, 84 Stat 314.

[64] See, e.g., *Kramer v Union Free Sch. Dist.*, 395 US 621 (1969). See also note 55.

[65] See *Mitchell*, 400 US at 117, 119–30 (opinion of Justice Black) (reasoning that Congress
had power to regulate federal elections under Article I, Section 4 and the Necessary and

Marshall and White, would have sustained the eighteen-year-old vote for all elections under the second rationale of *Morgan*, arguing that Section 5 empowers Congress to "determine whether the factual basis necessary to support a state legislative discrimination actually exists."[66] Although, as in *Morgan*, Justice Brennan and those in agreement with him endorsed broad language that arguably recognized Congress's definitional authority under Section 5, the emphasis of Justice Brennan's opinion in *Mitchell* was on Congress's superior fact-finding competence, which enables it to subject state restrictions on the fundamental right to vote to its own heightened scrutiny.

Morgan's first rationale—recognizing congressional power to act prophylactically "to secure" Fourteenth Amendment guarantees—appears to have survived *Mitchell* intact, and was reaffirmed in *City of Rome v United States*.[67] After *Mitchell*, however, the continued vitality of the second branch of the *Morgan* opinion, to the extent that it acknowledged congressional authority to define the reach of the amendment, was far from clear. Although *Mitchell*'s fractured holding cannot be said to have dealt a decisive death blow to the definitional theory, none of the Justices seemed prepared to sign on to the broadest possible reading of *Morgan*. The rationale's disuse in subsequent opinions, moreover, is unmistakable.[68] Nevertheless, the question whether Congress has authority under Section 5 independently to determine the meaning of the Fourteenth Amendment was not decided conclusively until the Supreme Court's 1997 decision in *City of Boerne v Flores*.[69]

Proper Clause, but that the power to determine qualifications for state elections was expressly delegated to states under Article I, Section 2).

[66] Id at 248 (Brennan, White, and Marshall concurring in part and dissenting in part).

[67] 446 US 156 (1980). Although recognizing that the Fifteenth Amendment prohibits only purposeful discrimination, the Court in *City of Rome* upheld the Voting Rights Act's ban on electoral changes that are discriminatory in effect only, see id at 167, reasoning that "Congress could rationally have concluded that, because electoral changes by jurisdictions with a demonstrable history of intentional racial discrimination in voting create the risk of purposeful discrimination, it was proper to prohibit changes that have a discriminatory impact." Id at 177.

[68] For example, the Court in *City of Rome* relied solely on *Morgan*'s remedial theory, although the case could easily have been decided on grounds of Congress's definitional authority. For a discussion of the Court's treatment of *Morgan*'s "substantive" theory, see Estreicher at 436–38 & nn 338, 340–42 (cited in note 61).

[69] 521 US 507 (1997).

B. CITY OF BOERNE V FLORES'S REJECTION OF THE
   DEFINITIONAL THEORY

In *Department of Human Resources v Smith*,[70] the Supreme Court
rejected the claim that the Free Exercise Clause requires that neutral, nondiscriminatory, generally applicable laws be subjected to
strict scrutiny whenever they impose a burden on religious activities. The *Smith* Court reasoned that the compelling state interest
test set forth in *Sherbert v Verner*[71] was unworkable in the context
of religious exemptions; however, the decision rested more fundamentally on the Court's view that it would be a "constitutional
anomaly" to use the compelling state interest test to secure for
religious believers "a private right to ignore generally applicable
laws."[72] Congress emphatically disagreed. With the Religious
Freedom Restoration Act (RFRA or Act),[73] Congress sought to restore the compelling state interest test as the operative standard for
neutral, generally applicable laws that burden religiously motivated
conduct.

RFRA, from its statement of purpose to its substantive components, had an undeniably constitutional tenor. The Act began by
stating that "[t]he framers of the Constitution, recognizing free
exercise of religion as an unalienable right, secured its protection
in the First Amendment to the Constitution."[74] Its substantive test
likewise was framed in patently constitutional terms. Faced with a
claimant whose religiously motivated conduct had been burdened
by a law of general applicability, a court applying RFRA would
ask, as it had under the Court's pre-*Smith* First Amendment jurisprudence, whether the claimant's "exercise of religion" had been
"substantially burdened," and, if so, would apply the "compelling
state interest" test.[75] For the purposes of the Act, the term "exercise of religion" was defined as "the exercise of religion under the

---

[70] 494 US 872 (1990).

[71] 374 US 398 (1963).

[72] *Smith*, 494 US at 886.

[73] Religious Freedom Restoration Act of 1993, Pub L No 103-141, 107 Stat 1488 (codified
at 42 USC § 2000bb (1994)).

[74] Id § 2000bb(a)(1).

[75] Id § 2000bb-1(a) to (b).

First Amendment to the Constitution."[76] Moreover, RFRA's express purpose was to "restore" the compelling state interest test rejected in *Smith* and "guarantee its application in all cases where free exercise of religion is substantially burdened."[77] Thus, in *Boerne*, the Court was confronted directly with the question whether Section 5 grants Congress the power to define the meaning of the Constitution. Not surprisingly, the Court's answer was an emphatic—and unanimous—no.[78]

The Court began with the obvious. After reaffirming its prior holdings according Congress broad discretion under Section 5 to remedy or prevent constitutional violations—"even if in the process it prohibits conduct which is not itself unconstitutional and intrudes into 'legislative spheres of autonomy previously reserved to the States' "[79]—the Court reiterated that, " '[a]s broad as the congressional enforcement power is, it is not unlimited.' "[80] It then squarely rejected the notion that Congress's authority to enforce Section 5 embraces the power to define the meaning of the Constitution:

> The design of the Amendment and the text of § 5 are inconsistent with the suggestion that Congress has the power to decree the substance of the Fourteenth Amendment's restrictions on the States. Legislation which alters the meaning of the Free Exercise Clause cannot be said to be enforcing the Clause. Congress does not enforce a right by changing what the right is.[81]

All this seems clear enough, and, indeed, fairly uncontroversial. RFRA rather obviously sought to change the operative meaning of the Free Exercise Clause; as Justice Ginsburg noted at oral argument, the question whether the Act *actually* redefined the clause

---

[76] Id § 2000bb-2(4).

[77] Id § 2000bb(b)(1). Indeed, when President Clinton signed it into law, he commented that RFRA "reverses the Supreme Court's decision [in] Employment Division against Smith." Remarks on Signing the Religious Freedom Restoration Act of 1993, II Pub Papers 2000 (Nov 16, 1993).

[78] *City of Boerne v Flores*, 521 US 507, 519 (1997). Justices Breyer and Souter expressed no view on the merits of the question whether RFRA was a valid exercise of Congress's Section 5 power and instead wrote separately to renew their objection to the holding in *Smith*. See id at 565–66 (Souter dissenting); id at 566 (Breyer dissenting).

[79] Id at 518 (quoting *Fitzpatrick v Bitzer*, 427 US 445, 455 (1976)).

[80] Id (quoting *Oregon v Mitchell*, 400 US 112, 128 (1970)).

[81] Id at 519.

was academic where its practical effect was to render *Smith* a dead letter.[82] Thus, the Court easily could have decided *Boerne* on the narrow ground that Congress's power to enforce the Fourteenth Amendment, while broad, does not allow it to compel the courts to adopt a particular construction of the Constitution.

On this view, the true infirmity of RFRA was one of congressional co-optation of judicial authority.[83] The Court long ago made clear that it will reject any attempts by Congress to prescribe a "rule of decision" for future cases. In *United States v Klein*,[84] the Court invalidated legislation providing that proof of a presidential pardon was to be deemed by the courts as conclusive evidence that the recipient had "given . . . aid or comfort" to the confederate forces during the Civil War.[85] The Court earlier had held that presidential pardons had precisely the opposite effect: They effectively erase whatever wrong the pardon's recipient had committed. As Professor Sager has explained, what was so displeasing to the *Klein* Court was that Congress had attempted to conscript the "articulate authority" of the judiciary; "the Justices were being asked to implicate themselves in what they saw as an injustice, and furthermore, to do so in the public light of judicial reason-giving for articulate reasons that went to the heart of the injustice."[86] Thus, Sager identifies as *"Klein's* first principle" the notion that "the judiciary will resist efforts to make it seem to support and regularize that with which it in fact disagrees."[87]

RFRA seems a particularly egregious violation of this principle. The fact that it, like the legislation at issue in *Klein*, created prohibitions grounded in a statute as opposed to the Constitution itself, does little to remove the sting. Sager has us consider the aftermath of *Boerne* had the Court upheld RFRA in full:

> Throughout the federal judiciary, judges in dozens or perhaps hundreds of cases would apply something called the Religious Freedom Restoration Act. They would determine whether the

---

[82] Oral Argument at *39, *Boerne* (No 95-2074) (statement of Justice Ginsburg).

[83] See Lawrence G. Sager, *Klein's First Principle: A Proposed Solution*, 86 Geo L J 2525, 2532 (1998).

[84] 80 US (13 Wall) 128 (1871).

[85] Id at 146–47.

[86] Sager at 2529 (cited in note 83).

[87] Id.

complainants' "exercise of religion" had been "substantially burdened." Then they would determine whether the offending governmental act was "the least restrictive means" of furthering "a compelling state interest." Each of these terms would be analyzed and given operational content, the application of one or more would be contested in each case, lawyers would plead these terms and argue to them, and judges would rule and offer these terms as central to the motivation of their ruling. In high visibility cases, newspapers would report on these terms as they appeared in courthouse step declamations, legal briefs, and judicial opinions.[88]

Such a picture clearly is inconsistent with well-accepted principles of separation of powers. The separation of powers difficulties, however, are both narrow in scope and rare.[89] The problem with RFRA was not that Congress had attempted, by statute, to create rights not required by the Constitution, but that Congress had defined those extra-constitutional rights in constitutional terms. Just as Congress has no power to change the content of the Constitution by ordinary legislation, so it is powerless to change the effective meaning of constitutional provisions by forcing the judiciary to act as its constitutional ventriloquist. Respect for separation of powers means, in this context, that Congress may not require the courts to say that the "exercise of religion under the First Amendment" means one thing when the Court has determined it means another. RFRA therefore violated the principle of *Klein* by enlisting the judiciary in Congress's constitutional misrepresentation. That alone was sufficient to render the Act unconstitutional, for reasons wholly unrelated to its status as Section 5–based legislation.

The *Boerne* Court did not, however, rest its decision on these grounds. Instead, it attempted to distinguish between a "substantive" and "remedial" role for Congress. In what has been aptly described as "the understatement of the Term,"[90] the Court noted that "the line between measures that remedy or prevent unconstitutional actions and measures that make a substantive change in the governing law is not easy to discern."[91] With this statement,

---

[88] Id at 2535.

[89] For discussion of another similarly rare and limited instance where separation of powers concerns are implicated in the context of Section 5–based legislation, see note 61.

[90] Cole at 46 (cited in note 4).

[91] *City of Boerne v Flores*, 521 US 507, 519 (1997).

the Court came face to face with the mystique of Section 5, and understandably left the encounter wholly mystified. It is indeed difficult—if not impossible—to distinguish between measures that properly can be deemed remedial or preventative and those that are appropriately viewed as substantive. *All* legislation, even that which is obviously remedial, works "a substantive change in the governing law." As a practical matter, there often is little difference between creating a new right and remedying or preventing the violation of an existing right. From the perspective of the rightholder, both types of legislation are "substantive" in that they enable her to assert a claim or obtain relief where previously she could not.[92]

If Congress has remedial authority to act in a prophylactic manner to prevent violations from occurring, as the Court repeatedly has held,[93] it necessarily exercises a substantive authority. But if we recognize that remedial or preventative legislation can and often does have substantive effects, must we conclude that Congress can, through ordinary legislation, define the meaning of the constitutional provisions it "enforces"?

1. *Demystifying Section 5: Separation of powers and federalism.* Much of the mystique of Section 5 lies in the notion that when Congress enacts legislation that might be termed "substantive"— for example, legislation that imposes statutory requirements above and beyond that which the Constitution requires on its own—it has somehow changed the meaning of the Constitution. This notion finds its roots in *Morgan*'s second rationale, which hinted at such a definitional role for Congress. However, a much more satis-

---

[92] This assumes, of course, that there may be a gap between right and remedy. The Court's distinction between substantive and remedial legislation might make sense if we imagined that the only rights individuals have under the Constitution are those they can vindicate in court; that the constitutional guarantee of equality, for example, is coterminous with the Court's enforcement of the Equal Protection Clause. On this view, Congress may remedy or prevent constitutional violations only to the extent that a court could do the same in, say, a nationwide class action. However, the Court consistently has rejected such a narrow view of Congress's Section 5 power. See note 35 and accompanying text. See also *United States v Morrison*, 120 S Ct 1740, 1755 (2000); *Kimel*, 120 S Ct at 644; *Boerne*, 521 US at 518–20.

[93] See *Boerne*, 521 US at 526 (noting that, "[a]fter *South Carolina v. Katzenbach*, the Court continued to acknowledge the necessity of using strong remedial and preventative measures to respond to the widespread and persisting deprivation of constitutional rights resulting from this country's history of racial discrimination" (citing *City of Rome v United States*, 446 US 156 (1980); *Oregon v Mitchell*, 400 US 112 (1970); *Katzenbach v Morgan*, 384 US 641 (1966))).

fying (and significantly less puzzling) interpretation of the Section 5 authority recognized in *Morgan* is that, rather than granting authority over the interpretation of the Constitution itself, Section 5 is simply a source of legislative authority to create statutory rights enhancing the constitutional values identified by the Court. Although these values, or areas of constitutional concern, are found in the Court's decisions, Congress's legislative authority is not tied to the particular resolutions struck by the Court. In effect, the Constitution—and the Court's authoritative interpretations of it—supplies an appropriate source of norms upon which legislation may rest.[94] The distinction is between what, for example, the Equal Protection Clause requires of its own force, and thus is a matter of self-enforcement through the courts, and what Congress may require in enacting appropriate legislation pursuant to that clause.

We will go a long way toward demystifying the question of congressional authority under Section 5 once we recognize that "substantive" and "definitional" are not synonymous. That Congress, under its authority to enforce the provisions of the Fourteenth Amendment, may reach conduct that the Constitution does not prohibit by its own force, does not, by itself, implicate the separation of powers concerns raised by RFRA and discussed above. The problem with RFRA was that it purported to change—effectively, if not literally—the meaning of the First Amendment. Rather than effectuate First Amendment values within the constitutional framework set forth by the Court, RFRA sought to change that framework by reviving a constitutional test the Court had rejected and mandating its application in every case involving the exercise of religion. The *Klein* problem raised by RFRA is not only rare, but also quite obvious: it arises only when Congress defines statutory rights using constitutional language and so requires the Court to act as its mouthpiece in explaining and applying terms like "exercise of religion."[95] Thus, if we revisit the Court's attempt to de-

---

[94] Compare Henry P. Monaghan, *The Supreme Court, 1974 Term—Foreword: Constitutional Common Law*, 89 Harv L Rev 1 (1975). Monaghan's theory of constitutional common law—in which the Court refers to the Constitution as a source of law permitting the development of supplementary common law rules—is, in a sense, the judicial version of the theory of legislative power advanced here.

[95] At oral argument in *Boerne*, Justice Souter asked whether the particular separation of powers concern identified by the petitioners was simply a question of congressional candor. See Oral Argument at *5–*6, *Boerne* (No 95-2074) (statement of Justice Souter) (suggesting that argument against RFRA "would be different had Congress simply kept its cards closer to its vest"). The answer should have been yes. The separation of powers problem at issue

lineate the bounds of Congress's Section 5 authority, substituting "definitional" for "substantive," it turns out that the line between preventative or remedial measures that give full effect to constitutional guarantees the Court has identified, and those that profess to (re)define the meaning of those guarantees, is not particularly difficult to discern after all.

But if "substantive" legislation that avoids the definitional problems of RFRA does not raise concerns about Congress usurping the power of the courts, it may raise a different set of concerns. The Court in *Boerne* reaffirmed the principle that Congress is entitled to deference, not only in its choice of legislative means, but also in its identification of appropriate legislative ends.[96] Yet the Court was well aware that, to the extent that Congress is granted discretion independently to identify a need for federal legislation under its Section 5 enforcement power, the sphere of federal power expands and that reserved to the states contracts. Thus, even if we recognize that the Court properly can defer to Congress's rational conclusions regarding the need for federal legislation to address matters of constitutional concern without intruding upon the province of the judiciary, we might still worry about ceding to Congress too much power to determine the bounds of its own authority vis-à-vis that of the states. It is crucial to understand that *this has nothing to do with separation of powers and everything to do with federalism.* Nor is this concern specific to Section 5. In this respect, Section 5 is no more mysterious than any of the provisions in Article I granting Congress authority to act. With regard to the latter provisions, courts consistently[97] defer to Congress's reasoned judgment regarding the appropriateness of federal legislation. It is true that in such circumstances Congress is in a sense independently interpreting the Constitution, but the Court remains the final arbiter of constitutional meaning, as is clear from its recent decisions overturning legislation based on what it saw as an un-

---

in *Boerne* was very simple, limited, and could indeed have been cured by a different choice of language. That is not to say that there were not other problems with RFRA. However, those problems had nothing to do with separation of powers. See Part I.B.2.

[96] *Boerne*, 521 US at 536 ("It is for Congress in the first instance to 'determin[e] whether and what legislation is needed to secure the guarantees of the Fourteenth Amendment,' and its conclusions are entitled to much deference." (quoting *Katzenbach v Morgan*, 384 US 641, 651 (1966))).

[97] Until recently, that is. See note 98.

reasonably broad congressional understanding of the Commerce Clause.[98] Those decisions rested on grounds, not of separation of powers, but of federalism.[99]

2. *Congruence and proportionality: The question of legislative ends.* The Court in *Boerne* proposed the following test to distinguish between acceptably remedial or preventative legislation, and that which is unacceptably "substantive": "There must be a congruence and proportionality between the injury to be prevented or remedied and the means adopted to that end. Lacking such a connection, legislation may become substantive in operation and effect."[100] This test, the Court explained, is designed to ensure that "the object of valid § 5 legislation [is] the carefully delimited remediation or prevention of constitutional violations."[101] It is, in other words, an inquiry into whether Congress's legislative ends are "legitimate."[102] But it is not immediately apparent how an inquiry into congruence and proportionality between legislative means and ends can provide any useful guidance in determining whether Congress has acted within its enumerated powers so as to maintain the proper balance of state-federal power.

The Court long has recognized that the purpose of the Fourteenth Amendment was to "limit[ ] the power of the states and enlarge[ ] . . . the power of Congress."[103] Accordingly, it is both inevitable and entirely appropriate that Section 5–based legislation will increase the power of the federal government in relation to

---

[98] See *United States v Morrison*, 120 S Ct 1740, 1747–54 (2000) (holding that Congress lacked power under the Commerce Clause to enact civil remedy provision of VAWA); *United States v Lopez*, 514 US 549 (1995) (holding that Congress exceeded its commerce power in enacting the Gun Free School Zones Act of 1990, 18 USC § 922(q)(1)(A)).

[99] See, e.g., *Morrison*, 120 S Ct at 1752–53 (expressing concern about potential intrusion of Congress's commerce power into traditional areas of state concern); *Lopez*, 514 US at 556–57 (warning against extending commerce power so as to "'effectively obliterate the distinction between what is national and what is local and create a completely centralized government'" (quoting *NLRB v Jones & Laughlin Steel Corp.*, 301 US 1, 37 (1937))). Compare *Printz v United States*, 521 US 898 (1997) (holding that the Tenth Amendment bars the federal government from commandeering state executive); *New York v United States*, 505 US 144 (1992) (holding that the Tenth Amendment forbids Congress to commandeer state government by forcing states to choose between legislating in accordance with federal scheme or taking title to radioactive waste).

[100] *Boerne*, 521 US at 520.

[101] *Fla. Prepaid Postsecondary Educ. Expense Bd. v College Savings Bank*, 527 US 627, 647 (1999).

[102] *McCulloch v Maryland*, 17 US (4 Wheat) 316, 421 (1819).

[103] *Ex Parte Virginia*, 100 US 339, 345 (1879).

that of the states. The question for the Court in any case concerning the validity of such legislation is whether the legislative end is legitimate, that is, whether the "injury to be prevented or remedied" is one properly understood to reside within the constitutional provision in question. If the legislation is a proper exercise of Congress's Section 5 authority, it will alter the federal balance in favor of the federal government and against the states. But the same will be true if the legislation is not a valid Section 5 enactment. We cannot assess the appropriateness of Section 5–based legislation by looking to whether the legislation intrudes on the provinces of the states, because *any* Section 5–based legislation, whether permissible or impermissible, necessarily will so intrude. Nor can we determine whether Congress has exceeded its power under Section 5 by reference to the magnitude of the intrusion on state affairs. The question whether a burden on the states is valid or invalid turns on whether Congress has the requisite Section 5 authority to impose it; If such authority exists, the imposition is valid even if it is quite significant; conversely, if such authority is lacking, the imposition is invalid no matter how slight.

Thus, in cases in which the legislative end is evident, either on the face of the statute or from the legislative record, the congruence and proportionality test is neither necessary nor sufficient to the determination of whether the end is a legitimate one. The test does have a proper role to play, however, in cases where it is unclear what constitutional concern informs a Section 5 enactment. As the Court has explained, its initial task in any case involving the constitutionality of Section 5–based legislation is to "identify the Fourteenth Amendment 'evil' or 'wrong' that Congress intended to remedy."[104] In some cases, it may be difficult for the Court to identify with any specificity the injury Congress is seeking to redress or prevent, because the legislative record may be devoid of any congressional findings with regard to the injury it has targeted.

It is, of course, preferable that Congress put its superior factfinding capabilities to use. Congress should, whenever possible, compile a detailed legislative record identifying the injury it hopes to remedy or prevent, and the ways in which its chosen means will help achieve its object. But in some situations, the object of Section

---

[104] *Florida Prepaid,* 119 S Ct at 2207.

5–based legislation—the injury to be remedied or prevented—is not well documented in the legislative record. In such circumstances, the congruence and proportionality test can prove useful: The Court is faced with post hoc rationalizations for congressional action, but it is unclear from the statute in question and its legislative history that Congress actually identified a problem of constitutional concern so as to bring the measure within its Section 5 power. The Court, however, wants to give Congress the benefit of the doubt. So it begins with the assumption that the legislative end is a legitimate one, that the injury to be prevented or remedied is within an area of constitutional concern, as identified by the Court. The Court then looks at the means Congress adopted to reach this hypothetical end; it attempts to identify what Congress intended to do by looking at what it did.[105]

The *Boerne* Court's application of the congruence and proportionality test, while unnecessary,[106] was consistent with this reasoning. In its brief and in oral argument before the Court, the United States attempted to characterize RFRA as a remedial measure aimed at rooting out intentional discrimination that might not be captured by the *Smith* test.[107] This characterization is more than a little implausible, but the Court correctly declined to dismiss it out of hand. It first examined RFRA's legislative record to assess whether Congress had reason to believe that legislation was necessary in order to remedy or prevent the sort of invidious discrimination the Constitution forbids. Finding that Congress had not identified any recent instances in which generally applicable laws were in fact passed because of religious bigotry,[108] the Court went on

---

[105] Professors Hamilton and Schoenbrod have defended the congruence and proportionality test on different grounds. See Marci A. Hamilton and David Schoenbrod, *The Reaffirmation of Proportionality Analysis Under Section 5 of the Fourteenth Amendment*, 21 Cardozo L Rev 469 (1999). They argue that the test may be justified by reference to the law of remedies, which requires that any judicially crafted remedy must respond proportionally to the wrong it seeks to redress. Hamilton and Schoenbrod's argument is both thoughtful and thought provoking. In our view, however, it is ultimately unpersuasive, for it fails satisfactorily to explain why Congress's power should be adjudged by the same standards that govern the ability of lower courts to fashion remedies for constitutional or statutory violations.

[106] As discussed above, the Court could have disposed of RFRA on the narrow ground that it violated the principle of *Klein*. See notes 74–83.

[107] Oral Argument at *53–*56, *Boerne* (No 95-2074) (statements of Acting Solicitor General Dellinger); Brief for the United States at 28–35, *Boerne* (No 95-2074). See also Brief for Respondent Flores at 30–34, *Boerne* (No 95-2074).

[108] See *Boerne*, 521 US at 530–31.

to inquire into the operation of the Act to determine whether the
ends it actually accomplished were, in fact, permissible. What it
found was a measure notable for its "sweeping coverage," which
promised to intrude into every level of government, displacing
countless laws of general applicability and unquestionable constitutionality.[109] In short, RFRA failed the congruence and proportionality test, and badly.[110] The costs it imposed on the states were
wholly out of proportion to any constitutional gains it might have
secured.

It is important to note here that the question for the Court was
not whether RFRA would result in exemptions for religiously motivated conduct that were not themselves required by *Smith*. If
RFRA had targeted only a certain category of state laws—say,
prison grooming requirements arguably burdening Muslim obser-
vance—that would have passed muster under *Smith*, the case
would have been a much closer one. The Court then would have
been forced to inquire whether it could "perceive a basis" on
which Congress could have concluded that the targeted group of
laws implicated First Amendment concerns. The congruence and
proportionality test, however, allows the Court to avoid this difficult inquiry in cases like *Boerne*, where there was an immense gap
between what Congress did and what Congress plausibly could
have done under the deferential *McCulloch* standard.

C. KIMEL AND FLORIDA PREPAID: CONGRUENCE
AND PROPORTIONALITY APPLIED

The Court's subsequent decision in *Kimel v Florida Board of Regents*[111] provides another useful example of the operation of the
congruence and proportionality test. The question for the Court
in *Kimel* was whether the Age Discrimination in Employment Act
(ADEA)[112] could be sustained as a valid exercise of Congress's
power under Section 5. Previous cases had established that the
Fourteenth Amendment permits states to discriminate on the basis

---

[109] Id at 532–34.

[110] See id at 532 ("RFRA is so out of proportion to a supposed remedial or preventative
object that it cannot be understood as responsive to, or designed to prevent, unconstitutional behavior.").

[111] 120 S Ct 631 (2000).

[112] 29 USC §§ 621–633a (1994).

of age as long as the age classification at issue is rationally related to a legitimate state interest.[113] Age-based classifications, the Court reasoned, do not raise the same constitutional concerns as classifications based on race or gender, as they often serve as a useful proxy for characteristics relevant to the state's legitimate interests. Moreover, given that old age happens to all of us, such classifications also are less likely to be based on the kind of irrational prejudice the Constitution forbids.

It was therefore no easy task for Congress to justify on Section 5 grounds the ADEA's comprehensive prohibition of all age-based employment decisions by the states.[114] The Court correctly recognized that the ADEA was not doomed simply because it prohibited conduct the Court had permitted (or would in the future permit) in the context of constitutional litigation.[115] Congress legitimately could "prohibit a somewhat broader swath of conduct, including that which is not prohibited by the [Fourteenth] Amendment's text" in the course of giving full effect to the rights guaranteed thereunder.[116] But if differential treatment of the elderly was not, according to the Court's equal protection precedents, an area of heightened constitutional concern, then the ADEA could qualify as "appropriate legislation" under Section 5 only if the Court could perceive a rational basis for a congressional judgment that broad prophylactic measures were necessary in order to protect the elderly from arbitrary and invidious discrimination.

Had Congress found that state employers had engaged in systematic arbitrary age-based discrimination, the Court's inquiry would have been limited to traditional highly deferential assessment of the means Congress employed to achieve the permissible goal of rooting out such discrimination. The problem in *Kimel* was that Congress had not identified any evidence that states generally were discriminating against their employees on the basis of age.[117] This made the Court's task significantly more difficult. Judicial

---

[113] *Kimel*, 120 S Ct at 645–46 (citing *Gregory v Ashcroft*, 501 US 452 (1991); *Vance v Bradley*, 440 US 93 (1979); *Mass. Bd. of Retirement v Murgia*, 427 US 307 (1976) (per curiam)).

[114] See 29 USC § 623(a)(1).

[115] See *Kimel*, 120 S Ct at 645.

[116] Id.

[117] See id at 648–49.

deference typically does not require legislative findings. Deference is owed not because of the state of the legislative record Congress compiles, but out of respect for the principle that Congress is entitled to decide in the first instance whether legislation is needed.[118] At the same time, however, Congress has no authority to act under Section 5 except to effectuate the constitutional values residing in the Fourteenth Amendment. Thus, before the Court can defer to Congress's judgment that Section 5–based legislation is needed to remedy or prevent constitutional harms or to ensure full enjoyment of constitutional rights, it must first satisfy itself that Congress did make—or rationally could have made[119]—such a judgment. When, having utilized its fact-finding capabilities to study the issue in question, Congress does decide that there exists a problem of constitutional proportions, the Court must defer to that judgment as long as it can "perceive a basis" for it.[120] But when, as in *Kimel*, Congress did not in fact legislate on the basis of a reasoned judgment, supported by appropriate findings, that the elderly generally were in need of statutory protections in order to ward off unconstitutional discrimination by state employers, the Court must ask whether Congress, had it studied the problem, could rationally have concluded that such legislation was needed. Rather than engage in an abstract hypothetical inquiry into Congress's subjective intent, in such circumstances the Court looks instead at the measures Congress adopted to determine whether they are plausibly designed to target an area of constitutional concern.

Consistent with this analysis, the Court in *Kimel* invoked the congruence and proportionality test as a means of assessing whether the ADEA could be seen as permissibly remedial or preventative or whether it was impermissibly "substantive"[121]—that

---

[118] *City of Boerne v Flores*, 521 US 507, 531–32 (1997).

[119] Admittedly, record evidence was absent in *Morgan*, but the Court was satisfied that Congress rationally could have made findings adequate to support its suspension of literacy tests for individuals education in U.S.-flag schools.

[120] *Katzenbach v Morgan*, 384 US 641, 656 (1966).

[121] *Kimel*, 120 S Ct at 644. The Court in *Kimel* appears to have repeated the mistake it had made previously in *Boerne* of conflating separation of powers concerns—that is, concerns over a definitional role for Congress—with federalism concerns. To the extent that the Court in either case meant to suggest that legislation that goes too far in overprotecting constitutional rights "effects a *substantive* redefinition" of the rights at issue, id (emphasis added), the Court's terminology should be revisited. The Fourteenth Amendment rights at issue have not changed one iota, and mean precisely the same thing before the ADEA's extension to the states as after it. What has changed, however, is the balance of state-federal power.

is, whether the Act strayed too far beyond the bounds of constitutional concern as identified by the Court.[122] Like RFRA, the ADEA failed the test. Of primary importance to the Court was that the ADEA, even with its "extremely narrow"[123] exception for bona fide occupational qualifications,[124] made a state employer's reliance on age presumptively unlawful. This across-the-board statutory presumption against the use of age-based classifications struck the Court as grossly disproportionate to the requirements of the Constitution. Because the means Congress had adopted to effectuate its legislative goal went so far beyond what the Constitution accomplishes of its own force, the Court refused to presume that the object of the ADEA was to enhance or protect constitutional values under Section 1.

The Court undertook a similar analysis in *Florida Prepaid Postsecondary Education Expense Board v College Savings Bank*,[125] in which it considered whether the Patent Remedy Act[126] could be sustained as an exercise of Congress's power under Section 5. The Court began its analysis by identifying the "evil" or "wrong" that Congress intended to remedy or prevent.[127] That evil, it appeared, was state infringement of patents and the use of state sovereign immunity to deny patent owners compensation for invasion of their patent rights.[128] In enacting the Patent Remedy Act, however, Congress had neglected to adduce any evidence of a pattern of patent infringement by the states, "let alone a pattern of constitutional [due process] violations."[129] Nor did Congress appear to have considered

---

[122] Concededly, the inquiry in *Kimel* did not follow the sequence we recommend. Rather, the Court first applied the congruence and proportionality test and, finding that the ADEA did not satisfy it, proceeded to ask whether the legislative record revealed that Congress had identified a problem the Court might have missed. That the inquiry was somewhat inverted, however, is not significant. What is important to note about *Kimel* is that the Court appeared prepared to defer to a reasoned congressional judgment regarding a legitimate object of Section 5 legislation. Finding that such a judgment had not, in fact, been made, the Court was forced to rely on the congruence and proportionality test to determine whether such a judgment, had it been made, would have supported the ADEA.

[123] *Western Air Lines, Inc. v Criswell*, 472 US 400, 412 (1985) (interpreting ADEA provision recognizing defense based on bona fide occupational qualifications).

[124] 29 USC § 623(f)(1).

[125] 119 S Ct 2199 (1999).

[126] 35 USC §§ 271(h), 296(a) (1994 & Supp IV 1998).

[127] Id at 2207.

[128] See id.

[129] Id.

the availability of state remedies for patent infringement, which, if adequate, would belie any suggestion that states were acting unconstitutionally by using their sovereign immunity to deprive individuals of their patent rights without due process of law.[130]

Because of the lack of findings to support Congress's purported conclusion that federal legislation was needed to remedy or prevent widespread due process violations by the states, the Court turned to the congruence and proportionality test. Congress, the Court maintained, had subjected the states to expansive liability, yet had done nothing to limit the coverage of the Act to cases involving arguable constitutional violations (where the state failed to offer adequate remedies for patent infringement, for example).[131] The Court concluded that the conduct Congress was attempting to remedy or prevent was almost entirely constitutional and thus could not serve as the basis for Section 5–based legislation: "The statute's apparent and more basic aims were to provide a uniform remedy for patent infringement and to place States on the same footing as private parties under that regime."[132] Such aims, while entirely proper, were the province of the Patent Clause of Article I,[133] not Section 5.

As *Kimel* and *Florida Prepaid* illustrate, the congruence and proportionality test can best be understood as implementing a judicial presumption of good lawmaking. The Court will assume, as a general proposition, that there typically is some proportionality between legislative means and ends. Thus, where the Court has no other good way to identify the legislative end in order to determine whether it is "legitimate"—whether federal legislation is needed to enhance or protect constitutional values identified by the Court—it will examine the operation of the legislation to see if it achieves some legitimate end.

Florida Prepaid suggests a second (albeit related) function for the congruence and proportionality test. It is difficult to read the case without being struck by the apparent incongruity of treating the Patent Remedy Act as Section 5–based legislation. As its name suggests, the Patent Remedy Act is first and foremost a patent law

---

[130] See id at 2209.

[131] See id at 2210.

[132] Id at 2211.

[133] US Const, Art I, § 8, cl 3.

and, as such, sensibly should be based on Congress's power under the Patent Clause. In the post–*Seminole Tribe* world, however, Congress could provide a patent infringement remedy against non-consenting states only if the Act could be shoehorned into a Section 5 framework. Thus, in *Florida Prepaid* we see the congruence and proportionality test with a twist: The question remains whether the congressional end is legitimate, but the emphasis now is on whether the end is legitimate for the purposes of Section 5.

The argument for allowing Congress to abrogate state sovereign immunity under Section 5 but not under Article I rests on the notion that it makes little sense to say that the Eleventh Amendment bars Congress from restricting state sovereignty when the Fourteenth Amendment grants Congress the power to enforce the substantive provisions of the Fourteenth Amendment, which "themselves embody significant limitations on state authority."[134] Thus, while Congress's ability to legislate under its Article I powers is inherently limited by the Eleventh Amendment, the reverse is true for Section 5–based legislation: "[T]he Eleventh Amendment, and the principle of state sovereignty which it embodies are necessarily limited by the enforcement provisions of § 5 of the Fourteenth Amendment."[135] If the basic premise of this argument is sound, it follows that Congress is authorized to abrogate state sovereign immunity only when it legislates with a rationally defensible purpose of effectuating one of the Fourteenth Amendment's prohibitions on state action. The Court's application of the congruence and proportionality test in *Florida Prepaid* suggests that the Court is not willing to permit Congress to circumvent this limitation simply by dressing Article I–based legislation in Section 5 garb. Rather, when it appears that Congress did not in fact have a legitimate Section 5 objective in mind when enacting the legislation in question—when it was driven by concerns about commerce rather than concerns about equality, for example—the Court will ask whether the means Congress has chosen are congruent and proportional to the prevention or remediation of an arguably *constitutional* injury as opposed to a merely commercial one. If the answer is no, the Court will reject Congress's attempt to abrogate state sovereign immunity.

---

[134] *Fitzpatrick v Bitzer*, 427 US 445, 456 (1976).

[135] Id.

Even as an inquiry of sorts into the legitimacy of Congress's legislative ends, the congruence and proportionality test should not be cause for great concern. Congress's conclusions regarding " 'whether and what legislation is needed to secure the guarantees of the Fourteenth Amendment . . . are entitled to much deference.' "[136] Deference, however, is premised on the assumption that Congress has in fact identified a problem within the realm of constitutional concern and has devoted its unique lawmaking expertise to crafting an appropriate response to the problem. That assumption will not always hold true. Indeed, the Court's recent Eleventh Amendment jurisprudence creates powerful incentives for Congress to find a Section 5 footing for legislation that was inspired by patently extra–Fourteenth Amendment concerns. Accordingly, the congruence and proportionality test may have an important role to play in ensuring that Section 5–based legislation be rationally grounded in such concerns rather than Article I legislation in disguise. It is equally important, however, that the test retain this limited role.

The congruence and proportionality test thus can play a salutary role in helping the Court monitor the state-federal balance, but only if the test is confined to settings where Congress either does not make clear it is invoking Section 5 authority or where the gap between what the legislation provides and plausible Fourteenth Amendment concerns suggests that the statute is not in fact animated by such concerns. As we shall see below, if the test is allowed to stray from its original purpose of ensuring that the *object* of Section 5 legislation is the prevention or remediation of constitutional violations, to an ill-defined inquiry into the appropriateness of Congress's legislative *means*, the promise of Section 5 as an alternative foundation for national civil rights protection soon will be lost.

II. Revisiting United States v Morrison

In the preceding part we argued that Congress has broad power under Section 5 to effectuate the rights secured by the Fourteenth Amendment. Section 5 is no different from other enforcement powers, such as Congress enjoys under Article I; under

---

[136] *City of Boerne v Flores*, 521 US 507, 536 (1997) (quoting *Katzenbach v Morgan*, 384 US 641, 651 (1966)).

the *McCulloch* standard, Congress is owed substantial deference as to both its identification of ends and its choice of means. But we recognize that this deference—at least as to ends—must have limits. Congress has no power to define for itself the bounds of the constitutional provisions it enforces; this remains the exclusive province of the judiciary. Accordingly, we proposed an additional limit to Congress's power under Section 5: While Congress is not limited simply to codifying those prohibitions the Fourteenth Amendment erects of its own force, it can act only in areas of constitutional concern identified by the Court.

All government classifications are subject to equal protection challenge in court at least for scrutiny as to their "rational basis."[137] A reading of Section 5 authority that gives Congress "authority . . . in the premises"[138] simply because the classification would be subject to rational basis scrutiny by a court would indeed endow Congress with the ability to federalize all law and thus threaten the federal-state balance. The only way to avoid this difficulty while still according the national legislature ample latitude to address national problems in the social arena—other than reviving disingenuous readings of the Commerce Clause to permit Congress to reach such issues—is to limit Section 5 authority to those areas the Court has identified (or is prepared to identify) as implicating the constitutional values that inhere in the Fourteenth Amendment.

With this conception of Section 5 authority in mind, we now address the Court's decision in *Morrison*, holding that the civil enforcement provision of the Violence Against Women Act (VAWA)[139] exceeds Congress's power under Section 5. *Morrison* rests on two fundamental mistakes: first, its reading of the "state action" limitation of the Fourteenth Amendment as it bears on congressional enforcement authority, and second, its application of the congruence and proportionality test to assess the propriety of Congress's choice of legislative means.

---

[137] As we demonstrate below in the context of disability discrimination, see Part III, while the fact that a government classification is subject to "rational basis" scrutiny is not, by itself, a sufficient predicate for Section 5 authority, not all classifications warranting only rational basis review when challenged in the courts fall outside of the purview of appropriate Section 5 legislation.

[138] *The Civil Rights Cases*, 109 US 3, 34 (1883) (Harlan dissenting).

[139] 42 USC § 13981.

A. STATE ACTION

The first, and most obvious, objection to VAWA is that it is addressed to purely private conduct. Because it is well settled that Section 1 of the Fourteenth Amendment "prohibits only state action"[140]—and therefore "does not . . . add anything to the rights which one citizen has under the Constitution against another"[141]— it appears at first blush that Congress has no power under Section 5 of the Amendment to reach private conduct.[142] This could mean one of two things, however. First, it could mean that the *object* of Section 5–based legislation cannot be the remediation or prevention of a purely private wrong. On this reading, the state action limitation contained in Section 1 translates into an ends-based limitation on Congress's power under Section 5. Simply put, private actors cannot, themselves, violate the Fourteenth Amendment. Thus, if Section 5 authorizes Congress to remedy or prevent constitutional violations, and if the Fourteenth Amendment is violated only by state action, then Congress has no power to premise Section 5–based legislation purely on the actions of private individuals. Because private wrongs are "evils not comprehended by the [Fourteenth] Amendment,"[143] targeting such evils is not a legitimate legislative goal.[144]

Second, the state action limitation in Section 1 could be under-

---

[140] *United States v Morrison*, 120 S Ct 1740, 1756 (2000).

[141] *United States v Cruikshank*, 92 US 542, 554–55 (1875); *Shelley v Kraemer*, 334 US 1, 13 (1948) ("[T]he principle has become firmly embedded in our constitutional law that the action inhibited by the first section of the Fourteenth Amendment is only such action as may fairly be said to be that of the States. That amendment erects no shield against merely private conduct, however discriminatory or wrongful.").

[142] See, e.g., Evan H. Caminker, *Private Remedies for Public Wrongs Under Section 5*, 33 Loyola L Rev 1351, 1359 (2000) (recounting common argument that, "because Section 5 merely authorizes Congress to 'enforce' Section 1, and Section 1 merely proscribes state conduct, Congress's Section 5 power is limited to directly proscribing state conduct").

[143] *South Carolina v Katzenbach*, 383 US 301, 326 (1966).

[144] Professor Sager has advocated a similar ends-based reading of the state action requirement of Section 1. See Lawrence G. Sager, *A Letter to the Supreme Court Regarding the Missing Argument in Brzonkala v. Morrison*, 75 NYU L Rev 150, 153–54 (2000). As Professor Sager correctly points out, a means-based understanding of the state action limitation such as that discussed below, see text accompanying note 145, applies the limitation not once, but twice (that is, to both the ends and the means of Section 5–based legislation). We break rank with Professor Sager in that we identify as the constitutional wrong VAWA permissibly could redress current state action denying the victims of gender motivated violence equal treatment in the criminal justice system, while he focuses primarily on historical discrimination against women.

stood to create a corresponding limitation on the *means* Congress permissibly may employ to achieve its legitimate ends. Therefore, because Section 1 prohibits only state action, Congress's power under Section 5 to "enforce" Section 1 is limited to proscribing state action. This reading was adopted by the Fourth Circuit in the *Morrison* litigation, where it reasoned that, "because Section 1 provides only rights against the States . . . Section 5 only grants Congress power to enforce the rights provided in Section 1 through legislation directed against state action, not a power to regulate purely private conduct."[145]

The constitutionality of VAWA turns on which of these competing understandings of the state action limitation is correct. Congress enacted VAWA in the face of evidence of widespread bias in state criminal and civil justice systems against the victims of gender-motivated violence; the purpose of the Act was to remedy the effects of such state bias so as to ensure practical enjoyment of the constitutional guarantee of equal protection of the laws. In order to effectuate this goal, Congress created a private right of action for women victimized by gender-motivated violence. Rather than subject themselves to discriminatory treatment at the hands of state officials, women could sue their attackers in federal court and recover compensatory and punitive damages as well as injunctive and declaratory relief.[146] Thus, if the state action requirement of Section 1 means simply that Section 5–based legislation must have as its object the prevention or remediation of unconstitutional state action, then VAWA easily passes constitutional muster. If, however, the state action limitation applies not only to legislative ends, but also to the means Congress adopts to achieve those ends, then VAWA must fall: Although Congress's goal was to remedy gender-based discriminatory treatment by state officials, VAWA's civil remedy operated directly upon private actors—the perpetrators of gender-motivated violence against women.

The Court in *Morrison* began its analysis by noting the "voluminous congressional record" containing evidence that "many participants in state justice systems are perpetuating an array of erroneous stereotypes and assumptions" that "often result in in-

---

[145] *Brzonkala v Va. Polytechnic Inst. & State Univ.*, 169 F3d 820, 865 (4th Cir 1999), aff'd as *United States v Morrison*, 120 S Ct 1740 (2000).

[146] 42 USC § 13981.

sufficient investigation and prosecution of gender-motivated crime, inappropriate focus on the behavior and credibility of the victims of that crime, and unacceptably lenient punishments for those who are actually convicted of gender-motivated violence."[147] The Court did not dispute Congress's determination that such "state-sponsored gender discrimination" could violate the Equal Protection Clause.[148] Instead, it went on to emphasize that "the language and purpose of the Fourteenth Amendment place certain limitations on the manner in which Congress may attack discriminatory conduct," foremost among which is the "state action" requirement of Section 1.[149]

From the perspective of the first, ends-based reading of the state action limitation discussed above, this is a non sequitur. On this reading, the appropriate question is whether the object of Section 5–based legislation is unconstitutional state action. The Court conceded that VAWA satisfied this requirement: It questioned neither the accuracy of Congress's findings of pervasive bias in state criminal and civil justice systems, nor the validity of Congress's conclusion that discriminatory treatment based on such bias is unconstitutional unless supported by, and substantially related to, an important state interest.[150] But, for the *Morrison* Court, the undisputed fact that Congress's legislative end was a legitimate one did not end the inquiry, for, in its view, the state action requirement also speaks to the *manner* in which Congress may permissibly act.

To support its acceptance of the second, means-based reading of the state action limitation, the Court relied on *United States v Harris*,[151] and the *Civil Rights Cases*,[152] two nineteenth-century decisions striking down antidiscrimination legislation as beyond Congress's Section 5 power.[153] However, it is far from clear that

---

[147] *Morrison*, 120 S Ct at 1755.

[148] Id.

[149] Id at 1755–56.

[150] See id at 1755.

[151] 106 US 629 (1883).

[152] 109 US 3 (1883).

[153] The continued validity of *Harris* and the *Civil Rights Cases* is open to question. Writing for the majority in *Boerne*, Justice Kennedy conceded that the holdings in the *Civil Rights Cases* and other early cases limiting Congress's power under Section 5 "had been superseded or modified." *City of Boerne v Flores*, 521 US 507, 525 (1997). In *Morrison*, the government argued (unsuccessfully) that *Harris* and the *Civil Rights Cases* were effectively overruled by the Court's subsequent decisions in *United States v Guest*, 383 US 745 (1966), and *District*

either of these cases supports the conclusion that Congress may not target private conduct as a means to remedy or prevent unconstitutional state action.

In *Harris*, the Court struck down Section 2 of the Voting Rights Act of 1871,[154] which sought to punish private persons for "conspiring to deprive any one of the equal protection of the laws enacted by the State."[155] The Court concluded that the law exceeded Congress's power under Section 5 because it was "directed exclusively against the action of private persons, without reference to the laws of the State, or their administration by her officers."[156] But the Court emphasized that the primary problem with Section 2 was one of ends, not means:

> When the state has been guilty of no violation of [the Fourteenth Amendment's] provisions, when it has not made or enforced any law abridging the privileges or immunities of citizens of the United States; when no one of its departments has deprived any person of life, liberty, or property without due process of law, or denied to any person within its jurisdiction the equal protection of the laws; when, on the contrary, the laws of the state, as enacted by its legislative, and construed by its judicial, and administered by its executive departments, recognized and protect the rights of all persons, the amendment imposes no duty and confers no power upon congress.[157]

This language is entirely consistent with the ends-based reading of the state action limitation. As explained in Part I, when assessing the validity of Section 5–based legislation, the question for the Court is whether the "injury to be prevented or remedied"[158] is one properly understood as residing within the constitutional provision in question. In other words, a necessary prerequisite for congressional power under Section 5 is the existence of a wrong con-

---

of Columbia v Carter, 409 US 418 (1973). See *Morrison*, 120 S Ct at 1756–58. Commentators likewise have questioned the appropriateness of "extract[ing] an account of the national government's powers from cases decided in 1883 and mechanically apply[ing] it to a federal civil rights statute enacted more than one hundred years later." Post and Siegel at 485 (cited in note 4). Post and Siegel argue persuasively that changes in our understanding of the role of the federal government in effecting civil rights guarantees suggest that *Harris* and the *Civil Rights Cases* are best understood as relics of a bygone era.

[154] Act of April 20, 1861, § 2, 17 Stat 13.

[155] *Harris*, 106 US at 639.

[156] Id at 640.

[157] Id at 639.

[158] *Boerne*, 521 US at 520.

templated by Section 1 of the Fourteenth Amendment. *Harris* makes clear that only wrongs committed by the states or their agents can satisfy this requirement: Because the Fourteenth Amendment does not address purely private wrongs, the "injury" of private discrimination, unsupported by state action, cannot be said to fall within the scope of the amendment, and hence standing alone gives Congress no warrant to act to prevent or remedy such private wrongs.

The Court reiterated this point in the *Civil Rights Cases*, where it struck down the public accommodation provisions of the Civil Rights Act of 1875,[159] which prohibited private discrimination against former slaves in "the enjoyment of the accommodations and privileges of inns, public conveyances, theaters, and other places of public amusement."[160] The Court began by noting that Section 1 "is prohibitory in character, and prohibitory upon the states."[161] Thus, the Court reasoned, the power of Congress to "enforce" the provisions of the Fourteenth Amendment means the power "[t]o adopt appropriate legislation for correcting the effects of such prohibited state law and state acts, and thus to render them effectively null, void, and innocuous."[162] Accordingly, valid Section 5–based legislation "must necessarily be predicated upon such [unconstitutional] state laws or state proceedings, and be directed to the correction of their operation and effect."[163] As in *Harris*, the Court in the *Civil Rights Cases* focused on the legitimacy of Congress's legislative ends, holding that, "until some state law has been passed, or some state action through its officers or agents has been taken, adverse to the rights of citizens sought to be protected by the fourteenth amendment, no legislation of the United States under said amendment, nor any proceeding under such legislation, can be called into activity."[164]

Both cases, therefore, stand for the limited proposition that "civil rights, such as are guaranteed by the constitution against state aggression, cannot be impaired by the wrongful acts of indi-

---

[159] Act of March 1, 1875, 18 Stat 335.

[160] *The Civil Rights Cases*, 109 US 3, 10 (1883).

[161] Id.

[162] Id at 11.

[163] Id at 11–12.

[164] Id at 13.

viduals, unsupported by state authority in the shape of laws, customs, or judicial or executive proceedings."[165] As such, while supporting the ends-based reading of the state action limitation, these decisions provide no basis for the conclusion that Congress lacks the power to legislate against private conduct as a means to remedy or prevent unconstitutional state action. This point did not escape VAWA's supporters, who argued in *Morrison* that *Harris* and the *Civil Rights Cases* could be distinguished on the ground that Congress had ample evidence of gender-based disparate treatment by state authorities, whereas there was no indication in either *Harris* or the *Civil Rights Cases* of such state action.[166]

The Court rejected this argument in a rather remarkable fashion: It reasoned that the legislative history of the Civil Rights Acts of 1871 and 1875 disclosed that the Congresses that enacted those laws were driven by similar concerns about discriminatory enforcement of state laws protecting the newly freed slaves.[167] One can search the opinions in *Harris* and the *Civil Rights Cases* in vain, however, for *any* mention of such discriminatory action on the part of state officials. Not only did the Court in those cases decline to reach the question whether congressional findings of unconstitutional state action could support legislation targeting private conduct, there is no hint in either case that the Court was even aware of the historical evidence cited in *Morrison*.

It is a well settled, if frequently ignored, rule of stare decisis that the Court will not consider itself bound by dicta in previous decisions. Indeed, the Court paid homage to this rule in *Morrison*, rejecting the government's argument that the validity of both *Harris* and the *Civil Rights Cases* had been called into question by dicta in subsequent cases.[168] Nevertheless, in concluding that *Harris* and the *Civil Rights Cases* support a limitation on Congress's power well beyond what their holdings require, the *Morrison* Court relied, not

---

[165] Id at 17.

[166] See *United States v Morrison*, 120 S Ct 1740, 1758 (2000).

[167] See id. The Fourth Circuit likewise engaged in an extensive description of the legislative history of the Civil Rights Acts of 1871 and 1875, concluding that the Reconstruction Congress was trying to "remedy" failures in state enforcement of the rights of African Americans. See *Brzonkala v Va. Polytechnic Inst. & State Univ.*, 169 F3d 820, 871 (4th Cir 1999), aff'd as *United States v Morrison*, 120 S Ct 1740 (2000).

[168] See *Morrison*, 120 S Ct at 1757 ("[I]t would take more than naked dicta . . . to cast any doubt upon the enduring validity of the *Civil Rights Cases* and *Harris*."); note 153.

merely on what the Court said in dicta in those earlier decisions, but on what the Court in 1883 presumably *would have said* had it considered an issue it apparently ignored. We are unaware of any other instance in which a court has gone to such lengths to derive controlling meaning from the presumed, yet unspoken, premises of century-old precedent.

If neither *Harris* nor the *Civil Rights Cases* compels us to adopt the means-based reading of the state action requirement, is there any other reason we should prefer that reading to one that requires only that state action be the object of Section 5–based legislation? One could argue that a state action limitation on the means Congress employs to accomplish its legitimate ends—the prevention or remediation of unconstitutional state action—is implied by the word "enforce" in Section 5.[169] "Enforce," the argument goes, means to "compel obedience to."[170] Section 5–based legislation therefore is not "appropriate" unless it will tend to compel state actors to obey the prohibitions set forth in Section 1. Because legislation that targets only private actors presumably will not lead state actors to conform their conduct to the requirements of the Equal Protection Clause, this understanding of "enforce" suggests that Congress can never reach purely private conduct under Section 5.

There are two obvious problems with this argument. The first is that the Court has never adopted such a cramped reading of Congress's power to "enforce" the provisions of the Fourteenth Amendment. The Court's repeated references to Congress's power to "remedy" *or* "prevent" constitutional violations[171] itself suggests that "enforce" must mean something more than "compel submission to." If one assumes that the Court has not simply been engaging in an exercise in redundancy, it follows that "some measures that redress but do not prevent unconstitutional state action must

---

[169] See, e.g., Brief for Respondent Antonio J. Morrison at 36–37, *Morrison* (Nos 99-5, 99-29).

[170] See id at 36 (quoting *Random House Unabridged Dictionary* 644 (2d ed 1993)).

[171] See, e.g., *Kimel v Fla. Bd. of Regents*, 120 S Ct 631, 644 (2000) (referring to Congress's "authority both to remedy and to deter violations of [constitutional] rights"); *Fla. Prepaid Postsecondary Educ. Expense Bd. v College Savings Bank*, 119 S Ct 2199, 2207 (1999) (holding that Congress must tailor remedial scheme to remedying or preventing unconstitutional conduct); *City of Boerne v Flores*, 521 US 507, 524 (1997) (discussing "remedial and preventative nature of Congress's enforcement power").

'enforce' Section 1 provisions, undermining the claim that prevention is the sine qua non of 'enforcement.'"[172]

Moreover, even in the *Civil Rights Cases*—seldom viewed as the
Court's most expansive moment with regard to the power of the
federal government to effectuate the guarantees of the Reconstruction Amendments—the Court embraced an understanding of
Congress's enforcement power that reached beyond the authority
to force state actors to comply with the prohibitions of the Fourteenth Amendment. The Court reasoned that Section 5's grant of
power to Congress to "enforce" the amendment meant that Congress could enact legislation to "correct[ ] the *effects*" of state actions prohibited by Section 1.[173] As VAWA illustrates, Congress
can act to redress the ill effects of unconstitutional state action
without directly and explicitly compelling state actors to obey the
strictures of the Constitution: The private right of action it creates
allows the victims of gender-motivated bias to obtain legal redress
against their attackers without subjecting themselves to discriminatory state justice systems.

VAWA likewise illustrates the second problem with the argument that Congress can never "compel obedience to" the Fourteenth Amendment by legislating against private conduct. VAWA's
enactment was well publicized,[174] drawing media and public attention not only to the problem of gender-motivated violence against
women, but also to the widespread bias in state criminal and civil
justice systems that gave rise to the need for federal legislation.
Such legislation can help "enforce" gender-neutral administration of
state laws by changing the legal culture to one more receptive to claims
of gender-based violence, much as the Civil Rights Act of 1964
changed the legal culture surrounding the acceptability of race discrimination in employment and public accommodations, even before
Congress applied the law to state and local governments.[175]

---

[172] Caminker at 1360 (cited in note 142).

[173] *The Civil Rights Cases*, 109 US 3, 11 (1883). See also text accompanying note 162.

[174] See, e.g., Michael Kranish, *Crime Bill Is Approved in Senate*, Boston Globe (Aug 24,
1994), at A1; Michael Ross, *House OK's Crime Bill*, LA Times (Aug 22, 1994), at 1; Robert
Shepard, *Female Agenda Takes Long Way to Become Law*, Chi Trib (Sept 25, 1994), at 1;
George F. Will, *Touchy-Feely Crime Bill*, Wash Post (July 14, 1994), at A23.

[175] Though not presented by the situation addressed by VAWA, private violence can also
effectively hamstring the efforts of state governments to meet their obligations under the
Fourteenth Amendment to, say, desegregate schools or other institutions. Even if the state
is not acting in collusion with the private parties, and thus state action cannot be found,
legislation visiting criminal and other sanctions on the perpetrators of such violence would

We have seen that neither precedent nor text compels acceptance of the means-based reading of the state action limitation.
This alone should be enough to suggest that the alternate, ends-
based reading is appropriate, for as a general matter courts will—
and should—refrain from setting limitations, not grounded in the
Constitution, on Congress's ability to perform its constitutionally
designated responsibilities. However, we have additional reason to
prefer the ends-based understanding of the state action limitation.
The Court in recent years has expressed considerable concern
about preserving the balance of federal-state power.[176] Considerations of federalism are furthered by federal legislation that secures
civil rights guarantees for citizens while intruding as little as possible on the sovereign powers of the states. VAWA did just that:
Rather than acting directly on state actors such as prosecutors,
judges, policemen, and caseworkers, Congress devised a way to
help women overcome the effects of state-sponsored bias by suing
their attackers themselves.

Perhaps recognizing the various deficiencies of the means-based
reading of the state action limitation, the *Morrison* Court stopped
short of stating that Congress can never target private conduct as a
means to remedy or prevent unconstitutional state action. Instead,
putting to the side the state action question, the Court turned to
the congruence and proportionality test to determine whether
VAWA's civil remedy was appropriately remedial or preventative
in character.

B. MORRISON'S APPLICATION OF THE CONGRUENCE
   AND PROPORTIONALITY TEST

The *Morrison* Court's application of the congruence and proportionality test is at best puzzling. The Court introduced the test in
Boerne—and applied it in *Kimel*[177] and *Florida Prepaid*[178]—as a way
to assess whether the object of Section 5–based legislation is legitimate. In other words, the congruence and proportionality test
speaks to the question of power in the premises: Is this an issue

---

represent an effort to "enforce" Fourteenth Amendment obligations and values. See Archibald Cox, *The Role of Congress in Constitutional Determinations*, 40 U Cin L Rev 199 (1971).

[176] See note 99.

[177] See notes 111–24 and accompanying text.

[178] See notes 125–33 and accompanying text.

with regard to which Congress is authorized to act? Understood
this way, the congruence and proportionality test is consistent with
the Court's traditional deference to Congress under the *McCulloch*
standard, pursuant to which Congress is afforded substantial discretion both in its identification of legislative ends and in its choice
of the means by which to carry out those ends. Though it is the
prerogative of Congress to decide, in the first instance, whether
national legislation is needed, concern for maintaining the proper
balance between state and federal power suggests that the Court
may properly play a role in policing the bounds of Congress's authority.[179] As we explained above,[180] the congruence and proportionality test allows the Court to engage in this sort of oversight
when it is unclear that Congress independently investigated the
issue in question to determine that an injury of constitutional proportion existed such that federal intrusion into the traditional prerogatives of the states was appropriate. By looking at what Congress has done so as to discern what Congress intended to do, the
test helps the Court assess whether the object of Section 5–based
legislation is "to prevent and remedy constitutional violations."[181]

It is difficult, however, to understand *Morrison* in these terms.
The Court did not dispute that gender-based disparate treatment
by state authorities constitutes the sort of equal protection violation that Congress may properly address under Section 5.[182] Nor
did the Court question the accuracy of Congress's findings—well
detailed in the "voluminous"[183] legislative record—that such disparate treatment was commonplace in state criminal and civil justice
systems. Accordingly, *Morrison* was precisely the sort of case in
which the congruence and proportionality test is unnecessary and
inappropriate. The object of VAWA was clear: The "injury to be
prevented or remedied"[184] was that of being subjected to biased
and discriminatory treatment at the hands of the state authorities
responsible for administering state laws proscribing violence.
Moreover, as the Court itself conceded, that injury fit quite com-

---

[179] But see note 3.

[180] See Part I.C.

[181] *City of Boerne v Flores*, 521 US 507, 535 (1997).

[182] See *United States v Morrison*, 120 S Ct 1740, 1755 (2000).

[183] Id.

[184] *Boerne*, 521 US at 520.

fortably within the recognized zone of equal protection concern. Thus, the initial question for the Court when it is called upon to determine the legitimacy of Section 5–based legislation—what is "the Fourteenth Amendment 'evil' or 'wrong' that Congress intended to remedy[?]"[185]—could be answered quite easily. Congress plainly had identified the evil, and the Court had no need to use the congruence and proportionality test as a way to infer congressional intent on that issue.

The use of the congruence and proportionality test in *Morrison* is puzzling precisely because it diverges so starkly from the Court's earlier explanations and applications of the test. Instead of using the congruence and proportionality test to identify the object of Section 5–based legislation where congressional intent is unclear—an exercise in superfluity, given the clarity (not to mention girth) of VAWA's legislative record—the Court proceeded on the assumption that the goal of VAWA was a legitimate one, and applied the test to evaluate the means Congress had adopted to achieve that goal.[186] Used in this fashion, the congruence and proportionality test is quite problematic.

As an initial matter, it bears mention that the test provides scant guidance for either Congress or lower courts as to the degree of congruence and proportionality required between legislative ends and means. But the indeterminate nature of the congruence and proportionality test is not its most serious failing. More fundamentally, the test is at odds with the long-standing principle that courts are not—and should not be—in the business of second-guessing Congress's reasoned judgment regarding how best to implement its valid legislative goals. That principle is no less applicable to Section 5–based legislation than to legislation enacted pursuant to Congress's Article I powers.

The history of the Fourteenth Amendment has been subject to exhaustive treatment elsewhere,[187] and we will not recount it in

---

[185] *Fla. Prepaid Postsecondary Educ. Expense Bd. v College Savings Bank*, 119 S Ct 2199, 2207 (1999).

[186] See *Morrison*, 120 S Ct at 1758.

[187] See, e.g., Horace E. Flack, *The Adoption of the Fourteenth Amendment* (1908); Joseph B. James, *The Framing of the Fourteenth Amendment* (1956); William E. Nelson, *The Fourteenth Amendment: From Political Principle to Judicial Doctrine* (1988); Jacobus TenBroek, *The Antislavery Origins of the Fourteenth Amendment* (1951); Michael P. Zuckert, *Congressional Power Under the Fourteenth Amendment: The Original Understanding of Section Five*, 3 Const Commentary 103 (1986).

detail here. The crucial point for the purposes of the present discussion is that it was widely understood—at the framing of the amendment, and by the Court in its earliest interpretations of it—that the word "appropriate" in Section 5 was meant to invoke the necessary and proper standard set forth in *McCulloch*, and therefore to apply to Section 5–based legislation the tradition of legislative discretion and judicial deference recognized under that standard. The original draft of the Fourteenth Amendment made this explicit, echoing the text of Article I, Section 8:

> The Congress shall have power to make all laws necessary and proper to secure to the citizens of each state all privileges and immunities of citizens in the several states, and to all persons in the several states equal protection in the rights of life, liberty, and property.[188]

The proposal met with substantial opposition, much of which, as the *Boerne* Court noted, focused on the fact that "[t]he proposed Amendment gave Congress too much legislative power at the expense of the existing constitutional structure."[189] Behind this general complaint, however, lay a wide variety of more specific critiques. For example, some expressed concern that the proposed language would grant Congress uncabined power to enact legislation concerning any matter touching on life, liberty, or property, and so would upset the balance of federalism.[190] Others worried that the equal protection language of the proposed amendment would vest Congress with the power to pass legislation equalizing laws among the states.[191] Still others complained that the proposal relied too heavily on Congress as the sole protector of constitutional rights.[192]

As a result of these critiques, a second version of the amendment was proposed. The new proposal contained several important changes. First, the newly minted Section 1 made the provisions of the amendment self-executing and limited to prohibiting only state

---

[188] Cong Globe, 39th Cong, 1st Sess, 1034 (1866).

[189] *Boerne*, 521 US at 520 (citing legislative record).

[190] See, e.g., Steven A. Engel, *Note: The McCulloch Theory of the Fourteenth Amendment: City of Boerne v. Flores and the Original Understanding of Section 5*, 109 Yale L J 115, 125 (1999).

[191] See id.

[192] See id at 125–26.

action. Second, Section 5 now read: "The Congress shall have the power to enforce, by appropriate legislation, the provisions of this article."[193] As such, it tracked the language of the Enforcement Clause of the Thirteenth Amendment.[194] Accordingly, any suggestion that the change from "necessary and proper" to "appropriate" signaled a constriction of Congress's enforcement power under Section 5 must contend with the settled view that Congress chose the word "appropriate" in the Thirteenth Amendment with the *McCulloch* standard in mind.[195] Moreover, from its first explication of Congress's Section 5 power in *Ex Parte Virginia*, the Court has reasoned that the grant of power to Congress to enact "appropriate legislation" suggested that Congress enjoyed the same broad discretion under Section 5 as under the *McCulloch* standard.[196] The link between the *McCulloch* necessary and proper standard and Section 5 was cemented in *Morgan*, where the Court stated that, "[b]y including § 5 the draftsmen sought to grant Congress, by a specific provision applicable to the Fourteenth Amendment, the same broad powers expressed in the Necessary and Proper Clause."[197]

The *McCulloch* standard requires courts to refrain from substituting their judgment for Congress's as to how to effectuate legislative goals:

> Congress must have a wide discretion as to the choice of means; and the only limitation upon the discretion would seem to be, that the means are appropriate to the end. And this must admit of considerable latitude; for the relation between the action and the end . . . is not always so direct and palpable as to strike the eye of every observer.[198]

Such deference to Congress's choice of means is grounded in the principle of separation of powers. For if the end is legitimate, Con-

---

[193] Cong Globe, 39th Cong, 1st Sess, 2286 (1866).

[194] US Const, Amend XIII, Section 2 ("Congress shall have power to enforce this article by appropriate legislation.").

[195] See, e.g., Akhil Reed Amar, *Intratextualism*, 112 Harv L Rev 747, 823–26 (1999); Engel at 131 & n 76 (cited in note 190). See also *Jones v Alfred Mayer Co.*, 392 US 409, 439 (1968) (recognizing that enforcement clause of Thirteenth Amendment "clothed 'Congress with power to pass all laws necessary and proper for abolishing all badges and incidents of slavery in the United States'" (quoting *The Civil Rights Cases*, 109 US 3, 20 (1883))).

[196] See *Ex Parte Virginia*, 100 US 339, 345–46 (1879). See also text accompanying note 29 (quoting *Ex Parte Virginia*, 100 US at 345–46).

[197] *Katzenbach v Morgan*, 384 US 641, 650 (1966).

[198] Joseph Story, *Commentaries on the Constitution of the United States* 417 (1883).

gress is in a far better institutional position than the judiciary to craft appropriate means to accomplish that objective.

The *Morrison* Court attempted to bring its analysis of VAWA into line with this principle by suggesting that VAWA's private remedy was obviously different from the legislation upheld in previous cases.[199] If this were correct, then the Court's invocation of the congruence and proportionality test would be significantly less startling: It would simply reflect a different nomenclature for traditional deferential rational basis scrutiny of congressional enactments. But VAWA was not, in fact, so easily distinguishable from previous remedial legislation as the Court implied. For example, the Court complained that VAWA's civil remedy "applies uniformly throughout the nation."[200] But so did the prohibition on literacy tests unanimously upheld in *Oregon v Mitchell*.[201] Similarly, though Congress did not gather evidence of discrimination against the victims of gender-motivated crimes in each and every state,[202] the absence of "state-by-state findings" did not trouble the Court in *Mitchell*. Indeed, Justice Stewart made clear in that case that the justification for a nationwide remedy "need not turn on" whether a constitutional violation could be found in every state, as Congress "may paint in a much broader brush than may this

---

[199] See *Morrison*, 120 S Ct at 1758–59.

[200] Id at 1759.

[201] 400 US 112, 131–34 (1970). The *Mitchell* Court upheld the prohibition as an exercise of Congress's power under Section 2 of the Fifteenth Amendment. See id at 132; id at 216 (Harlan concurring in part and dissenting in part); id at 235–36 (Brennan, White, and Marshall concurring in part and dissenting in part); id at 282 (Stewart concurring in part and dissenting in part). The Court has long interpreted Section 5 of the Fourteenth Amendment as coextensive with the parallel enforcement provision of Section 2 of the Fifteenth Amendment. See, e.g., *Katzenbach v Morgan*, 384 US 641, 651 (1966) (noting similarity between Fourteenth and Fifteenth Amendments).

[202] See *Morrison*, 120 S Ct at 1759. It is worth noting, moreover, that, contrary to the Court's assertion that "Congress' findings indicate that the problem of discrimination against the victims of gender-motivated crimes does not exist in all States, or even most states," the legislative record included, among other things, a letter signed by thirty-eight State Attorneys General supporting VAWA on the ground that "the problem of violence against women is a national one, requiring federal attention." Letter from Robert Abrams, Attorney General of New York, et al, to Jack Brooks, Chair, House Judiciary Committee (July 22, 1993), reprinted in *Crimes of Violence Motivated by Gender: Hearing Before Subcomm. on Civil and Constitutional Rights of the House Committee on the Judiciary*, 103d Cong, 34–36 (1993). Moreover, as Justice Breyer noted in dissent, Congress also "had before it the task force reports of at least 21 States documenting constitutional violations. And it made its own findings about pervasive gender-based stereotypes hampering many state legal systems, sometimes unconstitutionally so." *Morrison*, 120 S Ct 1779 (Breyer dissenting).

Court, which must confine itself to the judicial function of deciding individual cases and controversies upon individual records."[203]

There is, however, one way in which VAWA differed from other remedial legislation: its penalties were directed against private individuals who committed crimes motivated by gender bias. The Court seized on this factor, suggesting that although neither the text of the Fourteenth Amendment nor the Court's precedents interpreting Section 5 mandated a means-based reading of the state action limitation, the congruence and proportionality test did. VAWA, the Court explained, "visits no consequence whatsoever on any Virginia public official involved in investigating or prosecuting [plaintiff's] assault."[204] In the Court's view, this alone distinguished VAWA's civil remedy from the Section 5–based legislation upheld in *Morgan* and *South Carolina*, thus exposing the Act's lack of congruence and proportionality.[205]

It is hard to understand this argument as anything other than a flat rejection of Congress's judgment as to how best to effectuate its goals. Recall that the Court had declined to hold that the state action requirement of Section 1 sets limits on the means Congress may permissibly employ to achieve its legislative goals.[206] Instead, it proceeded on the assumption that VAWA was appropriately premised on unconstitutional conduct by state officials. Thus, the Court turned to the congruence and proportionality test on the premise that neither *Harris* nor the *Civil Rights Cases* compelled the conclusion that VAWA was invalid because it failed to satisfy the state action requirement. If we take the Court at its word (as presumably we must), the problem with VAWA's civil remedy was not a state action problem, but rather a lack of sufficiently narrow tailoring between legislative ends and means. It is far from obvious, however, that this is a necessary or even reasonable conclusion. As Justice Breyer noted in dissent:

> [W]hy can Congress not provide a remedy against private actors? Those private actors, of course, did not themselves violate the Constitution. But this Court has held that Congress at least sometimes can enact remedial "[l]egislation . . . [that]

---

[203] *Mitchell*, 400 US at 284 (Stewart concurring in part and dissenting in part).

[204] *Morrison*, 120 S Ct at 1758.

[205] See id.

[206] See id.

prohibits conduct which is not itself unconstitutional." . . . The statutory remedy . . . intrudes little upon either States or private parties. It may lead state actors to improve their own remedial systems, primarily through example. It restricts private actors only by imposing liability for private conduct that is, in the main, already forbidden by state law. Why is the remedy "disproportionate"? And given the relation between remedy and violation—the creation of a federal remedy to substitute for constitutionally inadequate state remedies—where is the lack of "congruence"?[207]

The fact that reasonable minds can disagree over whether the means Congress has chosen to achieve its goal will in fact be successful should itself put an end to the inquiry. If deference means anything—if the "presumption of constitutionality"[208] is not merely a phrase courts invoke out of politeness but ignore in fact—it means that courts must respect the institutional division of labor the Constitution creates. It is Congress's job to make law, to make difficult and complex judgments about when legislation is needed and what form it should take. When the Court agrees that Congress has acted within the bounds of its enumerated powers—that the end is legitimate, and that the means chosen plausibly are directed to achieving that end—the Court should sustain the law, whether grounded on Congress's Section 5 power or Article I.

III. Antidiscrimination Legislation after Morrison: The Americans with Disabilities Act

Morrison is troubling, not just for its rejection of the Violence Against Women Act, but for its implications for other antidiscrimination legislation. Until recently, such legislation has rested comfortably within the aegis of Congress's power under the Commerce Clause. However, the Court's recent decisions holding that Congress may abrogate state sovereign immunity under Section 5, but not under Article I,[209] have created powerful incentives

---

[207] Id at 1779 (Breyer dissenting).

[208] Id at 1748. See also id ("Due respect for the decisions of a coordinate branch of government demands that we invalidate a congressional enactment only upon a plain showing that Congress has exceeded its constitutional bounds.").

[209] See notes 12–13 and accompanying text.

to test the validity of federal antidiscrimination statutes as Section 5–based legislation.[210]

In this Part, we demonstrate how the theoretical framework we have proposed for analyzing Section 5–based legislation can be applied to such antidiscrimination statutes. We use as our model Titles I[211] and II[212] of the Americans with Disabilities Act (ADA).[213]

---

[210] See, e.g., *Holman v Indiana*, 211 F3d 399 (7th Cir 1999) (challenging Title VII); *In re Employment Discrimination Litig.*, 198 F3d 1305 (11th Cir 1999) (challenging Title VII); *Bd. of Trustees of Univ. of Ala. v Garrett*, 193 F3d 1214 (11th Cir 1999), cert granted in part, 120 S Ct 1669 (2000) (challenging ADA); *Fitzwater v First Judicial District of Pa.*, No Civ A 99-3274, 2000 US Dist LEXIS 4931 (ED Pa April 11, 2000) (challenging Title VII); *Sandoval v Hogan*, 197 F3d 484 (11th Cir 1999) (challenging Title VI); *Lesage v Texas*, 158 F3d 213 (5th Cir 1998) (challenging Title VI); *Litman v George Mason Univ.*, 186 F3d 544 (4th Cir 1999) (challenging Title IX), cert denied, 120 S Ct 1220 (2000).

[211] 42 USC §§ 12111–12117 (1994 & Supp IV 1998). Title I of the ADA targets discrimination by employers, including state and local governments. Id §§ 12111(2), (5)(A), (7). It provides that "no covered entity shall discriminate against a qualified individual with a disability because of the disability of such individual in regard to job application procedures, the hiring, advancement, or discharge of employees, employee compensation, job training, and other terms, conditions, and privileges of employment." Id § 12112(a). "Discriminate" is defined to include "limiting, segregating, or classifying a job applicant or employee in a way that adversely affects the opportunities or status of such applicant or employee because of [a] disability," as well as the use of employment criteria that "screen out or tend to screen out" persons with disabilities, unless the criteria are "job related for the position in question and [are] consistent with business necessity." Id §§ 12112(b)(1), (b)(6). Unlawful discrimination also includes the failure to make "reasonable accommodations to the known physical or mental limitations of an otherwise qualified individual with a disability," unless the accommodation "would impose an undue hardship" on the employer. Id § 12112(b)(5)(A). A "qualified individual with a disability" is a person who "can perform the essential functions of the job with or without reasonable accommodation." Id § 12111(8).

[212] Title II of the ADA addresses discrimination by governmental entities in the operation of public services, programs, and activities, including transportation. Id §§ 12131–12165. It prohibits "public entities"—defined to include "any State or local government and its components," id §12131(1)(A)-(B)—from discriminating against or excluding "qualified individual[s]" from participation in or enjoyment of the benefits of its services, programs, or activities "by reason of" their disability. Id §12132. Under Title II, a "qualified individual with a disability" is a person "who, with or without reasonable modifications . . . meets the essential eligibility requirements" for the governmental program or service, including employment. Id § 12131(2); 28 CFR 35.140. Title II normally does not require a public entity to make its existing physical facilities accessible, although alterations of those facilities and any new facilities must be made accessible. See 28 CFR 35.150(a)(1), 35.151. With the exception of new construction and alterations, public entities need not take any steps that would "result in a fundamental alteration in the nature of a service, program, activity or in undue financial and administrative burdens." 28 CFR 35.150(a)(3). See also 28 CFR 35.130(b)(7), 35.164; *Olmstead v L.C.*, 527 US 581, 606 n 16 (1999).

[213] 42 USC § 12101 et seq (1994 & Supp IV 1998). The Supreme Court granted certiorari in *Board of Trustees of the University of Alabama v Garrett*, 193 F3d 1214 (11th Cir 1999), cert granted in part, 120 S Ct 1669 (2000), to determine whether Titles I and II of the ADA are proper exercises of Congress's Section 5 power. Title III of the Act—which is not at issue in *Garrett*—addresses discrimination in public accommodations operated by private entities. See id §§ 12181–12189. We do not consider Title III because it does not

In one sense, a Section 5–based challenge to the ADA is entirely proper. Although the provisions we consider—which prohibit, respectively, disability-based discrimination by employers and by public entities providing public services—clearly bear some relationship to interstate commerce, it is equally clear that the concern driving those who passed the Act was not commerce as such, but equality. Thus, it seems desirable, from the perspective of legislative candor, that such legislation be linked explicitly to Congress's power to give full effect to the constitutional guarantee of equal protection.

In a different sense, however, the inevitable testing of the ADA and statutes like it is cause for great concern. Both Titles I and II of the ADA may be enforced through private suits against governmental entities.[214] Hence the need to determine whether the Act can pass muster as a Section 5 enactment: After *Seminole Tribe*, Congress can abrogate state sovereign immunity only when it acts pursuant to its Section 5 authority.[215] Accordingly, however valid the ADA may be as an exercise of Congress's commerce power, without the Section 5 footing Congress could not grant individuals a federal right of action for damages against nonconsenting states. Thus, the question whether the ADA and like legislation can be sustained as an exercise of Congress's Section 5 power is heavily laden with federalism concerns that threaten to obscure any attempt to discern appropriate and practicable limits on congressional enforcement authority.

The ADA is an appropriate candidate for testing our framework for another reason as well. The ADA imposes obligations on state governments that arguably exceed Fourteenth Amendment requirements. The legislation authorizes both disparate impact challenges that the Court has made clear are not available under the Constitution,[216] and an obligation to reasonably accommodate "qualified individuals with handicaps" that extends the antidis-

---

implicate the state sovereign immunity question and therefore is less likely to be the subject of a Section 5–based challenge.

[214] See 42 USC §§ 12117(a), 12133. Moreover, Congress unequivocally expressed its intent for the ADA to abrogate state sovereign immunity. Id § 12202 ("A State shall not be immune under the eleventh amendment to the Constitution of the United States from an action in Federal or State court of competent jurisdiction for a violation of [the ADA].").

[215] *Seminole Tribe v Florida*, 517 US 44, 55 (1996).

[216] See *Washington v Davis*, 426 US 229 (1976).

crimination principle considerably further than the Court has ever been prepared to do, even in race and sex discrimination cases, under the Equal Protection Clause.

Moreover, unlike *Morrison*, which involved gender discrimination, conduct which the Court has indicated merits a heightened judicial scrutiny, the ADA involves disability discrimination, a category of conduct that the Court has held warrants only rational basis review. In *City of Cleburne v Cleburne Living Center*,[217] the Court found that the zoning ordinance in question, which required a special use permit for a home for the mentally disabled but not, for example, for a boarding house or a hospital, was based on irrational prejudice and so violated the Equal Protection Clause.[218] Yet the Court explicitly rejected the argument that legislative classifications based on mental disability should be subject to anything other than traditional rational basis review.[219] At first blush, therefore, *Kimel*'s invalidation of legislation prohibiting age-based discrimination—which, like discrimination against the disabled, is reviewed under the rational basis standard—would seem to signal a similar fate for the ADA. However, on closer inspection, the differences between the two statutes become clear.

A. CONGRESSIONAL FINDINGS IN SUPPORT OF THE ADA

Like the Violence Against Women Act, the ADA is supported by a voluminous legislative record replete with findings of unconstitutional state action. Congress engaged in extensive fact-finding concerning the problem of discrimination against persons with disabilities, holding thirteen hearings devoted specifically to the consideration of the ADA,[220] and considering several reports and sur-

---

[217] 473 US 432 (1985).

[218] Id at 448–50.

[219] Id at 442–46.

[220] See Americans with Disabilities Act: Hearing on HR 2273 and S 993 Before the Subcommittee on Transportation and Hazardous Materials of the House Committee on Energy and Commerce, 101st Cong, 1st Sess (1990); Americans with Disabilities Act: Hearings on HR 2273 Before the Subcommittee on Surface Transportation of the House Committee on Public Works and Transportation, 101st Cong, 1st Sess (1990); Americans with Disabilities Act: Hearing Before the House Committee on Small Business, 101st Cong, 2d Sess (1990); Americans with Disabilities Act: Telecommunications Relay Services, Hearing on Title V of HR 2273 Before the Subcommittee on Telecommunications and Finance of the House Committee on Energy and Commerce, 101st Cong, 1st Sess (1990); Americans with Disabilities Act of 1989: Hearings on HR 2273 Before the House Committee on the Judiciary and the Subcommittee on Civil and Constitutional Rights, 101st Cong, 1st Sess (1989); Americans with Disabilities Act of 1989: Hearing on HR 2273 Before the Subcommittee

veys.[221] In addition, a congressionally designated Task Force held sixty-three public forums across the country, which were attended by more than 7,000 individuals.[222] The Task Force presented to Congress evidence submitted by nearly 5,000 individuals documenting the problems with discrimination faced daily by persons with disabilities—often at the hands of state and local governments.[223]

Moreover, the Congress that enacted the ADA brought to that legislative process decades of experience studying the scope and nature of discrimination against persons with disabilities and testing incremental legislative steps to combat that discrimination. Prior to enacting the ADA, Congress attempted to combat disability discrimination in a number of discrete areas, including architectural barriers to government buildings and courthouses,[224] education,[225] transportation,[226] voting,[227] and housing.[228] Only after witnessing the failure of more limited measures did Congress con-

---

on Select Education of the House Committee on Education and Labor, 101st Cong, 1st Sess (1989); Hearing on HR 2273, The Americans with Disabilities Act of 1989: Joint Hearing Before the Subcommittee on Employment Opportunities and Select Education of the House Committee on Education and Labor, 101st Cong, 1st Sess (July 18 & Sept 13, 1989) (two hearings); Oversight Hearing on HR 4498, Americans with Disabilities Act of 1988: Hearing Before the House Committee on Select Education of the House Committee on Education and Labor, 100th Cong, 2d Sess (1989); Americans with Disabilities Act of 1989: Hearings on S 933 Before the Senate Committee on Labor and Human Resources and the Subcommittee on the Handicapped, 101st Cong, 1st Sess (1989); Americans with Disabilities Act of 1988: Joint Hearing on S 2345 Before the Subcommittee on the Handicapped of the Senate Committee on Labor and Human Resources and the Subcommittee on Select Education of the House Committee on Education and Labor, 100th Cong, 2d Sess (1989).

[221] See S Rep No 116, 101st Cong, 1st Sess 6 (1989); HR Rep No 485, 101st Cong, 2d Sess Pt 2, at 28 (1990); Task Force on the Rights and Empowerment of Americans with Disabilities, From ADA to Empowerment 16 (1990) ("*Task Force Report*").

[222] See *Task Force Report* at 18 (cited in note 221).

[223] See 2 Staff of the House Committee on Education and Labor, 101st Cong, 2d Sess, Legis Hist of Pub L No 101-336: The Americans with Disabilities Act, 100th Cong, 2d Sess 1040 (Comm Print 1990); *Task Force Report* at 16 (cited in note 221).

[224] See Architectural Barriers Act of 1968, 42 USC 4151 et seq (1994).

[225] See Education of the Handicapped Act, Pub L No 91-230, Tit VI, 84 Stat 175 (re-enacted in 1990 as the Individuals with Disabilities Education Act, 20 USC 1400 et seq (1994)).

[226] See Urban Mass Transportation Act of 1970, 49 USC § 1612 (1994); Air Carrier Access Act of 1986, 49 USC § 41705 (1994).

[227] See Voting Accessibility for the Elderly and Handicapped Act, 423 USC § 1973ee-1 (1994).

[228] See Fair Housing Amendments of 1988, 42 USC § 3604 (1994).

clude that the ADA's "comprehensive national mandate for the elimination of discrimination against individuals with disabilities" was required.[229]

Congress found that, "historically, society has tended to isolate and segregate individuals with disabilities," and that "such forms of discrimination against individuals with disabilities continue to be a serious and pervasive social problem."[230] Specifically, discrimination against persons with disabilities "persists in such critical areas as employment, housing, public accommodations, education, transportation, communication, recreation, institutionalization, health services, voting, and access to public services."[231] Although most—if not all—states had enacted laws prohibiting discrimination against the disabled, such laws were "inadequate to address the pervasive problems of discrimination that people with disabilities are facing."[232] Even in the face of state antidiscrimination legislation, persons with disabilities:

> continually encounter various forms of discrimination, including outright intentional exclusion, the discriminatory effects of architectural, transportation, and communication barriers, overprotective rules and policies, failure to make modifications to the existing facilities and practices, exclusionary qualification standards and criteria, segregation, and relegation to lesser services, programs, activities, benefits, jobs, or other opportunities.[233]

"The continuing existence of unfair and unnecessary discrimination and prejudice," Congress concluded, "denies people with disabilities the opportunities for which our free society is justifiably famous."[234]

In light of these findings, the Court should have no difficulty finding that the ADA was animated by a purpose to address and

---

[229] 42 USC § 12101(b)(1).

[230] Id § 12101(a)(2).

[231] Id § 12101(a)(3).

[232] S Rep No 116 at 18; HR Rep No 485 at 47.

[233] 42 USC § 12101(a)(5). See also id § 12101(a)(7) (finding that people with disabilities have been "faced with restrictions and limitations, subjected to a history of purposeful unequal treatment, and relegated to a position of political powerlessness in our society, based on characteristics that are beyond the control of such individuals and resulting from stereotypical assumptions not truly indicative of the individual ability of such individuals to participate in, and contribute to, society").

[234] Id § 12101(a)(9).

remedy disability discrimination by state governments as employers and places of public accommodation, unless the fact that constitutional claims of disability discrimination merit only rational basis
scrutiny from courts changes the Section 5 analysis.

B. THE QUESTION OF RATIONAL BASIS REVIEW

Much ink has been spilled on the question whether the Court
in *Cleburne* in fact applied the rational basis standard, or whether
it subjected the ordinance at issue to some form of heightened
scrutiny under the guise of traditional rational basis review.[235] For
the purposes of determining Congress's power to remedy and prevent discriminatory treatment of the disabled, however, the answer
to that puzzle is irrelevant. What matters is not the verbal formulation the Court applies when determining whether a given classification violates the Equal Protection Clause, but rather the constitutional norms that inform the various tests.[236]

The great bulk of legislation, both state and federal, classifies

---

[235] See, e.g., Lawrence H. Tribe, *American Constitutional Law* 1612 (2d ed 1988) (describing Court's review in *Cleburne* as "covertly heightened scrutiny"); Philip P. Frickey, *The
Fool on the Hill: Congressional Findings, Constitutional Adjudication, and United States v. Lopez,*
46 Case W L Rev 695, 726 (1996) (suggesting that *Cleburne* applied something "more
stringent than garden-variety" rational basis review); Richard B. Saphire, *Equal Protection,
Rational Basis Review, and the Impact of Cleburne Living Center, Inc.,* 88 Ky L J 591, 598
(1999) ("While *Cleburne* purported to apply rational basis review, both its explication and
application of the rational basis standard proved difficult to square with the sort of judicial
deference that the paradigm clearly requires."); David O. Stewart, *Supreme Court Report:
A Growing Equal Protection Clause?* 17 ABA J 108, 112 (Oct 1995) (describing analysis in
Cleburne as "rational basis with teeth"). As one Justice noted at oral argument in *Garrett:*

> *Cleburne* does—the result seems at odds with the—with just anything goes, which
> had been what rational basis meant. I thought that the *Cleburne* decision was very
> much like *Reed v. Reed* in the gender area. That is, the Court purported to apply
> rational basis, but came to a result that didn't square with any prior rational basis
> decision.

Oral Argument at 52, *Univ. of Ala. v Garrett* (No 99-1240) (statement of unidentified
Justice).

[236] In its brief to the Court in *Garrett*, the United States argued that it is counterintuitive
to limit Congress's Section 5 authority on the ground that the classification in question is
subject to rational basis review by the courts. See Brief for United States at 38, *Garrett*
(No 99-1240). Given that rational basis scrutiny is premised on the principle of judicial
restraint, see *FCC v Beach Communications,* 508 US 307, 315 (1993) (observing that rational
basis review "is a paradigm of judicial restraint"), it does seem odd to suggest that the fact
that a *court* will review a given classification under the rational basis standard should translate into a limitation on what *Congress* can do with regard to that same classification. As
we argue below, however, it does not follow that the fact that a certain classification is
subjected to rational basis scrutiny under Section 1 is wholly unrelated to the question of
the scope of Congress's enforcement authority under Section 5.

individuals in some way.[237] All those classifications conceivably could be challenged on equal protection grounds, and most, if not all, would be reviewed under the highly deferential rational basis standard. This reflects, not only the "presumption of constitutionality" and corresponding principles of judicial restraint,[238] but, more fundamentally, the notion that "the prohibition of the Equal Protection Clause goes no further than . . . invidious discrimination."[239] The Equal Protection Clause simply is not concerned about every type of classification (or about classifications as such), even those that rest on rather dubious rationales.[240] To take the paradigmatic example of a classification subject to rational basis review, Congress surely lacks authority under Section 5 to enact regulations protecting opticians.[241] We reach this conclusion, however, not *because* courts review laws that distinguish between opticians and optometrists under the rational basis standard, but because of the typical reasons advanced for *why* such a classification merit only the most deferential scrutiny.

The applicability of rational basis review generally is related to the likelihood that the state has a legitimate reason for treating otherwise similarly situated individuals or groups differently. From an institutional perspective, it is entirely proper, indeed unavoidable, for courts to proceed on the assumption that the politically accountable branches of government (both state and federal) generally act constitutionally and in good faith.[242] Even if it were possible for a court to determine what *really* motivated legislators

---

[237] See *Romer v Evans*, 517 US 620, 631 (1996) ("The Fourteenth Amendment's promise that no person shall be denied the equal protection of the laws must coexist with the practical necessity that most legislation classifies for one purpose or another, with resulting disadvantage to various groups or persons.").

[238] See note 208.

[239] *Williamson v Lee Optical*, 348 US 483, 489 (1955).

[240] See, e.g., *Romer*, 517 US at 632 ("In the ordinary case, a law will be sustained if it can be said to advance a legitimate government interest, even if the law seems unwise or works tot he disadvantage of a particular group, or if the rationale for it seems tenuous."). See also *New Orleans v Dukes*, 427 US 297 (1976) (holding that tourism benefits justified classification favoring pushcart vendors of certain longevity); *Williamson*, 348 US at 488–89 (rejecting equal protection challenge to regulation, based on assumed health concerns, burdening opticians but not optometrists or ophthalmologists); *Railway Express Agency, Inc. v New York*, 336 US 106 (1949) (holding that potential traffic hazards justified exemption of vehicles advertising owner's products from general advertising bar).

[241] See *Williamson*, 348 US at 489.

[242] See, e.g., *Mueller v Allen*, 463 US 388, 394 (1983) (noting Court's "reluctance to attribute unconstitutional motives" to legislature).

when they passed a certain law containing a classification harming a particular group, it would be inappropriate for the judiciary customarily to second-guess the motivations of a coordinate branch of government. Accordingly, rather than inquire, in each case, whether the classification in question truly is based on rational, legitimate considerations, the Court will assume the truth of any explanations given, and will sustain the legislation if any plausible rational objective can be advanced for it.

The Court departs from this deferential approach when it has reason to be skeptical that legitimate objectives in fact inform the legislation, because it harms "discrete and insular"[243] minority groups whose participation in the political process is hampered by societal prejudice, or because the classification is such that it is likely to reflect irrational prejudice, "negative attitudes," or "vague, undifferentiated fears."[244] Classifications based on race and national origin, for example, are subjected to strict scrutiny not because individuals in the identified groups have different, or greater, rights under the Equal Protection Clause than do others, but because laws targeting those groups are extraordinarily unlikely to admit of any rational justification: Factors such as race or national origin "are so seldom relevant to the achievement of any legitimate state interest that laws grounded in such considerations are *deemed to reflect* prejudice and antipathy—a view that those in the burdened class are not as worthy or deserving as others."[245] The state may, in theory, overcome the presumption that race-based classifications and the like are illegitimately motivated by showing that such classifications are necessary to a compelling state interest, but it is generally understood that the required showing is almost impossible to make.

Other classifications, like those based on gender, call for a heightened, but somewhat less stringent, standard of review. Heightened scrutiny is appropriate because gender "generally provides no sensible ground for differential treatment."[246] However, to the extent that men and women are, in fact, different, there sometimes will be legitimate reasons for treating them differently.

---

[243] *Carolene Prods. v United States*, 304 US 144, 153 n 4 (1938).

[244] *City of Cleburne v Cleburne Living Ctr.*, 473 US 432, 448–49 (1985).

[245] Id at 440 (emphasis added).

[246] Id at 440–41.

Accordingly, while gender-based classifications are viewed with disfavor, we recognize that they do not always "reflect outmoded notions of the relative capabilities of men and women."[247] The state therefore bears a slightly less exacting burden of justification when it differentiates between individuals on the basis of gender: it must show that the gender-based classification is "substantially related" to an "important governmental objective."[248]

Finally, some classifications—such as those based on age—are far more likely than not to reflect legitimate legislative concerns. As a result, the state need show only that such classifications are rationally related to a legitimate governmental interest.[249]

It is important to recognize, however, that although rational basis review tends to reflect a judicial conclusion that the classification in question is unlikely to implicate concerns of constitutional stature, this is not always the case. Indeed, *Cleburne* aptly illustrates the prudential considerations that often drive the Court's application of the rational basis standard. The Court reasoned that disability discrimination should receive rational basis review by the courts, not because persons with disabilities lack the traditional indicia of a suspect class, but because heightened scrutiny would unduly restrict legislative solutions: "How this large and diversified group is to be treated under the law is a difficult and often a technical matter, very much a task for legislators guided by qualified professionals."[250] Thus, the Court's application of rational basis

---

[247] Id at 441.

[248] *Miss. Univ. for Women v Hogan*, 458 US 718, 724 (1982); *Wengler v Druggists Mut. Ins. Co.*, 446 US 142, 150 (1980); *Craig v Boren*, 429 US 190, 197 (1976).

[249] See, e.g., *Romer v Evans*, 517 US 620, 631 (1996) ("[I]f a law neither burdens a fundamental right nor targets a suspect class, we will uphold the legislative classification so long as it bears a rational relation to some legitimate end."); *Mass. Bd. of Retirement v Murgia*, 427 US 307, 314 (1976) (recognizing that legislative classifications are unavoidable, and stating that "[p]erfection in making the necessary classification is neither possible nor necessary," so legislation will be upheld so long as classification "rationally furthers the purposes identified by the State"); *Dandridge v Williams*, 397 US 471, 485 (1970) (stating that legislation "does not violate the Equal Protection Clause merely because the classifications [it makes] are imperfect"). See also *Cleburne*, 473 US at 441–42 ("[W]here individuals in the group affected by a law have distinguishing characteristics relevant to the interests the State has the authority to implement, the courts have been very reluctant . . . to closely scrutinize legislative choices as to whether, how, and to what extent those interests should be pursued.").

[250] *Cleburne*, 473 US at 442–43. See also id at 443–45 (expressing concern that heightened scrutiny of legislation singling out disabled for special treatment could dissuade legislators from passing laws to benefit disabled).

scrutiny in the disability discrimination context was explicitly tied to Congress's ability independently to address the problem.[251]

The probabilistic approach of the Court's tiered system of review—reflecting the recognition that some classifications are more likely than others to fall within the scope of equal protection concern—can be transferred to the context of Congress's Section 5 authority. The idea is generally the same, but the burden of justification is inverted: When Congress legislates to protect a group whose defining characteristics may, in some circumstances, merit differential treatment, it must explain why federal legislation is necessary in order to protect members of the group from the sort of invidious discrimination the Constitution forbids.[252] Congress's task, in other words, is to demonstrate that the injury it seeks to prevent or remedy is one of constitutional concern.[253] In the context of antidiscrimination legislation, this means, not that the Court would conclude that classifications involving the group in question should be subjected to heightened scrutiny, but that Congress has identified a problem that implicates constitutional values the Court has recognized, such as the guarantee that no citizen shall be subjected to "arbitrary and irrational"[254] discrimination based on "antipathy" or "prejudice."[255] Indeed, Congress's experience with regard to certain issues and its superior fact-finding ability will often enable it to identify, in a way courts cannot, instances of governmental action that violate the constitutional principles found in the Court's decisions.

The problem with the ADEA, the *Kimel* Court tells us, was that Congress failed to make such a showing: It "never identified any pattern of age discrimination by the States, much less any discrimination whatsoever that rose to the level of constitutional viola-

---

[251] See id at 439 (noting that rational basis scrutiny applies "absent controlling congressional direction"); id at 443–44 (citing with approval federal legislation prohibiting discrimination against mentally disabled individuals).

[252] Conversely, when Congress acts on behalf of a racial minority, for example, whose characteristics will seldom (if ever) be rationally related to a legitimate state interest so as to justify differential treatment, its bears a lower burden of justification, because one doesn't need extensive proof of unconstitutional discrimination to recognize that classifications based on race implicate constitutional concerns.

[253] See Part I.B.

[254] *Cleburne*, 473 US at 446.

[255] Id at 443.

tion."[256] The ADA, by contrast, is premised on Congress's finding—based on extensive evidence from across the country—that
"our society is still infected by the ancient, now almost subconscious assumption that people with disabilities are less than fully
human and therefore not fully eligible for the opportunities, services, and support systems which are available to other people as
a matter of right."[257] The result, Congress concluded, "is massive,
society-wide discrimination."[258] The Court repeatedly has emphasized that the Equal Protection Clause is violated by differential
treatment founded on such "invidious, overbroad, and archaic stereotypes" about the relative ability of certain individuals or
groups.[259] The object of the ADA, then, is a legitimate one: the
prevention and remediation of unconstitutional discrimination
against the disabled.[260]

C. IS THE ADA "APPROPRIATE LEGISLATION"?

Having determined that the injury Congress sought to address
with the ADA implicates the equality-based values embodied in
the Equal Protection Clause, as interpreted by the Court, we must
now assess whether the means Congress adopted are "plainly
adapted" to the goal of remedying or preventing that injury.[261]
Does the ADA "tend[ ] . . . to secure to all persons the enjoyment
of perfect equality of civil rights and the equal protection of the
laws"?[262]

The ADA's substantive provisions, on the whole, reflect the con-

---

[256] *Kimel v Florida Bd. of Regents,* 120 S Ct 631, 649 (2000).

[257] S Rep No 116, at 8–9.

[258] Id.

[259] *J.E.B. v Alabama ex rel. T.B.,* 511 US 127, 130–31 (1994); *United States v Virginia,*
518 US 515, 553 (1996); *Miss. Univ. for Women v Hogan,* 458 US 718, 725 (1982).

[260] The Court in *Cleburne* recognized that discrimination against the mentally disabled
could violate the Constitution: "Doubtless, there have been and there will continue to be
instances of discrimination against the retarded that are in fact invidious, and that are properly subject to judicial correction under constitutional norms." *Cleburne,* 473 US at 446.

[261] *McCulloch v Maryland,* 17 US (4 Wheat) 315, 421 (1819).

[262] *Ex Parte Virginia,* 100 US 339, 345–46 (1879). As discussed above, the congruence
and proportionality test is inapposite where, as here, it is clear from the legislative record
that "the object of [the legislation in question is] the carefully delimited remediation or
prevention of constitutional violations." *Fla. Prepaid Postsecondary Educ. Expense Bd. v College
Savings Bank,* 527 US 627, 647 (1999). See notes 100–104 and accompanying text; Part
II.B.

siderations that inform the Court's tiered system of review. The Act's principal provisions target only unreasonable discrimination, namely, discrimination in circumstances in which the government's interest in excluding an individual from a certain job or program "by reason of such disability" is minimal at most and is unlikely to bear a rational relationship to some legitimate interest.[263] Under the ADA, the states may exclude disabled individuals from employment, programs, services, or benefits for any lawful reason unrelated to their disability (after due consideration of the ameliorating effects of reasonable accommodation). Moreover, the ADA permits disqualification of a disabled individual if she is unable to perform "the essential functions" of the employment position,[264] or "meet[ ] the essential eligibility requirements" of the governmental program or service.[265] Thus, the ADA's core prohibition of discrimination applies only in those circumstances in which it is unlikely that differential treatment of the disabled can be justified by reference to valid, rational considerations.

Any debate over the ADA likely will center upon the Act's authorization of disparate impact challenges and its requirement of "reasonable accommodation" in employment[266] and "reasonable modification" in public services,[267] as these rules are not required by the Equal Protection Clause.[268] This is, in large part, a red herring. The Court repeatedly—and recently—has stated that Congress is not limited to prohibiting conduct the Constitution forbids of its own force.[269] Certainly, had Congress garnered little or no evidence of ongoing governmental discrimination against the disabled, it might be appropriate to inquire into the reach of the ADA to determine whether it is likely to achieve a legitimate end, or whether some unacceptable proportion of the conduct it prohibits falls outside the reach of constitutional protections. But such an inquiry is both inappropriate and unnecessary where Congress has

---

[263] 42 USC § 12132.

[264] Id § 12111(8).

[265] Id § 12131(2).

[266] Id §§ 12111(8), 12111(b) (5)(A).

[267] Id § 12131(2).

[268] This is, for example, the position taken by the petitioners in *Garrett*. Brief for Petitioners at 29–30, 42–44, *Garrett* (No 99-1240).

[269] See note 9.

found, based on the substantial evidence before it, that the disabled
have been subject to continuing unconstitutional discrimination.
In such cases, the proper question is whether Congress reasonably
could have concluded that broad prophylactic legislation was
needed to root out instances of discrimination that might escape
judicial attention, and to secure for the disabled full practical enjoyment of the constitutional guarantee of equality.

It seems clear that the ADA satisfies this deferential standard.
Given the nature of disability, to treat the disabled in precisely the
same way one would treat other citizens will often result in practical inequality.[270] Similarly, in light of the history of widespread
discrimination against the disabled,[271] to merely forbid future constitutional violations may accomplish little in the sense of guaranteeing disabled citizens the full equality the Constitution promises.
Thus, by targeting governmental practices with discriminatory impact, Congress has attempted to eliminate the "built in head-
winds"[272] faced by disabled individuals, as well as to smoke out
discriminatory treatment that may be based on "subconscious stereotypes and prejudices."[273] Indeed, it is through crafting legislative solutions that go beyond the minimum requirements of the
Constitution in order to ensure practical enjoyment of constitutional guarantees that Congress fulfills its role within the institutional division of labor envisioned by the Fourteenth Amendment.

Admittedly, the ADA's disparate impact and reasonable accommodation requirements will apply to some state employers who
have no previous history of discrimination. But that does not gain-
say the useful preventative role such requirements play in promoting general adherence on the part of covered employers and public
accommodations to legislation that seeks to promote the integration of groups previously excluded from employment and other
mainstream activities because of their disability. Whether Congress could have legislated in a narrower fashion, or should have
been more receptive to compliance costs in imposing these re-

---

[270] A similar argument was raised by amici in *Garrett*, who noted that, "[g]iving a person
who is mobility-impaired an equal right to vote or be a juror, without concomitant changes
in polling places or courtrooms, will accomplish nothing practical." Brief for Amici Curiae
Law Professors at 25, *Garrett* (No 99-1240).

[271] See Part III.A (discussing congressional findings of discrimination against disabled).

[272] *Griggs v Duke Power Co.*, 401 US 424, 432 (1971).

[273] *Watson v Fort Worth Bank & Trust*, 487 US 977, 990 (1988).

quirements—these are questions of legislative design and policy. Under *McCulloch*, and the principle of deferential review accorded actions of a coordinate branch of government that it stands for, they do not place in question whether ADA is an "appropriate" exercise of Section 5 authority.

IV. Conclusion

This article is, first and foremost, a call to demystify the Section 5 power of Congress. Correctly understood, Section 5 enactments raise no issue of separation of powers. The infirmity of the statute struck down in *Boerne* was not due to its provenance in Section 5. Rather, the statute sought directly to enlist the judiciary in implementing a congressional substitute for the equal protection analysis the courts ordinarily would perform; in effect, Congress was commandeering the courts to do its bidding in the course of engaging in constitutional adjudication. *Boerne* involved an unusual statute. Unlike RFRA, Section 5 legislation generally should be understood as providing supplemental protection of groups, supplemental regulation of conduct that implicate no separation of powers concerns. Thus, while Congress unquestionably exercises substantive authority under Section 5, it enjoys no definitional authority over the Constitution's meaning.

Section 5 enactments do raise federalism concerns, and the Court properly should inquire whether the ends of the legislation can be said plausibly to "enforce" the self-operative provisions of the Fourteenth Amendment. But enforcement authority is not limited to codifying, or providing additional sanctions, for conduct that courts on their own would find unconstitutional. Congress enjoys a remedial authority to act in a prophylactic fashion to prevent violations ever from occurring; to establish an environment conducive to the practical enjoyment of equal protection and due process of the laws. On the issue of permissible ends of Section 5 legislation, the question ordinarily should be whether Congress has acted in an area that the Court has identified (or will agree) is one warranting heightened constitutional concern. Classifications that the Court has subjected to intermediate or strict scrutiny are such areas, while classifications that are held to merit only rational basis scrutiny generally are not. However, classifications in the latter category may be proper subjects of Section 5 legislation when they are found to implicate the constitutional values that inhere in the Equal Protection Clause.

The Court's congruence and proportionality test plays a useful role in cases, like *Kimel*, where despite the invocation of Section 5, the absence of findings and the size of the gap between what the statute requires and what the Fourteenth Amendment requires of its own force raise the question whether Congress was, in fact, animated by Fourteenth Amendment concerns in passing the law. The test is unnecessary in cases like *Boerne;* it is inappropriate in cases like *Morrison*, for it results in a judicial scrutiny of the means Congress has chosen to advance an otherwise legitimate Section 5 objective.

On one level, we should welcome the renewed attention to Congress's Section 5 authority, for an appropriate set of ground rules can serve both to quiet legitimate concerns that Congress impermissibly will overtake state functions and to initiate a new era of candor in legislation, encouraging Congress to legislate in the service of equality and due process norms under Section 5 rather than under the guise of regulation of commercial activity under the Commerce Clause. *Morrison* gives pause, however, and presents a threat to the capacity of the national legislature to address national problems through national solutions.

JACK GOLDSMITH

STATUTORY FOREIGN AFFAIRS PREEMPTION

In November 1999, Florida fishermen found 6-year-old Cuban boy Elian Gonzalez drifting at sea off the coast of Florida. The boat carrying Elian, his mother, and eleven others from Cuba had capsized two days earlier. The Immigration and Naturalization Service (INS) took custody of Elian and then paroled him into the custody of his Miami uncle, Lazaro Gonzalez. Lazaro sought political asylum on Elian's behalf, but Elian's Cuban father represented that he wanted the application withdrawn. The INS eventually determined that the father, not the uncle, had the exclusive rights to control the asylum application. Because Lazaro's control over Elian extended only to the extent granted by the INS parole, Lazaro filed an action in a Florida state court seeking temporary custody over the child.

Family law is at the core of the states' reserved powers. Supreme Court jurisprudence suggests that Congress lacks the authority to regulate many aspects of family law, including the law of custody.[1] Moreover, nothing in the federal immigration statutes or regulations speaks to the validity of state power to award custody over

Jack Goldsmith is Professor of Law, University of Chicago.

AUTHOR'S NOTE: Thanks to Curt Bradley, Brannon Denning, Beth Garrett, Dennis Hutchinson, Daryl Levinson, Caleb Nelson, Eric Posner, Peter Spiro, Ed Swaine, Carlos Vasquez, and Adrian Vermeule for helpful comments and conversations, and Alex Gillette, Crista Leahy, and Nick Patterson for research and related assistance.

[1] See United States v Lopez, 514 US 549, 564 (1995) (asserting that Congress's power does not extend to "family law (including marriage, divorce, and child custody)"); id at 624 (Breyer, J, dissenting) (insinuating the same); but see Jill Elaine Hasday, Federalism and the Family Reconstructed, 45 UCLA L Rev 1297 (1998) (arguing the contrary).

an unaccompanied minor alien. Nonetheless, the Florida court had little difficulty in concluding that federal immigration law preempted Lazaro's state law custody action. The essence of the court's reasoning was as follows: "While the court recognizes the many, many authorities that establish that domestic relations, family law, is an area reserved to state courts, Petitioner fails to recognize the fundamental nature of this case—it is an immigration case, not a family case."[2]

The *Gonzalez* court's terse analysis reflects the conventional view that statutory foreign affairs preemption is a simple issue because foreign affairs statutes are easy to identify, and because these statutes carry a powerful presumption of preemption. But matters are more complex than this. As the distinction between domestic and foreign affairs blurs, and as international law comes to regulate issues formerly regulated by domestic law alone, the characterization of a case or issue as involving "foreign" or "domestic" affairs is often not obvious.[3] Even the application of a state's criminal law to crimes committed within the state can have profound international repercussions.[4] In addition, as foreign affairs and international law expand to include issues at the core of the states' reserved power, it is not at all clear that a presumption in favor of statutory foreign affairs preemption makes sense. Indeed, there may well be states-rights-based limitations on the federal government's power to regulate traditional state prerogatives that implicate U.S. foreign relations.[5]

In this article I will assume plenary federal power to preempt in this area, and will focus instead on difficult and largely unanalyzed issues concerning statutory foreign affairs preemption. One

---

[2] *In re Lazaro Gonzalez*, 2000 WL 492102 (Fla Cir Ct 2000). The federal courts eventually upheld the Attorney General's authority to determine that Elian's father was Elian's exclusive representative in applying for asylum. *Gonzalez v Reno*, 212 F3d 1338 (11th Cir 2000), cert denied, 120 S Ct 2737 (2000).

[3] See Jack L. Goldsmith, *Federal Courts, Federalism, and Foreign Affairs*, 83 Va L Rev 1617, 1670–80 (1997).

[4] This was true, for example, of *Breard v Greene*, 523 US 371 (1998).

[5] This issue has been vetted most thoroughly in the treaty context. See Curtis A. Bradley, *The Treaty Power and American Federalism*, 97 Mich L Rev 390 (1998) (arguing for federalism-based limitations on the treaty power); David M. Golove, *Treaty-Making and the Nation: The Historical Foundations of the Nationalist Conception of the Treaty Power*, 98 Mich L Rev 1075 (2000) (challenging this view); Curtis A. Bradley, *The Treaty Power and American Federalism—Part II* 99 Mich L Rev 98 (2000) (rebuttal).

issue concerns the proper interpretive default presumption. Should preemption analysis indulge a presumption in favor of the federal government's strong national interest in conducting foreign affairs? Should it instead be biased to protect traditional state prerogatives? Or should no presumption attach in either direction? I argue that neither an interpretive canon favoring federal foreign affairs interests, nor one favoring state interests, is warranted in this context. Considered separately, each canon rests on implausible institutional and empirical assumptions. When a foreign relations statute touches on traditional state prerogatives, both canons are implicated, and both lose coherence. The prudent course is for courts to apply "ordinary" principles of preemption without any presumption in favor of state or federal law, even when they think the statute concerns foreign affairs.

Of course, courts have an array of "ordinary" preemption doctrines at their disposal even after they have resolved the default presumption issue. Which preemption doctrine(s) should they apply in the foreign relations context? When a case involves a state law that appears to implicate foreign relations, options for preemption include express preemption, conflict preemption, obstacle preemption, field preemption, Dormant Commerce Clause preemption, dormant foreign affairs preemption, and the federal common law of foreign relations. These doctrines can be compared along two dimensions: (a) the degree to which the political branches have spoken to the preemption issue, and (b) the extent to which preemption doctrines require courts to engage in an independent assessment of the state law's effect on U.S. foreign relations. I argue that, for reasons of institutional competence and political process, and because of the waning of the domestic–foreign affairs distinction, courts should engage in minimalist statutory foreign affairs preemption. They should eschew independent judicial foreign policy analysis, and preempt state law only on the basis of policy choices traceable to the political branches in enacted law.

The occasion for this analysis is the Supreme Court's decision last Term in *Crosby v National Foreign Trade Council*, which held that federal sanctions on Burma (formerly Myanmar) preempted Massachusetts sanctions on Burma.[6] *Crosby* is the most important

---

[6] 530 US 363 (2000).

statutory foreign affairs preemption case in fifty years, and thus provides a good vehicle for analyzing the issue in the modern era. I argue that *Crosby* is best viewed as reflecting the minimalist approach to statutory foreign affairs preemption sketched here. The *Crosby* Court appeared sensitive to the difficulty of statutory foreign affairs preemption in a world in which the line between domestic and foreign affairs has blurred; it went out of its way to indulge no presumption whatsoever in favor of federal or state law, or to inject its own views of the foreign policy consequences of preemption versus nonpreemption; and it decided the preemption issue on the narrowest possible basis, leaving it to political process to work out the scores of other difficult issues about the relationship between state and federal law related to foreign affairs. We cannot be sure why *Crosby* embraced this minimalist approach. But whatever the Court's motivation, its analysis is a normatively attractive model for all statutory foreign affairs preemption cases.

A general caveat is in order at the outset. The Supreme Court's preemption jurisprudence is famous for its incoherence. The doctrines of preemption are vague and indeterminate. Their relations to one another are unclear. And the decisional outcomes are difficult to cohere. Only in passing does this article try to figure out what (if anything) is going on, behind the doctrines, in the preemption cases.[7] My primary aim is to take the Court's doctrines and justifications seriously and make the best normative sense of them I can in the context of statutory foreign affairs preemption.

I. Crosby

Since 1962, the nation formerly known as Burma and today known as Myanmar has been run by a repressive military regime.[8] Numerous public and private entities around the world have imposed various sanctions on Burma in an attempt to restore democracy there. In 1996, Massachusetts adopted "An Act Regulating State Contracts with Companies Doing Business with or in Burma (Myanmar)."[9] According to its sponsors, the act was designed to

---

[7] For an attempt at a positive theory of preemption, see David B. Spence and Paula Murray, *The Law, Economics, and Politics of Federal Preemption Jurisprudence: A Quantitative Analysis*, 87 Cal L Rev 1125 (1999).

[8] Like the courts and parties in *Crosby*, I will refer to the country as Burma.

[9] See Mass Ann Laws ch 7, §§ 22G–M, § 40 F1/2 (1997).

show disapproval of human rights violations in Burma, and to pressure the government there to reform.[10] The act barred state entities from buying goods or services from any person or firm on a "restricted purchase list" of persons and firms doing business with Burma.[11] The boycott did not apply if there was insufficient competition for important products, if the procurement concerned medical supplies, or if the highest bid from a noncovered firm was over 10 percent higher than a bid from a covered firm.[12]

Three months after Massachusetts imposed its sanctions, Congress passed a statute imposing federal sanctions on Burma.[13] (The record does not indicate whether Congress was influenced by the Massachusetts statute.[14]) The federal act banned most aid to Burma, required the United States to vote against assistance to Burma in international financial institutions, and prohibited entry visas for Burmese government officials unless required by treaty or needed to staff the Burmese mission to the United Nations.[15] It authorized the President to prohibit "United States persons" from "new investment" in Burma if he certified to Congress that the Burmese government committed violence against the Burmese democratic opposition or harmed, re-arrested, or exiled opposition leader and Nobel Peace Prize winner Daw Aung San Suu Kyi.[16] And it also required the President to develop "a comprehensive, multilateral strategy to bring democracy to and improve human rights practices and the quality of life in Burma," to file reports to Congress on Burma's progress, and to waive any sanction under the statute if doing so was in the national security interests of the United States.[17]

An organization representing several companies on Massachu-

---

[10] See *National Foreign Trade Council v Natsios*, 181 F3d 38, 47 (1999).

[11] Mass Ann Laws ch 7, § 22H(a), § 22J (1997). The statute exempts news organizations, telecommunications firms, and medical suppliers from its scope. See Mass Gen Laws ch 7, § 22H(e), § 22I (1997).

[12] See Mass Gen Laws ch 7, § 22H(b); § 22I.

[13] See Foreign Operations, Export Financing, and Related Programs Appropriations Act, 1997, § 570, 110 Stat 3009-166 to 3009-167.

[14] See Edward T. Swaine, *Crosby as Foreign Relations Law*, 41 Va J Intl L 481 (2001).

[15] Foreign Operations, Export Financing, and Related Programs Appropriations Act, 1997, § 570(a).

[16] Id at § 570(b).

[17] Id at § 570(c).

setts' restricted purchase list, the National Foreign Trade Council, brought a lawsuit against Massachusetts officials in federal district court seeking declaratory and injunctive relief from the Massachusetts Burma sanctions. The court granted the relief on the basis of dormant foreign affairs preemption, reasoning that the Massachusetts state law "unconstitutionally impinge[d] on the federal government's exclusive authority to regulate foreign affairs."[18]

The U.S. Court of Appeals for the First Circuit affirmed the district court on three independent grounds. It first agreed with the district court that the Massachusetts sanctions impinged on the foreign affairs power "vested exclusively in the federal government."[19] It then held that the Massachusetts statute violated the Dormant Commerce Clause because it discriminated against foreign commerce and interfered with the federal government's ability to speak with "one voice."[20] The court's third holding concerned statutory preemption. The court began with the premise that "when Congress legislates in an area of foreign relations, there is a strong presumption that it intended to preempt the field, in particular where the federal legislation does not touch on a traditional area of state concern."[21] Without making clear what brand of statutory preemption it was resting on, the court concluded that the federal statute preempted the state statute.[22]

A unanimous Supreme Court affirmed.[23] The Court declined to address the dormant preemption issues, and instead rested its decision to preempt solely on the ground that the state sanctions stood "as an obstacle to the accomplishment of Congress's full objectives under the federal Act" because they "undermine[d] the intended purpose and 'natural effect' of at least three provisions of the federal Act."[24] First, the state act undermined Congress's delegation of discretion to the President to control economic sanctions against Burma. The Massachusetts sanctions blunted the conse-

---

[18] *National Foreign Trade Council v Baker*, 26 F Supp 2d 287, 291 (Mass 1998).

[19] *National Foreign Trade Council v Natsios*, 181 F3d 38, 49–57 (1st Cir 1999).

[20] Id at 58–71.

[21] Id at 76.

[22] Id at 71–75.

[23] *Crosby*, 530 US 363. Justice Scalia filed an opinion, joined by Justice Thomas, concurring in the judgment. The opinion objected to the majority opinion's reliance on legislative history. See id at 371.

[24] Id at 361–62.

quences of this delegated discretion by limiting the President's ability to harness "fully the coercive power of the national economy" in calibrating sanctions against Burma.[25] Second, the state sanctions were broader that the federal sanctions. They prohibited contracts permitted by the federal act, prohibited more investment in Burma than the federal act, and applied to foreign companies not covered by the federal act. The inconsistency of the two sets of sanctions, the Court concluded, "undermines the Congressional calibration of force."[26] Third, Congress conferred authority on the President to develop, in the words of the federal statute, a "comprehensive, multilateral strategy to bring democracy to and improve human rights practices and the quality of life in Burma."[27] The state law interfered with this aim.

II. PRESUMPTIVE CANONS

Statutory preemption, we are told, "fundamentally is a question of congressional intent."[28] And yet in many statutory contexts, preemption analysis begins, and often ends, with general interpretive assumptions that appear to have nothing to do with congressional intent. Indian preemption provides a good example. In this context, courts reject "a narrow focus on congressional intent to pre-empt state law as the sole touchstone."[29] They instead base their analysis on "broader and less statute-focused considerations bearing on the nature of the state, federal, and tribal interests at stake, [thereby giving] preemptive effect to a broadly framed or highly abstract federal objective."[30]

There are two justifications for interpretive presumptions of this sort. The first is that courts should bias outcomes to serve constitutional values, leaving the final decision to the federal political branches.[31] In the Indian context, we might say that the Constitu-

---

[25] Id at 364.

[26] Id at 366.

[27] Id (internal quotations omitted).

[28] *English v General Electric*, 496 US 72, 79 (1990); see also *Medtronic v Lohr*, 518 US 470, 485 (1996).

[29] *New Mexico v Mescalero Apache Tribe*, 462 US 324, 334 (1983).

[30] Laurence H. Tribe, *American Constitutional Law* 1174–75 (Foundation, 3d ed 2000).

[31] Compare William N. Eskridge, Jr. and Philip P. Frickey, *Quasi-Constitutional Law: Clear Statement Rules as Constitutional Lawmaking*, 45 Vand L Rev 593 (1992).

tion evinces a preference for federal solutions to Indian relations. The second justification is that the presumption is a "majoritarian default" rule. Courts embrace the presumptive rule that they believe Congress would want in most cases.[32] In the Indian context, we might think that courts have determined that over the class of cases in which federal Indian law touches up against state law, Congress generally prefers federal law to triumph.

This section considers the two canons of presumption most relevant to the question of statutory foreign affairs preemption: the presumption against preemption of state law, and the canon that favors federal preemption for foreign relations statutes.

A. THE PRESUMPTION AGAINST PREEMPTION

The presumption against preemption has a number of formulations. Sometimes it is a mere "assumption that Congress did not intend to displace state law."[33] Other times the presumption is couched more narrowly not to protect all state law, but rather only "historic police powers of the States."[34] Yet other times the presumption is bolstered with the requirement that it can only be overcome with a plain statement or clear manifestation of congressional intent.[35] Although the presumption against preemption is nominally embraced by courts and widely hailed by commentators,[36] it is difficult to justify on either constitutional or majoritarian default grounds.

Consider the majoritarian default justification first. The notion of a "general" congressional intent not to preempt state law over a run of different statutory contexts makes even less sense than

---

[32] See Cass R. Sunstein, *Must Formalism Be Defended Empirically?* 66 U Chi L Rev 636 (1999).

[33] *Maryland v Louisiana*, 451 US 725, 746 (1981).

[34] *Rice v Santa Fe Elevator Corp.*, 331 US 218, 230 (1947).

[35] *Gregory v Ashcroft*, 501 US 452, 460–61 (1991); *Rice*, 331 US at 230.

[36] For commentators, see, e.g., Ken Starr et al., *The Law of Preemption: A Report of the Appellate Judges Conference, American Bar Association* 40–55 (ABA, 1991); Susan Raeker-Jordan, *The Pre-Emption Presumption That Never Was: Pre-Emption Doctrine Swallows the Rule*, 40 Ariz L Rev 1379 (1998); S. Candice Hoke, *Preemption Pathologies and Civic Republican Values*, 71 BU L Rev 685, 760–61 (1991); Paul Wolfson, *Preemption and Federalism: The Missing Link*, 16 Hastings Const L Q 69, 111–14 (1988). For challenges to the presumption against preemption, see Caleb Nelson, *Preemption*, 86 Va L Rev 225 (2000); Viet D. Dinh, *Reassessing the Law of Preemption*, 88 Georgetown L J 2085 (2000).

the notion of congressional intent in enacting a particular statute.[37] We can make the notion somewhat more coherent by recharacterizing it as a prediction about whether Congress would usually preempt state law if it were forced to consider the issue.[38] But this recharacterization requires intractable counterfactual analyses. With respect to the presumption against preemption, there is no empirical basis for predicting what Congress would have done had it addressed preemption in any particular statute, much less over the range of all statutes.[39] Certainly the actions Congress does take cut in no particular direction. Sometimes Congress makes clear that a federal statute does preempt; and sometimes it makes clear that a federal statute does not. The large majority of statutes in which Congress is silent provide no information—indeed, they are the very statutes we are trying to account for.

Public choice assumptions provide little assistance in the predictive enterprise. We might think that a Congress consisting of members seeking to maximize political support would "always exercise its power to preempt local law—either to regulate or to forbear from regulating—in order to obtain for itself the political support associated with providing laws to interested political coalitions."[40] If true, this assumption would attenuate the majoritarian basis for a presumption against preemption. But it is also plausible to think that in many circumstances federal legislators maximize political support by deferring to state regulation of particular issues.[41] When Congress is silent about its preemptive intent, therefore, public choice theory provides little guidance. Nor can we deduce a general congressional intent to preempt state law from the fact that Congress has for fifty years or so legislated against

---

[37] On the manifold difficulties with discerning congressional intent, see Frank H. Easterbrook, *Statutes' Domain*, 50 U Chi L Rev 533 (1983).

[38] Compare Richard A. Posner, *Statutory Interpretation—in the Classroom and in the Courtroom*, 50 U Chi L Rev 800 (1983) (advocating "imaginative reconstruction").

[39] I am not suggesting that such predictions are always impossible. For example, I believe that one can deduce from the various enforcement schemes in federal statutes that Congress generally legislates with domestic conditions—that is, conditions within the borders of the United States—in mind. See Jack L. Goldsmith, *The New Formalism in United States Foreign Relations Law*, 70 U Colo L Rev 1395, 1430–36 (1999). With respect to preemption, we have no such evidence of general congressional intent.

[40] Jonathan R. Macey, *Federal Deference to Local Regulators and the Economic Theory of Regulation: Toward a Public Choice Explanation of Federalism*, 76 Va L Rev 265, 266 (1990).

[41] This is Macey's thesis. See id.

the backdrop of a nominal judicial presumption against preemption. There is no actual evidence that Congress legislates with the canon in mind.[42] And there is little reason to think it would rely on such a presumption, since the presumption is applied so unpredictably.[43]

The presumption against preemption is no easier to justify on constitutional grounds. The Constitution allows states to regulate on any subject unless prohibited by the Constitution, statute, or treaty. In the absence of a controlling federal enactment, there is a conclusive presumption that state law governs.[44] But if the federal political branches make federal law within their delegated powers under Articles I or II, the Supremacy Clause makes these enactments "the supreme Law of the Land." The Supremacy Clause is a "constitutional choice of law rule . . . that gives federal law precedence over conflicting state law."[45] It does not contemplate any special requirement to trump state law over and above consistency with the lawmaking procedures in Articles I and II. Moreover, as Caleb Nelson has recently shown, the Supremacy Clause's *non obstante* clause—"any thing in the Constitution or Laws of any State to the contrary notwithstanding"—was designed precisely to eliminate any residual presumption against implied repeals of state statutes.[46]

For these reasons, it is difficult to see how a presumption against preemption follows from the Supremacy Clause or "the role of States as separate sovereigns" that inheres in the Tenth Amendment.[47] State sovereignty ends precisely at the point to which federal power, properly exercised, extends. This analysis does not tell us what types of conflicts should trigger preemption. But it does show that it is wrong, or at least question-begging, to infer a presumption against preemption from constitutional text.

The absence of a textual basis for the presumption against pre-

---

[42] See Nelson, 86 Va L Rev at 287–88 (cited in note 36).

[43] See id at 288–89. Nelson provides additional reasons for giving no credence to the feedback effect argument. See id at 289–90.

[44] This is the essence of the constitutional holding of *Erie R.R. v Tompkins*, 304 US 64 (1938), which follows from the vesting clauses, Art I, § 10, and the Tenth Amendment, among other provisions.

[45] Dinh, 88 Georgetown L J at 2088 (cited in note 36).

[46] See Nelson, 86 Va L Rev at 232 (cited in note 36).

[47] See *Geier v American Honda Motor Co.*, 529 US 861 (2000) (Stevens, dissenting).

emption leads many to rely on functional arguments. The leading functional argument is that the presumption is necessary to effectuate the "political safeguards of federalism" embraced in *Garcia*.[48] As the Court in *Gregory v Ashcroft* stated:

> Inasmuch as this Court in *Garcia* has left primarily to the political process the protection of the States against intrusive exercises of Congress' Commerce Clause powers, we must be absolutely certain that Congress intended such an exercise. "[T]o give the state-displacing weight of federal law to mere congressional ambiguity would evade the very procedure for lawmaking on which *Garcia* relied to protect states' interests."[49]

On this view, the presumption "pushes Congress to carefully consider the federal-state balance of power when making legislation."[50] Or, relatedly, the presumption gives the states notice of impending preemptive legislation and facilitates their efforts to marshal resources against the legislation.[51]

This set of arguments also fails to persuade. To the extent they rest on the absence of judicially enforced limits on Congress's Commerce Clause power, their force is attenuated by the Court's renewal of judicial review in this context.[52] The arguments also fail on their own functional terms. The concern here is that courts will erroneously interpret congressional ambiguity against states, where "error" means "contrary to congressional intent," however understood. This type of error is illegitimate, the argument goes, because in these cases authority for preemption flows from the judiciary (where the states are not represented) rather than Congress (where they are).[53]

If this were the only type of judicial error, it might well be a

---

[48] *Garcia v San Antonio Metro Transit Auth*, 469 US 528 (1985).

[49] *Gregory*, 501 US at 464 (quoting Laurence H. Tribe, *American Constitutional Law* 480 (Foundation, 2d ed 1988)).

[50] Paul E. McGreal, *Some Rice with Your Chevron? Presumption and Deference in Regulatory Preemption*, 45 Case W Res L Rev 823, 840 (1995).

[51] See *Gregory*, 501 US at 461; see also *United States v Bass*, 404 US 336, 349 (1971) ("In traditionally sensitive areas, such as legislation affecting the federal balance, the requirement of clear statement assures that the legislature has in fact faced, and intended to bring into issue, the critical matters involved in the judicial decision.").

[52] See *United States v Morrison*, 120 S Ct 1740 (2000); *United States v Lopez*, 514 US 549 (1995).

[53] See, e.g., Starr et al., *The Law of Preemption*, at 47–50 (cited in note 36); Wolfson, *Preemption and Federalism*, 16 Hastings Const L Q at 111–14 (cited in note 36).

reason to bias outcomes in favor of states. But it is not the only type of judicial error. Courts can also commit the opposite error of interpreting an ambiguous statute to preserve state authority when in fact Congress intended to displace it. This type of error, too, is illegitimate, for unelected judges fail to follow the wishes of the political branches and the dictates of the Supremacy Clause. Both errors, in other words, involve unauthorized judicial lawmaking.[54] There is no reason to believe that one error is more suspect under the Constitution than the other.

Nor is there any general reason to believe one type of judicial error is more prevalent than the other. If anything, nonpreemption errors that favor state power are likely to be more pervasive. States are among the most influential of interest groups in the federal legislative process, and thus are relatively well suited to convince Congress to revise unwanted judicial interpretations.[55] Erroneous judicial preemptions (which adversely affect states) are thus more likely, on balance, to be corrected than erroneous judicial nonpreemptions (which adversely affect groups that are in general less influential in Congress than states). This points to a similar error in thinking about the plain-statement requirement that is sometimes attached to the presumption against preemption. The plain-statement requirement is usually justified by the fact that it forces Congress to make clear its intent to preempt.[56] But the requirement only works if we can be confident that, along the general run of cases, congressional silence results from a design not to preempt rather than the usual factors informing congressional inertia. For reasons already given, there is no reason to think this is true.

The related notice argument for the presumption also runs into difficulties. A presumption against preemption can put states on notice of preemption by forcing Congress, in its lawmaking processes, to take discernible steps to overcome the presumption. But *any* default rule will put the states on notice as long as the rule is clear. Thus, for example, a presumption in favor of preemption

---

[54] Compare Dinh, 88 Georgetown L J at 263–88 (cited in note 36).

[55] See William N. Eskridge, Jr., *Dynamic Statutory Interpretation*, 101 Yale L J 331 (1991). This point holds for erroneous federal preemptions that harm the interests of all or most states; it has less force with respect to preemptions that adversely affect only one or a few states.

[56] See *Gregory*, 501 US at 461.

would give states notice that *all* federal legislation potentially preempts state law. This latter rule would require the states to monitor and lobby Congress much more extensively, and it would certainly result in more federal preemption than the opposite rule. But this is a point about the distributive consequences of the rule, not its notice-conferring effects. This is why the notice argument depends at bottom on a constitutional reason to bias outcomes in favor of states—a reason that is thus far lacking.

A final constitutional argument for the presumption against preemption is a translation argument. As a historical matter, modern statutory preemption doctrine's focus on congressional intent, as well as the rise of the presumption against preemption, occurred at the same time as, and probably in response to, the enormous expansion of federal regulatory power during the New Deal.[57] One might argue that these changes in preemption doctrine were needed to "translate" the Constitution's original commitment to limited federal government and state autonomy in a world in which the federal government has near-plenary authority to regulate.[58] Something like this argument is probably what underlies support for the presumption against preemption. Like all translation arguments, this one is difficult to evaluate because the object of translation (original meaning), the identification of the changed circumstances that warrant translation to preserve original meaning, and the selection of the proper translation are all generally contested.[59] Nonetheless, the translation argument is the most persuasive account we have for the presumption against preemption. We will return to it below.

B. THE FOREIGN AFFAIRS PRESUMPTION

Hines v Davidowitz is famous for its influential early articulation of the doctrines of field and obstacle preemption.[60] It is also a leading case in support of federal preemption for federal foreign relations statues. *Hines* held that a federal alien registration law preempted a similar state alien registration law. The *Hines* Court did

---

[57] See Stephen A. Gardbaum, *The Nature of Preemption*, 79 Cornell L Rev 767 (1994).

[58] Compare Lawrence Lessig, *Translating Federalism: United States v Lopez*, 1995 Supreme Court Review 125 (1996).

[59] See Michael Klarman, *Antifidelity*, 70 S Cal L Rev 381 (1997).

[60] 312 US 52 (1941).

not, as many maintain, establish that federal power in foreign relations, or even in immigration, is exclusive of the states.[61] Rather, it held that the Pennsylvania law "stands as an obstacle to the accomplishment and execution of the full purposes and objectives of Congress."[62] In explaining why the state law stood as an obstacle, the Court noted that Congress had regulated "in a field which affects international relations, the one aspect of our government that from the first has been most generally conceded imperatively to demand broad national authority."[63] The Court also noted that when a federal statute concerns foreign relations, "[a]ny concurrent state power that may exist is restricted to the narrowest of limits."[64] These and similar statements have led many to conclude that *Hines* establishes a rule that "preemption is much more easily found when Congress has passed legislation relating to foreign relations."[65]

In analyzing this canon, we begin with the constitutional arguments in its favor. The Constitution delegates broad foreign relations powers to the federal government. The Articles of Confederation experience demonstrated that the absence of a powerful national foreign relations apparatus would lead states to undersupply public goods (like military defense) and, relatedly, to pursue their parochial interests in various ways that harmed the national foreign relations interest.[66] But the clear need for federal control over foreign affairs says nothing about the manner in which control should be exercised—whether, for example, federal power should be exclusive, concurrent, or some combination of the two. The Framers chose a combined approach. And they chose to be

---

[61] The Court pointedly declined to address the argument that "federal power in this field, whether exercised or unexercised, is exclusive." Id at 62.

[62] Id at 67.

[63] Id at 68.

[64] Id at 67.

[65] *Natsios*, 181 F3d at 97, affd, *Crosby*, 120 S Ct 2298. See also *Maryland*, 451 US at 746 (citing *Hines* for proposition that an "Act of Congress may touch a field in which the federal interest is so dominant that the federal system will be assumed to preclude enforcement of state laws on the same subject."); *Boyle v United Technologies*, 487 US 500, 508 (1988) ("fact that the area in question is one of unique federal concern changes what would otherwise be a conflict that cannot produce preemption into one that can.").

[66] See Frederick W. Marks III, *Independence on Trial: Foreign Affairs and the Making of the Constitution* (LSU, 1973); Bradford Perkins, *The Cambridge History of American Foreign Relations: The Creation of a Republican Empire, 1776–1865*, at 54–80 (1993).

specific about which powers were exclusive and which were concurrent. Article I, Section 10 reflects a decided preference for federal over state regulation with respect to some of the traditional "high"-agenda foreign relations issues concerning war, peace, and diplomacy. But it does not suggest that the Constitution biases federal over state power in the many other regulatory contexts traditionally regulated by states that might cause (and throughout our history have caused) foreign relations controversy—contexts that include tort and contract law, criminal law, family law, procurement law, procedural law, education, and much more.[67]

These and other issues outside the scope of Article I, Section 10 fall within concurrent federal-state power. When the political branches enact statutes within this realm, their enactments trump inconsistent state law under the Supremacy Clause. But the Constitution provides no justification for courts to give extra preemptive weight to federal foreign relations enactments. The costly prerequisites to federal foreign relations lawmaking suggest the contrary. The Senate's supermajority veto was expressly designed to make it difficult to enter into treaties that impinged on state power;[68] and Article I's bicameralism and presentment requirements apply to "domestic" and "foreign relations" powers alike. Despite these provisions, one could imagine that the Framers made it costly to enact federal foreign relations law but wanted courts to construe the preemptive scope of this law generously once enacted. The U.S. Constitution suggests no such scheme, however. And one can read Article I, Section 10 to rule one out, for like a presumption of preemption, it reverses the states' usual burden of inertia in certain specified foreign affairs contexts, suggesting that no such reversal attaches in other contexts.

Many find this conclusion troubling because they believe that without the extra push of the judicial presumption, "normal" interpretive principles governing preemption will allow states acting selfishly to harm the national foreign relations interest at the margin. This worry is based on several unjustified assumptions. The first is that any state-provoked harm to the national foreign affairs interest is constitutionally unwarranted. This assumption rests on

---

[67] See Goldsmith, 83 Va L Rev at 1655–59 (cited in note 3).

[68] See, e.g., Jack N. Rakove, *Solving a Constitutional Puzzle: The Treatymaking Clause as a Case Study*, 1 Persp in Am Hist 233, 236–50 (1984).

the mistaken view that the accommodation of foreign relations concerns is an absolute value under our Constitution. The establishment of a powerful federal foreign relations apparatus was but one means to the Framers' goal of establishing a more perfect union.[69] Another important means was presumptive decentralization of regulatory authority subject to national override. The Constitution does not elevate the importance of one means over the other.

Nor does the Constitution suggest (outside of Article I, Section 10) that the potential public goods and externality problems produced by presumptive state authority to affect foreign relations are more worrisome than the many potential public goods and externality problems created by presumptive state authority of any number of important "domestic" interstate issues. In the former as well as latter context, there are benefits from decentralization— experimentation, information generation, maximizing preference satisfaction, local control, and the like[70]—that counterbalance these drawbacks. Thus, for example, state and local activities can put underscrutinized foreign activities on the federal agenda[71] and provide economic and political goods to local constituencies that are beyond the capacity of the federal government.[72] In addition, although we sometimes label state selective purchasing laws "foreign relations activities," they could also be described as self-governing decisions about how to spend local tax dollars on local ser-

---

[69] See US Const, Preamble; Alexander Hamilton, *The Federalist Papers* 1; see generally Curtis A. Bradley and Jack L. Goldsmith, *The Abiding Relevance of Federalism to U.S. Foreign Relations*, 92 Am J Intl L 675 (1998).

[70] For overviews, see David L. Shapiro, *Federalism: A Dialogue* 36 (Northwestern, 1995); Michael W. McConnell, *Federalism: Evaluating the Founders' Design*, 54 U Chi L Rev 1484 (1987).

[71] This is what happened, for example, with the dozens of state and local divestment laws with respect to South Africa in the 1980s, which resulted in pressure on the national government to do the same. See Michael Shuman, *Dateline Main Street: Courts v Local Foreign Policies*, 86 Foreign Policy 158, 160 (1992).

[72] For example, states have been aggressive in international economic affairs in areas where the federal government has either been unwilling or unable to provide adequate local assistance. See Earl H. Fry, *The U.S. States and Foreign Economic Policy: Federalism in the "New World Order,"* in Brian Hocking, ed, *Foreign Relations and Federal States* 124 (Leicester Press, 1993); John M. Kline, *State and Local Boundary Spanning Strategies in the United States: Political, Economic, and Cultural Transgovernmental Interactions*, cited in Jong S. Jun and Deil Spencer Wright, eds, *Globalization and Decentralization: Institutional Contexts, Policy Issues, and Intergovernmental Relations in Japan and the United States*, 329–37 (Georgetown, 1996).

vices consistent with local views of morality.[73] Finally, state and local "foreign affairs" activities sometimes "provide the federal government with additional leverage in addressing foreign policy issues," as arguably happened when threatened state sanctions on Swiss banks helped facilitate the Holocaust bank settlement.[74] As in the domestic interstate context, the costs of these "foreign relations activities" will sometimes outweigh their benefits. The Constitution provides the political branches with extensive power to resolve these trade-offs, in foreign and domestic contexts alike, subject to the burden of inertia.

The second unjustified assumption is that the political branches need the nudge of the presumption to fully protect U.S. foreign relations interests from intrusion by the states. The case for a bias in favor of federal foreign relations statutes seems particularly weak because the federal government's normal burden of inertia is easier to reverse when the nation's foreign relations are at stake. The federal government faces fewer collective-action hurdles to preemption because state-provoked foreign affairs controversy is likely to come to the attention of Congress, and because the President possesses extraordinary powers to preempt state law affecting foreign relations on his own constitutional authority and his authority delegated by Congress.[75] It is impossible to say for sure whether the political branches can fully protect U.S. foreign relations interests without the assistance of the presumption, for we lack settled criteria for the identification of such unprotected interests. But as suggested above, we should not assume that every state-provoked

---

[73] State and local governments often tailor their spending to comport with local conceptions of morality in numerous contexts beyond international human rights at issue in *Crosby*. For example, some state and local governments refuse to buy wood from rain forests, see, e.g., Ariz Rev Stat Ann § 34-201 (I) (West 1998); Tenn Code Ann § 4-3-1112 (1998), establish purchasing preferences for goods made from recycled content, see, e.g., NYC Admin Code § 6-122 (Law Co-Op 1999), and bar the purchase of products made in sweatshops, see, e.g., North Olmstead, Ohio, Resolution § 97-9 (1998).

[74] Curtis A. Bradley, *A New American Foreign Affairs Law?* 70 U Colo L Rev 1089, 1099 (1999); compare Lisa L. Martin, *Democratic Commitments: Legislatures and International Cooperation* (Princeton, 2000) (domestic democratic processes enhance international credibility).

[75] This includes the President's broad "emergency" powers to preempt under IEEPA, see 50 USC § 1702, his power to preempt pursuant to executive agreements, see *United States v Belmont*, 301 US 324 (1937), and his residual inherent Executive power, see *Dames & Moore v Regan*, 453 US 654, 673–74 (1981). For elaboration of this point, see Goldsmith (cited in note 3) at 1681–86.

foreign relations controversy constitutes a foreign relations interest that requires federal accommodation. Sometimes, perhaps often, the proper trade-off favors states.

This conclusion is bolstered by the steps actually taken by the federal political branches in federal foreign relations statutes. (Here we also begin to address the majoritarian default justification for the presumption of preemption.) Sometimes they expressly preempt. Usually they are silent. But often they expressly protect state law, even in important foreign relations contexts, and even where states appear to have incentives inconsistent with foreign relations harmony. Consider three recent examples. First, the United States made the GATT and NAFTA agreements non-self-executing; the implementing legislation for these agreements establishes a two-way consultative process between the state and federal governments, and precludes courts from preempting state law under these agreements except in actions initiated by the federal government.[76] Second, when Congress established federal law immunities for foreign sovereigns, it specified that cases against foreign sovereigns would in most instances be governed by state law.[77] Third, the treaty-makers (the President and the Senate) have consistently attached both "federalism understandings" and "non-self-executing declarations" to human rights treaties to ensure that the treaties do not trump state law or otherwise affect the federal-state balance.[78] There are many similar modern examples, as well as many historical precursors.[79]

Some believe that the federal political branches' frequent preference for statute authority over foreign relations interests represents illegitimate democratic decision making. Peter Spiro, for example, argues that "the politics of particular [state-provoked foreign relations] controversies will all too often cut against disciplining a state" because federal legislators will not want to be viewed as

---

[76] See the 1994 General Agreement on Tariffs and Trade (GATT), codified at 19 USC § 3512 (1994); North American Free Trade Agreement (NAFTA), codified at 19 USC § 3312 (2000).

[77] 28 USC 1608 (2000).

[78] See Curtis A. Bradley and Jack L. Goldsmith, *Treaties, Human Rights, and Conditional Consent*, 149 Penn L Rev 399, 416–23 (2000).

[79] For example, the Senate modified or denied consent to numerous treaties, both before and after the Seventeenth Amendment, on the ground that the treaties interfered with local state prerogatives. See Bradley, 97 Mich L Rev at 419–22 (cited in note 5). For other examples in this vein, see Goldsmith (cited in note 3).

"benefiting foreign actors at the expense of local actors," and concludes that "this is hardly democracy at work."[80] Spiro's is an inaccurate view of the federal legislative process, since (as *Crosby* shows) it is often very powerful U.S. interests who are the driving force behind suppression of state foreign relations activity. More fundamentally, the process Spiro bemoans could just as easily be described as democracy working well, with legislators responding to constituent preferences. As Ernest Young has noted in response to Spiro's argument: "if we are to take at all seriously the proposition that state prerogatives are remitted to the political process for their protection, then these are *precisely* the sort of political and structural impediments to federal preemption that courts must respect."[81]

It is possible, of course, that there is a truly destructive collective action problem here; legislators servicing constituent interests to gain reelection might in fact be producing suboptimal outcomes from the perspective of the national interest. But how can we tell? One suspects that complaints about underprotected national interests are based on the just-questioned belief that reduction of foreign relations friction is an absolute constitutional value. When the national interest is essentially contested, as it usually has been in federalism–foreign relations conflicts, the most accurate measure of the interest is the democratic political process—a process that, as just noted, faces fewer collective action hurdles to action than usual in foreign affairs.

These are all reasons to believe that courts should not indulge a special presumption of preemption for federal foreign relations statutes. Running against the grain of these arguments, however, is the claim in *Curtiss-Wright* that "the states severally never possessed international powers," and that the "investment of the federal government with the powers of external sovereignty did not depend upon the affirmative grants of the Constitution," but rather passed from Great Britain to the United States as a corporate entity by virtue of the law of nations.[82] Relatedly, a string of Supreme Court dicta suggests that all federal foreign relations

---

[80] Peter J. Spiro, *Foreign Relations Federalism*, 70 U Colo L Rev 1223, 1253 (1999).

[81] See Ernest A. Young, *"Dual Federalism," Concurrent Jurisdiction, and the Foreign Affairs Exception*, 69 GW L Rev (forthcoming).

[82] *United States v Curtiss-Wright Export Corp.*, 299 US 304, 316–18 (1936).

powers are exclusive,[83] and some commentators agree.[84] And beginning in the 1960s, the Supreme Court recognized an exclusive, though ill-defined, federal foreign affairs sphere beyond Article I, Section 10.[85] One might think that a presumption in favor of the preemptive force of federal foreign relations statutes follows from the fact that states have no residual authority in foreign affairs.

I will address the reality, and legitimacy, of a nontextual exclusive federal foreign affairs power in the next section. For now, it suffices to show that the existence of such a power would say little about a presumption in favor of statutory foreign affairs preemption. Within the scope of states' disability under the exclusive federal power, any state action would be *ultra vires*. Preemption would follow as a constitutional matter and there would be no need for statutory interpretation. There has been no such constitutional preemption for most of the issues of tension between federal enactments and state power; most difficult statutory preemption questions must therefore fall outside the exclusive federal power, whatever its scope. But if that is true, then the existence of an exclusive federal power need have no implications for a presumption in favor of statutory foreign affairs preemption beyond that exclusive realm, just as Article I, Section 10 need have no such implications outside its realm.

Nonetheless, the reasons for the development of an exclusive federal power beyond Article I, Section 10 might also support a presumption in favor of statutory foreign affairs preemption. Here we meet perhaps the best argument for such a presumption, an argument once again from translation. It is no accident that an aggressive regime of statutory foreign affairs preemption received its major impetus, in *Hines*, in the middle of World War II. Be-

---

[83] See, e.g., *United States v Pink*, 315 US 203, 233 (1942) ("Power over external affairs is not shared by the States; it is vested in the national government exclusively."); *Belmont*, 301 US at 331 ("In respect of our foreign relations generally, state lines disappear. As to such purposes the State . . . does not exist."); *The Chinese Exclusion Case*, 130 US 581, 606 (1889) ("For local interests the several States of the Union exist, but for national purposes, embracing our relations with foreign nations, we are but one people, one nation, one power.").

[84] See, e.g., Bradford R. Clark, *Federal Common Law: A Structural Reinterpretation*, 144 U Pa L Rev 1245, 1296–99 (1996); John Norton Moore, *Federalism and Foreign Relations*, 1965 Duke L J 248, 275–76.

[85] See *Banco Nacional de Cuba v Sabbatino*, 376 US 398 (1964); *Zschernig v Miller*, 389 US 429 (1968).

tween the beginning of World War I and the end of World War II, the United States emerged as a world superpower in a dangerous nuclear world. There was a general consensus beginning in this period, and continuing throughout the Cold War, that the these significantly changed circumstances required a much more centralized and flexible constitutional foreign relations apparatus than had previously been the case.[86] During this period the Supreme Court presided over, and indeed encouraged, an extraordinary and unprecedented centralization of foreign relations power in the federal government.[87] The extra thumb on the scales of a presumption in favor of preemption can be viewed as part of the broader need to establish federal control during the World and Cold Wars. Of course, because "foreign affairs" had a much narrower meaning then than today, foreign affairs centralization during this period did not extend nearly as far it would today. We will return to these points below.

C. THE CASE FOR NO PRESUMPTION

To determine when the presumptive canons apply, a federal statute must be characterized as involving a foreign affairs issue or an issue of traditional state prerogative. There is no reason in theory why the two categories of characterization need necessarily overlap. The issues traditionally governed by state law might have nothing to do with relations with other countries, and vice versa. Courts have made just this assumption in invoking the two canons during the last fifty years. Consider this passage from a wartime labor preemption case:

> [In *Hines*] we were dealing with a problem which had an impact on the general field of foreign relations. The delicacy of the issues which were posed alone raised grave questions as to the propriety of allowing a state system of regulation to function alongside of a federal system. . . . Therefore, we were more ready to conclude that a federal Act in a field that touched international relations superseded state regulation than we

---

[86] See G. Edward White, *The Transformation of the Constitutional Regime of Foreign Relations*, 85 Va L Rev 1 (1999); Joel R. Paul, *The Geopolitical Constitution: Executive Expediency and Executive Agreements*, 86 Cal L Rev 671 (1998).

[87] See sources cited in note 86. The leading cases were *Curtiss-Wright Export Corp.*, 299 US 304; *Missouri v Holland*, 252 US 416 (1920); *Pink*, 315 US at 229; and *Belmont*, 301 US 324.

were in those cases where a State was exercising its historic powers over such traditionally local matters as public safety and order and the use of streets and highways. Here, we are dealing with the latter type of problem. We will not lightly infer that Congress by the mere passage of a federal Act has impaired the traditional sovereignty of the several States in that regard.[88]

In this case, the court characterized the statute noncontroversially as one concerning a traditional state rather than a foreign relations concern. This choice of characterizations is necessary for the canons to work, even in cases when the choice is controversial. This is why the *Gonzalez* court characterized the case as about immigration rather than family law before proceeding to select the canon favoring federal preemption.[89] And it is why the court of appeals in *Crosby* characterized the case to concern foreign affairs rather than state procurement.[90]

The problem is that these latter two cases actually implicate both traditional state prerogatives and foreign relations interests. As the world becomes more interconnected—as international law increasingly regulates traditional "local" issues, as the category of "foreign affairs" expands to include traditional domestic "concerns," as local activities increasingly have foreign effects, and as state and local governments increasingly participate on the foreign stage in response to the growing influence of external activities on local communities[91]—this overlap in the canons will only grow. Consider other federal enactments that in recent years have simultaneously implicated both foreign affairs and traditional state prerogatives: the execution of Angel Breard (punishment for murder and alien rights to consul),[92] the New York City parking ticket

---

[88] *Allen-Bradley Local v Board*, 315 US 740, 749 (1942) (internal citations eliminated). See also *Hillsborough County v Automated Medical Laboratorie, Inc.*, 471 US 707, 719 (1985):

> [In *Hines*] the Court inferred an intent to pre-empt from the dominance of the federal interest in foreign affairs because "the supremacy of the national power in the general field of foreign affairs . . . is made clear by the Constitution," and the regulation of that field is "intimately blended and intertwined with responsibilities of the national government." Needless to say, those factors are absent here. Rather, as we have stated, the regulation of health and safety matters is primarily, and historically, a matter of local concern.

[89] See text at note 2 above.

[90] 181 F3d at 74.

[91] These points about the consequences of globalization for the distinction between domestic and foreign affairs are standard in the literature. For elaborations, see Goldsmith, 83 Va L Rev 1617 (cited in note 3); Spiro, 70 U Colo L Rev 1223 (cited in note 80).

[92] See *Breard*, 523 US 371.

controversy (traffic regulation vs. diplomatic immunity),[93] and California's unitary tax scheme (state tax vs. foreign protest).[94] There are many other examples.[95]

What should courts do when a federal foreign relations statute implicates a traditional state prerogative? In this circumstance, the competing presumptions against and for preemption lose coherence and usefulness. Consider the majoritarian default justifications for the two presumptions. It was difficult enough to determine "general congressional intent" about preemption on the assumption that the foreign-local distinction was mutually exclusive. The task becomes all the more challenging as the distinction blurs. As local affairs increasingly implicate foreign affairs, and as federal foreign relations statutes increasingly overlap with traditional state prerogatives, congressional preferences concerning the trade-off between foreign relations and localism necessarily become more difficult for courts to discern or predict. But without confidence in their ability to ascertain congressional intent across the run of foreign relations statutes, courts have no basis to indulge in general presumptions, at least on a majoritarian default rationale.

A similar conclusion follows for the constitutional arguments for the two canons. If a federal statute simultaneously implicates foreign affairs and a traditional state prerogative, the canons suggest that the Constitution creates both a presumption for and against preemption, which is nonsense.

One way out of this conundrum is for courts to decide that one of the two values at stake here—accommodation of foreign relations concerns, or protection of traditional state prerogatives—is more important, and simply choose the canon in support of that value across the board. The case for choosing the presumption against preemption would emphasize the following points: The justification for the foreign relations canon has diminished. The evaporation of the near-emergency circumstances of the World and Cold Wars suggests that our constitutional system need no

---

[93] See, e.g., Clifford J. Levy, *Giuliani May Again Trim Diplomatic Parking*, New York Times (April 20, 1997).

[94] *Barclays Bank PLC v Franchise Tax Bd*, 512 US 298 (1994).

[95] These clashes are not new. Numerous intractable foreign relations disputes in U.S. history have resulted from the application of state law. But they are more pervasive, and their resolution is more intractable.

longer depart from its "normal" assumptions about the relationship between state and federal power.[96] This is especially true because the category "foreign relations" has expanded in the last fifty years to include so much of what was once considered to be of local, and thus state, concern. On this view, the "translation" argument for a presumption against preemption is heightened by the waning of the distinction between domestic and foreign affairs, while the "translation" argument for the foreign affairs presumption is attenuated. This conclusion finds further support in the fact that the federal political branches have developed special means during the last fifty years to make their preemptive intent effective if they deem it necessary.

This argument has much force. But there are also arguments for choosing the foreign affairs presumption. Many believe that globalization increases the need for the nation to speak with a single voice before the world in order to better coordinate our activities with other nations with whom we have relations of unprecedented scope and depth.[97] If the presumption against preemption is chosen, then the federal government faces yet higher costs in conducting a unitary foreign policy when it so chooses. On this view, the protection of states qua states is simply less important than international harmony. And in any event, states are well enough organized in Congress to immunize themselves from preemption for issues that truly demand decentralized control.

I do not see how courts can choose between these two sets of arguments in a categorical fashion. Certainly the choice of either canon at the expense of the other is more controversial than the choice to embrace each canon separately in the 1940s, both because the already weak arguments for either canon are weakened by the blurring of the categories, and because the cost of choosing either canon—the suppression of the value represented by the other—increases. Moreover, courts lack competence or any plausible basis for identifying U.S. foreign relations interests as broadly conceived in modern times and weighing them in a categorical fashion against the continued viability of presumptive state regulatory authority. Categorical conclusions are infeasible, because the

---

[96] See White, 85 Va L Rev 1 (cited in note 86).

[97] Compare Louis Henkin, *Foreign Affairs and the United States Constitution* 150 (Oxford, 2d ed 1996).

case for federal versus state control depends on contested political priors and the vagaries of particular context-specific trade-offs. What is needed are fine-grained, not categorical, solutions. Politicians, who are both politically accountable and relatively expert in foreign relations, are much more likely than courts to provide intelligent solutions of this sort.[98]

It is of course possible to imagine more fine-grained characterizations than "foreign affairs statutes" and "traditional state prerogatives" to trigger application of the presumptive canons. But it is unclear what finer lines courts should draw. They could begin narrowly, perhaps leaving the presumption against preemption for foreign relations statutes that regulate the central operations of state government, and preserving the presumption of preemption for contexts in which the arguments for uniform national treatment are least controversial, such as immigration. Even these categories will present inevitable characterization problems. And even within these categories it will often be controversial whether state or federal regulation is most appropriate. *Crosby*, for example, concerned state procurement policies for state activities, a central government function. And even in federal contexts such as immigration, the Court has zigzagged in its commitment to presumptive federal regulation, recognizing that in some areas related to immigration there are good reasons to preserve presumptive state control.[99]

Another possibility would be to limit the presumption of preemption to state laws enacted with the purpose of influencing foreign relations. Purpose (or motive) review has gained wide approval in the constitutional law literature because it allows courts

---

[98] As Justice Breyer noted in a different context:

Courts cannot easily draw the proper basic lines of authority. The proper local/national/international balance is often highly context specific. And judicial rules that would allocate power are often far too broad. Legislatures, however, can write laws that more specifically embody that balance. Specific regulatory schemes, for example, can draw lines that leave certain local authority untouched . . . . That is why the modern substantive federalist problem demands a flexible, context specific legislative response.

College Savings Bank v Florida Prepaid Postsecondary Education Expense Board, 119 S Ct 2219, 2239 (1999) (Breyer, J, dissenting).

[99] The best example is *De Canas v Bica*, 424 US 351 (1976) (applying presumption against preemption, and invoking state police powers, in concluding that California law prohibiting employer from employing illegal alien not preempted by federal immigration laws).

to enforce important constitutional values without engaging in effects-based inquiries for which they are unsuited.[100] But there are problems with extending purpose review to the statutory preemption context. The biggest problem is that the narrower presumption begs the questions raised above whether the Constitution disallows state activities with a foreign relations purpose.[101] There are also problems of application. In the contexts in which purpose inquiry has flourished, the illicit purpose tends to be uncontroversial and easily identifiable. Not so with respect to state foreign relations activity. In many cases (*Crosby* probably is not one) the identification of the illicit purpose would be difficult and controversial.[102] In addition, many state activities that implicate the greatest international tensions (such the juvenile death penalty and state taxation schemes) and greatest constitutional concern are not motivated by the illicit purpose, and thus would be unaffected by the canon. A canon linked to foreign affairs purpose might be both difficult to apply and nonresponsive to the underlying constitutional value, whatever its scope.

All of this leads me to conclude that courts should perform preemption analysis without recourse to the presumptive canons. The canons have an uncertain justification in any event, and they probably conceal more than they enlighten about what drives the judicial decision to preempt or not. Courts are not particularly well suited to make the policy trade-offs needed to choose one canon over the other, or to develop more fine-grained canons. Perhaps most important, elimination of the presumptions leaves maximum room for political deliberation and compromise, which is appropriate in areas of contested constitutional policy where courts lack expertise.[103] This is especially so since there is little reason to fear

---

[100] For a summary and empathetic analysis of this trend, see Ashutosh Bhagwat, *Purpose Scrutiny in Constitutional Analysis*, 85 Cal L Rev 297 (1997).

[101] Compare Edward T. Swaine, *Negotiating Federalism: State Bargaining and the Dormant Treaty Power*, 49 Duke L J 1127, 1251 (2000) ("a purpose inquiry [for foreign affairs preemption] has the same problem as the effects approach: before considering how much state activity is too much, or what purposes are illegitimate, we must first establish more clearly the constitutional basis for the claim of interference").

[102] See id at 1250–51.

[103] See Cass R. Sunstein, *One Case at a Time: Judicial Minimalism on the Supreme Court* (Harvard, 1999); Mark R. Tushnet, *Taking the Constitution Away from the Courts* (Princeton, 1999); James Bradley Thayer, *The Origin and Scope of the American Doctrine of Constitutional Law* (Little, Brown, 1893).

a political process breakdown that would warrant a special thumb on the scale in this context; both the federal political branches and the states are well equipped to look after their interests in this context. Abandonment of the presumptive canons is not an abandonment of the interpretative enterprise. To the contrary, abandonment of these presumptions represents a flight *toward* statutory interpretation, since the presumptive canons have no discernible basis in statutory text or purpose.

Elimination of the presumptive canons in the foreign relations context would, however, raise two special difficulties. The first problem is that, as I have emphasized, the very category of "foreign relations statutes" is itself unclear. How can courts know when to abandon the presumptive canons and when not to? This difficulty arises only if there continues to be a justification for a presumption against preemption outside the foreign relations context, a proposition that I and others have questioned. But even if there remains a justification for the presumption against preemption when there is no conceivable foreign policy element in the case, and even if the presumption against preemption has real bite (a proposition many have questioned in recent years), courts should simply indulge no presumption whenever they are discerning whether a federal statute preempts state activity that they believe affects foreign relations.

The second problem is what to do when courts cannot decide whether a federal statute preempts state law using "normal" interpretive tools (which are discussed in detail in the next section). What, in other words, should courts to do when the interpretive materials do not indicate whether Congress intended to preempt state law? Such an outcome should rarely occur. But in any event, it is not a serious problem. If the party relying on federal law fails to demonstrate that federal law preempts, then state law applies by default in accordance with the usual enumerated power assumptions of our constitutional order. This is not at all the same thing as a presumption against preemption. The presumption against preemption weighs the interpretive scales in favor of states at the beginning of the analysis, and biases the interpretive project from the outset. A state law tiebreaker occurs at the end of the analysis in the rare case when there are no other federal interpretive principles on which to draw.

III. Preemption Doctrines and the Case for Minimalism

Even in the absence of presumptive canons, judges must choose among an array of statutory preemption doctrines, including express preemption, conflict preemption, obstacle preemption, field preemption, Dormant Foreign Commerce Clause, the federal common law of foreign relations, and dormant foreign affairs preemption. After sketching a framework for analyzing these doctrines, I argue for a particular form of interpretive minimalism: Courts should preempt state law only on the basis of foreign policy choices traceable to enacted federal law.

A. MAPPING THE DOCTRINES OF FOREIGN AFFAIRS PREEMPTION

The chart depicted in the Figure below maps the foreign affairs preemption doctrines along two dimensions. The horizontal axis in the chart measures the degree to which the preemption doctrines require courts to engage in an independent judicial analysis of the foreign relations consequences of applying state law. The vertical

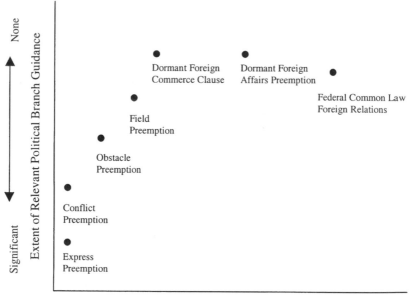

Extent of Independent Judicial Foreign Policy Analysis

None ⟵⟶ Significant

axis measures "the relative presence or absence of congressional action related to the matter regulated by the displaced state law."[104] (The significance of these measures will become clear presently.) The chart makes ordinal generalizations about foreign affairs preemption doctrines in order to make clear their broader relationships. There is much to quibble with in the precise location of each doctrine on the map, but I believe the relationships between the doctrines are, for reasons explained below, generally accurate.

1. *Dormant preemption doctrines.* We begin with the three dormant preemption doctrines in the foreign affairs context. The central one is dormant foreign affairs preemption. This is the doctrine relied upon by the district and (in the alternative) by the court of appeals in *Crosby.* Courts applying this doctrine preempt state law on their own authority in the absence of any federal enacted law. The justification for this doctrine is that certain state foreign relations activities concern "matters which the Constitution entrusts solely to the Federal Government."[105] In operation, however, courts apply this structural constitutional doctrine on the basis of a judicial determination that the state law or activity has sufficiently bad *effects* for U.S. foreign relations. The leading case of *Zschernig,* for example, preempted an Oregon statute that denied inheritance rights to certain East Germans because the statute "affect[ed] international relations in a persistent and subtle way" and had "a direct impact upon foreign relations."[106] The Supreme Court reached this conclusion even though there was no controlling enacted federal law, and even though the Executive branch denied that the Oregon statute adversely affected U.S. foreign relations. *Zschernig*'s "effects" analysis places great demands on courts. It requires courts to identify U.S. foreign relations interests, to determine whether and to what extent these interests are implicated by state law, and whether these interests are best accommodated by preemption.[107]

The second dormant preemption doctrine is the Dormant Foreign Commerce Clause. Like its "domestic" sister, the Dormant

---

[104] Dinh, 88 Georgetown L J at 2098 (cited in note 36). The vertical axis in the chart resembles, but is not identical to, Dinh's more general analysis of preemption doctrines.

[105] See *Zschernig,* 389 US at 436.

[106] Id at 440, 441.

[107] See Goldsmith, 83 Va L Rev 1617 (cited in note 3).

Foreign Commerce Clause asks whether a state law facially dis-
criminates against foreign commerce or has substantial discriminatory effects. But unlike its "domestic" sister, the Dormant Foreign
Commerce Clause also preempts state laws that prevent the federal
government from speaking with "one voice" in foreign relations.[108]
This one-voice test is functionally similar to dormant foreign affairs preemption.[109] It turns primarily on an independent judicial
assessment of the extent to which state law "offends" foreign nations and might provoke foreign retaliation.[110] The third dormant
preemption doctrine, the federal common law of foreign relations,
also relies on a foreign affairs effects test for preemption. The basic
difference is that the federal common law of foreign relations authorizes courts to go beyond mere preemption of state authority
and actually "legislate" the federal rule of decision.[111] Thus, for
example, the leading case of *Sabbatino* held not only that the act
of state doctrine was an exclusive federal concern, but also prescribed the content of that doctrine as a matter of federal law.[112]

The three dormant preemption doctrines share several features.
They all preempt state law in the absence of any congressional
legislation of the issue at hand. They do so on the basis of a judicial
analysis of the effects of state law on the judicially identified U.S.
foreign relations interest. Neither doctrinally nor in fact do judges
applying this "effects test" rely on political branch enactments or
even executive suggestions. As a result, even though the dormant
preemption doctrines purport to draw their authorization from
constitutional structure rather than written federal enactments,
they are functionally identical to statutory preemption because the
federal political branches retain the final say about whether state
law should be preempted and about the content of federal law that

---

[108] See *Japan Line Ltd v County of Los Angeles*, 441 US 434, 451 (1979).

[109] See Peter J. Spiro, *The States and Immigration in an Era of Demi-Sovereignties*, 35 Va
J Intl L 121, 164 (1994).

[110] Compare *Japan Line*, 441 US at 450–54 (invalidating state tax that poses "acute" risk
of offense to foreign nation) with *Container Corp. of America v Franchise Tax Bd*, 463 US
159, 194–95 (1983) (enforcing state law where offense to foreign nation is "attenuated at
best").

[111] See Henkin, *Foreign Affairs and the United States Constitution* 139–40 (cited in note 97)
(*Sabbatino* recognizes a "legislative" power in federal courts).

[112] See id.

preempts state law.[113] In effect, dormant preemption operates like statutory preemption without a statute.

Because the dormant preemption doctrines apply in the absence of direction from the political branches, they are all placed at about the same place at the north end of the vertical axis.[114] They are also all placed at the east end of the horizontal axis, which measures the degree of independent judicial analysis of foreign affairs effects. Along this dimension, however, there are differences of degree. The federal common law of foreign relations is the most demanding of the doctrines, because in addition to requiring courts to determine whether and to what extent judicially identified U.S. foreign affairs interests are implicated by state law and should be preempted, it also requires courts to legislate the federal rule of decision that best accommodates these interests. Dormant foreign affairs preemption and the Dormant Foreign Commerce Clause do not require this final step; they preempt without affirmative legislation. The Dormant Commerce Clause is somewhat less demanding along this dimension than dormant foreign affairs preemption, because it requires courts not to engage in an open-ended identification and assessment of U.S. foreign relations, but rather merely an assessment of whether the state law "offends" foreign nations and might provoke foreign retaliation.

2. *Statutory preemption doctrines.* There are four basic statutory preemption doctrines. Express preemption occurs when a statute on its face addresses preemption. Conflict preemption occurs when it is impossible to comply with a federal statute (which is otherwise silent about preemption) and a state statute. In this context preemption follows by necessary implication from the fact of conflict. Obstacle preemption first identifies the "purposes and objectives"

---

[113] Congress's power to revise dormant foreign affairs preemption decisions flows from the justification for the doctrine, namely, protection of political branch prerogatives. As in the dormant commerce context, it would make no sense to limit a power of the federal political branches in the name of protecting that power. See Henkin, *Foreign Affairs and the United States Constitution* at 164–65 (cited in note 97); Martin H. Redish, *Federal Jurisdiction: Tensions in the Allocation of Judicial Power* 137–38 (Michie, 2d ed 1990).

[114] The federal common law of foreign relations is placed somewhat lower than the other two in recognition of the fact that courts sometimes ostensibly point to enacted law in exercising this power. To the extent courts do this, their analysis becomes more like field or obstacle preemption. Since this form of "delegated" federal common law of foreign relations has not been the subject of academic focus, I will limit my remarks to consideration of "pure" federal common law of foreign relations.

of a federal statute that is silent about preemptive scope; preemption follows if the state statute "stands as an obstacle to the accomplishment" of these purposes and objectives.[115] Field preemption can occur in one of two ways. First, a federal regulatory scheme can be "so pervasive" as to imply that "Congress left no room for the States to supplement it."[116] Second, a "federal interest" in the field addressed by a federal statute may be "so dominant" that federal law "will be assumed to preclude enforcement of state laws on the same subject."[117]

These preemption doctrines are, to put it mildly, not "rigidly distinct."[118] Conflict, obstacle, and field preemption are all forms of "implied" preemption. In these contexts, courts rely on evidence of congressional intent to preempt that is not apparent on the face of the statute. The doctrines use different criteria to identify implicit congressional intent.[119] Even when courts interpret an express preemption (or savings) clause, they often look to implicit evidence of congressional intent in interpreting the scope of the preemption clause, or in ascertaining intended preemptive scope beyond the preemption clause.[120] In this respect, express preemption cases sometimes blur into obstacle preemption cases,[121] and for analytical purposes I will treat reliance on such purposes as examples of obstacle preemption.[122]

The four "statutory" preemption doctrines are lower on the vertical axis than the dormant preemption doctrines because they all have some basis in enacted law. Express preemption is lowest because Congress has made its preemptive intent plain. Conflict preemption comes next because it is impossible to comply with both state and federal law even though Congress has included no preemption clause. Obstacle preemption comes next. This form of

---

[115] See *Freightliner Corp. v Myrick*, 514 US 280, 287 (1995).

[116] *English v General Electric Co.*, 496 US 72, 79 (1990).

[117] *Rice v Santa Fe Elevator Corp.*, 331 US 218, 230 (1947).

[118] *English*, 496 US at 79 n 5.

[119] See id.

[120] See, e.g., *New York State Conference v Travelers*, 514 US 645, 655–67 (1995); *Medtronic, Inc. v Lohr*, 518 US 470, 484 (1996); *Freightliner Corp. v Myrick*, 514 US 280, 289 (1995); *Barnett Bank v Nelson*, 517 US 25, 31 (1996).

[121] As the Court has noted. See *Geier v American Honda Motor Co.*, 529 US 861 (2000).

[122] Compare Karen A. Jordan, *The Shifting Preemption Paradigm: Conceptual and Interpretive Issues*, 51 Vand L Rev 1149, 1178 (1998).

preemption, too, trumps only that state law inconsistent with a specific, identified federal law. But the conclusion of preemption is based on inferences of congressional purpose and federal interest that cannot always be deduced from the statute of the text alone. Field preemption is higher yet on the chart. It is below the dormant preemption doctrines because it is grounded ultimately in enacted law. But the federal purposes and interests that warrant preemption here are drawn more broadly not from any particular text, but rather from a broad regulatory scheme or from a federal interest not tied to text. Field preemption resembles obstacle preemption in this respect, but it is located just above obstacle preemption because the likelihood of reliance here on nontextual purposes and interests is greater, and because there is no particular federal statute identified to preempt state law.[123]

Placing the statutory preemption doctrines along the horizontal spectrum is somewhat more complicated. They are all to the west of the dormant preemption doctrines, which are based wholly on independent judicial foreign policy analysis. The statutory doctrines basically line up among themselves in the same order as they do on the vertical axis. Express and conflict preemption inherently involve little if any independent judicial foreign policy analysis. Obstacle and field preemption, however, can. These forms of preemption explicitly depend on the extent to which the state law in question adversely affects federal interests and congressional purposes underlying the legislation in question. As many have noted, judges performing these analyses often introduce their own independent assessment of the federal interests and purposes at hand.[124] Translated into the foreign affairs context, this means that courts performing obstacle or field preemption can draw on an independent judicial assessment of the U.S. foreign relations interests at stake, and consider the extent to which the state law in question

---

[123] Viet Dinh puts the point this way:

> Obstacle preemption stands at the midway point between conflict and field preemption. Like conflict preemption, it displaces only those state laws that are inconsistent with federal law. Like field preemption, the relevant law is not a specific provision or even a statute, but rather some broad regulatory scheme or independent interests external to the supremacy clause conflict analysis.

Dinh, 88 Georgetown L J at 2105 (cited in note 36).

[124] See, e.g., Jordan, 51 Vand L Rev 1149 (cited in note 122); Dinh, 88 Georgetown L J 2086 (cited in note 36); Nelson, 86 Va L Rev 225 (cited in note 36).

adversely affects these state interests.[125] At least one component of the obstacle and field preemption analysis, in other words, is often identical to dormant preemption analysis. Field and obstacle preemption nonetheless remain to the left of the dormant preemption doctrines because (*a*) unlike these latter doctrines, they do not necessitate the foreign affairs effects analysis, and (*b*) the foreign affairs effects analysis will be cabined to some extent by the presence of a statutory scheme.

With these many distinctions in mind, I turn to the case for a minimalist approach to statutory foreign affairs preemption.

B. THE NORMATIVE CASE FOR MINIMALISM

By "minimalism" in the statutory foreign affairs preemption context, I mean two things. First, courts should eliminate from their bag of interpretive sources any independent judicial consideration of the foreign relations consequences of preemption. Second, courts should make the decision to preempt on the narrowest possible ground, which I shall argue is rarely broader than obstacle preemption of a particular sort. In defending this conception of preemption minimalism, I begin with the dormant preemption doctrines. In recent years the Supreme Court has questioned the continued viability of these doctrines in the foreign affairs context on the ground that courts lack the authority or competence to make independent foreign policy judgments the doctrines require. My aim is to show that the reasons for attenuating the scope of the dormant preemption doctrines argue for minimalism in the statutory preemption context.

1. *Dormant preemption.* The historical-textual case for dormant preemption has always been problematic. The originalist claim that the states never possessed foreign affairs power and thus retain no such residual power rests on contested historical premises about the locus and transfer of "external sovereignty" during the period 1776–89.[126] As we saw above, this claim is belied by constitutional

---

[125] See Swaine, *Crosby as Foreign Relations Law* (cited in note 14).

[126] Some believe that the states retained powers of "external sovereignty" in the postrevolutionary period, and that the United States acquired these powers via the Articles and the Constitution rather than directly from Great Britain. See, e.g., David M. Levitan, *The Foreign Relations Power: An Analysis of Mr. Justice Sutherland's Theory*, 55 Yale L J 467, 478–90 (1946). Others believe, with Justice Sutherland, that the states never possessed foreign relations powers. See, e.g., Richard B. Morris, *The Forging of the Union Reconsidered: A Historical Refutation of State Sovereignty Over Seabeds*, 74 Colum L Rev 1056, 1088–89 (1974).

text. It is also belied by historical constitutional practice, for the states have always exercised residual powers to affect and even to conduct foreign relations.[127] Before the 1960s, courts never recognized a dormant foreign affairs preemption doctrine, even when states caused considerable foreign relations controversy.[128]

The best justification for the dormant preemption doctrines recognized in the 1960s is a functional one. It is no accident that the doctrines were applied by the Supreme Court in two cases in the height of the Cold War involving parties—Cuba and East Germany—who were our Cold War enemies.[129] In this milieu, courts deemed the foreign relations consequences of residual state power to affect foreign relations to be too high. Put differently, it seemed relatively uncontroversial for courts, on their own authority, to decide that there was no countervailing justification for residual state authority to cause foreign relations problems that potentially threatened the nation's existence. The dormant preemption doctrines came at a cost. Because the doctrines' applicability turned on a judicial identification and accommodation of U.S. foreign relations interests—a task that courts properly emphasize is beyond judicial competence[130]—courts are likely to err in their the identification and accommodation of U.S. foreign relations interests. But the "error" costs that inhered in the dormant preemption doctrines were thought to be outweighed by three countervailing considerations. First, federal courts were thought more likely to capture the national foreign relations interest than states. Second, and relatedly, the potential costs of unredressed state foreign relations activity were thought to be worse than the costs of judicial error

---

The truth is probably that the issue was contested during the period 1776–89. See Jack P. Greene, *Peripheries and Center: Constitutional Development in the Extended Politics of the British Empire and the United States, 1607–1788*, at 153–80 (University of Georgia, 1986).

[127] See Dennis James Palumbo, *The States and American Foreign Relations* 147–92 (1960) (unpublished Ph.D. dissertation); Goldsmith, 83 Va L Rev at 1643–58 (cited in note 3).

[128] See Henkin, *Foreign Affairs and the Constitution* 239 (cited in note 97).

[129] *Sabbatino*, 376 US 398; *Zschernig*, 389 US 429.

[130] See, e.g., *Container Corp. of America v Franchise Tax Bd*, 463 US 159, 194 (1983) (Court lacks capacity to "determine precisely when foreign nations will be offended by particular acts" and "nuances" of "the foreign policy of the United States . . . are much more the province of the Executive Branch and Congress than of this Court"); *Chicago & S Air Lines Inc. v Waterman SS Corp.*, 333 US 103, 111 (1948) (fine-grained foreign policy determinations are "of a kind for which the Judiciary has neither aptitude, facilities nor responsibility and have long been held to belong in the domain of political power not subject to judicial intrusion or inquiry").

in policing this activity. And third, the political branches retained the power to correct the judicial errors.

The dormant preemption doctrines were never robust, at least in the Supreme Court.[131] And for several reasons, the functional justifications for the doctrine outlined above are less compelling today than in the Cold War period in which it was announced. Some of these reasons have been mentioned above in connection with the presumptive canons, and some apply uniquely in this context.[132] The waning of the distinction between domestic and foreign affairs means that just about any state law, when applied in a case involving a foreign element, is potentially subject to judicial preemption.[133] The expanding array of preemptable state laws means that dormant foreign affairs preemption represents a potentially massive transfer of federal foreign relations lawmaking power to the federal courts at the expense of the states. It thus poses a greater threat than before to the federal structure. This concern is heightened by the fact that as the category of "foreign relations" expands, it is harder for courts to identify and weigh genuine U.S. foreign relations interests and to balance the trade-offs of those interests against the benefits of state control. Focusing on the federal side, the adverse consequences to the national interest are much less serious in these cases than in the cases that gave rise to the doctrine during the Cold War, especially in light of the Executive's independent unilateral preemption powers.[134] Moreover, the

---

[131] The Court has never again applied the dormant foreign relations preemption doctrine announced in *Zschernig*. Soon after *Zschernig*, the Court dismissed factually similar cases for lack of a substantial federal question, see *Gorun v Fall*, 393 US 398 (1969); *Ioannou v New York*, 391 US 604 (1968) (per curiam), leading some to question the Court's continuing adherence to the doctrine. See Harold G. Maier, *The Bases and Range of Federal Common Law in Private International Matters*, 5 Vand J Transnatl L 133, 141–45 (1971).

[132] What follows is a very compressed form of arguments made at length in Goldsmith, 83 Va L Rev at 1664–98 (cited in note 3); Goldsmith, 70 U Colo L Rev at 1410–24 (cited in note 39).

[133] In contrast to the Supreme Court, lower courts have expanded the doctrine significantly to justify federalization of various contract, tort, and property disputes as well as procedural issues (such as choice of law, forum non conveniens, and the enforcement of foreign judgments). See Goldsmith (cited in note 3), at 1632–39. Even when there is no obviously foreign element in a case (such as a foreign citizen or nation), commentators have urged courts to use a dormant foreign affairs preemption rationale to preempt various state laws (such as the death penalty and prison practices) that conflict with customary international law. See id at 1639–41.

[134] See Goldsmith, 83 Va L Rev 1617 (cited in note 3); Spiro, 70 U Colo L Rev 1223 (cited in note 80).

likelihood of preemptive federal foreign relations lawmaking by the political branches increases with the threat state activity poses to the federal foreign relations interest. A residual role for courts can only dissuade the more competent political branches from performing this constitutional role.[135]

Consistent with these concerns, and perhaps motivated by them, the Supreme Court beginning in the 1980s began to back away from dormant foreign affairs preemption doctrines.[136] The Court expressed its skepticism most clearly in *Barclays Bank PLC v Franchise Tax Bd. of Calif.*,[137] a case involving the validity of California's worldwide combined reporting tax for multinational firms. The California law violated no federal enactment. Plaintiffs nonetheless invoked *Zschernig*, the diplomatic controversy caused by the California law, and the complaints of foreign nations in arguing that the statute should be preempted because it "impaire[d] federal uniformity in an area where federal uniformity is essential" and prevented "the Federal Government from 'speaking with one voice' in international trade."[138] The Court rejected the challenge. It made clear that federal courts are "not vested with power to decide how to balance a particular risk of retaliation against the sovereign right of the United States as a whole to let the States tax as they please."[139] And it emphasized that it was the job of "Congress—whose voice, in this area, is the Nation's—to evaluate whether the national interest is best served by tax uniformity, or state autonomy."[140] The court emphasized that what mattered was whether a federal enactment preempted the state action; foreign relations effects were not an independent basis for preemption.[141] The court even went so far as to suggest that congressional inaction in the face of adverse state foreign relations activity indicates "Congress' willingness to tolerate" the state practice.[142]

---

[135] Compare Thayer, *The Origin and Scope of the American Doctrine of Constitutional Law* (cited in note 103).

[136] See *Container Corp. of America v Franchise Tax Board*, 463 US 159 (1983).

[137] 512 US 298 (1994)

[138] Id at 320 (internal citations omitted).

[139] Id at 328 (internal citations omitted).

[140] Id at 331.

[141] Id at 328–30.

[142] Id at 327; see also id at 326 ("Congress implicitly has permitted the States to use the worldwide combined reporting method."); id at 331 (Blackmun, J, concurring) (stating that

2. *Statutory preemption.* Many believe that *Barclay's Bank* marks the end of all dormant foreign affairs preemption doctrines.[143] Whether or not this is true remains to be seen, for the Court has not explicitly rejected the dormant foreign affairs doctrines. But the retrenchment in *Barclay's Bank* is consistent with a broader trend toward formalism in U.S. foreign relations law. The central characteristics of this trend are that in determining the content of nonconstitutional foreign relations law, courts eschew an independent role in identifying and accommodating foreign relations effects, and embrace of rules that narrow judicial discretion and leave resolution of these issues by the more competent and accountable federal political branches.[144]

Consider other examples of the trend toward this "new" formalism in U.S. foreign relations law. The Supreme Court backed away from its prior view that courts should determine the content of the act of doctrine based on a case-by-case judicial analysis of the foreign relations implications of examining the validity of a foreign act of state.[145] It eliminated this inquiry except, possibly, in the unusual case where the validity of the foreign act of state is an element in the case.[146] With the political question doctrine, the Court backed away from *Baker v Carr*'s invitation to courts to balance foreign policy factors, and suggested that it lacks competence and authority to abstain from an adjudication based on the adjudication's foreign affairs effects.[147] Finally, in two federal extraterritoriality cases, the Court in different ways rejected lower court analyses that required a case-by-case judicial assessment of foreign relations effects.[148]

Moving to the statutory preemption context, we have seen that here too courts can, under the rubric of obstacle or field preemption, insert independent judicial conceptions of U.S. foreign relations interests. These factors probably play a less decisive role in

---

majority opinion relies on "congressional inaction to conclude 'that Congress implicitly has permitted the States to use the worldwide combined reporting method' ").

[143] See, e.g., Spiro, 70 U Colo L Rev 1223 (cited in note 80).

[144] See Goldsmith, 70 U Colo L Rev 1395 (cited in note 39).

[145] This was the approach in *Sabbatino.*

[146] *W.S. Kirkpatrick & Co. v Environmental Tectonics Corp.*, 493 US 400 (1990).

[147] *Japan Whaling Ass'n v American Cetacean Society*, 478 US 221 (1986).

[148] *Hartford Fire Insurance Co. v California*, 509 US 764 (1993); *EEOC v Arabian Am Oil Co.*, 499 US 244 (1991).

statutory as opposed to dormant preemption. But these factors are no less inappropriate in the statutory context. It follows, I believe, that courts should preempt state law only when the justification for preemption is fairly traceable to the foreign policy choices not of the federal courts, but rather of the federal political branches. Returning to our chart, foreign affairs preemption of state law is more legitimate as the basis for preemption approaches the southwest quadrant, and less legitimate as it approaches the northeast quadrant.

This analysis argues for statutory over dormant preemption, and for statutory preemption approaches that eschew independent judicial foreign policy analysis. It also argues for express and conflict preemption over obstacle and field preemption. Field and obstacle preemption are not per se illegitimate. I have presented no arguments (subject to the caveat in the next paragraph) to suggest that field and obstacle preemption are illegitimate methods for ascertaining congressional intent to preempt. The danger with these forms of preemption, however, is that in practice they invite recourse to judicially created purposes and interests. My only claim is that the reasons underlying the move toward formalism in nonconstitutional foreign relations law demand that courts engaging in obstacle or field preemption trace the federal foreign relations purposes and interests harmed by state law to political branch and not judicial choices. This should make clear that minimalism in statutory foreign affairs preemption does not engage the debate between purposivists and textualists about the best mode of discerning congressional intent. It simply says that however else courts discern congressional intent, they should not do so by recourse to their independent assessment of the foreign policy consequences of preemption.

The final implication of minimalism is a modest preference for obstacle over field preemption. (This suggestion is consistent with the Court's attenuated use of field preemption in general in recent years.[149]) Both are forms of implied preemption. And yet obstacle preemption focuses more sharply on Congress's actual aims than field preemption, which draws inferences from patterns of legislation rather than from a particular statute. In addition, field pre-

---

[149] See *Cipollone v Liggett Group*, 505 US 504, 547–48 (1992) (Scalia, J, concurring).

emption less plausibly reflects congressional intent as the category "foreign relations" expands indefinitely. Finally, field preemption tends to sweep more broadly than obstacle preemption, thereby defeating minimalism's aim to maintain maximum room for political decision making. The claim here is not that field preemption is never appropriate in the foreign affairs context, for it is possible that traditional interpretive tools would yield that conclusion as the best reading of an array of statutes. The claim is merely that minimalism requires special caution before concluding that a particular foreign relations field preempts, for the danger of inappropriate judicial policy intrusion is greatest in this context.

This point applies even in a context, like federal immigration, that has long been viewed to preempt the field. Even here, the waning of the foreign/domestic distinction makes it difficult for courts to conclude, in the absence of clear congressional guidance or a fine-grained interpretive inquiry, that a state law implicates an exclusive federal interest. Consider *De Canas v Bica*, in which the Court declined to preempt a California law that prohibited California employers from employing illegal aliens.[150] The Court concluded that Congress had not occupied the pertinent field because neither the text nor legislative history of the Immigration and Nationality Act indicated that "Congress intended to preclude . . . harmonious state regulation touching on aliens in general, or the employment of illegal aliens in particular."[151] This minimalist approach—tying preemption to a decision traceable to Congress rather than on the basis of an immigration interest or policy identified by the Court—makes most sense in a world in which the regulation of aliens touches on any number of tradition state concerns.

Returning, then, to the *Gonzalez* case mentioned in the introduction: The court there may well have been right that the best reading of the immigration statutes preempted Lazaro's state law custody action. But it should have reached this conclusion, if at all, on the basis of a genuine interpretation of federal immigration law, not a cursory and ultimately question-begging characterization of the case as involving immigration rather than family law.

---

[150] 424 US 351
[151] Id at 358.

IV. Back to Crosby

Crosby is a very narrow decision in three ways. First, and most obviously, it decided very little. When *Crosby* was announced, it was heralded by some as the death knell for state international relations activities.[152] This is not true. The Court's obstacle preemption analysis concluded only that Congress's own Burma sanctions preempted the Massachusetts sanctions. Because the Court carefully avoided any ruling on dormant or field preemption grounds, it has no implications for state international relations activities beyond state laws regulating transactions with Burma. State foreign relations activities beyond this—including the scores of state human rights sanctions on countries not subject to sanction by the federal government—are technically untouched by the decision.[153]

Second, the decision was methodologically modest. Although the parties argued extensively about whether and to what extent dormant foreign affairs preemption survived *Barclay's Bank*, the court declined to address the issue.[154] It also declined to address the court of appeals' holding about the Dormant Commerce Clause.[155] Instead, the Court rested its decision to preempt solely on statutory grounds. The parties had argued extensively about whether a presumption for or against preemption was appropriate. Massachusetts maintained that a presumption against preemption was warranted because Massachusetts was exercising its traditional function of state procurement. The plaintiffs argued for a presumption in favor of preemption for foreign relations statutes. The Court, however, embraced neither presumptive canon. It expressly

---

[152] The president of the trade group that filed the lawsuit, for example, said the ruling would "help put an end to state and local efforts to make foreign policy." See USA*Engage Press Release, Supreme Court Rules Massachusetts Burma Law Unconstitutional, June 19, 2000.

[153] One possible implication of the decision is that pending alien tort statute litigation by Burmese plaintiffs against Burmese officials, see, for example, *Doe v Unocal*, 110 F Supp 2d 1294 (CD Cal 2000), is impliedly repealed by the federal Burma sanctions. The reasons the Court gave for concluding that Congress intended the President alone to construct a unitary foreign policy against Burma cut against allowing private parties to bring human rights suits pursuant to the ATS.

[154] 530 US at 362 n 8.

[155] Id.

declined to indulge the presumption against preemption (and claimed that it would have been ineffectual in any event).[156] And it never mentioned the presumption in favor of preemption for foreign relations statutes.[157] The Court also declined the invitation to rule that the federal statute preempted the "field" because it concerned foreign affairs.[158] It instead decided the case on obstacle preemption grounds, the narrowest of grounds presented to it.[159]

Third, and most important, in my view, the Court's obstacle preemption analysis appears to embrace the minimalist principles sketched above. The Court emphasized that the federal purposes and interests frustrated by the state scheme derived not from a judicial assessment of U.S. foreign relations, but rather from the statute and its purposes. To see the point, it is useful to contrast *Crosby*'s approach to preemption with *Hines*'s approach. Before the

---

[156] Id.

[157] Contrary to what some have suggested, the Court also declined to embrace any such "foreign affairs" preemption presumption earlier in the term in *United States v Locke*, 529 US 89 (2000). *Locke* held that Washington state regulations concerning remedies for oil spills were preempted by the federal Port and Waterways Safety Act of 1972 (PWSA). In the course of its analysis, the Court stated:

> The state laws now in question bear upon national and international maritime commerce, and in this area there is no beginning assumption that concurrent regulation by the State is a valid exercise of its police powers. Rather, we must ask whether the local laws in question are consistent with the federal statutory structure, which has as one of its objectives a uniformity of regulation for maritime commerce. No artificial presumption aids us in determining the scope of appropriate local regulation under the PWSA . . . .

Id at 108–09. This passage does not remotely embrace a presumption in favor of preemption for foreign relations statutes. First, the passage is concerned with maritime trade and navigation safety, a much narrower category than foreign affairs law. Second, the Court's conclusion is based not on its naked identification of federal interests, but rather on the fact that Congress had created an "extensive federal statutory and regulatory regime" that traces its provenance to the early nineteenth century. Id at 108. Third, the passage establishes that only (*a*) there is no presumption against preemption, and not that (*b*) there is a presumption in favor of preemption. These are not the same things.

[158] *Crosby*, 530 US at 362 n 8.

[159] Ernie Young claims that *Crosby* "departed from normal rules of preemption based on its view that the cases implicated foreign affairs." See Young (cited in note 81). By "normal rules," Young has in mind the presumption against preemption. He thinks the *Crosby* court "water[ed]-down" this presumption, and embraced a presumption a canon that favors preemption for "federal statutes that have a foreign affairs component." Id. Young's analysis rests on the mistaken premise that the presumption against preemption was the only relevant canon here. In fact, as explained in Section II, the *Hines* canon favoring preemption for foreign relations statutes has been around just as long as the presumption against preemption. Young's conclusion that the Court watered down the presumption against preemption thus begins from an inappropriate baseline. The Court was faced with conflicting canons and declined to rely on either.

Hines Court even considered the federal statute at issue, it devoted the bulk of the opinion to a discussion of the importance of federal authority in foreign relations generally and immigration in particular, as well as the need for uniformity in this area—all by way of establishing a presumption in favor of preemption.[160] The Court's analysis of the text and purposes of the federal alien registration law was curt and conclusory, almost an afterthought. The analysis in *Hines* was clearly driven by the Court's foreign relations characterization of the case and the Court's assessment of what U.S. foreign relations required, and not by congressional intent.

The contrast with *Crosby* is significant. From beginning to end, the Court tied its analysis self-consciously to the text and purposes of the statute. Unlike in *Hines*, there were no general preliminaries about the importance of federal uniformity in foreign relations. Instead, the Court jumped right into the three reasons why the state law was an obstacle to the accomplishment of the federal law's objectives. And it was scrupulous throughout to avoid any suggestion that the policies behind preemption came from any source other than congressional intent.

The Court's first reason for obstacle preemption was its conclusion, based on its reading of the text and legislative history of the statute, that "Congress clearly intended the federal act to provide the President with flexible and effective authority over economic sanctions against Burma."[161] The Court emphasized here and five additional times that the problem with the Massachusetts statute was not that it offended a free-floating federal foreign affairs power, or even presidential constitutional prerogatives, but rather the congressional policy, derived from the statute, of conferring discretion over U.S. Burma policy in the President.[162]

---

[160] *Hines*, 312 US at 401–03.

[161] *Crosby*, 530 US at 362.

[162] See id at 362–63 (referring to the "express investiture of the President with statutory authority to act for the United States in imposing sanctions with respect to the government of Burma, augmented by the flexibility to respond to change by suspending sanctions in the interest of national security"); id at 363 ("Within the sphere defined by Congress, then, the statute has placed the President in a position with as much discretion to exercise economic leverage against Burma, with an eye toward national security, as our law will admit"); id ("The President has been given this authority not merely to make a political statement but to achieve a political result, and the fullness of his authority shows the importance in the congressional mind of reaching that result. It is simply implausible that Congress would have gone to such lengths to empower the President if it had been willing to compromise his effectiveness by deference to every provision of state statute or local ordinance that might, if enforced, blunt the consequences of discretionary Presidential action."); id at 364

The Court's second basis for obstacle preemption was that "Congress manifestly intended to limit economic pressure against the Burmese Government to a specific range."[163] The state sanctions were inconsistent with this congressional intent, the court reasoned, because it swept more broadly than the congressional sanctions, including penalties for individuals and activities that the federal statute immunized. Throughout this portion of the analysis, the Court is once again careful to attribute the purposes warranting preemption to Congress, with no admixture of any independent judicial foreign policy input.[164]

The final basis for preemption was that the state act was "at odds with the President's intended authority to speak for the United States among the world's nations in developing a 'comprehensive, multilateral strategy to bring democracy to and improve human rights practices and the quality of life in Burma.'"[165] The emphasis in this part of the opinion was on how the state scheme interfered with the President's "explicit delegation" of authority from Congress to achieve an international diplomatic solution.[166]

It is true that in reaching this conclusion the Court credited the protests of "allies and trading partners," including the formal European Union and Japanese complaints against the United States in the World Trade Organization.[167] The important point, however, is that the Court considered these protests not in the course of applying an independent judicial foreign relations effects test, but rather because the federal act made such protests relevant. The Court invoked the protests only as "evidence" of the threat to the President's delegated authority from Congress to "speak and bargain effectively with other nations."[168] In at least five other decisions in the past decade, the Court has, as part of its general drift toward formalism in U.S. foreign relations law, declined to credit foreign protests as a basis for interpreting the scope of fed-

---

(state statute "undermines the President's intended statutory authority"); id ("the state Act reduces the value of the chips created by the federal statute").

[163] Id at 364.

[164] See id ("Congress's calibrated Burma policy is a deliberate effort 'to steer a middle path'").

[165] Id at 366 (citing § 570(c)).

[166] Id.

[167] Id at 367.

[168] Id.

eral law.[169] But in none of those decisions was there any plausible basis to conclude that Congress had made foreign protests relevant to the interpretive inquiry. And indeed, the *Crosby* Court distinguished one of these decisions—*Barclay's Bank*—precisely on the ground that the protests concerning the Massachusetts sanctions were relevant to "show the practical difficulty of pursuing a *congressional goal* requiring multinational agreement."[170] The Court ruled out any doubt about the reasons for considering the foreign protests when it disclaimed any competence or authority to weigh "foreign relations effects."[171] *Crosby* is in line with the Court's consistent disclaimer of competence or authority to gauge such effects, and in its confirmation that congressional intent is the touchstone for preemption.[172]

Very similar conclusions follow about the Court's invocation of Executive authority. In *Hines* and other "foreign relations effects" cases (including *Sabbatino* and *Zschernig*), the Court referred to exclusive presidential foreign relations powers as a basis for a judicial determination of the effects of state law on federal exclusive authority. In *Crosby* too the Court made much of the fact that the Massachusetts statute interfered with the Executive's international duties. But the reasons for doing so were much different than the reasons in *Hines*. The *Crosby* Court emphasized that its concern about interference with Executive power flowed from Congress's delegation to the President to achieve multilateral solutions to

---

[169] See *Breard*, 523 US 371 (upholding state right to execute foreign national in face of vigorous foreign protest and International Court of Justice provisional order); *Federal Republic of Germany v United States*, 526 US 111 (1999) (same); *Barclays Bank*, 512 US at 324–29 (1994) (foreign government protests against California tax irrelevant to Foreign Dormant Commerce Clause analysis); *Hartford Fire Insurance Co. v California*, 509 US 764, 798–99 (1993) (declining to credit British protests or, more broadly, to consider comity considerations in applying Sherman Act extraterritorially); *United States v Alvarez-Machain*, 504 US 655, 667 (1992) (foreign government objections to legality of abducting foreign national irrelevant).

[170] *Crosby*, 530 US at 369.

[171] See id ("We have, after all, not only recognized the limits of our own capacity to determine precisely when foreign nations will be offended by particular acts, but consistently acknowledged that the nuances of the foreign policy of the United States . . . are much more the province of the Executive Branch and Congress than of this Court.") (internal quotations and citations deleted).

[172] Ed Swaine has questioned whether the Court read Congress's intent accurately in this respect. See Swaine, *Crosby as Foreign Relations Law* (cited in note 14). The important point for present purposes, however, is that rightly or wrongly, the Court perceived the need to place responsibility for the relevance of foreign protests in Congress and not on its own authority.

Burma sanctions. The Court also made clear that Executive's views about the preemptive scope of the federal act were relevant because congressional purpose made them so.[173] The Court once again distinguished *Barclay's Bank*, which it cited for the proposition that "we do not unquestionably defer to legal judgments expressed in Executive Branch statements when determining a federal Act's preemptive character."[174] In *Crosby*, by contrast, the Executive's views (like foreign protests) were relevant only because Congress had made it so.[175] Once again, the Court ties its analysis of preemption to Congress's wishes.

At the end of the day there is no proof that *Crosby*'s minimalism was motivated by the normative concerns expressed in the article. Mark Tushnet is right that, as a technical matter, "[t]he opinion is self-consciously written as an exercise in neutral statutory interpretation," and it "leaves open nearly every possibility for preemption in the area of foreign affairs."[176] Moreover, as Ed Swaine has emphasized, *Crosby* relied on the canon of constitutional avoidance in declining to address the dormant preemption issues.[177] It certainly did not commit itself to a rejection of dormant preemption principles in cases where there is no statutory preemption.

And yet it is hard not to read *Crosby* as motivated by the concerns that inform the case for preemption minimalism. *Crosby* is a single data point, but it is directly in line with many other data points—namely, the half dozen or so foreign relations decisions in the last fifteen years that have eschewed judicial foreign relations inquiries in an effort to maximize political resolution of contested foreign relations issues. Nothing in the doctrine of constitutional avoidance would have led the Court to choose obstacle over field preemption, or the self-consciously narrow form of obstacle preemption the Court embraced. Rather, the Court seemed driven in this direction by a realization that it has no independent basis for choosing between federalism and foreign relations interests. More-

---

[173] See *Crosby*, 530 US at 362–64. On judicial deference to executive branch views in foreign relations, see Curtis A. Bradley, *Chevron Deference and Foreign Affairs*, 86 Va L Rev 649 (2000).

[174] *Crosby*, 530 US at 369.

[175] Id.

[176] See Mark Tushnet, *Globalization and Federalism in a Post-Printz World*, 36 Tulsa L J 11, 19 (2000).

[177] See Swaine, 41 Va J Intl L 481 (cited in note 14).

over, although the Court avoided a ruling on the continued viability of the dormant foreign affairs preemption doctrines, those doctrines should not survive the Court's pointed disavowal of any competence to identify, measure, and accommodate U.S. foreign relations interests.

It remains possible, of course, that the Court in *Crosby* was engaging in 1960s-style judicial foreign relations effects analysis, and masking this analysis by tying it to the statute itself. Even if this were true—and I think there is no basis in the opinion for such a conclusion—it remains significant that the Court believes that the judicial foreign relations effects test is sufficiently illegitimate that it requires masking. Moreover, even if the Court were hiding its true motive for analysis with an elaborate disavowal of an independent foreign policy role, surely at the margins, and perhaps much more broadly, the need to tie the preemptive scope of federal law to a congressional foreign policy purpose will limit the Court's independent role. In other words, even if we are skeptical that what the Courts say tracks what they really do, there is still reason to believe that the need to find a basis for preemption in a political branch policy judgment will in fact limit the scope of the foreign relations effects test.[178]

V. CONCLUSION

Some have characterized *Crosby* as the first foreign affairs opinion in the age of globalization.[179] This characterization is misleading to the extent it suggests that *Crosby* presented a novel set of interpretive problems. In fact, during at least the last fifteen years the Court has been struggling with a similar set of problems across a variety of foreign relations law doctrines. These doctrines, which were created in the middle years of the twentieth century, presupposed a sharp distinction between "domestic" law, to which "normal" constitutional and subconstitutional law doctrines applied, and "foreign relations" law, which developed its own set of constitutional and subconstitutional rules. As the line between domestic and foreign affairs has blurred, and as the category of

---

[178] Compare Jon Elster, *Alchemies of the Mind: Rationality and the Emotions* (1999) (discussing the "civilizing force of hypocrisy").

[179] See Tushnet (cited in note 176); Swaine, 49 Duke L J 1127 (cited in note 101).

"foreign relations" has lost distinctive meaning, the Court has been rethinking its approach across the many doctrines of U.S. foreign relations law.

The Court's basic move in these cases has been to embrace a particular brand of formalism that eschews independent judicial foreign policy judgments and that encourages the political branches to resolve contested issues of foreign relations law. *Crosby* joins this line of cases, extending the new formalism in U.S. foreign relations law to statutory preemption. There is every reason to think the Court will continue this approach as it works through related interpretive doctrines, including treaty preemption,[180] self-execution,[181] and delegated lawmaking.[182] In a world in which the category "foreign relations" has an indefinite scope, doctrines tied to the category make no sense.

---

[180] The Court has never focused on this issue extensively, but in various cases throughout its history it has sent mixed signals in passing. *Compare Guaranty Trust Co. v United States*, 304 US 126, 143 (1938) ("[E]ven the language of a treaty wherever reasonably possible will be construed so as not to override state laws or to impair rights arising under them.") and *Pink*, 315 US at 230 ("Even treaties . . . will be carefully construed so as not to derogate from the authority and jurisdiction of the States of this nation unless clearly necessary to effectuate the national policy.") with *El Al Israel Airlines v Tsui Yaun Tseng*, 525 US 155, 175 (1999) (rejecting claim that "federal preemption of state law is disfavored generally, and particularly when matters of health and safety are at stake" because "the nation-state, not subdivisions within one nation, is the focus of the [Warsaw] Convention and the perspective of our treaty partners," and thus "[o]ur home-centered preemption analysis . . . should not be applied, mechanically, in construing our international obligations.").

[181] See Goldsmith, 70 U Colo L Rev at 1413 (cited in note 39).

[182] See Julian G. Ku, *The Delegation of Federal Power to International Organizations: New Problems with Old Solutions*, 85 Minn L Rev 71 (2000).

JOHN F. MANNING

THE NONDELEGATION DOCTRINE
AS A CANON OF AVOIDANCE

The Supreme Court has often declared that Congress cannot validly delegate its legislative authority to the executive.[1] Rather than overturning administrative statutes on that ground, however, the Court has long enforced the nondelegation doctrine by narrowly construing administrative statutes that otherwise risk conferring unconstitutionally excessive agency discretion.[2] The nondelegation doctrine, in other words, now operates exclusively through the interpretive canon requiring avoidance of serious constitutional questions. This result is often hailed as a successful way to reconcile several competing concerns.[3] First, the Court recognizes that the nondelegation doctrine serves important constitutional interests, including the promotion of legislative responsibility for society's basic policy choices[4] and the preservation of a carefully

---

John Manning is Michael I. Sovern Professor of Law, Columbia University.

Author's note: I am grateful to Brad Clark, Debra Livingston, William Kelley, Henry Monaghan, Peter Strauss, and Adrian Vermeule for insightful comments on an earlier draft. I thank Keith Levenberg for excellent research assistance.

[1] See, for example, *Mistretta v United States*, 488 US 361, 371–72 (1988) ("[W]e long have insisted that 'the integrity and maintenance of the system of government ordained by the Constitution' mandate that Congress generally cannot delegate its legislative power to another Branch.") (quoting *Marshall Field & Co. v Clark*, 143 US 649, 692 (1892)).

[2] See *Mistretta*, 488 US at 373 n 7 ("In recent years, our application of the nondelegation doctrine principally has been limited to the interpretation of statutory texts, and, more particularly, to giving narrow constructions to statutory delegations that might otherwise be thought to be unconstitutional.").

[3] See text accompanying notes 99–105.

[4] US Const, Art I, § 1 ("All legislative Powers herein granted shall be vested in a Congress of the United States . . . ."); see, for example, *Loving v United States*, 517 US 748, 758 (1996); *Touby v United States*, 500 US 160, 164–65 (1991).

designed constitutional process for legislation—bicameralism and presentment.[5] Second, the Court fears that aggressive enforcement of the nondelegation doctrine would render modern government unworkable.[6] And third, it lacks confidence in its ability to make principled judgments about excessive delegations in the exercise of *Marbury*-style judicial review.[7] Narrow construction tries to secure the best of all worlds—promoting the interests served by the non-delegation doctrine, while avoiding many of the practical concerns raised by direct enforcement.

Last Term's decision in *FDA v Brown & Williamson Tobacco Corp.*[8] implemented this "narrow construction strategy" in rejecting the FDA's assertion of jurisdiction of tobacco under the broad terms of the Food, Drug, and Cosmetic Act (FDCA or Act).[9] The decision, as I explain below, is noteworthy because it offers a clear example of the narrow construction strategy—and an equally striking illustration of its conceptual weaknesses. In particular, the Court's opinion gives sharp focus to the following contradiction: If the nondelegation doctrine seeks to promote legislative responsibility for policy choices and to safeguard the process of bicameralism and presentment, it is odd for the judiciary to implement it through a technique that asserts the prerogative to alter a statute's conventional meaning and, in so doing, to disturb the apparent lines of compromise produced by the legislative process.

Brown & Williamson's facts are complex, but for present purposes they can be readily simplified. After a notice and comment period that generated more than 700,000 comments,[10] the FDA determined that the nicotine in tobacco constituted a "drug" subject to the agency's regulatory jurisdiction under the FDCA.[11] The agency rested its determination on the statute's explicit definition of "drug," which broadly extends to "articles (other than food) in-

---

[5] US Const, Art I, § 7 (requiring bicameralism and presentment); see also, for example, *Loving*, 517 US at 757–58; Cass R. Sunstein, *Nondelegation Canons*, 67 U Chi L Rev 315, 319–20 (2000).

[6] See text accompanying notes 93–95.

[7] See text accompanying notes 96–98.

[8] 529 US 120 (2000).

[9] 52 Stat 1040 (1938), codified as amended, 21 USC § 301 et seq (1994).

[10] Regulations Restricting the Sale and Distribution of Cigarettes and Smokeless Tobacco to Protect Children and Adolescents, 61 Fed Reg 44396, 44418, 44655 (1996).

[11] Id at 44628–50 (analyzing evidence collected in notice and comment period).

tended to affect the structure or any function of the body."[12] No doubt because of the importance of the question, or because the agency had previously asserted that it lacked jurisdiction over tobacco, the FDA supported its new position with an unusually detailed factual, policy, and legal analysis, including a separate "annex" on jurisdiction that occupied almost 700 pages in the Federal Register.[13]

In an extraordinary opinion, the Court rejected the FDA's assertion of jurisdiction on statutory grounds, but without ever interpreting the FDCA's operative language. Despite the statute's evident sweep, moreover, the Court declined to invoke *Chevron*'s established canon that a reviewing court must accept an agency's "reasonable" interpretation of a broad or open-ended organic statute.[14] In place of such analysis, the Court instead determined that "the FDA's claim to jurisdiction contravenes the clear intent of Congress."[15] The Court reasoned that if tobacco is a "drug," the FDA would have to ban it outright under various provisions of the Act.[16] Yet Congress could not possibly have intended such a result, given its passage of several post-FDCA statutes that regulate but do not ban tobacco.[17] The Court also emphasized that when Congress passed the post-FDCA tobacco statutes, it did so against a backdrop of committee hearings that included repeated executive branch disclaimers of FDA jurisdiction.[18] In view of this legislative history, the Court found that the post-FDCA legislation reflected a legislative intent to ratify the FDA's jurisdictional disclaimers, elevating that administrative understanding to the status of statute law.[19] Finally, the Court found that Congress's articulation of specific regulatory policies for tobacco in the post-FDCA legislation precluded the FDA from imposing further regulations under the FDCA's more general authority; by striking a specific policy bal-

---

[12] 21 USC § 321(g)(1)(C) (1994).

[13] See 61 Fed Reg 44396 (cited in note 10); id at 44619 (jurisdictional annex).

[14] *Brown & Williamson*, 529 US at 132–33; see also *Chevron USA, Inc. v NRDC, Inc.*, 467 US 837, 844 (1984).

[15] *Brown & Williamson*, 529 US at 132.

[16] Id at 133–43.

[17] Id at 137–39.

[18] Id at 143–56.

[19] Id at 155–56.

ance, Congress spoke directly to the precise question of appropriate tobacco regulation.[20]

If *Brown & Williamson* were viewed as a straightforward matter of statutory interpretation, much of its reasoning would be puzzling. For a Court that has become increasingly textualist in its orientation to statutes,[21] its heavy reliance on postenactment legislative history, in particular, seems out of character. Indeed, this use of legislative history is particularly striking when one considers that two of the five Justices in majority (Scalia and Thomas) are the Court's most committed textualists,[22] and the other three (Rehnquist, O'Connor, and Kennedy) have at least expressed sympathy with textualism.[23] While one might therefore be tempted to

[20] Id at 143–44.

[21] The current Court more often stresses the public meaning of an enacted text, rather than inferences of intent or purpose that might be extracted from legislative history. See, for example, Hans Baade, *Time and Meaning: Notes on the Intertemporal Law of Statutory Construction*, 43 Am J Comp L 319, 324 (1995); Gregory E. Maggs, *The Secret Decline of Legislative History: Has Someone Heard a Voice Crying in the Wilderness?* 1994 Pub Int L Rev 57, 58; Richard J. Pierce, Jr., *The Supreme Court's New Hypertextualism: An Invitation to Cacophony and Incoherence in the Administrative State*, 95 Colum L Rev 749 (1995); Peter L. Strauss, *On Resegregating the Worlds of Statute and Common Law*, 1994 Supreme Court Review 429; Samuel A. Thumma and Jeffrey L. Kirchmeier, *The Lexicon Has Become a Fortress: The United States Supreme Court's Use of Dictionaries*, 47 Buff L Rev 227, 252–60 (1999). Textualists typically cite several related grounds for excluding legislative history from statutory interpretation: legislative history is unenacted; a multimember legislature does not have any actual intent on matters that it has not clearly expressed; and even if it did, judges cannot know whether a constitutionally sufficient proportion of legislators read or agreed with the legislative history. See John F. Manning, *Textualism as a Nondelegation Doctrine*, 97 Colum L Rev 673, 684–89, 697 (1997) (discussing tenets of textualism).

[22] See, for example, *Bank American Trust & Sav Ass'n v 203 North Lasalle Street Partnership*, 526 US 434 462 (1999) (Thomas, joined by Scalia, concurring in the judgment) (noting that the legislative history "is irrelevant for the simple reason that Congress enacted the Code, not the legislative history predating it"); see also, for example, Thomas Merrill, *Textualism and the Future of the Chevron Doctrine*, 72 Wash U L Q 351, 351 (1994); Michael P. Van Alstine, *Dynamic Treaty Interpretation*, 146 U Pa L Rev 687, 717 (1998).

[23] See, for example, *Atherton v FDIC*, 519 US 213, 231 (1997) (O'Connor, joined by Scalia and Thomas, concurring in part and concurring in the judgment) ("I join all of the Court's opinion, except to the extent that it relies on the notably unhelpful legislative history to 12 U.S.C. 1821(k)."); *Public Citizen v US Dep't of Justice*, 491 US 440, 471 (1989) (Kennedy, joined by Rehnquist and O'Connor, concurring in the judgment) ("Where it is clear that the unambiguous language of a statute embraces certain conduct, and it would not be patently absurd to apply the statute to such conduct, it does not foster a democratic exegesis for this Court to rummage through unauthoritative materials to consult the spirit of the legislation in order to discover an alternative interpretation of the statute with which the Court is more comfortable."); Patricia M. Wald, *The Sizzling Sleeper: The Use of Legislative History in Construing Statutes in the 1988–89 Term of the United States Supreme Court*, 39 Am U L Rev 277, 306 (1990) (arguing that Justices Scalia and Kennedy are strong textualists and that Chief Justice Rehnquist and Justice O'Connor occasionally behave as textualists). For a contrary view of the jurisprudence of Chief Justice Rehnquist and Justice

view *Brown & Williamson* as being simply an idiosyncratic departure from the Court's usual assumptions, its reasoning is better
understood in light of what seemed to be the Court's broader concern—that the statute be interpreted to avoid significant nondelegation concerns that would result from a conventional reading of
its open-ended terms.[24] Although the Court did not explicitly invoke the nondelegation doctrine as such, portions of its opinion
clearly reflect significant nondelegation concerns. Because the FDA
had asserted "jurisdiction to regulate an industry constituting a significant portion of the American economy," the Court emphasized
that this was not "an ordinary case" of statutory interpretation.[25]
More specifically, the Court made clear that its interpretive
method was "guided by common sense as to the manner in which
Congress is likely to delegate a policy decision of such political
and economic magnitude to an administrative agency."[26] In short,
consistent with its approach in many other cases, the Court's narrow construction of the FDCA reflected an evident desire to avoid
otherwise serious nondelegation concerns.[27]

Kennedy, see Charles Tiefer, *The Reconceptualization of Legislative History in the Supreme Court,* 2000 Wis L Rev 205, 248.

[24] Viewing *Brown & Williamson* as a mere departure from standard practice, the Court's strong reliance on legislative history may bear resemblance to *Church of the Holy Trinity v United States,* 143 US 457, 459 (1892), which held that "a thing may be within the letter of the statute and yet not within the statute, because not within its spirit nor within the intention of its makers." Even if this characterization of the majority opinion is correct, however, it is still necessary to explain why the Court chose to invoke *Holy Trinity* here, given its increasing reluctance, as of late, to rely on *Holy Trinity*'s atextual and strongly purposive technique. See John F. Manning, *Textualism and the Equity of the Statute,* 101 Colum L Rev 1, 21–22 (2001) (describing the Court's recent approach to statutory interpretation). As discussed in the text, given the *Brown & Williamson* Court's repeated articulation of nondelegation concerns, it is reasonable to assume that such concerns—rather than an aberrational abandonment of textualism—explain the Court's approach.

[25] *Brown & Williamson,* 529 US at 159.

[26] Id at 133. In this regard, it is worth noting that the Court's nondelegation concerns related to the scope of the administrative authority that the FDCA would confer over the U.S. economy, rather than an absence of standards to guide such authority. Although this is not the paradigmatic basis for invoking the nondelegation doctrine, it nonetheless reflects an important element in the Court's nondelegation case law. See, for example, *Industrial Union Department, AFL-CIO v American Petroleum Institute,* 448 US 607, 645–46 (1980) (plurality) (noting that serious delegation concerns would be raised if the Occupational Safety and Health Act were construed to give the Secretary of Labor "unprecedented power over American industry"); *Wayman v Southard,* 23 US 1, 23 (1825) (suggesting that Congress may not delegate authority over "important subjects" but can do so with respect to "those of less interest").

[27] *Brown & Williamson,* 529 US at 133–34; see text accompanying notes 75–78.

This article contends that, contrary to the Court's assumptions, enforcing the nondelegation doctrine through the canon of avoidance undermines, rather than furthers, the constitutional aims of that doctrine. In particular, the Court typically narrows constitutionally doubtful delegations by restricting a broad statute in light of an imputed background purpose. Narrowing a statute in this way, however, threatens to unsettle the legislative choice implicit in adopting a broadly worded statute. Much legislation reflects the fruits of legislative compromise, and such compromises often lead to the articulation of broad policies for agencies and courts to specify through application. For that reason, the Court has recognized that, if "faithful agent" theories of statutory interpretation are to be given effect, the statutory text may well transcend the precise purposes that inspired it and that the judiciary must respect Congress's choice to legislate in open-ended terms. By artificially narrowing an open-ended statute to its background purpose, decisions like *Brown & Williamson* upset the terms of such a legislative compromise. If the point of the nondelegation doctrine is to ensure that Congress makes important statutory policy, a strategy that requires the judiciary, in effect, to rewrite the terms of a duly enacted statute cannot be said to serve the interests of that doctrine.

Part I frames the issues by describing *Brown & Williamson*'s reasoning. Part II discusses the Court's modern use of the canon of avoidance to vindicate nondelegation values. In addition, it examines the ways in which this practice of avoidance ultimately undermines the interests served by the nondelegation doctrine. Finally, Part III uses *Brown & Williamson*'s reliance on post enactment legislative history to illustrate the contradiction implicit in the Court's nondelegation strategy. Part III also suggests that a distinct aspect of the Court's decision—which construes the FDA's broad grant of authority in light of the more specific provisions of post-FDCA legislation—may offer a promising alternative for promoting the aims of the nondelegation doctrine.

I. Brown & Williamson Elaborated

In determining the scope of the FDA's authority, the Court in *Brown & Williamson* eschewed analysis of the FDCA's text. Instead, much of the Court's opinion attempted to narrow the FDCA's broad terms in light of imputed legislative intent, largely derived from postenactment legislative history. Because that strategy reflects an unconventional method of statutory interpretation, particularly for the current Court, it may reflect the Court's evident desire to narrow an otherwise questionable delegation of legislative authority. This part first describes the FDA's decision to extend its jurisdiction to tobacco; it then discusses the Court's rejection of that decision.[28]

A. THE FDA'S ASSERTION OF JURISDICTION

The FDCA grants the FDA authority to regulate (as a "drug") any "article[ ] (other than food) intended to affect the structure or any function of the body of man or animal."[29] For many years, the FDA asserted that it generally lacked jurisdiction over tobacco, reasoning that tobacco did not satisfy the "intent" requirement unless manufacturers made express claims of therapeutic value.[30] In 1995, however, the agency invited public comment on a proposal to reconsider that position.[31] After receiving more than 700,000 comments (the most ever submitted to the FDA), the agency found that scientific evidence indicated that nicotine in tobacco "affects the structure or any function of the body"[32] and that the tobacco manufacturers' conduct, in context, demonstrated that those companies "intended" such effects.[33]

First, the agency concluded that nicotine has "significant phar-

---

[28] I do not attempt here to address the question whether tobacco, in fact, falls within the FDCA's definition of a "drug," a matter that others have ably considered. Compare, for example, Richard A. Merrill, *The FDA May Not Regulate Tobacco Products as "Drugs" or "Medical Devices,"* 47 Duke L J 1071 (1998), with Cass R. Sunstein, *Is Tobacco a Drug?* 47 Duke L J 1013, 1034 (1998). Rather, my objective is merely to supply the context necessary to examine the Court's nondelegation strategy, as well as the limitations of that strategy.

[29] 21 USC § 321(g)(1)(C) (1994).

[30] See, for example, *Action on Smoking & Health v Harris,* 655 F2d 236 (DC Cir 1980) (affirming FDA's denial of petition to assert jurisdiction over tobacco); *U.S. v 354 Bulk Cartons * * * Trim Reducing-Aid Cigarettes,* 178 F Supp 847 (DNJ 1959) (sustaining FDA jurisdiction where cigarettes were marketed as weight reduction aids); *U.S. v 46 Cartons, More or Less, Containing Fairfax Cigarettes,* 113 F Supp 336 (DNJ 1953) (asserting jurisdiction where a particular brand was marketed as effective for reducing respiratory and other ailments).

[31] See Regulations Restricting the Sale and Distribution of Cigarettes and Smokeless Tobacco Products to Protect Children and Adolescents, 60 Fed Reg 41314, 41341 (1995) (notice of proposed rulemaking).

[32] 61 Fed Reg at 44664–85 (cited in note 10).

[33] Id at 44686–45204.

macological effects."[34] In particular, the agency found that it (a) "causes and sustains addiction," (b) produces "sedating or tranquilizing effect[s]" in some circumstances, (c) induces "a stimulant or arousal-increasing effect" in other contexts, and (d) "affects body weight."[35] In fact, the pharmacological effects of nicotine in cigarettes and smokeless tobacco greatly exceed those of nicotine products already regulated by the agency, such as the transdermal patch, nicotine gum, nicotine inhalers, and nicotine paper.[36] The FDA also found that "the powerful psychoactive effects produced by nicotine in cigarettes and smokeless tobacco are comparable to those produced by tranquilizers, stimulants, weight management agents, and drugs used for long-term maintenance of addiction, all of which are indisputably within FDA's jurisdiction."[37]

Second, and more important given the agency's previous position, the FDA cited several factors that, in its view, cumulatively supported a finding that tobacco manufacturers "intended" those effects. The agency found that nicotine's addictive, mood-altering, and weight-reducing effects were so widely recognized that any reasonable manufacturer would foresee that consumers use tobacco to satisfy their addiction or to produce the anticipated effects.[38] Because the law conventionally assumes that persons intend the natural and probable consequences of their actions, the FDA reasoned, such foreseeability satisfied the intent requirement.[39] The agency also concluded that "consumers actually use cigarettes and

---

[34] Id at 44651.

[35] Id at 44631–32.

[36] Id at 44665.

[37] Id at 44673.

[38] See id at 44634–35, 44698–744.

[39] See id at 44633:

> When Congress enacted the current definition of "drug" in 1938, it was well understood that "[t]he law presumes that every man intends the legitimate consequences of his own acts." Agnew v United States, 165 U.S. 36, 53 (1897). Consistent with this common understanding, FDA's regulations provide that a product's intended pharmacological use may be established by evidence that the manufacturer "knows, or has knowledge of facts that would give him notice," that the product is being widely used for a pharmacological purpose, even if the product is not being promoted for this purpose. 21 CFR 201.128, 801.4. Thus, FDA may find that a manufacturer intends its product to affect the structure or function of the body when it would be foreseeable to a reasonable manufacturer that the product will (1) affect the structure or function of the body and (2) be used by a substantial proportion of consumers to obtain these effects.

smokeless tobacco predominantly to obtain the pharmacological effects of nicotine,"[40] a further indicium of "intended" effect. Finally, the agency relied on tobacco companies' statements, research, and actions indicating that they have long known that consumers use tobacco for its pharmacological effects and that they designed cigarettes with those effects in mind.[41] Invoking the "ordinary meaning" of "intend," the agency concluded that this evidence satisfied the FDCA's intent requirement.[42]

Because nicotine was a "drug," the agency could treat the means of delivering it—cigarettes and smokeless tobacco—as "drug delivery devices" within the meaning of the FDCA.[43] This conclusion, in turn, allowed the FDA to invoke a statutory provision that required "a device [to] be restricted to sale, distribution, or use . . . upon such . . . conditions as [the FDA] may prescribe . . . if, because of its potentiality for harmful effect or the collateral measures necessary to its use, [the FDA] determines that there cannot otherwise be reasonable assurance of its safety and effectiveness."[44]

---

[40] Id at 44636; see also id at 44635–36, 44807–46. For example, the agency cited major recent studies concluding "that 77% to 92% of smokers are addicted to nicotine in cigarettes." Id at 44635. Other surveys, moreover, found that "over 70% of young people 10 to 22 years old who are daily smokers reported that they use cigarettes for relaxation," and "that between one-third and one-half of young smokers report that weight control is a reason for their smoking." Id at 44636.

[41] See id at 44847–45097. Specifically, the agency relied on evidence that manufacturers "have known for decades" that nicotine has significant pharmacological effects and that "consumers use cigarettes primarily to obtain the pharmacological effects of nicotine, including the satisfaction of their addition." Id at 44849. It also cited evidence that the manufacturers "have 'designed' cigarettes to provide pharmacologically active doses of nicotine to consumers," in part by conducting "extensive product research and development to establish the dose of nicotine necessary to produce pharmacological effects and to optimize the delivery of nicotine to consumers." Id at 44850. The agency found similar evidence for smokeless tobacco products. See id at 44643.

[42] See id at 44851 & n 413 (citing *The American Heritage Dictionary of the English Language* 668 (Houghton Mifflin, 1991) (defining "intend" to include "1. To have in mind; plan. 2.a. To design for a specific purpose. b. To have in mind for a particular use . . . .")).

[43] Id at 44397. The Act defines a "device," in relevant part, as "an instrument, apparatus, implement, machine, contrivance, . . . or other similar or related article, . . . which is . . . intended to affect the structure or any function of the body." 21 USC § 321(h) (1994). More precisely, the FDA determined that cigarettes and smokeless tobacco were "combination products," which the Act defines as a "combination of a drug, device, or biologic product." 21 USC § 353(g)(1) (1994). The agency concluded, however, that it could regulate combination products as drugs, devices, or both, depending on "how the public health goals of the act can be best accomplished." 61 Fed Reg at 44403 (cited in note 10). Because of the greater flexibility of the FDCA's provisions governing devices, the FDA chose to regulate cigarettes and smokeless tobacco as "devices." *Brown & Williamson*, 529 US at 129.

[44] 21 USC § 360j(e) (1994).

The FDA invoked that authority on the ground that tobacco use "was the single leading cause of preventable death in the United States" and that "[m]ore than 400,000 people die each year from tobacco-related illnesses."[45] Finding that such illnesses could be reduced only by addressing addiction and that "anyone who does not begin smoking in childhood and adolescence is unlikely ever to begin,"[46] the agency promulgated regulations specifically aimed at preventing children and adolescents from starting to smoke.[47] The regulations, for example, prohibited the sale of tobacco to persons under 18 years of age, required photo identification for sales to persons under 27, and prohibited selling tobacco through self-service displays or vending machines, except in adult-only locations.[48] The new regulations also imposed significant restrictions on tobacco advertising and promotion.[49] The FDA specifically concluded "that without the access and advertising restrictions imposed in this final rule, no finding that there is a reasonable assurance of safety for cigarettes and smokeless tobacco would be possible."[50]

B. THE COURT'S SEARCH FOR LEGISLATIVE INTENT

Initially, the FDA's interpretation seemed to present a straightforward application of *Chevron*'s familiar framework for judicial review.[51] With respect to an agency-administered statute such as the FDCA, a reviewing court asks first whether Congress has "directly spoken to the precise question at issue."[52] If so, principles of legislative supremacy compel the court and agency alike to respect Congress's clear instructions.[53] If, however, the statute is "silent

---

[45] 61 Fed Reg at 44398 (cited in note 10).

[46] Id at 44398–99.

[47] Id at 44615–18.

[48] Id at 44616–17.

[49] For example, the regulations required advertisements to appear in black-and-white and text-only formats, except in adult-only publications and facilities. See id at 44617. In addition, they banned outdoor advertising within 1,000 feet of schools and playgrounds, the distribution of various promotional products bearing a tobacco brand name or logo, and sponsorship in the tobacco company's name of any "athletic, musical, artistic, or other social or cultural event." Id at 44617–18.

[50] Id at 44407.

[51] See *Chevron USA, Inc. v NRDC, Inc.*, 467 US 837 (1984).

[52] Id at 842.

[53] Id at 842–43.

or ambiguous" regarding an interpretive question, the reviewing court must accept the agency's interpretation, if that interpretation is "reasonable."[54] In such instances, the Court emphasizes that the choice among reasonable alternative interpretations entails the exercise of policy-making discretion.[55] Because such discretion more appropriately lies with relatively accountable administrators, rather than relatively unaccountable judges, the Court treats silence or ambiguity in an administrative statute as an implicit delegation of law elaboration authority to the agency.[56]

Given the breadth of the FDCA's text, one might have thought that the FDA's decision to regulate tobacco would be a serious candidate for *Chevron* deference.[57] The FDA's findings made plain that nicotine "affect[s] the structure or any function of the human body," and its understanding of "intent" reflected at least a plausible interpretation of that term.[58] The *Brown & Williamson* Court, however, flatly rejected the FDA's interpretation without ever considering the meaning or scope of the FDCA's operative terms. Although much disagreement surrounds *Chevron*'s precise applica-

---

[54] Id at 843–44.

[55] See Lawrence Lessig, *Understanding Changed Readings: Fidelity and Theory*, 47 Stan L Rev 395, 436–37 (1995); John F. Manning, *Constitutional Structure and Judicial Deference to Agency Interpretations of Agency Rules*, 97 Colum L Rev 612, 625 (1996).

[56] See *Chevron*, 467 US at 865–66:

Judges . . . are not part of either political branch of the Government. . . . While agencies are not directly accountable to the people, the Chief Executive is, and it is entirely appropriate for this political branch of the Government to make . . . policy choices—resolving the competing interests which Congress itself either inadvertently did not resolve, or intentionally left to be resolved by the agency charged with the administration of the statute in light of everyday realities.

[57] See, for example, *Babbitt v Sweet Home Chapter of Communities for a Greater Oregon*, 515 US 687, 707 (1991) ("When Congress has entrusted the Secretary with broad discretion, we are especially reluctant to substitute our views of wise policy for his."); *Norfolk & Western Ry Co. v American Train Dispatchers' Ass'n*, 491 US 117, 218 (1991) (noting that *Chevron* deference is warranted where the statutory language is "clear, broad, and unqualified").

[58] The meaning of the term "intended" represented the only serious interpretive question. The evidence, however, clearly showed the tobacco companies' knowledge of nicotine's physical effects, and the law traditionally presumes that persons intend the natural and probable consequences of their acts. Although the agency had changed its interpretation of "intent" in promulgating its recent regulations, *Chevron* makes clear that such changes are permissible in cases of ambiguity, provided that the agency has adequately explained its change of position. See *Smiley v Citibank (South Dakota), NA*, 517 US 735, 742 (1996); *Chevron*, 467 US at 863. In addition, although the tobacco manufacturers argued that "intent," as used in the FDCA, was a term of art requiring companies to make express representations of therapeutic effect, see, for example, Brief of Respondent Brown & Williamson Tobacco Corp. 6–28, *FDA v Brown & Williamson Tobacco Corp.*, 529 US 120 (2000), the Court did not rely on or even address that premise in determining the scope of the FDCA.

tion,[59] the meaning of the statutory text is always a threshold question in determining the scope of agency power, particularly since the "new textualism" gained influence with (at least some of) the Justices in the 1980s.[60] *Brown & Williamson*, however, simply assumed arguendo that tobacco could satisfy the statutory definition and proceeded to determine congressional "intent" on the coverage of tobacco.[61] Perhaps most strikingly, the Court found that Congress had spoken to the precise question at issue, not on the basis of the FDCA, but on the basis of implied "intent" from legislative acts occurring decades after the FDCA's enactment.

First, the Court adopted a strong presumption of coherence among statutes passed over time; specifically, it reasoned that reading the FDCA's broad terms to cover tobacco would render that statute incoherent with subsequently enacted statutes that regulated tobacco in targeted ways. The Court explained that if tobacco qualified as a "drug," the FDA would have to ban it under various provisions of the FDCA.[62] A total ban, however, "would contradict

---

[59] See, for example, Clark Byse, *Judicial Review of Administrative Interpretation of Statutes: An Analysis of Chevron's Step Two*, 2 Admin L J 255 (1988); Peter L. Strauss, *When the Judge Is Not the Primary Official with the Responsibility to Read: Agency Interpretation and the Problem of Legislative History*, 66 Chi Kent L Rev 321 (1990); Cass R. Sunstein, *Law and Administration After Chevron* 90 Colum L Rev 2071 (1990).

[60] See, for example, *National R. Passenger Corp. v Boston & Maine Corp.*, 503 US 407, 417 (1993) ("If the agency interpretation is not in conflict with the plain language of the statute, deference is due. In ascertaining whether the agency's interpretation is a permissible construction of the language, a court must look to the structure and language of the statute as a whole.") (citation omitted); *K-Mart Corp. v Cartier, Inc.*, 486 US 281, 292 (1987) ("If the agency regulation is not in conflict with the plain language of the statute, a reviewing court must give deference to the agency's interpretation of the statute.").

[61] *Brown & Williamson*, 529 US at 132.

[62] In brief, the Court reasoned that the FDA's mission is to ensure that regulated products are "'safe' and 'effective.'" Id at 133 (quoting 21 USC § 393(b)(2) (1994)). That objective, the Court explained, "pervades the FDCA" and is central to the very provision on which the agency based its tobacco regulations. Id; see id at 134 ("Even the 'restricted device' provision pursuant to which the FDA promulgated the regulations at issue here authorizes the agency to place conditions on the sale or distribution of a device specifically when 'there cannot otherwise be reasonable assurance of its safety and effectiveness.'") (quoting 21 USC § 360j(e) (1994)). The Court also relied on the FDCA's provisions governing misbranded drugs. Because tobacco would be "'dangerous to health when used in the dosage or manner, or with the frequency or duration prescribed, recommended, or suggested in the labeling thereof,'" the Court found that they would be "misbranded" within the meaning of the Act. Id at 135 (quoting 21 USC § 352(j) (1994)). Tobacco would also be misbranded because the tobacco companies would not be able to provide "'adequate directions for use . . . in such manner and form, as are necessary for the protection of users.'" Id (quoting 21 USC § 352(f)(1) (1994)). Finally, the Court concluded that the FDA would have to classify cigarettes and smokeless tobacco in a category that would require premarketing approval. See

Congress's clear intent as expressed in its more recent, tobacco-specific legislation."[63] Since 1965, Congress has enacted six specific statutes addressing tobacco.[64] And, the Court noted, while the adverse health effects of tobacco were widely known when Congress passed these regulatory statutes, Congress always "stopped well short of ordering a ban."[65] Moreover, because Congress enacted certain labeling requirements with the express purpose of protecting commerce " 'to the maximum extent consistent with' " giving consumers adequate information about tobacco's health effects, the Court inferred a legislative "intent that tobacco products stay on the market."[66]

Second, the Court applied strongly purposive interpretive techniques to narrow the FDCA. Based upon the legislative history accompanying the later tobacco statutes, it concluded that Congress had ratified the FDA's prior assumption that tobacco fell out-

---

id at 136; see also 21 USC § 360(a) (1994); id § 360c(a)(1)(C) (1994); id § 360e (1994). In that context, the agency would have to deny approval, absent " 'reasonable assurance that such device is safe under the conditions of use prescribed, recommended or suggested on the labeling thereof.' " *Brown & Williamson*, 529 US at 136 (quoting 21 USC § 360e(d)(2)(A) (1994)).

The dissent argued that the statute gives the FDA greater discretion than the Court suggested. See id at 173–79 (Breyer dissenting). In addition, the FDA had specifically concluded that a total ban would not promote the Act's objectives; specifically, it would produce adverse net health effects by producing severe withdrawal symptoms and creating a black market for potentially more dangerous tobacco products. 60 Fed Reg at 44398, 44405, 44413 (cited in note 31). Based on those findings, the dissent concluded that the FDA had authority to forgo a complete ban based on statutory authority to consider comparative health effects in crafting its regulations. See *Brown & Williamson*, 529 US at 177 (Breyer dissenting) ("[S]urely the agency can determine that a product is comparatively 'safe' (*not* 'dangerous') whenever it would be *less* dangerous to make the product available (subject to regulatory requirements) than suddenly to withdraw it from the market. . . . Indeed, the FDA already seems to have taken this position when permitting distribution of toxic drugs, such as poisons used for chemotherapy, that are dangerous for the user but are not deemed 'dangerous to health' in the relevant sense.").

For purposes of analyzing the Court's interpretative method, it is unnecessary to consider whether it correctly determined this precise point. More important are the implications that the Court drew from that conclusion.

[63] *Brown & Williamson*, 529 US at 143.

[64] See Federal Cigarette Labeling and Advertising Act, Pub L No 89-92, 79 Stat 282 (1965); Public Health Cigarette Smoking Act of 1969, Pub L No 91-222, 84 Stat 87; Alcohol and Drug Abuse Amendments of 1983, Pub L No 98-24, 97 Stat 175; Comprehensive Smoking Education Act, Pub L No 98-474, 98 Stat 2200 (1984); Comprehensive Smokeless Tobacco Health Education Act of 1986, Pub L No 99-252, 100 Stat 30; Alcohol, Drug Abuse, and Mental Health Administration Reorganization Act, Pub L No 102-321, § 202, 106 Stat 394 (1992).

[65] *Brown & Williamson*, 529 US at 138.

[66] Id at 139 (quoting 15 USC § 1331 (1994)).

side its jurisdiction. In particular, when passing its six post-FDCA tobacco statutes, "Congress . . . acted against the backdrop of the FDA's consistent and repeated statements that it lacked authority under the FDCA to regulate tobacco absent claims of therapeutic benefit by the manufacturer."[67] One example will suffice: In 1965, Congress enacted the Federal Cigarette Labeling and Advertising Act ("FCLAA"),[68] which required cigarette manufacturers to place warning labels on all cigarette packages.[69] In a series of hearings preceding this enactment, FDA and other administration officials repeatedly advised the relevant congressional committees that the FDA lacked jurisdiction over tobacco products under the FDCA. The FCLAA also followed several unsuccessful legislative attempts to grant the FDA such jurisdiction.[70] In light of this history, the Court reasoned that statutes such as the FCLAA had "ratified" the FDA's position, thereby expressing a legislative "intent" to preclude the exercise of "significant policymaking authority on the subject of smoking and health."[71]

Third, because the six post-FDCA statutes "created a distinct regulatory scheme to address the problem of tobacco and health," the Court concluded that the resulting scheme "preclude[d] any role for the FDA."[72] In this respect, the Court emphasized the "classic judicial task of reconciling many laws enacted over time and getting them to make sense in combination."[73] Specifically, the Court explained that a specific policy found in a later statute controls the interpretation of an earlier and more general statute, even if the earlier statute has not been amended.[74]

The Court's approach reflects deeper assumptions about the proper allocation of power in the modern administrative state. Perhaps acknowledging the unconventionality of its decision to forgo

---

[67] Id at 144.

[68] Pub L No 89-92, 79 Stat 282.

[69] Id § 4, 79 Stat 283.

[70] See *Brown & Williamson*, 529 US at 144–46; see also HR 2248, 89th Cong, 1st Sess, 1 (1965); HR 9512, 88th Cong, 1st Sess, § 3 (1963); HR 5973, 88th Cong, 1st Sess 1 (1963); S 1682, 88th Cong, 1st Sess (1963).

[71] *Brown & Williamson*, 529 US at 149.

[72] Id at 144.

[73] Id (internal quotation marks omitted) (quoting *United States v Fausto*, 484 US 439, 453 (1988)).

[74] Id at 143–44.

all consideration of the FDCA's text, the Court recognized that the "nature of the question presented" had shaped its analysis of whether Congress had "directly spoken to the precise question at issue."[75] Specifically, the Court emphasized that the FDA had invoked its broad statutory authority to "to regulate an industry consisting of a significant portion of the American economy."[76] Even if *Chevron* ordinarily instructs courts to presume that a broad or ambiguous administrative statute effects an implicit delegation of lawmaking power to the agency, the Court felt "confident that Congress could not have intended to delegate a decision of such economic and political significance to an agency in so cryptic a fashion."[77] To avoid such an extraordinary delegation, the Court credited the implications of post-FDCA tobacco legislation that (in the Court's view) disclosed "a consistent judgment" to deny the FDA power over tobacco.[78] Thus, although the Court never explicitly invoked the canon of avoidance, *Brown & Williamson*'s reasoning fits neatly within the Court's practice of aggressively narrowing administrative statutes to avoid serious nondelegation concerns. Because this approach raises serious but as yet largely unexamined legitimacy concerns, the Court's practice merits closer examination.

II. MAKING SENSE OF THE NONDELEGATION DOCTRINE

More than a decade ago, the Court explained that "[i]n recent years, our application of the nondelegation doctrine principally has been limited to the interpretation of statutory texts, and, more particularly, to giving narrow constructions to statutory delegations that otherwise might be thought to be unconstitutional."[79] This practice seeks to accommodate the important constitutional interests promoted by the nondelegation doctrine, while avoiding certain pathologies thought to arise from its direct enforcement. Because others have thoroughly examined the competing consider-

---

[75] Id at 159.

[76] Id.

[77] Id at 160.

[78] Id.

[79] *Mistretta v United States*, 488 US 361, 374 n 7 (1989).

ations that inform the nondelegation debate,[80] a brief sketch of the
problem will suffice to frame the issue.

A. THE ILLUSORY NONDELEGATION DOCTRINE

Few doctrines have perplexed the Supreme Court more than the
nondelegation doctrine. The Court has repeatedly emphasized that
(at least in theory) this doctrine bars Congress from delegating its
legislative powers to the executive or, for that matter, the judiciary.[81] It has matter-of-factly attributed that principle to the constitutional separation of powers and, more particularly, to the fact
that Article I of the Constitution vests all legislative powers in
Congress.[82] Beyond these formal considerations, moreover, Congress presumably was vested with such authority on the basis of
its singular qualities.[83] More specifically, Article I, Section 7 fil-
ters congressional lawmaking powers through the carefully structured process of bicameral passage and presentment to the Presi-

---

[80] For varying perspectives, see, for example, Kenneth Culp Davis, *Discretionary Justice*
27–51 (Louisiana State Univ Press, 1969); David Schoenbrod, *Power Without Responsibility:
How Congress Abuses the People Through Delegation* (Yale Univ Press, 1993); Peter H. Aaran-
son et al, *A Theory of Legislative Delegation*, 68 Cornell L Rev 1 (1982); Lisa Schultz Bressman, *Schecter Poultry at the Millennium: A Delegation Doctrine for the Administrative State*,
109 Yale L J 1399 (2000); David Epstein and Sharyn O'Halloran, *The Nondelegation Doctrine
and the Separation of Powers: A Political Science Approach*, 20 Cardozo L Rev 947 (1999); Jerry
L. Mashaw, *Prodelegation: Why Administrators Should Make Political Decisions*, 1 J L Econ &
Org 81 (1985); Thomas O. Sargentich, *The Delegation Debate and Competing Ideals of the
Administrative Process*, 36 Am U L Rev 419 (1987).

[81] See, for example, *Mistretta*, 488 US at 371–72 ("[W]e long have insisted that 'the
integrity and maintenance of the system of government ordained by the Constitution' mandate that Congress generally cannot delegate its legislative power to another Branch.")
(quoting *Marshall Field & Co. v Clark*, 143 US 649, 692 (1892)).

[82] US Const, Art I, § 1 ("All legislative Powers herein granted shall be vested in a Congress of the United States . . . ."); see, for example, *Loving v United States*, 517 US 748,
758 (1996) ("The fundamental precept of the delegation doctrine is that the lawmaking
function belongs to Congress, U.S. Const., Art. I, § 1, and may not be conveyed to another
branch or entity."); *Touby v United States*, 500 US 160, 164–65 (1991) ("The Constitution
provides that '[a]ll legislative Powers herein granted shall be vested in a Congress of the
United States.' U.S. Const., Art. I, §1. From this language the Court has derived the nondelegation doctrine: that Congress may not constitutionally delegate its legislative power to
another branch of Government."); *Mistretta*, 488 US at 371 ("The nondelegation doctrine is
rooted in the principle of separation of powers that underlies our system of government.").

[83] *Loving*, 517 US at 757–58 ("Article I's precise rules of representation, member qualifications, bicameralism, and voting procedure make Congress the branch most capable of
responsive and deliberative lawmaking.").

dent.[84] By dividing legislative power among three relatively independent entities, that intricate and cumbersome process serves
several crucial constitutional interests: it makes it more difficult
for factions (or, as we would put it, "interest groups") to capture
the legislative process for private advantage,[85] it promotes caution
and restrains momentary passions,[86] it gives special protection to
the residents of small states through the states' equal representation in the Senate,[87] and it generally creates a bias in favor of fil-

---

[84] US Const, Art I, § 7.

[85] See, for example, *INS v Chadha*, 462 US 919, 951 (1983) (noting that bicameralism
addressed the "fear that special interests could be favored at the expense of public needs");
Federalist 62 (Madison) in Clinton Rossiter, ed, *The Federalist Papers* 378–79 (Mentor, 1961)
("[A] senate, as a second branch of the legislative assembly, distinct from and dividing power
with the first, . . . doubles the security to the people, by requiring the concurrence of two
distinct bodies in schemes of usurpation or perfidy, where the ambition or corruption of
one, would otherwise be sufficient."); Federalist 73 (Hamilton) in Rossiter, ed, *The Federalist
Papers* at 443 (noting that the veto "establishes a salutary check upon the legislative body,
calculated to guard the community against the effects of faction, precipitancy, or of any
impulse unfriendly to the public good which may happen to influence a majority of that
body"); 2 Joseph Story, *Commentaries on the Constitution of the United States* § 882, at 348
(Boston, Hillard, Gray, 1833) ("[T]he [veto] power . . . establishes a salutary check upon
the legislative body, calculated to preserve the community against the effects of faction,
precipitancy, unconstitutional legislation, and temporary excitements, as well as political
hostility.") (citation omitted); see also Richard J. Pierce, Jr., *The Role of the Judiciary in
Implementing an Agency Theory of Government*, 64 NYU L Rev 1239, 1249 (1989) ("The
Framers created two antidotes to factionalism in Congress: bicameralism and presentment.
Bicameralism forces a potential faction to capture both Houses of Congress simultaneously.
Presentment gives the president—the politically accountable entity least susceptible to cap-
ture by factions—voice in the legislative process.").

[86] *Chadha*, 461 US at 951 ("The division of the Congress into two bodies assures that
the legislative power would be exercised only after opportunity for full study and debate
in separate settings."); *The Pocket Veto Cases*, 279 US 655, 678 (1929) (arguing that it is an
"essential . . . part of the constitutional provisions, guarding against ill-considered and
unwise legislation, that the President, on his part, should have the full time allowed him
for determining whether he should approve or disapprove a bill, and if disapproved, for
adequately formulating the objections that should be considered by Congress"). The calm-
ing influence of bicameralism is nicely captured in an analogy attributed to George
Washington:

> There is a tradition that, on his return from France, Jefferson called Washing-
> ton to account at the breakfast-table for having agreed to a second chamber.
> 'Why,' asked Washington, 'did you pour that coffee into your saucer?' 'To cool
> it,' quoth Jefferson. 'Even so,' said Washington, 'we pour legislation into the sena-
> torial saucer to cool it.'

Max Farrand, ed, 3 *The Records of the Federal Convention of 1787*, at 21 (Yale Univ Press,
rev ed 1966).

[87] See, for example, *Garcia v San Antonio Metropolitan Transit Authority*, 469 US 528, 551–
52 (1985) (discussing the Senate's essential role in protecting interests of states); Manning,
101 Colum L Rev at 75–77 (cited in note 24); Sunstein, 67 U Chi L Rev at 319 (cited in
note 5).

tering out bad laws by raising the decision costs of passing any law.[88] The nondelegation doctrine protects those interests by forcing specific policies through the process of bicameralism and presentment, rather than permitting agency lawmaking on the cheap.

Despite these apparent virtues, the nondelegation doctrine has, with the exception of one brief moment, never gained traction with the Court—at least not when invoked to invalidate acts of Congress.[89] Under black-letter law, the Court will uphold any organic statute that supplies an "intelligible principle" to channel agency discretion.[90] Virtually anything, moreover, counts as an intelligible

---

[88] The bias in favor of blocking legislation did not go unnoticed during the debates over the Constitution's adoption. See, for example, Federalist 62 (Madison) in Rossiter, ed, *The Federalist Papers* at 378 (cited in note 85) (acknowledging that "this complicated check on legislation may in some instances be injurious as well as beneficial"); Federalist 73 (Hamilton) in Rossiter, ed, *The Federalist Papers* at 443 (noting that "the power of preventing bad laws includes that of preventing good ones"). And both the costs and benefits associated with a burdensome legislative process were frankly acknowledged in these debates. See, for example, Federalist 62 (Madison) in Rossiter, ed, *The Federalist Papers* at 378 (arguing that "the facility and excess of law-making seem to be the diseases to which our governments are most liable"); Federalist 73 (Hamilton) in Rossiter, ed, *The Federalist Papers* at 443 ("The injury which may possibly be done by defeating a few good laws will be amply compensated by the advantage of preventing a number of bad ones.").

[89] The Court only twice invalidated statutes on nondelegation grounds. *ALA Schechter Poultry Corp. v United States*, 295 US 495 (1935); *Panama Refining Co. v Ryan*, 293 US 388 (1935).

[90] *J.W. Hampton, Jr., & Co. v United States*, 276 US 394, 409 (1928) (articulating the "intelligible principle" test). The Court apparently believes that when a statute sets down an intelligible principle, the agency can be thought of as implementing legislative directions, rather than exercising legislative authority. See, for example, *Loving*, 517 US at 770 ("The intelligible-principle rule seeks to enforce the understanding that Congress may not delegate the power to make laws and so may delegate no more than the authority to make policies and rules that implement its statutes."); *Yakus v United States*, 321 US 414, 426 (1944) ("Only if we could say that there is an absence of standards for the guidance of the Administrator's action, so that it would be impossible in a proper proceeding to ascertain whether the will of Congress has been obeyed, would we be justified in overriding its choice of means for effecting its declared purpose."); *Marshall Field & Co.*, 143 US at 694 ("'The true distinction . . . is between the delegation of power to make the law, which necessarily involves a discretion as to what it shall be, and conferring authority or discretion as to its execution, to be exercised under and in pursuance of the law.'") (quoting *Cincinnati, Wilmington & Zanesville R. Co. v Commissioners*, 1 Ohio St 77, 88–89 (1852)). Under that view, the agency is engaged in law "execution," rather than receiving delegated legislative authority. See *Loving*, 517 US at 777 (Scalia concurring in part and concurring in the judgment) ("What Congress does is to assign responsibilities to the Executive; and when the Executive undertakes those assigned responsibilities it acts, not as the 'delegate' of Congress, but as the agent of the People. At some point the responsibilities assigned can become so extensive and so unconstrained that Congress has in effect delegated its legislative power; but until that point of excess is reached there exists, not a 'lawful' delegation, but no delegation at all.").

principle.[91] Two considerations appear to explain much of this attitude.[92]

First, the Court has suggested that if government is to function, Congress must have the power to delegate significant policy discretion to the law's executors.[93] And the appropriate limits of such delegation "must be fixed according to common sense and the inherent necessities of . . . governmental co-ordination."[94] Starting from that premise, the Court's hands-off approach reflects "a practical understanding that in our increasingly complex society, replete with ever changing and more technical problems, Congress simply cannot do its job absent an ability to delegate power under broad general directives."[95]

Second, the Court's reluctance to invalidate statutes on the basis of the nondelegation doctrine reflects serious concerns about its own competence to draw appropriate lines between permissible and impermissible delegations. All legislation necessarily leaves some measure of policy-making discretion to those who implement it.[96] Accordingly, enforcement of the nondelegation doctrine nec-

---

[91] See, for example, *Lichter v United States*, 334 US 742, 785–86 (1948) (sustaining agency authority to recoup "excessive profits" on war contracts); *American Power & Light Co. v SEC*, 329 US 90, 105 (1946) (SEC may reject corporate reorganizations that are not "fair and equitable"); *NBC v United States*, 319 US 190, 225–26 (1943) (Congress may grant FCC power to allocate broadcasting licenses in "the public interest, convenience, and necessity").

[92] See Richard B. Stewart, *Beyond Delegation Doctrine*, 36 Am U L Rev 323, 324 (1987) (discussing reasons for nonenforcement of the nondelegation doctrine).

[93] See, for example, *United States v Shreveport Grain & Elevator Co.*, 277 US 77, 85 (1932) (approving "directions to those charged with the administration of the act to make supplementary rules and regulations allowing reasonable variations, tolerances, and exemptions, which, because of their variety and need of detailed statement, it was impracticable for Congress to prescribe"); *Union Bridge Co. v United States*, 204 US 364, 387 (1907) ("[I]t is not too much to say that a denial to Congress of the right, under the Constitution, to delegate the power to determine some fact or the state of things upon which the enforcement of its enactment depends, would be 'to stop the wheels of government' and bring about confusion, if not paralysis, in the conduct of the public business.").

[94] *J.W. Hampton, Jr. & Co.*, 276 US at 406.

[95] *Mistretta*, 488 US at 372; see also, for example, *American Power & Light Co.*, 329 US at 105 ("The judicial approval accorded these 'broad' standards for administrative action is a reflection of the necessities of modern legislation in dealing with complex economic and social problems."); *Sunshine Anthracite Coal Co. v Adkins*, 310 US 381, 398 (1940) ("Delegation by Congress has long been recognized as necessary in order that the exertion of legislative power does not become a futility.").

[96] See *Mistretta*, 488 US at 415 (Scalia dissenting) (arguing "that no statute can be entirely precise, and that some judgments, even some judgments involving policy considerations, must be left to the officers executing the law and to the judges applying it"). The inevitability of interpretive discretion is not a new idea. See, for example, 1 William Blackstone,

essarily reduces to the question whether a statute confers too much discretion. Without a reliable metric (other than an I-know-it-when-I-see-it test), the Court has long doubted its capacity to make principled judgments about such questions of degree.[97] Consequently, even if the nondelegation doctrine does represent a fundamental premise of the constitutional structure, a growing judicial consensus assumes that "it is not an element readily enforceable by the courts,"[98] at least not by means of direct judicial invalidation of administrative statutes.

B. THE NONDELEGATION DOCTRINE AS A CANON OF AVOIDANCE

Despite the Court's apparent refusal to enforce the nondelegation doctrine directly, cases such as *Brown & Williamson* illustrate the Court's modern strategy of using the canon of avoidance to promote nondelegation interests.[99] Where a statute is broad enough to raise serious concerns under the nondelegation doc-

---

Commentaries on the Laws of England *61 (noting that "in laws all cases cannot be foreseen and expressed"); Federalist 37 (Madison) in Rossiter, ed, *The Federalist Papers* at 229 (cited in note 85) ("[I]t must happen that however accurately the objects may be discriminated in themselves, and however accurately the discrimination may be considered, the definition of them may be rendered inaccurate by the inaccuracy of the terms in which it is delivered.").

[97] As Chief Justice Marshall once put it:

> The difference between the departments undoubtedly is, that the legislature makes, the executive executes, and the judiciary construes the law; but the maker of the law may commit something to the discretion of the other departments, and the precise boundary of this power is a subject of delicate and difficult inquiry, into which a court will not enter unnecessarily.

Wayman v Southard, 23 US 1, 46 (1825). For further discussion of this point, see, for example, Manning, 97 Colum L Rev at 727 (cited in note 21); Sunstein, 67 U Chi L Rev at 326–28 (cited in note 5).

[98] *Mistretta*, 488 US at 415 (Scalia dissenting); see also *FPC v New England Power Co.*, 415 US 345, 352–54 (1974) (Marshall concurring) (noting that the Court has "virtually abandoned" nondelegation doctrine); Sunstein, 67 U Chi L Rev at 326–28 (cited in note 5). The Court itself recently suggested that courts cannot successfully draw the line between lawmaking and law implementation:

> The Government's distinction between "making" law and merely "enforcing" it, between "policymaking" and mere "implementation," is an interesting one. It is perhaps not meant to be the same as, but it is surely reminiscent of, the line that separates proper congressional conferral of Executive power from unconstitutional delegation of legislative authority for federal separation-of-powers purposes. This Court has not been notably successful in describing the latter line; indeed, some think we have abandoned the effort to do so.

Printz v United States, 521 US 898, 927 (1997) (citations omitted).

[99] For a description of this practice, see Cass R. Sunstein, *Interpreting Statutes in the Regulatory State*, 103 Harv L Rev 405, 470 (1989).

trine, the Court simply cuts it back to acceptable bounds.[100] This strategy, it is said, offers judges "a finer weapon" than *Marbury*-style judicial review.[101] If judges cannot draw principled lines between permissible and excessive delegations, they *can* interpret statutes.[102] And because judges routinely construe statutes to avoid grave constitutional doubts in other contexts,[103] they can rely on the same approach to avoid serious questions under the nondelegation doctrine.[104] As a canon of construction, the nondelegation doctrine has proven attractive to many who doubt its efficacy as a basis for judicial review.[105]

---

[100] I would distinguish this practice from cases in which the Court simply concludes that the text of an administrative statute, understood in context, has a specialized connotation that is narrower than the everyday meaning of the terms. For instance, sometimes a statutory phrase seems exceedingly broad on its face, but draws refinement from established traditions or practices associated with the phrase or subject in question. See, for example, *Fahey v Mallonee*, 332 US 245, 250 (1947) (reading authority to promulgate regulations for appointing conservators for savings and loan associations in light of "well-defined practices for the appointment of conservators"); *American Power & Light Co.*, 329 US at 104 (statute prohibiting police corporate practices that "unduly or unnecessarily complicate the structure" of a public utility or "unfairly or inequitably distribute voting power among [its] security holders" are intelligible to those "familiar with corporate realities"); *Federal Radio Comm'n v Nelson Bros Bond & Mortgage Co.*, 289 US 266, 285 (1933) (narrowing "public convenience, interest or necessity" in light of "its context [and] the nature of radio transmission and reception"). Often, this strategy involves the conventional idea that when Congress uses a term of art, "it presumably knows and adopts the cluster of ideas that were attached to each borrowed word in the body of learning from which it was taken." *Morissette v United States*, 342 US 246, 263 (1952). And such cases simply reflect the reality that statutes must be interpreted in context. See *Deal v United States*, 508 US 129, 132 (1993) (applying the "fundamental principle of statutory construction . . . that the meaning of a word cannot be determined in isolation, but must be drawn from the context in which it is used"). Such decisions do not involve the alteration of statutory meaning to avoid a serious question under the nondelegation doctrine.

[101] Paul Gewirtz, *The Courts, Congress, and Executive Policy-Making: Notes on Three Doctrines*, 40 L & Contemp Probs, Summer 1976, at 46, 72.

[102] Id.

[103] See, for example, *Jean v Nelson*, 472 US 846, 854 (1985); *NLRB v Catholic Bishop*, 440 US 490, 499–501 (1979); *Int'l Ass'n of Machinists v Street*, 367 US 740, 749 (1961). Professor Sunstein has suggested that, in general, applying the canon of avoidance to administrative statutes serves a special set of nondelegation interests; it compels Congress to speak explicitly when it wishes to push against constitutional boundaries. See Sunstein, 67 U Chi L Rev at 331–32 (cited in note 5). This paper does not address that broad claim as it relates to the avoidance of constitutional questions arising under provisions such as the First Amendment, which do not speak directly to the legislative process prescribed by Article I. Rather, it considers only those cases in which the Court invokes the avoidance canon to vindicate nondelegation concerns as such.

[104] Gewirtz, 40 L & Contemp Probs at 73–75 (cited in note 101).

[105] See, for example, Richard B. Stewart, *The Reformation of American Administrative Law*, 88 Harv L Rev 1669, 1697 (1975); Cass R. Sunstein, 103 Harv L Rev at 470 (cited in note 99).

In general, applying the canon of avoidance entails excluding a given statutory application because that application raises a serious question under a constitutional provision such as the First Amendment. This means that the Court's interpretation is driven by the underlying substantive protection (e.g., do not construe the NLRA to ban peaceful leafleting). But the underlying issue is far different in the nondelegation context. Here, the Court's task is simply to narrow what might otherwise be constitutionally excessive generality. To achieve that goal, the Court typically posits a plausible background purpose to restrict otherwise broad and unqualified statutory language. *Industrial Union Department, AFL-CIO v American Petroleum Institute*,[106] better known as the *Benzene* case, is perhaps the most famous illustration of this approach. Section 6(b)(5) of the Occupational Safety and Health Act ("the OSH Act") prescribed very open-ended regulatory criteria for "toxic materials or harmful physical agents."[107] In particular, Section 6(b)(5) required the Secretary of Labor to "set the standard which most adequately assures, to the extent feasible, . . . that no employee will suffer material impairment of health or functional capacity even if such employee has regular exposure to the hazard."[108] Benzene was a nonthreshold toxic material; scientific methods could identify no safe exposure level. In those circumstances, the Secretary of Labor interpreted Section 6(b)(5) to require the lowest level of benzene exposure that was not only technologically feasible but also economically feasible (in the sense that it would not threaten the financial viability of benzene-related industries).[109]

In an opinion concurring in the judgment, then-Justice Rehnquist contended that the phrase "to the extent feasible" provided no intelligible principle to guide the Secretary's discretion; it gave the Secretary "no indication where on the continuum of relative safety he should draw his line."[110] While agreeing that the OSH Act raised serious nondelegation concerns, Justice Stevens's plurality opinion invoked the canon of avoidance to narrow the Act to a constitutionally acceptable breadth.[111] Emphasizing that the Act

---

[106] 448 US 607 (1980).

[107] 29 USC § 655(b)(5).

[108] Id.

[109] *American Petroleum Institute*, 448 US at 637.

[110] Id at 675 (Rehnquist concurring in the judgment).

[111] Id at 642–46 (plurality opinion).

would "give the Secretary unprecedented power over American industry" if "limited only by the constraint of feasibility," the plurality imposed a threshold requirement that the Secretary find a "significant risk" to employee health before adopting a regulation.[112] Although the OSH Act itself nowhere explicitly required a "significant risk" element, the plurality derived that requirement largely from two sources. First, Section 3(8) of the Act generally defined "occupational safety and health standard" to mean measures "reasonably necessary or appropriate to provide safe or healthful employment and places of employment."[113] Focusing on the word "safe" in Section 3(8), the plurality reasoned that "a workplace can hardly be considered 'unsafe' unless it threatens the workers with a significant risk of harm."[114] The Court then read the Act's general definition of "occupational safety and health standard" into the more specific criteria prescribed by Section 6(b)(5) for standards governing toxic materials.[115] In addition, the plurality cited legislative history that (in its view) suggested a legislative purpose to eliminate only "significant" risks of harm.[116] The plurality then narrowed Section 6(b)(5)'s broad instructions to cover only the particular evil that the Act was said to address.

As others have argued, the plurality's imposition of a "significant risk" requirement seems to rewrite the OSH Act.[117] It surely does not reflect its most natural reading under established rules of construction. Because the phrase "safe or healthful" (as used in Section 3(8)) is nowhere defined, its *generally applicable* terms should

---

[112] Id at 645.

[113] 29 USC § 652(8).

[114] *American Petroleum Institute*, 448 US at 642 (plurality opinion).

[115] Id at 642–43.

[116] Id at 646–52.

[117] See, for example, Jerry L. Mashaw, *As If Republican Interpretation*, 97 Yale L J 1685, 1691 (1989) ("One common understanding of the Supreme Court's judgment in that case . . . is that the Court rewrote the Occupational Safety and Health Act in order to avoid affirming what it perceived to be an unreasonably costly health regulation."); Martin Shapiro, *Administrative Discretion: The Next Stage*, 92 Yale L J 1487, 1507 (1992) (noting that courts "may strike their own balance, declaring it the legislature's true intent," and that the *Benzene* plurality "read a requirement of 'significant risk' into the statute"); Richard B. Stewart, *Regulatory Jurisprudence: Canons Redux*, 79 Calif L Rev 807, 817–18 (1991) (noting the oddity of precluding an agency "from regulating a risk a court might deem not 'significant'—where the statute does not contain any requirement of 'significance' and, indeed, where it provides that toxic substance standards must ensure 'to the extent feasible . . . that no employee will suffer material impairment of health or functional capacity'") (book review of Cass R. Sunstein, *After the Rights Revolution* (Harvard Univ Press, 1990)).

have drawn content from the Section 6(b)(5)'s *specific* requirement that standards for toxins ensure "to the extent feasible . . . that no employee will suffer material impairment of health or functional capacity."[118] That is to say, Section 6(b)(5) specifies what counts as "safe or healthful" where toxins are concerned. Further, as the separate opinions in *Benzene* clearly establish, the legislative history did not speak with the clarity of purpose that the plurality suggests.[119] In light of these considerations, the Court's strategy must be understood as a decision to inject the OSH Act with a plausible, if not legislatively mandated, purpose that would civilize an otherwise " 'sweeping delegation of legislative power' that . . . might be unconstitutional."[120]

Although the Court has now identified this method as its preferred (if not exclusive) strategy for addressing nondelegation concerns,[121] it has failed to confront the question whether *judicial* narrowing of self-conscious statutory breadth reflects a legitimate means to enforce a doctrine that is designed to ensure *legislative* responsibility for making important policy choices. The answer to that question casts important light on *Brown & Williamson*.

---

[118] As Justice Marshall's dissenting opinion put it:

> The plurality's interpretation renders utterly superfluous the first sentence of § 655(b)(5), which . . . requires the Secretary to set the standard "which most adequately assures . . . that no employee suffer material impairment of health." . . . By so doing, the plurality makes the text for standards regulating toxic substances and harmful physical agents substantially identical to the test for standards generally—plainly the opposite of what Congress intended. And it is an odd canon of construction that would insert in a vague and general definitional clause a threshold requirement that overcomes the specific language placed in a standard-setting provision.

American Petroleum Institute, 448 US at 709 (Marshall dissenting).

[119] See *American Petroleum Institute*, 448 US at 676–82 (Rehnquist concurring in the judgment) (arguing that the "somewhat cryptic legislative history" does not impose a significant risk requirement or impose meaningful limits on the "feasibility" requirement); id at 710–11 (Marshall dissenting) (arguing that the plurality relied on "isolated statements in the legislative history," which in context do not support the requirement of a threshold finding of significant risk).

[120] Id at 646 (plurality) (citation omitted).

[121] See *Mistretta*, 488 US at 374 n 7. For other applications of this approach, see, for example, *National Cable Television Ass'n v FCC*, 415 US 336, 341–42 (1974) (reading the Independent Offices Appropriations Act "narrowly to avoid constitutional problems" raised by agency's open-ended authority to impose "fees" on regulated parties; holding that "fee" must reflect benefit to regulated party); *FPC v New England Power Co.*, 415 US 345 (same); *National Ass'n of Broadcasters v Copyright Royalty Tribunal*, 675 F2d 367, 376 n 12 (DC Cir 1982) (finding an intelligible principle to guide the tribunal in disbursing cable royalty fees in "specific statements in the legislative history and in the general philosophy of the Act itself").

C. THE LEGISLATIVE PROCESS IMPLICATIONS
   OF NARROW CONSTRUCTION

Because the nondelegation doctrine seeks to ensure that binding legislative commands are the product of the legislative process mandated by Article I, the narrow construction strategy is self-defeating unless the Court can somehow justify its creative interpretations as a faithful reflection of legislative, rather than judicial, commands. Otherwise, the narrow construction strategy does not place responsibility with Congress (as the nondelegation principle instructs), but merely substitutes judicial discretion for agency discretion in defining the statute's meaning. Until recently, this possibility raised little concern. Under the reasoning of decisions such as *Church of the Holy Trinity v United States*,[122] courts did not intrude upon legislative supremacy when they narrowed seemingly overbroad language to reflect the legislation's apparent background purpose.[123] The reason was this: Congress legislates against constraints of limited time, resources, and foresight; it must rely on imperfect language to express its intentions. Because statutes will therefore be overinclusive and underinclusive in some circumstances, a court was thought to promote, rather than disserve, legislative supremacy when it conformed an imperfect statutory text to its background purposes.[124] To the extent that this interpretive technique was otherwise legitimate, it assuredly made sense for the judiciary to invoke that method to prevent Congress from pressing "into dangerous constitutional thickets."[125]

Emphasizing the insights of public choice theory,[126] however,

---

[122] 143 US 457 (1892); see also, for example, *California Federal Savs & Loan Ass'n v Guerra*, 479 US 272, 284 (1987); *United Steelworkers v Weber*, 443 US 193, 202 (1979); *Train v Colorado Public Interest Research Group*, 426 US 1, 10 (1976).

[123] I have discussed *Holy Trinity*'s foundations in greater detail elsewhere. See Manning, 101 Colum L Rev at 10–15 (cited in note 24).

[124] In *Holy Trinity*, for example, Congress had broadly prohibited the importation of "labor or service of any kind." See Alien Contract Labor Act of 1885, ch 164, § 1, 23 Stat 332, 332. But the title of the act, its legislative history, and the circumstances surrounding its enactment suggested that Congress had done so for the apparent purpose of preventing "the influx of this cheap, unskilled labor." *Holy Trinity*, 143 US at 465. In light of this background purpose, the Court felt justified in clipping back the Act's broad prohibition to exclude professionals ("brain toilers") from its sweep. Id at 464; see also id at 459 (noting that judicial efforts to conform a broad text to its purpose are "not the substitution of the will of the judge for that of the legislator").

[125] *Public Citizen v U.S. Dep't of Justice*, 491 US 440, 466 (1989).

[126] Public choice theory is of course a branch of political science that uses the insights of economics and game theory to analyze the processes of governmental decision making.

modern textualism has in recent years challenged the legitimacy of this method of clipping back otherwise unqualified statutory texts.[127] For several related reasons, textualists believe that the legislative process is too complex and messy to permit reliable discernment of legislation's unexpressed purposes in the manner suggested by *Holy Trinity*:[128] First, statutes are often the product of compromise among competing interest groups,[129] and the statutory text may reflect a compromise that falls short of or exceeds the background purpose that apparently inspired it.[130] Accordingly, courts must enforce not a statute's background purposes but the outcomes reflected in the language adopted. Second, building on Arrovian social choice theory,[131] textualists argue that a statute's ultimate content may in fact reflect procedural factors, such as the sequence of alternatives presented (agenda manipulation) and the practice of strategic voting (logrolling).[132] For that reason, it is dif-

See Daniel A. Farber and Philip P. Frickey, *Law and Public Choice: A Critical Introduction* 21–33, 47–62 (Univ of Chicago Press, 1990).

[127] As discussed below, this challenge bears directly on the legitimacy of narrowing administrative statutes to avoid nondelegation concerns. See text accompanying notes 136–46.

[128] Because Judge Easterbrook has been the most consistent exponent of this position, much of the following discussion is drawn from his writings.

[129] Specifically, interest-group theory suggests that interest groups purchase legislation through "campaign contributions, votes, implicit promises of future favors, and sometimes outright bribes." William M. Landes and Richard A. Posner, *The Independent Judiciary in an Interest-Group Perspective*, 18 J L & Econ 875, 877 (1975).

[130] See, for example, Frank H. Easterbrook, *Foreword: The Court and the Economic System*, 98 Harv L Rev 4, 46 (1984) (noting that in such instances, "[w]hat Congress wanted was the compromise, not the objectives of the contending interests"). For helpful descriptions of the public choice critique of strong purposivism, see William N. Eskridge, Jr. and Philip P. Frickey, *Statutory Interpretation as Practical Reasoning*, 42 Stan L Rev 321, 335 (1990) (explaining public choice theory's contention "when a court uses purposivist analysis to elaborate a statute, it may actually undo a deliberate and precisely calculated deal worked out in the legislative process"); Philip P. Frickey, *From the Big Heat to the Big Sleep: The Revival of Theory in Statutory Interpretation*, 77 Minn L Rev 241, 251 (1992) (discussing the claim that judges could "reach the wrong results" by "promoting a public policy purpose gleaned from the statute rather than following the true lines of legislative compromise"); Manning, 101 Colum L Rev at 18 (cited in note 24).

[131] See generally Kenneth J. Arrow, *Social Choice and Individual Values* (Yale Univ Press, 2d ed 1963).

[132] See Frank H. Easterbrook, *Statutes' Domains*, 50 U Chi L Rev 533, 547–48 (1983):

Although legislators have individual lists of desires, priorities, and preferences, it turns out to be difficult, sometimes impossible, to aggregate these lists into a coherent collective choice. Every system of voting has flaws. The one used by legislatures is particularly dependent on the order in which decisions are made. Legislatures customarily consider proposals one at a time and then vote them up or down. This method disregards third or fourth options and the intensity with which legislators prefer one option over another. Additional options can be consid-

ficult (if not impossible) to know why a statute took the particular shape that it did—and thus artificial to alter the statute's clear text to promote the "true" legislative purpose.[133] Third, to the extent that (contrary to public choice theory) legislation reflects an accessible and coherent purpose, the breadth of a statute itself says something important about that purpose. Because Congress can (and does) legislate alternatively through open-ended standards or specific rules, shifting a statute's level of generality to conform to its background purpose dishonors an apparent congressional choice to legislate in broader (or narrower) terms.[134]

Although the Court has not fully embraced textualism,[135] it has assimilated certain important textualist assumptions that cast doubt on its nondelegation strategy. The Court has thus emphasized that

> Congress may be unanimous in its intent to stamp out some vague social or economic evil; however, because its Members

ered only in sequence, and this makes the order of decision vital. It is fairly easy to show that someone with control of the agenda can manipulate the choice so that the legislature adopts proposals that only a minority support. The existence of agenda control makes it impossible for a court—even one that knows each legislator's complete table of preferences—to say what the whole body would have done with a proposal it did not consider in fact.

See also id at 548 ("[W]hen logrolling is at work the legislative process is submerged and courts lose the information they need to divine the body's design."); Kenneth A. Shepsle, *Congress Is a 'They,' Not an 'It': Legislative Intent as Oxymoron*, 12 Intl Rev L & Econ 239, 244 (1992) ("Many policies, in principle, can topple an existing status quo. That some are more likely than others to actually do so is dependent on idiosyncratic, structural, procedural, and strategic factors, which are at best tenuously related to normative principles embraced by democratic theorists and philosophers.").

[133] In other words, if one accepts the premises of public choice theory, the very notion "that statutes have purposes or embody policies becomes quite problematic, since the content of the statute simply reflects the haphazard effect of strategic behavior and procedural rules." Farber and Frickey, *Law & Public Choice* at 41 (cited in note 126) (critically discussing the implications of Arrovian public choice theory).

[134] As Judge Easterbrook has explained, "[s]ometimes Congress specifies values or ends, things for the executive and judicial branches to achieve, but often it specifies means, creating loopholes but greater certainty." Frank H. Easterbrook, *Text, Structure, and History in Statutory Interpretation*, 17 Harv J L & Pub Pol 61, 68 (1994). Relying on "an imputed spirit to convert one approach into another dishonors the legislative choice as expressly as refusing to follow the law." Id.

[135] See Michael C. Dorf, *Foreword: The Limits of Socratic Deliberation*, 112 Harv L Rev 4, 6 (1998) (describing the Court's eclectic approach to statutory interpretation). For example, the modern Court sometimes engages in strongly purposive interpretation. See *Clinton v New York*, 524 US 417, 428–29 (1998) (broadening an expedited review provision because the literal meaning undermined the statutory purpose to provide "a prompt and authoritative judicial determination of the constitutionality of the [Line Item Veto] Act"); *Lewis v United States*, 523 US 155, 160 (1998) (refusing to enforce a statute's conventional meaning when "a literal reading of the words . . . would dramatically separate the statute from its intended purpose").

> may differ sharply on the means for effectuating that intent,
> the final language of the legislation may reflect hard-fought
> compromises. Invocation of the "plain purpose" of legislation
> at the expense of the terms of the statute itself takes no account
> of the processes of compromise . . . .[136]

This premise has been a recurring theme in many recent cases.[137] Perhaps more important, it has led the Court to conclude that, for unknowable reasons, Congress often adopts statutory texts that transcend the purpose that (apparently) inspired their enactment. Such breadth is a legislative signal that warrants judicial respect. Thus, the Court recently emphasized that "statutory prohibitions often go beyond the principal evil to cover reasonably comparable evils, and it is ultimately the provisions of our laws rather than the principal concerns of our legislators by which we are governed."[138] In another recent case, the Court made clear that "it is not, and cannot be, our practice to restrict the unqualified language of a statute to the particular evil that Congress was trying to remedy— even assuming that it is possible to identify that evil from something other than the text of the statute itself."[139] Statutory breadth

---

[136] Bd. of Governors of the Federal Reserve Bd. v Dimension Finance Corp., 474 US 361, 372 (1986).

[137] See, for example, MCI Telecommunications Corp. v FCC, 512 US 218, 231 (1994) (Scalia) (noting that judges "are bound, not only by the ultimate purposes Congress has selected, but by the means it has deemed appropriate, and prescribed, for the pursuit of those purposes") (Scalia); Landgraf v USI Film Products, Inc., 511 US 244, 286 (1993) (Stevens) ("Statutes are seldom crafted to pursue a single goal, and compromises necessary to their enactment may require adopting means other than those that would most effectively pursue the main goal."); West Virginia Univ. Hosps v Casey, 499 US 83, 98–99 (1990) (Scalia) ("The best evidence of . . . purpose is the statutory text adopted by both Houses of Congress and submitted to the President."); Pension Benefit Guaranty Corp. v LTV Corp., 496 US 633, 646–47 (1990) (Blackmun) ("'[N]o legislation pursues its purposes at all costs. Deciding what competing values will or will not be sacrificed to the achievement of a particular objective is the very essence of legislative choice—and it frustrates rather than effectuates legislative intent simplistically to assume that whatever furthers the statute's primary objective must be the law.'") (quoting Rodriguez v United States, 480 US 522, 526 (1987) (per curiam)).

[138] Oncale v Sundowner Offshore Servs, Inc., 523 US 75, 79 (1998).

[139] Brogan v United States, 522 US 398, 403 (1998). In Brogan, the Court refused to narrow 18 USC § 1001, which prescribes criminal penalties for any person who "knowingly and willfully . . . makes any false, fictitious or fraudulent statements or representations" concerning "any matter within the jurisdiction" of a federal agency. The courts of appeals had almost uniformly held that § 1001 incorporated an implied exception for the so-called "exculpatory no"—that is, falsely replying "no" to a federal investigator's question about culpability. Brogan, 522 US at 401 (collecting cases). Brogan defended that position by arguing that § 1001's purpose was to prevent the "perversion" of the governmental functions and that his simple denial of guilt did not produce that mischief. Although the Court had previously described § 1001's purpose in precisely such terms in United States v Gilliland, 312 US 86, 93 (1941), the majority in Brogan perceived "no inconsistency whatsoever between

may mean that the legislative majority wished to leave the statute's precise application to future resolution, that contending forces could not agree on a more precise expression of policy, or that legislators simply did not foresee all the implications of the text they adopted. Without knowing why Congress spoke in broad terms, the Court must accept that "the reach of a statute often exceeds the precise evil to be eliminated."[140] And textual open-endedness must be understood not as the likely reflection of un-anticipated overbreadth (as in *Holy Trinity*), but rather as the presumed exercise of legislative choice.[141]

Such principles have particular force in the context of administrative statutes. As discussed, the Court accepts broad delegations largely because Congress cannot always foresee and provide for a statute's detailed applications.[142] *Chevron* reflects precisely this assumption.[143] The *Chevron* Court thus explained that Congress might choose to enact an open-ended administrative statute for a host of reasons that are unknowable to a reviewing court:

> Perhaps [Congress] consciously desired the [agency] to strike the [specific policy] balance . . . , thinking that those with great expertise and charged with responsibility for administering the provision would be in a better position to do so; perhaps it simply did not consider the question at this level; and perhaps Congress was unable to forge a coalition on either side of the question, and those on each side decided to take their chances with the scheme devised by the agency. For judicial purposes, it matters not which of these occurred.[144]

If that assumption is correct, a reviewing court risks unsettling a legislative choice to leave a problem for another day when it imposes upon a statute determinacy that Congress itself did not sup-

---

the proposition that Congress intended to protect the authorized functions of governmental departments . . . from perversion . . . and the proposition that the statute forbids all the deceptive practices described." *Brogan*, 522 US at 403–04 (quotation marks omitted).

[140] Id; see also Sunstein, 47 Duke L J at 1044–46 (cited in note 28) (discussing the implications of *Brogan* and *Oncale* for the meaning of the FDCA).

[141] See *Pennsylvania Dep't of Corrections v Yeskey*, 524 US 206, 212 (1998); see also, for example, *NOW, Inc. v Scheidler*, 510 US 249, 262 (1994) (distinguishing between ambiguity and breadth); *United States v Monsanto*, 491 US 600, 609 (1989) (same); *Sedima, SPRL v Imrex Co.*, 473 US 479, 499 (1985) (same).

[142] See text accompanying notes 93–95.

[143] *Chevron USA, Inc. v NRDC, Inc.*, 467 US 837 (1984).

[144] Id at 865.

ply.[145] Especially in the administrative context (where constitutional presumptions are said to favor agency rather than judicial resolution of indeterminacy),[146] a court must respect a statute's lack of specificity, just as it must respect a statute's specificity when Congress has spoken clearly. Accordingly, when the Court narrows a broad administrative statute to reflect an unenacted purpose, as in *Benzene* (or, as we shall see, *Brown & Williamson*), its own precedents suggest that it is disturbing the very choice or compromise that the legislative process has produced.

To conclude that narrow construction contradicts legislative supremacy does not of course answer the separate question whether such a strategy reflects a legitimate means of avoiding serious nondelegation questions. As a general matter, the modern canon of avoidance instructs courts to interpret statutes to avoid serious constitutional questions if such an interpretation is "fairly possible."[147] Although this canon is increasingly controversial, its standard justification is relatively straightforward.[148] In the interests of majoritarian democracy and legislative supremacy, federal courts must refrain from needlessly exercising their *Marbury* power to

---

[145] For an excellent discussion of the premise that many administrative statutes effectively grant agencies common law powers to adapt broadly articulated policies to unforeseen circumstances, see Sunstein, 47 Duke L J at 1019 (cited in note 28).

[146] A constitutional preference for more accountable decision making is of course the standard explanation of *Chevron* deference. See, for example, Thomas W. Merrill, *Judicial Deference to Executive Precedent*, 101 Yale L J 969, 978 (1992) ("In order to make deference a general default rule, the Court had to come up with some *universal* reason why administrative interpretations should be preferred to the judgments of Article III courts. Democratic theory supplied the justification; agency decisionmaking is always more democratic than judicial decisionmaking because all agencies are accountable (to some degree) to the President, and the President is elected by the people."); Pierce, 64 NYU L Rev at 1256 (cited in note 85) (*Chevron*'s reasoning reflects "an effort to reconcile the administrative state with principles of democracy").

[147] *Crowell v Benson*, 285 US 22, 62 (1932) ("When the validity of an act of the Congress is drawn in question, and even if a serious doubt of constitutionality is raised, it is a cardinal principle that this Court will first ascertain whether a construction of the statute is fairly possible by which the question may be avoided."). Under classical avoidance doctrine, courts were to construe statutes, if possible, to avoid a conclusion of unconstitutionality. See John C. Nagle, *Delaware & Hudson Revisited*, 72 Notre Dame L Rev 1495, 1498–1504 (1997) (describing classical avoidance). The modern canon, in contrast, focuses on interpretations that "would raise serious constitutional problems." *Edward J. DeBartolo Corp. v Florida Gulf Coast Bldg & Constr. Trades Council*, 485 US 568, 575 (1988). This paper uses "the canon of avoidance" or "the avoidance canon" throughout to refer to the modern canon.

[148] The following points are outlined in Henry J. Friendly, *Benchmarks* 211 (Univ of Chicago Press, 1967).

hold statutes unconstitutional.[149] This means that courts should never invalidate a statute if a plausible alternative interpretation would sustain the law.[150] And if such a saving construction is available, courts must adopt it without first passing on the constitutional question; to do otherwise would be to issue an advisory opinion on the Constitution's meaning.[151] Finally, by assuming that Congress did not intend to "press into dangerous constitutional thickets,"[152] the Court also takes seriously the legislator's oath to the Constitution.[153] So understood, the canon is often defended as a doctrine of legislative supremacy.[154]

Recent scholarship, however, has shown that the legislative supremacy argument, at best, cuts two ways. It is true that the Court has stated that it will apply the canon of avoidance only when a statute is " 'susceptible' " of the saving construction,[155] and that the

---

[149] See, for example, *Spector Motor Serv. v McLaughlin*, 323 US 101, 105 (1944) ("If there is one doctrine more deeply rooted than any other in the process of constitutional adjudication, it is that we ought not to pass on questions of constitutionality . . . unless such adjudication is unavoidable."); *Ashwander v TVA*, 297 US 288, 346 (1936) (Brandeis concurring) ("The Court [has] developed . . . a series of rules under which it has avoided passing upon a large part of all the constitutional questions pressed upon it for decision.").

[150] See, for example, *Siler v Louisville & Nashville R Co*, 213 US 175, 191 (1909) ("[I]f a case can be decided on either of two grounds, one involving a constitutional question, the other a question of statutory construction or general law, the Court will decide only the latter.").

[151] See, for example, *United States v Rumely*, 328 US 41, 48 (1953) ("Grave constitutional questions are matters properly to be decided by this Court but only when they inescapably come before us for adjudication. Until then it is our duty to abstain from marking the boundaries of congressional power or delimiting the protection guaranteed by the [Constitution].").

[152] *Public Citizen*, 491 US at 466.

[153] See *Solid Waste Agency of Northern Cook County v U.S. Army Corps of Engineers*, 121 S Ct 675, 683 (2001) ("This requirement stems from our prudential desire not to needlessly reach constitutional issues and our assumption that Congress does not casually authorize administrative agencies to interpret a statute to push the limit of congressional authority."); *DeBartolo*, 485 US at 575 (noting that the canon of avoidance "not only reflects the prudential concern that constitutional issues not be needlessly confronted, but also recognizes that Congress, like th[e] Court, is bound by and swears an oath to uphold the Constitution").

[154] See, for example, William K. Kelley, *Avoiding Constitutional Questions as a Three-Branch Problem*, 86 Cornell L Rev (2001) (forthcoming) (describing the legislative supremacy justification for the canon of avoidance).

[155] *Jones v United States*, 526 US 227, 239 (2000) (" '[W]here a statute is susceptible of two constructions, by one of which grave and doubtful constitutional questions arise and by the other of which such questions are avoided, [a court's] duty is to adopt the latter.' ") (quoting *United States ex rel Attorney General v Delaware & Hudson Co.*, 213 US 366, 408 (1919)).

canon is "'not a license for the judiciary to rewrite language enacted by the legislature.'"[156] Still, these protestations hardly convey
the full picture. As others have noted, the canon of avoidance does
no work unless used to depart from the most likely or natural
meaning of a statute.[157] Indeed, the Court itself has often recognized that the avoidance canon may compel acceptance of a
"strained" interpretation or, by the same token, rejection of the
"most natural" reading of a statute.[158] Hence, in Professor
Schauer's words, the values served by the avoidance canon come
at a "cost to whatever systemic values lead a constitutionally unim-
peded interpreter to interpret a statute one way rather than
another."[159]

Indeed, critics of the avoidance canon suggest that its cost to
legislative supremacy can be quite substantial. Schauer, for example, has argued that "it is by no means clear that a strained interpretation of a federal statute that avoids a constitutional question
is any less a judicial intrusion than the judicial invalidation on constitutional grounds of a less strained interpretation of the same
statute."[160] More generally, Jerry Mashaw has invoked game theory
to suggest that willful misconstruction, if anything, intrudes on
legislative prerogatives more severely than outright invalidation of
an unconstitutional statute.[161] If the Court disturbs a legislative

---

[156] *United States v Monsanto*, 491 US 600, 611 (1989) (quoting *United States v Albertini*, 472 US 675, 680 (1985)).

[157] See, for example, *Feltner v Columbia Pictures Television, Inc.*, 523 US 340, 358 (1998) (Scalia concurring in the judgment) (noting that "'[t]he doctrine of constitutional doubt does not require that the problem-avoiding construction be the *preferable* one,'" for that "'would deprive the doctrine of all function'") (quoting *Almendarez-Torres v United States*, 523 US 224, 270 (1998) (Scalia dissenting)); Frederick Schauer, *Ashwander Revisited*, 1995 Supreme Court Review 71, 88 ("[A]voidance is only important in those cases in which the result is different from what the result would have been by application of a judge's or court's preconstitutional views about how the statute should be interpreted.").

[158] See, for example, *United States v X-Citement Video, Inc.*, 513 US 64 (1994) (rejecting the "most natural, grammatical reading" of a statute to avoid grave constitutional doubt); *Ullman v United States*, 350 US 422, 433 (1955) ("Indeed, the Court has stated that words may be strained 'in the candid service of avoiding a serious constitutional doubt.'") (quoting *Rumely*, 345 US at 47); see also, for example, *Textile Workers Union v Lincoln Mills*, 353 US 448, 477 (1957) (noting that the canon of avoidance "is normally invoked to narrow what would otherwise be the natural but constitutionally dubious scope of the language"); *United States v Lovett*, 328 US 303, 329 (1946) (Frankfurter concurring) ("'Words have been strained . . . to avoid that doubt.'").

[159] Schauer, 1995 Supreme Court Review at 82 (cited in note 157).

[160] Id at 74.

[161] Jerry L. Mashaw, *Greed, Chaos, and Governance* 105 (Yale Univ Press, 1997).

outcome by invalidating a statute, that action of course returns matters to the prestatutory status quo. The legislature might well reenact a policy relatively close to the one invalidated, since the process of reenactment, like the original enactment process, requires bargaining among all three constitutionally relevant actors (the House, the Senate, and the President).[162] If, instead, a court misconstrues a statute to avoid grave constitutional doubts, the misinterpretation will remain in place if any one of those three actors prefers it to the likely outcome of corrective legislation.[163] In other words, the avoidance canon may enshrine a result that could not have been adopted ex ante. Perhaps most importantly, because the avoidance canon is triggered by constitutional doubt (rather than unconstitutionality), any such intrusions upon the legislative prerogative merely protect a constitutional buffer zone, rather than a definite claim of constitutional right.[164]

Whether these (or other) criticisms of the avoidance canon justify its general abandonment is a matter for another day.[165] For

---

[162] See id.

[163] See id at 102–03 (discussing the game theoretic implications of faulty interpretation in general); see also Richard A. Posner, *Statutory Interpretation—In the Classroom and Courtroom*, 50 U Chi L Rev 800, 816 (1983) ("Congress's practical ability to overrule a judicial decision misconstruing one of its statutes, given all the other matters pressing for its attention, is less today than ever before, and probably was never very great.").

[164] See Posner, 50 U Chi L Rev at 816 (cited in note 163) ("The practical effect of construing statutes to avoid raising constitutional questions is therefore to enlarge the already vast reach of constitutional prohibition beyond even the most extravagant modern interpretation of the Constitution—to create a judge-made constitutional penumbra . . . ."). Justice Kennedy has voiced similar concerns:

> [The canon of avoidance] should not be given too broad a scope lest a whole new range of Government action be proscribed by interpretive shadows cast by constitutional provisions that might or might not invalidate it. The fact that a particular application of the clear terms of a statute might be unconstitutional does not provide us with a justification for ignoring the plain meaning of the statute. If that were permissible, then the power of judicial review of legislation could be made unnecessary, for whenever the application of a statute would have potential inconsistency with the Constitution, we could merely opine that the statute did not cover the conduct in question because it would be discomforting or even absurd to think that Congress intended to act in an unconstitutional manner.

Public Citizen, 491 US at 481 (Kennedy concurring in the judgment).

[165] For recent critiques of the canon of avoidance, see, for example, Kelley, 86 Cornell L Rev (forthcoming) (cited in note 154) (arguing that applying the canon of avoidance to administrative statutes ignores the lessons of *Chevron* and undervalues the executive's independent constitutional duty under Article II, § 3 to "take Care that the Laws be faithfully executed"); Adrian Vermeule, *Saving Constructions*, 85 Geo L J 1945, 1959–64 (1997) (arguing that the modern canon of avoidance and the doctrine of severability are in tension with each other both in purpose and effect).

present purposes, it suffices to note that the doctrine does not unambiguously serve legislative supremacy, as its defenders sometimes contend. Rather, it seems more accurate to suggest that it entails a trade-off. The Court sacrifices the most likely or natural meaning of a statute in order to advance extrastatutory values that have an uncertain constitutional pedigree but come close enough to the constitutional boundary to justify protection (at least in the Court's view).[166] In most contexts, the merits of this practice are at least debatable. If the Court narrows the broad terms of the National Labor Relations Act to avoid a serious First Amendment question,[167] it may well unsettle an apparent legislative outcome. In so doing, however, the Court promotes a competing constitutional interest. In such cases, there are constitutional values on both sides of the ledger.

Whatever the proper resolution of this trade-off generally, in the specific context of avoiding nondelegation concerns, the calculus is different. The nondelegation doctrine, as noted, seeks to protect the constitutional values embodied in Article I—specifically, that Congress sets legislative policy and that such policy passes through the filter of bicameralism and presentment prescribed by Article I, Section 7. As discussed, if the Court alters the meaning of an open-ended statute in order to avoid nondelegation concerns, it apparently disturbs whatever choice or compromise has emerged from that process. This creates the perverse result of attempting to safeguard the legislative process by explicitly disregarding the results of that process.[168] In other words, artificially narrowing a statute to avoid nondelegation concerns is at best self-defeating.[169]

---

[166] See, for example, Sunstein, 67 U Chi L Rev at 331 (cited in note 5) (defending the canon of avoidance as a means "to promote some goal with a constitutional foundation"); Vermeule, 85 Geo L J at 1963 (cited in note 165) (noting that the modern canon of avoidance "is a means of overprotecting constitutional values through statutory interpretation"); Ernest A. Young, *Constitutional Avoidance, Resistance Norms, and the Preservation of Judicial Review*, 78 Tex L Rev 1549, 1587 (2000) (noting that the avoidance canon does not further legislative intent, but "protects the constitutional values embodied in the provision that creates the constitutional 'doubt'").

[167] See *DeBartolo*, 485 US at 575–76 (applying NLRA's broad terms to ban peaceful, truthful leafleting would raise a serious constitutional question).

[168] See Bressman, 109 Yale L J at 1415 (cited in note 80) ("[T]o apply interpretive norms in such cases would frustrate Congress's intent.").

[169] Indeed, the avoidance of serious nondelegation questions is not merely self-defeating, but is a net detriment to the values sought to be preserved. Avoidance of nondelegation questions, as discussed, disturbs the outcome of the legislative process. By definition, however, such avoidance is sometimes—but not always—necessary to avoid an unconstitutional

The resulting interpretation reflects judicial, rather than legislative, lawmaking. To enforce the nondelegation doctrine through the canon of avoidance, then, contradicts the structure of Article I. To paraphrase Justice Scalia's remarks on a different subject, it is using the disease as cure.[170]

It is unnecessary to take a position here on whether the Court should "revive" the nondelegation doctrine as a doctrine of judicial review or simply permit its continued disuse, as some of its recent cases have suggested.[171] But if the Court *is* going to enforce the nondelegation doctrine, it should not employ the avoidance canon to do so.[172] It should displace a duly enacted statute only if it concludes that such statute has effected an unconstitutional delegation, not a potentially unconstitutional delegation.

The avoidance canon of course does seek to sidestep the practical concerns that make the Court unwilling to enforce the nondelegation doctrine directly. Those concerns, however, do not cut decisively between avoidance and *Marbury*-style judicial review. First, the Court's frequently expressed concerns about legislative (and,

---

delegation. Therefore, the certain detriment to the legislative process that flows from avoidance corresponds to an uncertain benefit of avoiding what might or might not ultimately be an unconstitutional delegation.

[170] See Antonin Scalia, *The Disease as Cure*, 1979 Wash U L Q 147 (1979).

[171] See, for example, *Whitman v American Trucking Ass'ns, Inc.*, 121 S Ct 903, 913 (2001) ("In the history of this Court we have found the requisite 'intelligible principle' lacking in only two statutes, one of which provided literally no guidance for the exercise of discretion, and the other of which conferred authority to regulate the entire economy on the basis of no more precise a standard than stimulating the economy by promoting 'fair competition.'").

[172] In this context, Jerry Mashaw's observations make particularly clear that outright invalidation would better serve the interests implicit in bicameralism and presentment. Consider the following example: If the Court narrows the OSH Act by requiring a threshold finding of "significant risk," that judicially imposed policy will be immune from legislative correction if the House, the Senate, *or* the President prefers that result to the likely outcome of the full legislative process. Conversely, if the Court were to declare the OSH Act unconstitutional on nondelegation grounds, that action would trigger a process that directly serves the interests of the nondelegation doctrine. By hypothesis, there is no question about the constitutionality of the underlying policy objective (workplace safety), merely the manner of its articulation. If judicial invalidation were to return matters to the pre-OSH Act status quo, then the House, the Senate, and the President would have an incentive to try again to bargain over an acceptable (but more specific) policy that all three prefer to the pre-Act status quo. If that process is successful, more precise policies will have passed through the filter of bicameralism and presentment, thereby addressing nondelegation concerns. If, however, the three relevant entities cannot agree on a more precise statute, that result also serves the interests of bicameralism and presentment, which aim in part to filter out laws that cannot secure the assent of the three constitutionally specified actors. In short, whereas using the avoidance canon disserves the goals of bicameralism and presentment, invalidation in appropriate circumstances would advance those goals.

more generally, governmental) flexibility go to the strictness with which the Court enforces the nondelegation doctrine, not to whether it enforces that doctrine through avoidance or judicial review. Second, with respect to concerns about the judicial administrability of the nondelegation doctrine, the avoidance canon offers no meaningful advantage. The administrability problem arises because there is no reliable metric for identifying a constitutionally excessive delegation. Yet there is no better way to identify whether a statute presents a sufficiently serious nondelegation question to trigger the canon of avoidance. In the judicial review context, the Court must draw a line between constitutional and unconstitutional delegations. In the context of avoidance, it must draw a similar line between questionable and nonquestionable delegations. Both turn on unquantifiable questions of degree. The move from judicial review to avoidance does not eliminate the difficulties in judicial line-drawing; it simply moves the line.[173]

Even if the canon of avoidance disserves nondelegation interests in a particular case, one might conclude that it serves a systemic interest in nondelegation by signaling Congress that overbroad statutes will be narrowed by the judiciary. Where the canon does not apply, *Chevron* authorizes relatively accountable administrative agencies to flesh out the meaning of broad or open-ended statutes. In contrast, by allowing judges to specify the meaning of the same open-ended terms, the avoidance canon shifts law elaboration authority to relatively insulated Article III courts.[174] Congress has in its arsenal many ways of influencing the manner in which agencies perform their functions but relatively fewer methods of influencing the federal judiciary in its disposition of particular cases or contro-

---

[173] This claim does not contradict Professor Sunstein's more general point that, in most contexts, applying the canon of avoidance to narrow an administrative statute will not raise the same administrability concerns as direct enforcement of the nondelegation doctrine. See Sunstein, 67 U Chi L Rev at 338 (cited in note 5). Consider, for example, the decision to construe the broad terms of the NRLA narrowly to avoid a serious First Amendment question. In such a case, the Court "do[es] not ask the hard-to-manage question whether the legislature has exceeded the permissible level of discretion, but pose[s] instead the far more manageable question whether the agency has been given the discretion to decide something that (under the appropriate canon) only legislatures may decide." Id. But when the canon of avoidance is invoked to avoid a serious question under the nondelegation doctrine as such, the hard-to-manage line-drawing questions return because the underlying constitutional question irreducibly involves matters of degree.

[174] See US Const, Art III, § 1 (assuring life tenure and salary protection during "good Behaviour").

versies.[175] Hence, if passing an overbroad statute will effectively shift law elaboration authority from agencies to courts, Congress may have a marginal incentive to supply the statutory details itself, rather than ceding that authority to courts that are less amenable to its control.

This argument is serious, but ultimately unavailing. As I have argued elsewhere, because Congress cedes substantial policy-making initiative to administrative agencies when it enacts open-ended rather than precise statutes, it already has a significant structural incentive to specify statutory policies.[176] The separation of powers, by prohibiting Congress from exercising direct control over agency lawmaking,[177] operates in effect as a structural nondelegation doctrine.[178] Even if the judicial specification of statutory meaning would marginally increase the resulting incentives for clarity,[179] this effect would not be meaningful, at least if it is restricted to cases raising serious nondelegation concerns. As noted, the trigger for the canon of avoidance in nondelegation cases (a serious question about excessive statutory breadth) is impossible to quantify. And federal courts do not frequently invoke the avoidance canon in the nondelegation context. Thus, it is speculative, at best, to suggest that Congress would have a systemic incentive to legislate more precisely because it faced an unpredictable risk, in extreme cases, of ceding law elaboration power to judges rather than agencies.

What is certain is that when the Court applies the canon of

---

[175] Congress exercises more effective control over administrative agencies than over the judiciary. See Landes and Posner, 18 J L & Econ at 879 (cited in note 129). It can more readily cut agency budgets, subject agency officials to discomfiting oversight hearings, and refuse to confirm or reconfirm top agency officials. See Richard A. Posner, *Theories of Economic Regulation*, 5 Bell J Econ & Mgmt Sci 335, 338 (1974); Barry R. Weingast and Mark J. Moran, *Bureaucratic Discretion or Congressional Control? Regulatory Policymaking by the Federal Trade Commission*, 91 J Pol Econ 765, 769 (1983). In contrast, Congress has relatively ineffective tools at its disposal to discipline judges who do not construe statutes to the liking of its members. See Jonathan R. Macey, *Promoting Public-Regarding Legislation Through Statutory Interpretation: An Interest Group Model*, 86 Colum L Rev 223, 260–61 (1986).

[176] See Manning, 97 Colum L Rev at 711–14 (cited in note 21).

[177] See *Washington Metropolitan Airports Authority v Citizens for the Abatement of Aircraft Noise, Inc.*, 501 US 252 (1992); *Bowsher v Synar*, 478 US 714 (1986); *INS v Chadha*, 462 US 919 (1983).

[178] See, for example, Richard J. Pierce, Jr., *Political Accountability and Delegated Power: A Response to Professor Lowi*, 36 Am U L Rev 391, 413–14 (1987).

[179] See Manning, 97 Colum L Rev at 712 (cited in note 21).

avoidance to further nondelegation objectives, it alters the enacted terms of an administrative statute in the interest of promoting legislative responsibility and preserving the integrity of the legislative process. It is equally clear that this practice, in contrast with straightforward judicial review, makes it less likely that *Congress* will ever clarify its unconstitutionally vague policies through the processes of bicameralism and presentment. Because application of the avoidance canon in the nondelegation context is therefore both self-contradictory and self-defeating, the Court should rethink its practice of enforcing the nondelegation doctrine through this means.

III. Brown & Williamson and the Canon of Avoidance

Brown & Williamson not only highlights concerns about treating the nondelegation doctrine as a canon of avoidance, but also suggests a more legitimate basis for using statutory interpretation to enforce nondelegation principles. As discussed, in denying the FDA jurisdiction over tobacco, the Court relied exclusively on the implications of later-enacted tobacco statutes. It did so in two respects. First, relying heavily on the legislative history accompanying post-FDCA legislation, the Court concluded that such legislation evinced an intention to ratify the FDA's long-standing position that it lacked tobacco jurisdiction. Second, the Court concluded that these post-FDCA statutes impliedly foreclosed FDA jurisdiction by adopting a comprehensive and detailed *legislative* scheme of tobacco regulation.

Although the Court conflated the two strands of analysis, they represent quite distinct approaches. The ratification arguments ultimately represent an unconvincing account of legislative intent, one that the Court almost surely would have rejected in the absence of nondelegation concerns. The Court's ratification analysis thus dramatically illustrates the double-edged legislative process concerns that arise when the Court uses avoidance to vindicate nondelegation principles. In contrast, by denying the FDA authority to invoke its open-ended authority to disturb the balance struck by Congress in explicit tobacco legislation, the Court arguably promoted the interests of bicameralism and presentment. Although the FDA might otherwise have enjoyed statutory authority under the FDCA to craft its own solution, nondelegation princi-

ples suggest that such a solution should give way when Congress
has itself spoken directly to the very questions that the agency
seeks to address. Such reasoning does not appear to rest on inferences of affirmative legislative "intent" to preclude agency authority; rather, it merely suggests that a settled canon of statutory interpretation—the specific governs the general—in fact promotes
the same interest as the nondelegation doctrine. I consider these
aspects of the Court's opinion in turn.

A. RATIFICATION AND THE AVOIDANCE
OF NONDELEGATION CONCERNS

To implement its avoidance strategy, the Court relied heavily
on postenactment legislative history to hold that Congress had ratified the FDA's (once) long-standing position on tobacco jurisdiction. Relying primarily on statements made by administration officials in hearings on the post-FDCA tobacco statutes, the Court
noted that Congress had passed those laws "against the backdrop
of the FDA's consistent and repeated statements that it lacked authority under the FDCA to regulate tobacco."[180] This pattern, in
turn, established that Congress had "ratified the FDA's long-held
position."[181] In addition, the Court attached further significance
to the fact that, in the same period, Congress repeatedly "considered and rejected bills that would have granted the FDA . . .
jurisdiction."[182]

In the absence of background nondelegation concerns, it is
highly unlikely that the majority would have relied on such evidence to determine the FDCA's meaning—and with good reason.[183] Except in narrow circumstances, the Court now regards
ratification and acquiescence arguments with suspicion. Classic
ratification occurs when Congress reenacts (or imports into a new
statute) a phrase that an agency or the judiciary has authoritatively
construed; in that context, the settled interpretation merely offers
a plausible point of reference for understanding the technical im-

---

[180] *Brown & Williamson*, 529 US at 144.

[181] Id.

[182] Id.

[183] For a thoughtful critique of the ratification argument as applied to the FDA's tobacco
jurisdiction, see Sunstein, 47 Duke L J at 1046–50 (cited in note 28).

port of the reenacted terms.[184] Although the Court has sometimes also inferred legislative ratification when Congress extensively amends a statute without disturbing the settled interpretation of a particular phrase,[185] all five Justices in the *Brown & Williamson* majority recently emphasized that this interpretive practice rests on mistaken assumptions about the legislative process.[186] The complexities of that process make it difficult if not impossible to know why Congress has failed to disavow an agency's interpretation of a statute. The precise question may not have been on the legislative radar; the leadership may have had other priorities; or perhaps the "correction" had insufficient support in a particular House or on a particular gatekeeping committee. Thus, even in the context of a statute's amendment, Congress's failure to "correct" a settled interpretation cannot be equated with an affirmative intention to ratify that interpretation.[187]

---

[184] See, for example, *Bragdon v Abbott*, 524 US 624, 644 (1997) ("When administrative and judicial interpretations have settled the meaning of an existing statutory provision, repetition of the same language in a new statute indicates, as a general matter, the intent to incorporate its administrative and judicial interpretations as well."); *Lorillard v Pons*, 434 US 575, 579 (1978) ("Congress is presumed to be aware of an administrative or judicial interpretation of a statute and to adopt that interpretation when it re-enacts a statute without change . . . .")

[185] See, for example, *Herman & MacLean v Huddleston*, 459 US 375, 384–85 (1983) (inferring ratification of cumulative interpretation of Section 10(b) of the Securities Exchange Act of 1934 when Congress extensively revised securities laws without changing that provision); *Lykes v United States*, 343 US 118, 127 (1951) ("Such a [Treasury] regulation is entitled to substantial weight. . . . Since the publication of that Treasury Decision, Congress has made many amendments to the Internal Revenue Code without revising this administrative interpretation . . . .").

[186] See *Central Bank of Denver, NA v First Interstate Bank of Denver, NA*, 511 US 164, 185–87 (1994) (Kennedy, joined by Rehnquist, O'Connor, Scalia, and Thomas); see also, for example, *Wells v United States*, 519 US 482, 495–96 (1997) (noting that claims of ratification were weak even though Congress had repeatedly amended a statute without "touching" the language that had been construed).

[187] The Court has reasoned:

> It does not follow . . . that Congress' failure to overturn a statutory precedent is reason for this Court to adhere to it. It is "impossible to assert with any degree of assurance that congressional failure to act represents" affirmative approval of the [courts'] statutory interpretation. . . . Congress may legislate, moreover, only through the passage of a bill which is approved by both Houses and signed by the President. U.S. Const., Art. I, § 7, cl. 2. Congressional inaction cannot amend a duly enacted statute.

See *Central Bank of Denver*, 511 US at 186 (quoting *Patterson v McLean Credit Union*, 491 US 164, 175 n 1 (1989), which quoted, in turn, *Johnson v Transportation Agency, Santa Clara County*, 480 US 616, 672 (1987) (Scalia dissenting)). Importantly, this reasoning relied on and extended *Patterson*'s conclusion that Congress does not acquiesce in a judicial or administrative interpretation simply by leaving it intact over time. Whereas *Patterson* applied that

The Court's reliance on post-FDCA history in *Brown & Williamson* extends even the more questionable version of the ratification doctrine. The post-FDCA legislation did not reenact, amend, or in any way address the FDCA's jurisdictional language. Rather, Congress merely passed distinct tobacco statutes in light of legislative history suggesting that such legislation was necessary and appropriate because of the FDCA's narrow scope. Far from satisfying any criteria for ratification, such evidence is simply postenactment legislative history. For good reason, however, the Court generally refuses to treat a subsequent Congress's interpretation of a statute as meaningful evidence of an earlier Congress's intent.[188] When subsequent legislation enacts language expressly approving a particular interpretation, the Court of course treats such explicit directions as authoritative.[189] But when the Court merely enacts new legislation based on a particular assumption about an earlier stat-

---

insight to Congress's simple failure to act, *Central Bank of Denver* extended it to Congress's failure to act in the context of a statutory amendment. Although acknowledging that its precedents were uneven on the question, the Court emphasized its present view that arguments ultimately predicated on legislative inaction "deserve little weight." *Central Bank of Denver*, 511 US at 187. For a differing view of congressional inaction, see, for example, Strauss, 1994 Supreme Court Review at 512–13 (cited in note 21) (arguing that legislative silence is a meaningful signal in the development of a consensus on statutory meaning through the cooperative interaction of Congress, agencies, and the courts over time).

[188] See, for example, *Reno v Bossier Parish School Dist.*, 520 US 471, 484–85 (1997) ("Our ultimate conclusion is also not undercut by statements found in the 'postenactment legislative record,' . . . given that 'the views of a subsequent Congress form a hazardous basis for inferring the intent of an earlier one.'") (quoting *United States v Price*, 361 US 304, 313 (1960)); *Mackey v Lanier Collection Agencies*, 486 US 825, 840 (1988) ("[T]hese views— absent an amendment to the original language of the section— do not direct our resolution of this case. Instead, we must look at the language of [the statute] and its structure, to determine the intent of the Congress that originally enacted the provision in question. 'It is the intent of the Congress that enacted [the section] . . . that controls.'") (quoting *Teamsters v United States*, 431 US 324, 354 n 39 (1977)); *Haynes v United States*, 390 US 85, 87 n 4 (1968) ("The views of a subsequent Congress of course provide no controlling basis from which to infer the purposes of an earlier Congress.").

[189] For example, in *Red Lion Broadcasting Co., Inc. v FCC*, 395 US 367, 369, 380 (1969), the Court held that Congress had subsequently given "explicit recognition" to the FCC's fairness doctrine. Through that doctrine, the FCC had implemented the Communications Act of 1934's "public interest" standard by requiring broadcasters to provide discussion of public issues and to ensure that both sides of an issue received fair coverage. When Congress amended the Act to compel broadcasters to give equal time to political candidates, it stated that the amendment left intact "the obligations imposed upon them under this Act to operate in the public interest and to afford reasonable opportunity for the discussion of conflicting views on issues of public importance." Act of Sept 14, 1959, § 1, 73 Stat 557, 557. In those circumstances, the amendment explicitly "vindicated the FCC's general view that the fairness doctrine inhered in the public interest standard." *Red Lion*, 395 US at 380.

ute's meaning, that understanding has little significance, particularly when it is merely reflected in the legislative history.[190] Simply put, enacting a statute based on an assumption about law does not amount to enacting that assumption.[191]

Quite apart from this general point, moreover, *Brown & Williamson* nowhere established that a legislative majority embraced the FDA's narrow position as the correct interpretation of the FDCA. Most of the Court's evidence involved administration testimony at legislative hearings on the post-FDCA tobacco statutes.[192] Although the Court has sometimes relied on such testimony to inform the meaning of a bill (specifically, when the administration has drafted the relevant language),[193] there is good reason to ques-

---

[190] See, for example, *Public Employees Retirement System of Ohio v Betts*, 492 US 158, 167–68 (1989) (rejecting an interpretation of the Age Discrimination in Employment Act found in legislative history accompanying amendments because the amendments did not modify the language being interpreted); *CPSC v GTE Sylvania, Inc.*, 447 US 102, 118 n 13 (1980) (refusing to credit a "mere statement in a conference report of [subsequent] legislation as to what the Committee believes an earlier statute meant"); *Rainwater v United States*, 356 US 590, 593 (1958) (holding that when a statutory amendment suggests an implicit understanding of prior legislation, that amendment "is merely an expression of how the [subsequent] Congress interpreted a statute passed by another Congress," and "such interpretation has very little, if any significance"). This premise now holds even when a committee of Congress interprets a prior statute during the course of that statute's reenactment. See *Pierce v Underwood*, 487 US 552, 566 (1988) ("[I]t is the function of the courts and not the Legislature, much less a Committee of one House of the Legislature, to say what an enacted statute means.").

[191] Indeed, the validity of legislation does not remotely depend on the correctness of any assumptions that underlay its enactment. See *Paris Adult Theaters I v Slaton*, 413 US 49, 61 (1974) ("From the beginning of civilized societies, legislators and judges have acted on various unprovable assumptions. Such assumptions underlie much lawful state regulation of commercial and business affairs."). Of course, legislative assumptions may illuminate the meaning of an ambiguous statutory term. In *Brown & Williamson*, however, the Court did not use Congress's assumptions to inform any particular language in the six post-FDCA tobacco statutes; rather, it reasoned the mere enactment of those statutes gave legal force to Congress's disembodied, general assumptions about the state of the law.

[192] See *Brown & Williamson*, 529 US at 144–61.

[193] See, for example, *United States v Sells Engineering*, 463 US 418, 439 (1983) ("In any event, we think the most reliable evidence of what Congress in 1977 understood to be standard Department practice was what Thornburgh, the Department's official representative at the Hearings, stated it to be."); *United States v Vogel Fertilizer Co.*, 455 US 16, 31 (1982); *Zuber v Allen*, 396 US 168, 192 (1969). In general, the Court gives testimony at legislative hearings little weight. See, for example, *Kelly v Robinson*, 479 US 36, 51 n 13 (1984) (declining to "accord any significance" to statements made in hearings when "none of those statements was made by a Member of Congress, nor were they included in the official Senate and House Reports"); *Ernst & Ernst v Hochfelder*, 425 US 185, 204, n 24 (1976) ("Remarks of this kind made in the course of legislative debate or hearings other than by persons responsible for the preparation or the drafting of a bill are entitled to little weight"); *S & E Contractors, Inc. v United States*, 406 US 1, 13 n 9 (1972) ("In construing laws [the Court has] been extremely wary of testimony before committee hearings and of debates on the floor of Congress save for precise analyses of statutory phrases by the spon-

tion the probativeness of the administration testimony relied on in *Brown & Williamson*. Even assuming that a requisite majority of Congress was aware of the testimony disclaiming FDA jurisdiction over tobacco, there is no reason to assume that those legislators agreed with the FDA. Because the administration's remarks on the FDCA did not purport to explain the meaning of any provision in the post-FDCA legislation (but rather offered background reasons for enacting it), legislators had no occasion to form a view about its correctness in deciding whether to vote for such legislation. Rather, to justify voting for the post-FDCA tobacco legislation, legislators simply had to conclude that the FDA had plausibly disclaimed jurisdiction over a problem thought to require attention.[194] In the administrative context, where an agency's position may reflect one of several permissible readings of the statute, this premise has particular force.[195] In the absence of any indication

---

sors of the proposed laws."); *McCaughn v Hershey Chocolate Co*,, 283 US 488, 493–94 (1931) ("Nor do we think of significance the fact . . . that statements inconsistent with the conclusion which we reach were made to committees of Congress or in discussions on the floor of the Senate by senators who were not in charge of the bill. For reasons which need not be restated, such individual expressions are without weight in the interpretation of a statute."); Reed Dickerson, *Statutory Interpretation: Dipping into Legislative History*, 112 Hofstra L Rev 1125, 1131 (1983) ("What is said at [committee] hearings is usually so unreliable, even when it appears to make good sense, that courts should pay little heed to it, except possibly for confirmatory purposes."). Since the rise of modern textualism, the Court had decreased its reliance on committee hearings. See William N. Eskridge, Jr. and Philip P. Frickey, *Cases and Materials on Legislation* 774 (West, 2d ed 1995).

[194] See *Brown & Williamson*, 529 US at 182 (Breyer dissenting) (noting that the postenactment legislative history "can be read either as (*a*) 'ratif[ying]' a no-jurisdiction assumption *or* as (*b*) leaving the jurisdictional question just where Congress found it") (citation omitted).

[195] Administrative agencies presumptively have the authority to change their positions provided that they offer a reasoned explanation for the change. See *Chevron USA, Inc. v NRDC, Inc.*, 467 US 837, 863 ("An initial agency interpretation is not instantly carved in stone."). Thus, even in the context of classic ratification, the Court has indicated that ratification connotes an acceptance of the agency's position as legitimate, not the adoption of the agency's position as the *only* legitimate interpretation of a statute. See, for example, *Motor Vehicle Mfrs Ass'n v State Farm Mutual Auto Ins Co.*, 463 US 29, 45 ("[E]ven an unequivocal ratification—short of statutory incorporation— . . . would not connote approval or disapproval of an agency's later decision to rescind [a] regulation."); *Trans World Airlines, Inc. v Hardison*, 432 US 63, 75 n 10 (1977) (noting that when Congress has ratified an administrative interpretation through positive legislation, that interpretation "is entitled to some deference, at least sufficient . . . to warrant our accepting the guideline as a defensible construction"); *Udall v Boesche*, 373 US 472, 483 (1963) ("The conclusion is plain that Congress, if it did not ratify the Secretary's conduct, at least did not regard it as inconsistent with the . . . Act."). Because the ratification doctrine typically arises in the context of defending administrative interpretations, invocation of that doctrine rarely even poses the question whether ratification precludes an agency from changing its position. But see, for example, *Telecommunications Research & Action Center v FCC*, 801 F2d 501, 517 (DC Cir 1986) ("We do not believe that language adopted in 1959 made the fairness doctrine a binding statutory obligation; rather, it ratified the Commission's longstanding position that

that key legislators or committees (much less Congress as a whole) agreed with, rather than merely understood, the administration's testimony about the FDCA, that testimony cannot support the Court's rejection of the FDA's subsequent change in position.[196]

Finally, the Court was mistaken in relying on Congress's failure to enact statutes granting the FDA jurisdiction over tobacco. The Court has recently emphasized that "[f]ailed legislative proposals are 'a particularly dangerous ground on which to rest an interpretation of a prior statute.'"[197] In particular, the Court has refused to treat the failure to pass legislation as evidence of legislative acquiescence in a regulatory practice that the proposal would have

---

the public interest standard authorizes the fairness doctrine."), cert denied, 482 US 519 (1987).

[196] To be sure, the Court cited a small number of statements by individual legislators agreeing with the administration's position, but those remarks are too sporadic and indefinite to support any inference that Congress affirmatively accepted the FDA's position. Specifically, the Court cited only three examples of legislative statements relating to post-FDCA tobacco bills. See *Brown & Williamson*, 529 US at 150–51, 154–55. First, in passing the Public Health Cigarette Smoking Act of 1969, Pub L No 91-222, which banned certain cigarette advertisements and strengthened warning label requirements, Congress extended an existing prohibition against any other required cigarette labeling. See § 5(a), 84 Stat 88. In connection with that legislation, the chairman of the responsible House committee remarked that "the Congress—the body elected by the people—must make the policy determinations involved in this determination—and not some agency made up of appointed officials." 116 Cong Rec 7920 (1970) (Rep Staggers). This open-ended statement, made in the context of a specific prohibition on agency-imposed labeling requirements, hardly supports the more general conclusion that Congress intended to adopt the FDA's narrow view of its tobacco jurisdiction.

Second, when Congress eliminated the Consumer Product Safety Commission's authority over tobacco in the Consumer Product Safety Commission Improvements Act of 1976, Pub L No 94-284, § 3(c), 90 Stat 503, codified at 15 USC § 1261(f)(2), a separate statement to a Senate Report explained that the statute "unmistakably reaffirm[ed] the clear mandate of Congress that the basic regulation of tobacco and tobacco products is governed by . . . legislation . . . and that any further regulation . . . must be reserved for specific congressional action." S Rep 251, 94th Cong, 1st Sess 43 (1975) (Sens Hartke, Hollings, Ford, Stevens, and Beall). Putting to one side the fact that this legislation dealt with the CSPC (rather than the FDA), it is noteworthy that these Senators were obliged to issue their views as a separate statement; this may suggest that such views were not shared by the relevant committee, much less by Congress as a whole.

Third, in connection with the Comprehensive Smoking Education Act, Pub L No 980474, 98 Stat 2200 (1984), Senator Hawkins argued that legislation was necessary because "[u]nder the [FDCA], Congress exempted tobacco products." 130 Cong Rec 36953. The statement of an individual legislator in the context of a floor debate carries little weight in interpretation.

I cite these examples not to establish the contents of the legislative history, but merely to show that the evidence of legislative sentiment relied on by the Court was sparse and highly attenuated.

[197] *Central Bank of Denver*, 511 US at 187 (quoting *Pension Benefit Guaranty Corporation v LTV Corp.*, 496 US 633, 650 (1990)).

repudiated.[198] The Court's reluctance is rooted in commonsense understanding of the legislative process: "A bill can be proposed for any number of reasons, and it can be rejected for just as many others."[199] Hence, little can be gleaned from Congress's failure to pass legislation granting the FDA authority over tobacco.

If the Court would otherwise regard the postenactment legislative history of the FDCA as an unreliable indicator of statutory meaning, it hardly serves nondelegation interests to give such history determinative weight. The Court's unwarranted extension of an already questionable version of the ratification doctrine raises similar concerns. If, in fact, the FDCA is broad enough to encompass tobacco (in light of the FDA's specific findings), one must acknowledge that the Court's interpretive method effectively rewrote Congress's command. It replaced a broad statute with a narrower statute, one of the Court's, and not Congress's, design. Taking such steps as a means to enforce nondelegation interests—specifically, to ensure legislative responsibility for policy decisions—was therefore self-defeating.

B. STATUTORY COHERENCE AS A NONDELEGATION DOCTRINE

Although my conclusions here are more tentative, a second aspect of *Brown & Williamson*'s reasoning may suggest a more promising interpretive strategy—enforcing nondelegation interests through the traditional canon of reading more general statutory commands in light of more specific ones. Although the Court principally relied on the post-FDCA tobacco legislation to support an (unwarranted) inference of legislative ratification, the Court also emphasized that this legislation had, in fact, crafted a "specific legislative response to the problem of tobacco and health."[200] In this connection, the Court applied the established principle that judges should promote coherence among statutes passed at different times, in part by reading the FDCA's general authority in light of the more specific commands in the post-FDCA statutes:

---

[198] See *Solid Waste Engineers of Cook County v Army Corps of Engineers*, 121 S Ct 675, 681 (2001).

[199] Id.

[200] *Brown & Williamson*, 529 US at 157.

At the time a statute is enacted, it may have a range of plausible meanings. Over time, however, subsequent legislation can shape or focus those meanings. The "classic judicial task of reconciling many laws over time and getting them to 'make sense' in combination, necessarily assumes that the implications of a statute may be altered by the implications of a later statute." This is particularly so where the scope of an earlier statute is broad but the subsequent statutes more specifically address the topic at hand.[201]

Given the detailed regulatory regime established by the six post-FDCA tobacco statutes, the Court found that Congress had "specifically addressed the question at issue"—that is, the appropriate level of tobacco regulation.[202] And it suggested that this specific *legislative* regime for tobacco effectively superseded the FDA's background authority to regulate the same subject matter differently.

In 1965, the FCLAA adopted a precisely defined requirement that cigarette manufacturers affix a specific warning label on all cigarette packages.[203] The statute explicitly sought to balance the competing goals of ensuring "that the public be informed that cigarette smoking may be hazardous to health" and protecting "commerce and the national economy to the maximum extent."[204] It further provided that "[n]o statement relating to smoking and health, other than the statement required by . . . this Act, shall be required on any cigarette package."[205] Although the FCLAA's prohibition against additional labeling requirements was to sunset on July 1, 1969,[206] the Public Health Cigarette Smoking Act of 1969 extended it indefinitely.[207] In the same Act, Congress amended the FCLAA not only to strengthen the labeling requirement, but also to ban all cigarette advertisements "on any medium of electronic communication subject to the jurisdiction of the [FCC]."[208] In 1984, Congress again modified the required warning

---

[201] Id at 145 (quoting *United States v Fausto*, 448 US 439, 453 (1988)).

[202] Id at 132.

[203] Pub L No 89-92, § 5(a), 79 Stat 283 ("Warning: Cigarette Smoking May Be Hazardous to Your Health.").

[204] Id § 2, 79 Stat 282, codified at 15 USC § 1331.

[205] Id § 5(a), 79 Stat 283.

[206] See id § 10, 79 Stat 284.

[207] Pub L No 91-222, § 5(a), 84 Stat 88, codified at 15 USC 1334(a).

[208] Id §§ 4 and 6, 84 Stat 88–89.

label.[209] And, in 1986, it extended the substance of the FCLAA to smokeless tobacco.[210] Finally, in 1992, the Alcohol, Drug Abuse, and Mental Health Administration Reorganization Act conditioned certain block grants to states on their prohibition of sales of tobacco products to minors.[211]

Quite apart from its more dramatic conclusion that the FDCA's remedial provisions required an outright tobacco ban if the FDA asserted jurisdiction at all (a premise sharply contested by the dissent), the Court suggested that the FDA's more limited exercise of regulatory authority threatened to disrupt the balance struck by these more specific statutes.[212] Although not free of doubt,[213] this conclusion has considerable force. For example, recall that the FDA's regulations banned the sale of tobacco to minors, required photo identification for sales to persons under twenty-seven, and largely prohibited sales of tobacco through self-service displays or vending machines.[214] Congress's 1992 legislation, however, provided that states will develop reasonable restrictions on sales to minors. In particular, that legislation conditioned block grants on a state's having "in effect a law providing that it is unlawful for any manufacturer, retailer, or distributor of tobacco products to sell or distribute any such product to any individual under the age of 18."[215] More importantly, it also provided that a state must agree to "enforce [such] law . . . in a manner that can reasonably be expected to reduce the extent to which tobacco products are available to individuals under the age of 18."[216] By specifying detailed measures to deny minors access to tobacco, the FDA's regulations appear to alter the balance struck by the 1992 statute. In particular, they unsettle Congress's apparent determination to

---

[209] Comprehensive Smoking Education Act, Pub L No 98-474, § 4(a), 98 Stat 2200, 2201–03.

[210] Comprehensive Smokeless Tobacco Health Education Act of 1986, Pub L 99-252, 100 Stat 30, codified at 15 USC § 4401 et seq.

[211] Pub L No 102-321, § 202, 106 Stat 394, codified at 42 USC § 300x et seq.

[212] See *Brown & Williamson*, 529 US at 144 ("Congress has created a distinct regulatory scheme to address the problem of tobacco and health, and that scheme, as presently constructed, precludes any role for the FDA.").

[213] See text accompanying notes 237–38.

[214] See text accompanying note 48.

[215] 42 USC § 300x-26(a)(1).

[216] Id § 300x-26(b)(1).

leave the development of such programs to reasonable state initiatives. Similarly, the FDA's regulations imposed significant new restrictions on tobacco advertising and promotion.[217] Congress, however, had arguably addressed that very issue by prohibiting all tobacco advertising on media regulated by the FCC.[218]

In light of these considerations, even if the post-FDCA statutes do not reflect an intent to ratify the FDA's original view of its authority, the Court may have properly furthered nondelegation interests by construing the FDCA's general provisions in light of the more specific tobacco statutes. This practice reflects a well-established interpretive canon. As the Court has explained, "it is a commonplace of statutory construction that the specific governs the general."[219] Thus, "[h]owever inclusive may be the language of a statute, . . . specific terms prevail over the general in the same or another statute which otherwise might be controlling."[220] The Court has applied this "specificity canon," moreover, to ensure the coherence of statutes enacted at different times. For example, although federal employees had traditionally enjoyed a cause of action for adverse personnel actions under the general authority of the Back Pay Act, the Court held that this authority was superseded by the "comprehensive and integrated" remedial scheme that the Civil Service Reform Act of 1978 specifically established for such actions.[221] Similarly, the Court recently held that the federal government's right to enforce a tax lien turned on the specific provisions of the Federal Tax Lien Act of 1966, rather than the

---

[217] See note 49.

[218] See 15 USC §§ 1335, 4402(f).

[219] *Morales v Trans World Airlines, Inc.*, 504 US 374, 385 (1992); see also, for example, *Gozlon-Peretz v United States*, 498 US 395, 406 (1991) ("A specific provision controls over one of more general application."); *Radzanower v Touche Ross & Co.*, 426 US 148, 153 (1976) ("'Where there is no clear intention otherwise, a specific statute will not be controlled or nullified by a general one, regardless of the priority of enactment.'") (quoting *Morton v Mancari*, 417 US 535, 550–51 (1974)).

[220] *Clifford F. MacEvoy Co. v United States*, 322 US 102, 107 (1944). This premise, moreover, also finds expression in the established maxim of *ejusdem generis*, which provides that "when a general term follows a specific one, the general term should be understood as a reference to subjects akin to the one with specific enumeration." *Norfolk & Western R. Co. v Train Dispatchers*, 499 US 117, 129 (1991); see also, for example, *Cleveland v United States*, 329 US 14, 18 (1946) ("Under the *ejusdem generis* rule of construction the general words are confined to the class and may not be used to enlarge it."); *Gooch v United States*, 297 US 124, 128 (1936) (noting that canon of *ejusdem generis* "limits general terms which follow specific ones to matters similar to those specified").

[221] *Fausto v United States*, 484 US 439, 453 (1988).

more generally applicable provisions of an older statute granting the United States priority in debt collection.[222]

Although its rationale is rarely explained, the canon preferring the specific over the general furthers nondelegation interests, even though it displaces statutory authority that an agency or court might otherwise enjoy. The central aim of the nondelegation doctrine is to promote specific rather than general legislative policymaking—that is, to induce Congress to filter more precise policies through the process of bicameralism and presentment rather than leaving such policies to be elaborated by agencies or courts outside the legislative process. Detailed legislation is more likely to reflect the results of a specific choice or compromise.[223] Permitting an agency to rely on general authority to disrupt the balance struck by a more specific statute may therefore undermine a precise outcome reached through bicameralism and presentment.[224] Consider the

---

[222] *United States v Estate of Romani*, 523 US 517, 532 (1998).

[223] In contrast with a general statute, a specific statute is more likely to reflect Congress's "detailed judgment" about the appropriate way to "accommodate" competing policy concerns relating to a particular subject. *Estate of Romani*, 523 US at 532; see Easterbrook, 50 U Chi L Rev at 547 (cited in note 132) ("A legislature that tries to approach the line where costs begin to exceed benefits is bound to leave a trail of detailed provisions, which . . . would preclude judges from attempting to fill gaps."). I have argued elsewhere that bicameralism and presentment require special respect for the specific results of such a compromise. See Manning, 101 Colum L Rev at 70–78 (cited in note 24). That process effectively establishes a supermajority requirement by allocating lawmaking authority among distinct institutions answering to different constituencies. See James M. Buchanan and Gordon Tullock, *The Calculus of Consent* 235–26 (Michigan, 1962). So understood, it gives minorities an exaggerated right to protect themselves against majority factions through their ability to block legislation or, as a condition of assent, to insist upon a compromise offering less than the full extent of what the majority might otherwise desire. See Manning, 101 Colum L Rev at 77–78 (cited in note 24).

[224] See, for example, *Gomez v United States*, 490 US 858, 871–72 (1989):

> Through gradual congressional enlargement of magistrates' jurisdiction, the Federal Magistrates Act now expressly authorizes magistrates to preside at jury trials of all civil disputes and criminal misdemeanors, subject to special assignment, consent of the parties, and judicial review. The Act further details magistrates' functions regarding pretrial and post-trial matters, specifying two levels of review depending on the scope and significance of the magistrate's decision. The district court retains the power to assign to magistrates unspecified "additional duties," subject only to conditions or review that the court may choose to impose. By a literal reading this additional duties clause would permit magistrates to conduct felony trials. But the carefully defined grant of authority to conduct trials of civil matters and of minor criminal cases should be construed as an implicit withholding of the authority to preside at a felony trial.

See also, for example, *International Paper Co. v Ouellette*, 479 US 481, 494 (1987) ("[W]e do not believe that Congress intended to undermine this carefully drawn statute through a general saving clause.").

following example: The OSH Act undoubtedly grants the Secretary of Labor general authority allowing her to issue a regulation prescribing maximum levels of benzene in the workplace. If, however, Congress were to enact the Benzene Control Act of 2001, providing that "benzene exposure in the workplace shall not exceed 10 parts per million," a court might find that this specific statute precluded the Secretary from promulgating a regulation setting the appropriate level at five parts per million. Although such a regulation may be viewed as supplementing, rather than contradicting, the specific statutory requirements, it might also be seen as unsettling the precise balance struck in a legislative process that presumably involved bargaining between labor and manufacturing interests. If the latter characterization is correct, applying the specificity canon promotes the nondelegation doctrine's aim of channeling specific policy decisions through the filter of bicameralism and presentment.

The Court's use of similar analysis in the context of federal common law making supplies a helpful analogy. Although the Court's post-*Erie* default position is that " '[t]here is no general federal common law,' "[225] the Court nonetheless continues to recognize "federal common law powers" in certain enclaves involving uniquely federal interests[226]—specifically, in areas involving "the rights and obligations of the United States, interstate and international disputes implicating the conflicting rights of States or our relations with foreign nations, and admiralty cases."[227] Even in these acknowledged enclaves, however, the Court has shown its readiness to find that federal common law authority is displaced

---

[225] *O'Melveny & Myers v FDIC*, 512 US 79, 83 (1994) (quoting *Erie R. Co. v Tompkins*, 304 US 64, 78 (1938)); see also, for example, *Northwest Airlines, Inc. v Transport Workers Union*, 451 US 77, 95 (1981) ("[I]t remains true that federal courts, unlike their state counterparts, are courts of limited jurisdiction that have not been vested with open-ended lawmaking powers."); *United States v Standard Oil Co.*, 332 US 301, 313 (1947) ("[I]n the federal scheme our part in that work [of law creation], and the part of the other federal courts, outside the constitutional area is more modest than that of the state courts, particularly in the freedom to create new common law liabilities . . . .").

[226] Professor Brad Clark has recently marshaled substantial historical materials suggesting that at least some of the "enclaves" can be re-rationalized as rules of decision designed to implement various aspects of the constitutional structure. See Bradford R. Clark, *Federal Common Law: A Structural Reinterpretation*, 144 U Pa L Rev 1245 (1996). For present purposes, I assume arguendo that the Court has properly characterized the relevant exercise of authority in these enclaves as federal common law making power.

[227] *Texas Indus. v Radcliff Materials*, 451 US 630, 641 (1980) (footnotes omitted).

when Congress has enacted a statute directly on point. In *Milwau-kee v Illinois*,[228] for example, the Court held that the Federal Water Pollution Control Amendments of 1972 (FWPCA)[229] superseded an established federal common law nuisance action for the abatement of interstate pollution.[230] Emphasizing that federal common law is a "'necessary expedient'" even in the recognized enclaves,[231] the Court explained that "when Congress addresses a question previously governed by a decision rest[ing] on federal common law the need for such an unusual exercise of lawmaking by federal courts disappears."[232] Of crucial significance here, in displacing federal common law, the Court has recognized that the relevant question is "whether the legislative scheme 'spoke directly to a question'" formerly addressed by federal common law, "not whether Congress had affirmatively proscribed [its] use."[233]

The *Milwaukee* Court's rationale rested squarely on the separation of powers; in our system of government, the federal courts are not the preferred locus of legislative policy-making authority.[234] Hence, when the FWPCA adopted "a comprehensive regulatory program," it removed the justification for judges to develop and apply "vague and indeterminate nuisance concepts and maxims of equity jurisprudence."[235] More fundamentally, the Court has fre-

---

[228] 451 US 304 (1981).

[229] 33 USC § 1251 et seq.

[230] The Court had recognized that common law nuisance action in an earlier incarnation of the same case, decided before the FWPCA's enactment. See *Illinois v Milwaukee*, 406 US 91 (1972).

[231] *Milwaukee v Illinois*, 451 US at 314 (quoting *Committee for Consideration of Jones Falls Sewage System v Train*, 539 F2d 1006, 1008 (4th Cir 1976) (en banc)).

[232] Id.

[233] Id at 315. It must be noted that the Court's approach is in some tension with the long-standing principle that "[s]tatutes which invade the common law or the general maritime law are to be read with a presumption favoring the retention of long-established and familiar principles, except when a statutory purpose to the contrary is evident." *Isbrandtsen Co. v Johnson*, 343 US 779, 783 (1952). The Court resolves that tension by holding that the statute must "'speak directly'" to the question previously covered by the common law before it may displace that prior law. See *United States v Texas*, 507 US 527, 534 (1993) (citation omitted); see also, for example, *County of Oneida v Oneida Indian Nation*, 470 US 226, 237 (1985) (holding that the Nonintercourse Act of 1793 does not displace federal common law relating to unlawful conveyance of Native American lands because it "does not speak directly to the question of remedies" for such conveyances).

[234] *Milwaukee v Illinois*, 451 US at 315 ("Our commitment to the separation of powers is too fundamental to continue to rely on federal common law by judicially decreeing what accords with common sense and the public weal when Congress has addressed the problem.") (internal quotation marks omitted) (quoting *TVA v Hill*, 437 US 153, 195 (1978)).

[235] Id at 317.

quently emphasized that when Congress prescribes a specific solution to a given problem, federal courts may not alter or supplement that outcome, lest they disrupt the balance struck by Congress.[236]

The context is somewhat different, but similar principles ultimately seem applicable to agency lawmaking as well. Initially, the difference in context highlights the fact that when the Court displaces federal lawmaking power in favor of a specific statute, it is disturbing judicial, rather than legislatively conferred, authority. In contrast, when the Court uses the specificity canon to narrow a broad delegation, it appears to be altering the prior understanding of an express statutory scheme. For example, *Brown & Williamson*'s use of the specificity canon is itself open to the charge that it disturbed a legislative choice to frame the FDCA in broad terms; indeed, if the Court would otherwise have read the FDCA to include tobacco, its use of the specificity canon to narrow the FDA's authority might be characterized as a species of implied repeal. This characterization of the specificity canon, if correct, would trigger some of the same concerns as the canon of avoidance. The Court restricts implied repeals to cases involving either an irreconcilable conflict between two statutes or an affirmative legislative intent in a later statute to alter a preexisting statutory scheme.[237] Hence, if the FDA regulations were thought to supplement, rather

---

[236] See, for example, *Middlesex County Sewerage Auth. v National Sea Clammers Ass'n*, 453 US 1, 14 (1981) ("In view of these elaborate enforcement provisions it cannot be assumed that Congress intended to authorize by implication additional judicial remedies for private citizens suing under [the Marine Protection, Research, and Sanctuaries Act of 1972] and FWPCA."); *Texas Indus.*, 451 US at 644 (refusing to recognize common law authority to supplement the remedies of the Sherman Act because "the remedial provisions in the antitrust laws are detailed and specific"); *Mobil Oil Corp. v Higginbotham*, 436 US 618, 625 (1978) ("The Death on the High Seas Act . . . announces Congress' considered judgment on such issues as the beneficiaries, the limitations period, contributory negligence, survival, and damages. . . . The Act does not address every issue of wrongful-death law, . . . but when it does speak directly to a question, the courts are not free to 'supplement' Congress' answer so thoroughly that the Act becomes meaningless."); *Arizona v California*, 373 US 546, 565–66 (1963) ("It is true that the Court has used the doctrine of equitable apportionment to decide river controversies between States. But in those cases Congress had not made any statutory apportionment."); cf. *Transamerica Mortgage Advisors, Inc. v Lewis*, 444 US 11, (1979) ("[I]t is an elemental canon of statutory construction that where a statute expressly provides a particular remedy or remedies, a court must be chary of reading others into it.").

[237] See, for example, *Morton v Mancari*, 417 US 535, 550 (1974) ("In the absence of some affirmative showing of an intention to repeal, the only permissible justification for a repeal by implication is when the earlier and later statutes are irreconcilable."); *Georgia v Pennsylvania R. Co.*, 324 US 439, 456–57 (1945) ("Only a clear repugnancy between the old . . . and the new [law] results in the former giving way . . .").

than conflict with, the post-FDCA tobacco legislation,[238] the Court could find an implied repeal only if it were able to conclude that the subsequent legislation reflected an affirmative intent to displace the FDA's background authority. As discussed in relation to the Court's ratification argument, one cannot convincingly impute such an intent to Congress in this case.

The well-established specificity canon, however, is broader than the doctrine of implied repeals. Properly understood, that canon in fact bears closer resemblance to the judicial practice of curtailing federal common law authority in the face of specific legislation. Although authorized by statute, agency lawmaking shares a crucial attribute with federal common law making: It departs from the constitutionally preferred method of lawmaking—bicameralism and presentment. As in the case of federal common law, the Court has indicated that it accepts delegated agency lawmaking as a necessary expedient in the modern administrative state. If the Court aggressively enforced the nondelegation doctrine, Congress would not be able to anticipate and resolve with specificity all the issues necessary to regulate modern industrial society. In addition, the Court lacks confidence in its ability to draw principled distinctions between permissibly and excessively broad statutes. Neither concern applies when Congress has otherwise spoken to an issue with particularity. In such cases, Congress has shown its capacity and desire to set a precise policy itself, and any effort by an agency to exercise its general authority on the same question threatens to disrupt the specific balance struck in the legislative process.[239] And

---

[238] Such a conclusion might be warranted if one accepts the background assumption that repeals by implication are disfavored. See *United States v United Continental Tuna Corp.*, 425 US 164, 168 (1976).

[239] The Court has thus explained that the specificity canon prevents a "narrow, precise, and specific" statute from being "submerged" by judicial or agency elaboration of a distinct statute covering "a more generalized spectrum." *Touche Ross & Co.*, 426 US at 153; see Theodore Sedgwick, *A Treatise on the Rules Which Govern the Interpretation and Construction of Statutory and Constitutional Law* 98 (Baker, Voorhis & Co., John Norton Pomeroy 2d ed 1874) (noting that the specificity canon seeks to preserve the fruits of a process in which "the mind of the legislator has been turned to the details of a subject, and he has acted upon it"). This consideration, moreover, distinguishes the Court's use of the specificity canon from its reliance on ratification arguments to narrow the FDCA. Although the ratification argument also serves the interest in specific, rather than general, policy-making, I have previously attempted to show that, in doing so, it rests upon erroneous assumptions about the discernment of legislative intent—assumptions that contradict the premises of bicameralism and presentment. The specificity canon, in contrast, narrows a broad delegation to preserve specific policies that Congress has properly enacted into law through bicameralism and presentment.

while the specificity canon presents its own line-drawing concerns (discussed below), they are not of the same order of magnitude as those involved in attempts to enforce the traditional nondelegation doctrine.

The practical difficulties in applying the specificity canon to narrow broad delegations are significant, but do not ultimately negate the utility of that canon. The touchstone for the canon's application, as *Brown & Williamson* suggests, is whether Congress has directly spoken to the precise question in issue. This fact will be most obvious when Congress has addressed a particular subject in a detailed and comprehensive way. In other cases, it will be less clear. But the inquiry is no more complicated than the threshold question posed when applying *Chevron* or, for that matter, the basic question posed in the federal common law cases.

In *Brown & Williamson* itself, if the Court correctly determined that the FDA would be obliged to ban tobacco if it asserted jurisdiction, then this result would plainly disrupt the balance that Congress specifically struck when it enacted tobacco regulations but stopped short of banning it. If, however, the Court misread the FDCA's remedial scheme in reaching that conclusion, the question of displacement would be more complex. Congress arguably tinkered at the margins in its tobacco statutes: imposing certain labeling requirements, banning advertising in certain media, and giving states inducements to regulate tobacco sales to minors. In contrast with the FWPCA's approach to water pollution, the post-FDCA legislation has not adopted a comprehensive and integrated program for regulating tobacco.[240] Still, despite Congress's limited steps into areas such as labeling, advertising, and sales to minors, it has arguably spoken to those particular issues by defining a precise level and method of regulating tobacco in such contexts. Indeed, one of the aims of bicameralism and presentment is to filter out laws that cannot secure a sufficient consensus to gain the assent of all three constitutionally specified participants in the legislative process. If Congress has addressed a subject, but has done so in a limited way, this fact itself may suggest that Congress has gone as far as it could, as far as the enacting coalition wished to, on the subject in question. If the Court permitted the FDA to

---

[240] See Sunstein, 47 Duke L J at 1050 (cited in note 28).

go farther under the FDCA's general authority, such action might disturb the more precise policies adopted by Congress through bicameralism and presentment.[241]

IV. CONCLUSION

The nondelegation doctrine serves important constitutional interests: It requires Congress to take responsibility for legislative policy and ensures that such policy passes through the filter of bicameralism and presentment. The Court, however, has been reluctant to enforce this doctrine directly, largely out of concern that aggressive enforcement of that doctrine will hamper Congress's ability to exercise its constitutional powers and will strain the Court's capacity to make principled judgments about excessive delegations. Although the Court has chosen instead to promote nondelegation interests through the canon of avoidance, this strategy produces significant pathologies of its own. As both *Benzene* and *Brown & Williamson* illustrate, when the Court departs from its usual methods of interpretation to avoid a serious nondelegation question, it runs the risk of departing from congressional commands in the process. If the aim of the nondelegation doctrine is to force Congress to take responsibility for legislative policy, the Court's avoidance strategy defeats, at least as much as it promotes, that constitutional objective.

---

[241] Of course, the specificity canon supplies only a default position. It does not apply when Congress has otherwise indicated its desire not to displace background agency authority through specific legislation on the same subject. In the context of tobacco, there may be an idiosyncratic reason to think that the Court's displacement of the FDA's tobacco authority contradicted legislative directions. In its post-FDCA legislation, Congress expressly foreclosed any "additional" labeling requirements. See, for example, 15 USC § 1334(a). One might infer from this legislation that when Congress wished to bar further agency action, it did so expressly. Because no similar statutory provision addresses tobacco advertising or sales to minors, the labeling provisions may themselves carry a crucial negative implication. Whatever the correct answer in the particular circumstances of *Brown & Williamson*, however, the specificity canon, properly applied, may suggest a basis for limiting delegations in the future.

EMILY BUSS

ADRIFT IN THE MIDDLE:
PARENTAL RIGHTS AFTER
TROXEL V GRANVILLE

In *Troxel v Granville*,[1] the Supreme Court held that a court order compelling visits between two young children and their paternal grandparents violated their mother's due process right to control her children's upbringing. Although the decision split the Court six ways, it revealed considerable consensus. Eight Justices recognized some constitutionally protected right of parents to control their children's private associations, but seven did so haltingly, reflecting their readiness to qualify that right in the face of competing relational claims more compelling than those asserted by the grandparents in this case. *Troxel* catches the Court in the awkward act of attempting to maintain a commitment to strong parental rights, while anticipating their serious compromise: It offers parental rights as the shield against state intrusions in family life, while discussing visitation regimes in terms that invite precisely such intrusions.

In this article, I will suggest that the line the Court is attempting to walk between the preservation of parental rights and the recognition of nonparental claims is untenable. The central problem

Emily Buss is Assistant Professor of Law, the University of Chicago.

AUTHOR'S NOTE: My thanks to William Buss, Mary Anne Case, Jack Goldsmith, and Martha Nussbaum for their helpful comments and to Erin Childress and Damon Taaffe for their excellent research assistance. The Max Rheinstein Research Fund and the Stuart C. and JoAnn Nathan Faculty Fund provided support for this research.

[1] 120 S Ct 2054 (2000).

with the Court's decision in *Troxel* is not that it affords parents too much protection, as some have argued, or that it affords parents too little protection, as others have argued, but that it tries to have it both ways. This attempt at compromise threatens to deprive children of the benefits they would derive from either the enforcement or the abandonment of constitutionally protected parental rights. Qualifying parental rights saps these rights of any special value they might have for children, and leaving parents with some, qualified, constitutional protection forces courts into a role of prominence in allocating child-rearing authority that they are ill equipped to assume.

After briefly reviewing the Court's decision in *Troxel*, I will consider the various approaches the Court might have taken in resolving the case and the benefits and harms to children that might flow from each of these approaches. I will begin by setting out a child-serving justification for recognizing nearly absolute parental rights. I will argue that children are likely to be best served by such an approach, an approach that limits state intervention to actions aimed at preventing a narrow set of harms. I will then consider the arguments for the other polar position—abandoning parents' constitutional protection altogether. I conclude that the considerable virtues of democratic decision making are likely to be seriously attenuated in this context. Then I will discuss the problems with any solution that falls between the two poles, the sort of solution advocated by a majority of seven, in four separate opinions, in *Troxel*. I will argue that the middle course for which the Justices aim in *Troxel* is conceptually unsound and problematic in its application. I will also suggest that the middle course is not supported by the Court's precedents, which, properly understood, tolerate significant state intervention in resolving competing parental claims but not in resolving competing relational claims where the identity of a child's parental figures is undisputed.

I. Troxel v Granville

While *Troxel* itself is a narrow ruling on a particularly problematic statute, it is the Supreme Court's first word, and perhaps only word, on a subject of considerable interest to courts and legislatures throughout the country. Third-party visitation statutes have been enacted in all fifty states, and *Troxel* has set in motion a nationwide project of assessing and retooling these statutes in an attempt to conform to the Court's apparent standards. Moreover, because the court so rarely expounds upon parental rights, *Troxel*'s significance extends well beyond the third-party visitation context. The Court's words, shaped as they clearly are by the specific issue before it, will inevitably be applied more broadly to a full range of cases in which parental rights are at issue.

The Washington statute challenged in *Troxel* provided that "any person" could petition a court for visitation rights "at any time," and authorized a court to compel visitation against parents' wishes whenever "visitation may serve the best interest of the child."[2] The Troxels, paternal grandparents of two children whose father had committed suicide, successfully invoked the law to expand visits beyond that allowed by the children's mother, Tommie Granville, and Granville challenged the court's visitation decree as a violation of her constitutional right to control the upbringing of her children. Ultimately, the Washington Supreme Court struck down the law,[3] finding that the statute violated the substantive rights afforded parents under the Due Process Clause.

The Washington Supreme Court's ruling was based on its conclusion that the Constitution protects parents from all significant state intervention in child rearing that is not narrowly designed to prevent harm to children or others. First and most significantly, the Washington Supreme Court ruled that the statute violated parents' constitutional rights by failing to condition court-compelled visits on a finding that denying visits would be harmful to the child. The court concluded that the statute's "best interest" standard was "insufficient to serve as a compelling state interest overruling a parent's fundamental rights."[4] Second, the Washington court faulted the statute for allowing "any person" to seek visitation at "any time," thereby extending the pool of potential claimants well beyond those who could credibly claim that maintaining their relationship with the child was necessary to protect the child from harm.

The Washington Supreme Court's approach is one that courts have commonly employed when domestic relations cases implicate

---

[2] Wash Rev Code § 26.10.160(3) (1996).

[3] *In re Custody of Smith*, 137 Wash2d 1, 969 P2d 21 (1998).

[4] 969 P2d at 30.

constitutional rights. Most custody and visitation disputes do not press constitutional issues, and in such cases courts have conventionally applied the open-ended "best interest" standard—simply asking what resolution best serves the child's interests. But when constitutional rights are at stake—most typically parents' First Amendment rights of religious exercise—courts have shifted to the more rigorous "harm" standard. They have refused to intervene unless convinced that inaction would expose the child to harm. In disputes between divorcing parents over the religious upbringing of their children, the effect of adopting a harm rather than a best interest standard has been a significant curtailment of the courts' involvement.[5] While a court might well conclude that exposing a child to two sets of conflicting religious practices and beliefs would cause a level of confusion inconsistent with the child's best interests, the harm standard prevents courts from limiting that exposure, absent affirmative proof of more definite and concrete harm.[6] By the time the Washington Supreme Court issued its decision in *Troxel*, courts in other states were increasingly employing this same harm standard to safeguard parents' constitutional right to control the upbringing of their children against well-meaning but unwelcome orders compelling visits with third parties.[7]

While the U.S. Supreme Court affirmed the Washington Supreme Court's holding that Tommie Granville's due process rights had been violated, the six opinions generated in the case reflect near unanimous rejection of the Washington Supreme Court's strongly protective approach. Only Justice Thomas endorsed a position similar to that of the Washington Supreme Court; he suggested that the Constitution bars most, if not all, third-party visita-

---

[5] See Lauren D. Freeman, *The Child's Best Interests vs. the Parent's Free Exercise of Religion*, 32 Colum J L & Soc Probs 73 (1998).

[6] *Zummo v Zummo*, 394 Pa Super 30, 574 A2d 1130, 1155 (1990) ("the speculative possibility of mere disquietude, disorientation, or confusion arising from exposure to 'contradictory' religions would be a patently insufficient 'emotional harm' to justify encroachment by the government upon constitutional parental and religious rights of parents, even in the context of divorce").

[7] See Joan Catherine Bohl, *Grandparent Visitation Law Grows Up: The Trend Toward Awarding Visitation Only When the Child Would Otherwise Suffer Harm*, 48 Drake L Rev 279 (2000) (concluding, shortly before *Troxel* was decided, that the vast majority of the third-party visitation decisions reflected a trend toward concluding that the Constitution required a finding of harm before visits could be ordered).

tion regimes.[8] At the other extreme, Justice Scalia argued against affording parents any constitutional protection whatsoever against third-party visitation claims.[9] Between these extremes, the seven remaining Justices, in four separate opinions, revealed their qualified support for parental rights.

These four opinions differed considerably in their approach to the specific issues in *Troxel*, but their analysis of parental rights was remarkably similar. Whether voting to reverse or affirm, all four recognized some constitutional protection for parental rights, but none suggested that the right is particularly strong. All four appeared open to third-party visitation schemes that would effect a considerable intrusion on parents' control over their children's upbringing.

Justice O'Connor, writing for a plurality of four, and Justice Souter, concurring, both purported to decide as little as possible. The plurality concluded that the statute, as applied, was unconstitutional because the mother's child-rearing choices were entitled to "at least some special weight." Justice Souter similarly rejected the statute's "any person" at "any time" language on the ground that it "sweeps too broadly."[10] But both the plurality and Justice Souter expressly avoided considering whether the Constitution requires the highly protective harm standard;[11] nor did they articulate any other standard that would minimize state intervention. Moreover, the plurality hinted, through extensive citations, at its approval of a broad range of state visitation statutes that would fail any such exacting standard.[12] And what the plurality and, to a lesser extent, Justice Souter signaled through omission and indirection, Justices Stevens and Kennedy conveyed more directly: Both of them rejected Washington's harm standard outright and concluded that a best-interest-based visitation scheme can be sufficiently protective of parental rights.[13]

---

[8] See 120 S Ct at 2068. Justice Thomas made clear that he is open to a reconsideration of the Court's whole line of substantive due process cases had the parties urged such a reconsideration in this case. See id at 2067.

[9] Id at 2074–75.

[10] Id at 2066.

[11] See id at 2064 (plurality opinion); id at 2066 (Souter concurring).

[12] See id at 2062–63 (plurality opinion).

[13] See id at 2070–74 (Stevens dissenting); 2077–79 (Kennedy dissenting).

Read together, these opinions, reflecting the views of seven Justices, convey a common mixed message. Despite the Justices' strong language trumpeting parents' fundamental rights, they stop short of affording parents any significant protection from state intervention. The Justices' attempt to find a middle ground between strong protection of parental decision making and full state authority to intervene in those decisions is easy to understand; it is clearly driven by their concern that children's interests in maintaining other important relationships be adequately protected. But while the Court[14] is right to aim for a constitutional regime that serves children well, it is wrong to think the middle course will take it there.

II. Allocating Child-Rearing Decisions Among Parents, Legislatures, and the Courts

There is broad agreement that deferring to parental decision making generally serves children's interests.[15] Parents commonly know their children better than anyone else and are most highly motivated, by their emotional attachment and considerable investment of time and attention, to pursue their children's interests aggressively. Children's parents are also, for the most part, readily identifiable, and deferring to them therefore eliminates potential confusion over control—or battles for control—that are likely to undermine child rearing.[16] The issue for a child-centered analysis of parental rights is not, therefore, whether parents should be afforded deference. Rather the question is under what condi-

---

[14] Throughout this article I will use "the Court" to refer to the views and approaches shared by a majority of the Justices, expressed in various combinations of Justice O'Connor's plurality, Justice Souter's concurrence, and Justices Stevens's and Kennedy's dissents.

[15] See, for example, *Parham v J.R.*, 442 US 584, 602 (1979) ("The law's concept of the family rests on a presumption that parents possess what a child lacks in maturity, experience, and capacity for judgment required for making life's difficult decisions. More important, historically it has recognized that natural bonds of affection lead parents to act in the best interests of their children."); Elizabeth S. Scott and Robert E. Scott, *Parents as Fiduciaries*, 81 Va L Rev 2401 (1995); Stephen G. Gilles, *On Educating Our Children: A Parentalist Manifesto*, 63 U Chi L Rev 937 (1996).

[16] As I will discuss, problems of parental deference are greatest when parents are not readily identifiable, and I will suggest that it is appropriate for the state to play a different, and I will argue a greater, role in sorting among potential parental claimants precisely because effective parental deference depends on the clarity of parental identity. See Part III.B.

tions, as determined by whom, that deference should be abandoned. It is with these questions that the Court struggles in *Troxel*, and it is its failure to bring any order to the struggle that sets it on its incoherent analytic path.

One can divide the options for allocating child-rearing authority under the law into three rough categories that distribute primary decision-making authority to parents, legislatures, and courts, respectively. At one extreme, we could afford parents an especially high degree of deference, deference only compromised upon a showing of particular, narrowly defined circumstances under which deference was believed to be particularly inappropriate. We commonly assure an individual this level of protection by recognizing a fundamental right, safeguarded by the Constitution, to engage in the protected action (here child rearing) without state intervention. Under the paradigmatic fundamental rights approach, parents would be the near-exclusive child rearer, and the state would play a minimal role in child rearing decisions. Courts would be actively involved as the protector of parental autonomy but not in the making of child-rearing choices, just as they are involved in safeguarding individuals' religious and expressive liberty, without assessing the merits of individuals' specific religious practices or speech.

Second, and at the other extreme, we might withhold all special constitutional protection from parents. While the Constitution would still shield parents, as it does all individuals, from purely arbitrary state action, states would be free to determine the proper scope of parental deference and the procedures to be followed to justify its compromise, so long as the state had some minimal non-arbitrary justification for its determinations. Because there is such widespread support for deferring to parents, legislatures would undoubtedly continue to enact parent-favoring laws, and laws that showed no deference to parents' choices in child rearing might even be struck down as arbitrary. Nonetheless, under this approach, the state legislatures would control the allocation of authority between parent, state, and other individuals. Courts would exercise little or no constitutional oversight over that allocation. But courts would play the role assigned to them by the legislature in resolving individual child-rearing disputes.

Third, and in between these two extremes, lies an interpretation of the Constitution that affords parents some special protection but that also allows for a compromise of parental authority in a relatively broad range of circumstances. Under any in-between scenario, the courts would assume a considerably greater role in assessing the merits of various struggles between parents and the state than they would under either the fundamental rights or rights-denying approach. Whereas a fundamental rights approach charges the courts with aggressively limiting state interference, and a rights-denying approach prevents the courts from blocking this interference, a qualified-rights approach leaves the allocation of child-rearing authority between parent and state to the courts. As with the rights-denying approach, the allocation of this authority between the parent and state would be determined issue by issue, but here the determiners would be the courts rather than the state legislatures. It is this in-between approach that a majority of the Justices embrace in *Troxel*.

In the sections that follow, I will consider the potential value to children of the more extreme options the Court avoids and the problems created by the Court's compromise solution. I will suggest that children are likely to be best served by a constitutional regime that shields most parental decision making from unwelcome state intervention, and considerably less well served by the complete abandonment of any special constitutional protection. Either of these more extreme approaches, however, offers more to children than any compromise that lies between them. In particular, I will suggest that the compromise attempted by the Court in *Troxel* is certain to produce an endless stream of constitutional litigation and likely to produce bad results for children.

In considering the extent to which the Constitution shields parents from state intervention, I will not debate whether it is in general appropriate to recognize unenumerated substantive rights under the Due Process Clause. I take this as a given, as does the Supreme Court, apparently, at least for now.[17] Nor do I address in detail the extent to which granting fundamental rights to parents conforms with general substantive due process doctrine as articulated in other areas of the law, although I will explain, in Part III,

---

[17] See, for example, *Troxel*, 120 S Ct at 2059–60 (plurality opinion); id at 2066 (Souter concurring); *Washington v Glucksberg*, 521 US 702, 719–20 (1997). But cf. *Troxel*, 120 S Ct at 2067 (Thomas concurring) ("express[ing] no view" on whether courts should enforce unenumerated rights, because the issue was not raised by the parties); id at 2074 (Scalia dissenting).

how the approach I suggest is fully consistent with earlier Supreme Court decisions dealing with parental rights. Recent substantive due process decisions have emphasized the importance of tradition in determining the existence and content of implied fundamental rights,[18] and the Justices agreed in *Troxel* that parents have traditionally been given great autonomy over their children.[19] But the issue the Justices struggled with in *Troxel*, appropriately, was the extent to which children's needs justify a departure from that tradition. The Justices in *Troxel* were concerned with what kind of constitutional regime would best protect children's interests and would, in general, make the most sense. I focus on that question as well.

A. AFFORDING PARENTS THE PROTECTION OF A FUNDAMENTAL RIGHT

Because fundamental rights are classically conceived as the rights of individuals to pursue their own interests, conventional analysis distinguishes between affording parents strong rights, on the one hand, and protecting children's competing interests on the other.[20] But children may be best served by a legal regime that bolsters their parents' rights and sharply restricts the state's authority to intervene on their behalf. Children are likely to benefit from such a system for two primary reasons, one straightforward and one counterintuitive. The first, already briefly acknowledged, is that parents are generally best situated to make good judgments on their children's behalf. The second is that parents, good and bad, can be expected to perform better as parents if afforded near absolute control over the upbringing of their children. Taken together, these arguments suggest that children may be best served by limiting state intervention to those circumstances where parental incompetence is most serious and demonstrable. Absent a showing of harm, and, more particularly, the sort of harm the state has

---

[18] See, for example, *Washington v Glucksberg*, 521 US at 721.

[19] 120 S Ct at 2060 (plurality opinion); id at 2066 (Souter concurring); id at 2071 (Stevens dissenting); id at 2076 (Kennedy dissenting).

[20] See Scott and Scott, 81 Va L Rev at 2405 (cited in note 15) (citing popular, academic, and judicial sources suggesting that the law affords parents too much protection, at the expense of their children).

superior competence to assess, state intervention is likely to make things worse for children.[21]

1. *Deference in recognition of parents' superior competence.* The basic, well-accepted argument for showing parents some deference translates readily to an argument for showing parents nearly absolute deference. If parents can be expected to know their children better and care about them more than does the state, parents ought to be given full authority over them, absent some showing that calls these expectations into serious question. Assuming that there is a wide range of reasonable disagreement on most child-rearing matters and that the best choices will require an individualized assessment of a child's needs, a strong system of parental rights ensures that the child-specific expert—the parent—is shielded from intrusions by well-meaning outsiders who are less likely to get things right.

The logic of this argument suggests that any exception to this rule of deference ought to be grounded, at a minimum, on a determination that the parent is making harmful choices. Where a parent can be shown to be harming her child, we might indeed question how well she understands her child's needs, or how devoted she is to meeting those needs. But when a parent's choices do not harm the child—when the only question is whether those choices are as beneficial to the child as some other choices might be—we have every reason to expect that the parents' decisions will be at least as good as those made by the less competent state. We also have no reliable means of disproving that expectation, and little reason to be particularly concerned even if we could. Of course, there is no clear line between "harmful" choices and choices that

---

[21] This argument has much in common with the argument of Elizabeth and Robert Scott, see id, who contend that the parent-child relationship can be viewed as a form of fiduciary relationship best fostered by affording parents considerable deference. While I embrace much of the Scotts' analysis, I fear that the fiduciary analogy, while conceptually illuminating, may invite precisely the sort of well-meaning intrusions by the state that this fiduciary analysis is offered to oppose. In my view, employing the "rhetoric" of rights that the Scotts criticize as undermining the fiduciary conception may be necessary to serve children's interests best. Because of the strong impulse of state actors to intrude where, in their view, children's interests are being disserved, grounding the protection firmly in parental rights and, in this sense, obscuring the connection between parental deference and children's interests may, in fact, increase the chance that these interests will be served. Any transparently child-focused legal construct is likely to afford inadequate protection against the temptation to depart from a generalized commitment to deference in the face of troubling particulars. By fixing that deference in the convention of rights, that deference is far less likely to be subject to such well-meaning compromise.

are not as beneficial as they might be; most child-serving goals could readily be recast as attempts to avoid some harm that could befall a child absent state intervention.[22] To prevent the exception from swallowing the rule, therefore, the harm required to justify intervention must be limited not only to the most severe and ascertainable harm, but also—and perhaps more important—to harm the state has some special competence to assess.

The state's relative competence in assessing harm is greatest in two sorts of circumstances where a community-focused viewpoint is especially relevant: first, where the alleged harm relates to the child's development as a public citizen, and, second, where the alleged harm is the subject of broad societal consensus. The state's expertise in assessing the first sort of harm comes from its superior knowledge of the political and economic community and, more particularly, what this community demands of its citizens as conditions of their participation and of the community's own survival. The state's expertise in assessing the second sort of harm comes from its superior knowledge of community views. But to remain faithful to the competence-based justification for deference, community views ought to trump parental views only when they reflect a broad consensus that the child-rearing practice in question is always harmful. Where there is no such consensus, the case for harm is too uncertain to justify displacing the parents' views with that of the state, and where the harm is child-specific, the relative expert on the question remains the parent.[23]

Under this analysis, the case for state intervention is particularly weak in the context of third-party visits. Indeed, cases like *Troxel* present a weaker argument for state intervention than do the core cases of *Meyer v Nebraska*,[24] *Pierce v Society of Sisters*,[25] and *Wisconsin*

---

[22] While such recasting has not occurred in the context of disputes over religious upbringing where parents' choices are protected by the Free Exercise Clause, see text at notes 5–6, it may be occurring where courts claim to be applying a type of harm standard in determining whether a parent's homosexuality justifies imposing limits on that parent's custody or visitation rights. See Julie Shapiro, *Custody and Conduct: How the Law Fails Lesbian and Gay Parents and Their Children*, 71 Ind L J 623, 641–45 (1996).

[23] Compare Scott and Scott, 81 Va L Rev at 2438–39 (cited in note 15) (arguing that the "pre-emptive conflict of interest rules" governing parents as fiduciaries should be limited to circumstances where "a societal consensus about the impact of the regulated conduct on children dictates a particular choice").

[24] 262 US 390 (1923).

[25] 268 US 510 (1925).

v Yoder[26]—cases that emphatically protected parents' rights to
make decisions about their children free from state interference.
A theory of parental rights grounded on an assessment of relative
competence should afford parents broadest authority over child-
rearing decisions such as visits, whose consequences are relatively
private, and more qualified authority over decisions with more significant public consequences, such as where and when their children go to school. And while this approach allows state intervention aimed at preventing child abuse (child-rearing conduct widely
perceived as harmful in all cases), it should shield parents from
intervention aimed at preventing the harmful disruption of relationships (conduct perceived only by some, and only in some circumstances, as harmful). This is not to say that depriving children
of particular relationships will never be harmful, but rather that
we simply cannot expect the state to have any comparative advantage over parents in assessing that harm.

But grounding deference on a confidence in parents' superior
child-rearing judgment, while theoretically sound, faces a significant problem in application. The vulnerability of the comparative
competence argument is that courts will find it least compelling
in precisely those circumstances where it is most needed—circumstances where the state disapproves of the judgments parents make.
This temptation to abandon institutional humility may be particularly great in the child-rearing context, where the stakes are high,
opinions are strong, and the issues are readily accessible to all.
Ultimately, deference based on parental competence is only as
strong as the courts' faith in that competence. The second argument for deference does not share this vulnerability, for it is premised on the assumption that parents' competence is limited and
easily undermined.

2. *Deference as a means of enhancing parents' competence.* While the
first argument for deference is that parents are more qualified than
the state to make child-rearing judgments for their particular children, the second is that the quality of those judgments will, on
balance, be better in the absence of state interference. This connection between state interference and parental competence can
be described in positive or negative terms. In positive terms, giving

---

[26] 406 US 205 (1972).

parents near absolute freedom to raise their children as they see fit may enhance their enjoyment of, and commitment to, the child-rearing task, thereby making them better parents. In negative terms, intruding on that freedom may undermine those parents' effectiveness, even where the intrusions are designed to help. While all parents may benefit from being given a greater freedom in child rearing, we can expect the worst parents to be least equipped to accommodate disruptive intrusions.

Unlike the first argument for deference, which essentially conceives of parents as their children's surrogates, this second argument takes more explicit account of parents' own interests, and in this sense it looks more like paradigmatic fundamental rights analysis. According to this paradigm, we afford individuals broad freedom in exercising choice in certain areas of their lives because we highly value autonomous action in certain contexts, and because we recognize that state intervention can readily inhibit these exercises of autonomy. Similarly, under our second justification for affording parents strong rights, the value and the fragility of parental autonomy are central concerns.

In other fundamental rights contexts, the value we place on autonomous action translates into a disregard for the actual choices made. The individual choice-making itself is thought to contribute significantly to individual well-being or, as it is sometimes more expansively described, to "human flourishing." We aggressively protect individuals' right to say what they want to say, worship as they choose, go where they want to go, and control their own procreation because we value individuals' freedom to do so, regardless of the perceived merits of those choices. Even wise, caring state intervention in these areas is harmful, for it compromises autonomy no less for being wise and well justified.

If we treat parents' authority to control the upbringing of their children as a fundamental right, we protect parents' autonomy in child rearing and shield those choices from the judgment and intervention of others. The challenge is to justify such a hands-off approach as a good means of serving precisely the interest that might inspire the state to intervene, namely, the interest in the well-being of children. The first justification for this approach depends on the objective quality of the judgments parents make (and the limited ability of the state to assess the quality of those judgments). The second justification, however, is more like the argument for freedom of religion or reproductive freedom: the individual's choice is better simply because it is the individual's, regardless of the objective quality of those choices. In other words, affording parents great freedom in making child-rearing choices, regardless of how good the particular choices are, may facilitate parenting that is, in fact, especially good for children. We might shield parents from an assessment of the choices they make, not because these choices do not matter, but because we conclude that the way to produce the best parenting overall is to avoid state scrutiny and intervention.

As unattractive as it sounds, children may benefit from an interpretation of the Constitution that conceives of parenting as an exercise in self-fulfillment and casts children as the objects of that exercise. Conceiving child rearing in these terms could quite plausibly inspire a greater level of commitment, creativity, and enthusiasm, a greater intensity of involvement and joy in execution, than would be inspired by job-like conceptions of parenting thought to be more respectful of children.[27] Even the proprietary implications of conceiving of child rearing as an exercise in self-fulfillment may serve children. The notion that children "belong" to their parents may have powerful, positive psychological value to parent and child alike.[28] It suggests a kind of inevitability, an absoluteness about the relationship that will help maintain the parent and child's sense of

---

[27] Compare Scott and Scott, 81 Va L Rev at 2456, 2463 (cited in note 15) (noting that affording parents special rights is a necessary part of the bargain that creates the incentive for parents to act responsibly toward their children and can be conceived as an "inducement to satisfactory parental performance"). This likely connection between the experience of parenting as self-fulfillment and the increased intensity of commitment to the parenting project suggests that even arguments for parental rights that claim to take no account of children's interests may, in fact, reveal a child-serving purpose. See, for example, Ferdinand Schoeman, *Rights of Children, Rights of Parents, and the Moral Basis of the Family*, 91 Ethics 6 (1980) (suggesting that parents' interest in forming and nurturing intimate relationships stands as a justification, independent of children's interests, for protecting parental decision making from state intervention).

[28] See Katharine K. Baker, *Property Rules Meet Feminist Needs: Respecting Autonomy by Valuing Connection*, 59 Ohio St L J 1523, 1576 (1998) (describing parents' "possessive sense" about their children as crucial to parents' devotion to the child-rearing process); Bruce C. Hafen, *Individualism and Autonomy in Family Law: The Waning of Belonging*, 1991 BYU L Rev 1, 31–33 (describing the value, to children, of the "sense of possession implicit in the concept of belonging"). The sense of loss experienced by many adopted children and the psychological problems sometimes associated with that sense of loss offer further evidence of the value, to children, of their sense of inevitable connection. See, for example, David M. Brodzinsky, *Adjustment to Adoption: A Psychological Perspective*, 7 Clinical Psychology Rev 25 (1987).

connection with one another even through fierce disagreements or failed parenting choices.[29]

This is not to suggest that parents will read court decisions declaring their rights to be nearly absolute and blossom as child rearers in response. But rights have the best chance of influencing behavior when they are strong and simple enough to be absorbed into popular culture. The average citizen knows he has a right to free speech in part because the right has been so boldly and unequivocally enforced. The effect of this awareness on behavior, however, will depend on the extent to which the potential for intervention is inhibiting. Ultimately, then, the positive case for affording parents expansive protection is entangled with the negative: We see what benefit parents derive from being given freedom, by considering what they would lose, and what they would fear losing, if that freedom were diminished.

As in other fundamental rights contexts, our justification for heightened protection is not just that individual choice making is valuable, but also that it is fragile. The process of child rearing, at its creative and self-fulfilling best, is a delicate process. Even relatively minor intrusions could wreak havoc on this parenting by introducing inhibitions, undermining authority, and forcing an awkward sharing of authorship.[30] But here, again, the child-serving focus twists the justification somewhat. Whereas with other rights we might worry that intervention will diminish an individual's achievement of life satisfaction, here we worry about the effect any such diminution will have on the children of these less satisfied parents.

While it would be difficult to try to assess, in general terms, the harm done to parenting by a scheme that diminishes parental autonomy, we can see, in more specific contexts, how intrusions can undermine the child-rearing process. When parents must comply with unwelcome intervention, they must accommodate their schedules and their attitudes to the intervention, modify other parenting choices to ensure consistency and continuity, and

---

[29] See Joseph Goldstein, Anna Freud, and Albert Solnit, *Beyond the Best Interests of the Child* (Free Press, 1973).

[30] See Andrew W. Watson, *Children, Families, and Courts: Before the Best Interests of the Child and Parham v J.R.*, 66 Va L Rev 678 (1980) (drawing on psychological literature to argue that even minor state intrusions, particularly judicial intrusions, on parental decision making can impair family functioning).

tolerate a relatively public display of their lack of authority. We can safely predict that the "best" parents, those most driven by their children's best interests and flexible, energetic, and imaginative in their child-rearing style, will be able to make these accommodations most successfully. The "worst" parents, in contrast, will be least able to weather the intervention without seriously compromising the quality of the care they provide.

In this sense, the second argument for deference to parents folds back on the first, though in a less idealized form. Parents' judgments about their children's interests may warrant deference simply because they are the judgments the parents have chosen to make. Because parents will inevitably be charged with implementing child-rearing choices, whether made by the state or parent, the value of these choices to children simply cannot be abstracted from the likelihood that parents will implement these choices properly. In other words, even if a choice is best for a child, in theory, it will often not be in fact, if a parent thinks otherwise. Moreover, no matter how successfully any particular choice is implemented, it will disserve children's interests if that implementation, in turn, undermines broader parental functioning.

Showing parents near unbounded deference will itself sometimes lead to abuse. To ground parenting on notions of possession and self-fulfillment is to admit as much. But this second argument for deference is premised on a view that giving parents this level of control over their children's upbringing can be expected, in most cases, to inspire them to act selflessly, to commit themselves more fully, and the like. Under this theory, the very constraints the state might impose in an attempt to improve parenting could have the effect of inhibiting what is best about parenting and attenuating the relationship between parent and child.

As with the first argument, this second argument for deference allows for exceptions when deference is least likely to serve this enabling function. But requiring a showing of harm will ensure that such exceptions are kept to a minimum and limited to circumstances where they are most justified.[31] The narrowness of the ex-

---

[31] The experience of courts in applying harm-based standards (as opposed to traditional best interest standards) in resolving certain custody issues suggests that such standards can be highly successful in constraining state intervention, See, for example, Lauren D. Freeman, *The Child's Best Interests v. the Parent's Free Exercise of Religion*, 32 Colum J L & Soc Probs 73 (1998) (noting that, where parents' religious rights are implicated, the courts

ception should leave parents considerable space in which to pursue the child-rearing project without the constant concern that their decisions will be second-guessed by the state, and the relative clarity of the standard should help define for parents the borders of that space. Moreover, this narrow approach ensures that whatever damage is done by the intrusion will be offset by the prevention of some identified harm on the other side.

Whether the harm avoided is sufficient to outweigh the harm imposed by the intrusion is, however, another question. This second argument for deference suggests that courts considering parental rights challenges should ask not only what harm the challenged state action is designed to prevent, but also what burdens the action would impose on parents' child-rearing performance.

As already noted, intervention designed to affect only a small number of parenting tasks can nevertheless infect the parents' overall attitude and effectiveness, and these psychological effects, as well as the more straightforward operational effects, must be taken into account. Because the disruptive effect is likely to be considerable but difficult to quantify, courts enforcing a fundamental right should assume that any intervention burdens parental functioning; to justify intervention, the state would need to demonstrate either that the intervention imposed no significant burden on parents or that the burden was outweighed by the harm avoided.[32]

Proper burden analysis, then, would make it even less likely that orders compelling third-party visitation would survive constitutional challenge. In addition to failing the harm standard imposed by the strong deference approach, compelled visitation orders can be expected to impose serious burdens on parenting. Even the best, most reasonable parents will experience an order compelling unwanted visits as a severe constraint on their fulfillment of their child-rearing responsibilities. Although visitation orders generally limit visits to a fraction of a child's time and do not qualify parental control of upbringing in any other way, compelled visits take away hours from the parent and limit the parent's flexibility in using

---

commonly employ a harm standard that significantly limits intervention in custody disputes involving religious practices).

[32] The procedural mechanism by which this would be accomplished would be the assignment to the state of the burden of persuasion on these points.

the hours that remain. At least as significantly, they send the message to children, extended family, and, to some extent, the entire community that the parent is not in control, indeed, that the parent has misjudged what is best for her children. Moreover, such visits set children up to be participants in the battle, inviting them to judge their parents' attitudes and choices before many of them are developmentally prepared to do so. It turns them, temporarily, into the hands of other adults sufficiently opposed to the child's parents to make them willing to fight the parents in court.

Where parents resist conforming to the visitation orders, the burden imposed on the family is likely to be greater still. The visits may introduce considerable stress and hostility into family relationships, effects the child would surely experience as well. To say that such resistance is bad, or reflects a parent's selfish motives, is beside the point, unless we go so far as to conclude that the resistance is bad enough to justify removing the child from the parent's control. Indeed, as noted, the value of showing deference to parents may be greatest for those parents who generally do less well, for they are the ones who will be least capable of working successfully around interventions to which they are opposed.

3. *The appropriate test to protect strong parental rights.* Both arguments for deference support an approach to parental rights that is near-absolute. They also rationalize the circumstances under which exceptions are appropriate. Read together, these exceptions suggest a test that courts could apply in enforcing strong parental rights: courts should forbid state intervention that burdens parental autonomy unless the intervention is necessary to prevent serious harm the state has special competence to assess.

This test would prohibit most state intervention with minimal court involvement in the substance of the child-rearing decisions, for it would point expectations heavily in the direction of preventing intervention. The test would serve the role commonly served by the strict scrutiny standard in enforcing other fundamental rights, but it offers a better fit than the strict scrutiny test in our context where the purpose behind giving such strong protection to parents' rights blurs with the state's interest in limiting those rights.

Because the primary justification for the fundamental rights approach, in our context, focuses on the protection of the interests of the child, the proper scope of exceptions cannot be determined by using the kind of tests often employed when other fundamental rights are asserted. In those other contexts, courts are called upon to balance a claim of right (such as the right of free speech or the interest in personal privacy) against the interests of others whom the state is charged with serving (such as the interest in national security or effective law enforcement). When a right is afforded particularly strong constitutional protection, the courts will use a test—the standard strict scrutiny approach, which asks whether the restriction on the right is necessary to promote a compelling state interest, is one example—that tilts the balance heavily in favor of the individual.

But this kind of approach offers an awkward fit when—as in dealing with a parent's right to raise her child as she sees fit—the individual's right and the state's asserted reason for limiting that right share the common purpose of securing a child's successful upbringing. A state's interest in ensuring the child's successful development can readily be cast as a compelling state interest,[33] and parents' interest in achieving that same goal by avoiding state interference can just as readily serve to justify strong protection for their rights. When the same interest is on both sides of the balance, courts will unavoidably find themselves weighing the relative competence of parent and state to assess and implement this single interest. Such weighing drags the court far deeper into the substance of child-rearing decisions than is appropriate where parents' authority over the substance is safeguarded as a fundamental right. Moreover, unlike in other rights contexts, where there may be little to guide courts' balancing other than the strength of the presumption favoring one interest over the other, here we can identify relevant criteria—harm, and the state's competence to assess various harms—that can give courts real guidance in resolving parental rights claims. In asking whether the state's action was needed to protect a child from some harm that the state had superior competence to assess and whether the states' purposes in intervening outweighed the likely harm associated with that intervention, the court can help ensure that any interferences with parents' decision making remain faithful to the child-serving purposes behind the general rule of deference.

---

[33] See, for example, *Prince v Massachusetts*, 321 US 158 (1944) ("It is the interest of youth itself, and of the whole community, that children be both safeguarded from abuses and given opportunities for growth into free and independent well-developed men and citizens").

Courts already apply a standard roughly like this in disputes between parents over their children's religious upbringing. The experience in that area suggests that the standard can be expected dramatically to reduce the frequency and extent of court intervention in parental decision making. Parents' free exercise rights have been construed to prohibit the court from making "best interest" judgments about their children's religious upbringing, even where the parents disagree sharply and one parent seeks the court's assistance in working things out. Relying on the harm standard, courts routinely eschew involvement in these controversies, which, but for their constitutional grounding, would entangle the court in complex assessments of parental attitudes, competitive scheduling concerns, and the ideal program of development for the child. As I will discuss below, the Supreme Court's very reluctance to embrace the harm standard in the third-party visitation context suggests that, in its eyes, this standard is both distinct from the "best interests" standard and a strong obstacle to state intervention.

B. LEAVING THE ALLOCATION OF CHILD-REARING AUTHORITY TO THE STATES

The arguments I offer for a fundamental rights approach rest on assumptions about parental competence and about how that competence is undermined. While these assumptions will ring true to many, they elude definitive proof. There is some support in the social science literature for the conclusion that state intrusions, even well-meaning intrusions, threaten family functioning,[34] but the literature is far from conclusive, and this is unlikely to change. The issues are too sensitive and complex to be tested in the laboratory setting, and real situations are too varied and volatile to produce clear answers. The strongest argument against this fundamental rights approach may well be that it rests on unprovable assumptions. We may not want to construe the Constitution to require near-absolute deference to parents in the absence of affirmative proof that children will benefit from such an approach.

This concern for proof argues for a full-scale abandonment of

---

[34] Joseph Goldstein, Anna Freud, and Albert Solnit are credited with drawing popular and political attention to the psychological risks associated with state intervention and family disruption in a series of books beginning with *Beyond the Best Interests of the Child* (cited in note 29).

parents' constitutional protection, which would leave the allocation of child-rearing authority to the states, to be determined by the legislative process. Under this approach, we would still expect to see considerable deference to parents, but the nature and extent of that deference would be left to the states to define. Such an approach might be preferable, not because state legislatures have better access to empirical evidence—there is no reason to believe that they do—but because their decision-making process may be perceived as more legitimate, in the absence of such evidence. To the extent legislation reflects majority views, allocating child-rearing authority through this process serves to legitimize the allocation, regardless of the soundness of the judgments made by the legislature.

But we ought not to be overly optimistic about the benefits that flow from this approach. Any value that comes from ensuring democratic control will be attenuated in at least three respects. First, children do not vote. As with individual decision making on behalf of children, the legislative process relies on surrogates to identify children's interests. The interest in self-government, generally advanced as a reason for allowing democratic decision making, is, therefore, weaker when those decisions affect children's interests.

Second, there is reason to be suspicious, at least in the context of third-party visitation, about whether the legislation even reflects the view of most adults. The explosion of grandparent visitation statutes appears to have been driven by interest group politics and may reveal not that most adults think that such compelled visits are good for children, but only that grandparents do. And, third, even to the extent that this legislation does reflect the majority's will, it leaves most of the policy-making undone. Legislation affecting child rearing commonly sets out policy at a high level of generality and defers implementation to courts and agencies. When, as in the third-party visitation context, states direct courts to ascertain children's "best interests," they shift the primary policy-making role to the implementing courts.

The legitimacy of legislative decision making derives at least in part from the common identity of legislative author and subject. Just as with individual decision making, we entrust lawmaking to the people in part because we think they are in the best position to ascertain what outcomes will be best for them. But, again as in the individual context, legislative decision making about children splits author from subject. The voters impose the rules, but do not experience the consequences. In the previous section I pointed to parents' superior, child-specific competence in assessing these consequences to argue for parental deference. A preference for a less individualized, more community-wide assessment of children's needs would argue for the legislative surrogate approach. Either way, choice making for children lacks one claim to legitimacy that we recognize where adults make choices for themselves.

Moreover, even if we conclude that the community of adults represents the best aggregate decision maker for children, we should not be confident that this community has endorsed all child-focused legislation enacted. There is much evidence to suggest that the vast majority of the support for these third-party visitation laws came from lobby groups representing the elderly, and that these groups have devoted considerable resources to getting these laws enacted.[35] The text of the visitation statutes reflects this bias, affording grandparents visitation rights in all fifty states, and including additional claimants, such as siblings and step-parents in only some, despite the comparable strength of their relational claims.

And finally, even where child-rearing legislation is, in fact, supported by a majority of adults, the routine involvement of agencies and courts in the implementation of such legislation ensures that considerable policy-making will occur at a distance from the law-making majority. The more absolute and defined the policies set out in legislation, the stronger the claim of democratic control.[36] But where the people's view set out in legislation is more equivocal and favors a departure from parental deference in only some cases, then the courts and agencies, in implementing the legislation, will play a much bigger policy-making role. Their policy-making role

---

[35] See Comment, Anne Marie Jackson, *The Coming of Age of Grandparent Visitation Rights,* 43 Am U L Rev 563, 564 (1994) (noting that third-party visitation statutes "are due largely to the well-organized efforts of grandparents and their supporters, who joined together to ensure that the law preserves the 'special' relationship between grandparents and grandchildren").

[36] This analysis echoes the analysis of appropriate exceptions under the deferential approach. In that context, I suggested that the state had superior expertise in assessing community attitudes about child rearing, but that these attitudes should only trump parents' individualized assessments where community attitudes were sufficiently absolute to render such individualization inappropriate. Here, I suggest that the case for legislative control is strongest where community standards are sufficiently absolute to leave little individualized policy-making to agencies and the courts.

will be especially great where they are directed to make "best interest" judgments. Whatever we might think of the best interest standard (I will discuss its problems below), its employment can hardly be characterized as the shifting of decision making from the courts to the people. Rather, legislation that relies on such best interest determinations shifts decision making from parents to courts, albeit with the people's approval.[37]

To put the point another way, the three alternative approaches to the issue presented in *Troxel* all, of necessity, assign some important role to the courts. But the roles differ sharply. The fundamental rights approach relies on the Supreme Court to articulate a nearly absolute parental right, and then on lower federal courts and state courts to enforce that right and ensure that parents' control is sufficiently protected. The lower courts may be called upon to block state intervention, but the approach is designed to minimize court involvement in the merits of child-rearing decisions by heavily favoring the parents in their disputes with the state. The second approach eliminates the courts' involvement in fundamental decisions about the allocation of child-rearing authority between parent and state—those decisions are made by the legislature—but it inevitably leads to extensive involvement by the courts in the case-specific determinations that will be needed to implement those standards. The middle ground that the *Troxel* Court sought, which I will address next, assigns to the courts a continuing role as constitutional interpreter that requires them to assess the merits of each parent-state dispute. As I will discuss, it is in this role of case-by-base constitutional policy-maker that courts are most likely to disserve children, by subjecting them to ongoing, standardless litigation that the courts have no special competence to resolve.

In his dissenting opinion in *Troxel*, Justice Scalia championed the superiority of leaving the articulation of parental rights to the democratic process rather than grounding those rights in the Constitution:

---

[37] Interestingly, legislatures' awareness of constitutional constraints has, if anything, reduced the extent to which policy-making is shifted to the courts. In imposing some constraints upon the courts' authorization of third-party visits, legislatures have simultaneously reserved control to parents (as child-rearing decision makers) and themselves (as the entity that defines the exceptions to that deference).

> I have no reason to believe that federal judges will be better at this than state legislatures; and state legislatures have the great advantages of doing harm in a more circumscribed area, of being able to correct their mistakes in a flash, and of being removable by the people.[38]

This argument is naive, both in its overweighing of the role of the legislature in the rights-denying approach and in its exaggeration of the courts' role under an approach that provides parents a near-absolute constitutional right. Justice Scalia's criticism nevertheless has considerable force, not as an argument against affording parents constitutional protection, but as an argument against his fellow Justices' foggy conception of that protection. It is these Justices' attempt to embrace an approach that falls between a full recognition of parents' constitutional rights and the abandonment of those rights that threatens to give unwarranted authority to the courts.

C. THE PROBLEM WITH THE MIDDLE WAY

A majority of the Justices in *Troxel*, as I have said, attempted to walk a middle course, suggesting that the Constitution establishes parents' rights to some deference, but that this deference can be qualified to serve children's needs. It is easy to see the appeal the middle holds for the Court: It recognizes some special authority in parents but allows the state to police how that authority is exercised. In application, however, the middle ground is standardless, offering no clear, principled basis on which to distinguish appropriate from inappropriate state interference. As a result, courts are left to make family law policy absent the constraints of either meaningful standards or the democratic process, and children can be expected to suffer a triple loss: they lose the individualized expertise of their parents and the community-wide expertise of democratic lawmaking, and in their place they gain the additional harm associated with this ongoing constitutional litigation.

1. *Something less than a fundamental right.* The Court's abandonment of the fundamental rights approach is not obvious on the face of its opinions. In addition to declaring their ongoing endorsement of the fundamental rights approach, the Justices' analy-

---

[38] 120 S Ct at 2075.

sis purports to require significant deference to parents. On closer look, however, the very details of this analysis reveal how far the court has strayed from the fundamental rights approach. Read together, the "in-between" opinions took four steps that are inconsistent with affording parental decision making the strong protection of a fundamental right: First, they sent a strong signal that the Constitution does not require a finding of harm to justify state intervention in a parent's child rearing. Second, they offered no alternative standard that would serve the same purpose of facilitating and rationalizing the courts' favoring of parents in parent-state disputes. Third, in their apparent embrace of the best interest standard, the Justices failed to recognize the comparative institutional competence of parents, over courts, in assessing the appropriateness of visits. And, fourth, they discounted the harm to parental effectiveness caused not only by compelled visitation, but also by the very litigation of third-party visitation claims.

a) The Court's failure to adopt the harm standard. As I have said, an approach that requires deference to parents must be safeguarded by high standards, and a harm standard offers a particularly strong and coherent means of screening out unconstitutional state intrusions. In rejecting the harm-based approach, the Court revealed its lack of commitment to such a strongly deferential approach. In showing no regard for the work done by the harm standard, or the void created by its absence, the Court suggested that it was paying little attention to the justifications behind the right it espoused.

While only dissenters Kennedy and Stevens expressly concluded that the Constitution does not require a finding of harm to justify unwelcome state intervention, the remaining in-between opinions sent the same message despite their protestations of avoiding the issue. This is, in part, because the very avoidance of an issue so squarely presented signals an unwillingness to endorse the approach. But the particular approaches the Justices took in analyzing parental rights served to strengthen the signal considerably. They did this, in part, by reading the harm rationale out of the aspects of the lower court's holding they claimed to embrace. The plurality went further, stopping just short of endorsing several third-party visitation statutes that impose no harm requirement.

The entire holding of the Washington Supreme Court was based on a conclusion that the Constitution protects parents from all state intrusions not designed to prevent harm. That conclusion, in turn, led the Washington court to reject the statute, both because the statute failed to premise visitation issues on a finding of harm and because it opened the courts to third-party claimants whose relationships with children are too attenuated to make a plausible case for harm.[39] But in interpreting the lower court's ruling, the Justices suggested that the Washington Supreme Court's rejection of the statute's breadth, of which they approved, was distinct from the Washington Supreme Court's reliance on the harm standard. In doing so, the Justices offered no alternative account of why the statute's breadth was constitutionally problematic.

The plurality also suggested that the Constitution imposes no harm requirement by citing, with apparent approval, to a number of state statutes that impose no such requirement. For an opinion designed to be as narrow as possible, it engaged in a strikingly lengthy exploration of other states' third-party visitation statutes to illustrate how the Washington legislature could have done better.[40] Later in this section I will address some of the problems created for parents and children by these statutes. Here, I simply note the significance, to legislatures and courts applying *Troxel*, of the plurality's apparent endorsement of any non-harm-based alternatives.[41] Among all the legislative efforts to conform third-party visitation statutes to *Troxel* since the case was decided, it appears that none has introduced a harm requirement, while a number have introduced language that mirrors that of statutes cited by the plurality.[42] Similarly, it appears that no court (among the many that have addressed third-party visitation since *Troxel* was decided) has interpreted the Constitution to impose a harm requirement, de-

---

[39] *In re Custody of Smith*, 969 P2d at 31 ("It seems that at a minimum such a showing [that the petitioner has a substantial relationship with child] should be required because harm to a child cannot reasonably be anticipated as a result of no contact with someone with whom the child has had no such relationship.").

[40] 120 S Ct at 2062–63.

[41] See, for example, *In re G.P.C.*, 28 SW3d 357, 363 (Mo App 2000) (interpreting the Court's citation to "differing provisions in the various statutes" as a "probable indication that the dissimilar terminology also affects their constitutionality"); *Rubino v DiCenzo*, 759 A2d 959, 975 (RI Sup Ct 2000) (citing *Troxel*'s citation of Rhode Island's statute as evidence that the Court approved of the Rhode Island approach to third-party visitation).

[42] See, for example, ND S.B. 2047 (proposing, among other things, the addition of language requiring a finding that visits would not interfere with the parent-child relationship before third-party visits could be ordered).

spite the evident trend in that direction prior to the *Troxel* decision.[43]

When a lower court interprets the Constitution to impose a harm requirement, and the Supreme Court declines to follow suit, legislatures and courts will construe the Supreme Court's action as a rejection of the harm requirement. Such a construction is clearly consistent with the views of two Justices, and probably consistent with the views of several more. If this construction misreads the Court's view, the result will be hundreds of unnecessary violations of constitutional rights. The Court's likely awareness of such consequences, particularly on issues, such as this one, which it is unlikely to revisit in the foreseeable future, offers still more evidence that the Court intended to reject the harm requirement.

b) The Court's failure to articulate any parent-favoring standard. The Court's failure to embrace a harm standard would be less significant if it offered some other standard affording parents comparable protection. But the Court offered no such standard, and it appeared deliberate in its refusal to do so. Despite Justice Thomas's explicit prodding, the Court was silent, neither adopting a standard nor explaining the omission. The result is a claim of protection with no apparent content—hardly a prescription for a fundamental constitutional right.

This refusal to articulate a standard (or even to justify the refusal to articulate one) is particularly striking in light of the guidance lower courts were clearly seeking from the Court in defining parents' substantive rights. The Court last articulated any standard thirty years ago, in *Wisconsin v Yoder*,[44] where it applied the strict scrutiny standard to state educational requirements challenged on free exercise and due process grounds.[45] But even there, the applicability of the strict scrutiny standard to purely secular parental rights claims was not clearly addressed. Since *Yoder*, the Court has had few opportunities to articulate a standard, despite a great deal of lower court activity considering the question. The *Troxel* Court surely must have understood the value, in preserving strong paren-

---

[43] See Joan Catherine Bohl, *Grandparent Visitation Law Grows Up: The Trend Toward Awarding Visitation Only When the Child Would Otherwise Suffer Harm*, 48 Drake L Rev 279 (2000); cf. *Rideout v Riendeau*, 761 A2d 291, 300 (Me Sup Ct 2000) (concluding, after *Troxel*, that a "harm element" was not constitutionally required).

[44] 402 US 205 (1972).

[45] Id.

tal rights, of articulating a standard through which such rights could be enforced. Its failure to do so is symptomatic of its lack of commitment to a strongly protective approach.

I note the apparent deliberateness of the Court's avoidance of standards because it suggests the Court's ambivalence and confusion about the right rather than simple sloppy drafting. In the seminal parental rights cases of *Meyer v Nebraska*[46] and *Pierce v Society of Sisters*,[47] the Court said very little to rationalize parental rights and barely articulated an ill-defined standard, the "reasonable relation" standard that has proved readily malleable. But the Court's endorsement of parental rights in *Meyer* and *Pierce* was by no means tentative. In those cases, standards may have seemed somewhat beside the point because the Court's message was so clear: Parents control the terrain of child rearing, and states should stay out. In *Troxel*, however, the Court's avoidance of standards signals no such brash confidence about parental rights. If the Court could have identified a standard with which it was comfortable, it surely would have named it. Having failed to do so, it left the right in a muddle, with no power to afford parents any meaningful protection.

The Court did not compensate for this lack of an articulated standard by revealing any principled means of determining when parental deference is appropriate through the details of its issue-specific analysis. In fact, the issue-specific detail provides two additional indications of the Court's departure from a fundamental rights approach.

The Court's refusal to embrace the harm standard, or to fashion some other highly protective standard, left it endorsing the best interest standard, at least under some circumstances. This is in part a product of convention: Custody jurisprudence generally divides all custody decisions into those governed by a harm standard and those governed by a best interest standard. But it is a convention that reflects real limits on the amount of parsing the law can contemplate if it wants its standards to have any meaning. One of the attractions of the harm standard is that it offers a fairly concrete standard to apply in making legal decisions on behalf of children. The best interest standard, itself considerably less concrete, can at least be defined to capture the rest of the field: What is in a child's

[46] 262 US 390 (1923).
[47] 268 US 510 (1925).

best interest is that which is good for the child, even if its denial would not cause the child harm.

The Court suggested that visitation schemes based on best interest findings can comport with affording parents strong constitutional protection, at least where those schemes embellish the best interest standard with some additional constraints. As I will discuss in the next two sections, however, these constraints cannot make up for the diminution of protection that comes with any embrace of the best interest standard. Moreover, the Court's very endorsement of these constraints provides additional evidence of the Court's lack of support for strong parental rights.

c) The Court's failure to recognize parents' superior competence. The problems with the best interest standard cannot be divorced from the problems with the courts as best interest decision makers. It is the courts' lack of any special competence in assessing best interests that makes reliance on that standard in judicial proceedings so troubling. While the Court acknowledged that deference to parental decision making is grounded in the law's expectation that parents are most qualified to assess their own children's interests, it demonstrated remarkable confidence in the courts' ability to know when such expectations should be abandoned. Indeed, by allowing courts the last word on children's best interests, the *Troxel* Court revealed its faith in the lower courts' ability to out-perform parents in judging what is best for their children, contrary to its purported endorsement of parents' rights. While the Court suggested that any concerns with the use of the best interest standard could be cured by making the sort of adjustments in standards and burdens of proof reflected in some of the statutory schemes it cited, these adjustments fail to change the basic question confronting the judge. Ultimately these statutes still allow a judge to trump a parent in determining which array of relationships, among a range of nonharmful options, best suits a child's needs.

Of course, any scheme that recognizes some limit to the deference afforded parents contemplates the second-guessing of a parent's judgments by legislatures or courts. But where those limits are grounded on nothing more than a different assessment of a child's interests, the protection afforded parents appears vanishingly thin. Unlike a harm standard—which limits departures from deference, both in conception and in practice, to a small group of the most extreme and provable circumstances—any best interest standard subjects all choices on the subject in question (here visitation) to challenge, thereby increasing the court's involvement in precisely those decisions it is least qualified to make.

In endorsing courts' use of the "entirely well-known best interests standard,"[48] in the visitation context, Justice Stevens took issue with the Washington Supreme Court's conclusion that the best interest standard "may be too boundless to pass muster under the Federal Constitution." Justice Stevens pointed to "698 separate references" to the standard and cited a number of cases applying the standard pursuant to ten different statutory requirements.[49] But these citations reflect Justice Stevens's confusion of competence with necessity. In most of these cases and all of the statutes, the best interest standard is applied to resolve conflicts between separating parents rather than between a parent and a third-party claimant. In both of these contexts, the best interest standard leaves the court with tremendous discretion, discretion the court is ill-prepared to exercise.[50] In the case of divorcing parents, the standard may well be the best the court can offer. Where two parents, with equal constitutional claims, cannot come to agreement, the constitutional claims cancel each other out, and the court, invited in by one or both parents, is left to guess at what arrangement will best serve the children.

In the third-party context, in contrast, the courts need not resort to such a second-best solution. Where there is no competition among parental claimants, the protection afforded parents by the Constitution directs courts to defer to the best interests judgments of the parents. The courts can then devote their limited competence to watching for those instances where those parents' judgments fail most clearly and at greatest cost to their children.

d) The Court's failure to account for the burdens imposed on parents. The Court's apparent openness to third-party visitation claims also reflects its disregard for the burdens imposed on parents, and, consequently, the harm caused to children, by compelled visits and the litigation pressing for those visits. This disregard, in turn, reflects, again, the Court's lack of appreciation for the purposes

---

[48] 120 S Ct at 2073 (Stevens dissenting).

[49] Id at 2069 n 5.

[50] See Robert H. Mnookin, *Child-Custody Adjudication: Judicial Functions in the Face of Indeterminacy*, 39 L & Contemp Probs 226 (Summer 1975).

served by affording parents deference. As noted, the argument suggests that parents deserve deference not only because they are likely to be the best assessors of what outcomes will be good for their children, but also because they will inevitably be charged with implementing those outcomes, however they are chosen. The Court's lack of attention to the effect visitation orders will have on that functioning—and the even greater disregard it showed for the effect the litigation will have on this functioning—is yet another indication of its weak support for parental rights.

As noted earlier, compelling parents to facilitate contacts, against their will, between their children and others is likely to be experienced as extremely disruptive to their child-rearing efforts. And the greater the antagonism and resistance, the greater that disruption will be. While the Court said very little about the burdens imposed on parents by compelled visitation, this inattention, itself, is somewhat striking in a decision purportedly grounded on parents' fundamental right to control the upbringing of their children. What the Justices did say on the subject appears to sell the burden short. Justice Kennedy cited with relative approval to cases that confine third-party visitation to circumstances in which parents are divorced or one parent is deceased.[51] But the burdens imposed by compelled visitation might be particularly great in such circumstances, where parental resources are already strained and emotions run high. And in her plurality opinion, Justice O'Connor cited with comparative approval to a number of statutes that limit the court's authority to compel visits to circumstances in which parents have denied all contact with a third party.[52] Making such a distinction between parental decisions to curtail or deny contact, however, reflects a cramped view of the parental interests involved. Parents' interest in exercising control over the nature of their children's contacts will be at least as great as their interest in controlling the scope and timing of those contacts. Under a fundamental rights approach, even a complete prohibition of contact should be protected in most cases, and when it is not, the compelled contact will impose at least as great a burden on parents' exercise of their child-rearing authority as a compelled expansion of visits.

While the Court's recognition of the burdens imposed by com-

---

[51] 120 S Ct at 2078.

[52] Id at 2063.

pelled visitations is thin, it is the Court's failure to recognize the serious burdens imposed by the litigation itself that most completely reveals the Court's distance from a parent-protective approach. Indeed, the very statutory constraints that the Court cited with approval invite the sorts of litigation burdens that ought to trouble the Court.

The plurality opinion cited a set of statutes that limit compelled visits to circumstances in which the court finds that such visits would not interfere with the parent-child relationship.[53] On its face, such an inquiry appears well designed to protect parents from destructive interference with their child rearing. But a judicial standard that assesses parental interference is considerably less protective than a law that shields a parent from assessment. The process of proving or disproving interference is likely to impose a considerable intrusion of its own.

If a court, in applying the noninterference condition, deferred to parents' views on the question (asking whether parents felt the visits would interfere with their control over the upbringing of their child), then the third party seeking visitation should never prevail. Parents who undertake court battles to resist visits clearly perceive these visits as an interference, and even if experts were to conclude that such visits ought not be disruptive, parents' expectation of interference, joined with their adversarial stance in the litigation process, are likely to be enough to render them so. If the courts take this approach, then the parent ought to prevail in all cases, and the condition amounts to an absolute prohibition against visits opposed by parents. Such a reading is unlikely, of course, for it would strip the third-party visitation laws of any effect.

If, on the other hand, courts made an independent assessment of parental interference, that assessment would require a fairly probing examination of the parents' attitudes about child rearing, relationships with the would-be visitors and others, and scheduling priorities, just to name some of the most obvious considerations. This is not to suggest that such an inquiry would be more intrusive than a straight best interest inquiry—which ought to take into account, among other things, the effect compelled visits would have on the parent-child relationship—but only that it would not be

---

[53] Id at 2062.

significantly less so. Even visitation statutes designed to minimize interference with parental autonomy cannot shield parents from the financial, temporal, emotional, and relational costs of the fight.

Concerns with the costs imposed by litigation on families, and particularly children, are certainly not limited to the third-party visitation context. Indeed, these concerns have led to widespread efforts to channel domestic relations cases into systems of alternative dispute resolution,[54] and to recraft custody standards to minimize the sorts of uncertainties that encourage litigation.[55] But, again, such efforts are the necessary, second-best options available for avoiding litigation where the dispute involves two parties whose legal claims rest on equal constitutional footing. Where disputants, such as third-party visitation claimants, lack that constitutional footing, another, more effective means of avoiding litigation is available: Their claims can be barred entirely from the courts.

While some of the Justices paid lip service to the burdens imposed by this litigation, their apparent support for statutes that impose no serious limitations on this litigation suggest that such comments had little effect on their analysis. Justice O'Connor's plurality opinion embraced Justice Kennedy's declaration that "the burden of litigation in a domestic relations proceeding can itself be 'so disruptive of the parent-child relationship that the constitutional right of a custodial parent to make certain basic determinations for the child's welfare becomes implicated,' "[56] but only as a reason for declining to remand *Troxel,* a case that had already passed through five courts over five years before coming before the Supreme Court. Parents can take little solace from a constitutional standard that will not protect them from litigation until after their case has been reviewed by the Supreme Court.

Taken together, the Court's refusal to embrace any specific parent-protective standard and its apparent openness to visitation statutes that require courts to make best interests assessments reveal how far the *Troxel* Court drifted from its fundamental rights

---

[54] See Ann M. Haralambie, *Handling Child Custody, Abuse and Adoption Cases* § 6.02 (describing broad-based support for the use of mediation, rather than litigation, in resolving custody disputes).

[55] The American Law Institute, *Principles of the Law of Family Dissolution,* Tentative Draft No. 4, p 1 (adopted May 2000) (noting that one of the primary aims, in developing the principles governing the allocation of custodial responsibility, was to minimize litigation).

[56] 120 S Ct at 2065 (quoting opinion of Kennedy at 2079).

course. But the Court took pains to preserve some constitutional protection, a protection whose ongoing force is at least great enough to reject the trial court's visitation order in this case. *Troxel* thus leaves parental rights adrift in the middle, neither afforded strong protection nor remitted to the democratic process. In the next section, I will consider the likely harm, to children, of setting parental rights adrift.

2. *The constitutional residue.* While it failed to afford parents the strong protection it claims, *Troxel* clearly kept some constitutional right alive. But how much protection the right affords, and in what contexts, is nowhere made plain. Indeed, all the Court was willing to say was that *some* right exists. This preservation of a standardless right offers nothing affirmative to children and, most significantly, it introduces a new source of harm: By fostering ongoing constitutional litigation, *Troxel* inflicts on children the harm that comes with any additional litigation compounded by the lack of standards and relevant expertise associated with the constitutional inquiry.

a) Standardless parental rights. In various ways, the Justices noted that the deference to parental decision making required by the Constitution is thought to serve children's interests, and that deference is no longer required when it would fail to serve those interests. But all seven of the "in-between" Justices failed to articulate how to disentangle the best interest calculation reflected in the deference requirement from a best interest calculation that would justify an abandonment of that deference. In one way or another, they all argued little more than that deference is appropriate, except when it is not.

A detailed search for some concrete criteria produces a handful of near contentless assertions about what the constitutional protection allows and requires. In the words of the plurality, the Constitution prohibits state visitation decisions that give "no special weight at all" to a parent's judgments, and requires them to give "at least some special weight" to these judgments.[57] In Justice Souter's words, the Constitution prevents a parent from being subject to "any individual judge's choice of a child's associates from out of the general population."[58] According to Justice Stevens, parents' constitutional rights "protect[] the parent-child relationship from

---

[57] Id at 2062.
[58] Id at 2067.

arbitrary impairment by the state,"[59] and Justice Kennedy specu-
lated that these rights might prevent the use of the best interest
standard to resolve visitation disputes "in the absence of other protection for the parent under state laws and procedures."[60]

Of course, the Justices did not claim that these assertions described the full extent of what is required or prohibited under the
Constitution, but the very lack of any other elaboration of the
scope of the right leaves us, and, more important, legislatures and
courts, sifting through these scraps. We should be most concerned
about the lack of guidance *Troxel* gives to state and federal courts,
charged with resolving the host of cases that *Troxel* will inspire.[61]

My criticism of *Troxel's* failure to articulate any standard is, for
the most part, derivative of my criticism of its in-between approach. To be sure, the Court might have named some standard,
such as the reasonableness standard, to guide courts' application
of the qualified constitutional approach.[62] But any such standard
designed to afford some middle level of protection will still leave
most of the right's description to the courts. Determining what is
reasonable, for example, would require a court to make substantive
assessments of the relative benefits and harms associated with allocating child-rearing authority to parent or state. Such judgments
are unlikely to look very different from those judgments made by
the court applying a standardless, qualified constitutional right.

b) Leaving the constitutional detail to the courts. Justice Kennedy
was most explicit in his acknowledgment of the potential burdens
imposed by the very litigation of third-party visitation claims. But
this awareness only led to the soft concession that "I do not dis-
count the possibility, that in some instances the best interests of
the child standard may provide insufficient protection to the
parent-child relationship."[63] More telling, he followed this weak

---

[59] Id at 2071.

[60] Id at 2075.

[61] See, for example, *In re G.P.C.*, 28 SW3d at 365–66 (noting that the Court "scarcely
mentions the appropriate standard of review for such cases," and concluding that this leaves
its state courts free to apply the rational basis test to its review of the constitutionality of
its grandparent visitation statute).

[62] See David D. Meyer, *The Paradox of Family Privacy*, 53 Vand L Rev 527, 575–91 (2000)
(endorsing the Court's employment of a reasonableness standard in resolving parental rights
claims).

[63] 120 S Ct at 2079.

declaration with a call for the Court to "proceed with caution." Ironically, it is this ethic of caution, echoed in the approach of a majority of the Justices, that imposes a particularly troublesome litigation burden of its own.

The Court's qualified approach to parental rights fosters two types of litigation, both raising issues of judicial competence, and both likely to undermine parental functioning. The first type is the best interest litigation already discussed, which could be authorized under either the rights-denying approach or, apparently, by the qualified constitutional approach endorsed by the Court in *Troxel.* While this litigation will disrupt family functioning and leave decisions in the hands of judges with lesser competence than parents and with an ill-defined standard to guide them, such litigation at least has the benefit of being produced and monitored through a democratic process. Moreover, because the judge's decision making is case-specific, any errors it makes will be limited to that single case.

But the second type of litigation, produced only by the qualified constitutional approach, has all of the problems and none of the virtues of the first type. Here, in the context of specific cases, the courts will be asked to determine whether particular allocations of child-rearing authority between parent and state are constitutionally permissible. This litigation will be just as disruptive to families, indeed, more so, to the extent it compounds rather than displaces the best interest litigation and increases the stakes.[64] The courts will be just as lacking in relevant expertise, indeed, more so, where the litigation is brought in federal court. The courts will be at least as unconstrained by standards, for their task is even less defined than that of courts applying the best interest standard. Nor will any democratic processes operate to constrain or alter the courts' judgments. And, finally, whatever errors courts make in determining a law's constitutionality will have implications that extend well beyond the individual case.

By insisting that parents have a fundamental right to raise their children as they see fit, while resisting an interpretation of the right that would afford parents nearly absolute protection, the Jus-

---

[64] Compare *Belair v Drew*, 770 So2d 1164 (Fla 2000) (remanding case for consideration of constitutional issues in the midst of proceedings addressing visitation claims pursuant to the challenged statutory provisions).

tices invited ongoing litigation about the constitutionality of fifty states' statutes, on their face and as applied. The openness of the issues, and the parties' stake in their resolution, guarantee that parents will frequently assert constitutional challenges and that the courts will need, in each of these cases, to engage the substance of the disputes. Presumably the courts must assess both the degree of intrusion a visitation scheme imposes on parents and the interests, particularly to children, served by the intrusion, though what it will look to in making these assessments is entirely unclear. The middle, standardless approach thus gives the courts more control over the allocation of child-rearing authority than either the fundamental rights approach or an approach that defers to the legislature. *Troxel's* retreat from parental rights is therefore worse for being halting.

The lack of any standard guiding the courts' constitutional interpretation is considerably more troubling than the lack of a standard guiding the courts' child-specific best interest judgments. The lack of standards guarantees that courts will produce conflicting constitutional interpretations, and the dominance of state courts in family law guarantees that the volume of those conflicting interpretations will be high. We can expect the Justices' equivocal support for parental rights to generate varying rulings not only in the state courts but among the federal courts as well. And if, as seems likely, the Supreme Court does not return to this issue, at least for some time, then the fifty states will be variously encumbered by diverse constitutional interpretations whose authority derives from a claim of universal right.

The long catalogs of statutes and cases included in the opinions reflects the Court's awareness of how many constitutional issues, in how many different courts, are left open by *Troxel's* refusal to embrace a strong form of parental rights or to abandon these disputes to the democratic process. Justice O'Connor's plurality opinion almost celebrates this lack of constitutional resolution:

> We do not, and need not, define today the precise scope of the parental due process right in the visitation context. In this respect, we agree with Justice Kennedy that the constitutionality of any standard for awarding visitation turns on the specific manner in which that standard is applied and that the constitutional protections in this area are best "elaborated with care." Because much state-court adjudication in this context occurs on

a case-by-case basis, we would be hesitant to hold that specific nonparental visitation statutes violate the Due Process Clause as a *per se* matter.[65]

There is much to be said for incremental constitutional adjudication in many contexts,[66] but considerably less so in this one. The advantage of case-by-case development of a protection is tied to our level of confidence in the case-by-case adjudicator, a confidence that should vary with the nature of the issues and the configuration of the reviewing courts. In the context of parental rights, the courts charged with constitutional interpretation are less expert in the subject matter, more diffuse in their composition, and less subject to the unifying influence of the federal appellate courts than they are in other constitutional contexts. While we might well, for example, want to leave the articulation of "reasonableness" in government searches to the courts, whom we can expect to be as competent as any institution in balancing an individual's interest in privacy against the state's interest in crime control, we have little reason to leave courts to grope their way through an assessment of dueling theories of children's associational developmental needs. Moreover, we have much reason to be concerned that any such incremental articulation of the constitutional protection will come at serious cost to the children required to endure each increment in court.

III. Consistency with Prior Cases

A number of the Court's prior parental rights cases appear, at first glance, to support *Troxel*'s qualified approach to parental rights. In a line of cases commonly known as the "unwed father" cases, the Court has tolerated state interference with claimants' exercise of parental authority that appears inconsistent with a fundamental rights approach. But a better understanding of those cases and their relationship to the Court's other parental rights cases makes clear that these cases provide no support for the Court's middle approach in *Troxel*. In these unwed father cases, the Court permitted states to intervene to identify parents, but not

---

[65] 120 S Ct at 2065 (citation and footnote omitted).

[66] See Cass R. Sunstein, *One Case at a Time: Judicial Minimalism on the Supreme Court* (Harv U Press, 1999).

to alter the child-rearing practices of identified parents. Where, as in the third-party visitation context, there is no question as to the identity of a child's parents, the Court's precedents clearly support the fundamental rights approach.

Courts and commentators conventionally group together all Supreme Court cases addressing parental rights, but these cases are better understood as two distinct sets of cases. In one set—what I will call the "core" parental rights cases—the identity of the parents (or the persons entitled to act as parents) is undisputed. In those cases, the Court has historically allowed only limited state interference in family decision making, generally restricting such interference to that aimed at protecting children or society from identifiable harms. In the second set of cases—generally cases involving unwed fathers—the identity of the adults who are entitled to act as parents is very much in dispute. In those cases, the Court has tolerated considerable state interference in the assignment of parental authority, particularly where that interference is aimed at defining and consolidating that authority. This greater tolerance does not reflect, as some of the Justices in *Troxel* suggest, a qualification of parental rights in the face of competing relational claims.[67] Rather, it reflects a recognition that resolving conflicting parental claims—something the state is in the best position to achieve—necessarily precedes the effective enforcement of parental rights.

A. THE STATE'S AUTHORITY TO INTERFERE WITH
    PARENTS' CHILD-REARING DECISIONS

The Court first afforded constitutional protection under the Due Process Clause to parents' interest in the care, custody, and control of their children in *Meyer v Nebraska*[68] and *Pierce v Society of Sisters*,[69] both of which invalidated laws that restricted parental freedom to make educational choices on behalf of their children. While the opinions in *Meyer* and *Pierce* are extremely brief, the Court in *Pierce* justified affording constitutional protection to parents by declaring that "[t]he child is not the mere creature of the

---

[67] See, for example, 120 S Ct at 2071–72 (Stevens dissenting).
[68] 262 US 390 (1923).
[69] 268 US 510 (1925).

State: those who nurture him and direct his destiny have the right, coupled with the high duty, to recognize and prepare him for additional obligations."[70] This language, repeatedly cited in cases analyzing parental rights, captures the basic rationale for a strongly deferential approach discussed above: The law places primary responsibility for child rearing with parents, and in order to ensure the effective satisfaction of those important responsibilities, it gives parents strong protection from outside interference.

Over the next fifty years, the Court added two more cases to this core. In *Prince v Massachusetts*[71] and *Wisconsin v Yoder*,[72] the Court reasserted the Constitution's strong protection of parental decision making, although its analysis of parental rights was somewhat obscured, in both cases, by its concomitant consideration of the parents' free exercise claims. In *Prince*, the Court made clear that the state could intervene, even in matters related to religious upbringing, to protect a child from harm, but in *Yoder*, the Court emphasized that such intervention would only be permitted when the state's concerns were found to be "compelling." As noted, the Court has said little to clarify the nature and extent of the protection the Constitution affords parents' secular decisions, but it has repeatedly cited to *Meyer, Pierce, Prince*, and *Yoder* to support the general claim that parents' child-rearing choices are entitled to strong protection.[73]

None of these four cases focuses, however, on the particular rights of parents as distinguished from other family members. Indeed, in *Prince*, the "parental rights" claimant was actually an aunt, who was filling the child-rearing role, apparently without competition from biological parents. The Court's lack of attention to this distinction between aunt and parent suggests that it was her role as family head, rather than her particular biological relationship to nine-year-old Betty, that gave strength to the aunt's claim against the state.

While the four core cases of *Meyer, Pierce, Prince*, and *Yoder* dif-

---

[70] Id at 535.

[71] 321 US 158 (1944).

[72] 406 US 205 (1972).

[73] See, for example, *Washington v Glucksberg*, 521 US at 720 (listing the "right to direct the education and upbringing of one's child" among those "fundamental rights and liberty interests provided heightened protection against governmental interference").

fer in many important respects, they share this important common attribute that distinguishes them from subsequent cases that implicate parental rights. All four cases represent a simple two-sided battle between parent (or unchallenged parent surrogate) and state. The litigation reflects no fragmentation of family interests, nor any ambiguity or conflict over lines of authority within the family. Rather, it reflects a dispute between the private family and the public state over the proper allocation of child-rearing authority between them. In this context, the Court has been consistent in its message that the balance of authority tips heavily in favor of parents.

B. THE STATE'S AUTHORITY TO INTERFERE IN
   THE ASSIGNMENT OF CHILD-REARING AUTHORITY

In contrast to these four core cases, it is precisely this distribution of child-rearing authority among competing familial claimants that is in dispute in most of the Court's recent parental rights decisions. In a string of cases, biological fathers asserted rights to some level of association with or control over their children that competed with others' state-sanctioned claims to such associations and control. Here, parental rights were asserted, not to prevent the state from interfering with the choices made by familial child rearers, but rather to prevent the state from depriving certain individuals of the status or authority of a parent. The Court has rejected most of these claims, affording states considerable latitude in assigning parental authority among competing claimants. While these cases denied the parental right claim pressed by the plaintiffs, the Court suggested that they served the purposes behind these rights more generally. By making clear which adults are entitled to protection (including protection against state intervention), these cases clear the way for the successful fulfillment of parental responsibilities.

Notably, the Court has been least willing to defer to state assignments of parental authority where the assignments do not appear to serve those interests. In *Stanley v Illinois*,[74] the first in the line of "unwed father" cases, the Court rejected a scheme that automatically placed all nonmarital children in state care upon the

---

[74] 405 US 645 (1972).

death of their mothers. The challenged law treated these children as parentless, without regard to the fitness of, or their relationship with, their biological fathers. Because there were no competing parental claimants in *Stanley* (the best the state could offer was the uncertain prospect of a future adoption, probably by strangers), there was no need for the state to play a parent-defining role. Indeed, the effect of the state's involvement was only to deprive the children of their one remaining parent. Where upholding parental rights could facilitate the fulfillment of parental duties, and where no competing parental claims threatened to undermine or surpass the father's achievement of those ends, the case for constitutional protection of the biological father's parental rights was straightforward and strong.

For similar reasons, the Court has also been unwilling to recognize constitutional claims asserted by private parties, where those claims threaten to interfere with the exercise of child-rearing authority by a clearly identified parent. In *Smith v OFFER*,[75] the Court rejected foster parents' attempts to secure greater procedural protections for their relationships with their foster children, noting that whatever relational claim they had was dwarfed by the claims of the legal (and usually biological) parents of the child. Critical to this ruling was the clarity with which state law identified the parent figure who was entitled to the Constitution's protections and limited the authority of the foster parent.[76]

The Court has taken a different approach, however, where the challenged action reflects the state's effort to select among competing parental claimants. In *Quilloin v Walcott*,[77] the Court denied constitutional protection to a biological father whose parental claim competed with the claim of a step-father whose decade-long marriage to the child's mother and assumption of child-rearing responsibilities established the strength of his own parental claim. Acknowledging that "the relationship between parent and child is constitutionally protected," the Court went on to suggest that the interests served by this protection could best be satisfied by

---

[75] 431 US 816 (1977).

[76] Id at 846 (noting that New York law limits foster parents' authority by contract and by statute, and gives a "natural" parent of a foster child in voluntary placement an "absolute right to the return of his child" under most circumstances).

[77] 434 US 246 (1977).

allowing an adoption that would give "full recognition to a family unit already in existence."[78] While only the biological father pressed a constitutional claim in *Quilloin*, there were clearly two competing paternal contenders in the litigation. So conceived, *Quilloin* amounts not to a rejection or curtailment of parental rights, but rather to a rejection of the preeminence of biology in assigning those rights, a point the Court reinforced in the subsequent cases of *Lehr v Robertson*,[79] and *Michael H. v Gerald D.*[80] The Court, in denying the claims of biological fathers in all three of these cases, did so in deference to the state's definitional choices, noting, in each, that such deference reinforced rather than undermined the purposes served by affording parents constitutional protection.[81]

Precisely how far the Court would allow a state to go in assigning or refusing parental status is an open question,[82] but it is clear that the Court allows the state a considerable defining role where disputes among parental claimants arise. This is not because the claims of parents are readily counterbalanced by others' claims to a relationship with their children (indeed, in these cases the Court has consistently allowed states to preclude certain adults from having relationships with children), but rather because determining who counts as a parent necessarily precedes the effective exercise of parental rights. Unless we simply defer to biology in resolving disputes among parental claimants (and assisted repro-

---

[78] Id at 255.

[79] 463 US 248, 261 (1982) (noting that it is when a man " 'come[s] forward to participate in the rearing of his child,' that 'his interest in personal contact with his child acquires substantial protection under the Due Process Clause.' ") (quoting *Caban v Mohammed*, 441 US 380, 392 (1979)).

[80] 491 US 110 (1989).

[81] See, for example, *Quilloin v Walcott*, 434 US at 255 (noting that, while the breakup of a "natural family" against the family members' wishes would offend the Due Process Clause, no such constitutional problems were created by the state's authorization of an adoption that gave "full recognition to a family unit already in existence").

[82] While there surely are limits to the state's authority to assign parental rights, these limits have not yet been well developed in the case law, in part, perhaps, because states have little inclination to press those limits. The cases suggest that any limits may be relative rather than absolute: A state may be barred from preferring a stranger to a biological parent, absent a showing of unfitness, but not from preferring a relational parent to a biological one. Some combination of biology and relationship will be sufficient to establish protection, but how much of each (assisted reproductive techniques allow biology as well as relationships to be distributed among multiple claimants) is required may depend upon whom the state is threatening to prefer.

ductive techniques prevent even this inquiry from yielding simple answers), then we need some decision maker to resolve them. The Court, in allowing states to fill this role, appears to acknowledge that the state, with all its intrusive force, may well offer the best prospect for neutral, peaceful, and authoritative decision making, where the private parties cannot resolve things on their own.

In sum, the unwed father cases differ from the core cases in two related, but distinct, respects. First, they consider the state's involvement in resolving conflicting claims among family members rather than a family's united claim against state interference. Second, they consider the state's authority as parent designator, rather than its authority to intervene in child-rearing decisions made by someone whose parental status is undisputed. *Troxel* shares with the unwed father cases the focus on family conflict. But unlike the unwed father cases, *Troxel* does not concern the state's parent-defining role. In this more important respect, *Troxel* belongs with the core cases, for it considers constitutional challenges to state intrusions on child-rearing decisions made by individuals whose authority as parents is unquestioned.

In this same respect, third-party visitation cases can be readily distinguishable from other claims that might be asserted by the same third parties if they were seeking adoption or perhaps full custody of a child. A concern for these claims, particularly cases where nonbiological parents have cared for children and wish to continue doing so, seems at least in part responsible for the Court's equivocal approach to parental rights in the third-party visitation context. As Justice Kennedy explained:

> My principal concern is that the holding seems to proceed from the assumption that the parent or parents who resist visitation have always been the child's primary caregivers, and that the third parties who seek visitation have no legitimate and established relationship with the child. For many boys and girls a traditional family with two or even one permanent and caring parent is simply not the reality of their childhood.[83]

If the core claim to parental authority is more protected than the details of its execution, then drawing a tough line on something as

---

[83] 120 S Ct at 2077.

small as visits would force the Court to provide even greater protection for parents fighting the far more intrusive custody or adoption claims. But the special role the Court has allowed the state to
play as parent definer suggests that the Court could reverse these
constitutional priorities. While more is at stake in determining
who is a parent, this does not mean it is clear who has the best
claim to that stake. Indeed, the state may well be needed to resolve
the conflict between the biological and relational claim.

There are surely constitutional limits in how the state can play
the role. As the Court has suggested in the unwed father context,
the state is on shakiest ground when its denial of a parental claim
leaves the child with no parent, and on firmest ground when there
is a conflict among parental claimants whose mix of biology and
relationship requires sorting out by some child-interested third
party. The highly publicized stories of "Baby Richard" and "Baby
Jessica" offer easy examples of cases in which unambiguous biology
competed against a strong parent-child relationship.[84] The Constitution imposes no bar to the resolution of such claims in favor of
relationship over biology. But once the state has chosen among
parental contenders, those parents, whoever they are, are entitled
to the same robust protection of their child-rearing authority as
other parents who have not faced any parental competition. Indeed, the importance of allowing those parents to have control,
including control over the child's relationships, will be at least as
great, if not greater, where the would-be visitors have asserted,
and lost, competing parental claims.

IV. Conclusion

There is no question that children benefit from the opportunity to develop an array of familial relationships. But there is
considerable disagreement about who should be allowed to sort
among potential familial relationships on behalf of a child. Affording constitutional protection to parents' control over the upbringing of their children means, at a minimum, that we should
leave such associational decisions to parents. If, on the other hand,

---

[84] *Petition of Kircher*, 649 NE2d 324 (Ill 1995); *DeBoer v Schmidt*, 496 NW2d 239 (Iowa
1992).

we disapprove of affording parents such deference, then we should abandon the pretense of affording their decisions the protection of a fundamental right. In embracing the right, while abandoning the deference, *Troxel* takes the authority for the sorting away from both parents and legislatures, leaving the courts with a mess they are ill equipped to clean up.

MARY ANNE CASE

LESSONS FOR THE FUTURE OF
AFFIRMATIVE ACTION FROM THE PAST
OF THE RELIGION CLAUSES?

Race and religion each have a privileged position in the American constitutional scheme: Both racial equality and religious freedom are central commitments of modern American constitutionalism. Similar awareness of historical abuses has led to a wariness about the uses of both racial and religious classifications by government actors. At the same time, the dangers of oppression and exclusion make acknowledgment of race or religion difficult to avoid. This tension between the importance and the danger of race and religion has led to similar oscillations in the constitutional case law, with a satisfactory equilibrium position difficult to attain in either field. Currently, the pendulum of case law is swinging in somewhat

Mary Anne Case is Professor of Law, University of Chicago Law School.

AUTHOR'S NOTE: Versions of this article were presented at a faculty workshop at Roger Williams University School of Law and the University of Chicago Law School, for students at Western New England College of Law as part of the Clason lecture series, and at Richard Rorty's University of Virginia Theory Center Colloquium "Does America Have a Democratic Mission?" I am grateful to participants in those events for their comments; to David Strauss for encouraging me to write on this subject; to Chris Eisgruber, Abner Greene, John Harrison, Daryl Levinson, John Monahan, Allyson Newton, Rick Pildes, Cass Sunstein, and Adrian Vermeule for comments on drafts; to Dick Badger, Len Baynes, Frank Easterbrook, Philip Hamburger, Alex Johnson, Pam Karlan, Michael McConnell, Linda McClain, Mike Seidman, and Frank Upham for brainstorming and bibliographic help; to Dan Shaviro and David Bradford, who, by inviting me to comment on Linda Sugin's paper for their 1999 Tax Colloquium at NYU, prompted me to think further about race, religion, aid, and symbolism; to Judge Diane Lebedeff for scheduling accommodation; and to Toby Heytens for outstanding research assistance. Research support for this project came from the Arnold and Frieda Shure Research Fund of the University of Chicago and the Class of 1966 Research Professorship of the University of Virginia.

opposite directions for race and religion. While the trend has been toward increasing explicit inclusion of religion and the religious (whether literally in the public square[1] or more broadly in funding and subsidy opportunities[2]), by contrast, recent cases seem increasingly to question any explicit use of race, even in areas of law, such as affirmative action and voting rights, where the intent of such use is to include rather than oppress or exclude minorities.

In this article, I want to press some analogies between the constitutional law of race and of religion, analogies I believe have implications for the future of both affirmative action and race-conscious districting.[3] My contention is that the Supreme Court's attitude toward race, at least in the two contexts of educational affirmative action and voting rights, should follow the same trajectory as its attitude toward religion already has.[4] The trajectory I have in mind is the following: For a period of time, on Establish-

---

[1] See, e.g., *Lynch v Donnelly*, 465 US 668 (1984), and its progeny; *Widmar v Vincent*, 454 US 263 (1981) and its progeny.

[2] See, e.g., *Rosenberger v Rector and Visitors of U. Va.*, 515 US 819 (1995).

[3] Numerous commentators over the past decade have suggested or contested analogies between the constitutional treatment of race and that of religion. See, e.g., Neil Gotanda, *A Critique of "Our Constitution Is Color Blind,"* 44 Stan L Rev 1, 64–68 (1991) (suggesting that "[t]he free exercise and establishment clause decisions provide a model for constitutional adjudication in the area of race to supplant the color-blind model" and introducing concepts of "free exercise of race" and "racial establishment"); Giradeau A. Spann, *Affirmative Action and Discrimination*, 39 Howard L J 1, 86–89 (1995) (arguing that *"Rosenberger* and *Adarand* involved the same basic constitutional problem but arrived at contradictory results"). Many have focused on whether governmental accommodation of the religious practice of minority religions through exemption from generally applicable laws can fruitfully be compared to affirmative action for racial minorities. See, e.g., Jesse Choper, *Religion and Race Under the Constitution: Similarities and Differences*, 79 Cornell L Rev 491 (1994); Frederick Mark Gedicks, *The Normalized Free Exercise Clause: Three Abnormalities*, 75 Ind L Rev 77, 95–103 (2000); Abner Greene, *Kiryas Joel and Two Mistakes About Equality*, 96 Colum L Rev 1, 58 (1996); Tseming Yang, *Race, Religion, and Cultural Identity: Reconciling the Jurisprudence of Race and Religion*, 73 Ind L Rev 119 (1997). Other commentators have compared majority-minority districting for racial and religious minorities. See, e.g., Thomas C. Berg, *Religion, Race, Segregation, and Districting: Comparing Kiryas Joel with Shaw/Miller*, 26 Cumb L Rev 365 (1996); James U. Blacksher, *Majority Black Districts, Kiryas Joel and Other Challenges to American Nationalism*, 26 Cumb L Rev 407 (1996); Christopher L. Eisgruber, *Ethnic Segregation by Religion and Race: Reflections on Kiryas Joel and Shaw v. Reno*, 26 Cumb L Rev 515 (1996).

[4] In an effort to reduce the number of moving parts in the discussion, I take the Court's current religion clause jurisprudence as a given. This jurisprudence seems to me (although not to everyone) to be comparatively settled, while the Court's jurisprudence of race is more open and confused at the moment. My objective is not to endorse or defend the holdings in *Widmar*, *Rosenberger*, or their progeny, or in any other case or line of cases involving religion. Rather, I start from the premise that these cases are the law and ask what implications the Supreme Court majority's approach in these cases has or should have for cases concerning educational affirmative action and majority-minority districting.

ment Clause grounds, the exclusion of religion and the religious from otherwise generally available opportunities was endorsed, indeed, was seen as constitutionally required. Then the Court came to realize that it worked a discrimination against those whose central organizing characteristic or salient trait was their religion to allow other such characteristics, but not religion, to form the basis for inclusion. Similarly, to allow every other basis for commonality or salience to count and not race may be seen to disadvantage those for whom race is a defining characteristic in a way that itself implicates the Equal Protection Clause.[5]

That the trend on the current Court is to exclude only race as the basis for forming a community of interest in voting rights cases and that this works a problematic discrimination against those whose basis for community is their race is clear to commentators on and off the Court. As Lani Guinier put it, "In contemporary discourse, colorblindness has come to mean that mere recognition of race, except to condemn intentional racial discrimination, is dangerous. Yet, because of the recognition and support our political system gives to other, non-racial groups, colorblindness, although ostensibly race-neutral, singles out race for special treatment."[6] And, as Justice Stevens first observed as a lower court judge, "an interpretation of the Constitution which afforded one kind of political protection to blacks and another kind to members of other identifiable groups would in itself be invidious."[7] Each of

---

[5] Compare *Washington v Seattle School Dist. No. 1*, 458 US 457 (1982) (holding unconstitutional state initiative allowing busing of schoolchildren away from their neighborhood school for virtually all reasons other than to achieve racial integration).

[6] Lani Guinier, *The Supreme Court, 1993 Term: [E]racing Democracy: The Voting Rights Cases*, 108 Harv L Rev 109 at 123, n 104 (1994). See also James U. Blacksher, *Dred Scott's Unwon Freedom: The Redistricting Cases as Badges of Slavery*, 39 Howard L J 633 (1996) ("The problem with the *Shaw* Cases is not simply that they have launched the federal courts into uncharted (indeed unchartable) political waters in an effort to restrain excessive gerrymandering, but that the only shoal they have marked as hazardous is racial classifications. By leaving legislative bodies free to squiggle district boundaries for partisan political purposes, to protect incumbents, or for any other nonracial reason, the Court has suggested—if it has not actually ruled—that it is black and Latino citizens alone who may not choose to associate with each other freely and try to optimize their legislative influence in pursuit of a common political agenda.").

[7] *Cousins v City Council of Chicago*, 466 F2d 830, 852 (7th Cir 1972) (Stevens dissenting). Although, in the context of *Cousins*, Stevens's point was that blacks should not be given a different and greater kind of political protection than members of other groups, in recent dissents from Supreme Court districting cases, Stevens has made clear his view is also that it would be invidious to offer different and lesser protection to blacks. See, e.g., *Shaw v Hunt*, 517 US 899, 949 (1996) (Stevens dissenting) ("Nor do I see how our constitutional tradition can countenance the suggestion that a State may draw unsightly lines to favor

the other habitual Supreme Court dissenters to the *Shaw v Reno*[8] line of majority-minority districting cases has made a similar point.[9]

Though the force of these observations has thus far escaped a majority of the current Court, that same majority has come to a similar realization in the context of the religion clauses. As Justice O'Connor put it in one of a line of recent cases mandating that the religious be afforded the "recognition and support" given other groups, "if a State refused to let religious groups use facilities open to others, then it would demonstrate not neutrality but hos-

---

farmers or city dwellers, but not to create districts that benefit the very group whose history inspired the Amendment that the Voting Rights Act was designed to implement"); *Bush v Vera*, 517 US 952, 1035 (1995) (Stevens dissenting) ("After the Court's decisions today, therefore, minority voters can make up a majority only in compact districts, . . . while white voters can be placed into districts as bizarre as the State desires. . . . Unaffected by the new racial jurisprudence, majority-white communities will be able to participate in the districting process by requesting that they be placed in certain districts, divided between districts in an effort to maximize representation, or grouped with more distant communities that might nonetheless match their interests better than communities next door. By contrast, none of this political maneuvering will be permissible for majority-minority districts, thereby segregating and balkanizing them far more effectively than the Districts here at issue, in which they were manipulated in the political process as easily as white voters. This result, it seems to me, involves 'discrimination' in a far more concrete manner than did the odd shapes that offended the Court's sensibilities in *Miller, Shaw II* and *Bush.*").

[8] 509 US 630 (1993).

[9] See, e.g., *Abrams v Johnson*, 521 US 74, 117–18 (1997) (Breyer dissenting) ("Thus, given today's suit, a legislator might reasonably wonder whether he can ever knowingly place racial minorities in a district because, for example, he considers them part of a 'community' already there. . . . And the legislator will need a legal principle that tells whether, or when, the answers to such questions vary depending on whether the group is racial or reflects, say, economics, education, or national origin. . . . Further, any test that applied only to race, ignoring, say, religion or national origin, would place at a disadvantage the very group, African Americans, whom the Civil War Amendments sought to help."); *Bush v Vera*, 517 US at 1066 (Souter dissenting) ("[I]t is in theory and in fact impossible to apply 'traditional districting principles' in areas with substantial minority populations without considering race. . . . It therefore may well be that the loss of the capacity to protect minority incumbency is the price of the rule limiting States' use of racial data. If so, it will be an exceedingly odd result, when the whole point of creating yesterday's majority-minority districts was to remedy prior dilution, thus permitting the election of the minority incumbent who (the Court now seems to declare) cannot be protected as any other incumbent could be."); *Miller v Johnson*, 515 US 900, 947 (1995) (Ginsburg dissenting) ("In adopting districting plans, however, States do not treat people as individuals. . . . Rather, legislators classify voters in groups—by economic, geographical, political, or social characteristics—and then 'reconcile the competing claims of [these] groups.' . . . That ethnicity defines some of these groups is a political reality. . . . Until now, no constitutional infirmity has been seen in districting Irish or Italian voters together, for example, so long as the delineation does not abandon familiar apportionment practices. . . . If Chinese-Americans and Russian-Americans may seek and secure group recognition in the delineation of voting districts, then African-Americans should not be dissimilarly treated. Otherwise, in the name of equal protection, we would shut out 'the very minority group whose history in the United States gave birth to the Equal Protection Clause.'") (citations omitted).

tility toward religion. The Establishment Clause does not license government to treat religion and those who teach or practice it, simply by virtue of their status as such, as subversive of American ideals and therefore subject to unique disabilities."[10]

To put the argument that follows in extremely compressed and referential form, if colorblindness is analogous to aggressive enforcement of the Establishment Clause, then, while the University of California's use of race in the plan struck down in *Bakke*[11] may resemble the New York legislature's use of religion in the districting legislation struck down in *Kiryas Joel*,[12] the inclusion of race in the Harvard admissions plan praised by Justice Powell[13] more closely resembles the inclusion of religion mandated by the Supreme Court for the University of Virginia's funding scheme in *Rosenberger*.[14] And, if the affirmative action claims of racial minorities are like the accommodation claims of religious minorities, then, while some voluntary pursuit of racial diversity by public educational institutions is like permissible accommodation, some majority-minority districting under the Voting Rights Act is like required accommodation. This is in part because the Equal Protection Clause itself may demand it, and in part because the Thirteenth and Fifteenth Amendments are like the Free Exercise Clause—counterweights to the presumption against state use of race or religion.

I wish to focus inquiry, not merely on any formal parallels in the structure of these arguments, but also on some of the common underlying concerns that special governmental treatment of the salient characteristics of race and religion may have. When "one of the [emerging] philosophical touchstones of the current Court's constitutional jurisprudence is giving content to the elusive line

---

[10] *Bd. of Ed. of Westside Community Schools v Mergens*, 496 US 226, 248 (1990) (citing Brennan's concurrence in *McDaniel v Paty*, 435 US 618, 641 (1978)).

[11] See *Regents of the University of California v Bakke*, 438 US 265 (1978) (striking down set aside of specified number of slots in state medical school class for disadvantaged members of minority groups).

[12] See *Bd of Ed. of Kiryas Joel v Grumet*, 512 US 687 (1994) (holding New York legislature's establishment of a special school district for a community of Satmar Hasidim unconstitutional).

[13] See *Bakke*, 438 US at 321 (1978).

[14] See *Rosenberger*, 515 US 819 (requiring university student activities' funding scheme to include a student publication dedicated to promoting an evangelical Christian viewpoint).

between 'equal rights' and 'special preferences,'"[15] it seems worth exploring how the Court may walk that line differently for race and religion. While the Constitutional and sociopolitical reasons for worrying about "special preferences" for race and religion are far from identical, similar distortions in the landscape may occur when race or religion are eliminated by Constitutional force from the picture, and there are similar risks of divisiveness surrounding the question of their inclusion.

Just as the drafters of the Establishment and Free Exercise Clauses had centuries of the established churches of Europe and of England as cautionary backdrop,[16] so the drafters of the Civil War Amendments had centuries of black chattel slavery.[17] In neither case did this history lead to an immediate abolition of state use of the dangerous categories: state religious establishment continued after the passage of the First Amendment and Jim Crow established both racial categorization and white supremacy for nearly a century after the passage of the Fourteenth Amendment. I use the term "established" advisedly—parallels can readily be drawn between the position of whites under Jim Crow and members of an established church. Compare, for example, the Bill Establishing a Provision for Teachers of the Christian Religion, which gave rise to Madison's *Memorial and Remonstrance Against Religious Assessments*[18] with the use of Southern state tax dollars to support public education for whites only.[19] Compare the degree of

---

[15] Richard Pildes, *Principled Limitations on Racial and Partisan Redistricting*, 106 Yale L J 2505, 2511 (1997).

[16] See, e.g., *Everson v Board of Ed.*, 330 US 1 (1946) ("The centuries immediately before and contemporaneous with the colonization of America had been filled with turmoil, civil strife and persecutions, generated in large part by established sects. . . . These practices . . . transplanted to the soil of the new America . . . shock[ed] the freedom-loving colonists into a feeling of abhorrence.").

[17] See, e.g., *The Slaughter-House Cases*, 83 US 36 (1873) ("[I]n the light of events almost too recent to be called history, . . . and on the most casual examination of the language of these amendments, . . . no one can fail to be impressed with the one pervading purpose found in them all, . . . we mean the freedom of the slave race, the security and firm establishment of that freedom, and the protection of the newly-made freeman and citizen from the oppressions of those who had formerly exercised unlimited dominion over him.").

[18] The Bill and Madison's *Memorial* are each reprinted as an appendix to Douglas's opinion in *Walz v Tax Commission*, 397 US 664, 716–26 (1970).

[19] See *Cumming v Bd. of Ed.*, 175 US 528 (1899) (unsuccessfully challenging use of black tax dollars for white high school).

concern the law accords marriage within an established church[20] with Virginia's concern, in the statute struck down in *Loving*, with the racial purity of marriages of whites only.[21] Is it too much of a stretch to hear in Harlan's insistence in his *Plessy* dissent that the white race "will continue to be for all time [the dominant race], if it remains true to its great heritage,"[22] the words of a true believer denying that establishment of his faith is necessary to its continued dominance?

By the mid-twentieth century, the Supreme Court mandated the end of both racial and religious establishment, incorporating the Establishment Clause against the states and putting an end to Jim Crow. It is perhaps no accident that many of the early contested cases in both spheres involved education. In the area of race and the schools, the Supreme Court moved from increasingly aggressive enforcement of separate but equal standards to the rejection of legally established separateness in *Brown*. It spent the rest of the century working through the required and permissible boundaries for the use of race in ending educational segregation. Among its leading affirmative action cases were two, *Bakke* and *Wygant*,[23] concerning the use of race in selecting, respectively, students and teachers.

Although the Supreme Court has not recently decided a case in the area, lower courts have continued to struggle with the use of racial affirmative action in the schools. Early in 2001, two district judges in the Eastern District of Michigan reached opposite conclusions with respect to the uses of race in admissions by two units of the same university. In the more recent case, *Grutter v Bollinger*,[24] Judge Bernard Friedman struck down the University of Michigan Law School's "race-conscious" admissions policy and

---

[20] See, e.g., An Act for the Better Preventing of Clandestine Marriages, popularly known as Lord Harwicke's Act or the Marriage Act of 1753 (recognizing only marriages performed by ministers of the established Church of England in accordance with prescribed rules).

[21] See *Loving v Virginia*, 388 US 1 (1967) (holding unconstitutional Virginia's antimiscegenation statute, which prohibited only racially mixed marriages in which one partner was white).

[22] *Plessy v Ferguson*, 163 US 537, 559 (1896) (Harlan dissenting).

[23] *Wygant v Jackson Bd. of Ed.*, 476 US 267 (1986).

[24] 2001 US Dist Lexis 3256 (ED Mich 2001). The Sixth Circuit issued a stay pending appeal so that the University of Michigan Law School could complete its admissions season. *Grutter v Bollinger*, 2001 US App Lexis 5606 (6th Cir 2001).

held that any future policy must be "race-neutral." Only a few months earlier, in *Gratz v Bollinger*,[25] his colleague Judge Patrick Duggan had upheld the University of Michigan's undergraduate admissions office's current use of race as a factor in admissions. The law school and the undergraduate admissions office did have somewhat different approaches to the use of race as a factor in admissions. Judge Friedman found that, for the law school, "race is not . . . merely one factor which is considered among many others in the admissions process" but rather "the law school places a very heavy emphasis on an applicant's race in deciding whether or not to accept or reject." More importantly, however, the two judges also reached significantly different conclusions as to the law they applied to their respective facts. In *Gratz*, Judge Duggan, following the path laid out in Powell's *Bakke* opinion, distinguished the Michigan undergraduate admissions office's most recent use of race as one of many factors, which he upheld, from its more rigid and singular use of race in earlier years, which he held to have been unconstitutional. In contrast, Judge Friedman, in addition to finding an absence of narrow tailoring in the law school's use of race in admissions, also held categorically, and directly contrary to Judge Duggan, that "the achievement of [racial] diversity is not a compelling state interest." The Ninth Circuit, in a case involving admission to the University of Washington School of Law, recently took the opposite position, holding that "educational diversity is a compelling governmental interest that meets the demands of strict scrutiny of race-conscious measures."[26] Federal circuit courts have recently become much more aggressive in their opposition to the use of racial classifications, with the Fifth Circuit in *Hopwood* banning any use of race in admissions decisions by the University of Texas Law School,[27] the Third Circuit in *Taxman* barring the use of race as a tiebreaker in determining which of two equally qualified teachers should be laid off,[28] the Fourth Circuit in

---

[25] 122 F Supp 2d 811 (ED Mich 2000).

[26] *Smith v Univ. of Washington*, 233 F3d 1188 (9th Cir 2000). The policy with respect to the use of race at issue in *Smith* was discontinued after the passage in 1998 of Initiative Measure 200, which, inter alia, forbade the State of Washington to "discriminate against, or grant any preferential treatment to, any individual or group on the basis of race . . . in the operation of . . . public education." Id at 1192.

[27] *Hopwood v Texas*, 78 F3d 932 (5th Cir 1996).

[28] *Piscataway Township Bd. of Ed. v Taxman*, 91 F3d 1547 (3d Cir 1996). The Supreme Court took cert in this case, but it was settled after briefing and before argument.

Podberesky striking down a scholarship program for exceptionally talented black applicants to the University of Maryland,[29] and the D.C. Circuit holding FCC pressure on broadcasters to recruit minorities unconstitutional.[30]

In so doing, these circuit courts claim to be responding to signals sent by a Supreme Court that appears to them to have both intensified its scrutiny of[31] and narrowed its list of acceptable justifications for governmental use of[32] racial classifications in efforts to benefit minority groups. While some of these signals came in traditional affirmative action cases involving employment opportunities of one sort or another,[33] a majority of the Court has also increasingly restricted the use of race in an effort to benefit minorities in the political process through the creation of majority-minority districts.

It is not my intent to summarize or analyze the full development of Supreme Court case law concerning either race or the religion clauses over the past several decades. Instead, for both educational affirmative action and the use of race in districting, I want to pursue parallels with the Supreme Court's religion clause jurisprudence in aid of my argument that the approach mapped out by the Powell opinion in *Bakke*, the Michigan District Court in *Gratz*, and the Supreme Court dissenters in the recent voting rights cases[34] makes more sense as a part of our constitutional law than

---

[29] *Podberesky v Kirwan*, 38 F3d 1884 (4th Cir 1994).

[30] *MD/DC/DE Broadcasters v FCC*, 2001 US App Lexis 570 (DC Cir 2001). I include the broadcasting cases within the scope of a discussion otherwise centered on educational affirmative action and districting because the broadcasting cases, unlike, for example, cases examining affirmative action in the construction industry, focus on issues of diversity and community rather than simply on remedying prior discrimination.

[31] For example, by holding that federal as well as state use of racial classifications for affirmative action was subject to strict scrutiny. *Adarand v Pena*, 515 US 200 (1995).

[32] For example, by rejecting the so-called role model justification for affirmative action in selecting teachers. *Wygant*, 476 US at 274.

[33] See, in particular, *Adarand*, 515 US 200, requiring strict scrutiny for all racial classifications, including those used by the federal government in an effort to aid minorities. It is worth noting that, on remand, the Tenth Circuit took to heart the notion that strict scrutiny need no longer be "fatal in fact" and held a revamped program for "disadvantaged business enterprises" in construction subcontracting to be narrowly tailored to achieve a compelling governmental interest in remedying the nationwide effects of past and present discrimination against racial minorities in the construction industry. *Adarand Constructors v Slater*, 228 F3d 1147 (10th Cir 2000).

[34] Because I believe the argument in the districting cases is stronger and simpler and has already been well laid out on the current Supreme Court by these dissenters, I will spend somewhat more time laying out the argument in the education context.

the sort of categorical opposition to the use of race in anything other than a strictly remedial context[35] that is rapidly becoming its chief competition.[36] The most direct religious parallel to the inclusion of racial communities of interest in districting and racial diversity in admissions comes in the line of cases from *Widmar* through *Rosenberger*, mandating the inclusion of religious groups in opportunities offered by public schools.[37] As I will discuss in detail below, a hallmark of these cases is their focus, not on discrimination between religions, or between religion and atheism or nonreligion, but rather between religion and other bases for inclusion or selection for governmentally provided opportunities.

The notion that religion and the religious cannot be singled out for extraordinarily unfavorable treatment extends beyond the *Widmar/Rosenberger* line of cases. Closely related to cases involving participation of religious groups in conceptual public fora like the *Rosenberger* funding scheme are those involving the inclusion of religious speech literally in the public square. As Scalia wrote in *Capitol Square Review Bd. v Pinette*,[38] "[T]he State may not, on the claim of misperception of official endorsement, ban all private religious speech from the public square, or discriminate against it by requiring religious speech alone to disclaim public sponsorship." Here again, analogies between extraordinarily discriminatory treatment for race and for religion spring readily to hand. Just as

---

[35] The distinct aspects of affirmative action and race-conscious districting as remedies for prior discrimination are not directly related to or addressed by my argument in this article. Although there may be disagreement about the appropriate circumstances, there is no disagreement on the Court that, in such circumstances, both racial affirmative action and the use of race in districting can be justified as such a remedy.

[36] I am not arguing that logical consistency necessarily demands parallel treatment of race and religion. One might well see analogies breaking down or see comparatively greater risk from either recognition of race or that of religion. But one should at least acknowledge and respond to the parallel structure of the argument to a greater degree than has yet been done by those Justices in the Court majority in both lines of cases.

[37] *Widmar v Vincent*, 454 US 263 (1981); *Mergens*, 496 US 226 (1990); *Lamb's Chapel v Steigerwald*, 508 US 384 (1993); *Rosenberger*, 515 US 819 (1995). The latest in this line of cases, *Good News Club v Milford Central School*, reported below at 202 F3d 502 (2d Cir 2000), is presently before the Court. The chief new wrinkle in *Good News Club* is that the school at which the club, led by an adult minister rather than students, wished to hold meetings of religious instruction immediately after the school day, was an elementary school; the prospective members included first graders. Largely because of these distinctions, the Second Circuit upheld the school's decision to exclude the club.

[38] 515 US 753, 769 (1995).

Scalia in *Pinette* sees it as "perverse"[39] to argue that religious speech should fare worse than pornography and commercial speech, given the special constitutional status of religion, so Stevens in *Shaw v Reno* sees it as "perverse,"[40] given African-Americans' special constitutional status, to have them fare worse in opportunities to obtain representation than Republicans and rural voters.[41]

And, just as in *Rosenberger* the Court held that the University of

---

[39] *Pinette*, 515 US at 766–67 ("Private religious speech cannot be subject to veto by those who see favoritism where there is none. The contrary view . . . exiles private religious speech to a realm of less-protected expression heretofore inhabited only by sexually explicit displays and commercial speech. . . . It will be a sad day when this Court . . . finds the First Amendment more hospitable to private expletives . . . than to private prayers. This would be merely bizarre were religious speech simply protected by the Constitution as other forms of private speech; but it is outright perverse when one considers that private religious expression receives preferential treatment under the Free Exercise Clause.") (citations omitted).

[40] *Shaw v Reno*, 509 US at 677 and n 4 (1993) (Stevens dissenting) ("Finally, we must ask whether otherwise permissible redistricting to benefit an underrepresented minority group becomes impermissible when the minority group is defined by its race. The Court today answers this question in the affirmative, and its answer is wrong. If it is permissible to draw boundaries to provide adequate representation for rural voters, for union members, for Hasidic Jews, for Polish Americans or for Republicans, it necessarily follows that it is permissible to do the same thing for members of the very minority group whose history in the United States gave birth to the Equal Protection Clause. . . . A contrary conclusion could only be described as perverse. . . . The Court's opinion suggests that African-Americans may now be the only group to which it is unconstitutional to offer specific benefits from redistricting. Not very long ago, of course, it was argued that minority groups defined by race were the only groups the Equal Protection Clause protected in this context.") (citations omitted).

[41] Scalia and Stevens elsewhere make arguments that mirror one another without acknowledging any resemblances or inconsistencies. As I have noted before, for example, other than the substitution of sex for race, the position on the relationship between remedy and standing that Scalia articulates in his *JEB* dissent is identical to what Stevens set forth in his *Shaw v Reno* opinion, a tension neither Scalia nor Stevens bothers to resolve or even acknowledge. Scalia's own focus on the individual in race cases is in substantial tension with his willingness to focus on the group in sex cases. This inconsistency is common among conservatives—Ted Olson, admittedly a hired gun, but one who frequently chooses his clients for the ideological appeal of their position, represented both Virginia in the Supreme Court argument of the VMI case, *U.S. v Virginia*, 318 US 515 (1996), and Cheryl Hopwood in her litigation successfully challenging the University of Texas's affirmative action policies. This put him squarely on both sides of the antistereotyping question. For women, Olson argued to the Supreme Court, individual merit was or should legally be irrelevant—group averages or tendencies could and should shape the law and exceptions be damned. But, in *Hopwood*, he successfully insisted on behalf of plaintiffs that all applicants to the University of Texas Law School be evaluated as individuals and not lumped with their racial group. Mary Anne Case, *"The Very Stereotype the Law Condemns": Constitutional Sex Discrimination Law as a Quest for Perfect Proxies*, 85 Cornell L Rev 1447, 1472 n 124 (2000).

Virginia could not single out for exclusion from funding religiously colored polemic, so in *Church of the Lukumi*[42] it held that a city cannot single out for disfavor religious reasons for killing animals. Again, importantly for the affirmative action and districting analogies I am pressing, in neither case was the relevant discrimination between religions[43] or even in a technical sense between religion and nonreligion or atheism, but rather it was between religious motivations and all others, like racial bases for community or diversity and all others.

The same notion of nondiscrimination against the religious underlies, according to Justice Scalia, the constitutionally mandated payment of unemployment compensation to those whose reason for unemployment is their religion: "[O]ur decisions in the unemployment cases stand for the proposition that where the State has in place a system of individualized exemptions, it may not refuse to extend that system to cases of 'religious hardship' without compelling reason."[44] When similarly individualized assessments are made of candidates for admissions or employment, excluding only their race from consideration as a factor may be, I would argue, similarly problematic. While I do not quite wish to argue that the makers of such individualized assessments "may not refuse to extend that system to [race] without compelling reason," their willingness to include race in the system, as those engaged in voluntary affirmative action do, should be seen as solving a potential constitutional problem, not just creating one. To pursue the religious analogy, such actions by admissions and hiring committees should be seen as at least comparable to permissible accommodation of religion, if not to required accommodation like that in the pre-

---

[42] *Church of the Lukumi Babalu Aye v City of Hialeah*, 508 US 520 (1993).

[43] The relevant contrast for the Court in *Church of the Lukumi* is not between religions, notwithstanding the care the statute's drafters took to protect kosher butchering. See id at 535.

[44] *Employment Division v Smith*, 594 US 872, 884 (1990), citing *Bowen v Roy*, 476 US 693, 708 (1986). In *Roy*, the plurality observed that, "The statutory conditions at issue in [*Sherbert* and *Thomas*] provided that a person was not eligible for unemployment compensation benefits if, 'without good cause,' he had quit work or refused available work. The 'good cause' standard created a mechanism for individualized exemptions. If a state creates such a mechanism, its refusal to extend an exemption to an instance of religious hardship suggests a discriminatory intent. Thus, as was urged in *Thomas*, to consider a religiously motivated exemption to be 'without good cause' tends to exhibit hostility, not neutrality, towards religion." Thus, the unemployment cases can be seen "as a protection against unequal treatment rather than a grant of favored treatment for the members of the religious sect." *U.S. v Lee*, 455 US 252, 263 n 3 (1981) (Stevens concurring).

Smith Supreme Court unemployment compensation cases.[45] This is particularly so given how narrowly states were otherwise permitted to define "good cause" for unemployment in these cases, excluding, for example, family obligations.[46]

Finally, although the case law is a thorny thicket into which I do not wish to wade deeply for present purposes, there are analogies in the Court's treatment of tax exemptions and direct and indirect governmental subsidies to religious organizations, notably sectarian schools: "[G]overnment grants exemptions to religious organizations because they uniquely contribute to the pluralism of American society by their religious activities. . . . [The] state encourages these activities not because it champions religion per se but because it values religion among a variety of private, nonprofit enterprises that contribute to the diversity of the Nation. Viewed in this light, there is no nonreligious substitute for religion as an element of our societal mosaic, just as there is no nonliterary substitute for literary groups."[47] (And no nonracial substitute for racial groups?)

One might argue that an important difference between the religion and race cases I am discussing, a difference that vitiates the force of my analogy, is that, in the race cases, but not in the religion cases, the state actor must be conscious of the suspect criterion and must use it in decision making. In other words, opponents of my argument would claim, while the religion cases require the state to be blind to the claimants' religion (religion-blind), to grant benefits without regard to religion, the race cases would require it to be conscious of the claimant's race (race-conscious), to grant benefits on account of race. I believe this difference to be overstated as a formal matter and, in any event, less than fully determinative as a conceptual matter.[48] Whether or not religious classifi-

---

[45] *Sherbert v Verner*, 374 US 398 (1963); *Thomas v Review Bd.*, 450 US 707 (1980); *Hobbie v Unemployment App. Commission*, 480 US 136 (1986).

[46] See, e.g., *Sherbert*, 374 US at 419 (Harlan dissenting).

[47] *Walz*, 397 US at 688, 693 (1970) (Brennan concurring).

[48] As a conceptual matter, it is, for example, important to remember that the constitutional equality guarantee is not textually or conceptually the same as, for example, the Title VII antidiscrimination guarantee. The Fourteenth Amendment does not ban race discrimination; it guarantees equal protection of the laws to persons of all races. The question to be asked is not whether prohibition on the use of the category of race in, for example, admissions or districting is race discrimination (it is not), but whether such a prohibition may work a denial of equal protection to some persons for whom race is a particularly salient characteristic.

cations are actually at work in a given case, it is important to remember that "we have rejected as unfaithful to our constitutionally protected tradition of religious liberty, any conception of the Religion Clauses as . . . stating a unitary principle that 'religion may not be used as a basis of classification for the purposes of governmental action, whether that action be the conferring of rights or privileges or the imposition of duties or obligations.' . . . Such rigid conceptions of neutrality have been tempered by constructions upholding religious classifications where necessary to avoid '[a] manifestation of . . . hostility [toward religion] at war with our national tradition."[49]

As a formal matter, in the *Widmar/Rosenberger* line of cases, not just any group can have access to facilities or funding, but only groups organized along appropriate dimensions. The state does, then, have to ask, "What sort of group is this?" and to use the answer in its decision making. That Wide Awake's activities are recognized by the state actor to be principally religious and not, for example, political, philanthropic, or social[50] is crucial to its claim of access in *Rosenberger*.[51] Thus, at a certain level, the group's central organizing characteristic, what it is that the members of the group have in common that distinguishes them from other groups, plays a role in governmental decision making and in the allocation of governmental benefits in both sorts of cases. Moreover, in both sorts of cases, it is generally in the first instance not the state but the individuals who identify themselves by classification, by applying as a group organized along a religious dimension in the access cases and through filling out census or application forms in the race cases.[52]

Similarly, in the unemployment compensation cases, in asking, as it must, "For what reason did a claimant become unemployed?"

---

[49] *McDaniel v Paty*, 435 US at 638 (1978) (Brennan concurring).

[50] See *Rosenberger*, 515 US at 825 (detailing groups eligible and ineligible for university funding).

[51] The funding Wide Awake gets is not that dissimilar from the admissions preference given to black applicants to university. Just as the pool for other funding candidates is marginally smaller if Wide Awake must be funded, so the odds of all other candidates go down marginally in the face of a thumb on the scales for blacks. In rejecting the categorical distinction between funding and access to facilities, the Court in *Rosenberger* shifted to the realization that all resources are scarce or none are.

[52] By contrast, in cases involving what are now seen as paradigmatically illegitimate racial classifications, such as *Plessy*, 163 US at 549, the state itself is in the first instance doing the classifications, for example, by telling Plessy he is colored despite his claim to the contrary.

and using the answer to distinguish between claimants, by treating religious reasons, but not, for example, family reasons, as acceptable, the state is at some level not "blind to" but "conscious of" the claimant's religion. At least after *Smith*, which rejects a broad free-exercise-based right of the religiously motivated to exemptions from generally applicable laws, it is not enough of an answer to invoke the distinctive requirements of the Free Exercise Clause to distinguish the race from the religion cases.[53] Rather, with both the equal access cases and the unemployment cases, the need to avoid inequality in treatment rather than any categorical right to the benefit at issue is doing the bulk of the work in cases benefiting the religious.[54]

In the public display cases, both menorahs and creches erected by the state on state property are chosen for display specifically as religious symbols, arguably unlike a Christmas tree (whose secular significance may predominate) and also unlike the cross in *Pinette* (erected by the Klan and not the state[55] and, in that context, having a significance historically more sinister than religious).

A particularly dramatic example of state use of a religious criterion in selection ironically comes from the same circuit that categorically prohibited the use of race in decision making in *Hopwood*. The Fifth Circuit, this time sitting en banc, very recently considered the constitutionality of the Beaumont, Texas, public school system's Clergy in the Schools program.[56] For this program, the school district on its own initiative enlisted local clergy by invitation to come to school to counsel groups of students on "secular issues including race, divorce, peer pressure, discipline and drugs." True to the name the school district had selected for it, the program refused to allow participation by nonclergy, even "profes-

---

[53] Nor is the availability of broader First Amendment speech clause arguments sufficient to distinguish religion cases like *Rosenberger* from race cases like *Bakke:* as the Court has repeatedly recognized, broad First Amendment concerns are implicated in virtually every aspect of a public university's intellectual activities, including, specifically, its freedom to determine "who may be admitted to study." T. X. Huxley quoted by Frankfurter in *Sweezy v New Hampshire*, 354 US 234, 263 (1957) and again by Stevens concurring in *Widmar*, 454 US at 279 n 2.

[54] In most of the equal access cases, equal protection claims were raised, but not addressed by the Supreme Court; there is little reason to think such claims would have been rejected had it been necessary to reach them.

[55] 515 US at 758.

[56] *Doe v Beaumont Ind. School Dist.*, 2001 US App Lexis 1153 (5th Cir en banc 2001).

sionals from secular counseling professions." And the only members of other professions participating as such in other school programs seemed to be law enforcement officers. Although my own view is that Judge Wiener's *Beaumont* dissenting opinion for himself and five colleagues, arguing that summary judgment should be entered against the school district, accurately represents the current state of the law of the religion clauses, five circuit judges astonishingly were prepared to issue summary judgment in the school district's favor and a controlling minority of three more remanded for further fact-finding. I find striking the contrast between the Fifth Circuit's willingness to let Texas schools be religion-conscious and its insistence that they be race-blind.

Although I am not arguing generally that if religious criteria can be used then so can race, I also find the contrast between the Supreme Court's apparent view of race and religion as criteria in districting nevertheless worthy of note.[57] When Kennedy wrote in his *Kiryas Joel* concurrence that "[t]he real vice of the school district, in my estimation, is that New York created it by drawing political boundaries on the basis of religion. . . . [I]n my view one . . . fundamental limitation [imposed by the Establishment Clause] is that government may not use religion as a criterion to draw political or electoral lines,"[58] he was speaking for himself alone; no other Justice joined any part of his opinion.[59] As noted above, the dissenting Justices in the *Shaw* line have contrasted uses of race in districting called into question by the majority with uses of religion that have not been so questioned.[60] Although both the lower court and the Supreme Court make a point in *U.J.O. v Carey* of insisting that "petitioners enjoyed no constitutional right in reap-

---

[57] Indeed, in districting it may be more to the point, as the habitual *Shaw* dissenters have argued, that if voters' national origin (e.g., Chinese-American or Russian-American) can be and is used in districting, race should and could be to at least the same extent. See, e.g., *Miller*, 515 US at 947 (Ginsburg dissenting).

[58] 512 US at 573, 577.

[59] Indeed, three of the other four habitual *Shaw* line majority—Scalia, Rehnquist, and Thomas—dissented in *Kiryas Joel*.

[60] See, e.g., *Shaw v Reno*, 509 US at 677 (Stevens, dissenting) ("If it is permissible to draw boundaries to provide adequate representation . . . for Hasidic Jews . . . it necessarily follows that it is permissible to do the same thing for [African-Americans]"). See also Ginsburg dissenting in *Miller v Johnson*, 515 US at 945 (citing newspaper report that "an Irish Catholic [State Assembly member] 'wanted his district drawn following [Catholic] parish lines so all the parishes where he went to baptisms, weddings and funerals would be in his district'").

portionment to separate community recognition as Hasidic Jews,"[61] neither did the courts suggest that the Hasidic community was precluded from such recognition on Establishment Clause grounds. There does seem to be a comparable suggestion in the recent voting rights cases that African-Americans may be precluded from "separate community recognition" because this would be to assume, stereotypically, that members of the same race have a community of interest.[62]

Is the argument I'm making in the affirmative action context dependent on establishing that diversity is a compelling governmental interest?[63] I don't think so. The relevant compelling governmental interest is in equal protection:[64] it would deny equal protection to racially defined groups to deny them an opportunity afforded other groups, in the same way as it denies equal protection to the religious to deny them opportunities afforded others to compete for funds or to use facilities. A public university can choose to admit on board scores alone, it can reject diversity entirely in favor of homogeneity[65] in its admissions process, but it cannot seek diversity without being allowed, perhaps in some instances required, to include racial diversity. Similarly, teachers can be laid off and people sorted into voting districts by lot, but perhaps not by criteria in pari materia with race to the exclusion of race.

Note that this argument is subtly different from an argument that diversity is a compelling interest—it does not so much argue for diversity, but to suggest that, if diversity is sought or mandated along other dimensions, the Constitution does not require ignoring racial diversity and might even compel racial diversity in cer-

---

[61] *U.J.O. v Carey*, 430 US 144, 153 (1977), describing holding of lower court in *UJA v Wilson*, 377 F Supp 1164, 1165–66 (ED NY 1974).

[62] Compare Richard H. Pildes and Richard G. Niemi, *Expressive Harms, "Bizarre" Districts and Voting Rights: Evaluating Election District Appearances After Shaw v Reno*, 92 Mich L Rev 483, 578 (1993) (discussing difficulty of distinguishing "legitimate communities of interest from the now-illegitimate one of race").

[63] A controversial and somewhat open question in current law, as noted above.

[64] Compare *Texas Monthly v Bullock*, 489 US 1, 39 (1989) (Scalia dissenting) ("[R]ather than reformulating the *Lemon* test in 'accommodation' cases . . . , one might instead simply describe the protection of free exercise concerns, and the maintenance of the necessary neutrality, as 'secular purpose and effect,' since they are a purpose and effect approved, and indeed to some degree mandated, by the Constitution.").

[65] Of course, not deliberate racial homogeneity.

tain circumstances.[66] Similarly, no one claims that the Free Exercise Clause mandates availability of student funds for religious activities or of rooms for student prayer, only that (*a*) the Establishment Clause does not categorically prohibit making such facilities available, and (*b*) the Equal Protection Clause and the antidiscrimination component of the First Amendment may require them to be made available to the religious for religious purposes if they are made available to others for a wide variety of other purposes. How do these claims differ from a claim that free exercise requires provision to the religious? First, the state actor need not establish a forum at all and can also restrict it to activities not remotely in pari materia with religion. For example, I know of no one who seriously suggests that if the only extracurricular activities a given school offers are sports, the exclusion of a Christian fellowship seeking to use the playing fields for prayer group meetings would create a constitutional problem. But, if a much broader spectrum of activities has access to school facilities and support, not only will the Establishment Clause not stand in the way, the Equal Protection Clause may require that the religious also have access to funding or space for their activities.[67]

Similarly, a university selecting on SAT scores alone need not add race to the mix (at least absent a history of discrimination or

---

[66] See *Bakke*, 438 US at 403, 404, 406 (opinion of Blackmun) ("The number of qualified, indeed highly qualified applicants to medical schools in the United States far exceeds the number of places available. . . . It is somewhat ironic to have us so deeply disturbed over a program where race is an element of consciousness, and yet to be aware of the fact, as we are, that institutions of higher learning, albeit more on the undergraduate level than on the graduate level, have given conceded preferences up to a point to those possessed of athletic skills, to the children of alumni, to the affluent who may bestow their largess on the institutions, and to those having connections with celebrities, the famous, and the powerful. . . . [G]overnmental preference has not been a stranger to our legal life. We see it in veterans' preferences. We see it in aid-to-the-handicapped programs. We see it in the progressive income tax. We see it in the Indian programs . . . . And in the admissions field, as I have indicated, educational institutions have always used geography, athletic ability, anticipated financial largess, alumni pressure, and other factors of that kind.").

[67] See, more generally, Michael McConnell, *Religious Participation in Public Programs: Religious Freedom at a Crossroads*, 59 U Chi L Rev 115, 189 (1992) ("The problem with the secularization baseline is that it is not neutral. . . . [W]hen the government owns . . . many of the principal institutions of culture, exclusion of religious ideas, symbols, and voices marginalizes religion in much the same way that the neglect of the contributions of African American and other minority citizens, or of the viewpoints and contributions of women, once marginalized those segments of the society. . . . When the public sphere is open to ideas and symbols representing nonreligious viewpoints, cultures, and ideological commitments, to exclude all those whose basis is 'religious' would profoundly distort public culture.").

a strong disparate-impact argument), but it is not precluded from so doing, and, depending on what all else it considers, one can imagine situations under which it may be required to include race. Consider, for example, an entering class selected to "look like America"[68] along every conceivable dimension but race. Or consider, more plausibly, in the voting rights arena, a redistricting plan in which every large concentrated group but blacks can elect a representative, but blacks cannot. Under certain circumstances the latter plan may violate the Voting Rights Act, it may constitute vote dilution, and it may be unconstitutional.[69]

Making sure that other constituencies[70] have their representatives, whether in the legislature (as in voting rights cases), in the classroom (as in admissions cases), or on the airwaves (as in the licensing cases), but excluding racially defined constituencies, works a discrimination so long as there still are racially defined constituencies.[71] This is especially so when racial constituencies are asymmetrically distributed throughout the relevant population—asymmetrically in two senses: first, in that racial identity means more to some than to others,[72] and second, in that those to whom racial identity is most salient are in the literal sense a minority group. Compare members of some minority religions, more intensely committed to religion and less likely to be in the political majority than the average citizen. Just as, predictably, more members of minority religions will find their employer's requirements

---

[68] In the phrase used by the Clinton administration to describe its ambitions for the Cabinet.

[69] Stevens, dissenting in *Miller v Johnson*, 515 US at 933 ("I have long believed [citing *Cousins*] that treating racial groups differently from other identifiable groups of voters, as the Court does today, is itself an invidious racial classification. Racial minorities should receive neither more nor less protection than other groups against gerrymanders. A fortiori, racial minorities should not be less eligible than other groups to benefit from districting plans the majority designs to aid them.").

[70] Even religious constituencies, as noted above.

[71] "[R]ace remains a defining characteristic of American life. Even in a world of racial equality, the educational imperative that Justice Powell identified in *Bakke* would exist as long as one's race was so prominent a part of one's experience." Introduction to the expert submissions of the University of Michigan in *Gratz v Bollinger*, No 97-75321 (ED Mich) 4–5.

[72] Consider, e.g., the high frequency with which members of racial minorities, compared to others, put race on even a very short list of their defining characteristics: when asked to describe themselves using only three adjectives, disproportionately many blacks and females as compared with whites and males listed their race and sex. See, e.g., Patricia A. Cain, *Feminist Jurisprudence: Grounding the Theories*, in Katharine T. Bartlett and Rosanne Kennedy, eds, *Feminist Legal Theory: Readings in Law and Gender* 263, 270 (1991).

incompatible with their religion and thus will be eligible for benefits, so predictably more members of minority racial and ethnic groups will find themselves underrepresented at state universities and will be eligible for admission on a diversity rationale.

In *Hopwood*, the Fifth Circuit lists a slew of characteristics an admissions office is permitted to consider: "A university may properly favor one applicant over another because of his ability to play the cello, make a downfield tackle, or understand chaos theory. An admissions process may also consider an applicant's home state or relationship to school alumni. Law schools specifically may look at things such as unusual or substantial extracurricular activities in college, which may be atypical factors affecting undergraduate grades. Schools may even consider factors such as whether an applicant's parents attended college or the applicant's economic and social background."[73] If all of these characteristics are indeed considered, and race may not be, a discrimination is worked against those who offer racial diversity.[74]

The Fifth Circuit in *Hopwood* strongly disagrees with this analysis, claiming that "the caselaw [i]s sufficiently established that the use of ethnic diversity simply to achieve racial heterogeneity, even as part of the consideration of a number of factors, is unconstitutional. . . ."[75] Among that court's premises is that, unlike other

---

[73] *Hopwood*, 78 F3d at 946 (5th Cir 1996).

[74] Interestingly, Scalia, dissenting in *Powers v Ohio*, 499 US 400, 423–24 (1991), seems to understand almost exactly this point in the context of race-based peremptory challenges. He insisted in that context that "When a particular group has been singled out in this fashion, its members have been treated differently, and have suffered the deprivation of a right and responsibility of citizenship. But when that group, like all others, has been made subject to peremptory challenge on the basis of its group characteristic, its members have been treated not differently but the same. In fact, it would constitute discrimination to exempt them from the peremptory-strike exposure to which all others are subject. If, for example, men were permitted to be struck but not women, or fundamentalists but not atheists, or blacks but not whites, members of the former group would plainly be the object of discrimination. . . . Unlike the categorical exclusion of a group from jury service, which implies that all its members are incompetent or untrustworthy, a peremptory strike on the basis of group membership implies nothing more than the undeniable reality (upon which the peremptory strike system is largely based) that all groups tend to have particular sympathies or hostilities—most notably sympathies toward their own group members. Since that reality is acknowledged as to all groups, and forms the basis for peremptory strikes as to all of them, there is no implied criticism or dishonor to a strike."

Because the Court's liberal wing, in the majority in *Powers*, disagrees with Scalia about the stigma of a strike and also disagrees with him about the constitutional difference between a "welcome mat" and a "no trespassing sign," they are less susceptible to a charge of inconsistency than Scalia and the Court's conservatives in this matter.

[75] *Hopwood*, 78 F3d at 945–46 (5th Cir 1996) (citations omitted).

characteristics, race may not constitutionally be used as an imperfect proxy and it is at best an imperfect proxy for characteristics a school may legitimately seek in applicants. But is it really imperfect here? I have elsewhere already questioned some aspects of the narrowness of the Supreme Court's remedial exception for racial classifications, arguing that, as the Supreme Court appears to have recognized with respect to sex, but notoriously not yet with respect to race, 100 percent of members of the historically subordinated group or suspect class, including those not demonstrably materially affected by discrimination, are subject to ambient discrimination on the basis of their membership in the group.[76]

And is race really a proxy here at all? Affirmative action in hiring and admissions need not proceed from the (stereotyping) assumption that blacks think alike or think differently from whites, but can instead proceed from exactly the opposite assumption.[77] It can proceed from the assumption that, by experience with black teachers and students who are no different than their white counterparts, students will realize the error of their previous stereotypic thinking about blacks: they will realize that there is no difference and will learn to reject " 'existing misconceptions and stereotypical categorizations which in turn lead to future patterns of discrimination.' "[78] In insisting that "[t]he use of race, in and of itself, to choose students simply achieves a student body that looks different [and that] Such a criterion is no more rational on its own terms than would be choices based on the physical size or blood type of applicants,"[79] the *Hopwood* court misses the point. It is an accident

---

[76] See Mary Anne Case, *"The Very Stereotype,"* 85 Cornell L Rev at 1454–55, 1460–61.

[77] To put it in Alex Johnson's terms, if admitted black students play bid whist, they can offer cultural diversity; but if they play bridge instead, they can demonstrate that blacks, too, play this card game like the white majority. Alex M. Johnson, Jr., *Bid Whist, Tonk, and United States v. Fordice: Why Integrationism Fails African-Americans Again*, 81 Cal L Rev 1401 (1993) (using the metaphor of bid whist and tonk, card games favored by African-Americans, to describe a unique African-American culture potentially threatened by forced integration).

[78] *Taxman*, 91 F3d at 1577 (Lewis dissenting) (citation omitted). Justice Stevens makes a similar argument in his *Wygant* dissent, 476 US at 315. And Justice O'Connor was quite right to note that, "The goal of providing 'role models' discussed by the courts below should not be confused with the very different goal of promoting racial diversity among the faculty. . . . [T]his latter goal was not urged as such in support of the layoff provision before the [courts below]." *Wygant*, 476 US at 288 (O'Connor concurring in part and in the judgment).

[79] Note that more than skin color was in fact at stake for the UT admissions officials, because they did not consider a black Nigerian to be a minority candidate. *Hopwood*, 78 F3d at 936 n 4.

of history that in the United States race has the sort of salience that leads to worrisome stereotypical categorizations and blood type does not, such that government here has a compelling interest in eradicating stereotypes with respect to race and not blood type, even through occasional affirmative use of racial classifications to do so. In a place like Japan, by contrast, where there has been a widespread popular belief that blood type does determine character, so that many believe one profitably could select employees, political candidates, and prospective mates by blood type,[80] it might make the same kind of sense to implement an admissions program seeking diversity by blood type, not in an endorsement of the ultimate rationality of blood type discrimination, but in an effort to eradicate such discriminatory impulses in the next generation.[81] The *Hopwood* majority is therefore wrong to claim so categorically that "Within the general principles of the Fourteenth Amendment, the use of race in admissions for diversity in higher education contradicts, rather than furthers, the aims of equal protection."[82]

One lesson of all the educational affirmative action cases from *De Funis* through *Hopwood* is that constitutional difficulties will arise when admissions officers "compar[e] minority applicants only with one another."[83] But there are two radically different ways to compare them with the whole of the applicant pool, as William

---

[80] See, e.g., Jennifer Trueland, *Japanese Search in Vein for Perfect Blood Type*, The Scotsman 12 (Aug 13, 1998); Associated Press, *"What's Your Blood Type?" Endures as one of Japan's Best Pickup Lines*, Chicago Tribune North Sports Final Edition N34 (Dec 18, 1997).

[81] See Bowen et al's evidence, adopted in *Gratz*, of benefit to white majority from exposure to minorities.

[82] *Hopwood*, 78 F3d at 945. The *Hopwood* majority appears to proceed from the assumption that the alternative to the use of race as a factor in admissions is the treatment of all applicants "as individuals." 78 F3d at 945, 940. But admission to law or medical school is not like bidding on a road contract. It is not even like admission to graduate school, where applicants can provide evidence of earlier academic work in the field. It is more like admission to a jury. Challenges are peremptory, rarely for cause. It is necessarily proxy thinking that gets one selected, because there is rarely available direct evidence of the ability to do what one is asking to do. It makes little sense to talk of treating people as individuals by, for example, taking their family circumstances into account, because we do not all react the same way to circumstance. An admissions officer can only bet that, for example, plaintiff Hopwood's own difficult family circumstances (including a severely handicapped child) will give her "a different perspective" (and hence make her a better bet) or "burden . . . her academic performance" (and hence make her a worse bet)—both possibilities considered by the *Hopwood* appeals court, 78 F3d at 946–47, in a tacit admission of the proxy character of any factor in the decision.

[83] *De Funis v Odegaard*, 416 US 312, 330 (1974) (Douglas dissenting).

Bowen points out in his expert testimony in the Michigan case, recapitulating what Powell cites him for in *Bakke*:[84] the first is to use a single metric for all applicants but to consider each individually and in isolation, and the second is to give some attention to the shape of the class as a whole, seeking diversity along a number of fronts—balancing the percentage of athletes and musicians, and, on a finer grain, making sure that, among musicians, there aren't a dozen cellists and no timpanist, and among athletes not a dozen linebackers and no quarterback. As Bowen acknowledges, this means that in any given year, as compared with any particular applicant pool, an individual's chances, given his or her mix of talents and attributes, will be affected by the talents and attributes of others in the pool in ways much more complicated and nuanced than in simple head-to-head competition.[85]

---

[84] Expert report of William G. Bowen in *Gratz* (1999) at 147.

[T]he task of an admissions officer is not simply to decide which applicants offer the strongest credentials as separate candidates for the college; the task, rather is to assemble a total class of students, all of whom will possess the basic qualifications, but who will also represent, in their totality, an interesting and diverse amalgam of individuals who will contribute through their diversity to the quality and vitality of the overall educational environment.

This concern for the composition of the undergraduate student body, as well as for the qualifications of its individual members, takes many forms. While a school is of course interested in enrolling students who are good at a great many things and not one-dimensional in any sense, it should also try to enroll students with special interests and talents in the arts and in athletics; it should seek a wide geographical representation; it should admit foreign students from a variety of countries and cultures; it should recognize the special contribution that the sons and daughters of alumni can make by representing and communicating a sense of the traditions and the historic continuity of the university; it should enroll students from a range of socioeconomic backgrounds; and it should work consciously and deliberately to include minority students, who themselves represent a variety of experiences and viewpoints.

We must accept it as a fact of life in contemporary America that the perspectives of individuals are often affected by race as by other aspects of their background. If a university were unable to take into account the race of candidates, it would be much more difficult to consider carefully and conscientiously the composition of an entering class that would offer a rich educational experience to all its members.

[85] Compare *Wygant*, 476 US at 318 (Stevens dissenting) (the loss "to petitioners is not based on any lack of respect for their race, or on blind habit and stereotype. Rather, petitioners have been laid off for a combination of two reasons: the economic conditions that have led Jackson to lay off some teachers, and the special contractual protections intended to preserve the newly integrated character of the faculty. . . . Thus, the same harm might occur if a number of gifted young teachers had been given special contractual protections because their specialties were in short supply. . . . A Board decision to grant immediate tenure to a group of experts in computer technology, an athletic coach, and a language teacher, for example, might reduce the pool of teachers eligible for layoffs during a depression and therefore have precisely the same impact as the racial preference at issue here.").

Does it follow that whites are entitled to comparable preferences? Ordinarily not. Whiteness is not the salient characteristic, the source of diversity or community for most whites. The claim is not that blacks denied an opportunity for affirmative action preference are disadvantaged vis-à-vis those of other races, but vis-à-vis those who offer another basis for inclusion. Just as in *Rosenberger*, *Lamb's Chapel* and the school club cases the claim is that the religious are disadvantaged, not as compared to the unreligious, atheists, or those of another religion, but as compared to, for example, chess players,[86] so here the claim is that blacks denied a preference opportunity in admissions are disadvantaged as compared with legacies, farm kids, Nebraskans,[87] tuba players, and quarterbacks; and in districting as compared with farmers, Republicans, city dwellers, and Polish-Americans. There might be a reason to offer scholarship opportunities or admission preferences for whites at historically black colleges ("HBC"s), but not at Texas, because whiteness is not a salient characteristic for applicants to Texas. There might also be some reason to consider concentrated groups of white supremacists to be a "community of interest" for districting purposes, for example, in Metairie, Louisiana, where electoral support for David Duke was concentrated.[88]

Of course, if excluding only religion or race is a problem, including it alone may also be.[89] In both districting and law school admissions, Texas paid unique attention to race.[90] This predominance

---

[86] See *Mergens*, 496 US at 254.

[87] Although there is something to be said for geographical diversity as a value, the sinister antisemitic origins of some of Harvard College's own emphasis on geographical diversity should not be forgotten. "Those aren't doughnuts, they're bagels," was the retort Harvard admissions dean Chase Peterson got from a Jewish faculty member in 1971, when he acknowledged that Harvard might be taking fewer students from what Peterson called the "doughnuts around the big cities." See Nora Sayre, *Sixties Going on Seventies* 107 (1973).

[88] See Neil Gotanda, *A Critique of "Our Constitution Is Color Blind,"* 44 Stan L Rev at 64–68 (suggesting "free exercise of race" includes "the attachment of many white southerners to the Confederate flag").

[89] Compare *Arizona Governing Committee v Norris*, 463 US 1073, 1077 (1983) (holding retirement scheme violated Title VII when "[s]ex is the only factor that the tables use to classify individuals of the same age; the tables do not incorporate other factors correlating with longevity such as smoking habits, alcohol consumption, weight, medical history, or family history"); *L.A. Dept. of Water and Power v Manhart*, 435 US 702, 712–13 (1978) (holding pension scheme with "an actuarial distinction based entirely on sex" violated Title VII).

[90] In *Bush v Vera*, it relied on the availability of uniquely detailed racial data, "at the block-by-block level, whereas other data, such as party registration and past voting statistics, were only available at the level of voter tabulation districts," 517 US at 961. In *Hopwood*,

or privileging of race, like a comparable predominance or privileging of religion, is harder to justify than the use of race as one of several factors,[91] even if sometimes it is then the determinative factor. The flip side of *Widmar*,[92] which allowed student groups to use school facilities for worship on the same terms as other student groups used the same facilities for other purposes, is *Santa Fe Ind. School Dist. v Doe*,[93] which prohibited selection of a single student specifically to lead a prayer before the assembled spectators at all school football games. The flip side of *Church of the Lukumi*, which prevents the legislature from singling out a religiously motivated activity for special disadvantage, is *Kiryas Joel*, which prevents the

---

although it used a larger number of more subjective factors in ultimate admissions decisions, it sorted all candidates initially only by race and by TI score (a weighted index of GPA and board scores), 78 F3d at 935–36.

[91] Compare *Widmar*, 454 US at 277 ("[T]here are over 100 recognized student groups at UMKC. The provision of benefits to so broad a spectrum of groups is an important index of secular effect. . . . At least in the absence of empirical evidence that religious groups will dominate UMKC's open forum, . . . the advancement of religion would not be the forum's 'primary effect.'") (citations omitted); *Mergens*, 496 US at 250 ("To the extent that a religious club is merely one of many different student-initiated voluntary clubs, students should perceive no message of government endorsement of religion."); *Estate of Thorton v Calder*, 472 US 703, 711 (1985) (O'Connor concurring) ("The statute singles out Sabbath observers for special, and, as the Court concludes, absolute protection without according similar accommodation to ethical and religious beliefs and practices of other private employees"). *Adarand*, 515 US at 258 (Stevens dissenting) ("Unlike the 1977 Act [at issue in *Fullilove*], the present statutory scheme does not make race the sole criterion of eligibility for participation in the program. Race does give rise to rebuttable presumption of social disadvantage which . . . gives rise to a second rebuttable presumption of economic disadvantage. . . . But a small business may qualify as a [Disadvantaged Business Enterprise] by showing that it is both socially and economically disadvantaged, even if it receives neither of these presumptions. . . . Thus, the current preference is more inclusive than the 1977 Act because it does not make race a necessary qualification."); *Metro Broadcasting v FCC*, 497 US 547, 621 (1990) (O'Connor dissenting) (citing *Bakke* for the proposition that "race conscious measures might be employed to further diversity only if race were one of many aspects of background sought and considered relevant to achieving a diverse student body" and noting that, by contrast, "of all the varied traditions and ideas shared among our citizens, the FCC has sought to amplify only those particular views it identifies through the classifications most suspect under the Equal Protection clause"). But see *Corporation of the Presiding Bishop v Amos*, 483 US 327, 338 (1987) ("We find unpersuasive the District Court's reliance on the fact that Section 702 singles out religious entities for a benefit. . . . Where, as here, the government acts with the proper purpose of lifting a regulation that burdens the exercise of religion, we see no reason to require that the exemption come packaged with benefits to secular entities.").

[92] See *Chess v Widmar*, 635 F2d 1310, 1316 (8th Cir 1980), aff'd sub nom. *Widmar v Vincent* ("In contrast with a neutral policy, UMKC's current regulation has the primary effect of inhibiting religion, an effect which violates the Establishment Clause just as does governmental advancement of religion. . . . The University's policy singles out and stigmatizes certain religious activity and, in consequence, discredits religious groups.").

[93] 530 US 290 (2000).

legislature from singling out a religiously motivated activity for unique advantage.[94]

Powell's vision in *Bakke*, by contrast, is like the Court majority's vision in *NEA v Finley*,[95] with race or decency, respectively, being a factor but not the predominant factor; given weight, but no fixed weight;[96] necessarily occasionally determinative (imagine two identical proposed museum shows, except one includes Serrano's "Piss Christ" and the other does not; or two otherwise identical candidates one of whom belongs to a racial minority[97]). Both *Bakke* and *Finley* are repudiations of the extremes of doctrinal purity, respectively, of colorblindness and of viewpoint neutrality, made possible by fuzziness around the edges.[98]

Perhaps my argument can only save affirmative action schemes where race really is just one of many salient characteristics.[99] It brings us back to Powell in *Bakke*: "The diversity that furthers a compelling state interest encompasses a far broader array of qualifications and characteristics of which racial and ethnic origin is but a single though important element. Petitioner's special admissions program, focused solely on ethnic diversity, would hinder rather than further the attainment of genuine diversity."[100] My argument

---

[94] It's no accident that Kennedy writes both *Church of the Lukumi* and *Romer v Evans*— both are about the extraordinary act of singling out. But Kennedy also writes a separate concurrence in *Kiryas Joel*, insisting that "This is not an action in which the government has granted a benefit to a general class of recipients of which religious groups are just one part." 512 US at 722. Compare *Committee for Public Ed. v Nyquist*, 413 US 756, 793 (1973) ("One further difference between tax exemption for church property and tax benefits for parents should be noted. The exemption challenged in *Walz* was not restricted to a class composed exclusively or even predominantly of religious institutions. Instead, the exemption covered all property devoted to religious, educational or charitable purposes. As the parties here must concede, tax reductions authorized by this law flow primarily to the parents of children attending sectarian, nonpublic schools. Without intimating whether this factor alone might have controlling significance in another context in some future case, it should be apparent that in terms of the potential divisiveness of any legislative measure the narrowness of the benefitted class would be an important factor.").

[95] 118 S Ct 2168 (1998) (upholding requirement that judging of NEA grant applications "tak[e] into consideration general standards of decency and respect for the diverse beliefs and values of the American public").

[96] Compare the notion in the districting cases that race may be "a factor" but not "the predominant factor."

[97] See *Taxman*, 91 F3d 1547.

[98] Note both vision metaphors.

[99] On the other hand, there may well be circumstances when no other characteristic has the same salience.

[100] *Bakke*, 438 US 265 at 314 (1978) (opinion of Powell). Let me insist again that a program excluding solely ethnic diversity, as the Fifth Circuit seems to be imposing in *Hopwood*, would also hinder genuine diversity, however.

may help save some nonremedial use of race in districting, but not the UT admissions scheme in *Hopwood*. And it supports the distinction drawn by the district court in *Gratz* between the University of Michigan's now abandoned admissions grids, in which "the only distinguishing factor . . . was the applicant's race," and its current system, which uses race as one of several enumerated plus factors.[101] Those who believe "[t]here are diversities of gifts but the same spirit"[102] may see this as all to the good—diverse conceptions of merit produce a better overall class than single metric reliance on test scores.

Kiryas Joel may set a limit on the religion analogies' usefulness in justifying existing affirmative action programs: a program intended to benefit only the Satmar Hasidim could not withstand scrutiny even when put in the form of a generally applicable benefit, as it has been in its last several incarnations before New York courts that struck each down (let alone when extended to the Satmar community by name, as it had been in the earlier case before the Supreme Court). Similarly, a program intended to benefit only blacks or only racial minorities may face difficulty, not only when this is apparent on its face, as in *Hopwood*, but also when they are the only true beneficiaries, as arguably they were in *Bakke*.[103] This may *a fortiori* be true of programs including other groups only after a legal challenge to preferences for racial minorities only. If we hew to the religion analogy, these newly redesigned programs may find themselves in the same trap as the New York legislature's repeated unsuccessful efforts to accommodate Kiryas Joel, in accordance with the Supreme Court's requirements, by

---

[101] To "flag" an application so as to keep it in the review pool even when it would not otherwise "pass . . . the initial admit threshold," counselors may use the characteristics, not only of "under-represented race" but also "high school class rank, unique life experiences, challenges, circumstances, interests or talents, socioeconomic disadvantage and geography." *Gratz* at 32 and n 17. In computing the selection index score, not only are twenty points added to an applicant's score for belonging to an underrepresented minority group, but "six for geographic factors, four . . . for alumni relationship, . . . three for an outstanding essay, five . . . for leadership and service skills, twenty . . . for socioeconomic status, [and] twenty . . . for athletes," up to a total of forty. *Gratz* at 33.

[102] I Corinthians 12:4. At the risk of stating the obvious, when I refer to believers in this proposition, I don't mean just believers in the New Testament.

[103] On some versions of the facts, for at least one of the years in which Alan Bakke applied to medical school, this was the case at U.C. Davis, where "disadvantaged whites . . . in large numbers" applied to be considered for one of the places set aside for the "disadvantaged" for which they were at least nominally eligible, but all of those admitted under the program were members of racial minorities. *Bakke*, 438 US 265, 273, 275.

laws of general applicability.[104] The New York Court of Appeals has repeatedly held that the legislative efforts are not "neutral law[s] of general application,"[105] because, despite their neutral form, their intent and effect are to "permit the statute's benefits to flow almost exclusively to the religious sect it was plainly designed to aid."[106]

Even if redesigned admission plans actually do benefit a broader group, they may be unconstitutionally tainted by their purpose to preserve the availability of racial diversity. If the use of race is as unconstitutional as the *Hopwood* court suggests, there is, for example, little reason under current disparate-impact doctrine to think that the solutions Texas proposes, such as the so-called 10 percent solution,[107] fix the problem. For, if these solutions do not have a disparate impact by race, they will have failed in their purpose, but if they do, they will have been undertaken "because of and not in spite of" their disparate impact, thus risking failure of the Supreme Court's test for measures that have a disparate impact upon an identifiable group.[108] To use other things as a proxy for race may be no more permissible under the *Hopwood* standards than to use race as a proxy for other things.[109]

---

[104] See *Grumet v Cuomo*, 90 NY2d 57, 76 (1997) (striking down law general in form, but on the facts covering only the single district of Kiryas Joel because it "would be perceived as an act of governmental favor for the sole benefit of the Satmar sect"); *Grumet v Pataki*, 93 NY2d 677 (1999) (striking down reworked general law, this time covering on its facts Kiryas Joel and only one other district); but cf. *Agostini v Felton*, 521 US 203, 227 (1997) ("Nor are we willing to conclude that the constitutionality of an aid program depends on the number of sectarian schools that happen to receive the otherwise neutral aid.").

[105] *Grumet v Pataki*, 93 NY at 686.

[106] Id at 690.

[107] See, e.g., David Montejano, *Maintaining Diversity at the University of Texas*, in Robert Post and Michael Rogin, eds, *Race and Representation: Affirmative Action*, 359, 363–67 (1998) (describing plan "for the automatic admission of the top ten percent of each graduating high school class" in the highly segregated Texas public school system "to the Texas university of their choice."

[108] See *Personnel Admr of Mass. v Feeney*, 442 US 256 (1977). But see *Grutter v Bollinger* (note 24 above) (holding that the University of Michigan Law School's "failure to consider . . . race-neutral alternatives" for "enrolling significant numbers of underrepresented minority students" such as "increasing recruiting efforts, decreasing emphasis for all applicants on undergraduate GPA and LSAT scores, using a lottery system for all qualified applicants, or a system, whereby a certain number or percentage of the top graduates from various colleges and universities are admitted . . . militates against a finding of narrow tailoring").

[109] Nor would it necessarily be determinative that the disparate impact is in favor of minorities. Although *Feeney* itself does speak of "adverse effects on an identifiable group," and although the plan was adopted to help the identifiable group of minority students rather than to hurt whites, the general emphasis on color blindness and a sense that, admissions being something of a zero sum game, some white applicants stand to lose put the plan at

Would the need to bring other groups into any affirmative action scheme to save its constitutionality resemble the addition of elves, santas, and candy canes to Christmas creche scenes in Establishment Clause cases? Compare *Lynch*,[110] rejecting an Establishment Clause challenge to a public display including, not only a creche, but also "a Santa Claus house with a live Santa distributing candy; reindeer pulling Santa's sleigh; a live 40-ft. Christmas tree strung with lights; statues of carolers in old-fashioned dress; candy-striped poles; a 'talking' wishing-well; a large banner proclaiming 'SEASONS' GREETINGS'; a miniature 'village' with several houses and a church; and various 'cutout' figures, including those of a clown, a dancing elephant, a robot and a teddy bear,"[111] with *County of Allegheny v ACLU.*, where a creche standing alone, framed by evergreens, on the grand staircase of the county courthouse was held an unconstitutional establishment. The fact that the grand staircase "occasionally was used for displays other than the creche (for example, a display of flags commemorating the 25th anniversary of Israel's independence)"[112] was found insufficient dilution of the religious message. This is not the paradox of *R.A.V.* redux—including racial hate speech as part of a generic prohibition on fighting words, as that case required,[113] may too greatly dilute the intended governmental message that racial hatred is particularly obnoxious, and being surrounded by elves may dilute the creche's spiritual message, but inclusion with violinists, farm kids, and athletes will still benefit minority applicants. If additions dilute the affirmative action message, like the Christmas message, beyond recognition, that may be undesirable from the perspective of racial or religious zealots, but acceptable, even desirable, from a civil constitutional perspective.

The creche cases have more cautionary parallels to recent voting rights cases, however.[114] Justice O'Connor has insisted for the ma-

---

legal risk. For discussion, see, e.g., Kim Forde-Mazrui, *The Constitutional Limitations of Race-Neutral Affirmative Action*, 2000 Georgetown L J 2331.

[110] 465 US 668 (1984).

[111] *County of Allegheny v ACLU*, 492 US 573, 595 (1989).

[112] Id at 599, n 50.

[113] See *R.A.V. v City of St. Paul*, 505 US 377 (1992).

[114] The creche and voting rights case also, unfortunately, have in common a tendency to partake of what Pam Karlan has aptly dubbed the new Redrupping. See Pam Karlan, *Still Hazy After All These Years: Voting Rights in the Post Shaw Era*, 26 Cumb L Rev 287, 288 (1996). The Court has shifted its particularistic examination of individual cases in an area

jority in *Shaw v Reno* that "reapportionment is one area in which appearances do matter."[115] For her, and increasingly for a majority of the Court, the Establishment Clause is another such area.[116] As she first said in her *Lynch* concurrence, "Endorsement sends a message to nonadherents that they are outsiders, not full members of the political community, and an accompanying message to adherents that they are insiders, favored members of the political community. Disapproval sends the opposite message."[117] This danger of making the favored feel like insiders and others like outsiders[118] carries over to problematic majority-minority districts in voting rights cases, according to O'Connor, and may even shift from perception to more concrete reality: "The message that such districting sends to elected representatives is equally pernicious. When a district obviously is created solely to effectuate the perceived common interests of one racial group, elected officials are

---

for which it has been unable to articulate a workable test of general applicability from the counting up of body parts and their distance from one another in dirty movies to the counting up of elves and candy canes and their distance from the creche in Establishment Clause cases involving use of public property for religious holiday displays; it also now scrutinizes individually the shape of voting rights districts as it used to scrutinize images on a screen.

[115] *Shaw v Reno*, 509 US at 647 (1993). The appearance O'Connor thinks dangerously reinforced by race-conscious districting is that of "resemblance to political apartheid. It reinforces the perception that members of the same racial group—regardless of their age, education, economic status, or the community in which they live—think alike. . . . We have rejected such perceptions elsewhere as impermissible racial stereotypes." Id.

[116] See Pildes and Niemi, *Expressive Harms*, 92 Mich L Rev at 512 (arguing that the "endorsement test" for the Establishment Clause "is grounded on the same concerns as those central to Shaw").

[117] 465 US at 687 (O'Connor concurring). Brennan, dissenting, quotes language from a lower court opinion to the effect that, "Those persons who do not share these holidays are relegated to the status of outsiders by their own government; those persons who do observe those holidays can take pleasure in seeing the symbol of their belief given official sanction and special status." *Lynch* at 702 n 7.

[118] Although articulating this endorsement test most clearly in *Lynch*, O'Connor does not think the *Lynch* creche flunks it. As a white Christian, and therefore accustomed to being a favored insider in matters racial and religious, she may have difficulty hearing the message outsiders may get. Compare the dissenting Brennan's observation in *Lynch* at 496 that "because the Christmas holiday seems so familiar and agreeable" the Court's majority is blinded to the "distinctively sectarian" nature of the creche with Pam Karlan's assertion that the Court majority can only describe "the most integrated districts in the country" as "segregated" examples of "political apartheid" because they begin, blindly, with the assumption "that only majority-white and, therefore white-controlled, jurisdictions *can* be integrated." Pamela S. Karlan, *Our Separatism? Voting Rights as an American Nationalities Policy*, 1995 Chi L Forum 83, 94, 95. Because they begin with a white, Christian default, some members of the Court find it as difficult to see the racialism of familiar white control as the sectarianism of familiar Christian symbols.

more likely to believe that their primary obligation is to represent only the members of that group, rather than their constituency as a whole."[119]

In order to avoid either a racial or a religious establishment, a majority of the Supreme Court, in, respectively, its *Shaw* and its *Lemon*[120] test, has decreed that neither race nor religion shall be a dominant consideration for legislative action. Thus, under *Shaw* and its progeny, the Court will strike down a districting plan when "race for its own sake, and not other districting principles, was the legislature's dominant and controlling rationale in drawing its district lines."[121] And, under *Lemon* and its progeny, it will strike down statutes when "the preeminent purpose of the . . . legislature was to advance [a] religious viewpoint. . . ."[122] If accommodating religion can qualify as secular purpose, to what extent will accommodating the Justice Department?

For race and religion, vocal minorities on the Court have belittled the Court's majority's fears of establishment, at least when racial minorities or minority religions attract the legislature's aid. Except perhaps in the extraordinary case of majority-minority government,[123] claiming that whites are marginalized and black supremacy established by affirmative action may be akin to claiming that "after escaping brutal persecution and coming to America with the modest hope of religious toleration . . . , the Satmar had

---

[119] *Shaw v Reno* at 648.

[120] See *Lemon v Kurtzman*, 403 US 602 (1971).

[121] *Miller v Johnson*, 515 US at 913. See also *Shaw v Hunt*, 517 US 899, 907 (1996) ("Race was the criterion that, in the State's view, could not be compromised; respecting communities of interest and protecting Democratic incumbents came into play only after the race-based decision had been made."). Note that this approach constructs "race" and "communities of interest" as mutually exclusive. Stevens in dissent replies that he cannot "see how our constitutional tradition can countenance the suggestion that a State may draw unsightly lines to favor farmers or city dwellers, but not to benefit the very group whose history inspired the Amendment that the Voting Rights Act was designed to implement." *Shaw v Hunt*, 517 US at 949. Compare *Walz*, 397 US at 696 (1970) (Harlan concurring) ("In any particular case the critical question is whether the circumference of legislation encircles a class so broad that it can be fairly concluded that religious institutions could be thought to fall within the natural perimeter.").

[122] *Edwards v Aguillard*, 482 US 578 (1987). The particular religious viewpoint there at issue was "that a supernatural being created humankind," advanced by a statute mandating the teaching of "creation science" whenever evolution was taught in Louisiana public schools.

[123] See *City of Richmond v Croson*, 488 US 469 (1989), where blacks were in the majority in the Richmond city government distributing affirmative action preferences.

become so powerful, so closely allied with Mammon, as to have become an 'establishment' of the Empire State," as Scalia mockingly suggests in his *Kiryas Joel* dissent.[124]

But the ability of various minorities to attract the legislature's attention has been a source of fear as well as of comfort in matters of both race and religion. The greatest fear is of civil discord brought on by competition for legislative favor. Compare the dissenting Brennan view of civic strife occasioned by competition among minority religions for government attention[125] with Powell's image in *Bakke* of the nation dissolving into a welter of ethnic minority groups each seeking special treatment.[126] As commentators have noted, however, systematic exclusion of racial or religious interests from legislative attention is at least as likely to lead to political strife.[127]

---

[124] *Kiryas Joel*, 512 US at 732 (Scalia dissenting).

[125] *Lynch v Donnelly*, 465 US at 702 (1983) (Brennan, dissenting) ("[A]fter today's decision, administrative entanglements may well develop. Jews and other non-Christian groups . . . can be expected to press government for inclusion of their symbols, and faced with such requests, government will have to become involved in accommodating the various demands. . . . Cf. *Nyquist* . . . 413 US at 796 . . . ('competing efforts [by religious groups] to gain and maintain the support of government . . . occasioned considerable civil strife')." See also *Lemon*'s emphasis on "potential for political divisiveness . . . [in] need for annual appropriations and the likelihood of larger and larger demands as costs and populations grow," 403 US at 623.

[126] *Bakke*, 438 US 265, 294 (1978) ("[T]he white majority itself is composed of various minority groups, most of which can lay claim to a history of prior discrimination. . . . Not all of these groups can receive preferential treatment and corresponding judicial tolerance of distinctions drawn in terms of race and nationality, for then the only 'majority' left would be a minority of white Anglo-Saxon Protestants. . . . Courts would be asked to evaluate the extent of the prejudice and consequent harm suffered by various minority groups. Those whose societal injury is thought to exceed some arbitrary level of tolerability then would be entitled to preferential classifications at the expense of other groups. . . . Disparate constitutional tolerance of such classifications well may serve to exacerbate racial and ethnic antagonisms rather than alleviate them."). For an alternate nightmare vision see the parade of horribles in Stevens's concurrence in *Goldman v Weinberger*, 475 US 503, 512 (1986). According to Stevens, "the interest in uniform treatment for the members of all religious faiths risks being compromised if an observant Jew's request to wear religious head covering in contravention of military uniform regulations is granted" but there is "the danger that a similar claim on behalf of a Sikh or a Rastafarian might readily be dismissed as 'so extreme, so unusual or so faddish an image that public confidence in his ability to perform his duties will be destroyed.'"

[127] See, e.g., Laurence Tribe, quoted in *Mc Daniel v Paty*, 435 US at 640 n 25 (Brennan concurring) ("To view such religious activity as suspect, or to regard its political results as automatically tainted . . . might not even succeed in keeping religious controversy out of public life, given the 'political ruptures caused by the alienation of segments of the religious community.'").

ADRIAN VERMEULE

THE JUDICIAL POWER IN THE STATE
(AND FEDERAL) COURTS

My subject is a common separation-of-powers claim: that a statute violates the constitutional grant of "judicial power" to the courts.[1] In the federal system this claim has been the subject of great cases known to every student of constitutional law and federal jurisdiction; *Hayburn's Case*,[2] *United States v Klein*,[3] *Crowell v Benson*,[4] and

Adrian Vermeule is Professor, University of Chicago Law School.

AUTHOR'S NOTE: Thanks to Richard Epstein, Beth Garrett, Jack Goldsmith, Saul Levmore, John Manning, Eric Posner, David Strauss, and Cass Sunstein for comments and suggestions, and to Susan Gihring and Stephanie Morris for excellent research assistance. Special thanks to Yun Soo Vermeule.

[1] I will call such claims "freestanding judicial power claims" to distinguish them from claims rooted in specific constitutional provisions that protect or regulate the judiciary's authority and jurisdiction—such as the provisions that grant federal judges life tenure and salary protection, and that limit the judiciary to the decision of "cases" and "controversies," see US Const, Art III, § 2—or specific provisions that establish independent constitutional rules, such as the right of jury trial, see US Const, Amend VI (criminal jury), Amend VII (civil jury).

[2] See *Hayburn's Case*, 2 US (2 Dall) 409 (1792) (declining to adjudicate veteran's statutory eligibility for pension benefits on the ground that a provision for subsequent review by the executive branch took the proceeding outside the ambit of the judicial power).

[3] See *United States v Klein*, 80 US (13 Wall) 128, 146–47 (1871) (invalidating statute that prescribed evidentiary effect to be given to presidential pardons, on the ground that Congress's attempt to prescribe rules of decision in pending cases had "passed the limit which separates the legislative from the judicial power").

[4] See *Crowell v Benson*, 285 US 22, 51, 54–57 (1932) (vesting of judicial power in Article III courts requires de novo review of jurisdictional and constitutional facts). See also *Northern Pipeline Constr. Co. v Marathon Pipe Line Co.*, 458 US 50 (1982) (plurality opinion) (invalidating statute that vested decision of common-law claims arising out of bankruptcy proceedings in nontenured bankruptcy judges); cf. *Granfinanciera S.A. v Nordberg*, 492 US 33 (1989) (holding that Seventh Amendment right of civil jury trial, see US Const, Amend VIII, may be coextensive with right to proceed before an Article III tribunal exercising the federal judicial power).

Plaut v Spendthrift Farm[5] are all familiar names. In its most recent Term the Supreme Court added another decision in this line, *Miller v French*,[6] which rejected a judicial power challenge to a provision of the Prison Litigation Reform Act that automatically stays injunctive decrees against prison systems until district judges apply the Act's new substantive standards.

The common problem these cases address—legislative encroachment on judicial prerogatives—has been exhaustively studied by scholars of the federal system.[7] This mountain of scholarship, however, rests upon only about a dozen decisions. To know the great cases mentioned above, and a few others, is to know almost all of the available material about the separation of the federal legislative power from the federal judicial power. Further parsing of the cases in this small sample is unlikely to yield net intellectual returns. In this article, I shall consider a large (and largely neglected) body of information about freestanding judicial power claims: separation-of-powers cases decided by the state courts.[8]

---

[5] See *Plaut v Spendthrift Farm, Inc.*, 514 US 211 (1995) (grant of federal judicial power requires invalidation of statute that retroactively reopened final judgments of Article III courts).

[6] 530 US 327 (June 19, 2000).

[7] The cases, and citations to the massive accompanying literature, are collected in chapters 2 and 4 of Richard H. Fallon et al, *Hart & Wechsler's The Federal Courts and the Federal System* (4th ed 1996). For recent examples of the continuing, largely inconclusive debate about this handful of federal precedents, see Exordium, *Suspension and Supremacy, Judicial Power and Jurisdiction: The Availability and Scope of Habeas Corpus after AEDPA and IIRIRA*, 98 Colum L Rev 695 (1998) (articles debating whether recent amendments to the federal habeas corpus statute violate the grant of judicial power to the federal courts); Symposium, *Congress and the Courts: Jurisdiction and Remedies*, 86 Geo L J 2445 (1998) (articles debating constitutional limits on congressional control over federal-court jurisdiction).

[8] There is a large body of literature on the resurgence of state constitutionalism, but it focuses largely upon individual rights and civil liberties, as opposed to structural constitutional law. See, e.g., G. Alan Tarr, *The New Judicial Federalism in Perspective*, 72 Notre Dame L Rev 1097 (1997); William J. Brennan, Jr., *The Bill of Rights and the States: The Revival of State Constitutions as Guardians of Individual Rights*, 61 NYU L Rev 535, 548 (1986). Some important recent exceptions to this general neglect of state separation-of-powers law are Jim Rossi, *Institutional Design and the Lingering Legacy of Antifederalist Separation of Powers Ideals in the States*, 52 Vand L Rev 1167 (1998), and the articles collected in Symposium, *Separation of Powers in State Constitutional Law*, 4 Roger Williams L Rev 1 (1998). These articles, however, focus principally upon the separation of legislative from executive powers, and the articles are not principally concerned with using state law as a source of comparative constitutional data for understanding federal constitutional law. If anything, the dominant concern is to assert the autonomy of state constitutionalism as a subject worthy of study in its own right. See, e.g., Robert A. Schapiro, *Contingency and Universalism in State Separation of Powers Discourse*, 4 Roger Williams L Rev 79, 80 (1998) (offering a "critique of the powerful influence that the federal Constitution exerts over state separation of powers doctrine").

State courts have long been vigorous defenders of the constitutionally vested "judicial power" against perceived legislative encroachments.[9] Recently that tendency has become even more marked;
in particular, a wave of cases has emerged from the constitutional
struggle over tort reform currently raging in the state courts,[10]
although the phenomenon is by no means confined to such cases.
The result is an enormous body of state court doctrine on freestanding judicial power claims. The state cases are worthy of study in
their own right, and one of my aims is to focus attention on these
developments. But from the standpoint of federal constitutional
law the state cases are particularly valuable as data about comparative constitutional law, in particular comparative separation-
of-powers law; the cases increase our information by an order of
magnitude. That advantage overwhelms the usual difficulties in
comparing constitutional processes across jurisdictions—especially
because the differences between the relevant state constitutions
and the federal constitution are much smaller than the differences
involved in the transnational comparisons that are a staple of comparative constitutional law.[11]

The state cases reach startling results. Some suggest that state
legislatures invade the judicial power merely by altering common-
law liability rules or common-law remedies; others suggest that
legislative prescription of a standard of review, a rule of evidence,
or any other "procedural" rule encroaches upon judicial authority;
in others, judges order state or local legislative bodies to increase
appropriations for judicial budgets, on pain of contempt.[12] More-

---

[9] See Schapiro (cited in note 8) at 104 ("state courts have asserted significant independent
authority in certain areas, especially matters pertaining to the courts themselves"); Robert
A. Schapiro, *Judicial Deference and Interpretive Coordinacy in State and Federal Constitutional
Law*, 85 Cornell L Rev 656, 690 & n 216 (2000) (stating that "state court deference to
state legislatures continues to be strong," but that "[p]erceived incursions on the judicial
domain provoke more assertive responses from state courts."); Carl Baar, *Judicial Activism
in State Courts: The Inherent-Powers Doctrine*, in Mary Cornelia Porter and G. Alan Tarr,
State Supreme Courts: Policymakers in the Federal System 129 (1982) (noting that, in cases
involving constitutional claims based upon "inherent" judicial powers, "state trial courts
have for many years been willing to challenge executive and legislative authorities, issue
mandatory writs to elected and appointed officials, and even hold those officials in
contempt").

[10] For a capsule summary of the current state of the tort-reform struggle, see *State Courts
Sweeping Away Laws Curbing Suits for Injury*, New York Times (July 16, 1999), pp A1, A13.

[11] See note 53 and accompanying text (describing the preference for transnational comparisons in comparative constitutional law).

[12] See Part II (collecting and analyzing state decisions).

over, opinions in these areas often provide fine examples of the paranoid style in American judicial review—they display a prickly sensitivity to any slighting of judicial prerogatives, a dismissive impatience toward legislative aims, and a general, brooding suspicion of legislative bad faith.[13] Taken as a whole, I shall argue, the state decisions articulate conceptions of judicial authority that sweep beyond any defensible conception of judicial power. That argument necessarily assumes some normative standpoint for assessing the proper scope of judicial authority, but it need not assume any particular or highly contentious normative standpoint; I shall suggest that a broad range of constitutional approaches and methodologies converge to support the conclusion.

So viewed, the state cases upset critical premises of the literature on the federal separation of powers.[14] In one prominent strand of that literature, functionalists argue that judges should assess claims of interbranch encroachment by means of a balancing test. They argue that balancing allows flexible adjustments of the separation of powers to accommodate social change while preserving the "core" or "essential" functions of each branch from invasion. Formalists, by contrast, charge that functionalist adjudication underprotects the separation of powers by allowing intrusions into the affected branch's core functions. On this view, judges applying core functions analysis tend systematically to overweigh the concrete exigencies that gave rise to the challenged legislation, while undervaluing the abstract and structural interest in the separation of powers. Formalists therefore propose a rule-bound approach, one that will prevent the gradual degradation of the separation of powers that they fear will occur in a functionalist regime.

The state decisions contradict the analysis of both camps. The cases are largely functionalist: most commonly, they enquire whether the challenged statute encroaches upon or unduly interferes with core judicial functions. Yet the pattern of outcomes in these cases suggests that the *direction* of systemic pressure is opposite to that predicted by the formalist critique of functionalism. The systemic pressure runs not toward judicial underprotection of the separation of powers, but toward judicial overprotection of judicial power and prerogatives. The principal causes of this overprotective

---

[13] See notes 104–14 and accompanying text.

[14] The literature is described in notes 23–25 and accompanying text.

posture are best described as cognitive rather than motivational. The judges in these settings possess detailed knowledge about the institutional needs of the litigation system; are extremely well informed about, and habituated to, the judge-made substantive doctrine and procedural rules that legislation attempts to alter; and decide controversies within institutional structures that highlight the apparent benefits of standard-based adjudication while concealing the benefits of rule-based statutory reform. By contrast, the judges often lack a system-wide view of substantive law-reform legislation and of legislative budgeting processes, with their accompanying trade-offs and compromises; lack information about, and experience with, the benefits of statutory reforms of substantive and remedial law; and are poorly positioned to appreciate the (sometime) virtues of adjudicative rules rather than adjudicative standards.

I shall therefore propose a decision-making strategy designed to correct for these systemic pressures. The rules for adjudicating judicial-power claims should reverse the direction of the formalist prescription: rather than safeguarding *judicial* authority, they should safeguard *legislative* authority from the predictable and insistent cognitive pressures that cause judges to press judicial prerogatives to implausible extremes. After considering various solutions, I will propose that state judges should declare nonjusticiable any claim that legislation intrudes upon the freestanding grant of the "judicial power" vested in state courts under a separation-of-powers scheme. Under this proposal, courts would still adjudicate claims that legislation either violates specific constitutional provisions governing judicial authority, such as a clause protecting judicial salaries from reduction, or violates independent constitutional rules, such as the right of jury trial.

The next question is whether to extend this nonjusticiability proposal to the federal system. The mechanisms that cause state judges to overprotect judicial prerogatives appear in some of the federal decisions as well. The argument for extending the nonjusticiability proposal is necessarily tentative, however, because the lower volume of federal caselaw makes it difficult to draw firm conclusions, and because examples of aggressive overprotection appear less frequently in the federal system. Yet overprotection in the federal system is more difficult to correct through the processes of constitutional amendment and judicial selection, and is therefore more damaging when it does occur. On net, therefore, the nonjusticiability proposal is a plausible recommendation for the federal system as well.

Part I situates the problem of freestanding judicial power claims within current judicial and scholarly debates over the separation of powers generally. Part II presents illustrative state cases that undermine widely held assumptions about the consequences of alternative decision-making strategies in judicial power cases. Part III presents the nonjusticiability proposal and considers important objections. Part IV examines freestanding judicial power claims in the federal system and considers the costs and benefits of applying the nonjusticiability proposal in that system as well as in the states.

I. Formalism, Functionalism, and Justice Black's Alarm Clock

On first inspection, the small set of separation-of-powers decisions from the federal Supreme Court divides naturally into two subsets. In one set are categorical, rule-bound decisions such as Justice Black's opinion for the Court in *Youngstown Sheet & Tube Co. v Sawyer*,[15] holding that the President may act only on the basis of affirmative constitutional or statutory authority. Any other presidential action, said Black, is an act of lawmaking, and thus a "legislative" act rather than an exercise of "executive" power. In the other set are looser decisions imbued with inchoate legal standards, such as *Morrison v Olson*,[16] in which the Court sustained a statute that created an independent federal prosecutor, dischargeable only for cause. Justice Scalia's dissent in *Morrison*, a dissent Black might have written, argued that prosecution is a purely "executive" function; all "executive" power is vested in the President; because the challenged statute vested executive power in an official other than the President, it was unconstitutional.[17] For the Court, however, the critical question was not the categorization of the independent prosecutor's authority, but whether the statute so greatly disrupted the balance of federal powers as to prevent the President from carrying out his constitutional functions.[18]

---

[15] See *Youngstown Sheet & Tube Co. v Sawyer*, 343 US 579 (1952).

[16] See *Morrison v Olson*, 487 US 654 (1988).

[17] See id at 705 (Scalia, J, dissenting).

[18] See id at 695 ("we do not think that the Act impermissibly undermines the powers of the Executive Branch, or disrupts the proper balance between the coordinate branches by

The literature labels these two approaches "formalist" and "functionalist."[19] Formalists argue for attention to text and original understanding, for rule-bound adjudication, and for clear lines of demarcation between the branches of the federal government (except insofar as the branches have explicit authority to participate in each other's activities; the President's veto power is an example).[20] For formalists, the critical threshold question is whether the challenged authority counts as an exercise of federal "legislative," "executive," or "judicial" power. Once that categorization is made, the Constitution attaches authorities and obligations to the relevant power, and the challenged action is then scrutinized for conformity to the constitutional allocation.

Functionalists argue for flexible adaptation of the separation of powers to the exigencies of modern government, for standard-based or balancing approaches to separation-of-powers adjudication, and for participation by each branch in the decision-making processes of other branches.[21] A critical functionalist claim is that the separation of powers must be implemented in light of its underlying purposes—to secure liberty by diffusing official power, and to increase the quality of political deliberation and federal lawmaking through an institutional division of labor. For functionalists, these purposes are best served by adhering to Madison's dictum that the separation of powers prevents the "whole power of one department" from falling into the hands of an official or institution that also exercises the "whole power" of another department.[22] The separation of powers does not prohibit interaction of branches or the commingling of their functions. It prohibits one branch from appropriating or intruding upon the "core functions" or "essential functions" of other branches.

What do formalists and functionalists disagree about, if anything? One possibility is that the two camps disagree about the

---

preventing the Executive Branch from accomplishing its constitutionally assigned functions") (internal citation and quotation omitted).

[19] See notes 23–25 (citing sources).

[20] See, e.g., Gary Lawson, *The Rise and Rise of the Administrative State*, 107 Harv L Rev 1231 (1994) (arguing for the "idea of a limited national government subject to a formal, tripartite separation of powers").

[21] See Martin S. Flaherty, *The Most Dangerous Branch*, 105 Yale L J 1725 (1996) (stating the "Federalist 'Case' for Functionalism" and the "Federalist 'Case' Against Formalism").

[22] See Federalist 47 (Madison) in C. Rossiter, ed, *The Federalist Papers* (Mentor, 1961).

meaning of the Constitution. On this view, when formalists and functionalists disagree in cases like *Morrison*, the dispute is whether the Constitution, correctly read, really does dictate that prosecutorial power is "executive" and, if so, whether it must necessarily be vested in the President.[23] Much of the literature is pitched this way. The ambition of this literature is, in the style of high doctrinalism, to synthesize the formalist and functionalist cases into a grand pattern premised upon a convincing, principled reading of the text, history, and structure of the Constitution, and of relevant precedents.[24] No two theorists agree about what that grand pattern is, not because each theory is flawed, but because there are so few separation-of-powers decisions from the Court that several incompatible theories may each successfully explain all of the data.

Here I shall pursue a different approach, focusing not upon the correct reading of the Constitution or the precedents, but rather upon the decision-making capacities of the judges who decide separation-of-powers cases. On this view, the disagreement between formalists and functionalists is not about constitutional meaning, but rather about a choice between alternative decision-making strategies.[25] At the level of constitutional meaning, both camps

---

[23] Compare Lawrence Lessig and Cass R. Sunstein, *The President and the Administration*, 94 Colum L Rev 1 (1994) (denying that prosecutorial power must necessarily be vested in the President) with Steven G. Calabresi and Saikrishna B. Prakash, *The President's Power to Execute the Laws*, 104 Yale L J 541 (1994) (arguing that all prosecutorial power is vested in the President).

[24] See, e.g., Harold J. Krent, *Separating the Strands in Separation of Powers Controversies*, 74 Va L Rev 1253 (1988) (reconciling the cases by advancing the principle that "the Constitution circumscribes the power of the branches by limiting the ways each can act"); Thomas M. Merrill, *The Constitutional Principle of Separation of Powers*, 1991 Supreme Court Review 225 (advancing a "minimal conception" of separation of powers that reconciles the formalist and functionalist cases); H. Jefferson Powell and Jed Rubenfeld, *Laying It on the Line: A Dialogue on Line Item Vetoes and Separation of Powers*, 47 Duke L J 1171 (1998) (reconciling cases through focus on congressional aggrandizement); Keith Werhan, *Normalizing the Separation of Powers*, 70 Tulane L Rev 2681 (1996) (proposing a doctrinal structure that attempts to integrate formal and functional approaches); *Public Citizen v Department of Justice*, 491 US 440, 484–86 (Kennedy, J, concurring) (attempting to reconcile functionalist and formalist decisions by reference to the specificity of the underlying constitutional text at issue in particular cases).

[25] This sort of understanding of the formalist-functionalist disagreement has been analyzed thoroughly in the context of statutory interpretation. See, e.g., Cass R. Sunstein, *Must Formalism Be Justified Empirically?* 66 U Chi L Rev 636 (1999) (examining formalism as a decision-making strategy in statutory interpretation); Adrian Vermeule, *Legislative History and the Limits of Judicial Competence*, 50 Stanford L Rev 1833 (1998) (arguing that formalism best suits judges' limited interpretive capacities). In the separation-of-powers context, the literature tends to be dominated by first-best readings of the legal materials, as set out in notes 23–24. For valuable exceptions to this generalization, see, e.g., William N. Eskridge,

subscribe to the basic principle that the separation of powers is maintained so long as no branch exercises the "whole power" of another branch, or seizes another branch's core functions. Formalists and functionalists disagree, however, about how judges should implement the core-functions norm. Functionalists desire judges to apply that norm directly to particular cases, statutes, and institutional innovations. Formalists fear that judicial implementation of core functions through case-specific balancing will underprotect the separation of powers, with the result that one branch will eventually arrogate to itself the core functions of the others.

This explains a principal strand in the formalism debate: the idea that formalism can serve as a useful corrective for failings of judicial cognition. We can also call this alarm-clock formalism, after one of Alexander Bickel's elegant put-downs of the free-speech opinions of Justice Hugo Black.[26] Black, said Bickel, kept insisting that the First Amendment's words—"Congress shall make no law abridging the freedom of speech"—are plain, that "no law" means no law and "speech" means any speech, and that judges should develop free-speech protections in a correspondingly rulelike way, as in the strong presumption that any content-based speech regulation is unconstitutional.[27] For Bickel, this was best understood not as simplemindedness but as subtle indirection on Black's part. Black's strategy was akin to setting an alarm clock one hour ahead of the time at which the sleeper must rise; even if the sleeper sleeps for an hour after the alarm goes off, he will awaken at the right time.[28]

Although Bickel seems to have thought alarm-clock formalism to be an unacceptably devious exercise, it is Black, not Bickel, who has carried the day. Something like Black's rationale for a rule-bound approach to free speech has been resuscitated in the work

Jr., *Relationships Between Formalism and Functionalism in Separation of Powers Cases*, 22 Harv J L & Pub Pol 21 (1998); Merrill (cited in note 24); Peter L. Strauss, *Formal and Functional Approaches to Separation of Powers Questions: A Foolish Inconsistency?* 72 Cornell L Rev 488 (1987).

[26] See Alexander M. Bickel, *The Least Dangerous Branch: The Supreme Court at the Bar of Politics* 93–98 (2d ed 1986).

[27] See *Simon & Schuster, Inc. v Members of New York State Crime Victims Board*, 502 US 105 (1991) (announcing rule of strict scrutiny of content-based regulation of speech).

[28] See Bickel (cited in note 26) at 96 ("[Justice Black] labors to set our alarm clocks one hour ahead, in the expectation that when we oversleep we may nevertheless wake, without quite knowing how it happened, at what is actually the right time").

of scholars such as John Hart Ely[29] and Frederick Schauer.[30] On this picture, free-speech doctrine is partly a judicial precommitment device[31] and partly a prophylactic rule.[32] It is a precommitment device insofar as judges devising free-speech doctrine at time 1 worry that at time 2 their own cognition or decision-making processes will be affected by some overpowering influence. (In the free-speech context, the influence might be the social exigency that provoked the political suppression of speech, or the offensiveness of the speech itself.) So the judges restrict their choices at time 2 by announcing, at time 1, a rule that will prevent their future selves from surrendering to the passions of the moment. It is a prophylactic device insofar as judges choosing free-speech rules at time 1 worry, not about their own future cognition, but about the cognition of other judges deciding future cases, either judges of subordinate courts or future members of the very court that devised the rule at time 1. Here the judges formulate legal doctrine in order to restrict other judges' future choices.

Both strands of alarm-clock formalism, precommitment and prophylaxis, are widely used decision-making strategies in the law. Free speech is one example;[33] others involve the coerced-confession rules set out in *Miranda v Arizona*,[34] justifiable in part by the judiciary's difficulties with the previous regime of case-specific "voluntariness" determinations,[35] and the use of per se rules in

---

[29] See John Hart Ely, *Flag Desecration: A Case Study in the Roles of Categorization and Balancing in First Amendment Analysis*, 88 Harv L Rev 1482 (1975).

[30] See Frederick Schauer, *The Second-Best First Amendment*, 31 Wm & Mary L Rev 1 (1989).

[31] A precommitment device is a mechanism by which a decision maker acting at time 1 restricts his choices at time 2, from fear of cognitive failure at time 2. See generally George Ainslie, *Picoeconomics: The Strategic Interaction of Successive Motivational States Within the Person* 123–79 (1992); Jon Elster, *Ulysses and the Sirens: Studies in Rationality and Irrationality* 37–47 (1979).

[32] See David A. Strauss, *The Ubiquity of Prophylactic Rules*, 55 U Chi L Rev 190 (1988).

[33] See id at 200 ("[I]f a court is permitted to balance the benefits of a content-based measure against its costs, it is too likely that the court will be influenced by its own reaction to the point of view expressed; that is why the Supreme Court uses relatively rigid categories instead of balancing in each case"); Vincent Blasi, *The Pathological Perspective and the First Amendment*, 85 Colum L Rev 449, 474 (1985) ("In crafting standards to govern specific areas of first amendment dispute, courts . . . should place a premium on confining the range of discretion left to decisionmakers who will be called upon to make judgments when pathological pressures are most intense").

[34] See *Miranda v Arizona*, 384 US 436 (1966).

[35] See Laurie Magid, *Questioning the Question-Proof Inmate: Defining Miranda Custody for Incarcerated Suspects*, 58 Ohio St L J 883, 917 (1997) ("In jettisoning the case-by-case volun-

antitrust law.[36] Unsurprisingly, alarm-clock formalism is also a critical strand of the separation-of-powers debate between formalism and functionalism. In *Plaut v Spendthrift Farms*,[37] the Court invalidated a federal statute that commanded the Article III courts to reopen damages judgments that had previously become final. Announcing a broad rule that any such command is unconstitutional, the Court swept aside Justice Breyer's concurring suggestion that legislative reopening of judgments should be declared invalid only where judges could discern, in the particular case, a concrete threat to the liberty-protecting purposes of the separation of powers, as where the reopening statute applied solely retroactively or targeted a small number of individuals.[38] Breyer's position, the Court wrote, overlooked that the separation of powers is "a structural safeguard."[39] But why protect the separation of powers through rules that may be triggered when none of the purposes of separation are implicated? One suggestion in *Plaut* is that the judges' decisional processes will predictably be affected by the drama of confrontation between the great branches of government; thus the judges must establish clear rules in advance of that confrontation. "In its major features," the Court said, the separation of powers "is a prophylactic device, establishing high walls and clear distinctions because low walls and vague distinctions will not be judicially defensible in the heat of interbranch conflict."[40]

Plaut's description of the separation of powers as a prophylactic rule leaves the cognitive justification for alarm-clock formalism implicit. Not so Justice Brennan's anguished dissent in *CFTC v Schor*.[41] The Court, effectively repudiating the formalist plural-

---

tariness standard in favor of *Miranda*'s prophylactic, bright-line rules, the Court decided to protect not only the core values of the Fifth Amendment itself, but also a secondary set of values associated with all bright-line or per se rules. This secondary set of values includes the provision of guidance to law enforcement actors and the conservation of judicial resources.").

[36] See Frank H. Easterbrook, *The Limits of Antitrust*, 63 Tex L Rev 1, 10–15 (1984) (explaining per se rules in antitrust law as judicial attempts to avoid the decision costs and error costs of fact-specific antitrust adjudication).

[37] 514 US 211 (1995).

[38] See *Plaut*, 514 US at 241–45 (Breyer, J, concurring).

[39] Id at 239.

[40] Id.

[41] *Commodity Futures Trading Commission v Schor*, 478 US 833, 859 (1986) (Brennan, J, dissenting).

ity opinion written by Brennan himself only four years earlier in *Northern Pipeline Construction Co. v Marathon Pipe Line Co.*,[42] held that Congress had constitutional authority to commit a state common-law counterclaim to initial adjudication by a federal agency, rather than to an Article III court. *Schor* announced that constitutional challenges to the vesting of judicial business in agencies would be judged by reference to a "number of factors, none of which has been deemed determinative,"[43]—in short, by the baldest version of functionalism. The Court "declined to adopt formalistic and unbending rules" precisely because those rules would "unduly constrict Congress' ability to take needed and innovative action."[44] For Brennan, this defense of functionalism ignored the insistent erosion in the power of Article III courts that would occur under a balancing test, an erosion made inevitable by pressure on the judges' cognition. The short-term benefits of "innovative action" would predictably appear far more appealing to the judges, in the setting of particular cases, than the seemingly abstract and speculative benefits of judicial independence. "The Court," wrote Brennan, "pits an interest the benefits of which are immediate, concrete, and easily understood against one, the benefits of which are almost entirely prophylactic, and thus often seem remote and not worth the cost in any single case."[45]

---

[42] 458 US 50 (1982) (plurality opinion).

[43] See *Schor*, 478 US at 851 (opinion of the Court). See Richard Fallon, *Of Legislative Courts, Administrative Agencies, and Article III*, 101 Harv L Rev 915 (1988) (concluding that in *Schor* the Court was employing an "ad hoc balancing test").

[44] Id at 851.

[45] Id at 863. Two plausible examples of this cognitive slippage are *United States v Nixon*, 418 US 683 (1974) (holding, inter alia, that the President could not assert executive privilege against a prosecutorial subpoena), and *Clinton v Jones*, 520 US 681 (1997) (holding that the Constitution does not confer immunity from suits brought against a sitting President based on nonofficial conduct). The *Nixon* Court rested its ruling on a balancing analysis that compared the President's interest in confidentiality to an asserted judicial interest in obtaining full disclosure of information relevant to a criminal trial. The President's interest in confidentiality, and therefore in executive privilege, was said to be "generalized" and "abstract," while the interest in full disclosure in criminal trials was said to be "specific" and "central to fair adjudication"; its denial would "gravely impair the basic function of the courts." *Nixon*, 418 US at 712–13. This looks like Brennan's cognitive effect in action: the President's interest in executive privilege, rooted (as the Court acknowledged) in the separation of powers, is eroded by judicial balancing that sees only the concrete needs of the case at hand and underestimates the systemic value of confidentiality. See Merrill (cited in note 24) at 235. A similar account explains *Clinton v Jones*. The Court's pragmatic balancing overweighed the importance of maintaining the judicial routine, overestimated the dis-

From examples such as *Morrison*, *Plaut*, and Brennan's dissent in *Schor*, formalists have generalized an account of the comparative effects of functionalism and formalism on the separation of powers. Functionalism, on this account, provides insufficient protection for the separation of powers;[46] functionalist judges will approve repeated departures from the separation-of-powers norm in the name of perceived social exigency.[47] Rule-bound versions of separation-of-powers doctrine are needed to overprotect the separation of powers in much the same way that, for example, the content-neutrality rule in First Amendment law is needed to prevent political encroachment on the core of free-speech protection.

With this background established, the significance of the state judicial power cases is apparent. The formalist thesis has been generalized from a startlingly small number of Supreme Court separation-of-powers cases. The state cases provide a much larger set of comparative constitutional law data against which to evaluate the formalist claims.

---

trict judge's competence to accommodate the relevant interests successfully, and underestimated the extent of disruption to the President's official duties that would result from the Court's holding. See Richard A. Posner, *An Affair of State* 225 (1999) (noting that Clinton "has come in for a good deal of ridicule because of the Justices' failure . . . to foresee that allowing the case to proceed could disrupt the Presidency").

[46] See, e.g., Martin H. Redish and Elizabeth Cisar, *"If Angels Were to Govern": The Need for Pragmatic Formalism in Separation of Powers Theory*, 41 Duke L J 449 (1991); Stephen Carter, *Constitutional Improprieties: Reflections on Mistretta, Morrison and Administrative Government*, 57 U Chi L Rev 357, 375–76 (1990). For discussion of the formalist contention by a sympathetic critic, see Peter L. Strauss (cited in note 25) at 513–18. Even commentators who do not necessarily subscribe to the normative claim that functionalism provides insufficient protection to the separation of powers agree that "[c]ases falling into the formalist category tend to invalidate efforts by one branch of government to exercise a power formally assigned to another, while functionalist decisions tend to permit novel arrangements." Michael C. Dorf, *The Relevance of Federal Norms for State Separation of Powers*, 4 Roger Williams U L Rev 51, 73–74 (1998).

[47] See, e.g., Peter L. Strauss (cited in note 25) at 513 ("At best, 'core function' analysis can guard against a sudden demarche, but not against the step-by-step accretion of reasonable judgments over time. The strength of flexibility is at the same time its weakness"); Merrill (cited in note 24) at 235 (footnotes omitted):

> The principal criticism leveled against functionalism is not that it is too rigid but that it is not rigid enough. The problem . . . derives largely from the substantive theory, and in particular from the nebulousness of the concepts of "diffusion of power" and "core functions." Because these concepts are so indeterminant [*sic*], the judicial reaction will almost always be to defer to the judgments of other branches when separation of powers controversies arise. The arguments in support of innovation will be concrete and immediate, while the case for preserving "diffusion" or the "core" will seem abstract and remote. Thus, the "core" functions notice is unlikely to achieve its stated aim: the preservation of a system of separated and balanced powers as a guarantee of liberty.

II. Functionalism and Judicial Prerogatives

A. THE OVERPROTECTION THESIS

An examination of the state judicial power decisions upsets the empirical assumptions of both the functionalist and formalist positions. In the setting of these cases, the functionalist assumption that judges can develop a stable and normatively defensible conception of core functions through case-by-case elaboration appears dubious; to that extent the formalist generalization is correct. The formalist claim that functionalism underprotects separation-of-powers concerns, however, is incorrect about the *direction* of departure from the core-functions norm. In the state decisions, functionalism overprotects separation-of-powers interests, or so I shall argue.

To speak of judicial "overprotection" of the judiciary's core functions and prerogatives is to assume some normative standard by which to measure overprotection. But the claim need not assume any particular normative standard. Rather, textual, historical, and consequentialist arguments converge to condemn the decisions examined here. So the normative baseline from which overprotection is measured need not be a controversial one; these cases articulate sweeping conceptions of judicial authority that press well beyond any defensible conception of the judiciary's core functions. That the criterion of "core functions" provides little barrier against systemic institutional and cognitive pressures is not equivalent to the nihilist claim that there simply are no identifiable core functions. More modestly, we can identify some distensions of the core that are clearly impermissible on an overlapping consensus of normative approaches.

Pursuing this modest aim, I shall call a freestanding judicial power holding "overprotective" if it cannot be generalized to new settings without contravening some settled premise of the constitutional order. Consider the position, adopted in various forms by some state courts,[48] that a statute encroaches upon the "judicial power" if it abolishes a cause of action, remedy, or procedure recognized by common-law precedent—a position that, absent some more specific provision elevating the precedent to constitutional

---

[48] See notes 55–84 and accompanying text.

status, contravenes the premise that statutes trump common law. That is the sort of minimal, universally accepted premise that gives substance to the idea of overprotection.

B. METHODOLOGICAL PRELIMINARIES

The claim that functionalism overprotects judicial prerogatives in the state cases is limited in several important respects. First, I do not advance a quantified empirical claim. The rigorous empiricism of the social sciences is poorly adapted to addressing questions that, although descriptive, rest upon evaluative predicates intertwined with legal conclusions.[49] The incidence of "functional" decisions that cause "overprotective" rulings cannot be identified by simple counting. It must instead be identified by legal argument, through a detailed evaluative analysis of decisions. Accordingly, I intend here to advance a descriptive claim that is intertwined with normative argument about reasonable or defensible conceptions of the judiciary's core functions. As the descriptive claim rests upon interpretive and evaluative predicates about reasonable conceptions of judicial authority, I substantiate the claim through a series of detailed, qualitative case studies, across several major areas of judicial power doctrine, rather than through an "empirical" study that would provide only an illusory precision.

From the standpoint of social-science empiricism, the great danger of this sort of qualitative description is selection bias, because detailed case studies provide no assurance that the sample cases are representative of the whole population of cases.[50] But there is ample middle ground between fully specified quantitative empiricism and solely normative argument, and I intend to explore that middle ground through an inquiry structured to minimize the dangers of a skewed sample. Whether a partial selection for qualitative study is useful must be judged relative to the questions that the selection is used to illuminate. In particular, the next section details

---

[49] See Adrian Vermeule, *Interpretive Choice*, 75 NYU L Rev 74 (2000).

[50] On the trade-offs involved in conducting qualitative case studies, see Gary King et al, *Designing Social Inquiry: Scientific Inference in Qualitative Research* (1994); *The Qualitative-Quantitative Disputation*, 89 Am Pol Sci Rev 454 (1995) (review symposium); David Collier and James Mahoney, *Selection Bias in Qualitative Research*, 49 World Politics 56 (1996). On the related problem of "data mining" in comparative law, see George G. Triantis, *The Careful Use of Comparative Law Data: The Case of Corporate Insolvency Systems*, 17 NY L Sch J Intl & Comp L 193 (1997).

(1) the *existence* of a set of functionalist state cases that overprotect judicial prerogatives, (2) the *extent* of the overprotection that occurs in such cases, and (3) the *causal mechanisms* by which overprotection occurs in these cases. All three inquiries minimize the concern about possible skew.[51] The existence inquiry shows that functionalism yields departures from widely held conceptions of the appropriate limits of judicial power, the extent inquiry shows that these outliers lie very far out indeed, and the inquiry into mechanisms identifies cognitive and institutional pressures that plausibly explain why functionalist analysis systematically overprotects judicial prerogative. And of course the concern with selection bias contains a core of good sense. It is misleading to omit evidence on one side of a descriptive question, so I shall describe a wide range of categories in which freestanding judicial power claims are made, examine cases from many states, and indicate contrary examples whenever relevant.

A second important limitation is that the category of state judicial power cases does not include other separation-of-powers issues, such as conflicts between state legislatures and executives, or the validity of legislative delegations to state administrative agencies, or state-level legislative vetoes. For that reason the state cases examined here cannot provide comprehensive evidence on the general formalist thesis that functionalism underprotects the separation of powers. That thesis might well remain true in the category of cases in which judges examine legislative encroachments upon the executive; cases such as *Morrison* strongly suggest that possibility. The claim here is just that the formalist thesis gets the cognitive effects backwards in the category of cases in which state judges adjudicate purported legislative encroachments on the judicial power. Third, it is possible that the formalist thesis describes the effects of functionalism at the federal level, even if not at the state level. In a later section I will discuss the implications of the state judicial power cases for federal separation-of-powers doc-

---

[51] The emphasis on the existence and extent of overprotection exploits a principal strength of small-n qualitative case studies: they bring to light new facts and new hypotheses that are not apparent from a large-n empirical study. See Collier and Mahoney (cited in note 50) at 71 & n 24. In particular, case studies demonstrate the existence of new causal mechanisms that explain correlations between variables. See id at 70 & n 21; King et al (cited in note 50) at 224–28; Daniel Little, *Varieties of Explanation: An Introduction to the Philosophy of Social Science* 15 (1991).

trine. It is clear, however, that any claim about the effects of functionalist adjudication must specify both a vertical domain (does the claim apply equally in federal and state systems?) and a horizontal domain (does the claim apply equally to cases of legislative-executive conflict and cases of legislative-judicial conflict?).

Finally, it is important to acknowledge both the variation in the judicial articles of state constitutions,[52] and the differences between state separation-of-powers systems and the federal separation-of-powers system. Some scholars emphasize these differences to such a degree as to disable any comparisons, but that outlook is parochial. Compared with the transnational differences between American and European judicial systems that are a staple of comparative law,[53] the intranational and interstate differences seem relatively minor. No American judicial system has an exclusive constitutional court, for example, although that arrangement is fairly common in Europe.[54] So I shall not hesitate to propose comparisons and generalizations, all of which might be subjected to further refinement by emphasizing local variation.

C. THE JUDICIAL POWER IN THE STATE COURTS

This section substantiates the twin claims that the state judicial power cases are functional decisions, and that they protect judicial prerogatives far beyond any defensible conception of the judiciary's core functions. Examples are drawn from four rough, and overlapping, categories of cases in which state courts have developed robust bodies of precedent: (1) statutes altering common-law

---

[52] See Jeffrey Parness, *Respecting State Judicial Articles*, in 3 *Emerging Issues in State Constitutional Law* 65 (1990).

[53] See, e.g., Mark Tushnet and Vicki C. Jackson, *Comparative Constitutional Law: Cases and Materials* (1999). The comparison to Europe is standard because "it is unusual for lawyers . . . to compare systems that did not overlap in time and that are unlikely to have shared a common influence." Saul Levmore, *Rethinking Comparative Law: Variety and Uniformity in Ancient and Modern Tort Law*, 61 Tulane L Rev 235 (1986). Given that practice (one that Levmore questions), it is odd that comparativists have not paid more attention to the states; maybe the states are too similar to the federal system to justify the comparativists' implicit claim to possess a distinctive disciplinary expertise.

[54] See Jackson and Tushnet (cited in note 53) at 456 (explaining that "in acting . . . as a 'generalist' court, and not primarily as a specialist in constitutional law, the U.S. Supreme Court differs from many European constitutional courts"); Jon Elster, Klaus Offe, and Ulrich K. Preuss, *Institutional Design in Post-Communist Societies: Rebuilding the Ship at Sea* 102–05 (1998) (surveying the role of constitutional courts in the recently-established democracies of Eastern Europe).

rules of liability or remedy; (2) statutes altering procedural and evidentiary rules; (3) statutes that alter the legal effect of judicial judgments; and (4) appropriations statutes that, in the judiciary's view, provide insufficient funding for the exercise of judicial functions. A final example illustrates the sweeping and sometimes intemperate rhetoric of the state cases.

1. *Liability and remedies. Best v Taylor Machine Works*, decided by the Illinois Supreme Court in 1997, has become a leading decision on the constitutionality of state tort reform, and it illustrates many of the traits common to the state cases.[55] At issue was the validity of the Illinois Civil Justice Reform Act of 1995, a statute that altered various rules of liability, remedy, and procedure applicable to personal injury actions. The statute's major reform was to impose a limit of $500,000 for "non-economic" compensatory damages, primarily damages for pain and suffering.[56]

The Illinois Supreme Court struck down the damages cap, on two alternative grounds. The first ground was that the cap constituted "special legislation"—what the federal constitutional lawyer would call a violation of equal protection.[57] The second ground,

---

[55] See *Best v Taylor Machine Works*, 179 Ill 2d 367 (1997). For other recent cases on the constitutionality of damages caps, see notes 58 and 59. Apart from civil damages, other recent examples of state courts invoking the judicial power to invalidate statutes that regulate liability and remedies have tended to involve judge-made rules of sovereign immunity or common-law remedies such as injunctions and stays, contempt sanctions, and bail. On sovereign immunity, see, e.g., *Office of the State Attorney, Fourth Judicial Circuit of Florida v Parrotino*, 628 So2d 1097 (Fla 1993) (dictum) (legislature may not abrogate prosecutorial immunity, because state attorneys are quasi-judicial officers); *Presley v Mississippi State Highway Comm'n*, 608 So2d 1288 (1992) (separation of powers bars statute directing state courts to apply only sovereign immunity precedents approved by the legislature). On remedies, see, e.g., *State v Hochhausler*, 668 NE2d 457 (Ohio 1996) (separation of powers gives judiciary authority to stay the administrative suspension of a driver's license, despite contrary statute); *People v Warren*, 671 NE2d 700 (1996) (legislature may not prohibit judicial imposition of civil contempt sanctions); *Walker v Bentley*, 678 So2d 1265 (Fla 1996) (striking down statute that restricted judicial authority to impose criminal contempts); *Burradell v State*, 326 Ark 182 (1996) (legislature may not restrict trial court's inherent authority to punish for in-court contempt); *In the Interest of J.E.S.*, 817 P2d 508 (Colo 1991) (invalidating statute that abrogated judicial power to incarcerate juveniles for contempt); *People v Williams*, 577 NE2d 762 (Ill 1991) (invalidating statute that restricted bail pending appeal).

[56] Noneconomic damages have become a prime target for tort-reform proponents and legislatures in many states, on the ground that those damages are difficult to measure and thus tend to provoke highly variable and unpredictable jury awards. See, e.g., Randall R. Bovbjerg et al, *Valuing Life and Limb in Tort: Scheduling "Pain and Suffering,"* 83 Nw U L Rev 908, 908 (1989) (criticizing awards of noneconomic damages as "ad hoc and unpredictable").

[57] See US Const, Amend XIV ("Nor shall any state . . . deny to any person within its jurisdiction the equal protection of the laws"); see also *Best*, 179 Ill 2d at 393. For cases from other states striking down damages caps on similar grounds, see, e.g., *Lakin v Senco*

the only one of interest here, was that the cap violated the separation of powers by arrogating to the legislature the judicial power of "remittitur"—the power to reduce juries' damages awards according to the highly discretionary standards of the common law.[58] There was no specific constitutional text, only the general grant of "judicial power" to the Illinois courts and a separation-of-powers clause covering all three branches. The Court gave content to these commands in a typically functional manner. The separation of powers was intended, not to prohibit overlapping spheres of governmental authority, but to secure core functions, preventing the "whole power of two or more branches [from residing] in the same hands."[59] The basic prohibition, then, reduced in operational terms to the familiar balancing standard of functionalism: "the legislature is prohibited from enacting laws that unduly infringe upon the inherent powers of judges,"[60] and the damages cap was found to "unduly encroach[ ] upon the fundamentally judicial prerogative of determining whether a jury's assessment of damages is excessive within the meaning of the law."[61]

Why, exactly, is the reduction of noneconomic damages a fundamentally judicial prerogative? The Court gave a congeries of hints, but no answer. It suggested first that the judicial power of remittitur is "traditional," indeed has been in place for "over a cen-

---

Products, 329 Or 62 (Or 1999) (statutory cap on personal injury damages violates right to jury trial); *Trovato v deVeau*, 736 A2d 1212 (NH 1999) (striking down statutory damages cap as violation of estate's right to recover for personal injuries); *Moore v Mobile Infirmary Ass'n*, 592 So2d 156 (Ala 1991) (statutory cap on noneconomic damages in medical malpractice actions violated right to jury trial); *Sofie v Fibreboard Corp.*, 112 Wash2d 636 (1989) (statutory cap on nonconmic damages violates right to trial by jury), opinion amended in unrelated respects, 780 P2d 260 (1989); *Arneson v Olson*, 270 NW2d 125, 137 (ND 1978) (statute regulating various aspects of medical malpractice claims violated right to jury trial). See generally Jennifer Friesen, *State Constitutional Law: Litigating Individual Rights, Claims, and Defenses* § 6-3 (2d ed & 1999 supplement).

[58] Id at 410. See also *Steinke v South Carolina Department of Labor*, 336 SC 373 (1999) (legislature usurped judicial power by attempting to retroactively reinstate statutory damages cap that the judiciary had earlier held to have been repealed by implication); *Sofie v Fibreboard Corp.*, 771 P2d 711, 720–21 (Wash 1989) (dictum) (cap on noneconomic damages is a legislative attempt to mandate a legal conclusion that may violate separation of powers). Compare *Smith v Department of Insurance*, 507 So2d 1080 (Fla 1987) (striking down statutory cap on noneconomic damages as invalid restriction on victims' access to the courts). But see *Kirkland v Blaine County Medical Center*, 2000 WL 861341 (Idaho 2000) (cap on noneconomic damages does not violate separation of powers).

[59] Id at 410.

[60] Id at 411.

[61] Id at 414.

tury";[62] and in the same vein it distinguished precedents in which the legislature had modified damages remedies on the ground that the underlying causes of action in those cases were themselves statutory, rather than judge-made.[63] But this failed to explain how a pedigree in tradition or judge-made law distinguishes remittitur of noneconomic damages from the run of common-law rules and practices that (the Court elsewhere acknowledged) the legislature may alter at will.[64] Later the Court gestured toward the right to jury trial.[65] But if that right prevents alteration of the jury's verdict, then it prevents judges as well as legislatures from doing so.[66] The question addressed in the Court's ruling was not whether jury verdicts should be inviolable, but rather who should have the power to violate them; and the Court answered, "we judges alone have that power."

There is another strand in the opinion, one that seems close to the core of the judges' concerns. This strand emphasized that the noneconomic damages cap was objectionable because it took the form of a rule, as opposed to the flexible, discretionary standards under which Illinois judges previously considered requests for remittitur: "Remittitur should be considered on a case-by-case basis . . . . The cap on damages is mandatory and operates wholly apart from the specific circumstances of a particular plaintiff's noneconomic injuries."[67] But the Court failed to explain what the rules-standards distinction has to do with the constitutional allocation of decisional authority. The former issue concerns the form of a legal directive, the latter concerns its source; if the statute had mandated the substitution of a balancing test for a judicially developed rule, a preference for standards and the concern for pro-

---

[62] Id at 411.

[63] A similar distinction is drawn in *Strukoff v Strukoff*, 76 Ill2d 53, 61 (1979) (rejecting claim that a statute requiring bifurcated trials in divorce proceedings unconstitutionally encroached upon the rulemaking powers of the judiciary, in part on the ground that the underlying proceeding was "statutorily created").

[64] See Michael J. Polelle, *Best v Taylor Machine Works: A Resounding "No" to the Tort Reform Act*, 22 SIU L J 825, 833 (1998) ("The logic of the majority's separation of powers argument would seem to reduce the legislature's authority to limit damages even in a non-discriminatory manner. . . . Arguably, this separation of powers holding effectively prevents the legislature from ever limiting or abolishing damages").

[65] See *Best*, 179 Ill2d at 413–14.

[66] See note 173 (discussing right to jury trial).

[67] *Best*, 179 Ill2d at 413–14.

tecting judicial prerogatives would cut in opposite directions. The Court's odd emphasis on the judges' previous case-by-case, standard-based approach, the approach disrupted by the statutory cap, is not legally relevant. But it is cognitively significant. The judges understood their practices and habits, understood the advantages of case-by-case approach remittitur (while seeming to ignore its disadvantages, or the advantages of the legislature's rule-based replacement), and they conflated the familiar remittitur regime, a regime overseen by judges in the comfortable mode of common-law adjudication, with a fundamental mandate of the separation of powers.

2. *Procedural and evidentiary rules.* Similar tendencies appear when litigants claim that statutes have usurped judicial power by altering the rules of judicial procedure and evidence, including the quasi-procedural rules that determine burdens of proof, standards of trial court review of jury verdicts, and appellate review of trial court determinations. In some of these cases the separation-of-powers claim is intertwined with claims arising under specific state constitutional provisions that vest rule-making authority in the judiciary,[68] but I shall focus upon the pure cases that invoke a bare constitutional grant of judicial power to defeat legislative modification of judge-made procedural rules.[69]

---

[68] See, e.g., Mich Const, 1963 Art 6, § 5 ("The supreme court shall by general rules establish, modify, amend and simplify the practice and procedure in all courts of this state"). Some recent examples are *Kittles v Rocky Mountain Recovery, Inc.*, 1 P3d 1220 (2000) (statute providing for ten-day appeal period from decision of county court is unconstitutional due to conflict with thirty-day period established by appellate rule); *Butterworth v Allen*, 756 So2d 52 (2000) (Death Penalty Reform Act invalid as legislative encroachment on Supreme Court's exclusive authority to adopt procedural rules); *McDougall v Schanz*, 461 Mich 15, 26–27 (1999) (holding that Michigan Supreme Court has exclusive authority to enact rules of procedure); *State v Napolitano*, 982 P2d 815 (Ariz 1999) (statute violated separation of powers by granting capital defendant less time to seek review than did the Supreme Court rules). In the federal system, by contrast, Congress has historically been understood to possess broad power over federal judicial procedure. See *Mistretta v United States*, 488 US 361, 387 (1989) ("Congress has undoubted power to regulate the practice and procedure of federal courts . . . .") (quoting *Sibbach v Wilson & Co.*, 312 US 1, 9 (1941)).

[69] Some recent examples, in addition to those subsequently discussed in text, are *Squillace v Kelley*, 990 P2d 497 (Wy 1999) (declaring invalid, on separation-of-powers grounds, a statute prescribing procedure for sanctioning unlawful court papers); *Fowler v Fowler*, 984 SW2d 508 (Mo 1999) (statute that treated judicial failure to issue decision before forty-five-day deadline as equivalent to denial of motion held to violate separation of legislative and judicial powers); *In re Interest of Constance G.*, 254 Neb 96 (1998) (separation of powers gives judiciary exclusive authority to determine whether admissible evidence is probative and how much weight it should receive); *Julian v State*, 966 P2d 249 (Ut 1998) (legislature violated separation of powers by enacting "inflexible catch-all" limitations period for habeas corpus claims); *Claypool v Mladineo*, 724 So2d 373 (Miss 1998) (separation of powers gives Supreme Court inherent authority to promulgate procedural rules); *Kunkel v Walton*, 179

A fine specimen is *Armstrong v Roger's Outdoor Sports.*[70] An Alabama statute commanded both trial and appellate courts to review juries' punitive damage awards de novo. The functionalist opinion by the Alabama Supreme Court described this statute as an "intrusion into the core of the judicial function," one that "attempt[s] to control some of the most inherently judicial functions exercised by the courts."[71] Approving, from an old precedent, the remarkable dictum that courts "cannot have their functions and their orderly processes disturbed by any legislative enactment," the Court found that judicial discretion to defer to the jury's punitive damages award constitutes "the very essence of a judge's power."[72]

The Court's objection was not based upon the right of jury trial, even though the new statute required jury verdicts to be scrutinized with no presumption of validity. The objection was that the statute deprived the courts of their previous discretion to decide whether such fresh scrutiny was warranted. The same complaint would have been implicated, indeed, a fortiori, had the statute supported the right to jury trial by making the jury's verdict conclusive on the court. Lacking any grounding in the right of jury trial, the Court's reasoning in support of the claimed judicial discretion had little to recommend it. As a dissenter pointed out, an unusual amendment to the Alabama Constitution specifically vested the "power to provide for and regulate the . . . remission of fines and forfeitures" in the legislature itself, not in the judiciary or even (as in most states) the executive.[73] Even if that provision were limited to publicly imposed fines, punitive damages serve deterrent aims, and are thus akin to fines imposed in civil or criminal enforcement proceedings brought by the state. Moreover, the legislature had long regulated the appellate jurisdiction of the Alabama courts and

---

Ill2d 519 (1997) (invalidating, on judicial power grounds, statutory rules regulating discovery and confidentiality questions in tort); *O'Bryan v Hedgespeth*, 892 SW2d 571 (Ky 1995) (legislative abrogation of collateral-source rule impermissible encroachment upon judicial power to declare rules of practice and procedure for the courts); *State v Almonte*, 644 A2d 595 (RI 1994) (statute making health care providers legally incompetent to testify about providers violates separation of legislative and judicial power); *Rutherford v Rutherford*, 414 SE2d 157 (SC 1992) (statute limiting scope of appellate review in domestic relations cases violates separation of powers).

[70] See *Armstrong v Roger's Outdoor Sports, Inc.*, 581 So2d 414 (Ala 1991) (per curiam).

[71] Id at 415.

[72] Id at 417, 420.

[73] Id at 428 (Houston, J, dissenting).

other rules of judicial administration and procedure; indeed, there was even a specific constitutional amendment that authorized the legislature to change any such rules by a statute of general applicability.[74] Against these specific grants of legislative power to regulate the very matters at issue, the Court could only oppose the general grant of the judicial power—that, and the conviction that somehow the legislature had tampered with a core, or essential, or fundamental, judicial function, simply by changing the way "courts have always exercised their judicial power and discretion."[75]

The Illinois and Alabama cases grew out of the tort-reform struggle. But the concern with judicial discretion, the elevation of common law to quasi-constitutional status, and the strong judicial preference for standards in place of (legislatively enacted) rules have appeared in a range of other contexts. A 1997 advisory opinion of the New Hampshire Supreme Court, *Opinion of the Justices (Prior Sexual Assault Evidence)*,[76] declared unconstitutional a proposed law creating a rebuttable presumption that evidence of a defendant's prior sexual assaults could be offered to prove motive or intent in prosecutions for rape and other crimes. The constitutional question, as the Justices saw it, was "whether the proposed legislation would prevent the judiciary from accomplishing its constitutionally assigned functions."[77]

One possible ground for decision was that the law contradicted the prevailing evidence rule previously promulgated by the judiciary under a general constitutional grant of rule-making authority. The Court had previously interpreted that grant to mean, not merely that it had authority to promulgate rules in default of supervening legislation, but also that contrary legislation would invade judicial prerogatives if it regulated "procedural" rather than "substantive" matters. Having gone this far, however, the Court suddenly changed the subject: the statute encroached upon the judicial power because it constricted judicial discretion, regardless of the substance/procedure distinction. "Prior sexual assault conduct

---

[74] Compare *State v Williams*, 938 SW 2d 456 (Tex Crim App 1997) (express constitutional grant of legislative authority to regulate judicial administration trumps general separation-of-powers clause).

[75] Id at 418.

[76] See Opinion of the Justices (Prior Sexual Assault Evidence), 688 A2d 1006 (NH 1997).

[77] Id at 1011.

may or may not be relevant, and the question whether it is relevant cannot be reduced to a legislative formula. To do so eliminates the inherent discretion of the judiciary as exercised on a case-by-case basis."[78] Citing *United States v Klein*, the case in which the U.S. Supreme Court famously declared that Congress may not "prescribe rules of decision to the Judicial Department of the government in cases pending before it,"[79] the New Hampshire Justices concluded that "the bill before us usurps the judicial function of making relevancy determinations by creating a rebuttable presumption . . . without regard for the particular facts or circumstances of a case."[80]

The basic objection to this analysis parallels the standard objection to *Klein* and to the Illinois decision in *Best v Taylor Machine*. *Klein* cannot seriously be taken to say that legislatures may not prescribe rules.[81] So too, in the New Hampshire case, there is not and cannot be any general principle that legislation interferes with essential judicial functions by constricting the judiciary's "inherent discretion . . . as exercised on a case-by-case basis." All statutes that modify or override common-law-making regimes do that. There is a hint that the proposed law would have usurped the judiciary's power to "determin[e] and evaluat[e] the facts of controversies it must adjudicate";[82] this is the narrow proposition for which the Court cited *Klein*. But all statutes, by defining law, make some facts relevant and others irrelevant, so the Court later retreated to the objection that the statute operated "without regard for the particular facts or circumstances of a case." The New Hampshire Su-

---

[78] Id at 1015.

[79] *Klein*, 80 US at 146.

[80] Opinion of the Justices (Prior Sexual Assault Evidence), 688 A2d at 101.

[81] See notes 212–14 and accompanying text.

[82] Id at 1006. See also *City of North Little Rock v Pulaski County*, 332 Ark 578 (1998) (statute declaring that municipal airports serve a public purpose violated separation of powers by usurping judicial authority to determine facts in particular cases); *San Carlos Apache Tribe v Superior Court*, 193 Ariz 195 (1999) (en banc). In *San Carlos Apache Tribe* the Arizona Supreme Court applied a classically functionalist four-factor balancing test to a separation-of-powers challenge to statutes that reallocated water rights. The challenge focused upon a provision instructing that certain minor water uses "shall be deemed" de minimis, and therefore exempt from a range of restrictions. By decreeing a "bright-line, legislative standard," the legislature had "remove[d] all possibility of meaningful judicial conclusions based on findings of fact" and left the court with "no power to hear the facts and make the ultimate conclusion in the context of each watershed." Citing *United States v Klein*, the court struck down this legislative exercise of judicial power.

preme Court, like its counterpart in Illinois, effectively decided the case upon the ground that legislation is subordinate to the common law.[83]

The outcome may not be wrong. The judgment might have been grounded upon substantive constitutional interpretation of the grant of rule-making authority, or (more promisingly) upon a holding that criminal defendants are constitutionally entitled to bar evidence of prior sexual assaults. But there simply is no general separation-of-powers principle that protects judicial discretion from legislative displacement, and the Court's suggestion of such a principle illustrates the systemic pressures for implausible assertions of judicial authority.

3. *Revision of judicial judgments.* The defense of judicial discretion is also a dominant theme in another area of legislative-judicial relations: the immunity of judicial judgments from legislative revision. One litigated issue concerns a question closely related to the *Plaut* rule that Congress may not abrogate final damages judgments of the Article III courts. The question is whether state legislatures may enact statutes that permit convicted criminal defendants, currently serving sentences, to apply for resentencing under a new, more lenient rule.

In the leading case, *Commonwealth v Sutley*,[84] the Pennsylvania Supreme Court held unconstitutional a statute that gave those convicted for possession of marijuana, and previously convicted under a harsh statute, the right to obtain resentencing under a more lenient scheme. The statute was said to interfere with the judicial discretion that inheres in traditional sentencing practice—that is, sentencing based upon statutes that merely specify a range within which the judge may choose, after considering the particular characteristics of the offender and the offense. "It is this exercise of

---

[83] Compare *Purdie v Attorney General*, 732 A2d 442 (NH 1991) (just-compensation case declaring that "the determination of common law questions is a judicial, not a legislative, function"). See also *Cronin v Sheldon*, 991 P2d 231 (Ariz 1999) (dictum) (statutory preamble violated separation of powers by purporting to leave courts with no authority to develop, modify, or expand common law); Parness (cited in note 52) at 72 (referring to the cases on statutory damage caps as posing the question of "the court's power to make common law rulings contravening statutes").

[84] See *Commonwealth v Sutley*, 378 A2d 780 (Pa 1997). For background on the extraordinary assertiveness of the Pennsylvania Supreme Court, see Comment, *Separation of Powers in Pennsylvania: The Judiciary's Prevention of Legislative Encroachment*, 32 Duquesne L Rev 539 (1994).

discretion that the rule of the 'inviolability of the final judgment' seeks to protect," wrote the Court, apparently because acts of legislative lenity subsequent to the sentence would "frustrate[ ] the sentencing decision [by] . . . introduc[ing] factors not considered at the time the sentence was imposed."[85]

As the Ohio Supreme Court commented in upholding a similar statute,[86] however, criminal sentences are, of all judicial judgments, the most susceptible to revision by the political branches, so long as the revision operates in the prisoner's favor. As the winning party to the previous judgment, the state should be able to waive the benefit of its judgment the way other parties may.[87] Moreover, in both Ohio and Pennsylvania the constitutional provision for executive pardon already authorized a nonjudicial abrogation of final sentences, and therefore authorized nonjudicial interference with judicial sentencing discretion. The right question in both cases, then, was not whether the judiciary's criminal judgments could be abrogated, but who could do so; in other words, whether the constitutional grant of the pardon power to the *executive* should be understood to exclude *legislative* lenity by negative implication. The Pennsylvania court's examination of the case through the lens of the judicial power, rather than the pardon power, was an error caused by its mistaken perception that fundamental prerogatives of the judiciary were at stake.[88]

4. *Judicial finances and the "inherent powers" doctrine.* In 1970 the mayor of Philadelphia (a city-county government) transmitted to the city council an annual budget proposal that allocated $16 mil-

---

[85] Id at 786–87.

[86] *State v Morris*, 378 NE2d 708 (Ohio 1978).

[87] Id at 715–16 ("[O]nly the state has a protected interest in the continuing punishment of convicted criminals and it is unquestionable that the state may waive its vested rights obtained through prior judgments."). The same holds for the federal system, where the United States may waive the benefit of a prior judgment in its favor, at least in civil cases. See *United States v Sioux Nation of Indians*, 448 US 371 (1980).

[88] For other separation-of-powers challenges to statutes that modify judicial judgments, see, e.g., *City of Providence v Employee Retirement Board*, 749 A2d 1088 (RI 2000) (separation of powers precluded city from vacating consent judgments previously entered into by city and retired city employees); *State v Murray*, 194 Ariz 373 (1999) (separation of powers bars the legislature from changing the rule of decision in completed cases); *Ex Parte Jenkins*, 723 So2d 649 (Ala 1998) (statute mandating reopening of final judgments of paternity held to unconstitutionally encroach upon the judicial power); *Quinton v General Motors Corp.*, 453 Mich 63, 77–78 (1996) (dictum) (adopting *Plaut* analysis under Michigan Constitution); *State v Mundie*, 508 NW2d 462 (Iowa 1993) (legislature lacks any power to change any valid judgment after it is entered).

lion to the Court of Common Pleas, a figure reduced from the presiding judge's earlier request of $19 million. The council approved the mayor's budget. Three months later a state trial judge ordered the mayor and council, on pain of contempt, to enact a judicial budget that awarded the Court of Common Pleas an additional $2.5 million, or almost the total of the court's initial request. The suit was brought by the same presiding judge who had made the request. The Pennsylvania Supreme Court affirmed the order, although it modified its terms and slightly reduced the total amount awarded. The legal basis for the proceedings was the doctrine of "inherent powers," as it has come to be known—the idea that (as the Pennsylvania Supreme Court put it)

> the co-equal independent Judiciary must possess rights and powers co-equal with its functions and duties, including the right and power to protect itself against any impairment thereof. . . . [T]he Judiciary Must [sic] possess the inherent power to determine and compel payment of those sums of money which are reasonable and necessary to carry out its mandated responsibilities.[89]

---

[89] *Commonwealth ex rel. Carroll v Tate*, 274 A2d 193 (Pa 1971). A related body of caselaw holds that the vesting of "judicial power" in the courts disables legislatures from regulating either the bar or the courts' administrative employees. Many states hold that admission to the bar and the supervision of lawyers are exclusive judicial powers immune from legislative regulation. See, e.g., *Turner v Kentucky Bar Ass'n*, 980 SW2d 560 (Ky 1998) (statute authorizing nonlawyers to represent parties in workers' compensation proceedings violated separation of legislative from judicial power); *Eckles v Atlanta Technology Group*, 485 SE2d 22 (Ga 1997) (Georgia Supreme Court is supreme authority on matters pertaining to practice of law in Georgia, contrary statutes notwithstanding); *Washington State Bar Ass'n v State*, 890 P2d 1047 (Wash 1995) (statute requiring state bar association to engage in collective bargaining with its employees violates separation of legislative and judicial power); *Lloyd v Fishinger*, 529 Pa 513 (1992) (statute prohibiting exploitative contingent-fee contracts unconstitutionally invade judicial power to regulate attorneys). Courts have also invoked the separation of powers to order governments to fund appointed counsel in amounts exceeding statutory fee caps. See, e.g., *Irwin v Surdyks Liquor*, 599 NW2d 132 (Minn 1999) (statutorily imposed limitations on attorneys' fees violate the separation of legislative and judicial powers); *State ex rel. Friedrich v Circuit Court for Dane County*, 192 Wis2d 1 (1995) (compensation for court-appointed attorneys should follow judge-made rules rather than statutory rules where the two conflict); *White v Bd. of County Commissioners of Pinellas County*, 537 So2d 1376 (Fla 1989) (judiciary has inherent power to exceed statutory fee caps for criminal defense attorneys). These decisions have stressed that lawyers are officers of the court, but courts have also invoked constitutionally grounded judicial authority to bar statutory regulation of purely administrative employees, such as court security officers, see *Petition of Mone*, 719 A2d 626 (NH 1998) (law requiring county sheriffs, rather than judicial-branch officers, to provide security in state courts held to encroach upon judicial power); court clerks and administrators, see *First Judicial District v Pennsylvania Human Relations Commission*, 556 Pa 258 (1999) (separation of powers bars agency, acting under statutory authority, from asserting jurisdiction over sexual harassment policies applied to employees in the judicial branch); *Judicial Attorneys' Ass'n v State*, 459 Mich 291 (1998) (statute designating county, rather than judiciary, as employer of court employees violates separation of powers); *McDon-*

This case, *Commonwealth ex rel. Carroll v Tate*, has come to represent an enormous and infrequently explored body of doctrine.[90] Courts in many states have asserted some form of "inherent power" to command state and local legislative bodies to provide resources and facilities to the judiciary, and to appropriate funds for judicial budgets in amounts determined by the judiciary itself.[91]

Several distinctions should be made here. The vast body of inherent-powers law encompasses several strands, not all of which are relevant to the subject of freestanding judicial power claims. One distinction is between inherent powers that are subject to statutory abrogation and those that are not. In the federal system, inherent powers encompass a range of activities said to be ancillary or necessary to the exercise of judicial power: examples are the powers to appoint special masters and auditors,[92] to sanction litigants,[93] and to appoint prosecutors in contempt proceedings.[94]

---

ald v Campbell, 169 Ariz 478 (1991) (application of general whistleblower statute to administrative employee of the Supreme Court violated separation of powers); *Maricopa County v Dann*, 758 P2d 1298, 1301 (Ariz 1988) (dictum); legal secretaries, see *Barland v Eau Claire County*, 216 Wis2d 560 (1998); stenographers, see *State ex rel. Schneider v Cunningham*, 101 P 962 (Mont 1909); and janitors, see *In re Janitor*, 35 Wis 410 (1874); *State ex rel. S. Howard v Smith, Auditor*, 15 Mo App 412 (1884).

[90] Important treatments of the "inherent powers" doctrine include Jeffrey Jackson, *Judicial Independence, Adequate Court Funding, and Inherent Judicial Powers*, 52 Md L Rev 217 (1993); Carl Baar, *Judicial Activism in State Courts: The Inherent-Powers Doctrine*, in Mary Porter and G. Alan Tarr, *State Supreme Courts: Policymakers in the Federal System* 129 (1982); Felix F. Stumpf, *Inherent Powers of the Courts: Sword and Shield of the Judiciary* (1994); Ted Z. Robertson and Christa Brown, *The Judiciary's Inherent Power to Compel Funding: A Tale of Heating Stoves and Air Conditioners*, 20 St Mary's L J 863 (1989).

[91] For an overview of the large body of relevant caselaw, see Stumpf (cited in note 90) at 47–61. A few recent examples are *State ex rel. Lambert v Stephens*, 490 SE2d 891 (W Va 1997) (finding inherent judicial power to order that a parking area on county property be designated for exclusive use by court personnel, despite contrary position of county commission); *County of Barnstable v Commonwealth*, 572 NE2d 548 (Mass 1991) (counties may be obligated to fund courthouses, in lieu of appropriations by state legislature); *Matter of Alamance County Court Facilities*, 405 SE2d 125 (NC 1991) (judiciary has inherent power to order local authorities to provide courthouse facilities); *Allen County Council v Circuit Court*, 549 NE2d 364 (Ind 1990) (adopting guidelines for judges issuing fiscal mandates against county governments); *County of Allegheny v Commonwealth*, 517 Pa 65 (1988) (Commonwealth, rather than counties, has constitutional obligation to fund unified court system).

[92] See *In re Peterson*, 253 US 300 (1920).

[93] See *Chambers v NASCO*, 501 US 32 (1991).

[94] See *Young v United States ex rel. Vuitton*, 481 US 787 (1987). Other cases claim inherent powers to award attorney's fees, see *Roadway Express, Inc. v Piper*, 447 US 752 (1980); vacate judgments, see *Hazel-Atlas Glass Co. v Hartford-Empire Co.*, 322 US 238 (1944); to ensure decorum in the courtroom, see *Illinois v Allen*, 397 US 337 (1970); and to dismiss lawsuits on various grounds, see *Gulf Oil Corp. v Gilbert*, 330 US 501 (1947) (forum non conveniens); *Link v Wabash R. Co.*, 370 US 626 (1962) (failure to prosecute).

Those powers are inherent in the sense that they are not traceable to affirmative statutory grants of authority. But the Supreme Court usually acknowledges that the inherent powers may be overridden by federal statute, at least when exercised by the lower federal courts, which are creatures of statute anyway.[95]

The same is true in many of the state inherent-power cases, although the basis for most state inherent-powers law is not the relatively narrow idea that the power is necessary to the adjudication of particular cases, but rather the broad idea, expressed in *Carroll*, that the existence of an independent judiciary entails certain judicial powers and political-branch obligations. When state courts invoke their inherent powers to increase judicial budgets above the level set by legislative appropriations, however, the inherent power is not merely a default power subject to legislative override, but a power of constitutional dimension that trumps the legislative appropriations decision. Such cases are easily understood as judicial-power rulings: by appropriating an amount inadequate to sustain necessary judicial functions, the legislature has attempted to curtail the judiciary's lawful exercise of its constitutional authority.[96]

A second important distinction is between state-level funding and local funding. Federal courts are nationally funded by congressional appropriations, but in many states the courts at the lower levels of the judicial hierarchy are funded by local or county governments, rather than the state government. Accordingly, a large fraction of the inherent-powers cases concerning judicial budgets present conflicts between state judiciaries and local legislative or administrative bodies that have provided "insufficient" funding for

---

[95] See *Peterson*, 253 US at 312 (stating that "[c]ourts have (at least in the absence of legislation to the contrary) inherent power to provide themselves with appropriate instruments required for the performance of their duties"); *Chambers v Nasco*, 501 US at 47 (stating that "the exercise of the inherent power of lower federal courts can be limited by statute and rule, for these courts were created by act of Congress") (internal quotation omitted); *Bank of Nova Scotia v United States*, 487 US 250 (1988) (suggesting that the federal judiciary's inherent "supervisory authority" over criminal prosecutions is subordinate to the Federal Rules of Criminal Procedure).

[96] See Geoffrey Hazard et al, *Court Finance and Unitary Budgeting*, 81 Yale L J 1286, 1287 (1972):

> The doctrine of inherent power runs essentially as follows: The courts are a constitutionally created branch of government whose continued effective functioning is indispensable; performance of that constitutional function is a responsibility committed to the courts; this responsibility implies the authority necessary to carry it out; therefore the courts have the authority to raise money to sustain their essential functions.

local courts—for example, trial courts with county-wide jurisdiction. In this respect many of the judicial funding cases are in practice cases about local governmental finance rather than cases about state-level separation of powers; moreover, state supreme courts have sometimes acted to restrain the more extravagant funding mandates of local trial courts. But some cases do see state-level courts, including state supreme courts, mandating judicial funding from state legislatures.[97] And the constitutional theory advanced by state courts in the judicial funding cases is based upon horizontal separation of powers rather than the vertical division of authority within states: the core theory is that state courts at any level, vested with the power of a co-equal branch, are constitutionally entitled to "reasonable" or "adequate" funding of their essential functions and activities.[98]

The subject of judicial funding and inherent powers is an enormous one that cannot be fully treated here. The narrow point is simply that in the funding cases the functional and open-ended character of the relevant adjudicative standards—"reasonable" funding for "necessary" or "essential" activities—encourages judicial prerogatives to swell beyond plausible limits. The basic outlook is captured perfectly by *State ex rel. Johnston v Taulbee*.[99] A juvenile-court judge brought a separation-of-powers challenge to an Ohio statute that instructed county commissions to appropriate a sum "reasonably necessary to meet all the administrative expenses" of the juvenile court system for that county, with the commission's decision subject to judicial review by writ of mandamus.[100] Under the predecessor statute, the county commission had been legally obliged to accept the juvenile court's proposed budget

---

[97] See Howard B. Glaser, *Wachtler v Cuomo: The Limits of Inherent Power*, 14 Pace L Rev 111, 112 (1994) (describing a suit brought against the state government by the Chief Judge of the New York Court of Appeals to compel funding of the state judiciary).

[98] See Baar (cited in note 90) at 130–31 (exploring connections between inherent judicial powers and the separation of powers). In a few states there are specific constitutional provisions that protect judicial budgets, and the supreme courts of those states have invoked those provisions to assert judicial control in funding cases, although the cases rely upon general claims about the judicial power as well. See, e.g., *Folsom v Wynn*, 631 So2d 890 (Ala 1993) (governor acted unconstitutionally by applying proration statute to cut 5% of judicial budget).

[99] See *State ex rel. Johnston v Taulbee*, 423 NE2d 80 (Ohio 1981). For similar examples, see note 91 (collecting recent cases).

[100] *Taulbee*, 423 NE2d at 81.

unless the commission could show that the court had abused its discretion.

The Ohio Supreme Court held that the new statute effected an "impermissible legislative encroachment upon the judiciary."[101] Its essential vice, in the Court's view, was that the General Assembly had "financially . . . inhibited," "restrict[ed]" and "imped[ed]" the judiciary in "the free and untrammeled exercise of their judicial functions."[102] The impediment was not that the legislature had denied the judiciary the ultimate authority to determine judicial budgets; a dissenting judge pointed out that the county commissions' appropriation could always be increased by judicial order after the statutorily authorized mandamus review.[103] The impediment, apparently, was simply that the county commissions were no longer obligated to accept any budget request that the relevant court decided to submit (with recourse only to abuse-of-discretion review by the judiciary itself). For the Ohio Supreme Court, the baseline for "reasonable" funding was whatever the judiciary said it was, and any reduction from that baseline amounted to a usurpation of judicial authority.

5. *The paranoid style in state judicial review.* Beyond these substantive areas there is a tendency to rhetorical excess, in particular a certain belligerence and defensiveness, that pervade the state judicial power cases. The tone is best illustrated, albeit in an extreme version, by another decision of the Ohio Supreme Court: its much-publicized 1998 decision in *State ex rel. Ohio Academy of Trial Lawyers v Sheward.*[104] The Ohio General Assembly, the Court declared while invalidating a major civil justice reform statute, had "usurped the judicial power," issued a "challenge to the judiciary as a coordinate branch of government,"[105] and had made a bid for "legislative omnipotence."[106] This usurpation took a particularly devilish form: not an alteration of the composition of the courts, nor of the judges' tenure, nor a diminution of their salaries, nor a reduction of their jurisdiction, nor an attempt to preclude judicial review

---

[101] Id.

[102] Id at 82–83.

[103] Id at 85.

[104] *State ex rel. Ohio Academy of Trial Lawyers v Sheward*, 715 NE2d 1062 (Ohio 1999).

[105] Id at 1073.

[106] Id at 1096.

of constitutional issues, nor even (as in *Plaut*) an abrogation of final judicial judgments. No, the General Assembly had made its bid for unchecked dominion by enacting a statute subject to full judicial review whose substantive provisions for tort reform were, in the Court's view, inconsistent with judicial precedent. The statute had the following critical features: (1) it enacted a fifteen-year statute of repose for certain product-liability and malpractice claims, despite a line of precedent holding that statutes of repose violated an Ohio constitutional provision that guarantees a "right to a remedy"; (2) it abrogated the common-law collateral source rule, despite a 1994 precedent declaring, very oddly, that such an abrogation would violate the right to jury trial;[107] (3) it enacted caps on punitive and compensatory damages, caps that were arguably inconsistent with precedent (not clearly so; the Court had to devote a few pages to rebutting proposed distinctions); and (4) it made various minor modifications to the summary-judgment standard and to evidentiary rules.

Of course most opinions that declare laws unconstitutional say that the law is inconsistent with precedent, and very few invalid laws can fairly be viewed as attempts to disrupt the constitutional order. The General Assembly provoked this explosion of judicial oratory by stating, in a statutory preamble and in legislative history, that it "respectfully disagree[d]" with certain of the relevant precedents and desired to "respond to the issues raised" by them.[108] This the Court saw as an attempt to "require the courts to treat as valid laws those which are unconstitutional."[109] The obvious formal rejoinder, as a dissenting judge pointed out, is that "[a]doption of a statute similar to one already struck down does not contradict a prior judgment of this court invalidating the first statute," and that the General Assembly's expression of disagreement does not violate the separation of powers.[110]

---

[107] The right to a jury trial is simply the right to have a jury, rather than a judge, decide the facts and the application of law to fact; it is not the right to have a jury, rather than the legislature, decide what the applicable law shall be. Legislative abrogation of a collateral-source rule no more violates the right of jury trial than does legislative abolition of a common-law cause of action, although either may be objectionable on other grounds. See notes 172–73 and accompanying text (discussing right to jury trial and *Sofie v Fibreboard Corp.*, 112 Wash2d 636 (1989)).

[108] Id at 1073.

[109] Id at 1086.

[110] See id at 1120.

But the critical point is a pragmatic one. Not even proponents of exclusive judicial authority to decide constitutional questions[111] have endorsed the rule seemingly made law in *Sheward:* that the very reenactment of a statute previously declared invalid is itself an independent violation of the separation of powers, quite apart from the statute's substantive invalidity or any interference with judgments between parties in previous cases. There are excellent consequentialist reasons for rejecting any such rule. It would prevent a court from ever changing its past constitutional rulings on the validity of legislation (putting aside the remote possibility of constitutional amendment), because the legislature would be constitutionally barred from supplying the reenactment needed to provide a case or controversy in which the reconsideration could occur.

In this light, the Ohio statute most closely resembles a legislative motion for reconsideration of precedent. The advantages of such motions are illustrated by *Helvering v Griffith*,[112] a decision of the reconstituted, post–New Deal U.S. Supreme Court. Justice Jackson's opinion said that the Court would find no constitutional offense or embarrassment in a congressional decision to reenact a tax statute that was flatly inconsistent with a restrictive constitutional precedent of the Old Court.[113] The mechanisms of legal change, Jackson observed, sometimes require legislatures to challenge existing precedent in exactly this way:

> There is no reason to doubt that this Court may fall into error as may other branches of the Government. . . . The Court differs, however, from other branches of the Government in its ability to extricate itself from error. It can reconsider a matter only when it is again properly brought before it in a case or controversy, and . . . the new case must have sufficient statutory support.[114]

---

[111] See, e.g., Frederick Schauer and Larry Alexander, *On Extrajudicial Constitutional Interpretation*, 110 Harv L Rev 1359 (1997) (defending "judicial primacy without qualification" in constitutional matters).

[112] See *Helvering v Griffiths*, 318 US 371 (1943).

[113] The precedent was *Eisner v Macomber*, 252 US 189 (1920). In *Helvering* itself Jackson's discussion was dictum; for unrelated reasons the Court construed the statute consistently with *Eisner v Macomber*.

[114] Id at 401. At the state level, an example of this sort of sensible interbranch cooperation is *Del Rio v Crake*, 87 Hawaii 297 (1998). The Court had previously held that a statute establishing tort thresholds under a no-fault law violated the state's equal protection guarantee. The legislature reenacted the statute in identical form; the Court overruled its earlier decisions and sustained the law, finding that its previous reasoning was in error.

The contrast between the pragmatism of *Griffith* and the bombast of *Sheward* is a consequence of the analytic failings of the *Sheward* opinion. The Ohio Supreme Court, concerned with a possible insult to the authority of its constitutional rulings, resorted both to declamations and to a prophylactic rule so broad that it protects the judicial power from perceived offense at the price of clogging an indispensable channel of constitutional change. As the legislature will sometimes guess incorrectly about whether the previously invalidated statutes it reenacts will be sustained by the judges, that channel will sometimes bring before the courts new statutes flatly inconsistent with well-founded precedent, rather than precedent deserving of reconsideration. That is just to say that legislatures are no more perfect than are courts; both institutions must tolerate errors, and must mitigate the effects of error through the ordinary processes of constitutional lawmaking.

D. THE MECHANISMS OF OVERPROTECTION

In these examples, the state cases undermine (where the judicial power is concerned) the formalist claim that judges conducting core functions analysis will systematically underweight abstract, "structural" separation-of-powers interests, and will systematically overweigh the immediate exigencies that provoked legislative action. In fact, the direction of systemic pressure is reversed in the state cases: freestanding judicial power claims trigger expansive conceptions of the judiciary's core functions and essential prerogatives.

It is difficult to isolate the precise causal mechanisms at work. Here I shall sketch three mechanisms that operate across cases; there may well be others. The first mechanism is habituation, which causes judges to confuse what they have always done with a fundamental component of the judicial power. The second is that judges' differential information about legislative policies and judicial prerogatives causes them to underestimate the benefits obtainable from the statutory scheme or even to dismiss legislative aims as unimportant. The third is that differential information, and the high salience of the particular cases that judges examine, together cause the judges to display a marked preference for case-specific judicial discretion—that is to say, for judicial authority to implement legal directives in the form of standards rather than rules.

1. *Habit.* Judges, like other people, become habituated to and invested in the tasks, activities, and procedures they customarily and repetitively perform.[115] They overestimate the disruption that would arise from switching to new tasks or activities.[116] The result is a strong tendency for judges to equate customary or habitual tasks with fundamental judicial functions. This theme is inescapable in the state cases. The high courts of Arizona, Alabama, Illinois, and New Hampshire, for example, seemingly suggest that it is a conclusive argument against reform that the legislative mandates would change the way judges have always done things.[117]

There are obvious connections between the idea of habituation and ideas about the role of tradition, and even the common law, in constitutional interpretation. Nothing here is intended to deny that tradition, common law, and other such sources have legitimate interpretive roles.[118] But it cannot be the case that all novel legislation affecting the courts is unconstitutional merely by reason of its novelty. Whatever the proper role of history and tradition in supplying content to separation-of-powers analysis, every plausible account recognizes that some traditions are not constitutionally dispositive, and that not all departures from tradition are constitutionally prohibited.[119] But prominent decisions of the state courts depict any novel legislative mandate as presumptively suspect, a likely usurpation of judicial authority. That untenable conception of judicial prerogative rests upon a strong judicial predilection to equate customary judicial tasks with rules of constitutional law.

2. *Information.* The judges in the state cases have far better information about the structural judicial interests affected by legislative

---

[115] See Gary S. Becker, *Accounting for Tastes* 119–22 (1996) (arguing that actors derive utility from following habitual patterns).

[116] This is a central point in the cognitive-psychology literature on the "status quo bias," under which "costs to switch from the status quo are perceived by decision makers but not actually borne by them." William Samuelson and Richard Zeckhauser, *Status Quo Bias in Decision Making*, 1 J Risk and Uncertainty 7, 41 (1988).

[117] See notes 55–83 and accompanying text.

[118] There is a large literature on the interpretive weight properly afforded to tradition and common law in constitutional interpretation. See David A. Strauss, *Common-Law Constitutional Interpretation*, 63 U Chi L Rev 877 (1996); A. C. Pritchard and Todd J. Zywicki, *Finding the Constitution: An Economic Analysis of Tradition's Role in Constitutional Interpretation*, 77 NC L Rev 409 (1999).

[119] Compare *Hurtado v California*, 110 US 516, 529 (1884) (although tradition is the touchstone of due process analysis, to hold every deviation from tradition unconstitutional "would be to deny every quality of the law but its age, and to render it incapable of progress or improvement.").

action than about the statute's aims and social consequences. The differential information affects their evaluation of those interests' importance. The inherent-power cases on judicial financing supply an example. There judges draw up a requested budget based upon concrete knowledge of the judiciary's financial needs, and assess their needs by reference to some ideal, "fully funded" judicial system. The judiciary also possesses concrete knowledge of plans that would improve judicial operations. Against this background of detailed information the judiciary encounters a budgeting process that is, to them, poorly understood and wholly abstract. In that process the legislature must develop a system-wide budget that accommodates an extraordinary range of trade-offs between competing client groups, institutions, agencies, and interests, of which the judiciary is only one, and none of which can reasonably expect to receive "full" funding relative to its self-perceived needs. These conditions generally cause the judges to take a partial, incomplete view of system-wide problems, one that demands ideal levels of judicial funding while describing the trade-offs inherent in a budget as "subordination" to the political branches.

The same effect operates with respect to cases that root judicial prerogative in substantive legal doctrine, in remedial and procedural rules, or in the inviolability of judgments. Recall *Commonwealth v Sutley*, the Pennsylvania decision that struck down a statutory procedure for reducing criminal sentences for marijuana possession on the ground that it interfered with the finality of judicial judgments. There the Court noted that the case at bar involved a conviction for *possession* under circumstances that suggested the defendant had in fact been *selling* marijuana, a far more serious offense; the trial judge had accepted the plea agreement for the lesser offense and simply issued a stiff sentence within the discretionary sentencing range.[120] To the Court, that sequence suggested that the statutory grant of leniency produced error in one class of cases. The impossibility of sorting those who merely possessed drugs from those who actually sold them, but pled to possession, meant that the new, reduced sentence would prove excessively lenient relative to the "true" underlying offense.[121] But the case at

---

[120] See *Sutley*, 378 A2d at 787.

[121] See id (arguing that if "a resentencing is required, the court is powerless to impose a new sentence which would be commensurate with the true nature of the offense").

bar supplied no information about the opposite type of error: absent the statutory scheme, many who had in fact merely possessed would remain in prison under excessively harsh sentences. The background suggested that the legislature, after investigation, had found the latter type of error to dominate the former. In this sense, differential information seems to have pushed the court toward overweighing the judiciary's need to address one type of error, thereby distorting the comprehensive overview needed to understand the trade-offs that provoked the legislation.

3. *Rules, standards, information, and the salience effect.* The choice of legal form is usually whether to embody legal directives as rules or as standards (categories that encompass many variants). But this problem has no general solution. Rules are costly because they are over- and underinclusive relative to their purposes, and because their formulation requires a great deal of information; standards are costly because they are unpredictable, and because their application requires a great deal of information.[122] Sometimes rules are best, sometimes standards, and from the standpoint of an omniscient institutional designer the choice turns upon considerations such as the value of legal certainty, the competence of decision makers, and the aggregate costs of decision and error (the point the *Sutley* court missed).

The hostility to statutory rules that is a defining feature of the state cases rests upon no such set of normatively relevant reasons. The judicial preference for judge-made standards is better seen as a product of the salience effect, a heuristic that causes decision makers to overweight the importance of vivid, concrete foreground information and to underweight the importance of abstract, aggregated background information[123]—and thereby to overweight the value of judicial authority to adjust legal directives to particular circumstances, an authority that rule-bound legislative schemes

---

[122] The literature on rules and standards is vast. The principal references, with citations to the propositions in text, are collected in Adrian Vermeule, *Interpretive Choice*, 75 NYU L Rev 74 (2000).

[123] See Scott Plous, *The Psychology of Judgment and Decision Making* 125–26, 178–80 (1993) (discussing the salience heuristic and the closely related heuristics of vividness and availability). Compare Robert M. Reyes, William C. Thompson, and Gordon H. Bower, *Judgmental Biases Resulting from Differing Availabilities of Arguments*, 39 J Personality & Soc Psychol 2, 5–12 (1980) (demonstrating that vivid, concrete information exerts greater influence on mock jury deliberations than abstract, pallid information).

deny.[124] *Sutley* illustrates this mechanism of overprotection as well, because there are close connections between the salience effect and the effects of differential information; the two are mutually reinforcing. The facts of the case at hand—the defendant's factual guilt for a more serious offense (sale) than the one to which he pled (possession)—supplied, in the Court's view, a *"graphic example"* that demonstrated the statute's tendency to "completely frustrate the judicial discretion" by making the court "powerless to impose a new sentence which would be commensurate with the true nature of the offense."[125] That focus upon the graphic example at hand is the salience effect in action.

A more detailed picture of the connection between the salience effect and the judicial preference for standards emerges from the Illinois Supreme Court's invalidation of a noneconomic damages cap in *Best v Taylor Machine Works*.[126] Consider the Court's repeated complaint that the noneconomic damages cap would fall most heavily upon the most badly injured plaintiffs, such as the burned and crippled industrial worker in the case at bar. There is an important relationship between that complaint and the Court's holding that the cap impermissibly encroached upon the judicial power by removing judicial discretion to tailor damage awards to particular cases when the cap was exceeded. Facing a stream of such cases in the concrete, rather than as part of an aggregate question of legal policy, plausibly causes judges to overweight the standard-based interest in tailoring damage awards to particular facts. The costs of the rule—here, the capping of damages for severely injured plaintiffs—are insistently visible to judicial actors. The

---

[124] There are also close connections here to the phenomenon of self-serving bias, which causes decision makers to "arrive at judgments of what is fair or right that are biased in the direction of their own self-interests," Linda Babcock and George Loewenstein, *Explaining Bargaining Impasse: The Role of Self-Serving Biases*, 11 J Econ Perspectives 109, 111 (1997), and to the tendency of experts to develop excessive confidence in their case-specific judgments relative to the performance of simple rule-like algorithms, see Robyn M. Dawes, *The Robust Beauty of Improper Linear Models in Decisionmaking*, in Daniel Kahneman, Paul Sloivc, and Amos Tversky eds, *Judgment Under Uncertainty: Heuristics and Biases* 391 (1982). Insofar as judges must pass upon the constitutionality of a legislative reform that displaces the judges' case-specific assessments with a simpler, although cruder, statutory rule, both cognitive tendencies are triggered: judges may interpret legislative curtailment of judicial discretion as particularly threatening or unfair (self-serving bias), and will overestimate their own performance in exercising professional discretion in particular cases (overconfidence).

[125] *Sutley*, 378 A2d at 787.

[126] See notes 55–67 and accompanying text.

benefits of the rule—here, the legal predictability that flows from eliminating high and highly variable, because largely unmeasurable, awards for pain and suffering damages—redound principally to the benefit of private actors, and are less visible to the judiciary.

The existence of such a salience effect cannot be proved from a few cases, but the claim should not be surprising. It is merely the obverse of the traditional justification for the constitutional requirement, applicable in the federal system and in many state systems, that the judicial power may be exercised only in the context of a concrete "case" or "controversy."[127] Proponents of the case-or-controversy requirement describe it as superior to alternatives (principally the system of advisory opinions used in a few states, and in several European judicial systems) because the presence of a specific factual record provides the judges with valuable information.[128] But as always there are trade-offs, and the salience effect is a major cost of concreteness: courts may have more information, but the information may have distortive effects. When the distortion outstrips the gains in information, judges will overweigh the visible costs of the policies under review and underestimate their systemic, less visible benefits. This is not always true, or it would supply a general argument against the case-or-controversy requirement; later I shall discuss a range of factors that may either dampen or exacerbate the distortions that operate in freestanding judicial power challenges. But salience-related distortion is an insistent pattern in the state cases.

III. Tethering the Judicial Power

It is important to emphasize the limited scope of the claims made to this point. There is a set of cognitive mechanisms that cause judges, assessing freestanding judicial power claims on functionalist standards, to arrive at implausibly broad conceptions of the judiciary's core functions. Examples from a range of doctrinal

---

[127] See, e.g., US Const, Art III, § 2 (limiting federal courts to the decision of "cases" and "controversies"); Robert L. Maddex, *State Constitutions of the United States* xxiv–xxix (Congressional Quarterly 1998) (showing that only ten state constitutions permit the judicial branch to issue advisory opinions).

[128] See, e.g., Bickel (cited in note 26) at 115 (arguing that case-or-controversy requirements permit "the judgment of courts [to] be had in concrete cases that exemplify the actual consequences of legislative or executive actions.").

settings illustrate those mechanisms. But those mechanisms do not necessarily dominate any other doctrinal, institutional, or political factors, and they need not operate uniformly in the face of local variation in constitutional provisions or judicial structure. Accordingly, this Part examines doctrinal and institutional correctives on the simplifying assumption that the mechanisms that cause overprotection may be addressed in isolation. Complicating factors, particularly questions about variation between state and federal systems with respect to freestanding judicial power claims, are taken up in Part IV.

A. THE PRESUMPTION OF CONSTITUTIONALITY

A corrective that sometimes surfaces in federal constitutional law is the presumption of constitutionality, or James Bradley Thayer's "rule of clear mistake."[129] Under this approach, judicial power claims would be sustained only if no reasonable understanding of the Constitution would sustain the legislation. Some state courts profess to use a similar approach in inherent-power cases, saying that the burden lies on the judiciary to show that an exercise of inherent power is reasonably necessary.[130]

In principle something like this is the right solution. The presumption of constitutionality is best understood as a device for coping with the expected costs of judicial error. The presumption might be defended on the view that a mistaken ruling of unconstitutionality is more damaging than a mistaken ruling of constitutionality, because the legislature may correct the latter through the ordinary lawmaking process, rather than through the cumbersome process of constitutional amendment.[131] The presumption might also be used to correct for judicial error if the probability of error

---

[129] See James Bradley Thayer, *The Origins and Scope of the American Doctrine of Constitutional Law*, 7 Harv L Rev 17 (1893). In the post–New Deal era, the Supreme Court sometimes says that the presumption of constitutionality applies only to legislation affecting "economic" rather than "social" affairs. See, e.g., *Usery v Turner Elkhorn Mining Co.*, 428 US 1, 15 (1976).

[130] The leading case is *Matter of Salary of Juvenile Director*, 552 P2d 163, 173–74 (Wash 1976). See also Stumpf (cited in note 90) at 73–73 (collecting cases from other jurisdictions). Some states say that the burden lies upon the political branches challenging the court's inherent-power order. See *Smith v Miller*, 384 P2d 738, 742 (Colo 1963); *County of Barnstable v Commonwealth*, 572 NE2d 548, 552–53 (Mass 1991).

[131] See Richard A. Posner, *The Problematics of Moral and Legal Theory* 147–49 (1999).

were greater in one direction or another, even if the harms from error were identical—and plausibly that is the tendency in the state judicial power cases. The basic insight is identical on either justification. The presumption is useful precisely because it is a standard of review that is sensitive to institutional effects.

But the great defect of the presumption of constitutionality is that it is a standard, not a rule; in application it requires a case-specific determination. As such it fails to address a pervasive problem in the judicial power cases: that informational and cognitive mechanisms operating with great force *in particular cases* cause the judiciary systematically to overweigh (its own) separation-of-powers interests relative to the "core functions" norm. To the extent that those mechanisms operate, we might expect to see judges reciting the presumption of constitutionality in judicial power cases, in all good faith, and then finding debatable infringements to be "clear" violations.[132]

That is exactly what the cases show. Many state courts recite the presumption of constitutionality in separation-of-powers cases. But there is no reason to think the presumption is doing any work: it is never said to be dispositive, opinions often invoke it formulaically and then proceed to issue ringing condemnations of purported legislative encroachment, and the presence or absence of an overprotective ruling, or the extent of overprotection that results, does not seem to depend upon the recitation of the presumption. It begs the question to suppose that the presumption influences litigants *ex ante*, inducing them to challenge fewer statutes than they otherwise would (thus leaving the pool of reported appellate cases to contain mostly statutes that are clearly unconstitutional). Litigants will not give the presumption any weight in their calculations if they realize that it does not influence judges in the first place. Probably the only effects of the presumption are perverse. Robert Nagel, for example, argues that the presumption causes judges to adopt an adversarial rhetorical and cultural pos-

---

[132] Compare Note, *The Courts' Inherent Power to Compel Legislative Funding of Judicial Functions*, 81 Mich L Rev 1687, 1697 (1983) (in inherent-power cases, "[i]f the reviewing court in fact harbors a pro-judicial bias, this favoritism will express itself as easily in the conclusion that the lower court 'met its burden' [of showing that the legislature granted the courts constitutionally inadequate funding] as in a finding that the lower court persuasively linked specific judicial functions threatened by low appropriation to the constitutional requirement of an independent judiciary").

ture toward the legislature, because it forces judges to describe every constitutional violation as "clear" and the legislature as "irrational."[133] All told, then, the presumption of constitutionality is an unpromising solution.

B. THE NONJUSTICIABILITY PROPOSAL

Despite its defects, the presumption of constitutionality is on the right track; an improved version would embody the same aims in the form of a rule rather than a standard. A better means to that end is the following: state courts should decline to adjudicate—should declare nonjusticiable—any freestanding "judicial power" claim. That category does *not* include either (1) claims that legislation violates express, or necessarily implied, provisions that protect or regulate judicial activity—for example, a provision that prohibits reduction of judicial salaries—or (2) individual-rights claims that happen to arise within the judicial process, such as the right to jury trial. Both categories of claims would, under this proposal, remain justiciable. I will provide some intellectual-history background for the nonjusticiability proposal, and then explore its advantages and disadvantages.

1. *The political process and the judicial process.* The nonjusticiability proposal might also be called the "reverse Choper" proposal. Jesse Choper famously argued that federal courts should declare nonjusticiable two categories of claims: (1) separation-of-powers claims that either Congress or the President has exceeded its authority, and (2) "division of power" claims (i.e., federalism claims) that the federal government as a whole has exceeded the scope of its enumerated powers vis-à-vis the states.[134] Both halves of the argument are rooted in a simple political process model. As far as the separation of national powers is concerned, the political branches can defend themselves from aggressive encroachments through political process mechanisms such as the veto power (in the case of the President) and the appropriations power (in the case of the Con-

---

[133] See Robert F. Nagel, *Name-Calling and the Clear Error Rule*, 88 Nw U L Rev 193, 201–02 (1993) (noting possibility that Thayerian judges "would tend to intervene often, to be unaware of the scope of the power they are exercising, and to be impervious to criticism").

[134] See Jesse H. Choper, *Judicial Review and the National Political Process* 175 ("Federalism Proposal," 263 ("Separation Proposal") (1980).

gress). As far as the division of power between federal and state governments is concerned, states are virtually represented in the congressional process by several mechanisms, notably state control over federal elections and the states' equal representation in the Senate. Because separation-of-powers interests and federalism interests will be adequately represented in the political process, the argument goes, courts should reserve their "political capital" for the adjudication of individual rights claims, at least those whose claimants, on the standard *Carolene Products* account, are underrepresented in the political process.[135]

A corollary to Choper's principal theses, which he labels the "judicial power proposal," holds that there is one category of separation-of-powers claims that must remain justiciable: claims that political branch action (principally legislation) has usurped the constitutionally assigned functions of the judiciary.[136] The judges' institutional interests are underrepresented in the political process, the argument runs, so the judiciary must defend itself from political branch aggression through constitutional review of judicial power claims—and this despite the seeming contradiction of the institutional design principle, fundamental to the separation of powers, that no institution should be the final arbiter of the limits of its own authority.[137]

---

[135] See *United States v Carolene Products Co.*, 304 US 144, 152 n 4 (1938) (suggesting strict judicial review of legislation that infringes explicit textual rights, that closes the channels of political change, or that burdens discrete and insular minorities).

[136] See Choper (cited in note 134) at 382 (advancing "Judicial Power Proposal— . . . that the Supreme Court should pass final constitutional judgment on questions concerning the permissible reach and circumscription of 'the judicial power.'").

[137] See id at 388 (acknowledging that his position "straightforwardly call[s] for the federal judiciary to act as final arbiter of its own constitutional power [ ] . . . unencumbered by any seeming contradiction with the axiom against any person or institution serving as judge in its own cause."); cf. Laura S. Fitzgerald, *Beyond Marbury: Jurisdictional Self-Dealing in Seminole Tribe*, 52 Vand L Rev 407, 483 (1999) (noting that the doctrine surrounding suits for injunctive relief against state officials "empowers the Court unilaterally to determine, in lawsuits against state interests, the terms and reach of its own constitutional authority. At the very least, this raises separation of powers issues . . . ."). Choper's position reflects the Supreme Court's assumption in the judicial power cases that federal judges should be final arbiters of their own constitutional authority; that assumption contrasts sharply with the Court's frequent claim that no *other* official or institution may be "allowed to be a judge in his own cause, because his interest would certainly bias his judgment," Federalist 10 (Madison) in C. Rossiter, ed, *The Federalist Papers* (Mentor, 1961), at 79. See, e.g., *Gutierrez de Martinez v Lamagno*, 515 US 417, 428–29 (1995) (holding that Congress provided for judicial review of the Attorney General's certifications of federal employment in tort suits against federal employees; the contrary position would make the federal executive judge of its own cause). In cases such as *Lamagno* the judiciary invokes the maxim to support broad judicial review of executive action, lest a conflict of interest occur. In other cases the

One line of critique would question the internal premises of Choper's argument. It might be said that judges are represented in the political process in exactly the same way that states are: virtually, through an alignment between political actors' interests and the judiciary's interests. Choper seems to think it important that judges neither participate *eo nomine* in the legislative process nor are formally represented there. But both these things are true of the states: state officials do not sit as such in the Congress, and as far as representation is concerned state officials have never chosen members of the House of Representatives, and have not chosen senators since the passage of the Seventeenth Amendment in 1913. Choper's real argument about federalism is that institutional structures and incentives align states' interests with the interests of federal legislators chosen by popular election. But it is also possible that other institutional structures and incentives, operating across rather than within branches, generally align legislators' interests with those of the judiciary. That is a vast topic; here I will simply mention a few critical political mechanisms that protect the judiciary from political attack.

One mechanism is virtual representation of the judiciary's interests by the organized bar—Bentham's "Judge & Co."[138] Subgroups within the bar, trial lawyers in particular, resist legislative alteration and (especially) simplification of judicial procedure and substantive legal rules and remedies because those changes reduce the trial lawyers' monopoly power over legal information and litigation skills.[139] Trial lawyers in Illinois, for example, fiercely opposed the

---

judiciary passes judgment, with unreviewable finality, on causes of action brought by federal judges to enforce the judges' own prerogatives. See, e.g., *Will v United States*, 449 US 200 (1980) (holding, in suit brought by Article III judges, that Article III forbade a congressional attempt to reduce judicial salaries). The conflict of interest in the latter sort of case is excused by the common-law "rule of necessity," see 449 US at 213–16, which holds that, because all the judges are equally affected by the conflict, the case must be reviewed by a biased judge if it is to be reviewed at all. The possibility implicitly rejected by this reasoning—the possibility that the judges should declare such a suit nonjusticiable precisely because of the structural conflict of interest—is never explored in the rule-of-necessity decisions. See also *Weinstock v Holden*, 995 SW2d 408 (Mo 1999) (holding that the legislature violated the separation of powers by enacting a statute that forbade judges from sitting to decide any case in which the judge could receive a direct or indirect financial gain from the proceeding; the statute's fatal flaw was that it abrogated the rule of necessity).

[138] See Gerald Postema, *Bentham and the Common Law Tradition* 274–75 (1986).

[139] See Peter Schuck, *Legal Complexity: Some Causes, Consequences and Cures*, 42 Duke L J 1 (1992). For an argument that downplays the interest-group influence of the organized bar, particularly the plaintiff's bar, see Frank B. Cross, *The Role of Lawyers in Positive Theories of Doctrinal Evolution*, 45 Emory L J 523 (1996).

Illinois statute that was held to have encroached upon the power of the Illinois judiciary by altering the collateral-source rule and instituting caps on noneconomic damages.[140] The bar is a heterogeneous category, and lawyers' interests generally are not perfectly congruent with those of the courts, but similar observations hold for the political actors who, on Choper's view, are adequate to virtually represent states' interests.

Other mechanisms also cause the judges' interests to receive virtual representation in the political process. The most practical safeguards of an independent judiciary are the competition between political coalitions within Congress, and the long-standing rivalry between Congress and the President. Within Congress, given that control of the legislature regularly alternates between two major parties, so that today's winner is tomorrow's loser, even the party that temporarily holds a legislative majority will tend to support the existence of an independent judiciary that protects legislative minorities. The forgone opportunity to oppress the current minority is more than compensated by the safeguard against future oppression by a future majority.[141] Between Congress and the President, the legislature often attempts to enlist the judiciary's aid in monitoring delegated executive authority. Federal legislation generally provides for broad judicial review of executive action, ensuring a judicial check upon presidential distortion of legislative policies,[142] and incidentally enhancing judicial authority. Most generally, a prominent account of the success of the independent judiciary in American law holds that pluralist political actors will generally desire the presence of an independent judiciary to enforce bargains embodied in constitutional and statutory provisions.[143] Choper seems to assume that a judiciary lacking either explicit representation in the national lawmaking process or constitutional authority to define the limits of its own power will prove an inviting

---

[140] On the role of the American Trial Lawyers' Association (ATLA) in the *Best v Taylor* litigation, see Richard D. Hailye, *ATLA's Constitutional Litigators Fight "Tort Reform,"* 34 Trial 9 (Feb 1, 1998).

[141] See Robert Cooter, *The Strategic Constitution* 59 (2000).

[142] See Peter L. Strauss (cited in note 25) at 524 ("Congress generally provides rather full [judicial] review of administrative action—one imagines, wishing the resultant control rather than seeking to avoid possible constitutional difficulty as such").

[143] See William M. Landes and Richard A. Posner, *The Independent Judiciary in an Interest-Group Perspective*, 18 J L & Econ 875 (1975).

target for political branch aggression, but this is at bottom an empirical claim, and it is hardly an overwhelming one.

The converse criticism is that Choper, arguing that judges are underrepresented in the political process, has overlooked that his position would commit final determination of judicial authority to a forum in which the judiciary's institutional interests are dramatically overrepresented, namely, the judicial process itself.[144] This point simply translates the cognitive mechanisms discussed above into Choper's simple political process model. In those terms, the adjudicative process will protect the institutional interests of the judiciary more assiduously than the institutional interests of other branches, not because of bad faith on the judges' part, but simply because the judiciary has better information about, and greater solicitude for, its own interests than about competing social interests.

The law already contains analogues to this inversion of Choper's process model. One is the Supreme Court's decision in *(Walter L.) Nixon v United States*,[145] which held nonjusticiable a federal judge's claim that the Senate procedures followed in the judge's impeachment violated the impeachment clauses of the Constitution; the Court was concerned, among other things, that judicial review of judicial impeachments "would place final reviewing authority with respect to impeachments in the hands of the same body that the impeachment process is meant to regulate."[146] The point generalizes beyond the impeachment context. Although the Court suggested that impeachment is the sole check on federal judicial excess,[147] another check on judicial power is the legislative power to control judicial behavior through valid enactments, and the danger is that adjudication of freestanding judicial power claims places final reviewing authority over such statutory controls

---

[144] This point draws upon Paul Verkuil's idea that the separation of powers is best viewed through the lens of institutional mechanisms for avoiding conflicts of interest. Paul R. Verkuil, *Separation of Powers, the Rule of Law, and the Idea of Independence*, 30 Wm & Mary L Rev 301 (1989). Verkuil, however, goes wrong by suggesting that "the purpose of an independent judiciary is to avoid the conflicts of interest inherent in a situation in which the deciders are dependent upon the litigants for their well-being and position." Id at 322. That claim ignores the conflicts of interest *produced* by judicial independence when a politically insulated judiciary passes upon a freestanding judicial power claim—that is, passes upon the constitutional limits of its own power under ill-defined constitutional standards.

[145] 506 US 224 (1993).

[146] Id at 235.

[147] See id.

in the hands of the same body that the enactment is meant to regulate. Likewise, the view advanced by a plurality of four Justices in *Coleman v Miller*[148]—that the procedural validity of constitutional amendments is not subject to judicial review[149]—is best defended on the ground that the amending process should be off limits to judicial oversight because the amending process is itself a principal check on judicial overreaching.[150] That rationale can also be generalized to the setting of freestanding judicial power claims.

Another analogue, one drawn from legal theory rather than doctrine, is John Hart Ely's argument for vigorous equal protection review.[151] For Ely, the principal danger to be feared in majoritarian legislation affecting underrepresented minorities was not malevolence, but poor information and flawed cognition. Majority-group legislators would develop stereotyped, largely inaccurate conceptions of minorities and their interests, and would systematically overweigh majority interests where the two conflict. The state cases suggest that a similar effect obtains when judges adjudicate ill-defined claims of freestanding judicial power: the judges stereotype and disfavor the interests advanced by legislative coalitions, while overprotecting their own, more familiar and better-understood interests.

2. *The nonjusticiability proposal as alarm-clock formalism.* The nonjusticiability proposal, then, is not a claim about the meaning of a textual grant of "judicial power." It is a formalist decision-making strategy that attempts to implement the core-functions norm without permitting systematic slippage toward an implausibly broad conception of judicial power. The nonjusticiability proposal thus shares the form of the deliberately overprotective, rules-based conception of the "judicial power" advanced in *Plaut v Spendthrift Farms* and in Justice Brennan's dissenting opinion in *CFTC v Schor*, but it reverses the direction of the formalist prescription. The nonjusticiability proposal aims to underprotect the judicial power be-

---

[148] 307 US 433 (1939).

[149] See id at 459 (Black, J, concurring, joined by Roberts, Frankfurter, and Douglas, JJ).

[150] See Laurence H. Tribe, *A Constitution We Are Amending: In Defense of a Restrained Judicial Role*, 97 Harv L Rev 433 (1983). Tribe, however, rejects total judicial abdication of review in this area; he supports modest judicial review of amendments' procedural validity.

[151] See John Hart Ely, *Democracy and Distrust* 135–79 (1980).

cause doing so is necessary to safeguard legislative authority to regulate non-core components of the judicial function—for example, legislative authority to override common-law tort rules—in the face of predictable judicial encroachments on that authority.

This sort of "underprotection" strategy is also a staple of formalist separation-of-powers doctrine, although it is not often recognized as such. Return to Justice Black's opinion for the Court in *Youngstown*. The opinion's holding that the President may act only on the basis of specific constitutional or statutory authority is deeply puzzling when the idea of "emergency" is introduced. It is easy to imagine contingencies in which executive power must be called into play, in which (precisely because of the unanticipated character of the emergency) there is no constitutional or statutory provision that expressly provides for the contingency, and in which there is no time for the President to convene Congress to request authorizing legislation. Can Black really mean to say that in such cases the President is helpless to act?[152] For that reason the other opinions in the case at least mentioned the possibility of an undefined residuum of presidential "emergency" power inherent in the grant of "executive" power.[153]

It is possible to understand Black's opinion as resting upon a naive, excessively narrow conception of presidential power. But it is also possible to see Black's opinion as a sophisticated example of alarm-clock formalism. On this conception, the Constitution might be understood as authorizing the President to act when there is either (1) a specific constitutional or statutory grant of authority to act or (2) when there is a genuine national emergency unanticipated by positive law. Embodying the latter constitutional authority directly as an adjudicative standard for courts to employ, however, might cause unacceptable, systemic departures from the constitutional norm itself when the President claims that an "emergency" requires executive action. Institutional incentives will

---

[152] "Whether, despite [the position defended in Black's *Youngstown* opinion,] the President possesses some narrow residuum of lawful authority to act in a genuine national emergency is a troublesome question that has existed since the foundation of the Republic." Henry P. Monaghan, *The Protective Power of the Presidency*, 93 Colum L Rev 1, 10 (1993).

[153] See id at 37 ("Although [*Youngstown*] seems to reject the existence of any executive emergency power, a careful examination of all seven opinions filed does not support such a definitive assertion. An analysis of the concurring and dissenting opinions indicates that a majority of the justices embraced the existence of some residual presidential emergency power").

cause the President to press the boundaries of the "emergency" category to ever-broader extremes, and that will be possible because the category of "emergency" is extraordinarily nebulous and difficult to specify through legal formulations. Cognitive limitations will induce the courts to acquiesce in this expansion. Because the courts will be aware of the limits of their information and of the high risks of error if they frustrate executive action in a genuine emergency, they will adopt a deferential stance.[154]

By contrast, the strategy of the *Youngstown* opinion does not aim to eliminate presidential power in genuine emergencies, but simply to confine the systemic institutional and cognitive pressures for its expansion. Under the *Youngstown* regime, it is predictable that the presence of high stakes will cause the executive and the courts to strain to bring unanticipated contingencies within the language of preexisting constitutional and statutory grants of presidential power,[155] so there will be some departures from the constitutional norm. The hope is that the extent of departure will, however, be less in the *Youngstown* regime than in a regime that attempts to implement the constitutional norm directly as an adjudicative standard. By setting the clock an hour early, we will get up close to the right time even if we oversleep.

The nonjusticiability proposal embodies an analogous decision-making strategy. Suppose that functionalists correctly identify the constitutional norms that govern separation-of-powers questions. Under those norms, interbranch interaction is subject to two important constraints: (1) no branch may act in a way that contradicts specific constitutional provisions; (2) no branch may act in a way

---

[154] See *Woods v Cloyd W. Miller Co.*, 333 US 138, 146 (1948) (Jackson, J, concurring) (describing the federal government's war power as "dangerous" because "[i]t is usually invoked in haste and excitement [and] . . . is interpreted by judges under the influence of the same passions and pressures. Always, [the] Government urges hasty decision to forestall some emergency or serve some purpose and pleads that paralysis will result if its claims to power are denied or their confirmation delayed"). For examples of the phenomenon of judicial deference to executive claims of emergency, see *In re Debs*, 158 US 564, 592 (1894) (approving the grant the President of an injunction, without statutory basis, against a massive railway laborers' strike and accompanying large-scale disturbances that created "a special exigency"); *Korematsu v United States*, 323 US 214, 223–24 (1944) (upholding internment of Japanese-Americans in special military zones in part because "[t]here was evidence of disloyalty on the part of some, the military authorities considered that the need for action was great, and time was short.").

[155] See *Dames & Moore v Regan*, 453 US 654 (1981) (engaging in aggressive construction of federal statutes to find authority for Presidential suspension of private claims against Iran).

that unduly encroaches upon another branch's "core" or "essential" functions.[156] The first constraint is reasonably stable, but the second proves radically unstable when the judiciary passes upon freestanding judicial power claims. In the face of a category—the "judicial power"—as nebulous as the executive's "emergency" power, direct judicial implementation of the second constraint is subject to systemic cognitive pressures that drive judges toward implausible assertions of judicial power.

The nonjusticiability proposal would address this problem by confining judges to ruling upon the scope of judicial power only when that power is embodied in specific constitutional provisions—either (1) provisions that govern the judiciary's authority and protect it from interbranch incursions, such as provisions granting judges life tenure and salary protection, or (2) provisions that guarantee individual liberties integrated with the judicial process, such as the right of jury trial. The proposal is not at all intended to eliminate the causes of judicial overprotection of judicial prerogatives, but simply to control their harmful effects. The empirical calculus behind the proposal is very rough, but it is just another example of alarm-clock formalism. Cognitive pressures will predictably cause expansive readings of specific provisions governing judicial power, perhaps so expansive that some decisions will depart from the constitutional norm of specific-provisions-plus-core-functions. But there will be readings that are not supportable on even the broadest interpretation of a particular provision. Confining the judiciary to the adjudication of specific judicial power provisions and guarantees of individual liberty will result in a legal regime closer to the core-functions norm than the regime that would result from direct judicial application of the norm.

3. *Objections.* One objection to this analysis rests on a type of legal-realist claim about the determinacy of the specific constitutional provisions that would remain justiciable. If those provisions are no more determinate than a nebulous grant of "judicial power," then limiting judges to the adjudication of those provi-

---

[156] See *Public Citizen v United States Dep't of Justice*, 491 US 440, 484–87 (1989) (Kennedy, J, concurring) (advocating similar framework for separation-of-powers adjudication); David A. Strauss, *Article III Courts and the Constitutional Structure*, 65 Ind L J 307, 309–10 (1990) ("Whenever the Supreme Court does not find an answer to a separation of powers issue in the plain language of the Constitution, it resolves the issue by deciding whether a measure has invaded the prerogatives of one of the branches to an unacceptable degree").

sions will change only the rationales of decisions, not their results; judges will simply distend those provisions to cover the same territory now encompassed by sweeping judicial definitions of judicial power. The problem with this objection is that the realist thesis is false. Of course determinacy is a matter of degree—"due process of law" is as open-ended as the "judicial power"—but some constitutional provisions are indeed more specific and more determinate than others. A provision forbidding the legislature to reduce the judges' salaries[157] simply cannot be construed to prohibit, for example, the statutory reopening of final judgments.[158] In general, the passionate legal realist can never be refuted, but the claim of universal indeterminacy need not be taken too seriously.

A second objection might be that the nonjusticiability proposal rests upon a false comparison between an idealized picture of the political process, on one hand, and a jaundiced view of the judicial process on the other.[159] Legislators no less than judges are subject to cognitive distortions and self-serving judgments. If the judges do not have the final say on the limits of their own power, the political process will. Is there any reason to believe that political control of judicial budgets, for example, is better than judicial control of judicial budgets?

But this objection mistakes the baseline from which the analysis begins. The nonjusticiability proposal does not introduce an asymmetry in favor of the political branches, but instead corrects the harmful effects of an asymmetry that is already present and that already runs in the judges' favor. It is a brute fact of American constitutional law, difficult to paper over with dialogic theories of judicial review,[160] that in a straightforward sense the judges have the final say over the scope of legislative power. A judicial decision that invalidates a statute stands unless and until someone enacts a constitutional amendment (which is extremely difficult and almost never happens) or else persuades the judges to change their minds,

---

[157] See US Const, Art III, § 2.

[158] See notes 37–40 and accompanying text (discussing *Plaut v Spendthrift Farm*, 514 US 211 (1995) (invalidating federal statute that retroactively reopened final Article III judgments)).

[159] See Neil K. Komesar, *Imperfect Alternatives: Choosing Institutions in Law, Economics and Public Policy* 6 (1994) (criticizing the fallacy of "single institutionalism").

[160] See, e.g., Barry L. Friedman, *Dialogue and Judicial Review*, 91 Mich L Rev 577 (1993) (denying that judicial review is countermajoritarian).

and although a sufficiently sustained public reaction may indeed change the Court's views in the long term, the change will often come too late for those affected.[161] The question is whether the judges should have the final say not only about the limits of legislative power, but about the limits of their own power as well. The nonjusticiability proposal allocates to the judges the power to check political branch violations of substantive constitutional restrictions. In turn, the proposal allocates to the political branches the power to check the judges' expansion of the judicial power itself. This system of mutual checks is just a rough attempt to "optimize the costs and benefits of judicial independence and judicial accountability,"[162] an optimization problem created by the imperfection of both political and judicial processes.

There is a final, more weighty objection. The nonjusticiability proposal does not address the causes of judicial overprotection of judicial prerogatives, but simply limits the harmful effects of overprotection. So the proposal advances a doctrinal solution to a problem with cognitive and institutional causes. This might be a grievous mismatch. In general, perhaps cognitive and institutional problems require solutions based upon institutional design, rather than legal doctrine. In particular, the nonjusticiability proposal is both addressed to judges and intended to constrain judges. But the same cognitive and institutional pressures that cause judges to construe "the judicial power" expansively might well cause them to reject the proposal; on the evidence of the state cases, the judges do not think they have construed the "judicial power" in an unacceptably broad way. So the proposal, on this view, is self-defeating.

If it is true that doctrinal changes cannot solve cognitive and institutional failings, or that judges will not accept such solutions when the failings are themselves judicial, it is a stunningly important discovery, one that cuts well beyond the present context. In many areas, as previously emphasized, alarm-clock formalism is best understood precisely as a solution to predictable problems of judicial cognition, a solution that is *adopted by the judges themselves when they become aware of distorted judicial cognition.* The cognitive account of the content-neutrality rule in free-speech rule, for example, supposes something like the following story: Judges issue

---

[161] See Ely (cited in note 151) at 45.

[162] David P. Currie, *Separating Judicial Power*, 61 L & Contemp Probs 7 (1998).

insufficiently speech-protective rulings at time 0. At time 1 the (same or other) judges evaluate the previous performance and elect to choose a strong content-neutrality rule in order to shield themselves from recurring cognitive pressures that will afflict the (same or other) judges deciding particular free-speech cases at time 2. The lesson is that "the judges" are not a unity, either over time or across courts, so that there is nothing strange about the possibility that some judges will at some times adopt strategies intended to ward off cognitive failings that will predictably afflict other judges, or even their future selves.

If the objection asserts that judges will never adopt such strategies because they will never become aware of the systemic pressures upon judicial cognition, either their own or that of other judges, the objection overlooks the possibility of learning effects. Judges learn of their cognitive failings, over time, and take steps to correct them. In free-speech cases, for example, it is possible that the content-neutrality rule gained adherents among the Justices because of the flaccidity of the balancing test used in many Vinson Court cases, and early Warren Court cases, concerning the speech rights of unpopular groups.[163] In separation-of-powers law, the Court's recent reinstatement of formal rules for distinguishing "principal" federal officers from "inferior" federal officers, for purposes of the Appointments Clause, is plausibly seen as a reaction to the disastrous consequences of the fact-specific approach taken in *Morrison v Olson*.[164] There is no a priori reason to exclude the possibility of a similar judicial reassessment of the courts' performance in deciding freestanding judicial power claims.

A narrower version of the objection would hold simply that where the judiciary's institutional self-interest is the particular cause of the decision-making distortions at issue, there is no reason to expect the judiciary to adopt (or abide by) doctrinal solutions.

---

[163] Compare *Dennis v United States*, 341 US 494, 510 (1951) (upholding convictions of communists, for conspiracy to overthrow the government, under a balancing test that asked "whether the gravity of the 'evil,' discounted by its improbability, justifies [the challenged] invasion of free speech as . . . necessary to avoid the danger") with *Brandenburg v Ohio*, 395 US 444 (1969) (announcing stiffer doctrinal protections for speech advocating unlawful action).

[164] See Nick Bravin, Note, *Is Morrison v. Olson Still Good Law? The Court's New Appointments Clause Jurisprudence*, 98 Colum L Rev 1103 (1998) ("*Edmond v. United States* [117 S Ct 1573 (1997)] . . . departed from the balancing approach [to Appointments Clause questions] employed in *Morrison* and articulated in its stead a bright-line test").

Even this version, however, assumes that the expansion of judicial power is what judges maximize. But that is a notorious puzzle;[165] some models depict (even unelected) judges as maximizing leisure, popularity, or some other variable, rather than simply maximizing the scope of their constitutional jurisdiction.[166] A simple model of judges as jurisdiction-maximizers has trouble explaining why judges would adopt so many self-imposed limitations on judicial power, such as the political question doctrine and the doctrines of standing, ripeness and mootness, and abstention. Accordingly, the critical mechanism discernable in the state judicial power cases cannot be personal or institutional self-interest in any narrow sense. The critical mechanisms appear to be cognitive, not motivational, and there is no particular reason to think that judges would be hostile to corrective changes in doctrine once they become aware of the cognitive problems.

Moreover, the alternative solutions are probably worse. The principal alternative to a doctrinal solution (such as the nonjusticiability proposal) is an institutional solution, such as changing the selection of judges, their tenure,[167] or the voting rules they use.[168] Such changes certainly might diminish concerns about the problem of freestanding judicial power claims, by enhancing political checks upon the judiciary; I shall take up this point in Part IV. But the large-scale, institutional character of these restructurings makes them dramatically overbroad as solutions to the narrower problem of judicial overprotection of the judiciary's core functions, so they must be justified, if at all, by some larger position on questions of institutional design. A shift from a life-tenured judiciary to an elected judiciary, for example, might eliminate judicial overprotection in freestanding judicial power challenges, but only at the cost of reducing judicial independence generally, with spillover

---

[165] See generally Lawrence Baum, *The Puzzle of Judicial Behavior* (1997) (examining competing accounts of the judicial utility function).

[166] See Richard A. Posner, *What Do Judges Maximize? (The Same Thing Everybody Else Does)*, 3 S Ct Econ Rev 1 (1993) (arguing that judges maximize not only or even chiefly their political power, but rather variables such as leisure time, professional respect, and so forth).

[167] On elected judges, see Steven P. Croley, *The Majoritarian Difficulty: Elective Judiciaries and the Rule of Law*, 62 U Chi L Rev 689 (1995).

[168] Compare Levinson, *Limiting Judicial Review by Act of Congress*, 23 Cal L Rev 591 (1935) (advocating statutory requirement that the Supreme Court may invalidate federal statutes only by vote of a supermajority of the Justices).

effects to substantive constitutional law, statutory interpretation, and so on. Those spillover effects might or might not be desirable, but the changes are poorly tailored to the more confined problems presented by adjudication of freestanding judicial power claims.

C. CONSEQUENCES OF THE NONJUSTICIABILITY PROPOSAL IN THE STATE COURTS

Here I shall sketch the consequences of the proposal for the state courts. Many of the state cases, especially those decided in the recent wave of tort reform litigation, cannot be squared with the proposal, although some might be reconstructed as cases about specific constitutional provisions. In general, the proposal would lop off much of the excessive growth in judicial power without exposing state judiciaries to political branch seizure of their core functions.

1. *Specific provisions governing judicial authority.* The nonjusticiability proposal is a technique of judicial self-restraint. As such, the proposal can be trumped by a constitutional command. Specific provisions that protect judicial authority or allocate lawmaking functions to the judiciary do not undermine the internal logic of the nonjusticiability proposal, but they do restrict its domain. If some particular, expansive conception of judicial authority is itself constitutionally mandated, on the best reading of the state constitution, there can be no objection that judicial implementation of the provision *over*protects the judiciary's core functions (although the provision might be objectionable from the standpoint of normative political theory).

Consider one sort of provision commonly found in the judicial articles of state constitutions: provisions that authorize state supreme courts to promulgate rules of judicial procedure or evidence. The state courts have, as previously described,[169] developed an active body of decisions striking down legislative modification of procedural rules on the ground that the legislature has encroached upon judicial functions. Under the nonjusticiability proposal, these cases could be litigated, if at all, only as cases about the best interpretation of the rule-making provisions themselves. Because state judicial articles vary on this question—some confer

---

[169] See notes 68–83 and accompanying text.

exclusive rule-making authority upon the judiciary, some confer authority subject to statutory override, and so forth[170]—decisions will vary. But in all cases the salutary consequence would be to confine the constitutional argument to a focal text that can be construed to protect judicial authority no more broadly than the broadest reasonable interpretation of that text.

The previously discussed New Hampshire decision supplies an example. That decision advised the legislature that a proposed bill broadening the categories of admissible sexual assault evidence would be invalid. Framed as a separation-of-powers case, the decision ultimately resorted to the sweeping position that "[a] court's constitutional function to independently decide controversies is impaired if it must depend on, or is limited by, another branch of government in determining and evaluating the facts of controversies it must adjudicate."[171] A narrower ground could have been achieved, under the nonjusticiability proposal, by casting the case solely as an interpretation of the rule-making provision granting the Court authority to promulgate procedural and evidentiary rules. Structure and precedent supported the idea that the rule-making provision might confer exclusive authority. In that case the legislation would be straightforwardly unconstitutional if it touched upon procedural or evidentiary subjects—a theory the court noticed, discussed, and then erroneously inflated into a grandiose account of the judicial function.

2. *Individual rights.* The same structure obtains when statutes arguably encroach upon individual rights. An example involves the right to jury trial. A neat contrast to the Illinois decision in *Best v Taylor Machine Works*, which held a cap on noneconomic damages unconstitutional on separation-of-powers grounds, is the Washington Supreme Court's ruling on the same issue in *Sofie v Fibreboard Corp.*[172] That court flirted briefly with the separation of powers, but then decided the case squarely on the ground that the damages cap invaded the right to jury trial.

To be sure, even the holding is dubious. The jury-trial right is a right to have the jury, rather than a judge, determine the facts

---

[170] See Parness (cited in note 52) at 67 (noting divergence in state constitutional provisions on the rulemaking authority of the judiciary).

[171] *Opinion of the Justices*, 688 A2d at 1006.

[172] See *Sofie v Fibreboard Corp.*, 771 P2d 711 (Wash 1989) (en banc).

and apply the law to those facts. And the statutory-damages cap is part of the applicable law. To say the jury has the authority to award damages in excess of the cap is no more plausible than to say that the jury has the authority to enforce a cause of action previously abolished by statute.[173] But at least the Washington Supreme Court did not hold, as the Illinois Supreme Court seems to have, that there is some substantive "judicial power" to establish common-law rules and accompanying remedies *immune from legislative revision*—a holding that applies in a far broader range of circumstances and contains more expansive, generative potential. For example, may courts grant equitable relief, in circumstances forbidden by statute, on the ground that the "judicial power" both authorizes the relief and condemns the statute as an unconstitutional encroachment? Under the nonjusticiability proposal, such indefensible expansions are precluded, but individual-rights provisions and associated judicial functions will (as in the Washington decision) receive robust protection.

In broad, the rough conclusion should be that application of the nonjusticiability proposal to the state courts would have desirable effects. Declaring freestanding judicial power claims to be nonjusticiable would prune the most outlandish excesses of judicial self-protection while leaving in place ample protections of both core judicial functions and related individual liberties.

IV. THE JUDICIAL POWER IN THE FEDERAL COURTS

This Part transposes the analysis of Parts II and III from the state judiciaries to the federal judiciary. I will suggest that the cognitive and institutional mechanisms evident in the state cases illuminate the small set of federal judicial power cases, bringing to light overprotective tendencies similar to those seen in the state courts. The more pointed question is whether federal courts

---

[173] See Jennifer Freisen, *State Constitutional Law: Litigating Individual Rights, Claims, and Defenses* § 6-3(d)(1) (2d ed 1996) ("The jury trial right is perhaps the least plausible of the various grounds for voiding legislation that alters remedies. . . . [T]he right to jury trial means that the jury decides all matters of fact made relevant by existing law; it does not mean that even after the legislature has modified the law, a party has the right to put to a jury any question he or she wishes"); Parness (cited in note 52) at 72 (criticizing the cases striking down statutes on jury-trial grounds, because "the jury only infrequently determines the substantive law. Typically the jury only applies the facts the jury finds to the law that others determine.").

should declare freestanding judicial power challenges to federal statutes nonjusticiable. I will argue that they should, although the case for that position is more difficult than in the state court setting.

Section A describes the federal courts' adjudication of freestanding judicial power claims. In general, the record is mixed. Federal courts have not distended the constitutional grant of "judicial power" to such an extreme as have the state courts, although several of the most prominent federal decisions display the same overprotective tendencies at work in the state cases. Extending the nonjusticiability proposal to the federal system would thus have some bite, but it would not prove radically destabilizing. Some of the prominent cases would have to be jettisoned. Many of the basic rules governing federal judicial authority, however, would survive as interpretations of specific constitutional provisions.

Section B examines the normative case for applying the nonjusticiability proposal in the federal system. Institutional differences between state and federal judicial systems affect both the relative frequency of overprotective decisions in the two systems and the relative magnitude of the resulting harms. Taken as a whole, these factors suggest that, while federal courts may be somewhat less susceptible to the systemic pressures discussed in Parts II and III than are state courts, the instances of overprotection that do occur in the federal system are more harmful because less easily corrected by the lawmaking process. On net, then, the nonjusticiability proposal might plausibly be extended to the federal system.

A. OVERPROTECTION IN THE FEDERAL COURTS

The analysis of Parts II and III suggests two critical descriptive questions about the federal caselaw: Do federal courts overprotect the federal judicial power? What would the landscape of federal separation-of-powers doctrine look like under a regime that declared those claims nonjusticiable?

The answer to the first question is yes, as I shall illustrate below; in several contexts, federal courts have announced sweeping conceptions of judicial prerogatives in decisions that display the same cognitive mechanisms and failures seen in the state cases. There are some important qualifications and exceptions to this answer, however, and I shall take them up subsequently. As for the second question, applying the nonjusticiability proposal in the federal system would alter the contours of federal judicial power doctrine in important ways. Claims about federal judicial prerogatives that are currently judged by reference to open-ended notions of essential judicial power would be transformed into ordinary legal questions about the interpretation of provisions in Article III that protect and regulate the federal judiciary, and of provisions both in Article III and elsewhere that guarantee individual liberties. On the whole, the new regime would capture many of the benefits promised by the nonjusticiability proposal. Some indefensible extensions of the federal judicial power would be pruned away, but many of the current precedents could fairly be reconstructed as interpretations of specific constitutional provisions.

To illustrate the operation of overprotective mechanisms in the federal caselaw and the effects of the nonjusticiability proposal in the federal system, this section examines three prominent areas of federal doctrine concerning the scope of judicial power: judicial rulings on the power of Congress to assign judicial business to non–Article III federal tribunals, to abrogate final judicial judgments, and to prescribe rules of decision for pending cases. Decisions in all three areas display the overprotective mechanisms identified in the state cases, although the tendency is less marked than in the states.

1. *Non–Article III federal tribunals.* Start with Justice Brennan's plurality opinion in *Northern Pipeline*,[174] which invalidated Congress's creation of bankruptcy courts staffed by judges lacking Article III's guarantees of life tenure and salary protection. The opinion began from a classic functionalist premise, Madison's dictum that the core command of the separation of powers is that the whole power of two branches must not be combined in the same hands.[175] But Brennan's opinion framed the legal issue in a curious way: "The question presented is whether the assignment by Congress to bankruptcy judges of the jurisdiction granted [in the challenged statute] violates *Art. III* of the Constitution" (emphasis added).[176] It is unclear what it might mean to say that a statute

---

[174] 458 US 50 (1982) (plurality opinion).

[175] See id at 52.

[176] Id.

violates a whole constitutional article, but the basic idea of the opinion seemed to be that the statute effected an "unwarranted encroachment[ ] upon the judicial power of the United States"[177]— a classic freestanding judicial power claim.

From these largely functionalist premises Brennan developed a rule-bound retrenchment of the doctrine concerning congressional authority to assign cases to non–Article III tribunals. The baseline constitutional command is that Congress may not assign jurisdiction over the cases and controversies mentioned in Article III to non–Article III courts—that is, courts staffed by judges who lack the signature protections of life tenure and salary protection. Brennan had to acknowledge that across a large range of governmental activity Congress had traditionally done just that. But he attempted to cabin these areas into three "narrow" categories (territorial courts, courts-martial, and cases involving public rights) in which "the grant of power to the Legislative and Executive branches was historically and constitutionally . . . exceptional."[178] Brennan's real objection was not that the bankruptcy statute effected a departure from the constitutional baseline he had identified, but that it effected a *novel* departure from that baseline.

Commentators were quick to leap upon the logical flaw. As Paul Bator put it in a famous demolition of the *Northern Pipeline* plurality, "Brennan's account is satisfying only if these exceptions can themselves be constitutionally legitimated. Why are these exceptions, and no others, in fact to be allowed?"[179] That criticism resembles the analysis in Part II above, because the fallacy that pervades the *Northern Pipeline* plurality opinion is also prominent in the state cases. The *Northern Pipeline* plurality generated an implausibly sweeping rule of judicial authority from functionalist premises by tacitly condemning novel assignments of adjudicative authority to non–Article III tribunals—that is, by equating customary practices with a constitutional command. That position rapidly proved unsustainable because it extended Article III au-

---

[177] Id at 84.

[178] Id at 64.

[179] Paul M. Bator, *The Constitution as Architecture: Legislative and Administrative Courts Under Article III*, 65 Ind L J 233, 244 (1989). See also Martin H. Redish, *Legislative Courts, Administrative Agencies, and the Northern Pipeline Decision*, 1983 Duke L J 197, 201 (describing "Justice Brennan's guidelines for determining the proper division of power among Article I and Article III courts" as "unacceptable").

thority too far beyond any reasonable conception of core judicial functions; the next two important cases in the area, *Thomas v Union Carbide*[180] and *CFTC v Schor*,[181] accordingly repudiated the *Northern Pipeline* plurality and its categories.[182]

Despite all this fuss, nothing in *Northern Pipeline* turns on the large questions about judicial power and judicial independence that the plurality sought to answer, and it is a major advantage of the nonjusticiability proposal that it would at least require asking the right questions in this line of cases. The two prosaic questions of constitutional interpretation at issue in the case were (1) whether, when, and to what degree the so-called Heads of Jurisdiction in Article III—the jurisdictional grants to Article III courts of authority to decide "cases" and "controversies" in various categories defined by subject matter or by party status—are implicitly exclusive, in the sense that they permit only the life-tenured, salary-protected federal officers mentioned in Article III (rather than federal administrative officers) to hear and determine cases in those categories, either as an initial or a final matter; and (2) whether and how the Due Process Clause, which may sometimes require a hearing before an Article III officer,[183] is relevant to question 1. Nothing in those questions turns upon what sort of power—"judicial" or "executive"—the tribunals that hear cases mentioned in the Heads of Jurisdiction are exercising, so Article III's initial clause vesting the "judicial power" in certain tribunals and not others is, in this sense, irrelevant to the case.[184] The nonjusticiability proposal, by remov-

---

[180] 473 US 568 (1985).

[181] 478 US 833 (1986).

[182] But see note 217 and accompanying text (discussing the partial resurrection of Brennan's position in *Granfinanciera, S.A. v Nordberg*, 492 US 33 (1989)).

[183] See *Crowell v Benson*, 285 US 22, 77 (Brandeis, J, dissenting).

[184] Compare A. Michael Froomkin, *The Imperial Presidency's New Vestments*, 88 Nw U L Rev 1346, 1353 (1994):

> Even on purely textual grounds it cannot be seriously suggested that the federal judiciary would lack the authority to decide cases if there were no Vesting Clause in Article III. One does not have to search very hard or far in Article III to find a firm textual basis for the federal courts' authority to act: it lies in the Heads of Jurisdiction.

For further debate on this claim, compare Steven G. Calabresi, *The Vesting Clauses as Power Grants*, 88 Nw U L Rev 1377 (1994) (arguing that the Article III Vesting Clause is not superfluous) with A. Michael Froomkin, *Still Naked After All These Words*, 88 Nw U L Rev 1420 (1994) (criticizing Calabresi's position). The position advanced here, that federal courts should declare the Article III Vesting Clause nonjusticiable as a freestanding restriction on federal legislative power, is a position concerned with institutional design rather

ing from the case the freestanding judicial power claim upon which the *Northern Pipeline* plurality focused, would tie the issue to specific constitutional provisions and would dispel the overheated idea that all novel jurisdictional assignments to non–Article III tribunals must necessarily be unconstitutional.

2. *Congressional revision of Article III judgments.* A similar analysis applies to *Plaut v Spendthrift Farm*,[185] the Court's most recent decision to invalidate an Act of Congress as a usurpation of federal judicial power. *Plaut* established the flat rule that legislation may never require courts to reopen damages judgments that had previously become final under then-obtaining statutory rules of finality. But *Plaut* combined two different types of justification to reach that holding, a combination that must be unbundled to get a clear view of *Plaut*'s significance for the nonjusticiability proposal. One type of justification in *Plaut* is the explicitly "prophylactic" strategy previously described—the Court's position that, even if it is sometimes impossible to discern any threat to separation-of-powers concerns when Congress instructs courts to reopen a final judgment, nonetheless "the doctrine of separation of powers is a structural safeguard rather than a remedy to be applied only when specific harm, or risk of specific harm, can be identified."[186] But the Court also offered a very different justification: that the flat rule against abrogation of judgments was not at all prophylactic, but rather was simply the best reading of the originalist sources.[187] On the latter view, the anti-abrogation rule is not a second-best device of overprotection, but simply an ordinary, first-best interpretation of the Constitution.

The nonjusticiability proposal bears on these two different justifications in different ways. To the extent that *Plaut* rests upon the first justification, the nonjusticiability proposal suggests that the Court's prophylactic strategy was unnecessary, even counterproductive. There is little reason to fear that case-specific inquiry would systematically underweight the judiciary's structural control over final judgments, and overweigh the exigencies alleged in sup-

---

than with a first-best reading of the Constitution; it does *not* entail that Froomkin's position is correct on the constitutional merits.

[185] 514 US 211 (1995).

[186] Id at 239.

[187] See id at 219–25.

port of the legislation. The more realistic fear is that a strong pro-phylactic rule will merely reinforce the systemic pressures that would operate in the judiciary's favor in any event. Exhibit A is the analysis in Justice Breyer's concurrence, precisely the analysis that provoked the Court's remarks on prophylaxis: Breyer both rejected the flat anti-abrogation rule and conducted a detailed fac-tual inquiry into the statute's background history, finding suspi-cious circumstances surrounding the statute's enactment that sug-gested a legislative attempt to "single out" particular individuals.[188] Breyer's vote to invalidate the statute after case-specific review provides a counterexample to the Court's fear that "low walls and vague distinctions will not be judicially defensible in the heat of interbranch conflict."[189] Nor was the majority itself immune from the overprotective fallacies so prevalent in the state cases. The opinion complements its affirmative originalist evidence with the negative suggestion that the statute's novelty might itself be a pow-erful indicator of unconstitutionality, because Congress's "pro-longed reticence would be amazing if such interference were not understood to be constitutionally proscribed."[190] That is some-thing like an originalist version of the idea, advanced by the Illinois Supreme Court in *Best v Taylor Machine* and by the plurality opin-ion in *Marathon*, that all novel regulation of judicial authority is constitutionally suspect.[191]

To the extent that *Plaut* rests straightforwardly on the second justification—a substantive reading of the Constitution that for-bids legislative abrogation of final judgments—the nonjusticiability proposal puts in question whether the anti-abrogation doctrine is traceable to any specific constitutional protection of judicial au-thority. The Court's originalist evidence was powerful; the harder question is whether and how that evidence related to anything in the constitutional text.[192] The Court described its holding as a logi-cal consequence of Article III's vesting of the "judicial Power" in the federal courts. That is hardly the only textual question, or even

---

[188] See id at 243 (Breyer, J, concurring).

[189] Id at 239.

[190] Id at 230.

[191] See notes 62–67, 174–84, and accompanying text.

[192] Compare Ernest A. Young, *Alden v Maine and the Jurisprudence of Structure*, 41 Wm & Mary L Rev 1601 (2000) (criticizing originalist decisions not linked to constitutional text).

the most obviously relevant one. A more tractable question would be whether the power to issue final judgments is a necessary incident of the judiciary's specific Article III power to decide "Cases" and "Controversies." It is a perfectly intelligible position to say that the power to decide a case is meaningless if the legislature may force the judiciary to re-decide that very case, perhaps as often as necessary; and the strong originalist evidence that the Court marshaled for its anti-abrogation rule does indeed suggest that the founding generation thought an anti-abrogation rule to be a necessary implication of the case-deciding power.[193] So the *Plaut* anti-abrogation rule would remain quite plausible, at least in originalist terms, if the opinion were recast in terms of Article III's specific textual reference to "cases" and "controversies," rather than in terms of the judicial power.

3. *Miller v French and the Prison Litigation Reform Act*. Finally, last Term's decision in *Miller v French*[194] illustrates the current limits of freestanding judicial power claims in the federal system. The background to *Miller* was a remarkably aggressive decision of the Seventh Circuit, titled *French v Duckworth*[195] in the lower court, that struck down a portion of the Prison Litigation Reform Act of 1995. The Act curtails the prospective relief, principally injunctive orders and consent decrees, that federal judges may grant in prison-reform litigation.[196] One provision of the Act says that if a state moves to modify or terminate an injunction for lack of compliance with the Act's new substantive standards,[197] and the court fails to rule upon the motion within a specified time (either thirty or ninety days), then the underlying prospective relief that binds the state is automatically stayed until the court rules.[198] The Seventh Circuit panel held that the automatic stay provision effected

---

[193] See *Plaut*, 514 US at 219–225

[194] 530 US 327 (June 19, 2000).

[195] See *French v Duckworth*, 178 F3d 437 (7th Cir 1999), reversed sub nom. *Miller v French* (US June 19, 2000) (No. 99-224, 99–582).

[196] See 10 Stat 1321–66 to 1321–77, codified at 18 USC § 3626 (1994 ed, Supp IV).

[197] The Act specifies that a court "shall not grant or approve any prospective relief unless the court finds that such relief is narrowly drawn, extends no further than necessary to correct the violation of a Federal right, and is the least intrusive means necessary to correct the violation of the Federal right." 18 USC § 3626(a)(1)(A). State officials may move to terminate any prospective relief, including existing orders, that do not meet this standard. See 18 USC § 3626(b)(2).

[198] See 18 USC § 3626(e)(2)–(e)(3).

"an unconstitutional legislative encroachment into the powers reserved to the judiciary."[199]

The lower court, and the prisoners' brief in the Supreme Court,
advanced two complementary theories to invalidate the automatic
stay provision. The first theory, based on *Plaut*, was that the provision

> places the power to review judicial decisions outside of the judi-
> ciary: it is a self-executing legislative determination that a spe-
> cific decree of a federal court [i.e. the underlying consent de-
> cree] must be set aside at least for a period of time, no matter
> what the equities, no matter what the urgency of keeping it in
> place.[200]

The second theory was that the provision "violate[d] the principle articulated in *United States v Klein*"; the principle was said
to be that "Congress does not have the power to impose a rule of
decision for pending judicial cases, apart from its power to change
the underlying applicable law."[201] (In fact, only the first clause of
that formulation is found in *Klein* itself; the second clause adds
a qualifier recently adopted by the Court.[202]) The automatic stay
provision in the Act "addresses what should happen during the
pendency of the case. For that time period, the statute does mandate a particular rule of decision: the prospective relief must be
terminated."[203] The panel held that stays of an underlying order
for prospective relief, when a ruling had not been produced by
the deadline, would be considered on a case-by-case basis under
"equitable" standards developed by the judiciary.

After rejecting an implausible proposal by the Solicitor General
to avoid the constitutional issues through statutory interpretation,[204] the Supreme Court reversed, holding the automatic stay
provision constitutional. Doctrinally, the *Miller* opinion adds very
little to existing precedent. The Court rejected the *Plaut* claim because *Plaut* had already stated clearly that federal statutes could

---

[199] *French*, 178 F3d at 446.

[200] Id.

[201] Id.

[202] See *Robertson v Seattle Audubon*, 503 US 429, 432–33 (1992) (stating that, whatever its
precise limits, *Klein* does not apply when the challenged statute changes applicable law).

[203] *French*, 178 F3d at 446.

[204] See *Miller*, 530 US at 336–41.

not abrogate final damages judgments but could alter the future effect of injunctive decrees.[205] *Miller* merely applied that rule to a statute that regulates a controversial area of public law. The Court rejected the *Klein* claim because the delphic pronouncement that Congress may not "prescribe rules of decision to the judicial department, in cases pending before it" applies only when Congress has failed to change the applicable law.[206] Here the Act had indeed changed the law by creating new substantive standards for courts to apply in prison-reform litigation.[207] The *Miller* opinion, however, assiduously avoided the most significant judicial power questions suggested by the case and by Justice Souter's dissent. The Court declined to address whether the Act's new substantive standards for injunctive relief—the provisions that do the statute's "heavy lifting," in the Court's words—encroached upon the judicial power.[208] The Court noted, but did not resolve, the question whether Article III might ever be violated by legislative imposition of time limits upon judicial decision making.[209] And the Court shunted aside the claim that the Act's relatively short time limit for judicial decision deprived the prisoners of a meaningful opportunity to be heard, in violation of Fifth Amendment Due Process.[210]

More interesting than the narrow holding of *Miller* is the larger sequence of the *Miller v French* litigation. The opinions of the Seventh Circuit and the Supreme Court illustrate both the forces that push federal courts toward sweeping overprotection of judicial prerogatives and also the mixed character of the ultimate pattern of decisions at the federal level. The Seventh Circuit decision displays all the symptoms of judicial self-protection, and overprotection, that appear in the state cases. The claim that the automatic stay provision violates the separation of powers because it establishes a rule, rather than leaving stays to the judiciary's equitable discretion, illustrates the characteristic judicial appreciation of the benefits of judge-made standards and discounting of the benefits of stat-

---

[205] See *Plaut*, 511 US at 232; *Miller*, 530 US at 341–44.

[206] See *Robertson*, 503 US at 432–33.

[207] See *Miller*, 530 US 344–45.

[208] Id at 345–46.

[209] Id.

[210] Id.

utory rules. Noting the benefits of "flexibility" in ruling on stays, the panel complained that the automatic stay provision would operate no matter what the "equities." Plausibly, however, the Act was itself passed because Congress thought the judges' perceptions of the equities to be systematically miscalibrated in structural reform cases. A group of judges dissenting from denial of en banc review suggested that Congress imposed a regime of strict time limits in the Act out of concern that federal judges had showed undue regard for their own work product (injunctions and decrees) in prison cases, and because case-specific treatment of the issues had produced long delays as judges declined to dispose expeditiously of states' motions to terminate prison-conditions decrees.[211]

The Supreme Court's subsequent opinion trimmed the lower court's excesses, but did little to check the impetus toward overprotection of the judicial power that is illustrated by *Plaut*, *Klein*, and other decisions. As for *Plaut*, that decision had already created a sweeping and expressly overprotective rule. *Miller* confirmed the location and dimensions of that rule, but did nothing to curtail it. Had *Miller* come out the other way on the point, of course, then both legal and equitable judgments would be forbidden subjects for congressional intervention. To say that the Act's automatic stay provision did not violate *Plaut*, then, is only to say that not every legislative regulation of federal judicial judgments violates the Constitution.

As for *Klein*, the *Miller* opinion failed to solve or even explain the basic puzzle of that decision. The puzzle is that if *Klein*'s pronouncements are taken seriously, the decision can be made applicable to any statute at all by describing the statute as one that directs the judiciary to rule in accordance with legislative instructions. So the Court has labored to identify some extra test, restriction, or factor that can coherently separate *Klein* violations from ordinary legislation. To date none of these efforts has succeeded. *Robertson v Seattle Audubon*,[212] for example, held that *Klein* does not apply when the underlying legislation amends applicable law. But that test fails to make *Klein* more coherent. Rather, it effectively abolishes the decision, because the *Robertson* test can always be invoked to defeat a *Klein* challenge. Any statute, even one that in

---

[211] *French v Duckworth*, 178 F3d at 448–49 (Easterbrook, J, dissenting).
[212] 503 US 429, 432–33 (1992).

terms instructs courts to decide claim C for Party P rather than Party Q, can be described as changing the applicable law.[213] If the new statute changes the law for only one case, *P v Q*, then it may be objectionable under constitutional rules that specify the minimum acceptable scope of legislative action—rules such as the Equal Protection Clause or the Bill of Attainder Clause—but according to *Robertson* it does not intrude upon the judicial power.[214] None of this suggests that there is some superior alternative to *Robertson*. The Court's failure to fashion a sensible test to implement *Klein* may simply show that *Klein* says nothing coherent about judicial power and should be ignored. At present, *Klein* remains an unstable land mine of judicial power doctrine; the *Miller* Court sidestepped the mine but missed an opportunity to disarm it.

In the end, although the *Miller* Court rejected a particularly aggressive application of *Plaut* and *Klein*, the sweeping declarations about the "judicial power" in those cases, and the potential applicability of *Klein* to any statute, will tend to provoke unwarranted extensions of the judicial power by other courts. Many of the state cases, for example, erratically invoke *Klein* to invalidate statutory rules,[215] and already a substantial body of state precedent extends *Plaut* in various directions.[216] The Seventh Circuit decision in *French v Duckworth* transposed those themes to the federal system; despite the correction in *Miller*, similar decisions should be expected in the future.

B. COMPARING STATE AND FEDERAL JUDICIAL SYSTEMS

In light of this background, the case for extending the nonjusticiability proposal to the federal system requires qualification,

---

[213] Compare Lawrence G. Sager, *Klein's First Principle: A Proposed Solution*, 86 Geo L J 2525, 2527 (1998) (noting that "*Robertson*, while paying nominal obeisance to *Klein*, in a unanimous stroke discarded the distinction [between forms of lawmaking] upon which *Klein*'s first principle seems to depend").

[214] Compare *Plaut*, 514 US at 227–28, 238–40 & n 9 (rejecting suggestions that the breadth of a statute's application is relevant to the judicial-power question, whatever its relevance to questions such as a challenge under the Bill of Attainder Clause).

[215] See notes 79–83 and accompanying text. The state analogue to *Miller*, although reaching the opposite result, is *Fowler v Fowler*, 984 SW2d 508 (Mo 1999) (statute that treated judicial failure to issue decision before forty-five-day deadline as equivalent to denial of motion held to violate separation of legislative and judicial powers).

[216] See note 88 (collecting cases).

because the small number of federal cases makes even the most modest generalizations contestable, and because decisions such as *Miller* emphasize that the federal courts' record on freestanding judicial power claims is not uniformly overprotective. *Miller* and *Robertson* reject claims based on *Plaut* and *Klein*, while cases such as *CFTC v Schor* undermined *Northern Pipeline*'s broad conception of federal judicial authority over federal claims (although that conception regained some of the lost ground in the later decision in *Granfinanciera S.A. v Nordberg*).[217]

The fairest summary is that the federal courts' record on freestanding judicial power claims is mixed. The frequency of overprotection is not so great as in the state systems, and perhaps the degree is not either; the outliers among the federal cases do not lie so very far out as the Illinois decision in *Best v Taylor Machine Works*.[218] But the mixed character of the record is only half the story. The normative question whether the nonjusticiability proposal should be extended to the federal system turns not only upon the frequency of systemic harms from the federal judiciary's overprotection of judicial prerogatives, but also upon the magnitude of the harms that result when overprotection does occur. Accordingly, this section considers institutional differences between the federal and state judicial systems and argues that the net harms from judicial overprotection are plausibly as great in the federal system as in state systems.

State and federal judicial systems differ in many respects. Four of the most important points of contrast are the different rules of judicial selection and tenure, differing caseloads and administrative responsibilities, the presence of courts with general common-law jurisdiction in the states but not in the federal system, and the greater difficulty of amending the federal constitution. If these differences either made it impossible to compare freestanding judicial power claims in the two systems, or else suggested that in the federal system there is no cause for concern about the systemic effects of judicial overprotection of judicial authority, then there would

---

[217] 492 US 33 (1989) (described in note 4). See Fallon et al, *The Federal Courts and the Federal System* (cited in note 7) at 433 (noting that, until *Granfinanciera* confused the issue, many observers thought that the Court had definitively rejected the categorical approach of Justice Brennan's plurality opinion in *Northern Pipeline*).

[218] See notes 54–68 and accompanying text.

be little reason to extend the nonjusticiability proposal to the federal system. I shall argue that none of the differences support those conclusions; there is no general reason to think that the nonjusticiability proposal is suitable only to state judicial systems.

1. *Judicial selection and tenure.* In the federal system, of course, judges take office by executive nomination and senatorial confirmation, and then serve for life (with constitutional immunity from any reduction of their initial salary). A significant fraction of state judges, by contrast, are once and future political candidates. In thirty-eight of the fifty states, judges are electorally accountable in some fashion. Within the group of thirty-eight, twenty-three states require judges to stand both for initial election and periodic reelection, while in fifteen states judges are initially appointed by a state's governor and then periodically stand for reelection. Only twelve states have any judges who enjoy life tenure after appointment.[219] The contrast is overdrawn, because in many state judicial elections the low visibility of issues and legal requirements of nonpartisan ballots for judicial elections ensure that state judges are routinely reelected. But commentators have discerned a trend toward increasingly contentious judicial elections,[220] and by comparison to the security of the life-tenured federal judge the prospect of any sort of election probably affects state judicial behavior to some degree.

This comparison suggests that judicial overprotection of judicial authority is at least as troubling in the federal system as in state systems. Judicial overprotection of judicial prerogatives poses the standard countermajoritarian difficulty in an aggravated form: it poses not only the usual question of the legitimacy of judicial review of democratic outcomes but also the question why judges should, unlike other institutions, be the arbiters of their own power. This argument does not rest on any contentious preference for unrestricted majoritarianism, so long as judicial "overprotection" is defined by reference to an overlapping consensus of interpretive approaches, as discussed in Part II. If anything, then, this contrast supports applying the nonjusticiability proposal in the federal system a fortiori.

The picture is more complicated, however. If the lack of politi-

---

[219] These figures are drawn from Croley (cited in note 167) at 725 & nn 110–14.

[220] See id at 697 & n 24.

cal checks in the federal system makes overprotection of judicial prerogatives by federal judges more damaging, the presence of political checks may—paradoxically enough—make overprotection of political prerogatives by state judges more *likely*. The standard assumption in the judicial-review literature has been that the prospect of reelection reduces state judges' independence from current politics, but there is an offsetting effect as well. Elected state judges possess something of a political constituency (at least a greater constituency then unelected federal judges do), and the stamp of public legitimacy that comes with election may just as easily embolden courts as enfeeble them. So there are crosscutting positive effects of varying selection and tenure rules. It is at least clear, however, that federal judges enjoy their offices for life and during good behavior, so in the federal system it is more difficult to correct overprotective decisions through the process of judicial selection than it is in the states.

2. *Caseloads and administrative responsibilities.* State courts hear many more cases than federal courts do, both in absolute and in relative terms, and the types of cases they hear are different as well. Both factors may affect the pressures at work in judicial power cases. First, "[s]tate courts, by conservative estimates, conduct ninety-five percent of the judicial business in this country."[221] In 1993, for example, 280,000 new cases were filed in the federal courts. In the same year the state courts received 35 million new filings, not counting an additional 55 million traffic and ordinance violations. Second, the cases state courts hear are heterogeneous and often quasi-administrative, especially at the lower reaches of the state court hierarchy. State trial courts often administer dockets that are, in effect, social service programs or adjuncts of law enforcement. Family courts, juvenile courts, drug courts, traffic courts, and other specialized tribunals are routine in state court systems.[222]

---

[221] Ellen A. Peters, *Getting Away from the Federal Paradigm: Separation of Powers in State Courts,* 81 Minn L Rev 1543, 1545 (1997); see also Roy A. Schotland, *Elective Judges' Campaign Financing: Are State Judges' Robes the Emperor's Clothes of American Democracy,* 2 J L & Pol 57, 77 (1985) (reporting that state courts handle about 98% of national judicial business).

[222] See Baar (cited in note 90) at 144 (detailing "the increasing variety of programs and personnel within the ambit of state trial courts"); Peters (cited in note 221) at 1562 ("Unlike federal courts . . . state courts also administer social services agendas that transcend classic judicial responsibilities").

This sort of quasi-administrative business is largely foreign to the federal courts. The federal judicial system, with its relatively trim vertical hierarchy of courts and relative paucity of specialized tribunals, is the consequence of the greater jurisdiction of federal administrative agencies and legislative courts. The federal judiciary has, both before and since the New Deal, acquiesced in the congressional creation of an extraordinary range of administrative and quasi-administrative agencies and tribunals that exercise adjudicatory power outside the Article III system. If some or all of those responsibilities had been vested in the federal judiciary, then the Article III system would probably resemble state judicial systems far more than it does today. Instead of the federal judiciary currently visible—an elite corps of several hundred life-tenured generalist judges sitting, for the most part, in courts possessed of the full range of federal jurisdiction—the federal judiciary would encompass a broader range and variety of courts, officers, and programs.

How might these differences affect the resolution of freestanding judicial power claims? It is hard to say anything general; here too there are crosscutting effects that are difficult to sum. On one hand, in state systems the development of large-scale managerial responsibilities increases the relative scale of state judiciaries and provides state supreme courts—who wield rule-making, administrative, and supervisory authority over a sprawling, heterogeneous institutional system—with distinctive client groups and alliances, and a measure of independent power. Plausibly, that base of support encourages judicial assertiveness vis-à-vis the political branches in separation-of-powers cases; consider the cases that strike down, on judicial power grounds, legislative attempts to regulate the bar or to regulate administrative employees of the courts.[223] But the opposite effect is that the blurring of lines between state judiciaries and state executive agencies dilutes the distinctiveness of the judicial power. In the federal system, by contrast, the line of demarcation between executive and judicial institutions has been maintained, in part, by judicial invalidation of statutes that either vest administrative functions in the courts[224]

---

[223] See note 89 and accompanying text.

[224] See *Keller v Potomac Electric Power Co.*, 261 US 428 (1923) (Congress may not require Article III courts to revise the discretionary decision of an administrative commission).

or that attempt to subordinate judicial functions to executive review.[225]

3. *Judicial review and common-law decision making.* In the federal courts, the Supreme Court tells us, there is no "general" federal common law.[226] Skeptics point out that the federal courts create common law more frequently than they admit.[227] "Pure" common law is brought into play when the courts find a sufficiently weighty "federal interest";[228] constitutional and statutory phrases are often interpreted according to common-law baselines, or elaborated in common-law-like ways;[229] it has even been claimed that most constitutional law is essentially judicial elaboration of precedent rather than interpretation of the written constitution.[230] But little in the federal system resembles, in kind or degree, the explicit, primary common lawmaking found in state court systems, in which there are courts of general jurisdiction open to hear any common-law claim.

Both constitutional and statutory interpretation in the state appellate courts have felt the pervasive influence of the simultaneous common-law jurisdiction. In statutory interpretation, the whole subject of implied statutory causes of action has a different significance in state than in federal courts, because the former possess acknowledged authority to create common-law actions for violations of statutory provisions.[231] State courts have often invoked the canon that statutes in derogation of the common law should be

---

[225] See, e.g., *Hayburn's Case*, 2 US (2 Dall) 408 (1792) (refusing to adjudicate veteran's pension claims subject to subsequent executive review); *Chicago & Southern Air Lines v Waterman S.S. Corp.*, 333 US 103, 113–14 (1948) (judicial decisions may not constitutionally be subjected to executive review).

[226] See *Erie R. Co. v Tompkins*, 304 US 64 (1938).

[227] See, e.g., Martha A. Field, *Sources of Law: The Scope of Federal Common Law*, 99 Harv L Rev 881, 890 (1986) (arguing for a broad definition of federal common law).

[228] *Texas Industries, Inc. v Radcliff Materials, Inc.*, 451 US 630, 640 (1981) (describing areas of "uniquely federal interest" in which federal courts may create federal common law).

[229] This claim is advanced with respect to constitutional law in Henry Monaghan, *Foreword: Constitutional Common Law*, 89 Harv L Rev 1 (1975), and with respect to statutory interpretation in Peter L. Strauss, *On Resegregating the Worlds of Statute and Common Law*, 1994 Supreme Court Review 429.

[230] See David A. Strauss, *Common Law Constitutional Interpretation*, 63 U Chi L Rev 877 (1996).

[231] See Peters (cited in note 221) at 1555–56 (noting that state courts, unlike federal courts, "have the opportunity to consider not only the entire body of statutory enactments but also the large reservoir of common law principles that continue to fall exclusively within the judicial domain").

narrowly construed, although that canon may be falling out of favor.[232] In constitutional interpretation, casual empiricism suggests
that state courts assume the validity of common-law baselines at
least as frequently as the federal courts do.

This difference suggests that judicial overprotection is likely to
occur more frequently in state than in federal judicial systems.
Conjoining common-law jurisdiction with the power of constitutional review predictably causes more vigorous assertions of judicial prerogative. State courts habituated to frequent and explicit
common lawmaking describe legislative modification of common-
law rules as illegitimate intrusion.[233] The magnitude of this differential effect should not be overstated, however. As previously discussed, federal courts adjudicating judicial power claims also tend
to conflate their habits and customary practices with fundamental
requirements of the separation of powers.[234] The absence of a general common-law jurisdiction reduces, but does not eliminate, their
opportunities for making that mistake.

4. *Costs of constitutional amendment.* The costs of constitutional
amendment are far lower at the state than at the federal level.
Under Article V of the federal Constitution, an amendment usually requires a two-thirds vote of the Congress and ratification by
three-quarters of the states;[235] the costs of assembling a national
coalition for amendment greatly outrun the costs of assembling
a statewide coalition. Unsurprisingly, state constitutions are, in
many cases, amended far more frequently than the federal. There
are twenty-seven (formal) amendments to the federal Constitution.[236] But South Carolina, for example, has already amended its
latest constitution—in fact, its seventh constitution—no less than

---

[232] See id at 1556.

[233] See notes 67–83 and accompanying text. See also Howard F. Twiggs, *Keeping the
Common Law: State Courts Have Fundamental Authority to Limit 'Tort Reform,'* Legal Times
(March 3, 1997), p 30 ("Contrary to the assertions of those horrified by the judicial scrutiny
applied to the new 'tort reform' statutes, state courts have been the articulators and the
keepers of the common law since the founding of the republic. Unlike federal courts established by statute, the states have common law courts with considerably greater authority
to define liability law.").

[234] See notes 115–27 and accompanying text.

[235] See US Const, Art V. The mechanism for amendment mentioned in text is not the
sole one—an amendment may also be adopted by a constitutional convention, for example,
see id—but it is the mechanism most frequently resorted to.

[236] On the question of how to count the number of federal amendments, see generally
Sanford Levinson, *How Many Times Has the United States Constitution Been Amended?* in

474 times; California has amended its second constitution 493 times; and Alabama leads all states with 618 amendments, made to its sixth constitution.[237]

The relative ease of state constitutional amendment makes any exercise of constitutional review less consequential in state systems than in the federal system. The cost of reversing judicial errors in constitutional cases, either erroneous invalidation of statutes or erroneous failures to invalidate, is always lower in the states. If anything, this suggests that the nonjusticiability proposal is especially appropriate in the federal system; it certainly does not suggest that it is less appropriate than in the states. Advocates of judicial restraint argue that the difficulty of amending the federal constitution means that erroneous invalidations by the federal judiciary are harder to overturn than erroneous failures to invalidate, because the former can be corrected by statute, while the latter can hardly ever be (formally) corrected at all.[238] Those who consider this a valid general argument about federal constitutional review should think that it applies a fortiori to freestanding judicial power claims, because (as argued in Part II) the risks of judicial error lean sharply toward erroneous invalidation in such cases. Conversely, those who do not subscribe to a general position of Thayerian restraint might plausibly make an exception for judicial power claims, for the same reasons.

On net, the undoubted institutional differences between federal and state judicial systems do not provide any convincing reason for restricting the nonjusticiability proposal to state judicial systems. Most simply, the existence of common-law jurisdiction in the states makes state courts somewhat more likely than federal courts to overweight judicial prerogatives. But the absence of political checks and the high costs of amendment in the federal system make systemic pressures toward overprotection more difficult to correct than in the states. Consequently, those factors increase normative concerns about the instances of overprotection that do occur. Accordingly, extending the nonjusticiability proposal to the federal system would prevent a smaller set of more serious harms.

Sanford Levinson, ed, *Responding to Imperfection: The Theory and Practice of Constitutional Amendment* (1995).

[237] These statistics are drawn from Robert L. Maddex (cited in note 127) at xxx–xxxv.

[238] See note 132 and accompanying text.

V. Conclusion

In general, legal scholarship on the judicial power has devoted far more attention to federal decisions and federal institutions than to state decisions and state institutions. And the
scholarship has generally overlooked cognitive and institutional
mechanisms that cause courts adjudicating open-ended constitutional grants of judicial power to overstate the harms to the separation of powers that flow from legislative reform of judicial action.
Those two failings are connected. The functionalist state decisions
that adjudicate freestanding judicial power claims display a systematic pattern of judicial overprotection of judicial authority; that
pattern then becomes apparent in the small and heavily analyzed
set of federal decisions as well. These conclusions undermine the
received view, which assumes that federal and state courts must
jealously scrutinize any purported encroachment on judicial authority. To the contrary, the comparative analysis of state and federal judicial power suggests that judicial scrutiny of purported encroachments upon the judiciary's constitutional powers frequently
results in *judicial* encroachment upon the core functions and responsibilities of the political branches. The appropriate doctrinal
remedy is to adopt a formal rule that prevents the most harmful
forms of overprotection: freestanding judicial power claims should
be declared nonjusticiable, thereby anchoring state and federal judiciaries to the interpretation of specific constitutional provisions
less susceptible to the distorting effects of judicial cognition.